The Feminist History Reader

Over the past thirty-five years, feminist historians have challenged, debated and transformed the way history is, and should be, written. This self-critical dialogue between women has resulted in the development of a richly reflexive historiography. *The Feminist History Reader* provides a clearly structured introduction to some of the very best writers in the field of feminist history, gathering together key articles that have shaped this vibrant historiography and introducing students to the major theoretical shifts and turning points in feminist historical discourse.

The *Reader* is divided into four parts. Part I looks at early feminist historians' writings following the move from reclaiming women's past through to the development of gender history. Part II focuses on the interaction of feminist history with 'the linguistic turn', addressing the challenges of poststructuralism and the responses it provoked. Part III examines the work of lesbian historians and queer theorists in their interrogation of the heterocentrism of feminist history writing. The fourth part of the *Reader* explores the concept of 'difference' in the work of black feminists, postcolonial critics and Third World scholars and the ways in which this scholarship has sought to decolonise feminist history. Each reading has a critical introduction and there is a guide to further reading for each part.

Including a specially written, comprehensive introduction by the editor, this is a wide-ranging guide to both past developments and future orientations in the theorising of feminist history and is essential reading for all students of history.

Sue Morgan is Principal Lecturer in History and Head of the School of Cultural Studies at the University of Chichester. She is the author of *A Passion for Purity: Ellice Hopkins and the Politics of Gender in the Late-Victorian Church* (1999), co-editor of *Masculinity and Spirituality in Victorian Culture* (2000) and editor of *Women, Religion and Feminism in Britain, 1750–1900* (2002).

The Feminist History Reader

Edited by

Sue Morgan

Routledge
Taylor & Francis Group

LONDON AND NEW YORK

First published 2006
by Routledge
2 Park Square, Milton Park, Abingdon, Oxon OX14 4RN

Simultaneously published in the USA and Canada
by Routledge
270 Madison Ave, New York NY 10016

Routledge is an imprint of the Taylor & Francis Group, an informa business

© Editorial matter and selection, 2006 Sue Morgan. Individual
contributions, the contributors (see individual chapters)

Typeset in Bell Gothic and Perpetua by
Florence Production Ltd, Stoodleigh, Devon
Printed and bound in Great Britain by
TJ International Ltd, Padstow, Cornwall

British Library Cataloguing in Publication Data
A catalogue record for this book is available from the
British Library

Library of Congress Cataloging in Publication Data
The feminist history reader/Sue Morgan [editor].
    p. cm.
  1. Women – History.   2. Women – Historiography.
  3. Feminism – Historiography.   I. Morgan, Sue, 1957–
HQ1121.F437 2006
305.42092–dc22   2005031180

ISBN10: 0–415–31809–2 (hbk)
ISBN10: 0–415–31810–6 (pbk)

ISBN13: 978–0–415–31809–9 (hbk)
ISBN13: 978–0–415–31810–5 (pbk)

Contents

Acknowledgements

THE IDEA FOR THIS *READER* has grown out of my teaching and research on feminist historiography during the past fifteen years at the universities of Gloucestershire, Bristol and Chichester. My particular thanks go to the many students at the latter institution who alerted me regularly to the need for just such a reader on debates in women's history. Teaching with so many of the texts included here has certainly facilitated the process of selection, but the wealth of thirty years of feminist scholarship still made the final choice of readings a difficult task. My warm thanks therefore to the anonymous referees of the original proposal whose comments helped to sharpen the focus and structure at an early stage, and to Jacqui de Vries, Clare Midgley and Alison Oram for their invaluable and timely suggestions on the Introduction. I am very grateful to Angela Sliwinski for her meticulous preparation of the final manuscript, to Carole Farnfield for her help with organising permissions and to the library staff at the University of Chichester for obtaining numerous articles with great speed and efficiency. I would like to thank Vicky Peters for commissioning this *Reader* and Eve Setch for her cheerful support (and great patience) in seeing the project through to completion.

My final thanks go to Keith Jenkins who has been a part of this work since its inception. *The Feminist History Reader* was originally to have been co-edited by us both until we realised that we had two quite different books in mind. His level of involvement has, nevertheless, remained significant. My profound thanks to him for the animated exchanges on feminist history and 'the linguistic turn' (which I always won!) for his rigorous and incisive critique of each version of the Introduction, for finding the wonderful image for the front cover and for his unfailing encouragement and support throughout, not just for this project, but for me.

The editor and publishers wish to thank the following for their permission to reproduce copyright material. Some of the extracts, including all of the roundtable discussions, have had the endnotes omitted due to reasons of space. The sources are listed as they appear in the *Reader*.

Sheila Rowbotham, 'The Trouble with "Patriarchy"' and Sally Alexander and
    Barbara Taylor, 'In Defence of "Patriarchy"', *New Statesman*, December
    1979. Reproduced by permission of the *New Statesman*;
Judith M. Bennett, 'Feminism and History', *Gender and History*, 1:3 (1989):
    251–72. Reproduced by permission of Blackwell Publishers Ltd;
Amanda Vickery, 'Golden Age to Separate Spheres? A Review of the Categories
    and Chronology of English Women's History', *Historical Journal*, 36:2
    (1993): 283–414. Endnotes omitted. Reproduced by permission of Cambridge
    University Press;
Ellen DuBois, Mari Jo Buhle, Temma Kaplan, Gerda Lerner and Caroll Smith-
    Rosenberg, 'Politics and Culture in Women's History. A Symposium', was
    originally published in *Feminist Studies*, Volume 6, Number 1 (Spring, 1980):
    26–64, by permission of the publisher, *Feminist Studies*, Inc. Endnotes
    omitted;
Gisela Bock, 'Women's History and Gender History: Aspects of an International
    Debate', *Gender and History*, 1:1 (Spring, 1989): 7–30. Endnotes omitted.
    Reproduced by permission of Blackwell Publishers Ltd;
Penelope J. Corfield, 'History and the Challenge of Gender History', *Rethinking
    History* 1:3 (1997): 241–58. June Purvis and Amanda Weatherill, 'Playing
    the Gender History Game: A Reply to Penelope J. Corfield', *Rethinking History*
    3:3 (1999): 333–8. Endnotes omitted. Reproduced by permission of Taylor
    and Francis Ltd. www.tandf.co.uk;
Joan Wallach Scott, 'Gender: A Useful Category of Historical Analysis', *American
    Historical Review*, 91:5 (1986): 1053–75. Reproduced by permission of the
    author;
Denise Riley, 'Does a Sex Have a History?', Chapter 1 in *Am I That Name?:
    Feminism and the Category of "Women" in History* (Minneapolis: University
    of Minnesota Press, 1988). Reproduced by permission of University of
    Minnesota Press. Copyright © Denise Riley, 1988;
Sonya Rose, Kathleen Canning, Anna Clark and Mariana Valverde, 'Gender
    History/Women's History: Is Feminist Scholarship Losing its Critical Edge?',
    Roundtable discussion in *Journal of Women's History* 5:1 (Spring, 1993):
    89–125. Endnotes omitted. Reproduced by permission of Indiana University
    Press;
Joan Hoff, 'Gender as a Postmodern Category of Paralysis', *Women's History
    Review* 3:2 (1994): 149–68. Responses by Susan Kingsley Kent and Caroline
    Ramazanoglu, *Women's History Review* 5:1 (1996): 9–23. Endnotes omitted.
    Reproduced by permission of the authors and Triangle Journals Ltd;
bell hooks, 'Postmodern Blackness' in her *Yearning: Race, Gender and Cultural
    Politics* (Boston: Southend Press, 1990): 23–31. Reproduced by permission
    of South End Press Ltd, Turnaround Publisher Services Ltd and Between the
    Lines;
Judith Butler, 'Contingent Foundations: Feminism and the Question of "Post-
    modernism"' in Judith Butler and Joan Scott (eds) *Feminists Theorize the
    Political* (New York and London: Routledge, 1992): 3–21. Copyright © 1992.
    From *Feminists Theorize the Political* by Judith Butler. Reproduced by
    permission of Routledge/Taylor & Francis Group, LLC;

Lillian Faderman, 'Who Hid Lesbian History?' in Bonnie Zimmerman and Toni A. H. McNaron (eds) *The New Lesbian Studies: Into the Twenty-first Century*, (New York: The Feminist Press, 1996): 41–7. Copyright © 1997 by Lillian Faderman. First appeared in THE JOURNAL OF LESBIAN STUDIES. Reprinted by permission of the author and the Sandra Dijkstra Literary Agency;

Sheila Jeffreys, 'Does it Matter if They Did It?' in Lesbian History Group (eds) *Not a Passing Phase: Reclaiming Lesbians in History 1840–1985* (London: The Women's Press Ltd, 1989): 19–28. Reproduced by permission of the author;

Martha Vicinus, 'Lesbian History: All Theory and No Facts or All Facts and No Theory?' in *Radical History Review,* Volume 60, pp. 57–75. Copyright, 1994, MARHO: The Radical Historians Organization, Inc. All rights reserved. Used by permission of the publisher;

Donna Penn, 'Queer: Theorizing Politics and History' in *Radical History Review,* Volume 62, pp. 24–42. Copyright, 1995, MARHO: The Radical Historians Organization, Inc. All rights reserved. Used by permission of the publisher;

'"Lesbian-like" and the Social History of Lesbianisms' by Judith M. Bennett, from the *Journal of the History of Sexuality* 9:1/2, pp. 1–24. Copyright © 2000 by the University of Texas Press. All rights reserved;

'Toward a Global History of Same-Sex Sexuality' by Leila J. Rupp, from the *Journal of the History of Sexuality* 10:2, pp. 287–302. Copyright © 2001 by the University of Texas Press. All rights reserved;

Elizabeth V. Spelman, 'Gender & Race: The Ampersand Problem in Feminist Thought' in *Inessential Woman: Problems of Exclusion in Feminist Thought* by Elizabeth V. Spelman. Copyright © 1988 by Elizabeth V. Spelman. Reprinted by permission of Beacon Press, Boston;

Valerie Amos and Pratibha Parmar, 'Challenging Imperial Feminism', *Feminist Review*, 17 (1984): 3–19, Palgrave Macmillan, reproduced with permission of the authors and Palgrave Macmillan. Bibliography omitted;

Audre Lorde, 'An Open Letter to Mary Daly': 66–71. Reproduced with permission from *Sister Outsider* by Audre Lorde. Copyright 1984 by Audre Lorde, The Crossing Press, a division of Ten Speed Press, Berkley, CA;

Elsa Barkley Brown, '"What Has Happened Here": The Politics of Difference in Women's History and Feminist Politics', *Feminist Studies* 18:2 (1992): 295–312;

Ania Loomba, 'Dead Women Tell No Tales: Issues of Female Subjectivity, Subaltern Agency and Tradition in Colonial and Post-colonial Writings on Widow Immolation in India', *History Workshop Journal*, 1993, Volume 36, pp. 209–27, by permission of Oxford University Press and the author;

Mrinalini Sinha, 'Gender and Nation' in Bonnie Smith (ed.) *Women's History in Global Perspective* (Bloomington, IN: University of Illinois Press, 2004): 229–74. Reproduced by permission of the American Historical Association and the author;

Catherine Hall, 'Introduction' to Hall, *Civilising Subjects. Metropole and Colony in the English Imagination, 1830–1867* (Cambridge: Polity Press, 2002): 1–22.

Reproduced with permission of Polity Press and the University of Chicago Press. Copyright © Catherine Hall, 2002;

Sanjam Ahluwalia, 'Rethinking Boundaries: Feminism and (Inter)nationalism in Early-Twentieth-Century India' with a response by Antoinette Burton, 'South Asian Women, Gender and Transnationalism', *Journal of Women's History* 14:4 (2003): 187–200. Reproduced by permission of Indiana University Press;

Cheryl Johnson-Odim, 'Actions Louder Than Words: The Historical Task of Defining Feminist Consciousness in Colonial West Africa' in Ruth Roach Pierson and Nupur Chaudhuri (eds) *Nation, Empire, Colony: Historicizing Gender and Race* (Bloomington, IN: Indiana University Press, 1998): 77–93. Reproduced by permission of the author;

Chandra Talpade Mohanty, '"Under Western Eyes" Revisited: Feminist Solidarity through Anticapitalist Struggles' in *Feminism Without Borders. Decolonizing Theory, Practicing Solidarity*, pp. 221–51. Copyright, 2003, Duke University Press. All rights reserved. Used by permission of the publisher. Endnotes omitted;

Scott, Joan W., 'Feminism's History', *Journal of Women's History* 16:2 (2004): 10–29. © *Journal of Women's History*. Reprinted with permission of the Johns Hopkins University Press and the author.

While every effort has been made to trace and acknowledge ownership of copyright material used in this volume, the Publishers will be glad to make suitable arrangements with any copyright holders whom it has not been possible to contact.

Introduction

Writing feminist history: theoretical
debates and critical practices

SUE MORGAN

The unresolved question of whether 'women' is a singular or radically diverse category, whether 'women' is a social category that
pre-exists or is produced by history, is at the heart of both feminist
history and the history of feminism.

Joan Scott, *Feminism and History*, 1996

The writing of history is not only not a transparent affair ... it
is not innocent either.

Himani Bannerji, 'Politics and the Writing of History', 1998

IN 1976 JOAN KELLY-GADOL announced enthusiastically that 'women's
history has revitalised theory, for it has shaken the conceptual foundations of
historical study'.[1] Her article identified three main historical approaches – period-
isation, social analysis and theories of social change – upon which feminist scholarship was likely to have the greatest methodological impact. Thirty years later, the
prodigious growth of feminist history alongside its counterparts, women's and
gender studies, has more than vindicated such predictions of its transformative
potential. The recovery of women as subjects of, and agents in, the making of history,
and the simultaneous decentring of the male subject has prompted widespread re-
examinations of the most fundamental of historical presumptions, not least through
vastly democratising the vision of who and what constitutes historical discourse.
As Joan Scott has recently cautioned, however, 'the achievement is not perfect' for
women are not yet 'fully equal players' in a profession where the extent of institutional and academic acceptance of feminist discourse still varies dramatically.
Nevertheless, if feminists have not rewritten all of history, they have successfully

'claimed a portion of the field' (Scott, Reading 29). For publications are now myriad and feminist analyses are acknowledged by many as a leading site of intellectual innovation.

The Feminist History Reader aims, therefore, to provide students and their teachers with an accessible introduction to some of the major theoretical and critical engagements that have animated feminist scholarship during the past thirty-five years. There are of course many excellent volumes already available that bring together feminist writings on specific historical themes, subjects, periods and events.[2] But this Reader differs from these in that its focus is not on the historical 'product' of feminist scholarship, but rather the main theoretical forms and directions it has taken. Many controversies have ensued throughout the years between feminist historians and their more traditional colleagues surrounding androcentric forms of history-writing, yet it is the internal debates and self-critical dialogue between women themselves that have done most to engender a richly theorised and reflexive feminist historiography. And it is the story of this historiography – understood not in the conventional sense as the study of historical writing on women but as an ongoing critical rethinking of the discourse as a whole – with which this Reader is concerned. How have feminists set about rewriting historical narratives through the insertion of women's stories? Through what categories, questions and intellectual frameworks have they been articulated? How have they sought to theorise a discourse that is typically (and unnecessarily) suspicious of theory? And how have feminists interrogated the ways in which various hierarchies of difference – gender, race, class, sexuality, ethnicity – have been traditionally constituted? This Reader aims to guide the student of history precisely through some of these most significant theoretical shifts and controversies in the development of feminist history-writing. This guide, organised through a four-part structure and an afterword, explores, in turn, early feminist theorisations of history, the impact of the post-structuralist challenge, lesbian reconstructions of the past and debates around 'difference'. The organisation of the volume is more thematic than chronological for no linear progression of analytical sophistication is proposed here. Instead we see a series of repeated or spiralling issues and concerns around the nature and purpose of feminist history occurring throughout.

Needless to say, the arrangement of three decades of feminist historical theory into these particular sections is an artificial although not, hopefully, an arbitrary one. Many different organisational structures could have been imposed upon this Reader.[3] My criteria for the selection of the twenty-nine readings in this volume was that each should be concerned primarily with reflections on the future theoretical direction of the field; in one sense, therefore, this is a collection of mini manifestos for feminist history. The extent to which these insights provoked further commentary and influenced the shape of the discourse was also an important determining factor concerning the matter of which reading to 'include' or 'exclude'. Given the increasingly global profile of feminist history – a development with which this Reader concludes – I am acutely aware of the resulting Anglo-American emphasis of many of the controversies referred to. This is due in part to the limitations of my own British expertise and location (I work on nineteenth-century British

gender and religion) and, in part, to the predominance of western anglophone feminist scholarship in driving forward many of the early debates that governed the
development of the field. I hope, however, that the critique of western feminism's
colonisation of the discourse (a major theme which occurs in several of the readings) and the references to comparative national perspectives wherever possible
throughout the volume go some way to indicating the thoroughly international
discourse that feminist history has now become.

Because the term 'theory' is used so frequently in the *Reader* it might help to
clarify, briefly, just what I understand by this term and its significance for feminist
(and indeed all) history. In offering a commentary on the ways in which feminists
have sought to theorise women's pasts, *The Feminist History Reader* is itself,
unavoidably, the product of a particular historical moment. That moment is one in
which Himani Bannerji's observation quoted at the beginning of this Introduction
– that the writing of history is neither innocent nor transparent – is more widely
acknowledged than ever before. Twenty-plus years on from the first 'shockwaves'
of poststructuralism, it is no longer possible to speak of 'an unmediated, uncon-
structed, non-perspectival account of the past'.[4] With impartiality and objectivity
successfully demystified, writing history has become recognised as a situated practice, by which I mean a self-aware reconstruction of the past circumscribed by the
subject position, theoretical intent and historical/political context of the writer.
Foregrounding the role of the historian as author in the way that this *Reader*
does presupposes a distinction between the past (the totality of humanity's previous
experiences) and history (the story or narrative ordering of that past). The past
does not present itself to us in a ready-made narrative form complete with explanations for social change. Thus, in order to give shape and meaning to the always
incomplete record of the past, historians, including feminists, must historicise it –
in other words they must re-present the past in the form of a narrative 'historical
discourse' it was never itself in.[5] All history-writing is therefore intrinsically theoretical because it cannot escape being artificially organised; formulated through
particular intellectual explanatory frameworks or epistemologies (theories of knowledge). If all history is thus inescapably theorised, then feminist history is so in very
particular and distinctive ways, for, as we shall see, feminists have been instrumental in exposing the gendered politics of knowledge production in history from
the research phase through to the writing process.

I make these by now somewhat over-familiar statements about the unavoid-
ability of theory in history because of what Catherine Hall has rightly referred
to as the 'tremendous resistance within the discipline to thinking theoretically'.[6]
Theory is ubiquitous, yet all too often it is simply identified by historians, including
feminists, with the development of postmodernism or 'the linguistic turn'. As a
result, theory is posited as a sort of optional layer on top of the solid base of
'proper' archival, empirical research. This empiricism/theory binary badly needs
disassembling. Not only is empiricism itself a theory but, as Ann-Louise Shapiro
has argued, because 'history is both a form of cognition and a form of writing,
historians cannot afford to absent themselves from these debates'.[7] I probably use
the term 'theory' in this *Reader* in a broader (some would say less rigorous)

sense than many might find acceptable or convincing, but my point, following Shapiro, is this: if feminist historians are to recover a leading role in producing even more wide-reaching strategies for change, they cannot afford to lose their theoretical edge.[8]

That feminists have never united around a single theoretical position or method- ological framework is evident from the multiplicity of positions that continue to disturb and enrich the field, many of which − socialist, Marxist, black, radical, liberal, lesbian, poststructuralist and postcolonial − are represented in this volume. In fact, such is the emphasis of this *Reader* upon theoretical controversy and conflict as it outlines attempts to dislodge gender as the primary cause of women's oppres- sion and to undercut the coherence of feminist identity itself, that readers might be tempted to ask why retain the term 'feminist' in the title at all? But, as every student knows, disagreement is the *sine qua non* of the academic profession. Such an absence of feminist unanimity is therefore neither a cause for concern nor for the dismissal of the integrity of the discourse itself. Rather, the consistent stance of self-critique and the destabilising of the familiar that is so characteristic of femi- nist critical practice is, to my mind, a source of tremendous creativity, optimism and analytical momentum. If a single common purpose *were* to be identified among such diverse approaches it would be, as Scott's quote suggests at the beginning of this Introduction, the inscribing and re-inscribing of what is meant by the term 'women'. Who is included or excluded in this category as the legitimate subject of feminist history? And what impact does this have upon the theoretical and political agenda of academic feminism? These are key questions that the readings in this volume seek to address.

Given that this *Reader* argues throughout for the heterogeneity of feminist historical discourse, it is also worth noting at the outset the important theoretical and methodological distinctions that have been made between women's, feminist and gender history. As Jane Rendall has commented, these approaches 'overlap yet are by no means identical'.[9] In a useful, clearly positioned discussion of these distinctions, June Purvis similarly recognises that while the links between women's and feminist history are strong they are not interchangeable terms. Whereas women's history is defined by its subject matter and need not evoke a feminist perspective at all, feminist history is defined by the very specificity of its theoret- ical agenda.[10] Gender history, the most recent approach undertaken by feminists, has shifted the debate away from a focus upon women to an examination of the interdependence and relational nature of female and male identities. The tendency has been to present these three approaches in terms of a progressive narrative of the displacement of women's and feminist history by gender history. I would argue instead that they continue to co-exist alongside each other in mutually productive ways; indeed, it is at the various points of intersection and overlap between them that much theoretical controversy and innovation has taken place. For this reason each of these approaches are represented in this *Reader* under the general rubric of 'feminist history'.

A practical point with which to conclude these preliminary observations. The remainder of this Introduction provides a synopsis of the main historiographical shifts and theoretical directions in feminist history during the past thirty-five years.

This has been organised as a guide to the four-part structure of the readings them-selves and follows exactly the same headings and debates. This structure has been adopted in the hope that readers will find it a helpful way to familiarise themselves with an overview of the main issues, many of which are quite complex, before turning to the actual excerpts.

Part I: Bringing the female subject into view

> ... our new understanding of the sexual division of labour, the organization of the family and the power relations between men and women meant that society could be transformed, that the world could be turned upside down by our new view of it.
>
> Catherine Hall, 'Feminism and Feminist History', 1992

What it meant to be a woman and how best that category might be represented historically was played out in numerous debates during the 1970s and 1980s. Early feminist historicisations of the meanings of sexual difference were immensely varied, and theories surrounding the nature and purpose of feminist history vigorously contested. In Part I, I examine a selected number of major controversies orientated around theories of 'patriarchy', 'separate spheres', 'women's culture' and 'gender', and the formative influence these discussions had on the initial theoretical trajec-tory of feminist history. These debates took place primarily, although not exclusively, within Anglo-American scholarship and were generated by the desire for a cohesive approach to women's historical experience. In order to produce women as subjects capable of historical agency, the consolidation of a recognisable women's identity was held to be paramount at this point although, as we shall see in subsequent sections, this was quickly opened up to successive challenges.

The development of feminist historical discourse from its dual parentage of the new social history and second wave feminism has been well documented, but it is worth reminding ourselves here of its overtly political and non-academic origins. Amidst a crucible of global social and political protest movements organised during the late twentieth century around a multiplicity of demands for equal opportunities, civil liberties and minority rights, the women's movement provided the radicalising spirit for feminist historians. Women's groups and adult education centres were important extra-academic sites for the initial exchanges of ideas in many coun-tries and a heady anticipation of the revolutionary potential of feminist theory was evident, as suggested by Catherine Hall's comment quoted above.[11] Catalysed by a growth in women's history courses and the simultaneous emergence of numerous professional associations, feminist history developed a steady academic presence during this period, albeit very unevenly. As the editors of *Writing Women's Histor-ies: International Perspectives* (1991) illustrate in their introduction to a germinal collection of essays from twenty-two countries, feminist history was an international phenomenon from the very outset. At the same time, however, its development along multiple and contradictory pathways was often nationally determined by 'local' and thus different 'historiographical contexts and institutional infrastructures'.[12]

Two contrasting examples of the development of feminist historiography can be seen with reference to France and Britain. As Cécile Dauphin and the authors of the essay 'Women's Culture and Women's Power' make clear, the influence of cultural anthropology and ethnology, the history of *mentalités* and the impact of the Annales school were particularly significant for women's history in France, factors reflected in the preference for cultural themes such as women's sexuality, the body and motherhood.[13] In contrast, 'British feminist history was fed and watered by the tradition of British Marxist historiography'.[14] Hall's much-quoted essay, 'Feminism and Feminist History', recounts the dominant influence of E. P. Thompson's classic espousal of the cultural formation and agency of the English working classes upon the work of British socialist feminists, leading to a central preoccupation with class struggle and gender.[15]

The question of patriarchy

It was the concept of 'patriarchy', however, that provided feminists with their first all-encompassing theory through which to identify the distinctive, gender-related forms of female subordination by men. Patriarchy may be defined, at its simplest, as 'a system of interrelated social structures through which men exploit women'.[16] Feminist analyses of male power took several different emphases, from social and economic forms of exploitation to male sexual violence. Despite its widespread usage the term has proved persistently controversial, criticised for encouraging a monocausal theory of women's condition. In an early exchange between three British feminist historians in 1979, Sheila Rowbotham expressed disquiet with the ahistorical presentation of patriarchy as the single determining cause of female subordination. Not only did this suggest a permanent oppositional antagonism between the sexes that left little analytical room for more positive, supportive male/female encounters but, Rowbotham argued, it also 'allow[ed] no space for the complexities of women's defiance' (Rowbotham *et al.*, Reading 1). Several years later, Joan Scott similarly warned against the inadequacies of any feminist meta-analysis grounded in biological difference: 'A theory that rests on the single variable of physical difference poses problems for historians', she argued, for 'it assumes a consistent or inherent meaning for the human body – outside social or cultural construction – and thus the ahistoricity of gender itself' (Scott, Reading 7). In response to Rowbotham, Sally Alexander and Barbara Taylor's defence of patriarchy was, in fact, a defence of theory. Feminist history, they contended, needed a distinctive theoretical framework through which to examine women's lives not least because '[h]istory only answers questions which are put to it' (Rowbotham *et al.*, Reading 1). Ten years later, Judith Bennett's call to arms for a restoration of feminist history's 'political nerve' propounded a fully historicised understanding of patriarchy as feminism's central theoretical problematic. Especially innovative was her departure from the 'male oppressor/female victim' binary suggesting, radically, that women themselves were part of the diverse historical operations of patriarchy: 'Women have not been merely passive victims of patriarchy; they have also colluded in, undermined and survived patriarchy' (Bennett, Reading 2).

Further nuanced appraisals of patriarchy have been prompted by gender histor-ians working on the history of masculinity. In their introduction to *Manful Asser-tions: Masculinities in Britain since 1800* (1991) Michael Roper and John Tosh provided what I think is still one of the best assessments of the 'middle ground' to be found between histories of masculinity and feminist analyses of patriarchy. The former need not be 'necessarily uncongenial to feminism' Roper and Tosh argue, because to 'understand women's position now or in the past requires not only an engagement with the experience of the oppressed, but an insight into the structures of domination'.[17] Thus, analysing the historical dimensions of male power should further feminist understanding of 'why men sought to control and exploit women'.[18] Whether or not patriarchy is the very life-blood of feminist history-writing, a useful theoretical shorthand for the multiple historical dynamics of female oppression or an overly ahistorical and essentialised account of female subjugation, remains unanswered at the beginning of the twenty-first century. It is clear, however, that if patriarchal theory is to be meaningfully revitalised it will need to include within it an exploration of the changing social relations between women and men as well as a more effective way to account for historical discontinuities.[19]

The separate spheres and 'women's culture'

An alternative analysis of patriarchy much in evidence throughout the 1970s and 1980s was based upon the metaphor of 'separate spheres' whereby feminist historians mapped the restrictions placed upon eighteenth- and nineteenth-century women's lives in accordance with ideological prescriptions concerning the gendering of private and public space. The 'separate spheres' argument would go on to become one of the most dominant organising tropes of European and American women's history for thirty years or more. In an important critical review of its development, Linda Kerber identified three distinct phases within feminist analyses of this influ-ential concept.[20] The first occurred in the 1960s, notably through the work of Barbara Welter who, contra Alexis de Tocqueville's approving observation in 1840 regarding the correlation between the elevated status of American women and their confinement 'within the narrow circle of domestic life',[21] interpreted the separate spheres in more derisory terms as a synonym for female incarceration within the home. Second, the publication in 1975 of Carroll Smith-Rosenberg's germinal essay, 'The Female World of Love and Ritual', marked a distinctively different theoret-ical approach to the separate spheres notion.[22] Smith-Rosenberg suggested that the rigid differentiation of nineteenth-century American gender roles gave rise to an autonomous, homosocial female world bound together through kinship networks and women's shared life experiences of marriage, family and religion. This evoca-tive depiction of a supportive and empowering female culture transformed previous negative readings of women's sphere. Consequently, a new theoretical framework for feminist history was engendered, that of a discrete 'women's culture'. This was an approach favoured particularly by American historians such as Nancy Cott and Estelle Freedman who reconstrued the domestic female sphere as a generative site of feminist identity formation that shaped the pattern of women's subsequent social and political activism.[23]

Debates around women's culture were a timely response to the growing sense of unease that, by continuing to work within a masculinist historical framework, feminists had so far inadvertently reinforced the subordinate status of women.[24] Theories of women's culture meant that new 'woman-centred' categories such as the familial and domestic realms assumed analytical centre-stage. The male public sphere was de-privileged as the main arena of authentic historical activity, and the relentless narrative of women's oppression was replaced by a more optimistic eliciting of the active female subject. But the 'turn to culture' did not go unchallenged. In 1980 a symposium was published in *Feminist Studies* that articulated wider concerns about the increasing cultural focus in feminist history, not least the recurrent theme of the depoliticising of feminist history. Those in favour of 'women's culture', such as Smith-Rosenberg and Mari Jo Buhle, pointed to the more radical aspects of a theory that broadened and democratised the vision of feminist history away from the study of a narrow cadre of female elites to the daily experiences of all women. But its critics, notably Ellen DuBois, regarded the sometime romanticised portrayal of female domesticity as an ineffective way to challenge patriarchal structures, reminding readers that any form of women's culture still existed in a world whose contours were largely determined by men (DuBois *et al.*, Reading 4).

Since the late 1980s, various analytical inadequacies of the 'separate spheres' have been identified, not least its geographical, racial and class-based limitations. In a 2002 retrospective analysis of Welter's original essay, Donna Guy observed, for example, that the opportunity to join the ranks of 'domestic femininity' did not arise until the twentieth century for Latin American women, inspired not by pious middle-class respectability but by nationalist ideologies and public health campaigns.[25] Moreover, as both a nineteenth-century metaphor *and* a historical analytical framework, the concept of the gendered separate spheres was heavily criticised for reproducing unproblematically the very assumptions that required interrogation. Historians' elision of prescriptive ideology with actual historical practice was just one aspect of Amanda Vickery's blistering attack on the dominance of separate spheres in British feminist historiography; the other was her demonstration of the sheer permeability and interrelatedness of the spatial locations inhabited by women and men in the past (Vickery, Reading 3). It was this latter argument, borne out by a wealth of scholarship in the 1990s which demonstrated the extensive political, civic and social activity of women and, conversely, the significance of the private and domestic world for men, that eventually toppled the dominance of the separate spheres as an overworked and overly mechanistic trope.[26]

Nevertheless, the longevity and durability of the metaphor is still apparent in feminist scholarship. Italian feminist research remains strongly focused around the public/private axis, and in German feminist historiography, according to Lynn Abrams and Elizabeth Harvey, there appears 'little inclination to abandon this approach'[27] because of the particular firmness of the boundaries of private and public in modern Germany. Recent retrospectives of Welter's work also testify to the staying power of her original analysis. The public/private divide continues, therefore, to prompt analytical refinements more sensitised to period, class and national identity and recent interrogations of the concept in Middle Eastern and Brazilian women's history have revealed a renewed enthusiasm for its potential to foster comparative and transnational feminist histories.[28]

Gender as a category of historical analysis

In 1990, the editors of the US-based *Journal of Women's History* suggested that feminist history was witnessing a 'Kuhnian revolution'. The separate spheres theory had 'outworn its usefulness' and was passing the epistemological baton onto a new analytical category of 'gender' that sought to locate women within a broader framework of their social, cultural and political relationships with men.[29] Calls for a historical analysis of gender had occurred as early as the 1970s in influential essays by Natalie Zemon Davis and Joan Kelly. For Zemon Davis it was self-evident that feminist historians should address the experiences of both sexes:

> ... it seems to me that we should be interested in the history of both women and men, that we should not be working only on the subjected sex any more than an historian of class can focus exclusively on peasants. Our goal is to understand the significance of the *sexes*, of gender groups in the historical past ... to discover the range in sex roles and in sexual symbolism in different societies and periods, to find out what meaning they had and how they functioned to maintain the social order or to promote its change.[30]

Previous reconstructions of 'women's culture' appeared on the surface to be prohibitive of the history of men, but the traces of a more relational gender theory were always evident within the concept of the separate spheres. As Kerber reflected, the 'need to break out of the restrictive dualism of an oppressive term (woman's sphere) and a liberating term (women's culture) ... propelled ... a third stage in the development of the metaphor of separate spheres':[31] how, in short, both private and public, female and male spheres influenced each other reciprocally. Kerber's 'third stage' was exemplified in Leonore Davidoff and Catherine Hall's *Family Fortunes: Men and Women of the English Middle Class, 1780–1850* (1987, rep. 2002) which quickly became a canonical, although not uncontroversial, text for feminist historians in the anglophone world. *Family Fortunes* was firmly located within a materialist, social-scientific understanding of gender despite the alternative cultural and linguistic definitions in circulation at this time, as we shall see in Part II. Davidoff and Hall placed gender relations at the very heart of the formation of early nineteenth-century middle-class identity, basing their formulation of the mutually constitutive forces of class and gender upon the separation of private and public spheres of activity for women and men. The work has consequently earned a reputation among some historians, unfairly in my opinion, as the high watermark of a somewhat triumphalistic reading of the dominance of the separate spheres. As the retrospective introduction to the 2002 edition of the book makes clear, the authors' intentions were always more far-reaching, aiming 'to move beyond the public/private divide'[32] to demonstrate the contested rhetoric of separate spheres in the negotiation of gender identities. Described by Jane Rendall as 'the most ambitious attempt to write a history uniting the variables of class and gender',[33] *Family Fortunes* epitomises the transformative potential of gender for the re-imagining of the existing social historical landscape. As Hall later explained:

> we wanted not just to put the women back into a history from which they had been left out, but to rewrite that history so that proper recognition would be given to the ways in which gender, as a key axis of power in society, provides a crucial understanding of how any society is structured and organized.[34]

The limitations of a 'compensatory' and 'separatist' approach to feminist history had already become increasingly apparent by the 1990s. As Scott observed in 1991, 'women's history was tolerated . . . by liberal pluralists . . . but it remained outside the dominant concerns of the discipline, its subversive challenge seemingly contained in a separate sphere'.[35] Gender theory accordingly appeared to offer a way out of this theoretical impasse. In a prescient 1982 discussion of its transformative potential as 'a fundamental category of historical analysis', Elizabeth Fox-Genovese outlined the cultural and relational constituents of gender and its primacy as a 'critical feature of all social relations'.[36] Both Scott in 1986 and Bock in 1989 were to reinforce the way in which the operations of gender, as a social and historical rather than biological category, could be analysed in relation to other cultural formations such as class, race age, sexuality and religion (Bock, Reading 5). Because of its capacity to intersect with so many areas of traditional historical enquiry, gender was heralded by Scott, Bock and others as a powerful means through which to refigure history (Bock, Reading 5; Scott, Reading 7).

The prospect of an approach that might genuinely reconceive not just the narrative content of mainstream history but also its theoretical underpinnings generated a tremendous sense of anticipation. Alongside this, however, ran a more sceptical feminist response. An important and controversial outcome of gender history was that it stimulated new areas of research into men, masculinity and male institutions. This was not the naturalised understanding of men that had for so long formed the normative subject of historical scholarship, but an approach that emphasised the variable, historically-specific meanings of male roles and behaviour. As the Japanese historian Ogino Miho observed, 'men are omnipresent' in history, but men as gendered, 'their bodies, minds, feelings, private lives and sexualities – remain[ed] transparent and unexplained'.[37] For some national historiographies such as that of Russia, the political neutrality of 'gender' and its disassociation with 'feminism' provided a more advantageous approach to the development of women's history.[38] But June Purvis and Amanda Weatherill expressed the concerns of many when they characterised the shift towards a more 'neutral', 'palatable' discourse of gender as a renewed silencing and marginalisation of women through restoring men to the narrative centre. For Purvis and Weatherill, the re-legitimation of men's history under the guise of gender signalled a dangerous 'malestream incorporation strategy' that depoliticised and deradicalised the original feminist challenge (Corfield *et al.*, Reading 6). Gender history could all too easily downplay men's privileged access to power allowing patriarchy, as Lois Banner described it, 'to engage in that disappearing act at which it has been so adept'.[39]

The cultural and linguistic specificity of this controversy was primarily the concern of anglophone feminist historians. As Rosi Braidotti alleged in an interview with the feminist philosopher Judith Butler, the notion of 'gender' was a particular 'vicissitude of the *English language*, one which bears little or no relevance to theoretical traditions in the Romance languages'.[40] Certainly in the Italian, French and German feminist movements, the term 'gender' found no direct, successful equivalent. The Italian term *genere*, according to Silvia Mantini, referred more to 'individuality' than 'sexuality', whereas the German word *geschlecht* – meaning both sex *and* gender – was unable to flag the cultural distinctiveness of the latter term[41] (Bock, Reading 5). The French historian Michele Riot-Sarcey argued, on the other hand, that the semantic difficulties raised by the term *genre* in France were merely a 'convenient pretext'[42] for the wider avoidance of gender theory in women's history.

Despite these linguistic anomalies and their varying justifications, gender history marked a significant theoretical re-orientation for feminists in the shift from a history of subjects to a history of relations. Whether or not it heralded a new epistemology is less clear according to Penelope Corfield, but in terms of theoretical and methodological innovation gender history remains unsurpassed (Corfield *et al.*, Reading 6). As Lynn Hunt wrote in 1998:

> gender history stands out not only for the sheer volume of new historical work that has been produced, but also for the pertinence of its internal debates for the future of the historical profession as a whole. Gender history is at the forefront of discussion about methods, periodization, the role of metanarratives, and the epistemological foundations of the discipline – in short, just about every general issue of concern to historians today.[43]

In addition, it should be noted that the global expansion of gender history during the past twenty-five years has been remarkable. Continuing the original internationalism of feminist history, many insightful theoretical contributions on gender have been articulated beyond Europe and the US, including India, Australia, Canada, Ireland and the Caribbean and, more recently, Africa, Latin America, Eastern Europe, Russia, China and Japan.[44] Much, though not all, of this scholarship has followed a parallel development to the Euro-American phenomenon moving from an explicitly politicised feminist history to gender history, as in Caribbean and Japanese historiography. Where 'feminism' has been signalled as representative of the hegemony of western intellectual discourse, for example, 'gender' has provided a more immediate and productive theoretical approach to recovering women's pasts and for analysing the relations between women and men.[45] As we shall see in Part IV, many black and Third World feminist scholars have explored the mutually constitutive formations of gender and race and the complex tensions between dominant and countercultural articulations of these. Patricia Mohammed's discussion of post-migrant Indian communities in Trinidad between 1917 and 1947, for example, illustrates the way in which dominant systems of gender were always open to subversion and reformulation by communities with a strong indigenous culture of their own.[46]

Concerns over the undermining of feminist history by gender enthusiasts have been largely unfounded. Unlike Hunt, who sees theories of 'patriarchy' and 'separate spheres' as important preliminary platforms for the development of later work on gender but having now 'dropped off the radar screen of most current studies',[47] I think that these earlier concepts are still capable of provoking important refinements in feminist history. In practical terms at least, publications remain prolific within each of the fields of women's, feminist and gender history, if indeed these approaches can be quite so clearly delineated. It is worth remembering that gender analysis is the *sine qua non* of all women's and feminist history, or, along with Bock, that 'women's history *is* gender history *par excellence*' (Bock, Reading 5). Some excellent critical work on masculinity has been produced by feminist and gender historians across different periods and cultures, and a potentially anti-feminist history of gender is only possible if a critical component of the definition of gender is lacking – its signification of the unequal power relations between women and men. I say this as a gender historian who works equally on constructions of femininity and masculinity from within an overtly feminist theoretical perspective and have always found it productive to do so.

Following Hunt's argument, however, it is possible to see how the theoretical dynamism of early feminist history produced 'paradoxical results'[48] in which the emergence of an increasing diversity of identity-based histories began to destabilise and undermine the original desire for a coherent, univocal feminist identity. Concerns over the marginalisation of women and feminism by gender history could only make sense in the context of a relatively unproblematic understanding of the category 'woman'. The entry of poststructuralist theories of identity and knowledge into feminist historical discourse through very particular readings of gender that held out no such certainties or presumptions about the female historical subject thus came to fuel a particular hostility towards the concept of gender. It is to these controversies that we now turn.

Part II: Deconstructing the subject: feminist history and 'the linguistic turn'

> Could it be argued that the only way of avoiding these constant historical loops which depart or return from the conviction of women's natural dispositions . . . would be to make a grander gesture – to stand back and announce that there aren't any women?
> Denise Riley, 'Does a Sex Have a History?', 1988

Poststructuralism came late to history – hardly surprising given the dominant positivist and empirical methods utilised by most historians. Yet, when it arrived, its impact was momentous. No approach has stimulated more controversy or brought the 'theoretical' into quite such sharp relief for feminist scholars during the last twenty years, controversies which I now outline and to which I add a critical commentary.

The nature of the poststructuralist challenge is an appropriately evasive one to define, given its resistance to totalising forms of expression. It incorporates elements as diverse as the decentring of the subject and the abandonment of 'grand narratives', but is probably best known for its affirmation of the inescapable centrality of language in the creation of historical meaning. Language, according to poststructuralist thought, simultaneously arises from, and inscribes, 'reality'. As Judith Butler and Joan Scott have observed, however, poststructuralism 'is not, strictly speaking, *a position*, but rather a critical interrogation of the exclusionary operations by which 'positions' [including feminist positions] are established'.[49] Feminist historians in the anglophone world became best acquainted with the major tenets of this so-called 'linguistic turn' through the American historian Joan Scott and the British philosopher Denise Riley whose works provided a central reference-point throughout the late 1980s and 1990s (Scott, Reading 7; Riley, Reading 8). Drawing upon leading French theorists such as Jacques Derrida and Michel Foucault, Scott and Riley proposed a radical reconceptualisation of existing readings of gender. Rather than recovering the historical experiences of women and men as evidence of sexual difference, they focused instead on how that difference was produced discursively as a normative system of knowledge and meaning and how identities of gender were disseminated variously over time. As Scott remarked in 1988 in the introduction to *Gender and the Politics of History*, a collection of essays that included her landmark 1986 article, 'Gender: A Useful Category of Historical Analysis':

> the story is no longer about the things that have happened to women and men and how they have reacted to them; instead it is about how the subjective and collective meanings of women and men as categories of identity have been constructed.[50]

According to Scott, such a paradigmatic shift was necessary because, as noted in Part I, the subversive potential of feminist history had failed to re-work and refigure the fundamental concepts and theoretical categories of the wider discipline. The 'add and stir' approach of women's history had perpetuated rather than challenged the essentialised, male/female binary structures of traditional history. Only by deconstructing those very categories that had been the constitutive of feminist historical analyses so far, argued Scott – women, identity, experience, agency, subjectivity – would such a transformation be possible (Scott, Reading 7). The relationship between a pre-given social experience and the formation of subject identity assumed by social scientific understandings of gender was thus ruptured by the deconstructionist 'methods' used by poststructuralist feminists. Butler's influential collapse of the sex/gender distinction was also a formative moment here. The female or male sexed body could not be seen as an essential, pre-discursive 'reality', she argued, for even orthodox formulations of the sex/gender distinction accepted gender as 'a multiple interpretation'[51] of sex and thus could not be said to follow directly from it. Rather gender, as a system of knowledge about sexual difference, produced various meanings of the body. 'Sex' was thus just as much a product of culture and of specific discourses as gender itself. Similarly, poststructuralist feminists argued that historical subjects were not constituted by a set of unmediated or self-evident experiences, but by particular discourses of gender, class or race that valorised and gave meaning to those experiences.

The refutation of sexual difference as an originary basis upon which cultural constructions of gender might then be formulated generated an extraordinary amount of feminist debate, ranging from the outright hostile to the more positively and strategically engaged. It is important to locate these debates within the broader context of discussions taking place on the nature of history per se at the time and to recognise that many of the following responses were also those of historians more generally.[52] Yet the undeniable fact that most leading poststructuralist thinkers were men – for the majority of whom neither gender nor feminism was the primary analytical concern – gave the feminist critique a particular edge. This gendering of poststructuralism as male is worth pausing to consider briefly before moving onto the particular theoretical and epistemological issues raised by this approach.

Concerns over the masculinism of the poststructuralist tradition were expressed in ways similar to parallel debates surrounding the 'turn to gender' referred to in Part I. In other words, that women might once again be eclipsed by men as both discursive subjects *and* mediators of the past. American historian Joan Hoff and the British sociologist Stevi Jackson were explicit in their condemnation of the theory's 'misogynistic'[53] origins, and even poststructuralist sympathisers such as the Canadian historian Mariana Valverde commented on Scott's uncritical tendency to 'pull Foucault and Derrida out of the methodological hat as offering solutions to the problems of women's history'[54] (Hoff *et al.*, Reading 10). Yet it would be difficult to think of any major feminist theorist, poststructuralist or otherwise, who had not drawn variously upon the work of a 'seminal' male thinker be that Marx, Nietzsche, Freud, Foucault, Lacan, Edward Said or E. P. Thompson, to name but a few. Here the salient point is not that feminist historians should avoid using male theorists on the grounds that they may be innately misogynist, but that they are not deflected from feminist causes by such appropriations, nor hesitant about refiguring male theorists for political purposes directed towards the interests of women.

Indirectly related to this critique was the rather more different claim that many radical poststructuralist insights had, in fact, long formed part of feminist epistemologies. 'We did not need post-structuralism to develop gender as a category of analysis' observed Catherine Hall, nor did feminists 'need Foucault to understand that power operates on many sites, or post-structuralism to understand that historical writing was a male centred form of knowledge'.[55] Hall has a point. It is undoubtedly the case that feminists had taken a leading role in the 1980s in exposing the subjectivity of 'truth' and the gendered politics of knowledge as well as revealing the dangers of essentialism via the proliferation of competing feminist identity politics. In her discussion of the turn to poststructuralist readings of gender, for example, Kathleen Canning begins by reminding us of the powerful challenge posed precisely along these lines by feminist scholars to the canon of social history (Rose *et al.*, Reading 9). But did this mean that poststructuralism was simply part of an already established legacy of feminist historical critique, or was it something more fundamentally discontinuous? I would contend that it was the latter. The challenge first thrown down by Scott and Riley was of a very different epistemological kind, moving from feminist theoretical critiques of narrative history to an interrogation of the historical project itself. Accordingly, three main areas of contention have surfaced repeatedly in feminist historians' discussions of poststructuralism: subjectivity and identity, women's historical and political agency and the language/experience dualism. The remainder of this Part will examine each of these in more detail.

Subjectivity and identity

Despite an awareness of the constructed nature of gender identities and the capacity of language/discourse to produce and legitimate social inequalities, the writing of feminist history had continued in the main to rest upon the assertion of a pre-existing, coherent female identity, the shared commonalities of which provided a secure foundation for historical analyses of the broader condition and status of women's lives. As will be seen in Part IV, black and Third World feminists had already mounted a significant critique of essentialism, demanding that western feminism take 'difference' seriously as an analytical category rather than falsely assuming the universality of the female subject. But the development of an increasing plurality of feminist histories had not, until now, sought to dismantle the pre-formed, foundational status of female subjectivity and deprive it of an underlying, experiential base. Denise Riley was to do exactly that. In her frequently quoted study of the category of 'woman' in history, Riley denied the existence of any core or originary 'woman' behind the historical contingencies of time and place. On the contrary, 'women' were a 'volatile collectivity' whose identities were constantly in process, defined and redefined through an endless series of conflicting discursive practices: 'Some characterisation or other [of woman] is eternally in play' she argued, 'the question then for a feminist history is to discover whose, and with what effects'. Such indeterminacy was the very basis for any meaningful history of women. It was neither postfeminist nor antifeminist Riley argued, articulating as it did the many constraints upon, and alliances of, differing feminist strategies (Riley, Reading 8).

The suggestion that women were cultural constructs 'all the way down', the 'effects' of historically variable discourses, generated a profound unease among many feminist historians who regarded this stance as an attack upon the self-understanding and identity of women and upon the very legitimacy of the feminist history project itself. Poststructuralists were accused of an extreme anti-essentialism where the actual experiences of women were denounced in favour of a representation of the female self as a series of ephemeral fluctuations, and where 'flesh-and-blood women' became social constructs (Hoff et al., Reading 10). The centrality to feminist theory of the material dimensions of women's oppression meant that poststructuralist readings of the female subject were perceived as diminishing the significance of bodily and physical suffering. This was compounded by what was perceived as an extreme form of cultural relativism denying any universally agreed foundations upon which to make moral judgements and undercutting the certainty of the feminist (or any other) ethical position. As Stevi Jackson demanded: 'What basis is there for arguing that a feminist reading of forced sexual intercourse as rape is any more valid than the rapist's interpretation of it as pleasurable seduction?'.[56] Grounded in the realist certainties of identity politics, many feminist scholars maintained that sexual difference could never be adequately mediated by language alone. 'If woman is just an empty category then why am I afraid to walk alone at night?' was the provocative title of an article by Laura Lee Downs who argued therein that:

> deconstruction . . . leaves aside the dilemmas of women, who must live as subjects in time . . . sexual difference is not something which can simply be argued into a corner and then left behind. Rather, individuals must inhabit those gendered categories, even as they strive to unmake them.[57]

Women's historical and political agency

Underpinning these sometimes rancorous exchanges was a key dilemma for feminists; namely, how is the history of women to be written without a common understanding of the terms 'woman' or 'women's experience'? Poststructuralists' disavowal of any one-to-one correspondence theory of 'truth' (in other words of a direct correlation between identity formation and social location) was a major theoretical obstacle for those feminists who felt that without a shared identity or set of experiences women's ability to mobilise themselves and to develop strategies for political change was compromised and undercut. As Purvis asserted, 'The emphasis on difference at the expense of what women have in common denies the existence of women as a political category and as a subordinate class'[58] (Hoff *et al.*, Reading 10).

The related problematic of political and historical agency or, as Anna Clark put it, 'how to link the elegant postmodernist play with language to the grubby historical questions of power', proved a persistent focus of debate throughout the 1990s (Rose *et al.*, Reading 9). In a rather acrimonious exchange of book reviews between Joan Scott and Linda Gordon, the impact of their contrasting understandings of the term 'agency' was all too evident. Gordon interpreted historical agency in conventional terms as that of a self-directed, autonomous act of will, whereas Scott's description was that of a 'discursive effect' in which individual or collective agency was constituted through the particularities of a given situation and a specific conjuncture of power relations. For Gordon, describing agency as 'a discursive effect' was not only to effectively 'drain that notion of any meaning' but also to problematise any direct relation to the women's lives under scrutiny. Her additional observation that a 'language-as-primary position produced a subtle deflection away from issues of political power' struck a chord at the time with feminist historians on both sides of the Atlantic.[59] Even those sympathetic to poststructuralist insights saw the emphasis on textual and linguistic analysis as undermining of the role of feminist political agency because of its perceived disregard for social historical context. Doubts were also expressed over whether or not a mere shift in discursive identities would ever be sufficient to explain social and political change. Words may well have the 'power to define reality', argued Claudia Koonz, but poststructuralists did not 'explore the process by which they can change reality . . . and transform the position of real women'.[60]

Language and experience

This critique of the depoliticising impact of poststructuralism has remained a key issue. Thus Chicana feminist, Paula Moya, has recently contended that 'a politics of discourse that does not provide for some sort of bodily or concrete action outside the realm of the academic text will forever be inadequate to change the difficult "reality" of our lives'.[61] I would suggest, however, that such claims have rested precariously on the tendency of some feminist historians – and anti-poststructuralist historians more generally – to dichotomise the linguistic/discursive and pre-discursive/material dimensions of analysis, deploying language as somehow situated outside of the material realm. In her 1987 review of Scott's essay 'On Language, Gender and Working-Class History', Christine Stansell's assertion that the constituency of nineteenth-century political radicalism was formed 'in the realm of a social experience quite distinct from the realm of speech and text'[62] typifies this approach. Given that the very legitimation of feminist history of the past lay in the explicit appeal to women's experience, this polarisation was perhaps not surprising. Yet the notion of some self-evident base of 'reality' upon which a 'superstructure' of discursive articulations might freely float was always a fallacious one, not least because, confronted with the wealth of women's different 'realities' revealed in the debates of the 1980s, the appeal to historical experience or subjectivity as if it were 'uncontestable evidence' had already been exposed as obscuring a whole range of exclusionary practices.

It is worth clarifying at this point, therefore, Derrida's (in)famous phrase '*il n'y a pas de hors-texte*' (there is nothing outside of the text) and the frequently mistaken reading of this by those historians who have insisted on bifurcating language and materiality in such an uncompromising way. The intrinsic interrelatedness of 'text' and 'context' can be illustrated in two ways. First, by Derrida who, rather than denying the existence of material reality, insisted that 'what I call "text" implies all the structures called "real", "economic", "historical", socio-institutional, in short: all possible referents'.[63] And, second, by Scott's reminder that the seemingly unproblematic status of a material context also always necessitates the selection of key events or circumstances, 'and so constitutes a textual moment'[64] itself. Interpreting the poststructuralist position as an anti-realist one (that the 'self' or 'reality' does not physically exist outside language) has proved a persistent misreading by historians, generating a series of unnecessarily defensive and digressive confrontations. For no poststructuralists, as far as I am aware, are anti-realist. Rather, they are all anti-representationalists, that is to say that they do not think that there is any direct correspondence between the world and human representations of it that could be described as 'true'. This does not mean that feminist historians cannot reconstruct or re-present women's pasts, but that such re-presentations will always be incomplete and imperfect (Butler, Reading 12). In order to make sense of the history of women and feminism we must, as I suggested previously, impose a linguistic shape upon the past that the past itself doesn't have – we must 'trope' and 'emplot' it, to use Hayden White's celebrated verbs. It is not that women have no existence outside language, then, but that that existence has no 'determinable meaning'[65] outside language – a very different emphasis. Thus the meaning of 'discourse analysis' may be better comprehended, as Louise Newman has pointed out, as circumventing rather than consolidating the language/reality binary:

> Discourses compose practices as well as beliefs, are both material as well as ideological, and may take a whole range of cultural forms: social institutions, aesthetic productions, political systems, popular cultures, economic structures, ideological belief systems, and so forth.[66]

As a system of knowledge about sexual difference, gender, like class and race, is always established through discursive sites of power located in social institutions, organisations and structures. According to Scott, therefore, being a subject, even in poststructuralist terms, means being 'subject to definite conditions of existence' for '[h]istorical explanation cannot ... separate the two'.[67]

With this clarification, it now becomes possible to rethink previous feminist assertions of poststructuralism's politically paralysing effects. In their introduction to *Feminists Theorise the Political* (1992), Butler and Scott intimate that deconstructionist methods are rich with political possibilities, enabling scholars to reveal the contradictions and instabilities inherent in any dominant discourse, exposing hitherto hidden operations of power and illuminating how oppression has been both perpetuated and resisted.[68] For them the refusal to critically examine the category of 'woman' or enquire into the construction of female agency had sanctioned all manner of racial and class privileges (Butler, Reading 12). Hence black feminist historians such as bell hooks and Evelyn Brooks Higginbotham, in her germinal article 'African-American History and the Metalanguage of Race',[69] find much to recommend in the interrogation of 'difference' proposed by poststructuralists as opposed to traditional definitions of identity that have left 'race' and 'ethnicity' as unhistoricised and essentialised categories (hooks, Reading 11).

And so in these postfeminist, post-poststructuralist times, how might the impact of poststructuralism upon feminist history be evaluated? The work of historians such as Judith Walkowitz, Kathleen Canning, Lata Mani, Cecilia Morgan, Lyndal Roper and Antoinette Burton, as well as Scott herself, is illustrative of a growing body of feminist scholarship seeking to engage critically with poststructuralist ideas in areas as diverse as late-Victorian narratives of sexual danger, female workers in the German textile industry, the formation of the Canadian colonial middle classes, and witchcraft and sexuality in early modern Europe.[70] New feminist theories such as 'strategic essentialism' and 'postpositivist realism' have also emerged as attempts to strategise ways in which women might appeal to common political interests to mobilise themselves, albeit in ways understood as partial and provisional.[71]

There can be no doubt, I think, that poststructuralism has therefore left a revolutionary and as yet incomplete legacy for the writing and theorising of feminist history. We now live in what Laura Lee Downs has described as a more 'theoretically heterodox era'[72] from which there can be no return to the unreflexive use of key analytical categories or, as Susan Kingsley Kent remarks, to a nostalgic desire for a unified female subjectivity (Hoff *et al.*, Reading 10). A new generation of feminist histories concerned with exploring the relationship between the discursive production of gender identities and the material context in which such discourses were naturalised and resisted have rethought what Mary Louise Roberts describes as the 'smooth surfaces' and 'optimism' of the modernist story.[73] Disrupting linear narratives of women's progress and advance (as dear to feminist hearts as that of any historian) in favour of histories of contradiction and ambiguity may be unsettling, but to remain indifferent to the epistemological and ontological challenges raised by poststructuralism is, even now, to risk reproducing, unexamined, the most fundamental of historical categories. The exclusionary consequences of a non-critical, non-interrogative approach to the category 'woman' are all too well highlighted in Parts III and IV wherein the challenges posed by lesbian and black feminist historians are examined and discussed.

Part III: Searching for the subject: lesbian history

> The word 'lesbian' must be affirmed because to discard it is to collaborate with silence and lying about our very existence, the closet-game, the creation of the UNSPEAKABLE.
>
> Adrienne Rich, 'It Is the Lesbian in Us', 1977

Lesbian history developed during the early 1980s within a political context of the women's and gay liberation movements and an academic context of an emergent history of sexuality. It constituted another major theoretical shift in the historicising of women's lives through its critique of the heteronormativity of feminist history and the consequent erasure of the lesbian subject. Historians of lesbianism have, from the outset, articulated their research on same-sex sexuality within an explicit political agenda that aims not only to restore the lesbian subject to history, but also to expose the ingrained homophobia of dominant patriarchal discourses such as religion, medical science, the law and even feminism itself. Over twenty-five years ago, in her classic essay 'Compulsory Heterosexuality and Lesbian Existence', the American poet and writer Adrienne Rich argued that heterosexuality was a central organising principle of patriarchy that prevented women from experiencing 'primary intensity' with other women. Rich's influential concept of the 'lesbian continuum', which she re-articulated in 2003 as 'the sharing of a rich inner life, the bonding against male tyranny [and] . . . the giving and receiving of practical and political support'[74] between women, provided feminist historians with one important, although not uncontentious, impetus in the mapping of lesbian desire. Over the last three decades a significant body of work has been produced on the origins of lesbian identity, as well as on the historical reconstruction of various manifestations of love and sex between women. Making particular use of oral testimonies, biographical and literary approaches, a rich legacy of lesbian-like behaviour and cultures has been identified which includes cross-dressers, romantic friends, student–teacher 'crushes', passing women, butch/femme partners, transgender politics and a diverse range of women-only communities.[75]

As with feminist history more generally, early approaches to lesbian history combined radical political aims with primarily recuperative historical objectives, seeking to bring to visibility a hitherto hidden lesbian past. Not surprisingly, it was white middle- and upper-middle-class women (those most likely to have left documentary evidence of their passions) that provided the focus of such historical narratives.[76] Yet the 'outing' of prominent women couples such as Lady Eleanor Butler and Sarah Ponsonby, or Emily Dickinson and Sue Gilbert, has not been without difficulty. Few unequivocal accounts have been left by those who chose to live at the sexual margins. Those accounts that have survived have often been subject to forms of 'homophobic vandalism, effacement and suppression'[77] either by the families of the women concerned or their heterocentric biographers (Faderman, Reading 13). This effective sanitisation of lesbian existence is compounded by its overwhelming legal invisibility, unlike lesbian history's male counterpart, gay history. As Jennifer Terry has commented: 'Lesbians have not had much of a public sexuality . . . often [being] seen more as a threat to the family than a threat to the streets'.[78] Despite encouraging signs of an increasing range of lesbian archival material as evidenced in Alison Oram and Annmarie Turnbull's, *The Lesbian History Sourcebook: Love and Sex between Women in Britain from 1780 to 1970* (2001), the relative absence and ambiguity of historical sources has had a significant effect upon lesbian theorisings of identity formation. Beset by a sense of what Judith Bennett stipulates as 'definitional uncertainty', a powerful but problematic politics of identity has come to dominate much lesbian historical discourse. Rich's call to affirm the 'lesbian' in the quote at the beginning of this section, when the term itself has no clear or agreed referent, has proved a considerable epistemological challenge. As Martha Vicinus has commented: 'The lesbian is an accepted subject for scrutiny – she exists, but how are we to define her history, who do we include and when did it begin?' (Vicinus, Reading 15).

Does it matter if they did it? Lesbian identity politics and sex

A key controversy surrounding this search for a lesbian subject identity has focused on the significance, or otherwise, of sexual activity. As Sheila Jeffreys asked in 1986, 'does it matter if they did it?' (Jeffreys, Reading 14). In what is arguably the most influential analytical concept in lesbian history to date, that of 'romantic female friendships', the answer was a resounding 'no'. Combining ideas drawn from Rich's 'lesbian continuum' with Carroll Smith-Rosenberg's influential account for lesbian historians of the intimate, homosocial women's culture of nineteenth-century America (previously discussed in Part I), Lillian Faderman's pathbreaking book, *Surpassing the Love of Men: Romantic Friendships and Love Between Women from the Renaissance to the Present* (1981), presented what was to become a significant historical 'orthodoxy' in lesbian scholarship; namely, the existence of an innocent 'golden age' of passionate, non-genital female friendships brought to an abrupt end by the pathologising discourse of late-Victorian sexologists who first categorised lesbian behaviour as sexually 'deviant'. The impact of sexological readings upon the formation of a modern lesbian identity has ever since been energetically debated.[79] But it was Faderman's de-eroticised reading of lesbianism that sparked the greatest single reaction. Many felt that to desexualise lesbian history in the way she did was an unacceptable betrayal of women who experienced daily oppression as a result of their sexual and political choices. According to a founder of the New York Lesbian Herstory Archives, Joan Nestle, Rich's assertion that 'every woman is a lesbian' was nothing but 'rhetorical posturing that obfuscated the material realities of all women's lives'.[80] As Jeffreys similarly argued, lesbian experience could not be 'subsumed beneath the good feelings of hand-holding sisterhood' (Jeffreys, Reading 14). In the romantic friendship archetype, passion between women 'regardless of whether or not the women . . . engaged in genital sex', had been essentialised and, in so doing, feminist scholarship had erased the distinctiveness and plurality of lesbian identity.[81]

The consequent general shift towards an increasingly sexualised reading of lesbian culture that occurred throughout the 1980s and 1990s did so under two main theoretical approaches; butch/femme role-playing and literary historical representations of lesbian sexual desire. Reconstructions of butch/femme culture through oral testimonies and community-based projects featured predominantly in American scholarship, providing an important twentieth-century working-class counterpart to the leisured, romantic friendships of earlier periods. Elizabeth Lapovsky Kennedy and Madeleine Davis's frequently cited *Boots of Leather, Slippers of Gold: The History of a Lesbian Community* (1993), for example, examined butch/femme roles in the New York bar communities of the 1940s and 1950s which they defended as a positive and alternative way of acting out the category 'woman'. Butch/femme communities, they argued, were historically significant as visible subcultures facilitating safe public spaces for lesbians long before the advent of the gay and lesbian liberation movements.

In the literary historical approach, scholars challenged not so much the class limitations of the 'romantic friendship' model but the assumed sexual naivety of both the women concerned and their surrounding culture. The number of references to sapphism, tribadism or cross-dressing in British print as early as the 1730s was justification enough for Emma Donoghue to argue that eighteenth-century writers did indeed perceive women who loved women as 'a distinct sexual and social group'.[82] According to Lisa Moore, the social wariness and prohibition that often surrounded these relationships also suggested a cultural awareness of female sexual transgression not present in Faderman's original thesis of socially condoned nineteenth-century romantic friendships.[83] The recovery of women's self-conscious narratives of lesbian sexual desire, as in Karen Hansen's account of the intimate references to 'bosom sex' between Addie Brown and Rebecca Primus, two nineteenth-century African-American women, was also important for a more sexualised reading of lesbian history, providing new theoretical possibilities for claiming lesbianism as an originary identity rather than just a reactionary discourse against hegemonic medical-scientific constructions of lesbian 'deviancy'.[84] Anna Clark's important and lively discussion of the early-nineteenth century English landowner, Anne Lister, makes precisely this point. Lister's sexually explicit diary, she argues, offers powerful evidence of lesbian passion, albeit coded, well before the advent of male sexological categories. Keen to emphasise the role of women's agency in lesbian identity formation, Clark points out that Lister would have 'naturally' drawn upon the cultural representations available to her at the time but that she ultimately 'invented her own fragmented lesbian identity and confused the categories of masculinity and femininity'.[85] Although not numerous, the recovery of such sexually self-aware texts have, in some ways, compounded the theoretical complexities of lesbian history not least because of the 'minoritising effect'[86] of an approach in which 'confirmed' lesbians end up as a tiny proportion of women. The rarity of such self-defined narratives also raises questions concerning the extent to which historians privilege self-identification in their definition of lesbian identity for, as Vicinus has asked: 'What kind of ahistorical presumption is it to speak of "lesbians" before the formation of either communities or individuals who used this word?'[87]

Queer theory

One way out of the 'identity dilemma' that the above debates had become immersed in – not least because it aimed to dismantle the category of 'lesbian' altogether – was provided by 'queer theory', which developed strongly in the wake of post-structuralism during the 1980s and 1990s. Queer theory is distinguished by an oppositional stance towards heteronormative readings of sexuality and gender, a thoroughgoing scepticism towards traditional identity politics and a refusal of the marginal status of homosexuality (Vicinus, Reading 15). Thus the notion of butch/femme role-playing as an inferior imitation of heterosexuality is vehemently rejected by queer scholars. In Judith Butler's celebrated formulation, hetero-sexuality, like all gender, is performative, and so merely produces the effect of being naturalised by establishing itself 'as the sign and the ground of all imitations'.[88] While cognisant of the political expediency of realist identity categories, queer theorists such as Butler, Lisa Duggan and Donna Penn, argue that all forms of sexual essentialism ghettoise theoretical horizons and replicate oppressive prac-tices[89] (Penn, Reading 16). As noted in Part II, fixed identity categories are seen as 'instruments of regulatory regimes' for Butler who prefers to leave what lives under the sign of 'lesbian' as 'permanently unclear'. 'What, if anything can lesbians be said to share?', she asks, '[a]nd who will decide this question, and in the name of whom?'[90] In this position 'definitional uncertainty' is not a concern; rather it is welcomed as a radical, open-ended theoretical device that avoids the pitfalls of reifying any sexual category as normative.

Instead of searching for the self-evident lesbian subject, therefore, queer theorists have focused upon the dynamic historical formation of lesbian and gay subjectivities through discourses of resistance and acts of transgression. Instead of reading for identity, queer theory challenges the heteronormativity of feminist histo-riography by reading for 'difference' in search of what Jennifer Terry refers to as 'deviant subjectivity'. Lesbian history cannot hope to free itself of the influence of discriminatory heterocentric discourses that, she argues, have relied parasitically upon lesbians and gays to establish their own authority.[91] Nevertheless, it is possible to queer the history of heterosexual hegemony by first 'reading against the grain' in order to establish the ways in which homosexuality has been produced as deviant and, second, by mapping the diverse methods of resistance to, and subversion of, such homophobia. Yet, despite Donna Penn's contention in 1995 that queer theory 'might provide the space in which to begin retheorising categories of inclusion and exclusion that guide our historical work', the tangible impact of queer theory over the past ten years in furthering lesbian historical work, as opposed to stimulating debates on theory and epistemology, has been a limited one[92] (Penn, Reading 16). Martha Vicinus acknowledges, for example, that queer theory has produced some 'immensely freeing notion[s] for historians', particularly its dismantling of the need to seek out a coherent identity, but that its emphasis upon the performative nature of gender has all too often proved unhelpfully ahistorical (Vicinus, Reading 15).

Queer theory has not passed unchallenged by feminist historians, therefore, not only because of its poststructuralist, presentist methods, but also because of its inclusion of gay as well as lesbian subjectivities. Male homosexuality is all too closely allied with patriarchy for Rosemary Auchmuty, Sheila Jeffreys and Elaine Miller who have warned of the need to remain vigilant about the possibility of gay sexism and the retention of an overtly feminist perspective on lesbian experience.[93] According to this approach the profound disparities in historical experience between lesbians and gays suggests that lesbian history needs to maintain its own distinct theoretical priorities. Yet, others have argued that there are limits to such a separatist agenda. Queer theorist Lisa Duggan, for example, deplores the generally 'strained relations' between queer theory and lesbian history that has produced 'devastating consequences' for the intellectual vitality of both discourses.[94]

Lesbians and 'difference'

From a quite different perspective black lesbian writers such as Barbara Smith have also argued that lesbian and gay history should be read and written as part of an integrated history of gender in which it is impossible to understand the experience of one group without the other: 'My own experience as a Black lesbian during the past two decades', she writes, 'indicates that Black lesbians and men are linked by our shared racial identity and political status in ways that white lesbians and gays are not'.[95] Smith was, of course, a founder member of the Combahee River Collective whose 'Black Feminist Statement' of 1979 was a pioneering manifesto for black lesbian politics. Unlike most single-identity groups organising around either gender *or* race, the Combahee River Collective acknowledged the need for a multiple analysis of oppression: 'Although we are feminists and lesbians, we feel solidarity with progressive Black men and do not advocate the fractionalization that white women who are separatists demand'.[96]

In addition to challenging white lesbians' prioritisation of sexuality over other identity categories (a theme to which I will return in Part IV), lesbians of colour have also written at length on the privileged status accorded to traditional family life within black communities as a supreme badge of respectability and upward mobility. As Makeda Silvera observes in her poignant reflections upon the invisibility of African-Caribbean lesbians, dominant racist representations of the hypersexuality of black women have led to a heightened suspicion of any form of sexual 'deviancy'. For many black heterosexual women, she argues, 'it is unconceivable, almost frightening that one could turn her back on credibility in our community

... by being lesbians'.[97] Such emphatic heteronormativity is also highlighted by Judy Tzu-Chun Wu in a recent 2003 discussion of Asian-American history. Tzu-Chun Wu explains the ways in which American immigration and anti-miscegenation laws obstructed the formation of Asian-American family life in the nineteenth and twentieth centuries. The subsequent enshrinement of heterosexual norms, she concludes, has made the public articulation of homosexuality particularly difficult for both Asian-American women and men.[98]

Scholarship such as this is a salutary reminder of the need for historians to consider the ways in which lesbian sexuality invariably intersects with other 'lived' and organising categories such as race, ethnicity and class. As noted, much lesbian history to date, certainly in Britain and Europe, has focused primarily on middle-class and elite literate women. Recently, however, there have been promising indications of an increasingly global focus on lesbian lives that builds upon the above-described debates to generate important questions as to how to theorise lesbian-like behaviour in historically specific and culturally diverse contexts such as Bolshevik Russia, modern China, medieval Italy and Australian Aboriginal society[99] (Rupp, Reading 18). This emergent work bodes well for an illumination of how dominant discourses of nationalism, race, ethnicity and colonialism have shaped expressions of lesbian experience and identity. For such work acknowledges that in many circumstances lesbians may not define themselves primarily by their sexuality at all. As Ruth Ford has argued with reference to Australian lesbian culture, 'Koori lesbians are more likely to identify themselves as Aboriginal survivors of a racist colonial society, defining themselves primarily as Koori or black rather than as lesbians'.[100]

Future perspectives in lesbian history

How do we thus assess the influence of lesbian theory on the wider realm of women's and feminist history; what differences has it made? In practical terms, Alison Oram has contended that, in British universities at least, lesbian studies continue to be less problematic in disciplines such as literary criticism, cultural studies and women's studies than in history, where it has gained only 'an insub-stantial foothold'.[101] In a similar vein, Adrienne Rich wrote in 2003 that a feminist critique of compulsory heterosexual orientation for women was still 'long over-due'.[102] But it would be wrong to conclude from these statements that hetero-normativity continues apace in feminist scholarship. Even this briefest of summaries demonstrates the significance of the lesbian challenge to feminist history and the complexity of theoretical reflection evinced by historians of lesbianism as they protest against the historical effacement of women who loved other women. More-over, it is clear that newer theoretical frameworks are emerging at some speed, driven by the desire to avoid the erasure of certain groups of lesbians through race, class, age and political differences, as well as the desire to further integrate lesbian history within the larger history of feminism, gender and sexuality. In the last few years an increased dissatisfaction with the identity model of lesbian history based on a language of self-identification – 'coming out' stories or distinctive lesbian markers and performances – has been evident. As Vicinus remarks in her *Intimate*

Friends: Women Who Loved Other Women, 1778–1928 (2004), 'identity history can be limiting; more interesting and difficult questions can be asked about friendship, intimacy, sexuality and spirituality than who had what kind of identity when'.[103] Despite the mixed reception that queer theory has had by historians of lesbianism, therefore, it is still possible to see the impact of poststructuralist thought in the recognition of the instability of all identity formations. As Cheshire Calhoun has argued:

> We cannot . . . get at lesbian difference by asking 'who is a lesbian?'
> Nor should we, since the . . . question invites a set of troubling assump-
> tions: that identity is an internal essence, that one is definitively and
> permanently either a lesbian or not a lesbian, and that real lesbians can
> never be correctly read for traces of heterosexuality . . . but perhaps we
> can get at lesbian difference . . . by instead asking 'who represents the
> lesbian?'[104]

Historical 'lesbian-spotting' and the privileging of the visible has thus steadily given way to more open-ended and fluid understandings of female sexual subjectivity alongside various radical deconstructions of the hetero–homo binary. Such approaches have invariably prioritised a study of behaviour over identity, as in Judith Bennett's preference for the term 'lesbian-like', in an attempt to recognise the variety of challenges posed by women of the past to the dominant gender system (Bennett, Reading 17). Lesbian sexuality can be 'both a part of and apart from normative heterosexual marriage and child-bearing', Vicinus reminds us, and historians need to find ways to theorise the experiences of women such as Mary Benson, the Archbishop of Canterbury's wife, whose lifestyles blurred the boundaries between heterosexuality and homosexuality[105] (Vicinus, Reading 15). It would appear that western dualistic notions of sexuality can all too often be a hindrance in analysing homoerotic practices in the past, not least through the privileging of the sexual over other complex identity factors. As Leila Rupp pertinently observes in her recent historical work on global aspects of 'same-sex sexuality', it is clear that in many such relations the evidence of genital similarity has been less determinative than factors such as differences in age or status. Without some way of theorising same-sex sexual practices that pays due regard to the indigenous cultural, spiritual and historical specificities within which they take place, asserts Rupp, we run the risk of over-simplifying and misreading their full significance (Rupp, Reading 18).

In their restoration of lesbians to history and history to lesbians – to paraphrase Joan Kelly-Gadol – scholars of lesbian-like behaviour have confronted women's, feminist and gender history with some significant epistemological dilemmas surrounding the formation of historical identities, the ambivalence of historical evidence, and authorial intention. Perhaps the most provocative challenge posed by this scholarship, however, is the exhortation to historians to deconstruct the hidden meanings of historical silences and omissions or, as Vicinus puts it, the 'unsaid' and the 'unseen' that characterises so much of lesbian history (Vicinus, Reading 15). The imaginative historicisation of the unspoken, or the 'creation of the unspeakable' – as Adrienne Rich describes it at the beginning of this discussion – is an epistemological challenge of considerable magnitude and one which, when attended to and fully envisioned, could and should locate lesbian history at the cutting edge of feminist historical theory.

Part IV: Centres of difference: decolonising subjects, rethinking boundaries

> Clearly, if you are poor, black and female you get it in three ways.
> Gayatri Spivak, 'Can the Subaltern Speak?', 1988

> The oppression of women knows no ethnic nor racial boundaries
> ... but that does not mean it is identical within those differences
> ... for then beyond sisterhood is still racism.
> Audre Lorde, 'Open Letter to Mary Daly', 1979

The concept of 'difference' has proved axiomatic for feminist historians as a means of interrogating essentialised readings of key categories such as 'women' or 'sisterhood' in favour of an increasingly complex and often contradictory plurality of feminist identities. Theorising differences between women as opposed to those between women and men has proved a protracted challenge. Although, as we have seen, feminist historians have not disregarded differences of race, class and sexuality among women, it has been primarily black and Third World feminist scholarship that has prioritised the theoretical ramifications of women's heterogeneity. Over the past three decades a burgeoning literature has laid bare the ethnocentric and imperialist proclivities of feminist history as well as the inadequacy of western epistemological frameworks generally as the basis for comprehending the historical and cultural locations of non-white or non-western subjects. In Part IV I consider the theoretical implications of racial and ethnic difference in the reconstruction of the category 'woman', illustrating how these debates have altered, arguably with more impact than any other, the theoretical trajectory of feminist history.

First though, a note on terminology. The terms 'black', 'women of colour' and 'Third World' used throughout this discussion remain contested ones. This is not least because, ironically, they appear to erase differences between women by homogenising vastly diverse cultural and historical experiences. As Ella Shohat has argued, the very notion of the 'three worlds' 'flattens heterogeneities, masks contradictions and elides difference'.[106] Cognisant of these conceptual limitations, black and Third World feminist scholars have nevertheless asserted that it *is* possible to argue for the intellectual coherence of such terms, not in any essentialist sense on the basis of racial or colour identifications, but as political categories forged out of what Chandra Talpade Mohanty has described as 'a common context of struggle'[107] against western colonial exploitation and racism. It is therefore in this latter sense that the terms are deployed here. Because of the sheer range and volume of work that has been produced in this area of feminist history I have structured the following discussion of 'centres of difference' (and the selected readings) around three broad sites of analysis: the black feminist challenge that was located mainly in the US and Britain, postcolonial feminist scholarship and, finally, transnational and comparative approaches to feminist history. Before turning to each of these examples, however, it is worth outlining one or two of the principal aspects of the epistemological challenge posed by 'difference' to feminist history.

Black and Third World feminist historians have sought primarily to impugn the theoretical colonisation and narrowness of the western feminist vision of women's emancipation. They have argued that the sometime dominant feminist focus on patriarchy and gender alone is inadequate for theorising the complexities of black women's simultaneity of oppressions in which gender may form just one aspect of a wider, multiple experience of inequity. As Africanist Cheryl Johnson-Odim has observed, 'gender discrimination is neither the sole nor perhaps the primary locus of the oppression of Third World women for these women's struggles are inextricably linked to those of their particular communities against racism and imperialism'.[108] The dislodging of gender as the fundamental cause of women's oppression has been radical indeed, rendering the term 'feminism' a problematic one for those who wish to signal a theoretical and political disjuncture with white feminist analyses. Some African-American women writers prefer to use Alice Walker's term 'womanist', for example, the definition of which underlines commitment not just to women but to the 'survival and wholeness of entire people, male *and* female'.[109] A more integrated vision of feminism as just one component of a more universal engagement with systemic forms of injustice is a theme that surfaces repeatedly throughout black and Third World scholarship. A second recurrent theme is the need to challenge the overwhelming theoretical imperialism exercised by western feminist historians that has frequently hindered the development of alternative, context-specific narrative strategies and methods. As Mahua Sarkar argued in 2004, although a seemingly transparent term, 'feminism' has figured in Third World women's histories 'as the epistemic ground that defines, indeed monopolises, the very terms within which we are obliged to pose questions of women's agency in *any* context'.[110] It is also worth noting that theoretical imperialism can also operate between western feminists as Ruth Roach Pierson makes clear in her article, 'Colonisation and Canadian Women's History', which describes how Canada, despite its own position as a coloniser of the First Nations' peoples, also occupies a colonised status in relation to its powerful American neighbours.[111]

How, then, does feminist history set about 'decolonising' or 'de-imperialising' its theory so as to find new ways of historicising indigenous women's pasts without reproducing other forms of exclusionary practices? This is the challenge at the heart of locating 'difference' as a central epistemological principle for feminist history, a challenge that requires both the reconstruction of black and Third World feminist histories and the simultaneous deconstruction of the hegemonic status of 'whiteness'. 'Race', like gender, is a primary system of meaning through which western thought (not least) has established hierarchical social classifications on a putative basis of biology and skin colour. As Pamela Scully remarks, as long as 'race' is perceived as synonymous with blackness, whiteness retains its 'naturalized, normative and unproblematic'[112] status and the potential for ethnocentric and imperialist discourse continues. Elizabeth Spelman's pioneering book, *Inessential*

Woman: Problems of Exclusion in Feminist Thought (1988), was a powerful salvo against the 'privileging-preserving posture' of liberal feminism vis-à-vis black women and an influential critique of the unexamined assumption of whiteness as normative. Spelman argued that one cannot separate out the various 'components' of human identity and arrogate to one – in feminism's case that of gender – an essentialised, pre-eminent status, for this relegates race and class as subsidiary components, rather than recognising that gender is itself constituted through these very categories (Spelman, Reading 19).

African-American feminist history

Debates over racial difference were first played out in the US and Britain from the 1970s onwards, catalysed by the emergence of the American civil rights movement. Scholars such as Hazel Carby, bell hooks, Valerie Amos and Pratibha Parmar were quick to point out that in privileging a white, middle-class norm of women's experience, feminist historians had failed 'to reach beyond the first patriarchal lesson', replicating the same exclusionary practices of traditional history that they had vowed to dismantle (Amos and Parmar, Reading 20). By universalising what was, in fact, a highly particularised construction of women's historical experiences, white feminists obscured the historical and cultural specificity of black women's pasts. As Evelyn Brooks Higginbotham reflected in 1989, the ethnocentrism of feminist history combined with the androcentrism of African-American history meant that the black woman's voice went 'largely unheard'.[113] Early attempts to recover black women's pasts frequently served to reinforce their 'otherness' or objectification by presenting them as superlative examples of heroic suffering or tantalising exoticism. As the black lesbian poet and writer Audre Lorde makes clear in her 'Open Letter to Mary Daly', this approach could lead to a fundamental distortion of black women's words and heritage while ensuring that dominant white theoretical frameworks remained unaffected (Lorde, Reading 21).

Throughout the 1980s and 1990s African-American women scholars exposed the longstanding racism of the women's movement in a series of penetrating critiques, arguing that the 'double jeopardy' of black women's identity – the simultaneity of being both black and female – had never proved a priority for first or second wave feminism.[114] As a result, mainstream feminist analyses of oppression and strategies for change were of limited value to women of colour. We have already seen in Part III, for example, that black feminists did not ally themselves with the separatist rhetoric of radical and/or lesbian feminism because of the primacy they accorded to racial solidarity with black men. Similarly, dominant analyses of key issues such as rape or contraception have also been met with greater circumspection by black women. Recalling the lynching campaigns against black men and the subjection of black and Third World women to experimental forms of population control, women of colour have identified the racist as well as misogynist connotations of such issues.[115] As a final example, women's right to a professional career outside the 'drudgery' and 'incarceration' of domestic life, arguably the defining strategy of second wave feminism, was clearly aimed at a white, educated audience and, as such, was extraneous to the circumstances of many black women for whom family life had been a key historical site of emotional strength and survival during slavery. As leading black feminist theorists bell hooks and Patricia Hill Collins observed, it was doubly ironic that the liberation of one group of women should so often be achieved upon the domestic labours of their black and working-class counterparts.[116]

Because of the inappropriateness of many Anglo-American feminist strategies surrounding male/female relations, family life, sisterhood and sexuality, black feminist historians have reconceptualised some of the most basic categories and assumptions of feminist history. In so doing they have put into place what Darlene Clark Hine has referred to as 'a quiet intellectual transformation'.[117] Studies have emerged on black women's experience of slavery, religion and family life, labour participation and a host of philanthropic associations. More recently, studies of gender have explored the construction of black manhood and masculinity.[118] We now know that black women such as Maria Stewart, Sojourner Truth, Harriet Tubman and Ida B. Wells played vital political roles as orators and activists redefining hegemonic constructions of womanhood. We know from Rosalyn Terborg-Penn's recent work that nineteenth-century black women suffragists were supporters of a universal as opposed to a women-only franchise throughout, while Hine has shown how pervasive historical representations of black female 'hypersexuality' produced a powerful 'culture of dissemblance' on the part of black women reformers who embraced middle-class values of moral respectability in order to erase demeaning stereotypes of their humanity.[119] Theorising difference primarily through the concept of racial solidarity has thus generated an exciting new field of feminist historical scholarship, although as Michele Mitchell's recent overview of African-American historiography makes clear, black solidarity has prevented as well as promoted theoretical innovation: 'writing about clashes between black women and men remains somewhat prickly', she remarks, 'because themes of collective survival, community mobilisation and institution building are of signal importance to the field'.[120] Critical analyses of intra-racial tensions, domestic violence and black male sexism have therefore been less well explored, although studies such as E. Frances White's examination of the highly conservative and oppressive attitudes towards gender and sexuality promoted by African-American nationalist discourses indicate a willingness to undertake such controversial themes.[121]

Women of colour have revolutionised previous assumptions not only of the historical agency of black women and men but also of the way in which gender formation rarely pivots around a simple oppositional binary of male and female. The notion that a woman's identity formation takes place not just in contrast to that of men's but over and against women of other racial and class-based statuses, has transformed feminist historical thinking on 'difference' and led to a series of innovative theoretical reflections on the potential for more relational analyses of gender. Two examples of this will suffice to conclude this section. Elsa Barkley Brown's frequently quoted proposal of the African-American practice of 'gumbo ya ya' (everyone talking at once) as a radically new way for feminists to write history, underlines the need for a relational analysis of racial difference. 'Gumbo ya ya' as a method has much to offer feminist history argues Brown, for it eschews western linear, historical narratives in favour of more realist asymmetrical and multiple stories in simultaneous dialogue (Brown, Reading 22). In 1992 Hine suggested similarly that feminists disassemble the boundaries between black and white women's lives and undertake 'crossover history'. In defence of why black women should abandon the historical recuperation of their foremothers in favour of yet more research on white women, she contended that only by examining each other's history would women 'register meaningful progress in the war against racism, sexism and class oppression'. 'In any event' she added, 'the time for cussing is past, now let's get busy'.[122]

Postcolonialism and feminist history

Feminist considerations of 'difference' also took place between British, European, Indian, African and Caribbean scholars with regard to the historical legacy of imperialism. These exchanges formed part of the wider intellectual movement of postcolonial studies during the 1980s and 1990s where new emphases upon the cultural as opposed to diplomatic and military dimensions of empire-building provided an opportunity for feminists to signal the value of gender to such analyses. In marked contrast to the predominantly experiential readings of difference utilised in African-American women's debates on race, postcolonial feminist analyses have been influenced more by poststructuralism, particularly the work of Edward Said and Michel Foucault.[123] Here, as Himani Bannerji remarks, difference is read as a discursive act of colonial power, understood 'not as what people intrinsically are, but what they are ascribed in the context of domination'.[124]

Throughout this discussion I use the term 'postcolonialism' in the sense of a continuous disengagement from colonialism, indicating an ongoing historical dynamic as opposed to the more literal (and inaccurate) sense of the term as the period 'after colonialism'.[125] As will become evident, the legacy of neo-colonialism lives on for many communities, lending the construction of 'new imperial histories' a particular urgency and acuity. As Clare Midgley identifies in a valuable overview of the field, feminist historians have been productive participants in the debates surrounding gender and imperialism. Initially, recuperative research on colonial wives, female missionaries, nurses, travellers and educators successfully challenged the notion that the empire was an essentially male enterprise, providing an important corrective to the gender myopia of early Subaltern Studies and of Orientalism.[126] As radical as this work genuinely was, however, concern was soon expressed at the continued Anglocentrism of both the subject matter and the theoretical approaches in these accounts. Jane Haggis, among others, observed that the bulk of this scholarship tended to overlook the substantial racial privileges enjoyed by British and European women in the colonies as well as perpetuating the historical invisibility of indigenous women.[127] Further accounts highlighted in more nuanced ways women's intellectual and political enmeshment with the civilising aims and mission of empire. As a result, western feminism's complicity with dominant imperial values became a new critical orthodoxy for postcolonialist feminist scholars. A flagship text in this regard, Antoinette Burton's Burdens of History: British Feminists, Indian Women and Imperial Culture (1994), argued that nineteenth-century British feminists colluded with imperial power by appropriating a racialised discourse that constructed

Indian and 'Oriental' women more generally as objects of oppression and pity in need of rescue by their white 'sisters'. In 1992 Kumari Jayawardena, Nupur Chaudhuri and Margaret Strobel had also concluded that western feminist attitudes encompassed a far more 'complex dynamic of complicity and resistance'[128] to imperialist values. These included both the veneration of Indian culture, an important strand of Orientalism that was perfectly compatible with colonial rule and, conversely, support for Indian national liberation.[129]

As Burton reflected in 2003, however, the original intention of Amos and Parmar's essay, 'Challenging Imperial Feminism' (1984), was not to generate the desired 'politically accountable historiography of Euro-American women's movements, but rather to make space for histories of black women, women of colour and . . . anti-colonial and nationalist women'.[130] Accordingly, the last twenty years have seen the emergence of a prodigious body of work by black and Third World scholars seeking to decolonise western feminist theory and prioritise difference. As with historians of lesbian culture, the politics of the archive and the paucity of available documentary sources have posed particular difficulties for the reconstruction of Third World women's histories. One creative response to this has been to radically redefine conventional understandings of what counts as historical evidence. Thus, innovative use has been made of oral testimonies, indigenous folk cultures, clothing, jewellery and tattoos in African women's history, while domestic architecture has been drawn upon in a recent examination of women's lives in twentieth-century colonial India.[131]

A related response by postcolonialist feminists, such as Antoinette Burton's innovative study *Dwelling in the Archive: Women Writing House, Home and History in Late Colonial India* (2003), has been to augment feminist historians' intrinsic suspicion of the powerful, patriarchal 'archive logic' that naturalises and renders 'official' highly random, fragmented traces of historical experience. 'Feminist historiography cannot be just additive', contends Janaki Nair, 'for if . . . already hampered by the nature of the archive, which disproportionately reflects the interests and concerns of the dominant classes, then the search for fresh 'evidence' could obscure the need for a critique of the techniques . . . by which patriarchies remain resilient'.[132] For feminist scholars such as Gayatri Spivak, the discriminatory colonial nature of the official archive is so acute that the recovery of the indigenous female subject's voice will always be eluded. Spivak's acclaimed essay, 'Can the Subaltern Speak?' (1988), has become an influential counterpoint to Euro-American feminist theories of agency and representation due to its (in)famous assertion that the subaltern woman cannot speak, or, more accurately, that her speech cannot be heard. Caught in the nineteenth-century contest between British colonial and Indian elite discourses on the prohibition of *sati* (Hindu widow sacrifice), the subject-position of the subaltern woman simply disappeared. Even the most empathetic western theorising will not restore her voice argues Spivak, for such constructions can never escape an 'imperialist subject-constitution, mingling epistemic violence with the advancement of learning and civilisation. And the subaltern woman will be as mute as ever'.[133] This is not to say (as some have done) that Spivak denies the lived existence or historical agency of the subaltern female. Rather, she contends that the historical and social conditions of representation at the time allowed her no place from which to speak. Thus, as Gyan Prakash notes, for Spivak the silence of the subaltern woman 'marks the limit of historical knowledge'.[134]

For historians such as Ania Loomba and Lata Mani, Spivak's silenced subaltern is unnecessarily pessimistic as well as being uncomfortably evocative of nineteenth-century colonialist discourse (Loomba, Reading 23). Mani's study, *Contentious Traditions: The Debate on Sati in Colonial India* (1998), attempts to restore the victims of *sati* to the narrative centre arguing that, while rarely the subject of primary concern, the suffering widow was still the site of conflicting struggles over the nature of Indian society and tradition in ways that 'unsettle the image of her as passive, willing or silent'.[135] As with the queering of feminist history discussed in Part III, Mani's reading strategy is one which seeks to foreground the historical and political conditions of discursive production:

> The issue ... may not be whether the subaltern can speak so much as whether she can be heard to be speaking in a given set of materials and what, indeed, has been made of her voice by colonial and postcolonial historiography. Rephrasing Spivak thus enables us to remain vigilant about the positioning of women in colonial discourse without conceding to colonial discourses what it did not, in fact, achieve – the erasure of women.[136]

Debates over whether or not, given the nature of the historical archive, it is possible to rehabilitate the voice of the subaltern female at all have raised important issues concerning the nature of historical representation and the colonising influence of western epistemological frameworks. Nevertheless, feminist narratives of indigenous communities' strategies for survival in an anticolonialist context have continued apace. Recent histories of colonised women and men such as Ruth Roach Pierson's and Nupur Chaudhuri's important collection, *Nation, Empire and Colony: Historicizing Gender and Race* (1998), have queried the analytical dominance of the coloniser/colonised binary, shifting from a single focus upon the impact of imperialism to greater awareness of the coterminous influences of regional conflicts or nationalist agendas upon the lives of indigenous women. As Ann Stoler and Frederick Cooper pointed out in 1997, scholars should not be writing as if 'the culture of the imperial power still sets the standard against which diverse national cultures must measure themselves'.[137] The ways in which feminists have begun to think beyond the bifurcated coloniser/colonised paradigm so as to further decolonise theory can be illustrated through two main approaches which will be examined briefly here; first, new research agendas that decentre imperialism in favour of analysing the gendered politics of national identity formations and second, feminist histories that have argued for the reciprocal shaping influences of metropole and colony.

As Mrinalini Sinha's comprehensive historiographical summary makes clear, histories of gender and national identity, although not exclusive to black and Third World scholarship, have reinforced the analytical significance of difference by asserting that 'gender is always already constituted by other forms of difference, such as those of class, race, ethnicity, religion and sexuality as well as of course, the nation' (Sinha, Reading 24). This scholarship provides powerful global evidence of the diverse and conflicting forms that a fully historicised, fully decolonised reading of feminism can take. Contrary to western feminism's tendency to present itself as somehow transcending national boundaries, Third World scholars have shown that 'nowhere has feminism ever been autonomous of the national context from which it emerged' (Sinha, Reading 24). Not surprisingly the historical relationship between feminism and nationalism belies any unitary analysis, although certain patterns do emerge such as that of the tension between the ubiquitous female iconography in nationalist discourse and women's thwarted claims for the right to full citizenship.[138] Historically, nationalist movements have made extensive use of gendered imagery in which women — their behaviour, dress-codes and, quite literally, their bodies — become eulogised as bearers of authentic, national or pre-colonial tradition, as in the previously mentioned contestations over *sati* or in Muslim debates over the *hijab*.[139] Yet, all too often nationalist discourses have castigated feminism as antithetical to national independence. As Hilary McD. Beckles has observed, in the masculinist Caribbean construction of the nation, 'radical feminists were prominent occupants of a discredited community that included Rastafarians, religious fundamentalists, communists, black power chanters and other advocates of allegedly "untenable" causes'.[140] Feminist historians have also shown that where women are involved in militant nationalist activity the ambiguities of gender norms will always dictate cultural and historical responses. Thus, women have mobilised themselves very successfully in various national political contexts around traditional female symbolism such as motherhood, as in the Argentinian Madres de la Plaza de Mayo or the Sri Lankan Mothers' Front.[141] According to Louise Ryan's work on women's involvement in the Irish militant nationalist campaigns between 1919 and 1923, however, the violent, transgressive female insurgent poses far greater contradictions to heroic accounts of national independence. As women's continued exclusion from Irish republican histories indicates, these narratives remain quintessentially male.[142]

Postcolonial and feminist scholarship on gender and national identity has long recognised that nations are neither fixed nor originary points of historical identity but 'imagined communities' whose traditions are reciprocally created and performed.[143] In a similar vein, Cooper and Stoler have argued that the single most determining 'tension of empire' was the mutually shaping influence of metropole and colony through which 'a grammar of difference was continually and vigilantly crafted as people in colonies refashioned and contested European claims to superiority'.[144] The influence of indigenous cultures upon the development of imperial policies in London, Paris or The Hague meant that each site, metropole and colony, was affected by the other in radically constitutive though not equal ways.[145] Thus the metropolitan, imperial sense of self-identity was rarely as secure as its public façade appeared to suggest. Instead, as Anne McClintock and Ann Stoler have variously argued, the racial and sexual values of the European bourgeois order were repeatedly constructed over and against the working classes at home as well as the colonised subjects of British India, French Indochina and the Dutch East Indies.[146]

Feminist historians such as Burton, Midgley, Susan Thorne and others, have thus rethought the relational narratives of metropole and colony in important ways exploring the impact of empire 'at home'. British feminist scholarship, for example, has examined the presence of Asian and black communities in the metropole as well as the impact of imperialism upon the formation of English/British identity, not least the origins of the nineteenth-century women's movement.[147] Here the work of Mrinalini Sinha and Catherine Hall has also been influential in tracing the simultaneity of colonial and indigenous formations of masculinity as indicative of the wider exercise of power relations between the coloniser and the colonised. Sinha's important work, *Colonial Masculinity: The 'Manly Englishman' and the 'Effeminate Bengali' in the Late Nineteenth Century* (1995), illustrates the perpetual negotiations between colonial and national elite discourses of gender. Hall's longstanding examination of the interconnected histories of Jamaica and England has similarly revealed how colonial encounters shaped imperial readings of masculinity and, most recently in her *Civilising Subjects: Metropole and Colony in the English Imagination, 1830–1867* (2002), she develops her influential thesis that English identity and 'whiteness' were thoroughly imbricated with the culture of empire.[148] Indeed, although a major moral imperative in the imperialists' civilising mission, whiteness was a peculiarly volatile category (Hall, Reading 25). As Marilyn Lake has argued in the case of Australian women, settler societies 'attached special significance to the status and meaning of "whiteness"'[149] because of their dual identity as both colonisers and, alongwith other indigenous peoples, colonised. Racial mixing, the most intimate manifestation of the inter-relatedness of metropole and colony, was the greatest challenge of all to whiteness and, as the pioneering critical work of Catherine Hall and others in this field have shown, a profound threat to the maintenance of imperial authority[150] (Hall, Reading 25).

Transnational, comparative and global feminist histories

So far in this emplotment of black and postcolonial feminist history-writing, we have seen the predominance of narratives structured around the binaries of white/other and coloniser/colonised in order to challenge the racially privileged epistemology of western feminist theory and foster alternative readings of women, feminism and history. Most recently, however, analyses of 'centres of difference' have been prompted by the renewed desire to build transnational alliances and solidarities between women across national borders and boundaries. The rapid global expansion of technology and communication systems, major demographic shifts due to economic migrations or political diasporas, the collapse of the socialist experiment in Eastern Europe, Central Asia and the Soviet Union, and the rise of multinational forms of capitalism, have altered our political and intellectual landscape dramatically. Such developments pose a number of urgent theoretical and methodological challenges for feminists at the beginning of the twenty-first century, demanding new formulations around global perspectives in women's history that capture the radically assymetrical power relations between nations.

Feminists already have a sound history of organising internationally around issues such as socialism, sexuality, citizenship rights, health and pacifism.[151] Sanjam

Ahluwalia's study of the transnational dimensions of the late nineteenth- and early twentieth-century birth control movement, for example, is a good illustration of the extent to which social reform movements have frequently brought together local, national and international forms of knowledge and activism (Ahluwalia and Burton, Reading 26). The developing field of African diaspora studies also indicates great promise for comparative global feminist analyses where in 1995 Rosalyn Terborg-Penn proposed the rudiments of a cross-cultural African feminist theoretical approach that might encompass the experiences of people of African descent throughout the Caribbean, Brazil, the US and Africa itself.[152] The ability to undertake such analytical 'border crossings' can just as easily occur between women within a single continent, of course, for as Asuncion Lavrin reminds us, twentieth-century Latin American feminism has demonstrated a 'strong vocation for internationalism'[153] as a means to confronting political regimes of immense diversity. According to Ahluwalia, the shift towards more interconnected global histories is a significant theoretical development allowing Third World scholars to interrogate western feminist political strategies and propose fully historicised, context-specific alternatives (Ahluwalia and Burton, Reading 26). Yet it is a theoretical approach fraught with difficulty. Transnational feminist histories require innovative comparative scholarship that neither diminishes 'difference' in the name of a falsely universalised feminism nor reifies it by taking refuge in relativist platitudes. In her response to Ahluwalia, Antoinette Burton agrees that the nation can often be an 'insufficient investigative category', not least because national boundaries are often 'a lingering effect of imperial power'. She is equally concerned, however, that in the rush to be fully transnational new forms of discursive colonisation wait just around the corner (Ahluwalia and Burton, Reading 26). How, then, to rethink a feminist history of 'solidarity across borders' that is firmly grounded in the local and particular experiences of women? This is the central theoretical challenge for a transnational feminist practice.

Chandra Talpade Mohanty's recent revisiting of her classic article 'Under Western Eyes' almost twenty years after it was first published, provides a salient case study of the shift in emphasis from, as the title of her book suggests, decolonising theory to practising solidarity (Mohanty, Reading 28). The discursive colonisation of Third World women still continues she explains but, confronted with the dominance of global capitalism and the normalisation of its increasingly oppressive values, it is time to move on from critique to reconstruction. What Mohanty refers to as the 'feminist solidarity' or 'comparative feminist studies' model provides a useful agenda for future feminist historical considerations of 'difference'. As she observes:

> differences are never just 'differences'. In knowing differences and particularities, we can better see the connections and commonalities because no border or boundary is ever complete or rigidly determining. The challenge is to see how . . . specifying difference allows us to theorise universal concerns more fully.
>
> (Mohanty, Reading 28)

Mohanty's response to this challenge is to advocate a historical materialist analysis of the marginalised communities of women from the Third World/South. Such

women form an epistemologically privileged site of reflection on difference and solidarity, she argues, because they provide the most 'inclusive paradigm and expansive
vision for thinking about universal social justice' as well as denormalising the
western viewpoint (Mohanty, Reading 28). Cheryl Johnson-Odim's study of twentieth-century Nigerian women's anticolonial protest movements offers just one
illustration of what a fully contextualised, indigenous reading of women's activism
might look like, which may or may not come under the name of 'feminism' (Johnson-
Odim, Reading 27). Scholars such as Susan Stanford Friedman and Mary E. John
have also called for further comparative work on women across the Third
World/South as a means of displacing western hegemony as the 'default frame of
reference'.[154]

As I think the above indicates, the prodigious growth of alternative histories by
black and Third World scholars has much transformed the theoretical landscape of
feminist history since Audre Lorde first wrote in 1979 that 'the oppression of women
knows no ethnic nor racial boundaries . . . but that does not mean it is identical
within those differences' (Lorde, Reading 21). 'Difference' has proved to be a potent
signifier for the inequitable relations of power between women and binary narratives of white women/women of colour, coloniser/colonised or First World/Third
World women have done much to expose and delimit the intellectual imperialism
of western feminist thought. Yet these models are not without their limitations.
As Susan Stanford Friedman has pointed out, 'white' and 'western' are not unitary
categories either, but all too often the heterogeneity of non-white women has been
premised on a monolithic construction of whiteness.[155] An array of new theoretical
challenges face feminists as they move now towards the production of increasingly
global, transnational forms of history-writing at the beginning of the twenty-first
century. As Himani Bannerji reminds us, in the attempt to reconceptualise feminist
solidarity across borders '[w]e need to be vigilant that our critical histories do not
themselves end up by creating reified subjects and narratival closures'.[156]

Afterword

I have chosen to conclude this *Reader* with an Afterword in the form of a 2004
retrospective on 'Feminism's History' by Joan Scott, an essay that raises some
thought-provoking reflections on the equivocal nature of feminist history's journey
from the academic borderlands into the disciplinary mainstream. This is perhaps
something that could only have been written from within a US context where feminist scholarship has received greater acceptance than just about anywhere else in
the academic world. Nevertheless, a consideration of feminist history's 'politics of
location' and the losses and gains to be made from institutional assimilation has
much to say about its future critical potential. Put simply, how possible is it to
continue the project of transformation, of revisioning and rewriting history, from
the 'safer' terrain of the centre? It is surely no coincidence that throughout
this summary of feminist historiography much critical questioning and innovative
analysis has come from those not yet in possession of the centre-ground. The black
feminist theorist bell hooks has argued that marginality is neither optional nor

something to surrender in haste as part of the move to the centre. It is, instead, a condition to remain in because it nourishes a critical stance of resistance: 'I am located at the margin', she writes, 'I make a definite distinction between that marginality which is imposed by oppressive structures and that marginality one chooses as a site for resistance – as a location of radical openness and possibility'.[157]

I would argue myself that the prodigious development and growth of feminist history over the past three decades has been due to precisely just such a location of marginality, not necessarily as a physical space (although it has been and still is this for many feminist scholars), but as a theoretical position. As we look to the future of feminist history in the twenty-first century, it becomes clear that it can never inhabit the historical mainstream in any epistemological sense, for that would be a disavowal of its fundamentally subversive practice. What characterises feminism's history and its perpetual interrogation of dominant categories is, as Scott notes, its 'radical refusal to settle down' and to call anywhere 'home' (Scott, Reading 29). To this sentiment I would add Diane Elam's observation on the need to write women's history in the future anterior tense 'which doesn't claim to know in advance what it is that women can do and be'.[158] This is the radical openness of feminist history's future that accepts that in rewriting and retheorising traditional history it must look to its own transformations and its own reimaginings, aware that the very best we produce will, in the future, be seen as 'not having been good enough'. 'Passion, after all', as Scott argues, 'thrives on the pursuit of the not-yet-known' (Scott, Reading 29).

Notes

1 Joan Kelly-Gadol, 'The Social Relations of the Sexes: Methodological Implications of Women's History', *Signs*, 1:4 (Summer, 1976): 809.

2 See the 'Guide to Further Reading: General Theoretical Surveys of Feminist History' at the end of this *Reader* for details.

3 A selection is always a process of exclusion as well as inclusion and there are many innovative feminist historical studies and approaches that I have not been able to incorporate, such as psychoanalytical and auto/biographical approaches to writing feminist history. See for example Carolyn Steedman, *Landscape for a Good Woman. A Story of Two Lives* (London: Virago, 1986); Liz Stanley, *The Auto/Biographical I: The Theory and Practice of Feminist Auto/Biography* (Manchester: Manchester University Press, 1992) and Lyndal Roper, *Oedipus and the Devil: Witchcraft, Sexuality and Religion in Early Modern Europe* (London: Routledge, 1994).

4 Ann-Marie Gallagher, Cathy Lubelska and Louise Ryan (eds) *Re-Presenting the Past: Women and History* (London: Longman, 2001): 5.

5 There are many useful discussions of the difference between the past and history, but see especially Susan Stanford Friedman, 'Making History: Reflections on Feminism, Narrative and Desire', in Diane Elam and Robyn Wiegman (eds) *Feminism Beside Itself* (London and New York: Routledge, 1995): 9–53; Keith Jenkins, *Rethinking History* (London: Routledge Classics edition, 2003) and Callum G. Brown, *Postmodernism for Historians* (London: Pearson Longman, 2005) for a useful introduction to this distinction.

6 Catherine Hall, 'Thematic Review: Politics, Post-structuralism and Feminist History', *Gender and History*, 3:2 (1991): 207.

7   Ann-Louise Shapiro, 'History and Feminist Theory; or, Talking Back to the Beadle' in Shapiro (ed.) *Feminists Revision History* (New Brunswick, NJ: Rutgers University Press, 1994): 19. See Stephen Davies, *Empiricism and History* (Basingstoke: Palgrave, 2003) for a discussion of the theory of empiricism as applicable to history.

8   Shapiro, 'History and Feminist Theory', p. 19.

9   Jane Rendall, 'Uneven Developments: Women's History, Feminist History and Gender History in Great Britain', in Karen Offen, Ruth Roach Pierson and Jane Rendall (eds) *Writing Women's History: International Perspectives* (Bloomington, IN: Indiana University Press, 1991): 46.

10 June Purvis, 'From "Women Worthies" to Poststructuralism? Debate and Controversy in Women's History in Britain', in Purvis (ed.) *Women's History, Britain 1850–1945: An Introduction* (London: UCL Press, 1995): 1–22.

11 See Mary Spongberg, *Writing Women's History Since the Renaissance* (London: Palgrave Macmillan, 2002): 172–88 for a useful overview of the political context of the development of feminist history. For the British scene see Catherine Hall, 'Feminism and Feminist History', in Hall, *White, Male and Middle-Class: Explorations in Feminism and History* (Oxford: Polity Press, 1992): 1–40; for the development of Italian women's history see Silvia Mantini, 'Women's History in Italy', *Journal of Women's History*, 12:2 (2000): 170–98; for the Australian context see Ann Curthoys, 'Gender Studies in Australia: A History', *Australian Feminist Studies*, 15:3 (2000):19–38; for the development of Russian women's history see Barbara Engel, 'Engendering Russia's History', *Slavic Review*, 51:2 (1992): 309–21 and for a wider international perspective see Offen, Pierson and Rendall (eds) *Writing Women's History*, pp. xix–xli.

12 Offen, Pierson and Rendall (eds) *Writing Women's History*, p. xix.

13 Cécile Dauphin, Arlette Farge, Genevieve Fraisse, Christiane Klapisch-Zuber *et al.*, 'Women's Culture and Women's Power: An Attempt at Historiography', *Journal of Women's History*, 1:1 (1989): 63–88. See also Karen Offen, 'French Women's History (1789–1940): Retrospect and Prospect', *French Historical Studies*, 26:4 (2003): 727–67 and Offen, *European Feminisms, 1700–1950: A Political History* (Stanford, CA: Stanford University Press, 2000) for an excellent comparative account of feminism in European societies.

14 Hall, 'Feminism and Feminist History', p. 11.

15 Ibid., pp. 1–40. Class has been a significant issue in feminist history. See for example, Sally Alexander, 'Women, Class and Sexual Difference: Some Reflections on the Writing of Feminist History', *History Workshop Journal*, 17 (Spring, 1984): 125–49 and Anna Davin, 'Imperialism and Motherhood', *History Workshop Journal*, 5 (1978): 9–65. See also Laura Lee Downs, *Writing Gender History* (London: Hodder Arnold, 2004): 30–42 and, for the American context, see Elizabeth Fox-Genovese, 'Socialist-Feminist American Women's History', *Journal of Women's History*, 1:3 (Winter, 1990): 181–210.

16 Sylvia Walby, *Patriarchy at Work* (Cambridge: Polity Press, 1986): 51. See also Joan Kelly, 'The Doubled Vision of Feminist History', *Feminist Studies*, 5:1 (Spring, 1979): 216–27 for an early analysis of the various forms of patriarchy.

17 Michael Roper and John Tosh (eds) *Manful Assertions: Masculinities in Britain since 1800* (London: Routledge, 1991): 7.

18 Ibid., p. 10.

19 According to Sue Clegg, patriarchy fails 'because it generalises about the primacy of a specifically patriarchal mechanism in explaining oppression, and that mechanism cannot explain discontinuities'. Sue Clegg, 'The Feminist Challenge to Socialist History', *Women's History Review*, 6:2 (1997): 205.

20 Linda Kerber, 'Separate Spheres, Female Worlds, Women's Place: The Rhetoric of Women's History', *The Journal of American History*, 75:1 (1988): 9–39. See Nancy Isenberg, 'Second Thoughts on Gender and Women's History', *American Studies*, 36

(1995): 93–103, however, for a refutation of Kerber's three-stage schema of the separate spheres.

21   Kerber, 'Separate Spheres', p. 10. See Barbara Welter, 'The Cult of True Womanhood 1820–1860', *American Quarterly*, 18 (1966): 151–74.

22   Carroll Smith-Rosenberg, 'The Female World of Love and Ritual: Relations Between Women in Nineteenth Century America', *Signs*, 1:1 (1975): 1–18.

23   See Nancy Cott, *The Bonds of Womanhood: Woman's Sphere in New England 1780–1835* (New Haven: Yale University Press, 1977); Estelle Freedman, 'Separatism as Strategy: Female Institution Building and American Feminism 1870–1930', *Feminist Studies*, 5:3 (1979): 512–29.

24   Gerda Lerner for example commented in 1979 that 'to light up areas of historical darkness we must, for a time, focus on a *woman-centred* inquiry, concerning the possibility of the existence of a female culture within the general culture shared by men and women'. Lerner, *The Majority Finds Its Past: Placing Women in History* (New York: Oxford University Press, 1979): 178.

25   Donna Guy, 'True Womanhood in Latin America', in Mary Louise Roberts, Nancy A. Hewitt, Tracy Fessenden and Donna J. Guy, 'Women's History in the New Millennium: A Retrospective Analysis of Barbara Welter's "The Cult of True Womanhood"', *Journal of Women's History*, 14:1 (2002): 170–3.

26   For a useful survey of this scholarship see Jane Rendall, 'Women and the Public Sphere', in Leonore Davidoff, Keith McLelland and Eleni Varikas (eds) *Gender and History: Retrospect and Prospect* (Oxford: Blackwell, 1999): 57–70. For the significance of the private and domestic sphere for men see John Tosh, *A Man's Place: Masculinity and the Middle-Class Home in Victorian England* (New Haven, CT: Yale University Press, 1999).

27   Lynn Abrams and Elizabeth Harvey (eds) *Gender Relations in German History: Power, Agency and Experience from the Sixteenth to the Twentieth Century* (London: UCL Press, 1997): 19. See also Silvia Mantini, 'Women's History in Italy'.

28   See Sandra Lauderdale Graham, 'Making the Private Public: A Brazilian Perspective' and Elizabeth Thompson, 'Public and Private in Middle Eastern Women's History' in 'Women's History in the New Millennium: Rethinking the Public and Private', *Journal of Women's History*, 15:1 (2003): 11–69 and Mary Louise Roberts, Nancy A. Hewitt, Tracy Fessenden and Donna J. Guy, 'Women's History in the New Millennium: A Retrospective Analysis of Barbara Welter's "The Cult of True Womanhood"', *Journal of Women's History*, 14:1 (2002).

29   Christie Farnham and Joan Hoff-Wilson, 'Femininities and Masculinities – New Metaphor for the Nineties? An Editorial', *Journal of Women's History*, 2:2 (1990): 6.

30   Natalie Zemon Davis, '"Women's History" in Transition: the European Case', *Feminist Studies*, 3:3/4 (Spring/Summer, 1976): 88. See also Joan Kelly, 'The Doubled Vision of Feminist History', *Feminist Studies*, 5:1 (Spring, 1979): 216–27.

31   Kerber, 'Separate Spheres', p. 18.

32   Leonore Davidoff and Catherine Hall, *Family Fortunes: Men and Women of the English Middle Class 1780–1850* (London: Routledge, 2002 edition): xvi.

33   Rendall, 'Uneven Developments', p. 49.

34   Hall, 'Feminism and Feminist History', p. 12.

35   Joan Scott, 'Women's History', in Peter Burke (ed.) *New Perspectives on Historical Writing* (Oxford: Polity Press, 1991): 55.

36   Elizabeth Fox-Genovese, 'Placing Women's History in History', *New Left Review* 133 (1982): 15.

37   Ogino Miho, 'Writing Women's History in Japan: Traditions and New Trends', *Historical Studies in Japan* (Tokyo: Yamakawa Shuppansa, 1995): 17–32, cited in Andrea Germer, 'Feminist History in Japan: National and International Perspectives', *Intersections: Gender, History and Culture in the Asian Context* 9 (August 2003) www.sshe.murdoch.edu.au/ intersections/issue9_contents html (accessed 9 April 2005).

38 See Irina Korovushkina, 'Paradoxes of Gender: Writing History in Post-Communist Russia 1987–1998', in Davidoff, McLelland and Varikas (eds) *Gender and History: Retrospect and Prospect*, pp. 151–64. See also Marilyn Lake, 'Women, Gender and History', *Australian Feminist Studies*, 7–8 (1988): 1–9.

39 Lois Banner, 'A Reply to "Culture and Pouvoir" from the Perspective of United States Women's History', *Journal of Women's History*, 1:1 (1989). See also Mary Evans, 'The Problem of Gender for Women's Studies', in Jane Aaron and Sylvia Walby (eds) *Out of the Margins Women's Studies in the 1990s* (London: The Falmer Press, 1991): 67–74.

40 Rosi Braidotti with Judith Butler, 'Feminism by Any Other Name', *differences: A Journal of Feminist Cultural Studies*, 6:2 (1994): 37.

41 Mantini, 'Women's History in Italy', p. 173.

42 Michele Riot-Sarcey, 'The Difficulties of Gender in France: Reflections on a Concept', in Davidoff, McLelland and Varikas (eds) *Gender and History: Retrospect and Prospect*, p. 71. See also Karen Offen, 'French Women's History', p. 755.

43 Lynn Hunt, 'The Challenge of Gender. Deconstruction of Categories and Reconstruction of Narratives in Gender History', in Hans Medick and Anne-Charlotte Trepp, *Geschlechtergeschichte und Allgemeine Geschichte: Herausforderungen und Perspektiven* (Gottingen, 1998): 59.

44 Space permits only a limited selection of titles from numerous publications in this field, but see for example, Louise Tilly (ed.) 'Women in Central and Eastern Europe', special issue, *Women's History Review*, 5:4 (1996); Susan Brownell and Jeffrey N. Wasserstrom (eds) *Chinese Femininities/Chinese Masculinities. A Reader* (Berkeley, CA: University of California Press, 2002); Wendy Z. Goldman, *Women at the Gates: Gender and Industry in Stalin's Russia* (Cambridge: Cambridge University Press, 2002); Linda Edmondson (ed.) *Gender in Russian History and Culture* (Basingstoke: Palgrave, 2001); Angela Zito and Tani E. Barlow (eds) *Body, Subject and Power in China* (Chicago, IL: University of Chicago Press, 1994); 'Themed Issue on Eastern Europe', *Signs*, 29:3 (Spring, 2004); Asuncion Lavrin, *Women, Feminism and Social Change: Argentina, Chile and Uruguay, 1890–1940* (Lincoln, NB: University of Nebraska Press, 1995).

45 See Korovushkina, 'Paradoxes of Gender'.

46 Patricia Mohammed, 'Writing Gender into History: The Negotiation of Gender Relations Among Indian Men and Women in Post-Indenture Trinidad Society, 1917–47', in Verene Shepherd, Bridget Brereton and Barbara Bailey (eds) *Engendering History: Caribbean Women in Historical Perspective* (London: James Currey Publishers, 1995): 20–47.

47 Hunt, 'The Challenge of Gender', p. 64.

48 Ibid., p. 62.

49 Judith Butler and Joan Scott (eds), *Feminists Theorize the Political* (New York and London: Routledge, 1992): xiv.

50 Joan Scott, *Gender and the Politics of History* (New York: Columbia University Press, 1988): 6. For contrasting reviews of Scott's and Riley's work, see Mariana Valverde, 'Poststructuralist Gender Historians: Are We Those Names?', *Labour/Le Travail*, 25 (Spring, 1990): 227–36 and Karen Offen, 'The Use and Abuse of History', *The Women's Review of Books*, VI:7 (1989): 15–16. For useful overviews of the deconstructionist turn to gender from different national perspectives see Isabel Hull, 'Feminist and Gender History through the Literary Looking Glass: German Historiography in Postmodern Times', *Central European History*, 22:3–4 (1989): 279–300; Nancy Isenberg, 'Second Thoughts on Gender and Women's History', *American Studies*, 36 (1995): 93–103 and Joy Parr, 'Gender History and Historical Practice', *The Canadian Historical Review*, 76:3 (September 1995): 354–76. See also Laura Lee Downs, 'From Women's History to Gender History', in Stefan Berger, Heiko Feldner and Kevin Passmore (eds) *Writing History: Theory and Practice* (London: Hodder Arnold, 2003): 261–81.

51   Judith Butler, *Gender Trouble: Feminism and the Subversion of Identity* (New York: Routledge, 1990): 6.

52   The controversies among historians over postmodernism have been extensively aired in many publications. For useful introductory interviews see Kevin Passmore, 'Poststructuralism and History', in Stefan Berger, Heiko Feldner and Kevin Passmore, *Writing History*, pp. 118–40; Callum G. Brown, *Postmodernism for Historians*; Alun Munslow, *The New History* (London: Longman, 2003) and Keith Jenkins, *Refiguring History: New Thoughts on an Old Discipline* (London: Routledge, 2003). The classic summary of the major debates is probably Keith Jenkins (ed.) *The Postmodern History Reader* (London: Routledge, 1997).

53   Stevi Jackson, 'The Amazing Deconstructing Woman', *Trouble and Strife*, 25 (1992): 25.

54   Valverde, 'Poststructuralist Gender Historians', p. 232.

55   Hall, 'Politics, Post-structuralism and Feminist History', p. 209.

56   Jackson, 'The Amazing Deconstructing Woman', p. 28. See also the sociologist Liz Stanley, 'Recovering Women in History from Feminist Deconstructionism', *Women's Studies International Forum*, 1:2 (1990): 151–7 for a similar critique.

57   Laura Lee Downs, 'If "Woman" is Just an Empty Category, Then Why Am I Afraid to Walk Alone at Night? Identity Politics Meets the Postmodern Subject', *Comparative Studies in Society and History: An International Quarterly*, 35:3 (April 1993): 436 with a response by Scott, 'The Tip of the Volcano', pp. 438–43.

58   Purvis, 'From "women worthies" to Poststructuralism?', p. 13.

59   See the exchange between Joan Scott and Linda Gordon in *Signs*, 15:4 (Summer, 1990): 848–60.

60   Claudia Koonz, 'Review of Gender and the Politics of History', *Women's Review of Books*, 6:4 (January 1989): 19.

61   Paula M. L. Moya, 'Postmodernism, "Realism," and the Politics of Identity: Cherrie Moraga and Chicana Feminism', in M. J. Alexander and C. T. Mohanty (eds) *Feminist Genealogies, Colonial Legacies, Democratic Futures* (New York and London: Routledge, 1997): 135.

62   Christine Stansell, 'A Reply to Joan Scott', *International Labor and Working-Class History*, 31 (1987): 26.

63   What Derrida means by *il n'ya pas de hors texte* has been outlined in many places, but never better than by Simon Critchley in his *The Ethics of Deconstruction* (Edinburgh: Edinburgh University Press, second edition, 1999): 31–44. Thanks to Keith Jenkins for this reference.

64   Scott, 'The Tip of the Volcano', response to Laura Lee Downs, p. 442.

65   Louise M. Newman, 'Dialogue: Critical Theory and the History of Women: What's At Stake in Deconstructing Women's History', *Journal of Women's History*, 2:3 (Winter, 1991): 62.

66   Ibid., p. 62.

67   Joan Scott, 'Experience', in Butler and Scott (eds) *Feminists Theorize the Political*, p. 34. See also Joan Scott, 'The Evidence of Experience', *Critical Inquiry*, 17:4 (1991): 773–97.

68   Butler and Scott (eds) *Feminists Theorize the Political,* pp. xiii–xvii. Wendy Brown also argues that postmodernity pulls us towards an increasingly politicised future, but one which is a politics of diversity, not individuality. See Brown, 'Feminist Hesitations, Postmodern Exposures', *differences: A Journal of Feminist Cultural Studies*, 3:1 (1991): 63–84.

69   Evelyn Brooks Higginbotham has been especially receptive towards postmodern theory and discourse analysis, arguing that the language of race was 'double-voiced' because it was subverted by black communities into a language of power. See Higginbotham, 'African-American Women's History and the Meta-language of Race', *Signs*, 17:2 (Winter, 1992): 251–74.

70   Kathleen Canning, 'Feminist History after the Linguistic Turn: Historicizing Discourse and Experience', *Signs*, 19:12 (Winter 1994): 368–404; Kathleen Canning, *Languages of Labor and Gender. Female Factory Work in Germany, 1850–1914* (Ithaca, NY and London: Cornell University Press, 1996); Cecilia Morgan, *Public Men and Virtuous Women: The Gendered Languages of Religion and Politics in Upper Canada, 1791–1850* (Toronto: University of Toronto Press, 1996); Joan Scott, *Only Paradoxes to Offer. French Feminists and the Rights of Man* (Cambridge, MA: Harvard University Press, 1996) and Judith Walkowitz, *City of Dreadful Delight: Narratives of Sexual Danger in Late-Victorian London* (London: Virago, 1992). Laura Lee Downs has a useful chapter on 'Gender and History in a Post-poststructuralist World' in her *Writing Gender History* in which she proposes Lyndal Roper's *Oedipus and the Devil* as a 'most suggestive set of essays that plays off many of the debates around poststructuralism without ever really becoming entangled in their philosophical snares', p. 166.

71   See Mary Maynard, 'Beyond the "Big Three": the Development of Feminist Theory in the 1990s', *History Review*, 4:3 (1995): 259–81 for a discussion of 'strategic essentialism' and Paula Moya, 'Chicana Feminism and Postmodernist Theory', *Signs*, 26:2 (2001): 441–83 for a consideration of 'postpositivist realism'.

72   Downs, 'From Women's History to Gender History', p. 275.

73   Mary Louise Roberts, 'Review Essay: Only Questions to Offer', *Journal of Women's History*, 19:3 (Autumn, 1998): 180.

74   Adrienne Rich, 'Retrospective on "Compulsory Heterosexuality and Lesbian Existence (1980)"', *Journal of Women's History*, 15:3 (2003): 27. Details of Rich's original article are: Adrienne Rich, 'Compulsory Heterosexuality and Lesbian Existence', *Signs*, 5:4 (1980): 631–60.

75   A brief selection of key titles in this body of scholarship include: Martha Vicinus, '"They Wonder to Which Sex I Belong": The Historical Roots of the Modern Lesbian Identity,' *Feminist Studies*, 18 (1992): 467–97; Martin Bauml Duberman, Martha Vicinus and George Chauncey (eds) *Hidden from History: Reclaiming the Gay and Lesbian Past* (New York: New American Books, 1989); Hall Carpenter Archives Lesbian Oral History Group, *Inventing Ourselves: Lesbian Life Stories* (London: Routledge, 1989); Laura Doan, *Fashioning Sapphism: The Origins of a Modern English Lesbian Culture* (New York: Columbia University Press, 2001). This section has drawn upon Alison Oram's excellent overview, '"Friends, Feminists and Sexual Outlaws": Lesbianism and British History', in Gabrielle Griffin and Sonya Andermahr (eds) *Straight Studies Modified: Lesbian Interventions in the Academy* (London: Cassell, 1997): 168–83.

76   See for example, Lesbian History Group (eds) *Not a Passing Phase: Reclaiming Lesbians in History, 1840–1985* (London: The Women's Press, 1989); Estelle B. Freedman, '"The Burning of Letters Continues": Elusive Identities and the Historical Construction of Sexuality', *Journal of Women's History*, 9:4 (1998): 181–200; Alison Oram, 'Telling Stories about the Ladies of Llangollen: the Construction of Lesbian and Feminist Histories' in Gallagher, Lubelska and Ryan (eds) *Re-Presenting the Past. Women and History*, pp. 44–62.

77   Jennifer Terry, 'Theorizing Deviant Historiography', *differences: A Journal of Feminist Cultural Studies*, 3:2 (1991): 59. See Blanche Wiesen Cook, 'The Historical Denial of Lesbianism', *Radical History Review*, 20 (Spring/Summer, 1979): 60–5 for a pioneering analysis of the heterocentric suppression of the lesbian relations between the female academics Mary Woolley and Jeannette Marks.

78   Terry, 'Theorizing Deviant Historiography', p. 69.

79   See for example Lillian Faderman, 'The Morbidification of Love between Women by Nineteenth-Century Sexologists', *Journal of Homosexuality*, 4 (1986): 73–91; Sheila Jeffreys, *The Spinster and Her Enemies: Feminism and Sexuality, 1880–1930* (London: Pandora Press, 1985); Valerie Traub, 'The Perversion of Lesbian Desire', *History Workshop Journal*, 41 (1996): 23–49; Lucy Bland and Laura Doan (eds) *Sexology in Culture: Labelling Bodies and Desires* (London: Polity Press, 1998) and

Lisa Duggan, *Sapphic Slashers: Sex, Violence and American Modernity* (Durham, NC: Duke University Press, 2000).

80 Joan Nestle, 'Wars and Thinking', in Adrienne Rich, Joan Nestle, Judy Tzu-Chun Wu, Mattie Udora Richardson and Alison Kafer, 'Retrospective on "Compulsory Heterosexuality and Lesbian Existence (1980)"', p. 52.

81 Cheshire Calhoun, 'The Gender Closet: Lesbian Disappearance under the Sign "Women"', *Feminist Studies*, 21:1 (Spring, 1995): 7–34.

82 Emma Donoghue, *Passions Between Women: British Lesbian Culture, 1668–1801* (London: Scarlet Press, 1993): 2. See also Alison Oram, 'Cross Dressing and Transgender', in H.G. Cocks and Matt Houlbrook (eds) *Palgrave Advances in the Modern History of Sexuality* (London: Palgrave, 2005): 256–85.

83 Lisa Moore, '"Something More Tender Still Than Friendship": Romantic Friendship in Early Nineteenth Century England', *Feminist Studies*, 18:3 (1992): 499–520. See also Lisa Moore, *Dangerous Intimacies: Toward a Sapphic History of the British Novel* (Durham, NC: Duke University Press, 1997). Liz Stanley also argues that Faderman proceeded from a reductionist equation of 'sexual' with 'genital', 'thereby defining much erotic behaviour as non-sexual'. Stanley, 'Romantic Friendship? Some Issues in Researching Lesbian History and Biography', *Women's History Review*, 1:2 (1992): 196.

84 Karen Hansen, '"No Kisses Is Like Youres": An Erotic Friendship between Two African-American Women during the Mid-Nineteenth Century', *Gender and History*, 7:2 (1995): 153–82.

85 Anna Clark, 'Anne Lister's Construction of Lesbian Identity', *Journal of the History of Sexuality*, 7:1 (1996): 50. See also Helena Whitbread, *I Know My Own Heart: The Diaries of Anne Lister, 1791–1840* (London: Virago, 1988).

86 Eve Kosofsky Sedgwick, *The Epistemology of the Closet* (Berkeley, CA: University of California Press, 1990): 40.

87 Martha Vicinus, *Intimate Friends: Women Who Loved Women, 1778–1928* (Chicago, IL: University of Chicago Press, 2004): xvi.

88 Judith Butler, 'Imitation and Gender Insubordination', in Diana Fuss, *Inside/Out: Lesbian Theories, Gay Theories* (New York: Routledge, 1991): 21. See also Harriet Malinowitz, 'Lesbian Studies and Postmodern Queer Theory', in Bonnie Zimmerman and Toni A. H. McNaron (eds) *The New Lesbian Studies: Into the Twenty-First Century* (New York: Feminist Press, 1996): 262–8. It is interesting to note in this regard, Martha Vicinus's section on eighteenth- and nineteenth-century lesbian 'husband and wife' couples in her recent book *Intimate Friends: Women Who Loved Women, 1778–1928*, in which the women discussed did not consider their imitative versions of heterosexual marital and familial relationships inferior ones. Thanks to Alison Oram for pointing this out to me.

89 Butler, 'Imitation and Gender Insubordination' and Lisa Duggan, 'Making it Perfectly Queer', *Socialist Review*, 22:1 (January–March 1992): 11–31.

90 Butler, 'Imitation and Gender Insubordination', pp. 14–15.

91 Terry, 'Theorizing Deviant Historiography', p. 53.

92 Thanks to Alison Oram for this useful observation.

93 Rosemary Auchmuty, Sheila Jeffreys and Elaine Miller, 'Lesbian History and Gay Studies: Keeping a Feminist Perspective', *Women's History Review*, 1:1 (1992): 89–108.

94 Lisa Duggan, 'The Discipline Problem: Queer Theory Meets Lesbian and Gay History', *Gay and Lesbian Quarterly*, 2 (1995): 181. See also Lisa Duggan, 'History's Gay Ghetto: The Contradiction and Growth in Lesbian and Gay History', in Susan Porter Benson, Stephen Brier and Roy Rosenweig (eds) *Presenting the Past: Essays on History and the Public* (Philadelphia, PA: Temple University Press, 1986): 281–302. For a more encouraging assessment of the mutually beneficial interaction between cultural studies, cultural history and queer theory in the construction of a new 'lesbian cultural history', see Laura Doan, 'Lesbian Studies After the Lesbian Postmodern: Towards a

New Genealogy in Twenty First Century Lesbian Studies', *The Journal of Lesbian Studies*, 10 (2006). My thanks to Laura Doan for allowing me to see a copy of this article before publication.

95   Barbara Smith, 'African-American Lesbian and Gay History: An Exploration', in *The Truth that Never Hurts: Writings on Race, Gender and Freedom* (New Brunswick, NJ: Rutgers University Press, 1998): 84.

96   Combahee River Collective, 'A Black Feminist Statement', in Cherrie L. Moraga, and Gloria E. Anzaldua (eds) *This Bridge Called My Back: Writings by Radical Women of Color* (Berkeley, CA: Third Woman Press, 2002 edition): 237.

97   Makeda Silvera, 'Man Royals and Sodomites: Some Thoughts on the Invisibility of Afro-Caribbean Lesbians', *Feminist Studies*, 18:3 (Fall, 1992): 531.

98   Judy Tzu-Chun Wu, 'Asian American History and Racialized Compulsory Deviance', in Adrienne Rich, Joan Nestle, Judy Tzu-Chun Wu, Mattie Udora Richardson and Alison Kafer, 'Retrospective on "Compulsory Heterosexuality and Lesbian Existence (1980)"', pp. 58–61.

99   Tze-Ian D. Sang, *The Emerging Lesbian. Female Same-Sex Desire in Modern China* (Chicago, IL and London: University of Chicago Press, 2003); Ruth Ford, 'Speculating on Scrapbooks, Sex and Desire: Issues in Lesbian History', *Australian Historical Studies*, (1996): 111–26; Dan Healey, 'Evgeniia/Evgennii: Queer Case Histories in the First Years of Soviet Power', *Gender and History*, 9:1 (1997): 83–106; Dan Healey, *Homosexual Desire in Revolutionary Russia* (Chicago, IL: University of Chicago Press, 2001); Judith C. Brown, *Immodest Acts: The Life of a Lesbian Nun in Renaissance Italy* (New York: Oxford University Press, 1986).

100 Ford, 'Speculating on Scrapbooks, Sex and Desire', p. 125.

101 Oram, '"Friends, Feminists and Sexual Outlaws": Lesbianism and British History', p. 179.

102 Rich, 'Retrospective on "Compulsory Heterosexuality and Lesbian Existence (1980)"', p. 13.

103 Vicinus, *Intimate Friends*, p. xxiii.

104 Calhoun, 'The Gender Closet', p. 21.

105 Martha Vicinus, '"The Gift of Love": Nineteenth-Century Religion and Passion', in Sue Morgan (ed.) *Women, Religion and Feminism in Britain, 1750–1900* (Basingstoke: Palgrave, 2002): 73–88.

106 Ella Shohat, 'Notes on the Postcolonial', *Social Text*, 31:32 (1992): 100. 'Black feminism' or 'women of colour' are terms used most frequently in the US and British contexts to refer to women of African descent, whereas 'Third World' refers to a more diverse configuration of women's geographical, often ex-colonial circumstances. See Inderpal Grewal and Caren Kaplan (eds) *Scattered Hegemonies. Postmodernity and Transnational Feminist Practices* (Minneapolis, MN and London: University of Minnesota Press, 1994) and Chandra Talpade Mohanty, 'Cartographies of Struggle: Third World Women and the Politics of Feminism', in Mohanty, *Feminism without Borders, Decolonizing Theory, Practicing Solidarity* (Durham, NC and London: Duke University Press, 2003): 43–84 for useful discussions and problematicisations of these terms.

107 Mohanty, 'Cartographies of Struggle', p. 49.

108 Cheryl Johnson-Odim, 'Common Themes, Different Contexts: Third World Women and Feminism', in Chandra Talpade Mohanty, Ann Russo and Lourdes Torres (eds) *Third World Women and the Politics of Feminism* (Bloomington, IN: Indiana University Press, 1991): 315.

109 Alice Walker, *In Search of Our Mothers' Gardens: Womanist Prose* (San Diego, CA: Harcourt Brace Jovanovich, 1983): xi.

110 Mahua Sarkar, 'Looking for Feminism', *Gender & History*, 16:2 (August 2004): 324.

111 Ruth Roach Pierson, 'Colonization and Canadian Women's History', *Journal of Women's History*, 4:2 (Fall, 1992): 134–56. A similar accusation could be made, of course, about the dominant Anglocentrism of British scholarship with regard to the Celtic 'fringe' of Wales, Scotland and Ireland.

112   Pamela Scully, 'Race and Ethnicity in Women's and Gender History in Global Perspective', in Bonnie E. Smith (ed.) *Women's History in Global Perspective* (Urbana, IL and Chicago, IL: University of Illinois Press, 2004): 197. See also Gerda Lerner, 'Reconceptualizing Differences Among Women', *Journal of Women's History*, 1:3 (Winter 1990): 106–22 for an early discussion of the inadequacies of certain models of 'difference' and race that omitted issues of power. Ruth Frankenberg, *White Women, Race Matters: The Social Construction of Whiteness* (Minneapolis, MN: University of Minnesota Press, 1993) is an early and well-known deconstruction of 'whiteness'.

113   Evelyn Brooks Higginbotham, 'Beyond the Sound of Silence: Afro-American Women in History', *Gender and History*, 1:1 (1989): 50. See Hazel W. Carby, 'White Women Listen! Black Feminism and the Boundaries of Sisterhood', in Centre for Contemporary Cultural Studies, *The Empire Strikes Back: Race and Racism in 70s Britain* (London: Hutchinson, 1982): 212–35; bell hooks, *Ain't I a Woman?: Black Women and Feminism* (Boston, MA: South End Press, 1981) and bell hooks, *Feminist Theory: From Margin to Center* (Boston, MA: South End Press, 1984) for early formative critiques of white feminist theory.

114   bell hooks, *Ain't I a Woman?*; Paula Giddings, *When and Where I Enter: The Impact of Black Women on Race and Sex in America* (New York: William Morrow, 1984); Angela Davis, *Women, Race and Class* (New York: Random House, 1981); Gloria Hull, P. Scott and B. Smith, *But Some of Us Are Brave* (New York: The Feminist Press, 1982); Louise Newman, *White Women's Rights: The Racial Origins of Feminism in the United States* (New York: Oxford University Press, 1999).

115   See for example, Angela Davis, 'Rape, Racism and the Myth of the Black Rapist', in her *Women, Race and Class*; Darlene Clark Hine, 'Rape and the Inner Lives of Black Women in the Middle West: Preliminary Thoughts on the Culture of Dissemblance', *Signs*, 14 (1989): 912–20; Lourdes Beneria and Gita Sen, 'Accumulation, Reproduction and Women's Role in Economic Development: Boserup Revisited', *Signs*, 7:2 (1981): 279–98 and Evelyn M. Hammonds, 'Toward a Genealogy of Black Female Sexuality: The Problematic of Silence', in M. Jacqui Alexander and Chandra Talpade Mohanty (eds) *Feminist Genealogies, Colonial Legacies, Democratic Futures* (New York: Routledge, 1997): 170–82.

116   bell hooks, *Feminist Theory*; Patricia Hill Collins, *Black Feminist Thought: Knowledge, Consciousness and the Politics of Empowerment* (New York: Routledge, 1990).

117   Darlene Clark Hine, 'Black Women's History, White Women's History: The Juncture of Race and Class', *Journal of Women's History*, 4:2 (Fall, 1992): 126.

118   See for example, Jacqueline Jones, *Labor of Love, Labor of Sorrow: Black Women, Work and the Family from Slavery to the Present* (New York: Basic Books Inc., 1985); Glenda Elizabeth Gilmore, *Gender and Jim Crow: Women the the Politics of White Supremacy in North Carolina, 1896–1920* (Chapel Hill, NC: University of North Carolina Press, 1996); Gail Bederman, *Manliness and Civilization: A Cultural History of Gender and Race in the United States, 1880–1917* (Chicago, IL: University of Chicago Press, 1995); Darlene Clark Hine and Earnestine Jenkins (eds) *A Question of Manhood: A Reader in US Black Men's History and Masculinity* (Bloomington, IN: Indiana University Press, 1999).

119   Rosalyn Terborg-Penn, *African-American Women in the Struggle for the Vote, 1850–1920* (Bloomington, IN: Indiana University Press, 1998); Darlene Clark Hine, 'Rape and the Inner Lives of Black Women in the Middle West: Preliminary Thoughts on the Culture of Dissemblance'. See also Hammonds, 'Toward a Genealogy of Black Female Sexuality'.

120   Michele Mitchell, 'Silences Broken, Silences Kept: Gender and Sexuality in African-American History', in Davidoff, McLelland and Varikas (eds) *Gender and History: Retrospect and Prospect*, p. 22.

121   E. Frances White, 'Africa On My Mind: Gender, Counter Discourse and African-American Nationalism', in Cheryl Johnson-Odim and Margaret Strobel (eds)

Expanding the Boundaries of Women's History: Essays on Women in the Third World (Bloomington, IN: Indiana University Press, 1992): 51–73.

122 Hine, 'Black Women's History, White Women's History', p. 132. See also Evelyn Brooks Higginbotham, 'African-American Women's History and the Metalanguage of Race' for a discussion of the significance of class. For another view on the need for studies in relationality between black and white women see Linda Gordon, 'On Difference', *Genders*, 10 (1991): 91–111.

123 See for example, Verene Shepherd, Bridget Brereton and Barbara Bailey (eds) *Engendering History: Caribbean Women in Historical Perspective*; Nancy Rose Hunt, Tessie R. Liu and Jean Quataert (eds) *Gendered Colonialisms in African History* (Oxford: Blackwell, 1997); Jean Allman, Susan Geiger and Nakanyike Musisi (eds) *Women in African Colonial Histories* (Bloomington, IN: Indiana University Press, 2002). For helpful overviews of the significance of Said and Foucault to postcolonialist feminist theory and the role of the influential Subaltern Studies Group in the development of postcolonial studies see Clare Midgley, 'Gender and Imperialism: mapping the connections', in Midgley (ed.) *Gender and Imperialism* (Manchester: Manchester University Press, 1998): 1–18 and Catherine Hall, 'Introduction: Thinking the Postcolonial, Thinking the Empire', in Hall (ed.) *Cultures of Empire. A Reader: Colonizers in Britain and the Empire in the Nineteenth and the Twentieth Centuries* (Manchester: Manchester University Press, 2000): 1–33.

124 Himani Bannerji, 'Politics and the Writing of History', in Ruth Roach Pierson and Nupur Chaudhuri (eds) *Nation, Empire, Colony: Historicizing Gender and Race* (Bloomington, IN: Indiana University Press, 1998): 289.

125 See Hall, 'Introduction: Thinking the Postcolonial, Thinking the Empire', p. 3. See also Ania Loomba, *Colonialism/Postcolonialism* (London: Routledge, 1998); Jane Haggis, 'The Social Memory of a Colonial Frontier', *Australian Feminist Studies*, 16:34 (2001): 91–9; Ruth Frankenberg and Lata Mani, 'Crosscurrents, Crosstalk: Race, "Postcoloniality" and the Politics of Location', *Cultural Studies*, 7 (Spring, 1993): 292–310 for discussions of the postcolonial.

126 See Clare Midgley, 'Gender and Imperialism: Mapping the Connections', pp. 1–18 for an authoritative overview of this scholarship. See also Reina Lewis, *Gendering Orientalism: Race, Femininity and Representation* (London and New York: Routledge, 1996) and R. Kabbani, *Europe's Myths of Orient* (London: Pandora, 1986).

127 Jane Haggis, 'Gendering Colonialism or Colonising Gender?', *Women's Studies International Forum*, 13:2 (1990): 105–15. See also Jane Haggis, 'White Women and Colonialism: Towards a Non-recuperative History', in Midgley (ed.) *Gender and Imperialism*, pp. 45–75.

128 Nupur Chaudhuri and Margaret Strobel (eds) *Western Women and Imperialism: Complicity and Resistance* (Bloomington, IN: Indiana University Press, 1992): 7. See also Kumari Jayawardena, *The White Women's Other Burden: Western Women and South Asia During British Colonial Rule* (London: Routledge, 1995). See also the 'Guide to further reading' at the end of this *Reader*.

129 My thanks to Clare Midgley for clarifying the distinction between the veneration of Indian culture and an anti-imperialist stance.

130 Antoinette Burton, 'Some Trajectories of "Feminism" and "Imperialism"', *Gender and History*, 10:3 (November 1998): 562.

131 See the special themed issue 'Revising the Experiences of Colonized Women: Beyond Binaries', *Journal of Women's History*, 14:4 (Winter, 2003). See also Antoinette Burton, *Dwelling in the Archive: Women Writing House, Home and History in Late Colonial India* (Oxford: Oxford University Press, 2003).

132 Janaki Nair, 'On the Question of Agency in Indian Feminist Historiography', *Gender and History*, 6:1 (April 1994): 84. For a discussion of patriarchal 'archive logic' see Antoinette Burton, 'Thinking beyond the Boundaries: Empire, Feminism and the Domains of History', *Social History*, 26:1 (January 2001): 60–71.

133 Gayatri Spivak, 'Can the Subaltern Speak?', in C. Nelson and L. Grossberg (eds) *Marxism and the Interpretation of Culture* (London: Macmillan, 1988): 295.

134 Gyan Prakash, 'Subaltern Studies as Postcolonial Criticism', in Hall (ed.) *Cultures of Empire. A Reader*, p. 131.

135 Lata Mani, *Contentious Traditions: The Debate on Sati in Colonial India* (Berkeley, CA: University of California Press, 1998): 190.

136 Ibid., p. 190.

137 Frederick Cooper and Ann Laura Stoler, 'Between Metropole and Colony. Rethinking a Research Agenda', in Cooper and Stoler (eds) *Tensions of Empire, Colonial Cultures in a Bourgeois World* (Berkeley, CA: University of California Press, 1997): 33. Ruth Roach Pierson and Nupur Chaudhuri's *Nation, Empire and Colony: Historicizing Gender and Race* (Bloomington, IN: Indiana University Press, 1998) was the conference volume of the International Federation for Research in Women's History, Montreal, 1995.

138 See for example, Kumari Jayawardena, *Feminism and Nationalism in the Third World* (London: Zed Books, 1986); 'Gender, Nationalisms and National Identities', *Gender and History*, themed issue, 5:2 (Summer, 1993); Margot Badran, *Feminists, Islam and Nation: Gender and the Making of Modern Egypt* (Cairo: The American University Press, 1996); Ida Blom, Karen Hagemann and Catherine Hall (eds) *Gendered Nations: Nationalism and Gender Order in the Long Nineteenth Century* (Oxford: Berg, 2000) and Tamar Meyer (ed.) *Gender Ironies of Nationalism* (New York: Routledge, 2000).

139 For discussion of the *hijab* see Badran, *Feminists, Islam and Nation;* Hammed Shahidian, 'Islam, Politics and Problems of Writing Women's History in Iran', *Journal of Women's History*, 7:2 (Summer, 1995): 113–44; Bronwyn Winter, 'Fundamental Misunderstandings: Issues in Feminist Approaches to Islamism', *Journal of Women's History*, 13:1 (2005):1–22; Lama Abu Odeh, 'Post-colonial Feminism and the Veil: Thinking Difference', *Feminist Review*, 43 (Spring, 1993): 26–37; Leila Ahmed, *Women, Gender and Islam: The Historical Roots of a Modern Debate* (New Haven, CT: Yale University Press, 1993).

140 Hilary McD. Beckles, 'Historicizing Slavery in West Indian Feminism', *Feminist Review*, 59 (Summer, 1998): 48–9.

141 See Rita Arditti, *Searching for Life: the Grandmothers of the Plaza de Mayo and the Disappeared Children of Argentina* (Berkeley, CA: University of California Press, 1999) and Malathi de Alwis, 'Motherhood as a Space of Protest: Women's Political Participation in Contemporary Sri Lanka', in Amrita Basu and Patricia Jeffrey (eds) *Appropriating Gender: Women's Activism and the Politicization of Religion in South Asia* (New York: Routledge, 1997): 185–202. See also Suruchi Thapar-Bjorkert and Louise Ryan, 'Mother India/Mother Ireland: Comparative Gendered Dialogues of Colonialism and Nationalism in the Early 20th Century', *Women's Studies International Forum*, 25:3 (2002): 301–13 on the symbolism of motherhood.

142 Louise Ryan, 'Splendidly Silent: Representing Irish Republican Women, 1919–23', in Gallagher, Ryan and Lubelska (eds) *Representing the Past: Women and History*, pp. 23–43.

143 Benedict Anderson, *Imagined Communities: Reflections on the Origin and Spread of Nationalism* (London: Verso, 1983).

144 Cooper and Stoler, 'Between Metropole and Colony. Rethinking a Research Agenda', in Cooper and Stoler (eds) *Tensions of Empire*, pp. 3–4.

145 See Julia Clancy-Smith and Frances Gouda, *Domesticating the Empire: Race, Gender and Family Life in French and Dutch Colonialism* (Charlottesville, VA and London: University Press of Virginia, 1998).

146 Anne McClintock, *Imperial Leather: Race, Gender and Sexuality in the Colonial Context* (New York: Routledge, 1995); Ann Laura Stoler, *Carnal Knowledge and Imperial Power. Race and the Intimate in Colonial Rule* (Berkeley, CA: University of California, 2002).

147   Antoinette Burton, *Burdens of History: British Feminists, Indian Women and Imperial Culture* (Chapel Hill, NC: University of North Carolina Press, 1994); Antoinette Burton, *At the Heart of the Empire: Indians and the Colonial Encounter in Late Victorian Britain* (Berkeley: University of California Press, 1998); Clare Midgley, *Women Against Slavery: The British Campaigns, 1780–1870* (London: Routledge, 1992); Susan Thorne, *Congregational Missions and the Making of an Imperial Culture in Nineteenth-century England* (Stanford, CA: Stanford University Press, 1999).

148   See also Hall, '"Going-a-Trolloping": Imperial Man Travels the Empire', in Midgley (ed.) *Gender and Imperialism*, pp. 180–99 and 'Competing Masculinities: Thomas Carlyle, John Stuart Mill and the Case of Governor Edward Eyre', in her *White, Male and Middle Class* (Cambridge: Polity Press, 1992): 255–95.

149   Marilyn Lake, 'Colonised and Colonising: the White Australian Feminist Subject', *Women's History Review*, 2:3 (1993): 377–86.

150   See Hall, 'Introduction: Thinking the Postcolonial, Thinking the Empire', pp. 1–33 and Adele Perry, *On the Edge of Empire, Gender, Race and the Making of British Columbia 1849–1871* (Toronto: University of Toronto Press, 2001) for discussions of racial mixing.

151   See Leila J. Rupp, *Worlds of Women: The Making of an International Women's Movement* (Princeton, NJ: Princeton University Press, 1997). Other recent examples of global women's history include Sarah S. Hughes, 'Gender at the Base of World History', in Ross E. Dunn (ed.) *The New World History* (Boston, MA: St Martin's Press, 2000); Bonnie E. Smith, (ed.) *Global Feminisms Since 1945* (London: Routledge, 2000).

152   Rosalyn Terborg-Penn, 'Through an African Feminist Theoretical Lens: Viewing Caribbean Women's History Cross-Culturally', in Shepherd, Brereton and Bailey (eds) *Engendering History: Caribbean Women in Historical Perspective*, pp. 3–19. See also Sandra Gunning, Tera Hunter and Michele Mitchell, 'Gender, Sexuality, and African Diasporas', *Gender and History*, 13:3 (2003): 397–408.

153   Asuncion Lavrin, 'International Feminisms: Latin American Alternatives', in Mrinalini Sinha, Donna Guy and Angela Woollacott (eds) 'Special Themed Issue: Feminisms and Internationalism', *Gender and History*, 10:3 (1998): 520.

154   Susan Stanford Friedman, 'Beyond White and Other: Relationality and Narratives of Race', *Signs*, 21 (1995): 1–49 and Mary E. John, 'Feminisms and Internationalisms: A Response from India', *Gender and History*, 10:3 (1998): 546.

155   Friedman, 'Beyond White and Other'.

156   Bannerji, 'Politics and the Writing of Writing History', p. 293.

157   bell hooks, *Yearning: Race, Gender and Cultural Politics* (Boston, MA: South End Press, 1990): 153.

158   Diane Elam, *Feminism and Deconstruction. Ms. en Abyme* (London: Routledge, 1994): 41.

PART I

Bringing the female subject into view

Sheila Rowbotham, Sally Alexander and Barbara Taylor

THE TROUBLE WITH 'PATRIARCHY'

Originally published in *The New Statesman* in December 1979, this early exchange on patriarchy between the three British socialist-feminist historians, Sheila Rowbotham, Sally Alexander and Barbara Taylor, generated themes that would continue to be debated throughout succeeding decades, notably the relationship between gender and class conflict (patriarchy and capitalism), and the (in)flexibility of patriarchal theories. For Rowbotham, patriarchy is too blunt an analytical tool to do justice to the more supportive forms of male/female relations. Because it is presented in an overly universalised and ahistorical manner as the 'single determining cause' of female oppression, she argues, the concept of 'patriarchy' will never provide a sufficiently historical understanding of sex/gender relations. In addition, it denies historical agency to women in favour of a permanently victimised stance of 'fatalistic submission'. Alexander and Taylor respond to Rowbotham's critique by pointing out that patriarchy is a necessary theory in order to profile the distinctiveness of sexual conflict and avoid it becoming subsumed within class antagonism. The concept of patriarchy should not be regarded as hostile to men, they argue. Rather, it exposes the inequitable web of 'psycho-sexual relations in which masculinity and femininity are formed'. The recovery of women's diverse historical experiences cannot be achieved without an appropriate perspectival framework through which to order such an analysis they explain: 'sexual antagonism is not something which can be understood simply by living it: it needs to be analysed with concepts forged for that purpose'. For Alexander and Taylor, therefore, theories of patriarchy are the first systematic attempt to do just this.

Sheila Rowbotham

WHEN CONTEMPORARY FEMINISTS began to examine the world from a new perspective, bringing their own experience to bear on their understanding of history and modern society, they found it was necessary to distinguish women's subordination as a sex from class oppression. Inequality between men and women was not just a creation of capitalism: it was a feature of all societies for which we had reliable evidence. It was a separate phenomenon, which needed to be observed in connection with, rather than simply as a response to, changes that occurred in the organisation and control of production. So the term 'patriarchy' was pressed into service – as an analytical tool which might help to describe this vital distinction.

The term has been used in a great variety of ways. 'Patriarchy' has been discussed as an ideology which arose out of men's power to exchange women between kinship groups; as a symbolic male principle; and as the power of the father (its literal meaning). It has been used to express men's control over women's sexuality and fertility; and to describe the institutional structure of male domination. Recently the phrase 'capitalist patriarchy' has suggested a form peculiar to capitalism. Zillah Eisenstein, who has edited an anthology of writings under that heading, defines patriarchy as providing 'the sexual hierarchical ordering of society for political control'.[1]

There was felt to be a need (not confined to feminists) for a wider understanding of power relationships and hierarchy than was offered by current Marxist ideas. And with that came the realisation that we needed to resist not only the outer folds of power structures but their inner coils. For their hold over our lives through symbol, myth and archetype would not dissolve automatically with the other bondages even in the fierce heat of revolution. There had to be an inner psychological and spiritual contest, along with the confrontation and transformation of external power.

However, the word 'patriarchy' presents problems of its own. It implies a universal and historical form of oppression which returns us to biology – and thus it obscures the need to recognise not only biological difference, but also the multiplicity of ways in which societies have defined gender. By focusing upon the bearing and rearing of children ('patriarchy' = the power of the father) it suggests there is a single determining cause of women's subordination. This either produces a kind of feminist base-superstructure model to contend with the more blinkered versions of Marxism, or it rushes us off on the misty quest for the original moment of male supremacy. Moreover, the word leaves us with two separate systems in which a new male/female split is implied. We have patriarchy oppressing women and capitalism oppressing male workers. We have biological reproduction on the one hand and work on the other. We have the ideology of 'patriarchy' opposed to the mode of production, which is seen as a purely economic matter.

'Patriarchy' implies a structure which is fixed, rather than the kaleidoscope of forms within which women and men have encountered one another. It does not carry any notion of how women might act to transform their situation as a sex. Nor does it even convey a sense of how women have resolutely manoeuvred for a better position within the general context of subordination by shifting for themselves, turning the tables, ruling the roost, wearing the trousers, henpecking, gossiping, hustling, or (in the words of a woman I once overheard) just 'going drip, drip at him'. 'Patriarchy' suggests a fatalistic submission which allows no space for the complexities of women's defiance.

It is worth remembering every time we use words like 'class' and 'gender' that they are only being labelled as structures for our convenience, because human relationships move with such complexity and speed that our descriptions freeze them at the point of understanding. Nancy Hartsock[2] recalls Marx's insistence that we should regard 'every historically developed social form as in fluid movement'; thus we must take into account its 'transient nature not less than its momentary existence'. Within Marxism there is at least a possibility of a dialectical unity of transcience and moment. But it seems to me that the concept of 'patriarchy' offers no such prospect. We have stretched its meaning in umpteen different ways, but there is no transience in it at all. It simply refuses to budge.

A word which fails to convey movement is not much help when it comes to examining the differences between the subordination of women, and class. The capitalist is defined by his or her ownership of capital. This is not the same kettle of fish at all as a biological male person. Despite the protestations of employers, their activities could be organised quite differently and, in this sense, the working class carries the possibility of doing without the capitalist and thus of abolishing the hierarchies of class. But a biological male person is a more delicate matter altogether and is not to be abolished (by socialist feminists at least).

It is not sexual difference which is the problem, but the social inequalities of gender – the different kinds of power societies have given to sexual differences, and the hierarchical forms these have imposed on human relationships. Some aspects of male-female relationships are evidently not simply oppressive, but include varying degrees of mutual aid. The concept of 'patriarchy' has no room for such subtleties, however.

Unless we have a sense of these reciprocities and the ways they have changed among different classes, along with the inequalities between men and women, we cannot explain why women have perceived different aspects of their relationship to men to be oppressive at different times. We cannot explain why genuine feelings of love and friendship are possible between men and women, and boys and girls, or why people have acted together in popular movements. In times of revolution (such as the Paris Commune, the early days of Russian communism, or more recent liberation struggles in developing countries), women's public political action has often challenged not only the ruling class, the invader or the coloniser, but also the men's idea of women's role. Less dramatically in everyday life, men's dependence on women in the family, in the community and at work, is as evident as women's subordination – and the two often seem to be inextricably bound together. Some feminists regard this as an elaborate trick, but I think it is precisely within these shifting interstices that women have manoeuvred and resisted. We thus need an approach which can encompass both the conflict and the complementary association between the sexes.

If we could develop an historical concept of sex-gender relationships, this would encompass changing patterns of male control and its congruence or incongruence with various aspects of women's power. It would enable us to delineate the specific shapes of sex-gender relationships within different social relationships, without submerging the experiences of women in those of men, or vice versa. If we stopped viewing patriarchy and capitalism as two separate interlocking systems, and looked instead at how sex-gender as well as class and race relations have developed historic- ally, we could avoid a simple category 'woman' – who must either be a matriarchal stereotype or a hopelessly down-trodden victim, and whose fortunes rise and fall at the same time as all her sisters. We could begin to see women and men born into relationships within families which are not of their making. We could see how their ideas of themselves and other people, their work, habits and sexuality, their participation in organisation, their responses to authority, religion and the state, and the expression of their creativity in art and culture – how all these things are affected by relations in the family as well as by class and race. But sex-gender relationships are clearly not confined to the family (we are not just sex-beings in the family and class-beings in the community, the state and at work): like class relations, they permeate all aspects of life.

Equally, we inherit the historical actions and experience of people in the past through institutions and culture – and the balance of sex-gender relations is as much a part of this inheritance as is class. The changes which men and women make within these prevailing limitations need not be regarded simply as a response to the reorganisation of production, nor even as a reflection of class struggle. Indeed, we could see these shifts in sex-gender relationships as *contributing* historically towards the creation of suitable conditions for people to make things differently and perceive the world in new ways.

Rosalind Petchesky has argued that: '. . . if we understand that patriarchal kinship relations are not static, but like class relations, are characterised by antagonism and struggle, then we begin to speculate that women's consciousness and their periodic attempts to resist or change the dominant kinship structures will themselves affect class relations'.[3] Relations between men and women are also characterised by certain reciprocities, so we cannot assume the antagonism is a constant factor. There are times when class or race solidarity are much stronger than sex-gender conflict and times when relations within the family are a source of mutual resistance to class power. Nonetheless, the approach suggested by Petchesky opens up an exciting way of thinking about women's and men's position in the past, through which we can locate sex-gender relations in the family and see how they are present within all other relationships between men and women in society.

However, we need to be cautious about the assumptions we bring to the past. For instance, women have seen the defining features of oppression very differently at different times. Large numbers of children, for example, could be regarded as a sign of value and status, whereas most Western women now would insist on their right to restrict the numbers of children they have, or to remain childless. Feminist anthropologists are particularly aware of the dangers of imposing the values of Western capitalism on women of other cultures. But we can colonise women in the past, too, by imposing modern values.

We also need to be clear about which groups we are comparing in any given society, and to search for a sense of movement within each period. For instance, the possibilities for women among the richer peasantry in the Middle Ages were clearly quite different from those of poor peasants without land. And presumably these were not the same before and after the Black Death. Change – whether for better or worse – does not necessarily go all one way between the classes, nor even between their various sub-strata, and the same is true of changes which varying modes of production have brought to sex-gender relationships. The growth of domestic industry, for example, is usually associated with the control of the father over the family. But it could also alter the domestic division of labour, because women's particular work skills were vital to the family economy at certain times in the production process. This might have made it easier for women in domestic industry to question sexual hierarchy than for peasant women.

Similarly, nineteenth-century capitalism exploited poor women's labour in the factories, isolated middle-class women in the home, and forced a growing body of impecunious gentlewomen on to the labour market. Yet at the same time it brought working-class women into large-scale popular movements at work and in the community, in the course of which some of them demanded their rights as a sex while resisting class oppression. Out of domestic isolation, the extreme control of middle-class men over their wives and daughters, and the impoverished dependence of unmarried women, came the first movement of feminists.

An historical approach to sex-gender relations could help us to understand why women radicalised by contemporary feminism have found the present division of domestic labour and men's continued hold over women's bodies and minds to be particularly oppressive. These were not really the emphases of nineteenth-century feminism. What then are the specific antagonisms we have encountered within sex-gender relationships? And what possibilities do they imply for change?

It has often been said that as women we have come to know that the personal is 'political' because we have been isolated in the personal sphere. I think this is only half the story. We *were* isolated in the personal sphere, but some of us were hurtled dramatically out of it by the expansion of education and the growth of administrative and welfare work, while some (working-class and black women) were never so luxuriously confined. What is more, modern capitalism has created forms of political control and social care, and has produced new technologies and methods of mass communication, which have disturbed and shifted the early nineteenth-century division of private and public spheres. As a result, the direct and immediate forms through which men have controlled women have been *both* reinforced *and* undermined. Kinship relations have increasingly become the province of the state (we have to obey certain rules about the way we arrange our private lives in order to qualify for welfare benefits, for example). Contraceptive technology has enabled women to separate sexual pleasure from procreation. And the scope for sexual objectification has grown apace with the development of the visual media. Men are being sold more strenuously than ever the fantasy of controlling the ultimate feminine, just as their hold over real women is being resisted. Women are meanwhile being delivered the possibility of acting out male-defined fantasy of ultimate femininity in order to compete with other women for men. All the oppressive features of male culture have been thrown into relief and have served to radicalise women: who does the housework, unequal pay and access to jobs, violence in the home, rape, the denial of abortion rights, prostitution, lack of nursery provision, and male-dominated and exclusively heterosexual attitudes towards sex and love.

This convoluted state of affairs has created a new kind of political consciousness in socialist feminism. In tussling with the specifics of sex-gender relations in modern capitalism, feminists have challenged the way we see our identities and experience our bodies, the way we organise work and childcare, and the way we express love and develop thoughts. In other words, they have challenged the basic components of hierarchy to create a vision of society in which sexual difference does not imply subordination and oppression.

Just as the abolition of class power would release people outside the working class and thus requires their support and involvement, so the movement against hierarchy which is carried in feminism goes beyond the liberation of a sex. It contains the possibility of equal relations not only between women and men, but also between men and men, and women and women, and even between adults and children.

Notes

1　For critical accounts of how the word 'patriarchy' has been used see: Paul Atkinson, 'The Problem with Patriarchy', *Achilles Heel*, 2, 1979; Zillah Eisenstein & Heidi Hartman, *Capitalist Patriarchy and the Case for Socialist Feminism*, Monthly Review Press, 1978; Linda Gordon & Allen Hunter, 'Sexual Politics and the New Right', *Radical America*, November 1977, February 1978; Olivia Harris & Kate Young, 'The Subordination of Women in Cross-Cultural Perspective', *Patriarchy Papers*, Patriarchy conference, London, 1976. Published by PDC and Women's Publishing Collective, 1978. Roisin McDonough & Rachel Harrison, 'Patriarchy and Relations of Production', *Feminism and Materialism*, Kuhn & Wolfe, eds, Routledge, 1978; Gayle Rubin, 'The Traffic in Women', *Towards an Anthropology of Women*, Reiter, ed, Monthly Review Press, 1975; Veronica Beechey, 'On Patriarchy', *Feminist Review*, 3, 1979.

2&3　See *Capitalist Patriarchy and the Case for Socialist Feminism*.

Sally Alexander and Barbara Taylor

IN DEFENCE OF 'PATRIARCHY'

THE MAJOR PROBLEM WITH THE theory of patriarchy, Sheila Rowbotham claims, is that it ascribes women's subordination and men's domination to their respective biological roles – a politically dangerous position which can only lead to a call for the abolition of all 'biological male persons'. Feminists must realise, she says, that 'it is not sexual difference which *is* the problem, but the social inequalities of gender': it is not men we want to eliminate, but male power.

Like Sheila, we are socialist feminists. But we believe that sexual difference is the problem, or at least a fundamental part of it. Does that mean that we are busy training for a final day of sexual Armageddon, when all 'biological male persons' will receive their just deserts (castration or annihilation, as we choose at the time)? No doubt every woman has had moments when such a vision seemed attractive, but what we have in mind is (to use Sheila's words) 'a more delicate matter altogether'.

Throughout her article Sheila assumes that sexual difference is a biological given, linked to reproduction. Clearly if it is defined in this way, it is hard to see how it can be changed. However, one of the most important breakthroughs in feminist theory occurred when women began to question this commonsense definition of sex, pushing past all the old assumptions about 'natural' womanhood and manhood to examine how deep the roots of women's oppression really lay. What was needed, then, was a theory of gender itself, a new way of thinking about reproduction and sexuality. The search drew some of us towards structural anthropology and psycho-analysis. From a feminist reading of anthropology we learned that the social meaning of maleness and femaleness is constructed through kinship rules which prescribe patterns of sexual dominance and subordination. From psychoanalysis we learned how these kinship rules become inscribed on the unconscious psyche of the female child via the traumatic reorientation of sexual desire within the Oedipal phase away from the mother and towards the father ('the law of the father'). The two arguments combined, as in Juliet Mitchell's highly influential *Psychoanalysis and Feminism*, provide a powerful account of the 'generation of a patriarchal system that must by definition oppress women'.

This account remains controversial within the women's movement, but it has greatly expanded our theoretical and political horizons. For if the mechanisms by which women's subordination are reproduced are also those which reproduce family structure and gendered individuals, then a revolution to eliminate such subordin-ation would have to extend very widely indeed. It would need to be, as Juliet says, a 'cultural revolution' which not only eliminated social inequalities based on sexual difference, but transformed the meaning of sexuality itself. We would need to learn new ways of being women and men. It is this project, not the annihilation of 'biological male persons', which the theory of patriarchy points towards.

Constructing a theory of patriarchal relations is hazardous, not least because it analyses gender in terms wholly different from those of class. But without a theory of gender relations, any attempt to 'marry' the concepts of sex and class will simply do for theories of sex what marriage usually does for women: dissolve them into the stronger side of the partnership. It was precisely because a Marxist theory of class conflict, however elaborated, could not answer all our questions about sexual conflict that we tried to develop an alternative. If we need to keep the two areas of analysis apart for a time, so be it. Theories are not made all at once.

However, Sheila's own anxiety about this theoretical dualism conceals a greater anxiety about the whole attempt to construct a theory of sexual antagonism. She seems to view any such theory as an iron grid of abstractions placed over the flow of direct experience; and, as an alternative, she appeals to history to answer ques-tions about female subordination which the 'fixed' and 'rigid' categories of theory cannot answer.

As feminist historians, we share Sheila's desire for more research into women's lives and experience. But this is no substitute for a theory of women's oppression. History only answers questions which are put to it: without a framework for these questions we shall founder in a welter of dissociated and contradictory 'facts'. Nor can women's own testimony about their relations with men be taken as unprob-lematic. Women have dwelled within their oppression at all times, but it is only occasionally that some have become sharply aware of it. Our analysis of women's consciousness must (as Sheila says) explain the periods of quiescence, as well as the times of anger. Simply recording how women behaved or what they said cannot give us this analysis, any more than recording what workers do gives us a theory of class: it is the underlying reality which must be examined.

Finally, Sheila is unhappy with the concept of patriarchy because it seems to discount all the good things which happen between men and women. She reminds us that women love men, that men need women, and that both sexes often find real support in each other, especially in moments of class confrontation –

all true (at least of heterosexual women). But does all this loving and needing and solidarising prove there is no general structure of sexual antagonism, only bad times and good times? Does it mean that loving men is unproblematic for women, something to be gratefully accepted rather than critically investigated? Surely not. Learning to love men sexually is a social process not a natural one, and in a patriarchal society it involves at least as much pain as joy, as much struggle as mutual support. Again, it is the analysis of kinship rules and unconscious mental life — not the study of biology — which helps us to understand how this channelling of desire towards reproductive heterosexuality occurs, and also what some of its costs have been: not only in terms of the systematic repression of homosexual love and lovers in most cultures, but also in terms of 'normal' feminine sexuality. Did not Freud help us to understand that in learning to love men we learn also to subordinate ourselves to them? The ropes which bind women are the hardest to cut, because they are woven with so many of our own desires.

The concept of patriarchy points to a strategy which will eliminate not men, but masculinity, and transform the whole web of psycho–social relations in which masculinity and femininity are formed. It is a position from which we can begin to reclaim for political change precisely those areas of life which are usually deemed biological or natural. It allows us to confront not only the day-to-day social practices through which men exercise power over women, but also mechanisms through which patterns of authority and submission become part of the sexed personality itself — 'the father in our heads', so to speak. It has helped us to think about sexual division — which cannot be understood simply as a by-product of economic class relations or of biology, but which has an independent dynamic that will only be overcome by an independent feminist politics. Finally, it has allowed us to look past our immediate experiences as women to the processes underlying and shaping that experience. For like class, sexual antagonism is not something which can be understood simply by living it: it needs to be analysed with concepts forged for that purpose. The theories which have developed around 'patriarchy' have been the first systematic attempts to provide them.

Judith M. Bennett

FEMINISM AND HISTORY

This is the first of two extracts by Judith Bennett in this *Reader*. A historian of medieval women, Bennett has also written at length on theorising feminist history and the history of sexuality. 'Feminism and History' was published in the journal *Gender and History* in 1989. It deals with two of the major themes in Part I of this *Reader* – 'patriarchy' and 'gender'. Bennett begins by highlighting the potentially debilitating effects of the institutionalisation of women's history, which, she argues, has come at the cost of the field's steady 'severance from feminism'. Under the assault of gender history, feminist analytical language has become more neutral and the term 'patriarchy' has virtually disappeared. Although the study of gender, class and race has enriched women's history in many ways admits Bennett, it has ignored the study of 'women as women' and therefore cannot 're-invigorate the influence of feminism'. According to Bennett, the challenge for feminist history now is to regain its 'moral vision ... political nerve ... [and] feminist indignation', aims that cannot be delivered by the study of gender. The primary question for feminist history in the 1990s is 'why and how has the oppression of women endured for so long and in so many different historical settings?' – in other words – a historical study of patriarchy. Bennett defends the academic use of patriarchy both as a single, uncluttered word and as a conceptual term that (contra Rowbotham's definition) can be endlessly historicised in a multiplicity of contexts. One of Bennett's most significant contributions to this debate is to reject the female victim model of patriarchal history, arguing that any study of patriarchy must include women and their collusion with the dominant social formation wherever relevant. 'Patriarchy' is as theoretically essential to women's history as capitalism is to labour history, or racism to African-American history Bennett argues; only through its revivification will we regain our feminist vision.

[. . .]

IN THE LAST TWO DECADES, the relationship between feminism and history has grown stronger than ever, with the nascent field of women's history providing a new forum for feminist investigations of the past. Yet, the place of feminism in history remains unstable; for even within the field of women's history, feminism has an insecure and eroding foothold. In this essay, I will examine what I see as the major challenge to women's history as it approaches the 1990s: the trend towards increasingly less explicit feminist perspectives in our scholarship. [. . .]

* * *

In the last twenty years, women's history has become a field of intense research, writing, and teaching in the United States. The results are impressive. We now have departmental positions in women's history (in some cases even chaired professorships), undergraduate majors and graduate fields in women's history, several programs that offer master's and/or doctoral degrees in women's history, regular conferences in women's history, prizes for articles and books in women's history, and now two new journals to serve the field.[1] Given the generally slow pace of change in academia, these achievements are quite remarkable, and they testify not only to the importance that feminists have placed on educational institutions as agents of change but also to the relative flexibility and openness of the university system in the United States. For better or for worse, women's history in the United States has matured into a conventional historical field.

Yet, despite the extraordinary institutional advances of the last two decades, perhaps the most discussed aspect of women's history in the United States is its ambivalent place within the larger discipline. Although women's history has become an institutionalized part of many departments, it has gained that place too often at the cost of isolation and segregation. This 'ghettoization' has allowed women's history a separate but not equal enclave within the historical profession. In advising students, for example, counselors sometimes ignore or trivialize women's history offerings as 'light history' or recommend them only to female students. In day-to-day decisions and activities of faculty, too many historians of women find themselves isolated, ignored, and subjected to covert ridicule. In hiring new faculty, historians of women are treated as exceedingly specialized and hence incompetent to fill positions in their geographical and chronological areas. And perhaps most troublesome of all, in both teaching and writing, women's history has not effectively reached other historians. There is precious little treatment of women or gender issues in courses not specifically devoted to such topics; despite modifications in standard textbooks and the availability of packets specifically designed for the purpose, survey courses in Western Civilization and U.S. history, for example, remain fundamentally unchanged. And there is some, but not enough awareness of women or gender in presentations, articles, and books by historians who specialize in other fields of history.[2]

These are certainly important problems that stunt the growth of historical knowledge and blight the professional lives of women's historians. Yet these problems are not surprising. Most historians are not feminists, and as either nonfeminists or antifeminists, few are likely to welcome enthusiastically an approach to history that criticizes their profession and seeks to transform it, just as few are likely to welcome a politics that challenges the fundamental presumptions of their private lives. These problems, moreover, cannot belie the very real advances women's history has made in the last two decades. Although many subtle and silent obstacles remain, the days of struggle against *overt* institutional hostility in the United States are largely gone. And although we might argue about whether or not women's history has fully 'arrived,' it is undeniably established as a permanent part of the historical profession in the United States.[3]

The greatest challenge to women's history may come, indeed, from the debilitating effects of institutionalization itself, which has nurtured the field's slow and ongoing severance from feminism. Women's history (defined as historical work on women) and feminist history (defined as historical work infused by a concern about the past and present oppression of women) are, of course, not identical. [. . .] Nevertheless, the ties between women's history and feminist history have always been strong; the institutionalization of women's history in the past twenty years owes a great deal to feminist pressure, and the field of women's history has always attracted the bulk of feminist historical scholarship.

Slowly, however, the force of feminism within women's history seems to be waning. As the field has gained institutional sanction in the United States, many historians of women have succumbed to pressures to produce studies that are palatable to their nonfeminist colleagues – studies that avoid hard feminist questions and that are seemingly more 'objective' than 'political.' One symptom of this trend away from feminism is the very language we have used and now use. When women's history was a nascent and marginalized activity in the United States, its founding mothers wrote freely and often about patriarchy and women's oppression. [. . .]

As women's history has become more entrenched in the academy (and hence, more dependent upon approval from the academic establishment), such strong language has become less common. 'Oppression of women' with its implication of male agency has been replaced by the more neutral 'subordination of women' (even Gerda Lerner now prefers this latter phrase) or better yet by the rather obfuscating 'inequality of the sexes' (a phrase which doesn't even specify which sex is disadvantaged by inequality).[4] And, since to focus on the systems through which women have been oppressed seems to 'blame men' in awkward and unappealing ways, the term 'patriarchy' has all but disappeared from most women's history. Indeed, I was recently told that I could not use this word in the title of a collection of essays about medieval women because it might offend some readers.

As our language has shifted, so has our thinking. Some of our very best historians of women continue to publish hard-hitting feminist analyses, but much work now published in women's history lacks explicit feminist content. In my field, there is a burgeoning market for books on women in the Middle Ages, but many are largely descriptive – texts of saints' lives, editions of women's writings, biographies of female saints, queens, and heroines, histories of individual nunneries or orders.[5] The authors of such books are making available very useful information about medieval women, but they are also usually avoiding difficult questions about the sexual dynamics of power within medieval society.[6] Even an interpretive tour-de-force like Caroline Bynum's *Holy Feast and Holy Fast: The Religious Significance of Food to Medieval Women* rarely deals forthrightly with the oppression of women within the medieval Church.[7] On the one hand, that oppression is taken for granted; on the other hand, it is almost disguised by being neither analyzed nor critiqued. As we know from our very first explorations into women's history, what is muted is soon obscured, and what is obscured is eventually forgotten. [. . .]

From the perspective of feminist scholarship within the academy, women's history has also lost considerable influence. In the developing years of feminist studies, women's history was in the forefront of the field – defining issues for research, contributing to feminist theory, and convening some of the very first university-level courses on women. In the last decade, history has lost that leadership role, yielding way particularly to the new frameworks provided by feminist literary criticism.[8] While feminist scholarship has been greatly enhanced by feminist literary criticism and is properly enriched from many directions, the erosion of historical influence is striking and (from my perspective) regrettable.[9] This loss of historical influence in feminist studies might be symptomatic of general academic fashions (with the pendulum swinging away from history and towards literary studies), but it is a trend probably aggravated, in this particular case, by the increasing de-politicization of women's history.

The really profound predicament for women's history in the United States, then, lies not in the ambivalent reception the field receives in most history departments (although we can wish it would be otherwise), but rather within the field itself. The most fundamental challenge for historians of women is to regain our moral vision, our political nerve, our feminist indignation. I do not mean to imply here that women's history should become a poor and oddly politicized step-child of history in general, for all history, of course, is political.[10] Moreover, some of the very best scholarship in women's history in the United States continues to be strongly and explicitly feminist; consider, for example, Linda Gordon's recent *Heroes of Their Own Lives* or Jacqueline Jones' *Labor of Love, Labor of Sorrow*.[11] But increasingly, these works seem to be exceptions – important and influential exceptions, to be sure, but exceptions in a field in which the bulk of published research is becoming more 'women's history' than 'feminist history.' Nor do I think that most women's historians are not feminist (or worse yet, that most don't measure up to my personal standards of feminism). Instead, I think that our feminism has been diverted, redirected away from broader issues (such as economic and legal equity, physical health, freedom from violence) and refocused (more comfortably) on internal, academic feminism: we seek to integrate women's experiences into mainstream history, to hire more women faculty, to create curricula that serve the needs of female as well as male students, and to improve the status of women on our campuses. These are important, indeed crucial issues, and they rightly absorb the attention and energy of many feminist scholars. But they are not sufficient. As feminist academics, we must have two agendas: first, to eradicate the misogynistic traditions of academia in its many, entrenched forms, and second, to contribute – through our privileged position as educated people, as research scholars, as teachers – to the understanding of (and hence, final eradication of) women's oppression.

* * *

As we approach the 1990s, women's history in the United States seems to be headed in three main directions. Scholars are variously studying the intersection of race, class, and gender, exploring the meanings of gender, and working to integrate women's history into mainstream scholarship. These endeavors are not discrete, but instead overlap with and complement one another. Together, they have enriched and expanded women's history, but they, nevertheless, cannot by themselves re-invigorate the influence of feminism within the field. Let me briefly discuss some of the possibilities and problems presented by each approach.

The effort to achieve greater inclusivity by studying not merely women but also the 'intersection of race, class and gender' has several clear advantages. By placing race and class on equal footing with gender, we can incorporate into feminist scholarship the hard lessons of practical feminist politics (which in the 1970s were often though not exclusively based on the needs of middle-class, white women). By treating gender as part of a complex of factors, we can better approximate the real experiences of women, whose identities are formed not by sex alone. By focusing on the *intersection* of several factors, we can study linkages between systems of oppression that are too often treated as discrete and independent. And by explicitly linking historians of women with their most natural allies within the profession (such as labor and African–American historians), we can try to break down part of the ghetto of women's history, getting at least some other fields of history thinking about gender.

Clearly, the concept of the intersection of race, class, and gender has enhanced and deepened women's history, but it also presents us with certain problems; for it is both unnecessarily exclusive and potentially hierarchical. 'The intersection of race, class and gender' has been rapidly enshrined as a politically correct approach, but it frankly often strikes me as a politically correct compromise that accommodates the interests of the more powerful while excluding the more silent. With its almost mantra-like status, the litany of race, class, and gender implies that these three factors do it all, and that is manifestly not true. What about ethnicity (something that is occasionally whispered at the end as a fourth category)? What about sexual orientation (something almost studiously ignored)? What about marital status? And so on. [. . .]

Other historians of women are focusing especially on the study of gender *per se*, using gender to signify those aspects of relations between women and men that are socially induced. 'Sex' denotes biological differences between women and men; 'gender' the differences that are created by societies.[12] Gender analysis, then, has the advantage of integrating both women and men into any subject studied. Instead of treating women as a separate, peculiar subject (i.e. instead of always implicitly asking, 'how were women's lives different from the (male) norm?'), we can seek, by focusing on gender, to understand the social constructions of both femaleness and maleness. [. . .]

The historical study of gender has some very real advantages; it reminds us that many seemingly 'natural' ideas about women and men are, in fact, socially constructed, and it has the potential to demolish entirely the academic 'ghetto-ization' of women's history. But the study of gender as advocated by Joan Scott and others must be pursued carefully and never in isolation from other feminist historical work. Pursued on its own, the Scottian study of gender ignores women *qua* women (a subject that still deserves greater attention); it evinces very little interest in material reality (focusing on symbols and metaphors rather than experi-ence);[13] and it intellectualizes and abstracts the inequality of the sexes. The hard lives of women in the past; the material forces that shaped and constrained women's activities; the ways that women coped with challenges and obstacles – all of these things can too easily disappear from a history of gender as meaning.[14]

The third major approach taken by historians of women in the United States has been to 'mainstream' women's history into general historical writing. At its crudest, mainstreaming simply means adding material on women to the current corpus of historical 'facts,' and almost everyone agrees that this sort of crude, nontransformative use of historical information about women is undesirable. But Louise Tilly has recently called for a new relationship between women's history and traditional history which, while not properly mainstreaming, draws neverthe-less upon the same integrative ideal. Tilly has argued that women's historians must begin answering other historians when they ask such questions as, 'Now that I know that women were participants in the French Revolution, what difference does it make?'[15] I agree with Tilly that women's history would be strengthened by connecting our analytical findings to the concerns of other historians. This requires a return, in part, to the agenda set by Joan Kelly who in the 1970s urged us to write women's history with an eye to transforming the very practice of history (historical description and periodization as well as explanation).[16] [. . .]

* * *

I do not propose that historians of women quit studying the historical intersection of race, class, gender, and other related factors, or cut short their search for the meanings of gender, or curtail their efforts to deal with general historical questions. These endeavors will take us far. But they will not bring moral and political vision back into women's history, unless also accompanied by a return to feminism and to the grand feminist tradition of critiquing and opposing the oppression of women. The historical task in this tradition is to study the oppression and subordination of women in the past, not just to detail women's oppression but also to understand the means through which that oppression has been accomplished. Historians of women must begin researching answers to this fundamental question: 'Why and how has the oppression of women endured for so long and in so many different historical settings?' This question should be at the top of the agenda for women's history as it moves into the 1990s.

If we accept this question as our central question, we will be setting out to study patriarchy as a historical phenomenon. This is a controversial agenda, since the historical study of patriarchy has been undercut not just by the de-politicizing effects of the institutionalization of women's history, but also by three other factors: by an ambivalence about the term 'patriarchy,' by a concern about overemphasizing the 'origins' of patriarchy, and by a deliberate decision on the part of some histor-ians of women to focus less on women's oppression and more on women's agency. Despite these problems, I think that the historical study of patriarchy deserves our intense and careful scrutiny. Let me discuss each problem in turn.

In a series of complex and sometimes arcane arguments, some feminist scholars have attacked the term 'patriarchy,' arguing that we should, instead, use such alternatives as 'male dominance' or 'the sex-gender system.'[17] I continue, however, to prefer patriarchy for five specific reasons. First, patriarchy originally denoted the legal powers of a father over his wife, children, and other dependents, and it is still used by some historians in this specific sense; Linda Gordon, for example, defined patriarchy in her recent book on family violence as 'a form of male dominance in which fathers control families and families are the units of social and economic power.'[18] But I use it here in its broader meaning to denote, in the words of Adrienne Rich,

> a familial-social, ideological, political system in which men – by force, direct pressure, or through ritual, tradition, law, and language, customs, etiquette, education, and the division of labor, determine what part women shall or shall not play, and in which the female is everywhere subsumed under the male.[19]

I adopt this expanded definition quite self-consciously. Although patriarchy originally derived from a specific familial meaning, it is now commonly used by feminists in its broader sense; when demonstrators at last April's feminist march on Washington, D. C. chanted 'Hey, Hey, Ho, Ho, Patriarchy's Got To Go,' they weren't talking about a specific form of paternal domination, but instead about the system through which women in the United States are regularly disadvantaged vis-à-vis men. Historians should accept this semantic development in the meaning of patriarchy; we can find better words to describe the specific forms of male dominance that have occurred and do occur within families ('familial patriarchy' might do just fine). Moreover, patriarchy is not just commonly used in this fashion by feminists; it is also, in fact, the *best* available word (or phrase) to denote the system described by Rich. 'Male dominance' and 'male supremacy' suggest not only that such systems rest in biological differences but also, through analogy with such terms as 'white supremacy,' that patriarchal institutions are strictly equivalent to racist and other oppressive institutions; 'sexism' suggests mere prejudice; 'oppression of women' and 'subordination of women' fail to convey the full complexity of systems in which many women have colluded and from which some women have benefited. And, patriarchy is a *single* word, a not insignificant asset. As long as we use a phrase like 'male dominance,' we'll slip into using roughly equivalent phrases like 'male supremacy' or 'male domination,' and such a multitude of terms will lead to unclear thinking and unclear writing.[20]

Second, patriarchy (used in the broad sense that I have adopted) has been misrepresented as a transhistorical, fatalistic term which implies that women's oppression is unchanging, natural, and inevitable. But patriarchy clearly has existed in many forms and varieties, and its history will, in fact, be a history of many different historical patriarchies (a point I will return to later). Nor should the apparent historical ubiquity of patriarchy (despite all its various forms) lead to fatalistic conclusions; as Zillah Eisenstein has put it, 'The reason patriarchy exists is because a nonpatriarchal sex-gender system could exist if allowed to.'[21] Indeed, unless feminist scholars historicize patriarchy by studying its many varieties, it will remain a bugbear for feminists, an ignored but ever-present spectre that suggests (however falsely) that the oppression of women is natural and ineradicable.

Third, patriarchy has been maligned as an offensively anti-male term. On the one hand, Rosalind Coward has suggested that patriarchy implies the 'literal over-powering' of a woman by a man. On the other hand, Sheila Rowbotham has argued that patriarchy ignores all the positive, happy interactions of women and men. I see nothing in the term patriarchy that evokes such images any more power-fully than such alternatives as male dominance. And, in any case, I concur with Sally Alexander and Barbara Taylor who responded specifically to Rowbotham that 'all this loving and needing and solidarising [does not] prove there is no general structure of sexual antagonism.'[22]

Fourth, patriarchy has been rejected as a term that falsely applies modern femi-nist assumptions to the past, an accusation reminiscent of attacks on all sorts of politically informed history.[23] Yet, we can certainly study the underlying reality of historical patriarchy without looking everywhere for female anger, female resist-ance, even female awareness of the systems through which women were oppressed. It is the business of historians to try to understand the past not only on its own terms but also through the prism of the present; to do so, we have regularly inter-preted the past with words and concepts – such as 'renaissance' and 'capitalism' as applied to the sixteenth century – that were unknown at the time.

And fifth, patriarchy has been attacked as a too-encompassing term that ignores the many different experiences of women of different times, countries, religions, races, sexualities, classes, and the like. But patriarchy highlights the pervasiveness and durability of women's oppression, without denying the differences generated by such other oppressions as imperialism, racism, feudalism, capitalism, and hetero-sexism.[24] Patriarchy is, to my mind, a perfectly good (and indeed, absolutely necessary) term to describe the systems – with multi-faceted and varying forms – through which the superordination of men has been established and preserved.

Aside from disputes about the meaning and utility of the term patriarchy, the historical study of patriarchy has also been inhibited by a focus upon the *origins* of patriarchal institutions. The search for origins has a distinguished history, motivated at least in part by the desire to prove that patriarchy – because it has an origin – is neither ahistorical nor timeless. From Frederick Engels and Johann Bachofen in the nineteenth century to Gerda Lerner in 1986, the search for the origin of patriarchy has been a compelling and uncertain one.[25] It has not been a fruitless search – we've learned a great deal both conceptually and practically – but it is a search that is doomed not only because the sources are too fragmentary but also because there was almost certainly no single origin of patriarchy. Fortunately, this doomed search is not essential: we do not need to find the origin (or origins) of patriarchy in order to establish its historicity. Patriarchy has clearly existed in many different manifesta-tions in many past societies, and these different manifestations constitute a history.

Finally, the historical study of patriarchy has been undermined by the un-appealing nature of the subject. To many feminist historians, it has seemed a depressing and pointless endeavour. Instead of looking at how women have coped and survived, created their own discourses and standards of beauty, nurtured their friends and frustrated their enemies, the study of patriarchy looks at the mechan-isms through which women have been oppressed, kept down, put in 'their place.' This is certainly not an inspiring history either to research or (especially) to teach.

This is also potentially a history that focuses more on men than women and that insofar as it does treat women, must consider the most unpleasant fact of women's collusion in their own oppression (since the oppression of women could not have endured so long and in so many places without their cooperation).[26] Hence, in the last decade, some historians of women have consciously opted to forgo the study of women as victims under patriarchy in favor of the study of women as agents in creating their own spaces, own cultures, own lives.

I think, however, that this division between women as victims and women as agents is a false one: women have always been both victims and agents. To emphasize either one without the other, creates an unbalanced history. Women have not been merely passive victims of patriarchy; they have also colluded in, undermined, and survived patriarchy. But neither have women been free agents; they have always faced ideological, institutional, and practical barriers to equitable association with men (and indeed, with other women). By creating a false dichotomy between victimization and agency and then eschewing the study of victimization, historians of women have sometimes created an almost idyllic history of a medieval 'golden age' for working women, of a renaissance for learned women in the sixteenth century, of a 'female world of love and ritual' in nineteenth-century America.[27] In celebrating the agency of women in the past, we have sometimes lost sight of their very real oppression.

What I want to propose, then, is that we bring the concept of patriarchy back into the mainstream of feminist scholarship by studying its *workings* throughout history. We might well never know *where* and *when* patriarchy began, but we can reconstruct *how* patriarchy has adapted, changed, and survived over time and place. Women have a large part to play in this historical study of patriarchy, not merely as victims, but also as agents. Women's support has always been crucial to the endurance of patriarchy; hence, we must examine and understand the motivations of women who have colluded in their own oppression. Women's agency *per se* is part of the strength of patriarchy; as Margaret Ezell has recently argued for seventeenth-century England, the very endurance of partriarchy must be explained, in part, by the 'very looseness of its structure' which insured that 'conditions were not intolerable to the point of open rebellion for the majority of women in their everyday lives.'[28] And the linking of women's agency to women's vulnerability (as in, for a modern Western example, the 'freedom' of women to walk the streets at night and their vulnerability in such environments to rape) is a crucial part of patriarchal endurance; we must examine the patriarchal ideologies and realities that have assured women that there is safety in protected subordination and danger in vulnerable freedom.[29]

I have thus far discussed the concept of patriarchy in the singular, but as we examine its historical workings, we will write many histories of many patriarchies – of its many manifestations and the many systems through which it has thrived. In time, I hope that we might be able to distinguish various sorts of historical patriarchies, particularly as they have interacted with various economic systems; we might someday be able to distinguish analytically, say, 'feudal patriarchy' from 'capitalist patriarchy' from 'socialist patriarchy.'[30] As we work towards this goal of better understanding patriarchy through studying its many forms, we must also keep two other perspectives in mind; we must trace not only how the mechanisms of any given patriarchy changed over time but also how those mechanisms affected different women in different ways. To approach this vast and complex subject, I suggest that we begin with three preliminary strategies: first, that we undertake case studies to analyze the many mechanisms of patriarchy in specific historical contexts; second, that we examine times of exceptional crisis to determine how patriarchal institutions adapted and hence, survived; third, that we risk generalization (cutting across differences of time, region, class, race, marital status, sexuality, and the like) to identify the most common mechanisms of patriarchy.

The first of these strategies is relatively unproblematic. Historians like case studies, and they are a proven method of analyzing complex subjects. Because the mechanisms of patriarchy are embedded in many institutions – religious, political, ideological, economic, cultural, familial, social, and the like – case studies provide an ideal method for reconstructing and evaluating their richly-textured and intertwined characters. [. . .] But very few of these completed case studies take patriarchy as their central focus. My own work on Brigstock, for example, argued against other historians who held idyllic notions of a rough-and-ready sexual equality in the medieval countryside; what I had to say about the mechanisms of the inequality I found in the records – about the workings of a rural patriarchy in the Middle Ages – was almost an aside in my main argument. I believe, in fact, that I never used either the noun patriarchy or the adjective patriarchal in the entire book. As a result, my book contains some information about rural patriarchy in the Middle Ages, but very little direct analysis of patriarchal institutions and no analysis at all of how these institutions might fit into the context of a historiography of patriarchy. What we need, then, are not only case studies *per se* but also case studies that are directed explicitly at problematizing historical patriarchies.

Crisis studies can give us another sort of perspective on patriarchy – one that will enable us to examine the causes of the remarkable durability of patriarchal structures. Patriarchy has endured not only in many settings but also through many great transitions – political (such as the decline of Rome or the growth of nation states), economic (such as the decay of trade in the early Middle Ages or the growth of capitalism in the modern world), religious (the triumph of Christianity in late Antiquity, the Reformation of the sixteenth century), social (as caused, for example, by the devasting plague of 1347–9 or the two World Wars of this century), even intellectual (the Renaissance, the Enlightenment). We need to examine how these transitions challenged patriarchies, how patriarchies changed in response to these challenges, and how patriarchies nevertheless endured.

[. . .]

The results justify the risks. Some of my recent comparative work has suggested, for example, that medieval women encountered many obstacles in their working lives that resemble the experiences of working women in modern economies; medieval women clustered, as do women today, in low paid, low status, low skilled jobs. Clearly, some essential aspects of the low working status of women predated the emergence of modern industrialism, predated the rise of capitalism in the early modern era, and indeed, predated the growth of a commercial, urbanized economy in the High Middle Ages.[31] Other work has shown how many aspects of public life in the Middle Ages were open to women, with the single resounding exception of formal politics. Medieval patriarchy, it seems, could tolerate women in markets, law courts, and a wide variety of social settings, but it could not tolerate (except in the most unusual circumstances) the exercise of formal political power by women. This rule extended across the social classes of the Middle Ages, limiting alike peasant women, townswomen, and feudal women.[32] Generalizations such as these identify common threads – in these cases, economic and political constraints on women – that might be vital to the sustenance of many historical patriarchies.

By advocating generalization, I do not mean to suggest that we should ignore differences in women's lives, differences related to class, race, sexuality, and the like. Indeed, once we risk generalization, distinctions within broad trends will be absolutely crucial to our understanding of historical patriarchy. Consider, for example, the economic generalization just mentioned above: that in medieval towns, women were generally second-rank workers. Within this general trend, different women had different working experiences – for example, the economic status of a woman differed dramatically according to whether she was a single-woman, wife, or widow. The patterns shown by these variations within the generally low economic status of women suggest that economic structures not only discriminated against women as women but also discouraged female autonomy and encouraged women to marry.[33]

All of these specific examples – about women's work in preindustrial Europe, about the exclusion of medieval women from formal politics, about women in the crises of the Reformation and the two World Wars, about women workers in the twentieth-century United States – are meant to be more suggestive than conclusive. We haven't yet looked hard enough at patriarchies as *patriarchies* to be able to reach many firm conclusions. But our tasks are clear; we must historicize patriarchy not only by identifying its main mechanisms (both those specific to only a few societies and those common to most) but also by examining how it has managed to survive and endure. In this endeavour, we must not forsake the three alternatives that I have described earlier – the exploration of the multiplexity of women's experiences, the examination of gender as a cultural and ideological representation, and the effort to nurture dialogues with historians in other fields. But I would like historians of women to start from a consciousness of the need to study patriarchy and to return, in the end, to that same consciousness; I would like a concern for historicizing patriarchy to be both our starting point and our destination.

If we make patriarchy (and its mechanisms, its changes, its endurance) the central problem of women's history, we will write not only feminist history but also better history. Our history will be more analytic and less descriptive; it will address one of the greatest general problems of all history – the problem of the nature, sustenance, and endurance of power structures; and it will eschew simplistic notions of times getting 'better' or 'worse' for women and grapple instead with the pressing problem of overall constancy in the (low) status of women. As we develop a more historical understanding of patriarchy, historians of women will also contribute in substantive ways to both feminism and feminist scholarship. By identifying the nature and causes of women's oppression in the past, we can directly enhance feminist strategies for the present. The history of women's work, for example, suggests that present-day feminists should be very cautious about the long-term efficacy of such programs as affirmative action or comparable worth; for, if economic constraints are a crucial buttress of patriarchy, they are unlikely to be overcome by strategies that do not attack the entire structure. By giving patriarchy a full history, we can also directly influence feminist scholarship in other disciplines. [. . .]

Few people like to study oppression and subordination, but the study of patriarchy is, to my mind, as central to women's history as is the study of capitalism to labour history or the study of racism to African–American history. And the study of patriarchy promises to revitalize women's history in the United States. Despite its many advances, women's history is still somewhat marginalized; while we should properly seek to break down that marginalization by integrating the history of women with the histories of class and race, by looking at the uses of gender as a universal signifier of power, and by considering the questions of mainstream historiography, we must also create our own historiography, centered on the crucial question of the endurance of patriarchy. Despite its feminist origins, women's history has lost much of its nonhistorical feminist audience in the United States; by addressing a central concern of all feminists – the nature, structures, and endurance of patriarchy – we can try to regain their attention. In making the central issue of feminism the central subject of women's history, we will be working not only within the very best traditions of history (for the greatest historians have always been motivated by moral and political commitment) but also within the very best traditions of feminism which, from its origins with Christine de Pizan in the early fifteenth century, has sought inspiration and understanding from the past.

Notes

1   *Gender and History*, published by an Anglo-American collective and *The Journal of Women's History*, based entirely in the United States.
2   For a recent discussion of some aspects of 'the powerful resistance of history' to women's history, see Joan Wallach Scott, *Gender and the Politics of History* (Columbia University Press, New York, 1988), esp. pp. 15–50 (quote from p. 18).
3   This more upbeat assessment of the place of women's history in the United States was taken, for example, by Louise A. Tilly in her paper on 'Women's History, Gender and Social History,' delivered at the 13th annual meeting of the Social Science History Association in November 1988 (and in the Winter 1990 volume of *Social Science History*).
4   Gerda Lerner, *The Creation of Patriarchy* (Oxford University Press, New York, 1986), pp. 233–5. Lerner eschews 'oppression' in favour of 'subordination' because oppression (a) inadequately describes the mutuality of paternalistic dominance, (b) implies victimization of women, and (c) 'represents the consciousness of the subject group that they have been wronged.' Despite my own inclination (after eight years of assimilation into academia) to prefer subordination to oppression, I have used oppression consciously in this essay, for as Lerner herself notes, oppression, defined as the victimization of women who recognize that they have been wronged, is part 'of the historical experience of women.' Since subordination inadequately describes the experiences of such women and since we can't yet ascertain the balance of oppression and subordination in the history of the relations between the sexes, the use of 'oppression' by historians has two advantages. First, it expresses the *consciousness of historians* that the sexual relations under examination are oppressive (no matter what the consciousness of the actors themselves might have been). Second, it creates more conceptual space for the analysis of subjects that many historians might be inclined to ignore – evil intent on the part of men, suffering on the part of women, hatred between the sexes, and the like.

5   For example, the publishers' advertisements in the program for the 24th International Congress on Medieval Studies (May, 1989) include 14 books on women, of which three are editions of texts by women, four are books on individual 'women worthies,' and two explore women in the writings of John Milton.

6   A similar tendency towards non-critical description can be seen in most recent surveys published on medieval women, such as: Angela M. Lucas, *Women in the Middle Ages: Religion, Marriage and Letters* (St. Martin's Press, New York, 1983); Frances and Joseph Gies, *Women in the Middle Ages* (Harper & Row, New York, 1978); and Margaret Wade Labarge, *A Small Sound of the Trumpet: Women in Medieval Life* (Beacon Press, Boston, 1986). The recent survey that deals most straightforwardly with women's oppression nevertheless lacks a theoretical overview: Shulamith Shahar, *The Fourth Estate: A History of Women in the Middle Ages*, trans. Chaya Galai (Methuen, London, 1983).

7   Caroline Walker Bynum, *Holy Feast and Holy Fast: The Religious Significance of Food to Medieval Women* (University of California Press, Berkeley, 1987).

8   See, for example, the entire issue of *Feminist Studies* devoted to deconstruction and its uses in feminist research, vol. 14, no. 1 (Spring, 1988).

9   For a useful discussion of some of the pitfalls of feminist scholarship that is insufficiently informed by historical understanding, see Karen Offen's review of Denise Riley, *Am I That Name?* and Joan Landes, *Women and the Public Sphere in the Age of the French Revolution*, 'The Use and Abuse of History,' *Women's Review of Books*, vol. 6, no. 7 (April 1989), pp. 15–16.

10   As Peter Novick has recently shown so clearly in his *That Noble Dream: The 'Objectivity Question' and the American Historical Profession* (Cambridge University Press, Cambridge, 1988), many historians in the United States have been (and are) obsessed with the appearance of objectivity in history and quite fearful of explicitly political interpretations. Yet, historians properly have many politics, many perspectives, many different audiences. In this respect, I hope that an assertive revitalization of feminist analysis in women's history will be an exemplar for the re-construction of history as a moral and political (but many-voiced) part of society in the United States.

11   Linda Gordon, *Heroes of Their Own Lives: The Politics and History of Family Violence, Boston 1880–1960* (Viking, New York, 1988); Jacqueline Jones, *Labor of Love, Labor of Sorrow: Black Women, Work, and the Family from Slavery to the Present* (Basic Books, New York, 1985).

12   Gisela Bock has recently questioned the biological basis of this distinction. See her 'Women's History and Gender History: Aspects of An International Debate,' *Gender and History*, 1 (1989), p. 15.

13   In saying this, I obviously disagree with Scott's argument that 'experience' can be reduced to something 'discursively organized' by 'plays of power and knowledge.' See *Gender and the Politics of History*, p. 5.

14   For a fuller critique of Scott's approach to the study of gender, see Claudia Koonz's review, 'Post Scripts,' *Women's Review of Books*, vol. 6, no. 4 (January, 1989), pp. 19–20.

15   Tilly, 'Women's History, Gender and Social History.'

16   See particularly, Kelly's 'The Social Relations of the Sexes: Methodological Implications of Women's History,' first published in 1976 and reprinted in *Women, History and Theory* (Univ. of Chicago Press, Chicago, 1984), pp. 1–18.

17   See, for example, Elizabeth Fox-Genovese, 'Placing Women's History in History,' *New Left Review*, 133 (1982), pp. 5–29, esp. p. 7 and pp. 22–3; Gayle Rubin, 'The Traffic in Women: Notes in the "Political Economy" of Sex,' in *Toward an Anthropology of Women*, ed. Rayna Reiter (Monthly Review Press, New York, 1975), pp. 157–210; Joan Scott, *Gender and the Politics of History*, esp. pp. 33–4; and Sheila Rowbotham, 'The Trouble with "Patriarchy",' 1979, reprinted in *People's History and Socialist Theory*, ed. Raphael Samuel (Routledge, Kegan & Paul, London, 1981), pp. 364–9. Many of these definitions of patriarchy have evolved in debates about the nature of the relationship between feminism on the one hand and Marxism and/or socialism on the other. I cannot enter into this debate here; for my purposes, the salient point has

been how various scholars have defined or maligned the term 'patriarchy.' For a useful summary of some parts of the debate, see Walby, *Patriarchy at Work* (Polity Press, Cambridge, 1986), pp. 5–49. For a fine example of an attempt at synthesis, see Lise Vogel, *Marxism and the Oppression of Women: Toward a Unitary Theory* (Rutgers University Press, New Brunswick, 1983).

18   Gordon, *Heroes of Their Own Lives*, p. vi. *The Oxford English Dictionary* defines patriarchy as 'government by the father or eldest male of the family' (a definition curiously unchanged in the new second edition). For Gerda Lerner's reservations about this narrow definition, see *Creation of Patriarchy*, pp. 238–9.

19   Adrienne Rich, *Of Woman Born* (1976: UK edition by Virago, London, 1977), p. 57.

20   Unlike most of its alternatives, 'patriarchy' also boasts simple adjectival and adverbial forms.

21   Zillah Eisenstein, *The Radical Future of Liberal Feminism* (Longman, New York, 1981), pp. 21.

22   See Rosalind Coward, *Patriarchal Precedents: Sexuality and Social Relations* (Routledge & Kegan Paul, London, 1983), p. 272 and repeated p. 273; Rowbotham, 'The Trouble with Patriarchy,' p. 366; Sally Alexander and Barbara Taylor, 'In Defence of "Patriarchy",' 1979, reprinted in *People's History and Socialist Theory*, pp. 370–3, quote from p. 372.

23   For example, see Brian Harrison and James McMillan's charge that feminist historians are especially susceptible to historical anachronisms, 'Some Feminist Betrayals of Women's History,' *The Historical Journal* 26 (1983), pp. 375–89. For this charge against patriarchy, see Rowbotham, 'The Trouble with "Patriarchy",' and responses by Alexander and Taylor, 'In Defence of "Patriarchy".'

24   The supposed narrowness of 'patriarchy' forms the basis of Elizabeth Fox-Genovese's dismissal of the term. Most theorists of patriarchy, however, insist that systems of sexual oppression must interact with other systems; see, for example, Sylvia Walby, *Patriarchy at Work*, and Zillah Eisenstein, *The Radical Future of Liberal Feminism*.

25   Frederick Engels, *The Origin of the Family, Private Property and the State*, ed. Eleanor Leacock (International Publishers, New York, 1972); Johann J. Bachofen, *Das Mutterrecht* (Krais & Hoffman, Stuttgart, 1861); Gerda Lerner, *The Creation of Patriarchy*.

26   In 1975, Gerda Lerner complained that 'Such inquiry fails to elicit the positive and essential way in which women have functioned in history,' *The Majority Finds its Past. Placing Women in History* (Oxford University Press, New York, 1979), p. 147. Carroll Smith-Rosenberg noted in 1980 her feeling that 'an exclusive emphasis on male oppression of women had transformed me into a historian of men.' See 'Politics and Culture in Women's History: A Symposium,' *Feminist Studies*, 6 (1980), p. 61.

27   For some examples of this trend toward overemphasis on women's agency in the past, see: David Nicholas, *The Domestic Life of a Medieval City: Women, Children and the Family in Fourteenth-Century Ghent* (University of Nebraska Press, Lincoln, 1985); Patricia H. Labalme (ed.), *Beyond Their Sex: Learned Women of the European Past* (New York University Press, New York, 1984); and Carroll Smith-Rosenberg, 'The Female World of Love and Ritual: Relations Between Women in Nineteenth-Century America,' *Signs*, 1 (Autumn, 1975), pp. 1–29. Note, however, that Smith-Rosenberg has disassociated herself from much of the work on 'women's culture' that has derived from her seminal article (see discussion by Smith-Rosenberg and others in 'Politics and Culture in Women's History').

28   Margaret J. M. Ezell, *The Patriarch's Wife: Literary Evidence and the History of the Family* (University of North Carolina Press, Chapel Hill, 1988), p. 163.

29   See, for example, Anna Clark's interesting discussion of the emergence of an ideology that linked vulnerability to rape with movement in public, in *Women's Silence, Men's Violence: Sexual Assault in England 1770–1845* (Pandora, London, 1987).

30   Sylvia Walby might be right in arguing that 'patriarchy is never the only mode in a society but always exists in articulation with another, such as capitalism.' Yet, we

can only establish the veracity of her argument through historical and comparative study of patriarchies. See Walby *Patriarchy at Work* p. 50.

31   Judith M. Bennett, '"History that Stands Still": Women's Work in the European Past,' *Feminist Studies*, 14, no. 21 (1988), pp. 269–83.

32   See particularly, Mary Erler and Maryanne Kowaleski, *Women and Power in the Middle Ages* (University of Georgia Press, Athens, 1988).

33   See, for example, chapters IV to VI in Bennett, *Women in the Medieval English Countryside: Gender and Household in Brigstock before the Plague* (Oxford University Press, New York, 1987). Barbara A. Hanawalt (ed.), *Women and Work in Preindustrial Europe* (Indiana University Press, Bloomington, 1986); and Maryanne Kowaleski and Judith M. Bennett, 'Crafts, Gilds, and Women in the Middle Ages,' *Signs*, 14 (1989), pp. 474–88.

Amanda Vickery

GOLDEN AGE TO SEPARATE SPHERES?
A review of the categories and chronology of English women's history

In this article, published in the *Historical Journal* in 1993, the British historian Amanda Vickery attempts to dismantle what she accurately describes as 'one of the fundamental organizing categories, if not *the* organizing category of modern British women's history' – that of the 'separate spheres'. As an eighteenth-century specialist, Vickery's challenge to the dominance of this trope is both chronological and theoretical. First, she queries historians' assumptions as to the particular significance of the early nineteenth-century period for the emergence of a class-based society steeped in evangelical values and a pious, submissive ideal of femininity. Second, Vickery finds much to criticise theoretically in the undiscerning use of the metaphor of the separate spheres by historians. Rather than problematising the relationship between prescriptive literature and the daily realities of women's and men's lives, she argues, the pervasiveness of the separate spheres' ideology is assumed rather than interrogated. Did women's affinity with the private sphere and the moral ethics that shored up the nineteenth-century middle classes really strip women of previous freedoms she asks? Surely it would be equally possible to invert the separate spheres model and declare that the revival of religious activity in the 1800s saw an *expansion* in women's public role not a diminution of it? The metaphor of the separate spheres has been subject to extensive review over the past decade as noted in the Introduction to this *Reader*. Greater appreciation of the complex, uneven meanings of both private and public space has led to the realisation that fewer Victorian women took their 'didactic medicine' quite so literally as first suspected. Following Vickery, therefore, feminist historians now agree that the metaphor of the separate spheres 'fails to capture the texture of female subordination and the complex interplay of emotion and power in family life'.

I

'**PUBLIC AND PRIVATE**', 'separate spheres' and 'domesticity' are key words and phrases of academic feminism. The dialectical polarity between home and world is an ancient trope of western writing; the notion that women were uniquely fashioned for the private realm is at least as old as Aristotle. But the systematic use of 'separate spheres' as *the* organizing concept in the history of middle-class women is of more recent vintage. Formative for American feminist historians in the 1960s and 1970s was the idea that gender oppression, the experience of sisterhood and a feminist consciousness have a natural, evolving relationship. Resulting studies undertook a quasi-marxist search for this developing consciousness. Nineteenth-century advice books, women's magazines, evangelical sermons and social criticism provided chapter and verse on the bonds of womanhood at their most elaborate, although such literature was prescriptive rather than descriptive in any simple sense. Thus a particularly crippling ideology of virtuous femininity was identified as newly-constructed in the early to mid-nineteenth century. What Barbara Welter dubbed the 'cult of true womanhood' prescribed the attributes of the proper American female between 1820 and 1860. She was to be pious, pure, submissive and domesticated, for the true woman turned her home into a haven for all that was civilized and spiritual in a materialistic world. The assumption that capitalist man needed a hostage in the home was endorsed by subsequent historians who linked the cult of true womanhood to a shrinkage of political, professional and business opportunities for women in the years 1800–40. In this way, the glorification of domestic womanhood became associated with the deterioration of women's public power, which was itself presented as a function of industrialization. Consequently, the early nineteenth century assumed its present status as one of the key, constitutive periods in the history of gender. [. . .]

In the meantime, the analysis of manuscripts written by middle-class women themselves prompted a more sophisticated understanding of the cult of domesticity. Instances were found of American women using notions of domestic virtue for their own purposes, particularly in the attempt to justify their efforts at moral reformation both within the family and outside the home. Furthermore, it was argued that in accepting the conventional message as to their domestic mission, women saw themselves increasingly as a group with a special destiny and their consciousness of sisterhood was therefore heightened. In other words, the bonds of 'womanhood bound women together even as it bound them down'. However, life in a separate sphere was not in all senses impoverished, for it was in the private sphere that historians such as Carroll Smith Rosenberg discovered and celebrated a rich women's culture of sisterly cooperation and emotional intimacy.

> Women's sphere had an essential integrity and dignity that grew out of women's shared experiences and mutual affection . . . Most eighteenth and nineteenth-century women lived within a world bounded by home, church, and the institution of visiting – that endless trooping of women to each others' homes for social purposes. It was a world inhabited by children and by other women. Women helped each other with domestic chores and in times of sickness, sorrow, or trouble.

Implicit in Carroll Smith Rosenberg's account [. . .] is the theory that the private sphere nurtured a sense of gender-group solidarity which was ultimately expressed in mid-Victorian feminism, a sisterhood which foreshadowed the culture and ideals of the 1970s women's movement. Thus, by now it should be apparent that these various chapters in the history of women can be incorporated into a long positive story, making sense of a swathe of time from the establishment of the first textile mill to the Nineteenth Amendment to the Constitution, and beyond. For many, the foregoing elements fused together to create the most powerful and satisfying narrative in modern American women's history. As Nancy Hewitt regretfully concluded in 1985, despite the fact that Barbara Welter, Nancy Cott and Carroll Smith-Rosenberg all regarded their work 'as speculative and carefully noted parameters of time, region and class, the true woman/separate spheres/woman's culture triad became the most widely used framework for interpreting women's past in the United States'.

Although the foundation of the separate spheres framework was established through a particular reading of didactic and complaint literature, ensuing primary research was rarely designed to test the reliability or significance of this sort of evidence. Many women's historians neglected to ask the questions posed by early modern family historians: Did the sermonizers have any personal experience of marriage? Did men and women actually conform to prescribed models of authority? Did prescriptive literature contain more than one ideological message? Did women deploy the rhetoric of submission selectively, with irony, or quite cynically? And to quote Keith Wrightson, did 'theoretical adherence to the doctrine of male authority and *public* female subordination' mask 'the *private* existence of a strong complementary and companionate ethos'? Those modernists who reminded us that 'the attitudes of ordinary people are quite capable of resisting efforts to reshape or alter them' had little impact on the development of the field. Instead, research confidently built on the sands of prescription. The old sources predetermined the questions asked of the new. The process is here illuminated by Nancy Cott describing the evolution of the historical characterization of the 'woman's sphere' from domestic cage, to ambivalent arena of both constraint and opportunity, to the safe haven of a loving female subculture:

> The three interpretations primarily derived from three different kind of sources; the first from published didactic literature about woman's place and the home, the second from the published writings of women authors, and the third from the private documents of non-famous women. It is worth pointing out that the more historians have relied on women's personal documents the more positively they have evaluated woman's sphere.

However different these successive interpretations might seem, the conceptual importance of a constraining 'women's sphere' is constant. Rather than conclude from positive female testimony that women were not necessarily imprisoned in a rigidly defined private sphere, the dominant interpretation simply sees the private sphere in a better light. Moreover, the assumption prevails that it is helpful and appropriate to examine culture and society in terms of intrinsically male and female spheres.

And indeed the dichotomy between the home and the world continued to structure the bulk of work on nineteenth-century American women until the mid to late 1980s. Recently, however, crucial criticisms of the American historiography have been offered by Linda Kerber, leading her to ask 'why speak of worlds, realms, spheres at all?' and American research now in progress seems more sceptical in its approach. Yet this interpretive tradition was by no means restricted to American women's history, having predetermined the way historians have conceptualized the experience of middle-class women in England. And as British historians were slower to elaborate this conceptual framework, so now they are slower to abandon it.

Of course, elements of the interpretations were hardly new in British historiography. After all, in popular understanding 'Victorian' has long served as a general synonym for oppressive domesticity and repressive prudery. But more specifically, as early as the 1940s and 1950s cultural historians such as Walter Houghton, Maurice Quinlan and Muriel Jaeger had seen the assertion of a new model of femininity as a central component in the rise of Victorianism – a shift in standards and behaviour which Quinlan and Jaeger saw in process from the closing decades of the eighteenth century. Using the same sources (the sanctimonious novels and sermons of Evangelicals like Hannah More, Mrs Sherwood and Mrs Trimmer, the didactic manuals of Sarah Stickney Ellis and her ilk, and the sentimental or chivalric fantasies of Coventry Patmore, John Ruskin, Alfred Lord Tennyson, and so on), a younger generation of women's historians told essentially the same story but with greater rhetorical flourish, arguing that a new ideology of ultra-femininity and domesticity had triumphed by the mid-Victorian period. The first studies painted a highly-charged picture of the typical woman of the nineteenth-century middle class. A near prisoner in the home, Mrs Average led a sheltered life drained of economic purpose and public responsibility. As her physicality was cramped by custom, corset and crinoline, she was often a delicate creature who was, at best, conspicuously in need of masculine protection and, at worst, prey to invalidism. And yet she abjured self-indulgence, being ever-attentive and subservient to the needs of her family. Only in her matronly virtue and radiant Christianity did she exercise a mild authority over her immediate circle. She was immured in the private sphere and would not escape till feminism released her.

Thereafter, the rise of the ideology of domesticity was linked, as in the American case, to the emergence of middle-class cultural identity. It was separate gender spheres which allegedly put the middle in the middle-class. [. . .] Of course, as organizing characteristics go, class had long been seen as central to history of nineteenth-century England. In adding gender to the picture of class society, historians of women confirmed a vision of the past shared by most social historians in England in the 1960s and 1970s. And indeed class was to remain a more powerful category in English women's history than in its American counterpart, and as a result the notion of a universal sisterhood which triumphantly bridged the gulf between mistress and servant, prosperous philanthropist and poor recipient never took a firm hold in English historiography.

Less pronounced in the English literature than in the American was the argument that life in a confined sphere could be emotionally enriching for early Victorian women, although there is some work on the support networks and intense friendships of late Victorian rebels. However, the argument that women in prosperous families were robbed of economic and political function and incarcerated in a separate private sphere in the early years of the century came to serve as useful prelude to accounts of feminist assault on public institutions in the later period. Implicit and sometimes explicit in such accounts was the assumption that the private sphere operated as a pressure cooker generating pent-up frustrations which eventually exploded as mass female politics. Revealingly, the first significant history of the English women's movement, written by the activist Ray Strachey in 1928, had opening chapters entitled: 'The prison house of home, 1792–1837', 'The stirring of discontent, 1837–1850', 'The widening circle, 1837–1850' and 'The demand formulated, 1850–1857'. [. . .]

Buttressed therefore by three types of evidence – didactic literature, contemporary feminist debate and post-Victorian denunciations – the separate spheres framework has come to constitute one of the fundamental organizing categories, if not *the* organizing category of modern British women's history. Moreover, through the medium of women's studies, the orthodoxy has been communicated to adjacent disciplines, where 'public and private', 'separate spheres', and 'domesticity' are rapidly becoming unquestioned key words.

Of course, interpretations have developed over time. Proponents of the British separate spheres framework have revised many of their early generalizations. Sceptics have debated particular aspects of the framework, with varying degrees of effectiveness. Most are now at pains to present women as sentient, capable beings rather than as passive victims, emphasizing the ways in which women shaped their own lives within a male-dominated culture. The Angel-in-the-House model of Victorian ladyhood has proved most vulnerable to criticism. Using household manuals aimed at the lower middle-class wife managing on about £200 a year, Patricia Branca contested the representativeness of the pure and passive stereotype. Only prosperous upper middle-class ladies, she argued, idly received callers and supervised staff with cool aplomb. The vast majority of middle-class housewives coped with heavy housework and quarrelsome servants, while simultaneously struggling with the nervous art of creative accounting. [. . .]

The breathless inadequacy model of bourgeois femininity has also been questioned in studies of intrepid emigrants, formidable travellers and driven philanthropists. Feeble females would simply not have been capable of the courageous enterprise and conscientious administration that recent work reveals. In fact, as Pat Thane has astutely argued, it is actually rather difficult to reconcile the 'strong sense of social responsibility, purpose and commitment to hard work with which Victorians of both sexes and all classes were socialized' with the conventional story of *increasing* female passivity.

In fact, where historians have researched the activities of particular individuals and groups, rather than the contemporary social theories which allegedly hobbled them, Victorian women emerge as no less spirited, capable, and, most importantly, diverse a crew as in any other century. Not that diversity should surprise us. Early modern family historians have long stressed the unique role of character and circumstance in shaping a woman's freedom of manoeuvre in marriage. Assuredly, stern patriarchs sometimes married biddable girls, but by the same token strong women sometimes married weak men. [. . .]

The endless permutations in matrimonial power relations that can result from the accidents of circumstance and character have led some scholars to argue for the unpredictable variety of private experience, in any given period, whatever the dominant ideology. But even if we reject such extreme particularism, the history of ideas tell us that in every era alternative 'ideologies' are usually on offer. Another look at Victorian sexual debate, for instance, reveals it may not have been so universally 'Victorian' as we have been led to believe. Wherever angelic uniformity was to be found, it was not in Victorian sitting rooms, despite the dreams of certain poets, wistful housewives and ladies' advice books.

Most historians now concede that few women actually lived up to the fantasies of Ruskin and Patmore, but still differ as to how seriously the Victorians took their didactic medicine. Martha Vicinus, for instance, reflects that if 'nineteenth-century women were not always the passive, submissive and pure creatures of popular idealizations . . . neither were they completely free from this stereotype'. However, much recent scholarship has refused to see the domestic ideal as a force which, in and of itself severely limited a woman's freedom of manoeuvre. Most vehement in this vein is Jeanne Peterson, who concludes that the ideal of the domesticated Madonna was simply an irrelevance in upper middle-class households. The imposition of such a constraining behavioural model, she suspects, would have made rebellious New Women of an entire generation. 'Instead the freedom, the adaptability, the choices inherent in genteel family life laid the basis for a profound conservatism'. [. . .] Similarly, a thorough conversance with conservative assessments of woman's proper place (worried over in her diary) failed to keep Lady Charlotte Guest from translating the Mabinogian from medieval Welsh and managing the Dowlais iron works after her husband's death, while simultaneously mothering her ten children. Of course, these particular examples are culled from the records of the socially exalted, who were better placed than most to flout convention or indulge exciting enthusiasms if they chose, nevertheless their experience still serves to remind us of the elementary, but crucial, point that women, like men, were eminently capable of professing one thing and performing quite another. Just because a volume of domestic advice sat on a woman's desk, it does not follow that she took its strictures to heart, or whatever her intentions managed to live her life according to its precepts.

Nevertheless, faith in the constitutive power of domestic precepts still lingers in the explanation of the achievements of mid-Victorian heroines. The heroic narrative assumes that a model of domestic femininity was *actively imposed* on women, who experienced feelings of entrapment of such strength that they were led fiercely to resist their containment, resulting in a glorious escape from the private sphere. To be sure, extraordinary women like Florence Nightingale have left passionate writings which ask us to see public heroism as an inevitable reaction to a previous period of mind-numbing cloistration. However, while Nightingale felt her early career aspirations cruelly thwarted, she herself had been taught Latin and Greek by her father, and was expected to engage in a ceaseless round of good works and charitable visiting in young adulthood. Although Nightingale undoubtedly lacked scope for her great ambitions, she was hardly locked in the parlour with nothing but advice books for nourishment. [. . .]

In consequence of recent work both theoretical and empirical, doubts now circulate within women's history about the conceptual usefulness of the separate spheres framework. As Jane Lewis remarked in 1986: 'while such a separation of spheres appears to fit the recent historical experience of western women well, anthropologists have found, first that the dichotomy conflates too easily with public/

private and reproduction to be a useful conceptual tool and second that it has more descriptive than analytical power'. But despite the dissenting voices, the questions, focus and chronology of the separate spheres framework still holds an uneasy sway. At conferences and seminars, participants raise queries and criticisms, while defendants of 'separate spheres' acknowledge the weaknesses of many aspects of the framework, yet still 'separate spheres' is believed to be of central importance in the history of nineteenth-century women and remains the model taught to students. To add to the confusion, the vocabulary of separate spheres also overlaps with that deployed by political historians to rather different ends; specifically, in the argument that the eighteenth century saw the creation, through the market in print, of a public sphere of politics, in contrast to the previously closed political world of Westminster and the royal court. A major study by Leonore Davidoff and Catherine Hall has tried to take account of recent doubt and debate, but still asserts the historical significance of the ideology of separate spheres. As a result, *Family fortunes: men and women of the English middle class* offers the most complex use of separate spheres as an organizing concept to date. Indeed, many see the book as the last word on the subject. Unquestionably, therefore, a landmark of English women's history, *Family fortunes* is an appropriate focus of detailed critical attention.

The explicit aim of *Family fortunes* is to insert an awareness of 'the constitutive role of gender into the main agenda of social and historical analysis'. This is achieved by bringing the analysis of gender relations to bear on the question of mid-Victorian class formation. To this end, *Family fortunes* offers an account of the economic, associational, religious and domestic lives of middle-class families in Birmingham, Essex and Suffolk, between the years 1780 and 1850. And indeed the study impresses as a massively detailed and richly elaborated account of gender relations in a certain religious and institutional milieu. It offers much invaluable illumination of the complexities which lie beneath the stereotypes: the hidden investment of female knowledge, labour and capital in apparently male-only enterprises; the varying organization of the different churches and religious associations which offered women a place, albeit circumscribed; the role of wider kin in the life of the supposedly intensely nuclear bourgeois family; and the contradictory nature of middle-class taste and aspiration – even in the papers of the pious families studied, the scandalous Lord Byron was cited almost as often as the unexceptionable William Cowper and Hannah More. If anything, however, the richness and singularity of the picture Davidoff and Hall reconstruct refuses the general structure they seek to impose. The picture still stands although the claims they make for it, in my opinion, do not. In brief, they argue that gender played a crucial role in the structuring of an emergent, provincial, middle-class culture, for it was the ideology of domesticity and separate gender spheres which gave distinctive form to middle-class identity. Yet this claim rests upon a series of problematic assumptions which must be explored if women's historians are truly to assess the usefulness of the modified separate spheres framework and to build on the research of Davidoff and Hall in creative ways.

First and foremost, *Family fortunes* rests on the conviction that a class society emerged between 1780 and 1850. For many historians of women, E. P. Thompson's inspirational masterpiece, *The making of the English working class* celebrated the making of a class with the women left out. *Family fortunes*, by contrast, presents the making of the middle class with women and the family emphatically in the spotlight. Without reference to the ever-growing literature on the culture and consequence of the early-modern middling sort, Davidoff and Hall assert that the provincial middle class took shape in the late eighteenth and early nineteenth centuries. Set apart from aristocracy and gentry by virtue of evangelized religion, a domestic value-system and non-landed wealth, the middle classes experienced a 'growing desire for independence from the clientage of landed wealth and power' which culminated in the political incorporation of the first reform act. Despite internal differences in income and outlook, the nineteenth-century middle class were bound together by a distinctive culture; moderate, rational and commercial, but above all moral and domesticated. These cultural values stood in marked contrast to the lavish and licentious mores of the aristocracy and gentry, although eventually the middle-class world view would become 'the triumphant common sense of the Victorian age'.

[. . .]

In the assertion that modern class and gender relations were made in the period from 1780 to 1850, Davidoff and Hall call into play vintage assumptions about the impact of economic change. The period from 1780 to 1850 is a conventional choice for nineteenth-century historians and in characterizing these seventy years as formative, Davidoff and Hall are not unusual. They do not aim to examine the late eighteenth century in any detail; in fact their close focus is saved for the period 1820–50. Again the eighteenth century is the sketchy before-picture, the primeval sludge out of which modern, industrial society emerges. There seems to be a consensus in the literature about nineteenth century society that 1780 is a key social and economic moment. Implicitly this derives from an old idea of a late eighteenth-century industrial 'take off' which enabled historians to cite the industrial revolution as the *deus ex machina* accounting for most social developments. But in the light of a revised economic history which has variously stressed the vigour of seventeenth-century and early eighteenth-century international commerce and domestic manufacturing, and/or down-played the socio-economic contrast between 1750 and 1850 in England as a whole, it is surprising that social historians should continue to present, with relatively little qualification, an apocalyptic industrial revolution, 1780–1850, as the midwife of modernity. After all, seventeenth- and early eighteenth-century wealth creation was sufficiently impressive for there to be plenty of commercial families supporting non-earning wives, prospering long before Hannah More and William Wilberforce took up their campaigns. Similarly, the ideas and institutions which allegedly defined both economic man and a manly economy: accounting, banking, an investment market, a complex retail network and so on were also well-established before 1780.

If the economic changes of the period 1780 to 1850 were not as dramatic as *Family fortunes* implies, it cannot be said that the same years were unmomentous in terms of politics. Davidoff and Hall stress the role of the shock-waves of the French revolution and the campaigning zeal of the evangelicals in creating a new moral climate in English social and political life discernible from the 1790s. In the turbulent decades ahead, it is argued, the image of pure womanhood unsullied by public cares, was to offer the English middle class a vision of harmony and security in an uncertain world. What should we make of this version of events? Firstly, it is clear that texts extolling domestic virtue and a clear separation of the realms of men and women circulated long before 1789, so it cannot be the case that political fears begat this particular theory of social organization. Secondly, while no-one would deny that evangelicalism was a crucial force in nineteenth-century society, the extent to which evangelicalism was an exclusively middle-class project is unclear: the Clapham sect themselves hailed from lesser gentry, while the appeal of Methodism was obviously felt far down the social hierarchy. Thirdly, it would be mistaken to see evangelical enthusiasm thriving in every middle-class home, just because the history of the tepid, the backsliding and the utterly indifferent nineteenth-century household remains to be written. And fourthly, the extent to which shifts in public morality actually stripped women of important powers and freedoms is also obscure. Of course, it is beyond question that the Victorians were different from the mid Georgians in their public reactions to sex. [. . .] Assuredly, the behaviour of both women *and* men became more constrained in certain public contexts. Yet does the onset of prudishness necessarily signal the haemorrhage of important powers for women? That so many of us have presumed it does, *ipso facto*, is perhaps more of a testimony to the continuing strength of the 1960s belief that sexual adventure and social liberation are synonymous, than the result of research on early nineteenth-century social practices. Still, evangelical fervour *may* have resulted in the discrediting of certain public arenas within which privileged women had once been active, like the theatre auditorium, the assembly room and the pleasure garden, although research on this issue is in its infancy. Nevertheless, if evangelized religion took from some women's public lives with one hand, it undoubtedly gave with the other in the burgeoning of religious associations, moral campaigns and organized charity. Certainly, this was Wilberforce's rather self-serving conclusion:

> There is no class of persons whose condition has been more improved in my experience than that of unmarried women. Formerly there seemed to be nothing useful in which they could naturally be busy, but now they may always find an object in attending the poor.

Moreover, Linda Colley has recently argued that the conservative backlash of the 1790s offered opportunities for *greater* female participation in a new public life of loyalist parades, petitions and patriotic subscriptions. Viewed from this angle, in fact, reactionary politics offered these 'angels of the state' a higher public profile, not an upholstered private cage.

And this brings us back to the vexed question of separate spheres. Taking account of feminist revisionism, Davidoff and Hall recognize that the prescriptions of sermons and conduct books can never offer a perfect design for living. (In fact, Davidoff herself suggested in an important essay in 1977 that the ideal system laid out in sermons and manuals was belied by the complexity of lived experience.) Davidoff and Hall argue that the spheres could never be truly separate and that it was impossible for Victorians to live as if that separation was absolute. Nevertheless, they still assert that the ideology of separate spheres had a powerful hold on the imagination of the Victorian bourgeoisie and that negotiating this ideology was a central middle-class concern. It was the middle-class belief in appropriate spheres which shaped the formal organization (if not the day-to-day running) of their emergent institutions. Their argument for, the ideological significance of 'separate spheres' rests upon the existence of a large body of nineteenth-century texts extolling the strict separation of the public and private, and the fact that religious institutions tended to segregate the formal activities of men and women. But does this juxtaposition offer sufficient proof that the Victorians exerted themselves to live up to the rhetoric of separate spheres? Davidoff and Hall do not offer evidence from personal manuscripts of a constant dialogue between precept and practice. Instead, they detail the attempts of churchmen of all denominations to ensure a proper division of labour between the sexes: women were allotted subsidiary roles, directed to single-sex committees and for the most part expected to content themselves dispensing liquid and emotional refreshment. However, this raises a crucial question – is the maintenance of a sexual division of labour within institutions *the same thing as* the separation of public and private spheres? If we decide it is, then we must conclude that the drive to create separate spheres is universal, transcending class and time, for throughout history and across cultures there are virtually no institutions which have not differentiated between men and women when it comes to dispensing power and prestige. Of course, if the segregation of men and women within church organization can be shown to be a novel development, then it might be read as another manifestation of the forces that spawned the separate spheres literature, thereby confirming the status of 'separate spheres' as a powerful ideology. And in this vein, Davidoff and Hall assume: 'as so often, increased formality led to the increasing marginalization of women'. Yet, few eighteenth-century historians would claim that women enjoyed an institutional heyday in their period. If anything, the early nineteenth-century growth of female committee work and the like looks like an expansion of the female role, not a diminution. Indeed, one might go further and argue that the stress on the proper female sphere in Victorian discourse signalled a growing concern that more women were seen to be active *outside* the home rather than proof that they were so confined. In short, the broadcasting of the language of separate spheres looks like a conservative response to an unprecedented *expansion* in the opportunities, ambitions and experience of late Georgian and Victorian women.

In questioning the ideological power of the separate spheres rhetoric in the making of the middle class, or the confinement of women, this essay does not argue that the vocabulary of public and private spheres had no currency in nineteenth-century society. Linda Colley's female patriots used the rhetoric of separate spheres to legitimize their actions. 'Posing as the pure-minded Women of Britain was, in practice, a way of insisting on the right to public spirit.' Equally, philanthropists deployed this rhetoric to justify their non-domestic activities. That they should call on the language of true womanly duty is hardly surprising. After all, even St Paul conceded that good works became good women. [. . .] Demonstrably, also, the language of separate spheres was deployed in the late Victorian controversy about women's citizenship. Numerous campaigners stated categorically that they wanted access to the public sphere, by which they clearly meant the universities, the professions, local and central government. Gissing's fictional New Women called for 'an armed movement, an invasion by women of the spheres which men have always forbidden us to enter' and categorically rejected 'that view of us set forth in such charming language by Mr Ruskin'. [. . .]

It should be emphasized that none of this is to argue that Victorian women had a fine time of it. It is beyond question that they laboured under great disadvantages:

legal, institutional, customary, biological and so on. Nor should one suppose that all was happiness and harmony in the middle-class family. Clearly, if a husband was deaf to persuasion, resolved to push his prerogatives to the utmost, then marriage could mean miserable servitude for his unlucky wife. But it is to say that the metaphor of separate spheres fails to capture the texture of female subordination and the complex interplay of emotion and power in family life, and that the role of an ideology of separate spheres in the making of the English middle class, 1780–1850, has not been convincingly demonstrated. It is also to suggest that our preoccupation with the ideology of separate spheres may have blinded us to the other languages in play in the Victorian period. As a sociological study of a particular set of gender relations at a particular historical moment, *Family fortunes* has much to offer to the next generation of women's historians, but the overarching historical narrative it seeks to tell should he discussed and debated, not given the unwarranted status of holy writ.

II

The unquestioned belief that the transition to industrial modernity robbed women of freedom, status and authentic function underlies most modern women's history. One can hardly pick up a text on women's lives in the nineteenth century which is not founded on the conviction that things ain't what they used to be. But were the work opportunities and public liberties enjoyed by propertied women before the factory so much greater than those of the Victorian period? Much of the literature on early modern women's work and social lives would have us believe so.

[. . .]

The wives of the merchants and manufacturers I have studied were definitely not idle, but it cannot be said that they enjoyed extensive commercial opportunities which their Victorian equivalents subsequently lost. Nor should the eighteenth century be seen as a golden age of female public life. And this point takes us back to my earlier discussion of separate spheres. In no century before the twentieth did women enjoy the public powers which nineteenth-century feminists sought – the full rights of citizenship. Public life for the gentlemen I have studied invariably incorporated some form of office, but there was no formal place for their wives in the machinery of local administration. Customarily, a wealthy woman wielded power as a mother, kinswoman, housekeeper, consumer, hostess and arbiter of polite sociability. If all this adds up to a separation of the public sphere of male power and the private sphere of female influence, then this separation was an ancient phenomenon which certainly predated the misogyny of the 1690s, evangelicalism, the French revolution and the factory.

The public/private dichotomy may, therefore, serve as a loose description of a very long-standing difference between the lives of women and men. What is extremely difficult to sustain, however, is the argument that sometime between 1650 and 1850 the public/private distinction was constituted or radically reconstituted in a way that transformed relations between the sexes. The shortcomings of the public/private dichotomy as an analytical framework are many, but most obviously there is little unanimity among historians as to what public and private should be held to mean in this context. Current interpretations of 'the public' vary enormously. In a historian's hands, a public role can mean access to anything from politics, public office, formal employment, opinion, print, clubs, assembly, company, the neighbourhood, the streets or simply the world outside the front door. However, we should take care to discover whether our interpretation of public and private marries with that of historical actors themselves. Take the excellently documented experience of Elizabeth Shackleton of Alkincoats. She resorted often to the 'publick papers', perpetuated her dead husband's 'publick spirit' by selling his famous rabies medicine at an affordable price, witnessed her second husband's 'publick humiliation' in the house of a tenant, and saw her own kitchen become 'very publick' with a stream of unexpected visitors. [. . .] It seems likely that eighteenth-century conceptions of publicity were different from those of nineteenth-century feminists and twentieth-century historians. All of which underlines the deficiencies in our knowledge of the distinctions between public and private in language, never mind as social practice.

III

This then, is the contradictory inheritance of seventeenth- and nineteenth-century women's history. In essence, the rise of the new domestic woman (whether in her seventeenth or nineteenth-century guise), the separation of the spheres, and the construction of the public and private are all different ways of characterizing what is essentially the same phenomenon: the marginalization of middle-class women. Like the insidious rise of capitalism, the collapse of community, the nascent consumer society and the ever-emerging middle class, it can be found in almost any century we care to look. When confronted with the numerous precedents, nineteenth-century historians of this phenomenon may claim that early modern developments represent only the *germ* of what was to come on a grand scale for the Victorian middle class. But the obvious problems of periodization which result cannot be brushed aside with the explanatory catch-all of 'uneven development'. The problem is exemplified if we try to reconcile Susan Amussen's work on early-modern Norfolk and Leonore Davidoff's on nineteenth-century Suffolk. Are we to believe that women were driven out of a public sphere of production and power in one district in the seventeenth century, while just over the county border the same development was delayed by well over a hundred years? Surely uneven development of this magnitude would have raised some contemporary comment, or at the very least female migration.

As a conceptual device, separate spheres has also proved inadequate. The economic chronologies upon which the accounts of women's exclusion from work and their incarceration in domesticity depend are deeply flawed. At a very general level, eighteenth and early nineteenth-century women were associated with home and children, while men controlled public institutions, but then this rough division could be applied to almost any century or any culture – a fact which robs the distinction of analytical purchase. If, *loosely speaking*, there have always been separate spheres of gender power, and perhaps there still are, then 'separate spheres' cannot be used to explain social and political developments in a particular century, least of all to account for Victorian class formation.

To conclude, this paper suggests that the orthodox categories of both seventeenth-century and nineteenth-century women's history must be jettisoned if a defensible chronology is to be constructed. Of course, such a renunciation carries a cost. A belief in the wholesome transformation wrought by capitalism on the economic role of women has provided early-modern women's history with an alluring big picture. Without that faith, we must accept a less heroic and more provisional chronology. Nevertheless, the notion of separate spheres in particular has done modern women's history a great service. With this conceptual framework women's history moved beyond a whiggish celebration of the rise of feminism, or a virtuous rediscovery of those previously hidden from history. In asserting the instrumental role of the ideology of separate spheres in modern class formation, historians asserted the wider historical significance of gender. Thereby the interpretation offered powerful justification for the study of women when the field was embattled. Yet strategic concerns do not in themselves justify the deployment of an artificial and unwieldy conceptual vocabulary. In the attempt to map the breadth and boundaries of female experience, new categories and concepts must be generated, and this must be done with more sensitivity to women's own manuscripts.

The burden of this piece has not been to argue that the discourses of femininity and masculinity, space and authority, found in printed literature are not important. Yet their power to shape female language and behaviour needs to be demonstrated not taken as read. Otherwise virtually any printed text we come across can be deemed to have ideological potency regardless of the form of the publication, its popularity with the readers, or the currency of the ideas contained within it. In short, 'intertextuality' must be researched, not simply asserted in the abstract. Case studies are needed of the economic roles, social lives, institutional opportunities and personal preoccupations of women from the seventeenth to the nineteenth centuries. In parallel, we need a long span, but integrated, history of the full range of debates about women's proper role covering the same period. (For too long it has been assumed that domestic ideology hogged the discursive stage unchallenged.) All this needs to be undertaken with especial sensitivity to changes in the range of language and categories employed. Only then will we establish with any precision the extent to which women accepted, negotiated, contested or simply ignored, the much quoted precepts of proper female behaviour in past time. Only then will we establish whether the rhetoric of domesticity and private spheres contributed to female containment, or instead was simply a defensive and impotent reaction to public freedoms already won.

Ellen DuBois, Mari Jo Buhle, Temma Kaplan, Gerda Lerner and Carroll Smith-Rosenberg

POLITICS AND CULTURE IN WOMEN'S HISTORY
A symposium

According to Ellen DuBois in her thoughtful, retrospective essay 'The Last Suffragist' (1998), this 1980 symposium published in *Feminist Studies* constituted one of the 'first theoretical debates' surrounding the purpose, method and subject matter of women's history.[1] This is a spirited exchange in which all five participants reflect upon the meaning of, and relationship between, 'feminist politics' and 'women's culture'. In an argument not dissimilar to that of Judith Bennett's in Reading 2, DuBois makes her case for the centrality of suffrage and organised politics in feminist history based on a wider concern surrounding the overall subordination of politics to culture in US women's history at the time. Thus DuBois depicts the relationship between women's culture and feminism as a somewhat oppositional one, suggesting that romanticised portrayals of a separate women's culture in fact conceal 'a very sneaky kind of antifeminism'. Mari Jo Buhle and Gerda Lerner point out instead that nineteenth-century American feminist politics was frequently grounded in the values and discourse of women's culture, as witnessed by the mass mobilisation of women in numerous reform crusades. Temma Kaplan provides European, African and Russian examples of ways in which women's cultural practices could take a politicised form and argues for a sharper class analysis of both concepts. Carroll Smith-Rosenberg, whose study of women's culture is central to DuBois's critique, reiterates the fact that 'culture' and 'politics' are not hermetically sealed categories and that feminist history should include the everyday experiences of ordinary women rather than restricting itself to 'a pantheon of ideologically correct heroines'. Although generated within a particular moment in the development of US feminist history-writing, this important exchange anticipates many later controversies surrounding 'equality' versus 'difference' in women's historical discourse.

Ellen DuBois

THIS ESSAY CONCERNS THE RELATIONSHIP between the history of feminism and the history of women. It rests on two propositions that I believe are closely related: A feminist perspective is necessary to make women's history a vital intellectual endeavor, and women's history should give special attention to the history of the feminist movement. My approach is basically historiographical: What have contemporary women's historians had to say about the history of feminism and how has this affected their interpretations of other matters?

[. . .]

The most significant theoretical formulation coming from these discoveries has been the concept of women's culture. The term 'women's culture' has been used by historians to refer to the broad-based commonality of values, institutions, relationships, and methods of communication, focused on domesticity and morality and particular to late eighteenth- and nineteenth-century women. The concept of women's culture shares a great deal with the concept of slave culture and probably derives in part from it. Reacting to a historical theory of slavery that saw black people only as their masters' ideas of them, historians of slavery have analyzed the social structures and belief systems that slaves formed for themselves and discovered the existence of a semiautonomous slave culture. Although this slave culture did not directly challenge the slave system, it did encourage blacks to resist the masters' power and established limits to their exploitation. It is this 'resistance' aspect of slave culture on which historians have focused.

The analogy to women's culture is obvious. Like slaves, nineteenth-century women have been ignored in favor of their images – passive, dependent, content, dedicated to home and family. The investigation of women's culture is a reaction to this, a way to see women creating themselves and not just being created. Here too the emphasis has been on resistance. In woman's culture, women developed group solidarity and some degree of psychic autonomy from men. Women's culture itself did not constitute an open and radical break with dominant sexual ideology any more than slave culture openly challenged slavery. Indeed, it was part of the dominant system, sharing most of its assumptions about women and men – separate spheres, women's domesticity, male dominance.

The pressing historical questions about the concept of women's culture center on its relation to feminism. At what point can we say that feminism surfaced out of women's culture? How was feminism in conflict with, as well as a development of, women's culture? What was the impact of feminism, and particularly of the emergence of a women's politics, on the course of women's culture? Women's historians are just beginning to address these questions. In *The Bonds of Womanhood: 'Women's Sphere' in New England, 1780–1835*, [Nancy] Cott stresses that 'woman's sphere [was] the basis for a subculture among women' in the 1830s, and that it led to the development of women's consciousness of themselves as a group, which was a necessary prerequisite for the emergence of a feminist movement. Yet, as Cott herself suggests, it is important not to confuse women's culture and feminism, or to assume a simple and direct development out of one into the other. [. . .]

From the point at which the woman's rights movement began to develop, it is impossible to understand the history of women's culture without setting it in dialectical relation to feminism. On the one hand, some defenders of women's culture saw in feminism a serious threat to their conception of women's place. In her biography of Catherine Beecher, Kathryn Sklar writes that Beecher 'began the task that was to occupy her for the rest of her career – that of interpreting and shaping the collective consciousness of American women' in direct reaction to the feminism of Sarah and Angelina Grimke, to counter any influence they might have had on women's thinking. The culmination of this was that Beecher published one of the first antisuffrage tracts. On the other hand, the mammoth and powerful Woman's Christian Temperance Union of the 1870s and 1880s developed out of Frances Willard's very creative efforts to synthesize the militance and political outlook of woman's rights with the traditional values and intense loyalties of women's culture.

However, the dominant tendency in the study of women's culture has not been to relate it to feminism, but to look at it in isolation and to romanticize what it meant for women. Another way to put it is that the concept of women's culture, the discovery of the humanity and historical activity of all those whom we once dismissed as 'true women' threatens to satisfy the impulse that led us into women's history; it may forestall further inquiry into the system that structured women's historical activity and shaped their oppression.

These tendencies can be seen in the pioneering study of women's culture, Carroll Smith-Rosenberg's 'The Female World of Love and Ritual: Relations Between Women in Nineteenth-Century America.' Smith-Rosenberg vividly portrays the quality of women's culture and the nature of women's attachment to it and to each other. However, she never really gets outside the female world, to see the larger social and historical developments of which it was a part. She is not concerned with how women's culture arose in history, or how it was transformed. Above all, she takes the separateness of the women's world at face value and does not investigate its relation to the dominant male culture. Conflict between the two worlds is underplayed, so much so that the concept of women's oppression begins to seem irrelevant; and Smith-Rosenberg says explicitly that, despite the discrimination, inequality, and misogyny rife in the nineteenth century, women's historical experiences were too rich, the evidence of their power and autonomy too impressive, to call them an 'isolated and oppressed subcategory in male society.' Nor does she address the limitations of the values of women's culture, the ways that they restrained and confined women, for instance, by being hostile to both politics and sexuality. Such a picture of women's history has little to do with classical woman's rights feminism, with its focus on political equality, and elsewhere, Smith-Rosenberg has dismissed the woman's rights and woman suffrage movement as 'of little importance either to American politics or to American women.'

The consequences of interpreting women's social history without reference to feminist politics can be seen very clearly by comparing two recent histories of birth control and women: Daniel Scott Smith's 'Family Limitations, Sexual Control, and Domestic Feminism in Victorian America,' which ignores the role of political feminism, and Linda Gordon's *Woman's Body, Woman's Right: A Social History of Birth Control in America*, which stresses it. Daniel Scott Smith argues that mid-nineteenth-century American women gained increasing control over marital intercourse, and this enabled them to reduce the number of children they had. He attributes this to the spread of 'domestic feminism,' by which he means an ideology that encouraged women to win greater freedom and control within their families and through their individual efforts. [. . .] Clearly Smith's domestic feminism is very close to the concept of women's culture, and indeed some subsequent historians have used it that way. Smith explicitly contrasts domestic feminism with the woman's rights movement, which he describes as having a 'narrow social base among women,' and dismisses because he considers its focus on equality and individuality in public life 'limiting as a political ideology' for most nineteenth-century women.

Linda Gordon's approach to the history of birth control and women is very different. Her focus is on the history of political struggles over birth control, and particularly on the rise and fall of a feminist political movement committed to winning reproductive freedom for women. [. . .] Unlike Smith, Gordon believes that 'public' feminism in the woman's rights movement had a great deal to do with the spread of these beliefs among average nonpolitical women. Furthermore, she recognizes that the widespread existence of a pro-birth control attitude among women was not sufficient to win them birth control freedom. What was necessary was a feminist political movement, committed to that goal and capable of struggling with other forces in the political arena over who would control reproduction and to what ends. She traces the rise of that movement in the 1870s, its transformation into a socialist movement in the early twentieth century, and its ultimate collapse in the 1920s.

Gordon's political focus has subjected her book to much more intense criticism than just about anything else written in women's history. In addition to attacking Gordon because of her explicitly feminist and Marxist point of view, the critics all challenge the prominent role that she gives the political history of birth control. They charge that she has taken the ideas of a few irrelevant birth control ideologues and political activists and offered them as a substitute for what the reviewers believe is the real history of birth control use and ideology among 'average' women. Here the critical attacks on Gordon come very close to Daniel Scott Smith's approach, in that they all categorically dismiss any impact that woman's rights feminist politics had on the birth control history of the average woman. The critics prefer to concentrate either on the changing character of family and marriage, or technological breakthroughs in contraception to explain why and how women's use of birth control changes.

There is a very sneaky kind of antifeminism here, that criticizes feminism in the name of the common woman, and political history in the name of social history. Underlying all the criticisms of Gordon's book is a challenge to the feminist perspective on contemporary society on which it is based. The question Gordon asks is the one posed by the contemporary feminist movement: Why do women today lack real reproductive freedom, especially in light of the modern technological capacity for contraception? Gordon's critics do not accept the validity of this question. For them, the birth control 'revolution' is over, because they see it as a matter of 'sexual liberation' or 'population control,' and not as a question over which people have and will struggle politically: women's freedom.

As we have seen, the interest that women's historians have shown in questions of culture parallel similar concerns in black and labor history. So too do my criticisms, that questions of culture may have come to replace questions of politics, and that it may be time to return to the study of politics from the more sophisticated perspective which the study of culture has afforded us. [. . .] Like labor history and black history, women's history was deeply 'political' in its origins, arising in connection with contemporary political movements and holding certain political perspectives without any need for apology. As these developments have coalesced into the new field of 'social history,' many of us have felt some anxiety that these intellectual projects will become 'depoliticized' and academic in the worst sense of the word. One way to work against this tendency is to insist that in our own writing, we give adequate attention to political questions, and thereby insure that the women's history – or black history or working-class history – which we produce retains its focus on social change.

Mari Jo Buhle

THE RELATIONSHIP OF WOMEN'S CULTURE and feminism is a major issue in contemporary scholarship. Ellen DuBois has made a strong case against historians who limit their studies to women's culture alone. I would like to suggest, in turn, how historians might utilize the knowledge provided by these students of women's culture to recast the history of late nineteenth-century feminism.

The promise is great for that relatively uncharted period, the seeming hiatus between the valiant woman's rights campaigns of the antebellum era and the well-organized and skillful woman suffrage movement of the early twentieth century. Whereas the early and late waves of the women's movement have attracted scholars, the middle period between 1870 and 1890 has, in contrast, drawn relatively few. Two historians have touched upon this era, both to offer dismal assessments of its significance. Aileen Kraditor, in *The Ideas of the Woman Suffrage Movement, 1890–1920*, traced the devolution of political ideology over the course of the nineteenth century by comparing the philosophical integrity of the natural rights basis of antebellum feminism with the expedient, hence pragmatic, arguments employed by latter-day suffragists. William O'Neill, in *Everyone Was Brave: The Rise and Fall of Feminism in America*, invented the term 'social feminists' to describe a generation of activists at the close of the century who sacrificed the struggle for women's equality to the 'unfeminist' aspiration to reform society. Although O'Neill and Kraditor offered necessary counterpoints to the heroic emphasis, common to most histories of the women's movement written prior to the 1960s and usually by former activists, their revisionist message motivated few scholars to pursue the subject further.

By virtue of sheer magnitude and measurable political influence, the Gilded Age women's movement nevertheless remained a troubling detail. Above all, there was the persistent legacy of Frances Willard, acclaimed by her contemporaries as the century's greatest woman. Willard had aroused masses of women presumed indifferent to woman's rights, had created a national organization of women unprecedented in scale and coordination, and had managed to challenge the concept of male hegemony in all sectors of society.

The suffrage movement itself had flagged until the Woman's Christian Temperance Union (WCTU) touched a responsive chord in hundreds of thousands of Protestant women, white and black, small town and urban, from coast to coast. Although historians could not fail to note Willard's remarkable achievement, its significance evaded them. [. . .]

Only recently has the study of the WCTU at last come into its own. Ruth Bordin, who examined the origins of the movement in the 1870s, concluded that women participating in the temperance crusade experienced a 'baptism of power and liberty.' Barbara Easton, in a forthcoming book on women's experiences in religious revivalism and in temperance, documents fully the process by which women moved into political activism via the WCTU, how they emerged as prime agitators for political rights, economic equality, and sundry causes to elevate women's status in civil society. My own research has led me to believe that training in the WCTU prepared a sector of native-born Protestant women for leading positions in the American Socialist movement at the turn of the century.

This new wave of sympathetic analysis flows directly from the interpretive advances of the mid-1970s. The concept of women's culture, as DuBois rightly points out, is undoubtedly one of the most significant theoretical formulations of recent years. Nancy Cott's *The Bonds of Womanhood: 'Women's Sphere' in New England, 1780–1835* has been especially instrumental in establishing the relationship between women's emerging awareness of themselves as a distinct group and the formation of a women's movement. Historians must resist, as Cott advises, assuming simple causal relationships between culture and politics. Yet it is clear that the heuristic scholarship of Cott and others already allows us to look past the abstractions of previous historians and to view the nineteenth-century woman reformers and their demands within the context of their own constituency's sensibilities. [. . .]

We will not find feminist role models in the Gilded Age, but we may find something ultimately more valuable. By situating the reform crusades amidst the real experiences of mid-nineteenth-century women, we begin to understand the mediation between the presence of distinct cultural values and their transformation into a political arsenal for the self-advancement of a sex. The significance of leaders' ability to tap latent resources and to foster thereby an unprecedented women's mobilization, becomes a compelling scholarly goal.

[. . .]

DuBois says rightly that we cannot stop at studying women's culture alone without endangering larger purposes. I would like to add a corollary, that only through a study of women's culture can we assess nineteenth-century feminist consciousness and activity within its social context. The new scholarship on women's culture is therefore crucial if we wish to gain a new perspective on the postbellum women's movement, for its leaders spoke directly to the values that historians have only recently described. We may now see beyond the unfamiliar rhetoric and take seriously the activists' desire to forge, as they said, a political sisterhood to advance women's 'entry' into public life. We cannot judge this political expression unless we understand the culture from which it sprang. [. . .]

Temma Kaplan

SPECIFICITY ABOUT CLASS RELATIONS is relevant in all discussions of feminism or women's culture in Europe and the Third World, as it ought to be in any examination of the history of women in the United States. Feminism appears to have two different strains. The more familiar strain includes feminist organizations or ideologies designed to win gains for women. The other tendency emerges as female collective action in pursuit of generalized human goals, which we would do well to examine for implicit feminist overtones.

Women have organized to win equality with men of their class, and this has been the source of feminism among the aristocracy and bourgeoisie in Europe. Female-centered networks and institutions take on political organizational form to assure the survival of groups to which peasant and working-class women belong. Under extreme conditions, in which the ability of women to provide food for their families is impaired, females often mobilize to preserve their community rather than to win gender equality. Until quite recently, this may have been the prevalent form of female political action among working-class and peasant women throughout the world.

[. . .]

It is impossible to speak of 'women's culture' without understanding its variation by class and ethnic group. Women's culture, like popular or working-class culture, must appear in the context of dominant cultures. Sometimes it is a variation upon the ruling culture. Sometimes it is created from the shards of broken tribal or peasant cultures. Sometimes the alternative culture grows in opposition to the dominant culture. Female aristocrats in seventeenth-century France and nineteenth-century Germany formed salons with men of their class or sometimes apart from the men to develop and assert their class culture against that of a growing bourgeoisie to whom they felt socially, if no longer economically or politically, superior. Under such circumstances, class issues prevailed over feminism.

Women's rituals may provide the context for enormous social solidarity within ethnic groups. The proletarian, female Jewish community of Frankfurt, Germany, had principal responsibilities for preserving Jewish life and for financially supporting their talmudic scholar husbands and sons in the seventeenth century. The ancient female ritual, 'measuring the ground,' invoked the power of ancestors to aid women during difficult labors and to protect the community against plagues and pogroms. Women used this ritual to mobilize the female population of the community when anti-Semitic female, as well as male, artisans invaded their ghetto in 1614. They failed to ward off their Christian enemies, and ultimately, they were driven from their homes, which were sacked. But their cultural form, here applied defensively, permitted them to mobilize *as women* and implicitly to proclaim women's right to preserve human life.

Female cultural practices sometimes take on a direct political form. West African women, for example, have a variety of ways to make their wills known to husbands, and they adapted these tactics in struggles against imperialism. Traditionally Bakweri women use escalating shame rituals in dealing with men of their village. When a woman has been insulted by a man, she uses other women as witnesses and calls forth the offender. If he fails to satisfy her claims, the women demand that the village head hear their case. If the judge rules in favor of the women, the culprit must pay a fine and submit to female shaming rituals. [. . .]

Igbo women had such a ritual, too. When women wanted to punish a man who had stinted in his provisions to a wife, or had taken concubines, they called the other wives of the village together and humiliated him by singing outside his hut. If the man refused their demands, no woman would cook for him. If he continued to hold out, the women burnt down his hut.

Judith Van Allen has written extensively about the Aba Women's War of 1929 during which Igbo women of Eastern Nigeria adapted such shaming rituals to their struggle against the British. Several years before, British rulers of the Igbo district had taxed men's production and livestock just after they took a census. When the British attempted to assess women's possessions, the women became alarmed, and word traveled along the female market networks that women would be taxed. Black officials, who represented the British, could not convince the women that their fears were groundless.

In mid-December 1929, ten thousand peasant/market women converged on the administrative center of Aba, sang humiliating songs in front of Barclays Bank, attacked British shops, and burnt down administrative centers. When the movement escalated, the police panicked and shot eighteen women. The attempt by peasant/market women to signal the British about the collective rights of women through rituals demonstrated female efforts to speak a cultural vocabulary that the British not only misunderstood, but also reacted against with force.

Ellen DuBois argues that in the United States, domestic and political feminism sometimes represented alternatives to one another. But she does not specify the class of the women for whom this was true. European examples indicate that domestic feminism was not so much an alternative as a stage from which some bourgeois women emerged to participate in moral reform movements or socialist struggle. The vast majority of bourgeois women appear to have led lives of 'quiet desperation,' as Emily Dickinson described it. [. . .]

During the First World War, working-class women in Russia struggled with problems of economic survival that led them to confront the state and indirectly helped them bring down the Czar. On February 3, 1917, poor women in St. Petersburg demanded bread, stole food from the bakeries, and then joined female textile workers in a general strike the Bolsheviks opposed. When ordered by the Czar to restore order, the generals called in the cossacks. The women pitted their bodies against the soldiers who retreated. By March 12, Czar Nicholas II had fallen.

The extent to which feminism is limited to organizations exclusively dedicated to improving the lot of women and the implicit feminism of mass mobilizations of women to preserve or win human rights remain to be explored. Ellen DuBois stresses that in the United States, theories of women's culture and domestic feminism underestimate the way in which some women, notably suffragists and birth control reformers, attempted to undermine the systematic oppression of all women and the exploitation of working-class women. Although it is obvious, it never hurts to reiterate that suffragists wanted the vote because they hoped to influence legislation, particularly as it could improve the social conditions of women. Birth control reformers attempted to assist poor women whose life expectancy was severely limited by overexploitation of their bodies through excessive childbearing. Emphasis upon the goals for which suffragists and birth control reformers fought should counteract what Ellen DuBois calls a 'sneaky kind of antifeminism . . . that criticizes feminism in the name of the common woman. . . .'

Nineteenth-century working-class women needed all the help they could get, although they allied with bourgeois women for common goals only under certain conditions. What emerges from studies of organizations such as the Women's Trade Union Leagues in Britain and the United States, the Ladies' National Association for Repeal of the Contagious Diseases Acts in Britain, and the Catholic feminist organizations in Spain and Belgium is that working-class women might accept public assistance from middle-class women, but they would not mobilize around strictly middle-class issues such as equal property rights for women. However, when middle-class women used their political skills to aid working-class women to protect themselves from economic and sexual exploitation, they won the solidarity of working-class women.

Class analysis of organizations, movements, and cultures in which women are principal participants illuminates female lives in ways that focusing solely upon women's culture or feminism does not. The original task of women's history – to explore the totality of female experience – requires some investigation into how class in the United States, as well as elsewhere in the world, structured differences in women's experiences and thus in women's culture and in the fortunes of feminism.

Gerda Lerner

ELLEN DUBOIS RAISED A NUMBER of interesting and valuable questions, yet I find it impossible to address her questions in the terms in which they were posed. For example, regarding her proposition that 'women's history should give special attention to the history of the feminist movement,' and her question, 'How was feminism in conflict with, as well as a development of, women's culture?' the answers really depend on how we define the terms. All the words we use derive from a language based on andocentric thought and from academic scholarship that tends to subsume, trivialize, or marginalize women and their activities. Therefore, the problem of redefinition is a basic problem of feminist scholars in our search for an appropriate conceptual framework. The terms we use define the questions we can ask. [. . .]

The traditional meaning of the word 'feminism' is so generalized that its use defies precise analysis and tends to obliterate distinctions and stages of development. Here are a few current definitions:

Feminism means a) a doctrine advocating social and political rights of women equal to those of men; b) an organized movement for attainment of these rights; c) the assertion of the claims of women as a group and d) belief in the necessity of large-scale social change to increase the power of women. Definition a), which describes a belief system, is frequently combined with definition b). Definition c) implies the concept of the oppression of women, which makes of them a distinct group seeking redress. Most persons using the term subsume under it definitions a–c, but d), the necessity for basic social change in the system to which women demand equal access, is not necessarily accepted by feminists. To add to the vagueness and complexity of the term, there is unclarity about what is meant under b), since the organized movement for women's rights encompasses in fact a number of distinct historical movements, i.e. the nineteenth century suffrage movement, the nineteenth century woman's rights movement, the twentieth century women's liberation movement. The imprecision and looseness of the term demands clarification and more disciplined definitions.

Just what do we mean, then, when we say feminist? I have some time ago called attention to the utility of more precise definitions in an effort to distinguish between the nineteenth- and twentieth-century woman's movements. I then suggested that, as a first step, we distinguish between 'woman's rights' and 'woman's emancipation' [liberation].

The *woman's rights* movement means a movement concerned with winning for women equality with men in all aspects of society and giving them access to all rights and opportunities enjoyed by men in the institutions of that society. Thus, the woman's rights movement is akin to the civil rights movement in wanting equal participation for women in the status quo, essentially a reformist goal.

Woman's emancipation means: freedom from oppressive restrictions imposed by sex; self-determination; autonomy.

Freedom from oppressive restrictions imposed by sex means freedom from biological and societal restrictions. Self-determination means being free to decide one's own destiny, being free to define one's own social role; having the freedom to make decisions concerning one's own body. Autonomy means earning one's own status, not being born into it nor marrying it; it means financial and cultural independence; freedom to choose one's own lifestyle and sexual preference, all of which implies a radical transformation of existing institutions, values, and theories.

The striving for women's emancipation predates the women's rights movement. It is not always a *movement*, for it can be a level of consciousness, a stance, an attitude, as well as the basis for organized effort. Where woman's rights advocates ask for equality with men, emancipationists seek women-defined goals and process. Many women, who do not consider themselves feminists or part of any woman's movement, are emancipationists. [. . .] Most emancipationists also advocated woman's rights. Thus, I would argue, that 'woman's emancipation' is a more advanced stage of consciousness than 'woman's rights.'

Returning to Ellen DuBois's 'the feminist movement,' the term is inadequate, for it can mean the suffrage movement or the woman's emancipation movement of the nineteenth century. Both were 'feminist,' but each represented feminism of a different kind. I would suggest, as a useful beginning, that we separate 'woman's rights feminism' and 'woman's emancipation feminism.' The latter would, in the nineteenth century, embrace the social and cultural transformations sought by utopians, advocates of free love, reproductive freedom, and self-determination for women, and revolutionary feminist thinkers such as Charlotte Perkins Gilman. Was Catharine Beecher a feminist? Yes, and so were Mary Lyon and Dorothea Dix, all three opponents of the organized woman's rights movement. They were feminist in working for the emancipation of women from educational and institutional restrictions; as such their impact on the development of feminist consciousness was perhaps more decisive than was the impact of the early suffrage movement. Yet their feminist consciousness remained on the first level, that of 'rights.' In the post-Civil war period, the true distinction between Stanton and Anthony and the American Woman Suffrage Association (AWSA) was not so much their embracing different political strategies, but the fact that Stanton and Anthony worked for woman's emancipation, defining their feminism more radically and thus embracing sexual and cultural transformation, whereas the AWSA worked for woman's rights. [. . .]

Applying the terms to twentieth-century feminism, the distinctions are more complex, since the modern women's movement [. . .] embraces both woman's rights and woman's emancipation demands. Still, the terms help us to distinguish between those individuals and groups who define their goal as wanting into the system on an equal basis (or better, who want into the system in male-defined terms) and those emancipationists who want that and more – the transformation of patriarchy into a different system. [. . .]

Keeping these complexities in mind, I believe it is desirable to be as specific as possible, when discussing a particular historical situation or movement. To come back to Ellen DuBois's initial question, I would recast it to read: 'Was the feminist ideology of the nineteenth-century woman's rights movement in conflict with the concept of woman's culture?' This brings us to yet another troublesome term.

Ellen DuBois uses the term 'woman's culture' as though it were meant to define 'woman's sphere.' The important distinction here, as elsewhere, is whether we use the term within a male-defined context or within a female-defined context. Historically, 'woman's sphere' is a nineteenth-century term, denoting those aspects of activity and function men determined appropriate to women. The fact that many women, through social conditioning, also accepted that definition as 'natural,' does not make it a woman's definition. Despite the rhetorical claims of its advocates, that the domestic sphere women were to occupy was a 'higher sphere,' the essence of the doctrine of 'separate spheres' is that it consigned women to activities which are subordinate in importance and power to those of men.

If one speaks of women's activities and goals from a woman-centered point of view, one calls that which women do and the way in which they do it, woman's culture. Confining the term to the nineteenth century, which I think is appropriate and useful, 'woman's culture' is women's redefinition in their own terms. The term implies an assertion of equality and an awareness of sisterhood, the communality of women. Carroll Smith-Rosenberg has shown particularly well how this process worked in the case of the women in the moral reform societies in 1830s. Similarly, women in the antislavery movement stepped outside their male-defined auxiliary role, challenged the limitations of this role openly, and found their own mode of work and organizing in petitioning, educational work and fundraising.

The term 'woman's culture' has also been used in its anthropological sense, to encompass the familial and friendship networks of women, their affective ties, their rituals. It is important to understand that 'women's culture' is not and should not be seen as a subculture. It is hardly possible for the majority to live in a subculture. As Joan Kelly has so aptly put it, 'woman's place is not a separate sphere or domain of existence but a position within social existence generally.' Women live their social existence within the general culture and, whenever they are confined by patriarchal restraint or segregation into separateness (which always has subordination as its purpose), they transform this restraint into complementarity (asserting the importance of woman's function, even its 'superiority') and redefine it. Thus, women live a duality — as members of the general culture and as partakers of women's culture. What happens to women's culture in periods of relative egalitarianism and the opening to women of access to most institutions of the society, remains to be studied. It is, at all events, a most useful and specific term applied to the nineteenth century United States.

To state, as DuBois does, that (Daniel Scott) Smith's 'domestic feminism is very close to the concept of women's culture' is confusing and misleading. The term 'domestic feminism' is based on Smith's assertion that nineteenth century women in making birth control decisions (a factual assertion which is in itself open to question), exercised some kind of real power. He observes slight shifts in status and decision making of a powerless group and interprets these as power. 'Domestic feminism' is not close to 'women's culture,' it is simply good old 'woman's sphere,' updated. It is an objectionable term, like the media-engendered shift from 'house-wife' to 'homemaker.' [. . .]

If we call what women do in a patriarchal world and the way they do it 'woman's culture,' then there is no point in counterposing this concept to 'feminism.' Woman's culture is the ground upon which women stand in their resistance to patriarchal dominance and their assertion of their own creativity in shaping society. Out of this ground rise different levels of feminist consciousness: first, the recognition of a collective wrong suffered; then, efforts to remedy these wrongs in political, economic, and social life. These efforts, when institutionalized, become 'movements.' Movements in turn give rise to new forms of woman's culture, for example, sex-segregated or separatist institutions or modes of living. Finally, feminist consciousness gives rise to autonomously defined demands and theory. At a certain level of thought and activity, women make the shift from the andro-centricity, in which they have been schooled, to 'woman-centeredness.' In the field of scholarship, woman-centered scholarship seeks to find a new framework of inter-pretation from within women's historical culture, leading to their emancipation.

As Ellen DuBois observed, as long as historians stay within the confines of androcentric thought while viewing women in history, they are not generally subject to attack and distortion. They may even receive a pat on the back for 'schol-arly impartiality.' But when we begin to practice woman-centered scholarship, stepping outside of androcentric question-setting and value judgments, then we are likely to be, as Linda Gordon was, attacked for injecting 'political judgments' into supposedly value-free scholarship. Nevertheless this must be done, not by all historians of women's history, but by those whose consciousness works at that level. The terms of our discourse and our definitions are our tools in the struggle for our intellectual emancipation. Let's keep them clean; let's keep them sharp.

Carroll Smith-Rosenberg

ELLEN DUBOIS'S ARTICLE ATTEMPTS a new feminist critique of women's history. Questioning the close ties that have linked women's history and contemporary social history, it espouses a revisionist women's history that would focus upon political issues and elite cadres of activists. Central to this critique is an evaluation of the relation of women's history to feminism and to 'women's culture.' Although many of us have found these three phenomena mutually reinforcing, the author argues that 'women's culture' is extrinsic to feminism and, indeed, frequently opposed to it. Within the author's revisionist framework, 'women's culture' thus becomes an aberrant factor within the canon of women's history. Rather than studying women's interaction with each other, the author admonishes, we should focus our attention on feminists' resistance to male oppression.

I take issue with this article on three grounds. First, I cannot accept a revisionist women's history that views with suspicion an analysis of the experiences of the average woman. Second, as a historian, I disagree with an analytic framework which insists on the causal centrality of the political and ignores the economic, demographic, and institutional factors that helped shape the political. Third, I reject both the author's argument that women's culture is dialectically opposed to feminism and her warning of the dangers inherent in the continued exploration of women's culture. We cannot understand the public acts of a few women without understanding the private world that produced them. Women's interaction with each other formed an intrinsic component of the female experience and of feminism. It constitutes, consequently, a legitimate and fruitful category within women's history.

While ostensibly advocating a women's history that does not overemphasize women's 'unchanging oppression,' ignore the 'breadth and complexity of women's historical experience,' or confuse 'men's image of women' with women's 'historical reality,' the article ends by proposing just such an analytic framework. The author urges historians of women to focus primarily upon 'men's oppression of women and women's efforts to understand and overcome it [that oppression].' Historians of women, we are told, ought to answer the question 'How did . . . women experience their lives?' by examining women's 'traditions of protest and resistance.' But just as the reality of our world is not limited to men's image of us, so the parameters of our experience are not set by male exploitation, either direct or indirect. To insist, as Ellen DuBois does, on the centrality of the male–female oppressive dyad, ironically maintains men as the central actors in women's past and thus transforms women's history into a subcategory of the history of male values and behavior.

This insistence upon a political focus causes additional problems. The author refers approvingly to a second major criticism of earlier histories of women – that they focused primarily upon the exploitation experienced by white middle-class women and upon bourgeois definitions of oppression. Yet, at the same time, by urging us to direct our attention primarily at political issues such as birth control, temperance, abolition, socialism, which had little appeal to the Catholic and black women who comprised a majority of the nineteenth-century working classes, she ends by advocating the bourgeois analysis she commenced by condemning. [. . .]

To define women's history as the study of male oppression and of women's organized resistance challenges the basic direction that women's history has taken over the past decade. One of the principal goals of women's history has been to so redefine the canons of traditional history that the events and processes central to women's experience assume historical centrality, and women are recognized as active agents of social change. Indeed, a historical analysis that fails to do so distorts our understanding of past societies. A second goal of women's history has been to explore the complexity of the female experience. The purpose of women's history, thus, is not to create a pantheon of ideologically correct heroines, but to analyze the evolution of women's roles, in the context of the effect of economic change upon a society's allocation of economic resources and power, institutional developments, and ideological conceptualizations.

The stated goal of this article is to evaluate current historical scholarship from the perspective of contemporary feminism. Yet at no time does the author clarify her usage of 'feminism.' She comes closest when discussing Linda Gordon's *Woman's Body, Woman's Right: A Social History of Birth Control in America.* A 'feminist' orientation seems there to involve first a stress upon 'the role of political feminism' (later referred to as '"public" feminism') and second, a primary concern with issues of women's reproductive freedom. In contrast, the investigation of women's relations with other women is categorized as counterproductive. None can question the centrality of reproductive freedom to the contemporary women's movement. But physiological and sexual autonomy cannot be defined in such limited and simplistic terms. It is wedded to female economic autonomy and involves issues and options of behavior far broader and more fundamental in their challenge to power relations and social structure than the simple prevention of conception. This focus on birth control not only reinforces traditional views of female sexuality, it again posits men as the active agents in women's lives. It says, in effect, that the key feminist sexual issue is how to control the effect of sperm. Even more fundamentally, to fail to include the concept of female solidarity in a definition of feminism ignores what is probably the most central component of both nineteenth-century and contemporary feminism. This omission compounds the article's male orientation and its emphasis on women's victimization.

How can we understand this adherence to men and politics? The answer may be discerned in the author's fear of and condemnation of 'women's culture.' She envelops the phrase in innuendo and foreboding. DuBois tells us that 'The concept of women's culture threatens to satisfy the impulse that led us into women's history. . . .' 'Questions of culture,' she says later 'may have come to replace questions of politics. . . .' No trend could be more dangerous, we are warned, because 'women's culture,' far from forming the keystone of feminism, constitutes its dialectical opposite. The crux of this argument, as I understand it, is as follows. Historians and feminists have recently turned their attention away from an analysis of men's political exploitation of women to an exploration of the 'female world.' To study the sources of our strength and solidarity, however, the article implies, will lead us to withdraw from the struggle with and against men. We are in danger of becoming modern Narcissae and, like the unicorn, entrapped by the impassioned contemplation of ourselves.

Although a discussion of 'women's culture' lies at the center of the author's argument, her definition is unclear and contradictory. The article begins by defining 'women's culture' as 'the broad-based commonality of values, institutions, relationships, and methods of communication, focused on domesticity and morality particular to late eighteenth- and nineteenth-century women.' The article later defines the study of 'women's culture' as 'a way to see women creating themselves and not just being created.' But the author proceeds to undercut her own definition of 'culture' by arguing that 'women's culture' shares most of the dominant values of male culture – especially men's view of women's proper place. 'Indeed,' the author states, 'it was part of the dominant system, sharing most of its assumptions about women and men . . . and reinforcing them in the process.' These definitions are contradictory and confusing. DuBois, while choosing to use the term 'culture,' ignores the very attributes that define that term. A culture must have its own autonomous values, identities, symbolic systems, and modes of communication. If this putative 'women's culture' accepted and reinforced the values of the dominant, male culture to such an extent, it cannot be classified as a 'culture' at all – or even as a subculture. [. . .]

The one constant in this shifting definition of 'Women's culture' is the author's juxtaposition of 'women's culture' and feminism. Indeed, this tenacity provides the key to understanding the implications of her argument. Although the author asks us to examine how political feminism emerged out of the female world, DuBois preempts such an analysis by insisting on their dialectical opposition. 'From the point at which the women's rights movement began to develop, it is impossible to understand the history of women's culture without seeing it in dialectical relation to feminism.' One's first response is simply to dismiss the author's statement as a confused use of the term culture. But far more is implied in the author's argument than is overtly stated. By not clarifying her definition of women's culture, the author is able to imply a causal relation between two unrelated meanings. If women's culture is equated both with the Cult of True Womanhood and with female-identified institutions, relationships, and methods of communication, then the argument is implicitly made that women's networks and communities, separate from men, will generate neither a sense of female solidarity and strength nor a radical critique of society. Rather, such female interaction will encourage conservative collaboration with the dominant male power system. This is DuBois's real message. [. . .]

Woven into the article's criticism of 'women's culture' is an analysis of my work. Yet it is difficult to recognize my own analyses in this critique. On the most fundamental level, my words are quoted out of context and terms are attributed to me that do not appear in any of my writings. I never stated explicitly or implicitly that 'despite the discrimination, inequality, and misogyny rife in the nineteenth century, women's historical experiences were too rich, the evidence of their power and autonomy too impressive, to call them an "isolated and oppressed subcategory of male society".' The part of that statement that is attributed directly to me is quite brief: 'an isolated and oppressed subcategory. . . .' I did not write these words as part of an argument for the autonomy of female culture, but rather as part of a methodological discussion in which I argued that advice books written by men about women did not encompass the totality of the female experience. 'Women, however,' I wrote, 'did not form an isolated and oppressed subcategory of male society. Their letters and diaries indicate that women's sphere had an essential integrity and dignity that grew out of women's shared experiences and mutual affection.' 'To interpret such friendships more fully,' I continued, 'they must be related to the structure of the American family and to the nature of sex-role divisions and of male–female relations both within the family and in society generally. The female friendship must not be seen in isolation. . . .' [. . .]

At no time did I criticize the study of feminism or of the feminist movement. Nor have I ever used the term 'women's culture'. I have never asserted that women's sphere was free from male oppression or that it existed separately from the economic and ideological forces that shaped its society. In my article to which the author so prominently refers, 'The Female World of Love and Ritual: Relations Between Women in Nineteenth-Century America,' I analyzed not women's culture but female sexuality. I began with a question. How can we understand the nature of the emotionally intense and erotic friendships between eighteenth- and nineteenth-century married women and society's benign approval of such relationships? To answer this question, I explored the nature of women's emotional, physical, and social interaction across the life cycle. I made no claim for this world being a separate culture or being free from male control. Indeed, in my work over the past ten years, I have frequently explored male ideology concerning women and male modes of female oppression. Gradually, however, I had come to realize that such an exclusive emphasis on male oppression of women had transformed me into a historian of men. Indeed, my research convinced me that the most complex and suggestive questions we can ask about the female experience or women's location in the power structure do not necessarily revolve around an analysis of overt exploitation.

The debate over this article does raise fascinating and complex questions. What terms can we use to describe the type of world women form when forcibly segregated along gender lines? What relation exists between the values, rituals, and symbols women expressed among themselves and those of the larger society to which they also gave allegiance? How is power distributed within a segregated female world and how does this distribution reflect power relations between women and men?

In hundreds of cultures around the world and across time, women have lived in highly sex-segregated communities; spending their time with other women; developing female rituals and networks; forming primary emotional, perhaps physical and sexual, ties with other women. Such women develop visions of the world, values, and, indeed, I would argue, even symbolic and cosmological systems different in highly significant ways from those of the men with whom they shared sex, food, and children. This is true among Tiwi aborigines, Victorian ladies, Nazi women, and working-class women of London in the 1960s. What do these patterns of differentiation and separation tell us about cultural evolution and the relation of cultural forms to modes of production, women's economic productivity, institutional organization, and the distribution of economic power? [. . .]

An analysis of the sex-segregated world of bourgeois women in nineteenth-century American society provides an ideal historical laboratory for the exploration of these issues. American society changed radically during the middle period of the nineteenth century. Rural communities were disrupted, the function and structure of the family was fundamentally altered, and daughters were pulled into roles their mothers had no knowledge of (factories, the world of the urban bourgeoise, academies, and the frontier). Immigrant ghettoes and destitution marked not only the major seaports, but also interior towns and cities. Tens of thousands of women used prostitution – the imposition of a cash nexus upon relations between the sexes and the division of sex from family – to symbolize these disruptive changes. [. . .] At these times, these bourgeois and socially conservative women identified with the prostitute and vilified their same class males. It was male exploitation of women, they argued, and male acceptance of new capitalist and commercial values that threatened women, their families, and communities. But this identification with women across class and the denigration of same class males did not carry with it either a sustained radical critique of society or an insistence on nonhierarchical relations between women. These women sought escape from the power of male-controlled capitalism in a retreat to a mercantile patriarchal world which women knew to contain spaces of safety for women, but not places of power. Symbolically, they insisted on mothers' rights to control their daughters and, implicitly, on bourgeois women's rights to dominate working-class women. This was a world in which identification as a woman was complex indeed.

The world of women does not automatically produce feminism. But can feminism develop outside a female world? 'The pressing historical questions about women's culture,' I would argue do not 'center on its relation to feminism,' but rather the pressing questions about feminism center on its relation to the existence of a female world. [. . .]

Note

1   Ellen Carol DuBois, 'The Last Suffragist: An Intellectual and Political Autobiography', in DuBois, *Woman Suffrage and Women's Rights* (New York: New York University Press, 1998): 1–29.

Gisela Bock

WOMEN'S HISTORY AND GENDER HISTORY
Aspects of an international debate

Gisela Bock is a leading historian of comparative European women's and gender history who has worked extensively on Nazi Germany. This frequently cited article was initially published in the journal *Gender and History* in 1987, and provides a very useful articulation of gender for historians as both an 'intellectual construct' and as a 'complex set of relations' between women and men that require historical analysis. Bock is very clear that gender is a social, cultural and historical category rather than a biological one. Indeed, her research on National Socialist Germany makes her particularly sensitive to the use of the term 'biology' as some unproblematic 'given'. She reminds readers of the ways in which cultural and quasi-scientific appropriations of biology have served to legitimate numerous racist and sexist atrocities throughout history and urges the elimination of the term 'biology' in favour of a more comprehensive understanding of 'gender' that recognises the culturally constituted origins of even physiological categories. Bock regards gender history as the logical successor of women's history, opening up new possibilities for studying men as gendered beings and thus transforming some of the most conventional histories of military warfare and politics. Rather than positing gender over and against class, as some social historians have done, Bock argues that we must examine the ways in which social formations such as race, age, language and religion are mutually constitutive of each other. In contrast to those scholars who accuse gender of diluting feminist approaches to history writing, Bock asserts that gender is not a neutralising approach but an all-encompassing one given its ability to affect so many facets of human relations.

A FEW YEARS AGO, the question, 'Is there a history of women?' was far from being a rhetorical one. Traditional historiography has excluded women not only inadvertently, but sometimes programmatically from 'universal' or 'general' history. Meanwhile, the question has been answered in part by an expansion of research and by the impact, though still modest, which women's history and women historians have had on the historical profession. Some well-established historical journals in the United States, Switzerland, Italy, Sweden and Denmark have even risked the double step of dedicating issues to women's history and to a new generation of women historians. We have discovered that women's history has not only emerged in the last two decades, but that there has been a long tradition of female historians studying the history of women, a tradition which had been extinguished or pushed into the background by the academic establishment of the historical profession. The search for women's history has encouraged reflection on what such history could be, what implications it holds for the rest of historiography, and what its relationship to a truly general history should be, a history in which women and men equally have a place.

The pursuit of 'restoring women to history' soon led to that of 'restoring history to women'. Women and female experience have a history which, though not independent from men's history, is nonetheless a history of its own, of women as women. To explore it, the hierarchies between the historically important and unimportant had to be overturned. What women have done, should do and want to do is being scrutinized and re-evaluated. Despite the numerous, heterogeneous and sometimes controversial results, there are two common features which have recently been pointed out by Maité Albistur: 'There is no doubt that the plot of women's history is no less complex than that of men's. But we may assume that time as lived by the female part of humanity does not pass according to the same rhythms and that it is not perceived in the same way as that of men'. The history of women equals that of men insofar as it is just as rich and complicated, and that it is not linear, logical or cohesive. On the other hand, it is different from the history of men, and it is precisely because of this difference that it deserves to be studied – a difference that may embrace not only the contents of historical experience, but also the experience of time itself.

The autonomous character of women's history, its difference from the history of men, does not mean it is less important or just a 'special' or 'specifically female' problem. Rather, we must recognize that, on the one hand, general history has up to now essentially been male-specific, and on the other hand, that the history of women must count as just as general as that of the 'other' sex. But more than this, the difference between women's and men's history does not imply that the history of women is identical for all women: women do not all have the same history. Awareness of the otherness, the difference, the inequality between female and male history has been complemented by an awareness and historical study of the otherness, the differences and inequalities among women themselves. In this vein, the Italian journal for women's history, *Memoria*, devoted an issue to the subject '*piccole e grandi diversità*' (small and great differences).

[. . .]

Gender as a social, cultural, historical category

In studying women's past, one important point of departure has been the observation that women are half of humankind and in some countries and times, even more than half; indeed, an important and influential contribution bears the title *The Majority Finds Its Past*. In conceptual terms, this observation implies the following principle: it is no less problematic to separate the history of women from history in general than to separate the history of men – and even more so, truly general history – from the history of women. Women's history concerns not merely half of humankind, but all of it.

The most important step in efforts to link the history of one half to the other half, and both to history in general, has been to conceptualize women as a socio-cultural group, i.e. as a sex. As a result, men also become visible as sexual beings, so that the new perspective turns out to be not just about women and women's issues but about all historical issues. Since the mid-1970s, gender (*Geschlecht, genere, genre, geslacht*) has been introduced as a fundamental category of social, cultural and historical reality, perception and study, even though the new terminology, which in some languages indicates a shift from a grammatical concept to a broader socio-cultural one, has different linguistic and cultural connotations in different tongues. One of the major reasons for the introduction of the term 'gender' in this broader sense as well as for its relatively rapid diffusion in place of the word 'sex' (at least in English), has been the insistence that the 'woman question', women's history and women's studies, cannot be reduced solely to sex in the sense of sexuality, but must embrace all areas of society including the structures of that society. Hence the concept gender implies that history in general must also be seen as the history of the sexes: as gender history (*Geschlechtergeschichte, storia di genere or storia sessuata, histoire sexuée*).

To the same extent that the need to study gender has for many people become self-evident, gender or the sexes are no longer perceived as something self-evident: neither as an obvious matter nor as an *a priori* given. It is now clear that the concepts, the underlying assumptions and the consequences of historical research in gender terms, must be created, conceived and investigated anew, since they have not been part of the historiographic vocabulary. Thus, for instance, in the important multi-volume *Geschichtliche Grundbegriffe* (Fundamental Historical Concepts), the entry *Geschlecht* does not appear alongside such other terms as 'work', 'race' or 'revolution', nor does 'woman', let alone 'man'. Despite centuries of philosophical speculation about the sexes, *Geschlecht* likewise fails to appear in the *Historisches Wörterbuch der Philosophie* (Historical Dictionary of Philosophy), and under the entry *Geschlechtlichkeit* (sexuality) we find cell plasma, genes and hormones.

But gender history rejects both these approaches: the omission of gender and its reduction to an object of apparently natural science. We have learned to see that, on the one hand, all known societies have gender-based spaces, behaviours, activities and that gender-based differentiation exists everywhere. On the other hand, the concrete manifestations of gender difference are not the same in all societies; they are not universal, and the variations within the status of the female sex are just as manifold as those within the status of the male sex. Secondly, we have learned to separate the question of gender-based difference from the question of gender-based hierarchies; i.e. the power relations between men and women. The differentiation and the hierarchies are not always necessarily connected with one another nor are they identical: for instance, a sexual division of labour does not necessarily imply a sexual division of social rewards and of power. Thirdly, it has become clear that the perception of male and female scholars, most of whom are West Europeans or North Americans, is often profoundly shaped by the gender, relations of their own culture, by widespread ethno- or Euro-centrism, and by differing assumptions about the status and the emancipation of women. The current perceptions of the sexes and the terms used to describe them are to a large extent a product of the history of culture, science and of gender relations themselves, particularly since the eighteenth century. Therefore, the sexes and their relations must be perceived as social, political and cultural entities. They cannot be reduced to factors outside of history, and still less to a single and simple, uniform, primal or inherent cause or origin.

When we speak of gender as a 'category' in this context, the term refers to an intellectual construct, a way of perceiving and studying people, an analytic tool that helps us to discover neglected areas of history. It is a conceptual form of socio-cultural inquiry that challenges the sex-blindness of traditional historiography. It is important to stress that the category gender is, and must be perceived as, context-specific and context-dependent. While it does offer fundamental possibilities for a more profound understanding of virtually all historical phenomena, it should not be used as a static pattern, a myth of origins for explaining the panorama of histor-ical events. Its power is not one of elimination − by reducing history to a model − but of illumination, as a means to explore historical variety and variability. Gender is a 'category', not in the sense of a universal statement but, as the Greek origin of the word suggests, in the sense of public objection and indictment, of debate, protest, process and trial.

This public objection is directed above all at the category 'biology', a static, reductionistic model, and thus a major obstacle to historical understanding. In order to take gender as a sociocultural category seriously, historians must above all do away with the sociocultural category 'biology' and abandon the notions attached to it. For a common language among historians who study women in culture and society, this means doing without the word biology. Mireille Laget's book, *Naissances*, is one example of how to treat a subject eminently bound up with the female body without reverting to biology. Critical studies of precisely those histor-ical figures and processes that made use of 'biology' (such as, for instance, German National Socialism), should analyse, translate and not simply repeat the term.

On the level of conceptualization, it must be recognized that 'biology', as commonly used in historical writing, usually does not really refer − as the term is meant to suggest − to something non-social, pre-social, and even less to an object of natural science, but is itself a sociocultural category which has marked and distorted the perception and relation of the sexes, as well as other groups. The word *biology* was invented by German and French male scholars in the early nineteenth century, later acquiring many diverse meanings, some of which no longer exist. It came into circulation and common use at the turn of the century, earlier in the German- and English-speaking world, later in the Romance languages, particularly in and through the 'nature vs. nurture' debate of that period. Previously, biology did not exist, and the terms used to describe the female sex were of a different kind and context than the later gender-linked biology. In the twentieth century, the word *biology* became part of the common language of the right as well as of the left. Yet, the earlier women's movement, significantly, did not use this word and usually expressed visions of gender, including ideas on motherhood, in cultural terms.

Today, biology has such a variety of meanings that the use of the term by historians is more confusing than explanatory. It may mean a natural science, especially genetics, with which historians do not deal professionally. It also means the objects of this science, ranging from life and death to anatomy and bodies, to genes and brains, from plants and biological food to animals and human beings. Today the question even arises as to whether a biological mother is the genetic or the pregnant mother. Biology may refer to a way of thinking and acting upon human and other beings, matters and activities, ranging from physiological determinism to physiological change. Since the period when the term *biology* came to be commonly used, particularly in the latter sense, it referred to an inherent, unchanging constant behind cultural phenomena (as was often, but not always the case with the concept *nature*). Possibly even more often, it also implies a perspective of social change through 'biological', meaning bodily, intervention.

The sociocultural character of the idea of 'biology' is visible on various levels. It carries a clear gender bias, since it is regularly used in speaking about the female sex, but not about the male sex. Long before biology existed, Jean-Jacques Rousseau, for example, made a similar point, but in exclusively cultural terms: 'The male is male only at certain moments, the female is female all her life' (he was cautious enough to add a small but revealing reservation: '. . . or at least during her youth'). Biology is a modern metaphor for the old assumption that men are ungendered and women are gendered beings, that men are the 'one' and women the 'other sex' or even, as in the nineteenth century, 'the sex'.

Most importantly, this assumption implies a value judgement. Biology can be loaded with hopes and fears, can be viewed as an obstacle and as a resource; it has specific, though varying contents. The content which has been historically and politically the most powerful, is one which carries a negative judgement on human value; here, biology is a metaphor for the lack of value, for inferiority (*Minderwertigkeit*). This is why it has been used for those areas and activities of women's lives which are assigned less value than male areas and activities, such as child-bearing, child-raising and housework, which do not usually count as work, even though *Gebärarbeit* ('bearing work') was a common term in traditional German gynaecology, and in English, French and Italian giving birth is referred to as work (*labour, travail, travaglio*).

This use of the term *biology* is based on the notion that physical differences among persons justify social and political inequality, and that such equality should be granted only to those who are physically equal. The problem of biology proves to be one of economic, social and cultural relations between the sexes: 'the peculiar arrangement whereby many women receive economic rewards for their social contribution (in child care, homemaking, and community work) only indirectly, via their husband's income, is neither morally nor practically required by the fact (if indeed it were a fact) that women are biologically better parents than men'. It is not anatomy that brings inferior rewards to those women, but culture in the form of *biology*, of biological value judgements.

That biology is above all a value judgement is also visible in the fact that thinking in terms of biology did not initially relate only to women, but also to other social phenomena which came to be excluded from the social: for instance, the issue of the insane and the feeble-minded, the ill, of life and death, of (genetic or other) hereditary traits, of the body and of embodiment, of ethnic groups and races.

One might say that the emergence of biology as a sociocultural category and perspective of social intervention since the end of the nineteenth century extended to all those phenomena which transcended the traditional 'social question' and those objects which could be grasped within traditional social science and policy. In this context, the racist notion of biology is particularly illuminating about its sexist version, for both developed simultaneously and overlapped.

It is self-evident that black people are not physically equal to whites in all respects, but are different in one respect. It is self-evident that women are physically not equal to men in all respects, but rather, different in four or five respects. But this partial and physical difference is neither the cause nor an explanation for the relation between whites and 'alien' races or between one and the 'other' sex: 'Biology itself is mute'. Sexism and racism are not derived from physical differences. Rather, certain physical differences are used to legitimate pre-existing social relations and, in particular, power relations. So-called biological differences become metaphors for actual or alleged different lifestyles. Both modern racism and modern sexism classify the 'alien' or the 'other' group as inferior, denying not only the right of such groups to be equal, but also – and probably more important – the right to be different without being punished for it. [. . .]

Even more important for historical thought, however, is the problem that such notions and values, when projected back into the past, are anachronistic and fail to do justice to women's actual experiences in and of history. For instance, the 200,000 women sterilized in National Socialist Germany by no means experienced this removal of their '*fatalités biologiques*' as a liberation. Their case, and that of many other victims of National Socialism, demonstrates clearly that sexist and racist biology was a perspective of social change through biological measures, through intervention in body and life. Moreover, the fact that some thousands of women died as a result of compulsory sterilization was not due to female biology. Instead, it was the result of the power relations between the predominantly male agents of Nazi racism and their victims, half of whom were women. And if in such cases, historians should not attribute childlessness and death to biology, in other cases it is child-bearing that should not be attributed to biology, but to gender relations.

The frequent reduction, by feminists as well as non-feminists, of (female) embodiedness, and specifically of maternity, to 'biology' or 'biological sex' is misleading because it obscures what women's and gender history is attempting to render visible: the concrete, manifold and changing forms of women's and men's bodily experience, activity and representation, which is not neatly separable from other kinds of experience, activity and representation.

This same problematic reduction is put forward and theorized in the dichotomy, proposed between '(biological) sex' and '(social) gender', and in the hypothesis of the 'transformation of raw biological sex into gender' including the ensuing debate about what and how much is to be attributed to the one or to the other. This sex/gender distinction does not resolve, but only restates, for the sexes, the controversy 'nature vs. nurture', a more embracing opposition. It is ambivalent and problematic because, while postulating gender as a sociocultural category, it simultaneously reduces sex to a 'biological' category and thereby confirms traditional visions of gender. Often, and for good reasons, the dichotomy has been found to be analytically and empirically false. Even eminent theoreticians of gender realize this but insist that it cannot be dismissed because of politically inspired fears of biologically deterministic backlash. Political motives, however, that lead us to refuse important intellectual insights, may not lead to the best political results for women. Perhaps it is time to realize – particularly in view of an ever better-known past – that sociocultural conditions are by no means easier and faster to change than those which are called biological. Indeed, it should be realized that the sex/gender dichotomy as well as the biologically deterministic backlash are both rooted in the opposite assumption, that sociocultural conditions are amenable to change while biology remains immutable.

In any case, political motives which block theoretical insights do not lead to historical insights. As to the study of the past in a gender perspective, it seems more useful to do without 'biology' and to use gender in a comprehensive way: comprehending not only that part of women's and men's life which is proven to be culturally constructed, but also that part which falls, or is assumed to fall, outside it. Only then can gender become a historical category in the full sense.

As to the impact and power of the material and bodily world inside and outside of us which may seem to defy human reason and historical reasoning, we should be able to find other words than those dictated by the biological tradition. Some of these words can be found in precisely those historical studies which sometimes are perceived as focusing on women's biology (such as the history of maternity, child-bearing, midwives, wet-nurses, prostitutes) and which have demonstrated that the female (as well as the male) body is shaped by culture and history. Here, surely, is a domain not of biology, but of women's and gender history.

Gender as social, cultural, historical relations

Gender or the sexes refer neither to an object, nor to various objects; rather, they refer to a complex set of relations and processes. 'Thinking in relations' is needed in order to understand gender as an analytical category as well as a cultural reality, in the past as well as in the present. Such a vision of gender has implications for all forms of history as they are now practiced:

Women's history as gender history

Perceiving gender as a complex and sociocultural relation implies that the search for women in history is not simply a search for some object which has previously been neglected. Instead, it is a question of previously neglected relations between human beings and human groups. In the words of the late anthropologist Michelle Zimbalist Rosaldo, 'Women must be understood . . . in terms of relationship – with other women and with men – (not) of difference and apartness'. Rosaldo pointed to an important and often ignored dimension which goes beyond the now obvious insistence that women's history be integrated into general history through the study of relations between women and men. Not only must we study the relations *between* the sexes, but also the relations *within* the sexes, not only those of women to men, and of men to women, but also relations among women and among men.

Many relations among men have been the focus of historical writing, those emerging in the political, military, economic and cultural realms, and those between kin and friends, but rarely have they been studied as intra-gender relations or as to their impact on women. On the other hand, it is also vital to look at women's relationships with each other: between housewives and female servants, between mothers and daughters, between mothers, wet-nurses and midwives, between social workers and poor women, between female missionaries and the women of colonized peoples, among women in the professions and in politics, and to be aware of relations of conflict as well as solidarity. The history of female kin, friendship and love between women has become an important area of research. Such studies have usually focused strongly on intra-gender relations as well as on their signifi-cance to men.

Insisting on the importance of studying the relations within the sexes and particularly between women becomes all the more crucial in the 1980s as the concept of gender, *Geschlecht*, *genere*, *genre* threatens to become high fashion, which seeks to soften the challenge of women's history by developing a kind of gender-neutral discourse on gender. But if it is forgotten that the discovery of the social, cultural and historical relations between and within the sexes was the result of women studying women and men, we have fallen far short of our goal: not a gender-neutral but a gender-encompassing approach to general history. Women's history is gender history *par excellence*.

The fact that it is still not evident for scholars to view gender history, particu-larly in respect to women, also as a history within the sexes was recently shown by the eminent British historian Lawrence Stone. Expert on, among other areas, *Family, Sex and Marriage*, he has studied a field where gender relations are of conspic-uous importance and where women are half of the group to be examined. In his article, 'Only Women', he set himself up as a historians' god and handed down 'Ten Commandments' for the writing of women's history which – surprising for a historian – were to apply: 'at any time and in any place'. The first of them: 'Thou shalt not write about women except in relation to men and children'. Whereas the author correctly recognized that the new approaches deal essentially with relations and their history, he failed to see that women are not conditioned solely by their relations to men, that the relations of women to other women are just as important as those of women to men, that children are not genderless beings, and that the history of men should also include their relations to women.

Gender history as men's history

Examining men's relations to women means viewing what previously counted as an object of 'history in general' in gender-conscious and thus 'male-specific' terms: the history of men as men. Questions about gender have mainly focused on the female sex, on 'the woman question'. Men appear to exist beyond gender relations to the same degree that they dominate them. While the imperative that women's history always be related to men's has become commonplace, up to now the reverse has hardly been true.

Military history and the history of warfare are a case in point. They have dealt exclusively with men – and for good reason, since warfare in the Western world (at least within Europe) has generally been a form of direct confrontation between groups of men. Nonetheless, explicitly male-specific issues have not been raised in this field, for example its connection with the history of masculinity. Furthermore, wars have had an enormous significance for women and for the relations between and within the sexes. We need only think of the strongly gender-based and sexual war symbols and language in wars of liberation as well as in civil wars, in aggressive as well as in defensive wars, of women camp followers in the early modern armies, of the women's peace movement before, during and after the First World War or of the new forms of prostitution which appear in the First and Second World Wars.

The past few years have seen a rise of 'men's studies', mainly carried out by men, which deal with the relations between men and women, and among men. Some authors have examined the relation between war and the social construction of masculinity, and they have underlined that the latter should not be understood as a 'biological given'. What women's studies have shown is now being confirmed by men's studies: gender norms and gender realities are not identical and they are subject to historical change. According to a French historian, masculinity meant not only power but also grief and suffering for nineteenth century men. Fatherhood has also become a focus of interest for historians. Some of these studies – those being done by men – draw inspiration from a current call for male participation in female experiences and work ('Pregnant Fathers: How Fathers can Enjoy and Share the Experiences of Pregnancy and Childbirth') or for 'men's rights', a tendency not merely corresponding to feminist demands for women's rights, but – as might be expected – also at odds with them. Although these men's studies have illuminated some topics, much remains to be done, particularly in the field of history.

An issue which is still often considered as 'women's history', namely the ways in which famous – that is, male – philosophers and other thinkers have thought about women, the sexes, sexuality and the family, must in fact be viewed as men's history. It is men's, not women's history for reasons which have been discussed in various contexts, i.e. the fact that these writings present primarily men's views on women, that their image of the sexes is rarely descriptive but normative and proscriptive, and that the norms for women are usually not only different from the norms for men, but also from the realities of women's lives. The study of men's thinking on gender has come to be very diversified and it has brought to light many and unexpected complexities and contradictions, between different philosophers as well as within individual men's thought.

Such studies have also promoted the awareness of a specifically historical question of method: the problematic character of a historiography which limits itself to the presentation and repetition of the misogynous pronouncements which were said and written by men over the centuries. This often leads from outrage and denunciation to a kind of fascination. It risks becoming anachronistic as it neglects the analysis of such texts against the background of their historical context and significance, of their role within the complete works of an author and how they were judged by their female contemporaries.

Studies in intellectual history which turn, to the fewer and often less known female philosophers or to the thought and judgements of other women regarding gender as well as other relations, often uncover important differences from male thinking. Here one might consider Hannah Arendt's central concept of political thought, 'natality' – the principle and capacity of human beings to act in new ways, beyond whatever happened in history, by virtue of their being born – and her notion of human plurality which she saw symbolized in the plurality of the sexes, or in the case of Carol Gilligan's insights into women's 'different voice' in moral judgements. Thus, intellectual history also demonstrates that the history of men as men becomes visible only when seen in relation to women's history and women's thought and hence in a perspective of gender history.

Gender history and social history

If we perceive women's and gender history as a history of social relations, then we need to think about its relation to social history. Given that gender is a social category and that the sexes are social entities, all of women's and gender history is in some sense social history. But this definition is starkly at odds with what has emerged since the 1960s as the 'new social history'. Its classic objects are the (social) classes. Accordingly, the social is essentially viewed in terms of class stratification, and history in general is perceived as the history of society as determined by class structure. From the perspective of women, traditional social history, therefore, operates with a too narrow understanding of the 'social'. The frequent equation of the notion 'social' with 'class-based' or 'class-specific' (often expressed in the terms 'sexual and social') has contributed to the view that other social relations – for instance those between races and between the sexes – are something non-social, pre-social, or even 'biological'.

During the last few years, historians have often debated the relation between class and gender. Frequently it has been asserted that class was more important than gender; as an eminent social historian has argued:

> Perhaps certain socially relevant commonalities do exist between women as women at certain times after all. However, more important for an understanding of self and practical living, for the experiences and inter-ests of most women (despite their similar experiences of socialization and exclusion) were and are the concretely and highly variable mani-festations which can be traced back to class. Didn't the young, educated aristocratic woman in the capital of the newly-founded Bismarckian Reich have much more in common with her brother of the same age group than with the old, widowed Polish woman seasonal worker – working during the summer in Saxony – who lived in dire poverty and could neither read nor write?

While this image certainly points to deep and real differences between women, it does so by using features which are in fact *not* class differences. The noble lady is young; the woman worker old; the lady educated, the worker can neither read nor write; the lady is unmarried, the worker widowed; the lady is German, the worker is Polish; the lady lives in a city, the worker in a rural area. But age, marital status, ethnic-national status, living in an urban or rural milieu are not criteria of class, nor can this be said to any great extent of literacy in the late nineteenth century. If the image intends to demonstrate that working-class women had a bad time of it compared to women of the aristocracy, one can also turn it around, comparing, e.g. a young, German, light-hearted urban housewife, happily married to a German worker, who is relatively securely covered by social insurance to a poor widow of the declining Polish rural aristocracy. If then the image says nothing about the relation between class and sex, it nonetheless reveals something different and important: that differences within a sex are just as large as those within a class.

In fact, neither class nor gender refer to homogenous groups and even less to necessary bonds of solidarity, but both class and gender are important context-specific and context-dependent categories and realities of social relations between and within social groups. Thus, women's history also deals with class, and there are important studies of women workers, workers' wives, middle-class and noble women. Many of these focus on, and attempt to solve, three problems: the different conceptualization of class for men, where the main criterion is their relation to capital, production, the market, or employment, and for women, where it is their relation to the men of their family, particularly husband and father; secondly, the different and gender-based experience of class which, in the case of women, includes their work for family members; thirdly, relations between women of different classes, which may be different from those between men. [. . .]

Gender relations and other socio-cultural relations

Looking at gender as a sociocultural relation enables us to see the links between gender and numerous other sociocultural relations in a fresh light; in addition to class there are, for example, race, age, sexuality, culture, language, freedom, religion, family, economy. Just as in the debate 'class vs. gender', a kind of competition has been set up between gender and other dimensions, so that it is not the inter-action of different relations that is sought, but rather, which is considered as more fundamental, more real, more important. For instance, in Stone's Seventh Commandment: 'Thou shalt not exaggerate the importance in the past of gender over that of power, status, and wealth, even if all women experienced the same biological destiny'.

However, the assertion that (apparently) gender-neutral factors carry more weight than gender-based ones ('biological' ones according to Stone), disregards the fact that each such factor has historically meant something different for women than for men. This is obvious, for instance, in the case of power and of wealth. In the case of power not just because men have usually had more power than women and power over women at that. Under the surface of formal cleavages of power between the sexes, women have also had their own forms of power, often of a more informal kind, power – or rather, as French historians say, 'powers' – of various kinds, such as participation in men's power, power vis-à-vis other women, self-assertion as women. Gender studies have contributed to seeing the phenomenon of power as highly differentiated, and one of the forms of legitimization of power has been gender.

The gender dimensions in the case of wealth are strikingly clear. Women as a social group have had a smaller income than men and namely – at least in the nineteenth and twentieth centuries – in three respects: as houseworkers or homemakers, they had no income, as lower- and middle-class wage earners, they had a smaller income than the men of their class, and in higher income brackets they represent only a small proportion (for instance, making up four per cent of history professors at West German universities today).

Hence, each sociocultural relation means something different for women and for men. We must, however, go beyond even this insight and recognize that each one of the apparently gender-neutral relations between human beings is *also* conditioned by gender relations; gender is one constituent factor of all other relations. The history of religion, from the ancient gods to those of the twentieth century, is incomprehensible if treated as gender-neutral. The same is true of ethnic minorities, whose gender history has been studied particularly in the United States; more recently, the history of Jewish and Gypsy women as well as of other women who have suffered racist discrimination has been taken up in Germany. These women differ not only from those of the majority, but also from men in their respective minority groups.

On the other hand, the language of racism is obsessed with the sexes and sexuality, and it contains a characteristic mixture of sexuality, blood and violence. Contemporaries rightly diagnosed National Socialist anti-Judaism as also being 'sexual anti-semitism'. Historians of European and particularly German racism – more specifically, men who belonged to its victims – have shown that in the racist world view, the 'Aryan' or 'Nordic' person was a 'Westerner of the male sex'. Racism cannot be understood without understanding its gender dimension, which is one of its constituent factors. And if, conversely, the analysis of gender relations or sexism includes an analysis of race relations or racism, we may arrive at new and unexpected results. One of these might be the insight that the specifically National Socialist policy towards women did not consist – as is usually assumed – in 'pronatalism and a cult of motherhood'. Rather, it was antinatalism, a cult of fatherhood, virility and mass extermination of women as well as men.

* * *

History, then, is not only one of male, but also of female, experience. It should not be studied only in male or apparently gender-neutral perspectives, but also in female and gender-encompassing perspectives. This should not mean a simple inversion of the traditional postulate that other human relations are more important than gender relations, by setting up a counter-claim that gender is more important than everything else, although it is clear that inversion first opened our senses to many historical discoveries. Rather, it means that gender relations are equally as important as all other human relations, and that gender relations contribute to and affect all other human relations. Conversely, all other human relations contribute to and affect gender relations.

To insist on the hypothesis that other relations are more fundamental than gender relations is both ideological and historically unproductive. It recalls the situation of Cassandra, the king's daughter, in Christa Wolf's narrative. Cassandra dreamt that she had to judge as to whether 'the moon or the sun could shine brighter'. A humble and wise woman taught her that this was a misguided 'attempt to find an answer to a completely absurd question'. When Cassandra finally understood that she 'had the right, perhaps even the duty to reject it' she had taken a crucial and liberating step in comprehending her own history.

Penelope J. Corfield, June Purvis and Amanda Weatherill

HISTORY AND THE CHALLENGE OF GENDER HISTORY

This exchange on the challenges posed by gender history was published in the journal *Rethinking History* and brings our Part I readings to a close. Penelope Corfield's 1997 essay is a reflective overview of gender history at the end of the twentieth century, a development that she believes has enriched immeasurably the study of history. What is interesting about this piece is Corfield's assertion that, despite its original intention to effect a fundamental recasting of the discipline, neither women's nor gender history has lived up to their optimistic claims to deliver an 'ambitious new epistemology'. Gender has raised significant interpretive issues concerning many central axes of historical analysis, argues Corfield, such as chronologies, period-isation and, echoing Vickery's point in Reading 3, the tension between prescriptive literature and material reality. Although gender 'will continue to be one of the most challenging areas of future [historical] research', it has not achieved a 'seismic epistemological shift in cognition' nor, she reassures us, is it necessary to do so to generate theoretical innovation. June Purvis's and Amanda Weatherill's response to this upbeat assessment of gender history's future focuses on Corfield's claim that women's history has 'mutated' into gender history. They critique Corfield for her imprecise and interchangeable use of terms such as 'women's history' and 'feminist history' and they remind us that women's history can often be antifeminist in scope and purpose. They also reject Corfield's positive reading of the assimilation of gender studies into traditional history departments. Gender history is a 'malestream incorp-oration strategy' for Purvis and Weatherill that decentres the study of women *as* women. Mainstreaming gender is a nice idea, they argue, but for feminist academics in the late 1990s the institutional reality suggests a bleaker reading in which women feel obliged to suppress their feminist politics in order to gain academic respectability and to access permanent institutional positions.

Penelope J. Corfield

ONE FIRST GENERAL QUESTION may be posed before all others. Has studying the history of women – and now the history of gender – enriched the study of history? And the answer is unequivocally in the affirmative. Indeed, to avoid misunderstanding, it should be repeated: the answer is unequivocally and enthusiastically in the affirmative. Moreover, the recent publication of a key reader on *Feminism and History* (Scott, 1996) provides a helpful guide to the theoretical and empirical sophistication of the field. With twenty contributions on the variable conceptualizations of men, women and gender over time, it presents a range of stimulating approaches in response to questions that would have not been deemed answerable or even worth asking only twenty-five years ago. The reader also demonstrates in its diversity that there is not an agreed feminist 'line' on the mutabilities of the past. Gender history is eclectic, with a diverse range of intellectual inputs. It is therefore timely to take a critical overview of the field.

Despite much initial controversy, the history of gender has quickly established itself within the discipline. It has not only furnished new data and intense new debates but it has become accepted as an essential component of holistic analysis. Furthermore, women's history is not static. The field is transforming itself – again not without continuing controversy – into the study of historical gender. That shift suggests that the subject has its own internal dynamic as well as sharing in wider changes within the discipline. The advent of 'gender' is thus a highly significant development, which has recharged the focus rather than ended the radical impetus of the subject. Specialist studies into either men or women are not outlawed. But such studies can now be located within the variable history of gender roles. A stark male/female dichotomy is ceasing to be viewed as a static 'given'. Moreover, students of historical gender tend to show a welcome awareness of the wider framework that informs their analysis. Theory is not spurned but, at best, incorporated into the detailed picture.

Women's history, in other words, has moved rapidly from a fringe interest into a mainstream one. Whereas in the early 1970s it was viewed as a raffish or eccentric subject, it has now become normalized. The very speed of its assimilation may even prove disconcerting to the bold pioneers. They have scarcely had time to enjoy their success before their role has been transformed from that of pathbreaking iconoclasts into established icons, ripe for challenge in turn by the next research generation. This progression has already happened, sedately enough, in other subfields, such as urban history and social history (both beginning their modern boom in the 1960s) and it is now overdue in the case of econometric history (inaugurated in the 1970s).

At the same time, the process of renewal is liable to be contentious in the case of gender history because the specialism has a high potential for ideological, political and personal commitment. That has decisively moved the subject in from the margins – and promises to keep it in the spotlight.

Clearly, one of the major reasons for the success of women's history has been its speedy inclusion within the new and broadly-based social and cultural history. The tides and times were favourable to the change. Once a narrow political history was gradually widened and a mechanistic economic history was rejected in favour of a broader approach, then a loose-jointed and ecumenical social history began to hold sway. Moreover, the vibrant field of women's history itself helped to force these changes onto the intellectual agenda. It raised explicit questions about how social history should be studied. What was the key to understanding people's lives in the past?

Specifically, were women to be commiserated for their historic burdens? Or celebrated for their resistance to repression? Or studied simply because they were part of the past? Put very schematically, women's history has provided examples of all these approaches.

[. . .]

A new epistemology?

Given the creative richness of women's history, a second general question can then be formulated: has this new focus for study in itself transformed the analytical under-pinning of the discipline? That at least was the hope of at least some pioneers. 'Herstory' would not just update 'history' but would launch historical studies onto a distinctive and innovatory pathway. The subjective and personal would be welded into the public and impersonal. Hence would follow 'not only a new history of women but also a new history'. The whole intellectual landscape would change. 'Clio, the muse of history, is now a liberated woman', added [S. R.] Johansson cheerfully. As such, she would renovate the profession by introducing more women into academe and at the same time rethinking the whole project.

A 'terrible beauty' would be born. An ambitious new epistemology, a whole new way of knowing, would promote a 'reconceptualization of historical practice', in Joan Wallach Scott's influential and controversial formulation. What was needed was nothing less than 'a more radical epistemology' that would lead simultaneously to a radicalized feminist history and to a radicalized feminist politics. In arguing that all cultural practices were human-made and mutable, Scott also endorsed the post-modernist critique of traditional history. The old form of the discipline, she argued, had erred in allegedly dealing in value-free absolutes. Her formulation encapsulated the sense that sweeping changes were nigh (widely expressed by feminist theorists), even if not all accepted the precise form of Scott's philosophical revisionism.

An exemplary indicator of the new approach was the popularization of a novel verb. Henceforth history was to be 'gendered'. This term was more frequently invoked than closely defined. It did, however, signal the new creed. Cultural forma-tions could not be studied without a central awareness of gender roles. Indeed, to hammer home the point, some of the most eminent male pioneers of a left-leaning social history were criticized for their neglect of this perception. [. . .]

Yet has the new research into gender history achieved a conceptual recasting of history (as opposed to enriching it with a vital dimension)? The answer to the second general question, by contrast, must be in the negative. Women's history, or gender history as it is becoming, does not operate within a new epistemology. It does not require an intellectual quantum leap to understand the works of its practitioners. Gender historians tend to be aware of theory. They can, however, readily communicate with their peers, under the capacious mantle of 'history'. Moreover, although a few gender specialists do express their theoretical meditations too abstrusely, such a style is not an intrinsic requirement of the field. There is no fundamental conceptual or linguistic barrier between gender history and the rest of history.

Indeed, it is easier to call for a new epistemology than to create one. At this point, however, it is appropriate to pause for a moment. What would in fact constitute a new epistemology for the study of the past? Does it consist in a new mindset? a new style of thinking? in new answers? a new prevailing theorem? new techniques of analysis? a new language of communication? or some combination of any or all of these? In the history of physics, the Newtonian and Einsteinian revolutions each time introduced a new set of paradigmatic 'grand theories' within the discipline. These could not be ignored by later physicists. In each case, it was possible to talk of an intellectual quantum leap, once the new world-view had been fully assimilated. The discipline of history does not, however, proceed in a directly comparable manner. Historians do not seek to formulate general 'laws' for general acceptance. They do not follow hegemonic authorities, whose interpretations come to be endorsed and developed by virtually all practitioners in the field.

[. . .]

Interpretative problems

Gender history, moreover, has so far been notable for raising yet more analytical problems rather than for adopting one settled viewpoint. Such an achievement is, of course, an admirable index of vitality. The pluralist exploration of historical gender is generating new debates, not new doctrine.

For example, one perplexing issue relates to the significant chronologies of continuity/change. When historians abandoned a narrow political perspective upon the past, many hoped that a new temporal framework could be constructed. After all, what real significance did dates such as 1066 or 1689 or 1832 (say) have for gender identities in England? And the same sceptical question could be asked about the history of gender in all countries with reference to their own key political moments. It has, however, not proved easy to construct alternative chronologies.

Some historians resolve the problem by excluding change entirely. Women's history may be 'the history that stands still'. From this viewpoint, deep continuities ensure that, whatever the changing outer framework, the structural repression of the world's child-bearers remains unchanged. It means too that the lost 'Golden Age' of woman-power never existed. Discarding nostalgia for a non-existent past is helpful to scholarship. But a model of eternal stasis is not a satisfactory alternative. 'No change' conceals too much cultural and historical variation to be convincing as an overall interpretation. [. . .]

Required therefore is a more nuanced categorization and chronology. There is, however, no sign as yet of this emerging. In common with much recent social and cultural history, women's history has been stronger in short-term synchronic exposition than in diachronic interpretation. When general long-term trends are invoked, such as the separation of work from the household and the banishment of women from a public world of production into a private sphere of demure domesticity, there is no agreement as to how, why and especially when change occurred. [. . .]

These debates will no doubt prompt more much-needed research. What, if anything, did change significantly? and how, when and why? Excellent questions. But the lack of synthesis in reply means that women's history has not so far produced a commanding new temporal framework. As Natalie Zemon Davis noted in 1976, there is disagreement not only about significant dates but even about the nature of the trends. Despite the torrent of exciting new work, her verdict on the diversity of chronologies and key developments still remains valid in the 1990s.

And that is without men. Once the problematic timetable of historical masculinity is added into the equation, things become yet more complicated. Were changes in the historic roles for women always, often, sometimes, or never correlated with concomitant changes for men? These are crucial questions, to which there are as yet no answers.

Incidentally, it should be noted that this marked thematic and chronological uncertainty is by no means unique to gender history. On the contrary. It closely matches the absence of consensus across the subject generally about both the nature and timing of 'grand trends' over the very long term. In particular, the concern with meaning and/or with micro-history has tended to produce a synchronic focus that has distracted attention from debating as opposed to invoking the long term. These difficulties are also multiplied when comparing and contrasting trends within the many different cultures across the world. The globalization of historical studies still has a very long way to go.

Identifying gender

That said, gender historians have other conceptual problems of their own to preoccupy them. There is a rumbling and important debate over what exactly is being studied. Its basic concepts have been formidably problematized. How is gender identity, as opposed to biological sex, formed and expressed? And how therefore should it be analysed in the past? Is it a biological and/or a psychological 'given'? Should it be viewed as an *a priori* philosophical category that can be applied objectively to the past? Or is it a conceptual variable that is humanly derived from social and cultural expectations about gender roles? Or is it generated by some possibly or probably fluctuating combinations of both inheritance and adaptation? How fluid and mutable can gender be?

Then, if formed or at least strongly influenced by social expectations, how can those key factors best be studied? Can public rhetoric be taken as direct proxy for communal beliefs in action? Or, alternatively, could the official discourse – for example, clerical advice about sexual restraint – sometimes or always represent the inverse of actual behaviour? Certainly, moral and social codes could be broken as well as endorsed.

Again, these are fascinating questions that deserve further debate. Initially, some feminists implied that there was a given woman's nature that could be traced through history. This view is known as 'essentialist'. Currently, it is out of fashion, although it may have some lurking adherents among the feminist ranks. Lyndal

Roper in 1994 has notably urged greater attention to the biological constraints upon womanhood whereas ten years earlier, in an essay on attitudes towards prostitution, she had discussed 'masculinity' and 'femininity' as cultural creations. Instead, the new emphasis is strongly in favour of a social 'constructionist' view, derived ultimately from the writings of Michel Foucault on the history of sexuality. He himself was not particularly interested in the history of women. But he stressed the potential plasticity of gender roles. Those were not (and are not) innate, in Foucault's view, but were (and are) socially constructed through discourse. Indeed, the essays reprinted in *Feminism and History* demonstrate the great variety of factors that impinge upon personal identity.

It was this approach in particular that has helped to transform women's history into gender history. By no means all feminists were happy with this development. But the new impetus to the field was difficult to deny. The quest became an examination of how gender roles were created and sustained historically. It need not be an exclusively feminist agenda. Hence the discourse about masculinity was just as relevant as that about womanhood.

However, the shift in emphasis and methodology within the subject has raised its own problems. Can gender history best be studied by reference to the public discourse? And what constitute satisfactory sources for such a study? Do prescriptive works, such as sermons and advice books, really provide an unproblematic picture of everyday behaviour at every social level? Certainly, they do not. Hence it is as misleading to deduce the history of gender from conduct books as it is to derive the history of food preparation from published recipes; or the history of child-care from child-rearing manuals; or the history of morals from sermons; or the history of manners from etiquette books; or the history of everyday dress from fashion magazines; or the history of motoring from a close reading of the Highway Code. It could well be that conventional advice either preceded or followed or contradicted directly the changing patterns of social practice.

Furthermore, as literary experts remind historians, it is also important to allow for varieties of 'reader response'. Elite conduct books might propose, but they could not automatically dispose. Men and women were not ciphers. The stuffier conventions were often more honoured in the breach than in the observance. Indeed, historians who argue that gender roles are socially constructed do not have to imply thereby that men and women perform parrot-fashion on the authority of literary texts. Human socialization is much more variegated than that, as indeed is language. [. . .]

Discourse or diversity?

Where does this leave gender history? These new theorizations of sexuality and new approaches to reading texts have manifestly enlivened the debates. Indeed, women's history was ready for a stimulus to new research. The dramatic impetus derived from 1970s feminism was beginning to fragment, reflecting also the diversification of political feminism. Once success had been achieved in the important initial effort to get women's history taken seriously, the subject moved on to new issues. (Incidentally, there is a scope for a good study of the changing dynamic between academic and political feminisms over the last thirty years.)

Rousing denunciations of 'patriarchal oppression' have gradually given ground to explorations of 'inequalities between the sexes' – a development that has been strongly deplored by some. Similarly, the influential contributions of Marxist-influenced historians, who added gender to class, have run into problems, as the Marxist interpretative schema (including Marxist concepts of class itself) has been contested. Here too an intellectual tradition is in the process of diversification. Of course, the fuzziness of 'class' as a concept does not mean it has no historical meaning; but it does pose problems for a Marxist interpretation that assumed an irreducible and unmistakable class struggle throughout history. As issues became more complex, a new focus upon sexuality and the body became a bold and attractive way to change the analytical focus.

With such interesting themes to explore, it is not difficult to predict that the study of gender will continue to be one of the most challenging areas of future research. It is already becoming global in scope. The cross-currents between gender and class can now be compared with those between gender and race, and between gender and national identity. For example, a significant number of essays in *Feminism and History* confront these wider themes. And there is much else to be done. Indeed, it becomes more and more apparent that the subject, far from being exhausted, has hardly begun. The ultra-modish discussions of 'the body' in history, for example, have so far focused mainly upon attitudes to the female body. But the male and masculinity are new hot topics. Such is the enthusiasm for the body that bookshops are now positively strewn with tomes on 'mangled members, tormented torsos, bodies emblazoned or incarcerated, disciplined or desirous', complains [Terry] Eagleton, in a knockabout critique. He views the trend as a sad displacement of radical political analysis – turning away from the public body politic merely to dally with the fleshly body personal. His discussion also probes the relationship between mind and matter. Can the role of men and women be deduced from the history of the body? Or does it have its own history/histories? Can 'the body' (usually studied as the young, healthy body, as Eagleton points out) stand proxy for the range of human sexualities? All this indicates academic gender's admirable capacity not only to innovate but equally to goad.

Hitherto, much discussion has been couched in terms of dichotomous alternatives. The contrast between biological man and woman has perhaps subconsciously encouraged a dualistic approach. Women's history has particularly attracted dichotomies. But these may be – indeed, often are – false. How helpful are either/or scenarios? Should historians of gender have to choose between nature/culture, work/family, public/private, equality/difference, integration/autonomy as rigidly opposed alternatives? These debates are not, of course, confined to women's history. Currently (1997), the Habermas-derived distinction between the 'public' and the 'private' is also disputed within a wider social history. This dualism indeed awaits a thorough critique; and there are already signs that it is too schematic to be fully convincing.

Overthrowing the dominance of the 'two' will provide scope for a more ambitious and pluralist analysis. It will also chime more sympathetically with human experience, since both past and present societies have seen more than two forms of sexual identity and more than two varieties of possible gender roles. Gay studies in particular highlight the far-from-static history of homosexual orientations. And heterosexualities are just as complex.

The study of gender therefore offers a range of challenging questions within the wider subject of history, that do not lend themselves to easy answers. It is a field that remains in a constant process of adaptation and renewal. As a result, its theoretical and research richness will continue to provide a stimulus for all historians. But what is required to generate innovation? It is not necessary to claim a seismic epistemological shift in cognition to achieve that. Moreover, feminist discussions as to whether there is a separate feminist philosophy, and way-of-knowing have remained notably inconclusive. Some assert that there should be, although without revealing what it is. Others are doubtful. Yet surely it is far too simplistic to invoke a warm, female intuition in lieu of a cold, male logic. That would endorse a crude stereotyping of gender attributes that historical research has done much to combat.

Similarly, there is no need to reject the possibility of achieving a reasoned understanding of the past, even if there are many acknowledged problems in the task. The fact that not everything can be known with certainty does not mean that nothing can be known. There are plenty of analytical options between an overconfident omniscience and an unduly pessimistic nescience.

So gender history does not depend for its credibility upon the acceptance of a postmodernist dismissal of a universalist 'Enlightenment reason'. There have been a significant number of meditations upon this question by feminist theoreticians. They tend to be sympathetic to the argument that women's history (more specifically than gender history) does need to reject many old intellectual assumptions. But they are less certain that postmodernism provides the right new answers. Indeed, there have been strong warnings from other feminists against accepting that case too readily. Academic history before gender studies has not been one intact monolith, based on the worship of Reason. As already noted, conservatives like Gertrude Himmelfarb have instead complained that the subject has already strayed too far from the paths of universalist rationalism. Consequently, gender history does not have to kill a lumbering, one-eyed Goliath Reason in order to progress.

Posing the options in such terms deals again in false polarities. Gender analysis, like feminism, is not a unitary body of thought. Nor, certainly, is postmodernism. Thus the two cannot be simply identified together as alternative sides of the same intellectual coin. If gender history shares with postmodernism an awareness that social categories are mutable and 'slippery', postmodernism also tends towards a general scepticism that accords ill with the enthusiasm and commitment generated by women's history in particular. These are complex cross-currents within the current turmoil and questioning within the Humanities. Meanwhile, it is relevant to note that Keith Jenkins's postmodernist appeal for a new history based upon 'a sceptical, critically reflexive approach' does not make his case on the strength of gender history. The field is hardly mentioned, although Foucault is invoked with approval. All that Jenkins does say is that feminist history should remain outside the historical mainstream where it can offer a separate 'her-story'. That would be a valid contribution to a decentred model of knowledge. But it is doubtful whether most feminists, let alone most gender historians, would be truly happy with settling for a role that could be so easily marginalized.

Instead, the important issue at stake is that of a pluralist inclusion. Not a tame 'redomestication' as Jenkins would see it. Women and men are inescapably part of the past/present. The study of history, as a route to complex knowledge, must therefore incorporate the history of gender as part of the contentious mainstream, not as a separate but equal alternative.

Exactly how significant a factor it is deemed to be will remain a matter for argument. Gender identity may not always be the most important question. But it must be examined in all its complexity and diversity, including also its limits and constraints. These pluralities can then be fitted into the big picture(s) of time and space. After all, the quest for a conceptual holism does not intrinsically imply a monolithic model, but can and should incorporate the full diversity of human society. Within that, to ignore gender is to sacrifice depth, breadth, realism. And, happily, to include it is a task that has been stirringly begun but emphatically not completed. [. . .]

Reference

Scott, Joan (ed.) (1996) *Feminism and History* (Oxford: Oxford University Press).

June Purvis and Amanda Weatherill

PLAYING THE GENDER HISTORY GAME: A REPLY TO PENELOPE J. CORFIELD

PENNY CORFIELD'S ARTICLE on 'History and the Challenge of Gender History' in the Winter 1997 issue of *Rethinking History* raises important themes in so far as it not only explores some of the complexities of 'gender history' but also covertly illustrates some of the problems when attempting to assimilate women's history and gender history. For the purposes of this response, we shall focus primarily on the implications for women's history of Corfield's claim that it is 'mutating' into gender history. We write as feminists who are involved in researching women's lives in the past and who are employed in a British university.

First, however, throughout her article, Corfield uses the terms *women's history* and *feminist history* interchangeably, implying a shared homogenous field of study. This is not the case. Although the ties between women's history and feminist history have been strong, as [Judith] Bennett acknowledges, women's history is not necessarily feminist history. As Purvis argues, *women's history* takes women as its subject matter and may be written by men and women alike. Indeed, some women's history is anti-feminist or non-feminist whilst some women writing women's history prefer to distance themselves from the label 'feminist'.

If *women's history* is defined by its subject matter, *feminist history* may be defined by its approach and the forms of analyses that are adopted. As the label implies, *feminist history* is informed by the ideas and theories of feminism, and such an approach may be applied to any topic in history, including the study of men. When feminists study women in the past, rather than men, we should strictly use the term *feminist women's history*; however, few people follow such conventions and the term *feminist history* is usually used instead. What unites all feminist histories, however, is a concern to make women visible where they had been hidden in the 'male' view of the past; an intention to challenge the traditional ways in which women had been represented stereotypically as wives and mothers who are supportive towards, and supported by, their menfolk; to present women as individuals in their own right, active agents in the making of history; to question the concepts and analyses of mainstream history; and, above all, to explore the ways in which women were disadvantaged/oppressed by the personal and institutionalized power of men in past patriarchal societies. *Feminist history* was, and is, therefore linked to the modern feminist movement in a way that was/is not necessarily so for *women's history*. It is a serious omission on Corfield's part to fail to draw such distinctions clearly and to use the two terms as if they were synonymous. Indeed, Corfield confuses the issue further by using a similar homogeneity of categorization for the terms *gender history* and *history of gender*, which, yet again, are not clearly defined.

Whatever meaning Corfield attaches to the term *gender history*, we find it a problematic term since it implies an equivalence of consideration to women and men, femininity and masculinity, within the field of study. This is a naive position to take. At present, we do not know enough about women's lives in the past nor about cultural constructions/representations of femininity and masculinity to write a fully fledged gender history. There is the danger, therefore, that gender history is yet another variation of men's history, peppered with frequent references to 'gender' but with little reference to women's lives. In our view it is important for women's history and feminist women's history to continue as academic fields of study, even in the changing times of the 1990s.

Corfield seems to confuse the terms *gender history* and the *history of gender*, using them interchangeably. In our view, while *gender history* entails an egalitarian consideration of women and men, masculinity and femininity, the *history of gender* moves us away from this towards an historiography of gender relations, in all their diversity, hidden and unhidden. Here we concur with Corfield that much more research is needed into the social constructions of femininity and masculinity. Men writing history must begin to identify their standpoint within the research process for, as [Bev] Skeggs reminds us, many men are 'normalized' when undertaking research so that they are able to leave their gender, and its accompanying institutionalized power positions, 'unquestioned'. It is no secret that the majority of male historians have not voiced their masculinist standpoints and, until they do so, we cannot hope to drop the 'invisible' prefixes assigned to *History*; nor can we adopt 'gender' as an egalitarian indication. We believe this to be a fundamental political aim within the *history of gender*, without which it will become just another extension of malestream history.

That being said, it is Corfield's assertion that women's history is 'mutating' into gender history, a belief that is reiterated throughout her article that we particularly challenge. Furthermore, Corfield posits that this mutation 'is notably broadening and enriching historical studies' presenting such a position as 'incontestable'. If feminism and women's history has taught us anything, it is that everything is contestable. Thus in regard to Corfield's 'incontestable enrichment' – we contest it! Corfield articulates the malestream incorporation strategy which has been adopted within the Western academy in these most anti-feminist of times. In so doing however, she fails to explore fully the implications for women of incorporation. Incorporation, in the terms that Corfield describes, rapes women of the legitimacy to historicize women since, as Purvis notes, it 'decentres the study of women *as* women'. It is a male tool used in an attempt to dissipate women's power whereby women become historically viable subjects only when placed alongside men, thus reinforcing their position as 'other'. Whereas feminist historians researching women's lives in the past were concerned to explore the causes of the social construction of gender in history, the post-structuralist emphasis upon exploring the meanings of gender in language and discourses, run the risk, as Bennett so eloquently asserts, of intellectualizing and abstracting the inequalities of the sexes. [Joan] Hoff sums up the concerns of many critics of the poststructuralist approach when she notes that they use gender as a category of analysis to 'reduce' the experiences of women, struggling to define themselves and better their lives in particular historical contexts, 'to mere subjective stories'.

A further point made by Corfield in regard to the supposed mutation of women's history into gender history, needs to be discussed, namely that such a mutation has 'recharged the focus rather than ended the radical impetus of the subject' with gender history enabling the incorporation of '[t]heory . . . into the detailed picture'. Feminist women's histories, in all their diversity, were formed upon the theoretical position of women. Indeed, they continue to be theoretically and politically charged through the continual reformulation of feminist epistemologies which are constructed upon theoretical differences and similarities between women as well as their material circumstances.

Corfield is critical of analyses such as that by Himmelfarb who suggests a growing gulf between an 'old' rationalist political history on the one hand and a 'new' anti-rationalist, structuralist composite of economic, social, cultural, psychoanalytical and gender history on the other. These polarities are 'too melodramatic' claims Corfield, '[h]istorians do not have to choose from stark either/or alternatives'. Whilst it is a nice idea to reject dualisms in a shift towards pluralities, the reality for feminist academics in higher education, at least in Britain and the USA, does not always mirror this utopian ideal. Gender history, like gender studies, is regarded by many men who hold key positions of power in the academy as more neutral and balanced than women's history or women's studies. As [Mary] Evans, a professor of women's studies, perceptively comments, 'gender' is seen as less threatening since it seems to add 'an aura of "complexity" to what might otherwise be seen as a narrow or restricted field'. Corfield seems unaware that many feminist academics in higher education today face a very real either/or situation where they have to choose between Corfield's 'stark either/or alternatives'. As such, gender history does not move women's history, as Corfield claims 'from a fringe interest into a mainstream one'. Instead it maintains a politics of subterfuge, resulting in feminists overtly exhibiting a loss of feminist convictions in order to covertly exist.

For feminist academics within the historical disciplines, the role of subterfuge is an important one; they will continue the 'constant interrogation of what is being silenced and why' and, since the study of man remains the only really respectable tradition, they gain 'respectability' as [Ann] Oakley notes, by naming what they do as 'about gender' rather than as 'about women'. Thus, 'gender' becomes an academic euphemism for 'women' in that it leaves open an avenue in which feminists can continue to study women within malestream academe. Feminist women's history has not mutated into gender history; it has gone underground, striking wherever and whenever it can. Indeed, Corfield is right to conclude from Keith Jenkins that there are problems for feminist history in maintaining a position outside the historical mainstream where it can offer a separate 'herstory'. However, this is more acceptable to us than incorporation into gender history on the anti-feminist terms she presents.

In conclusion, it would seem to us that there are two main ways in which to play the gender history game. You either play for the 'tootsies' or you side with the 'women'. [Kathleen] Barry, drawing on the film *Tootsie*, with Dustin Hoffman in the eponymous role, identifies what she terms 'The Tootsie Syndrome' where a man could be nominated for Academy Awards for playing the role of acting as a woman, which was established as much harder and more demanding a role to act than that of those of the human species who merely *are women through no effort of their own* (Barry's italics). If one plays for the 'tootsies' then this presents many strategies and ways to historicize women but all are constrained by the need to score in the interests of men. The 'women' on the other hand, allow for an infinite number of representations sharing a common goal, to score in the interests of women. We are not sure which team Penny Corfield is in. Upon first reading, it appears she is playing alongside the 'tootsies' and she would indeed be in infamous company with the likes of George Dangerfield. However, whilst it is obvious that she is not playing in a feminist position, Corfield could actually be a 'woman' team player, posing as a 'tootsie'. It is a role that many academic women are forced to play as viability for the women's team is still very much dependent on malestream versions of history, theory, truth and knowledge supported by anti-feminist allegiance to patriarchal power. [. . .]

Corfield is right to argue that dichotomous models in history are giving way to more complex and pluralistic accounts, but this is not to argue that dichotomous models do not exist, nor that they do not influence the experiences of feminist academics. Nowhere is this more evident than in the ambiguous relationship of some academic women to 'gender history'. Corfield should take note that gender history can be feminist, can be about women, and can be political. It may be a game of double bluff, playing the male game by the male rules – in the interests of women.

Penelope J. Corfield

FROM WOMEN'S HISTORY TO GENDER HISTORY: A REPLY TO 'PLAYING THE GENDER HISTORY GAME'

I THANK JUNE PURVIS and Amanda Weatherill for their comment 'Playing the Gender History Game', which provides a close reading of my article 'History and the Challenge of Gender History'. [. . .]

There does not in fact appear to be substantive disagreement about my analysis of the achievements/failures of women's history to date. We do, however, diverge markedly in our assessments of the nature and merits of current research trends. This seems worth exploring further.

Briefly, I argued that the field of women's history, having begun by rescuing the history of women from undue oblivion, has now begun to broaden into a wider gender history. The extended perspective includes the history of men/ women/gender identities and all forms of gender relationships. There are lots of reasons for this shift, not least the fact that no separate 'herstory' has emerged. In my view, the capacity of the subject to broaden itself is a sign of intellectual vitality.

By contrast, Purvis and Weatherill argue that women's history both is not – and should not be – mutating into gender history. They believe that a clear distance should be kept. The maintenance of women's history as a separate field will offer, in their view, the best chance for the formulation of a specifically feminist 'herstory', outside the 'malestream'. As context for this view, Purvis and Weatherill see feminist academics within British and American higher education as imperilled [. . .], and they buttress their case by reference to the poor representation of women among the professoriat.

Our debate therefore centres around two questions. First, is women's history shifting towards a broader gender history? On that, the best reply is that time will show.

And, second, is such a shift, if occurring, a 'bad thing' (by implication, either for understanding the history of women – or for women's position in academe)? I think not.

The details of my reply are summarized under three definitional headings. *Feminist history*: An explicit feminism, concerned with the just appreciation, advancement and theoretical understanding of the roles of the *quondam* 'second sex', was and remains a common motivation for the study of women's history. Indeed, the changing interaction between feminist theories and research praxis is a wonderful topic for investigation in its own right.

Yet there is no easily identifiable and separately feminist women's history. The dividing lines between feminist and non-feminist versions are highly subjective. No single approach has been established to act as a litmus test. Modern feminism has become a very pluralistic and argumentative affair. As a result, one historian may consider herself to be feminist; yet not be so accepted by others. [. . .]

Feminism therefore provides an approach (or, rather, a range of approaches) that may be applied to history, as to many other subjects especially within the humanities and social sciences. That being so, it seems just as feasible to apply feminist perspectives to the history of gender as it does to apply them to the history of women.

Women's history is a field of study that is defined by its subject matter. It contains a range of approaches; but the most common shared assumption is that women must be regarded as independent historical agents in their own right. 'Anti-womanism' as a motivation for studying women's history is very rare, no doubt because historians who believe women to be historically insignificant do not wish to waste time in studying such trifling beings.

Overall, the advent of women's history has been admirably effective in broadening and deepening historical research. It has not led, however, to a new 'grand narrative' or to a separate 'herstory' as some (though not all) pioneers had hoped. Women's history remains enmeshed in the rest of history. It interacts particularly strongly with social and cultural studies. Incidentally, the widespread terminology of 'gender' has itself been much encouraged by women's history specialists. They often refer, for example, to social structures as being 'gendered', or displaying an uneven gender balance of power. Such linguistic creativity, if now sometimes hackneyed, showed that analysts of women's history were early aware of the way that women's status was located within wider contexts.

Gender history is thus not a cuckoo in the nest. It is instead a logical development, signalling the explicit consideration of men and of gender relationships. In particular, it indicates that 'man' is no longer deemed to be an ahistorical concept that is beyond analysis. 'Gender history' thus refers to the history of gender in all its aspects, just as 'women's history' is the name commonly given to the history of women.

Reconfiguring the field emphasizes the adoption of a broad perspective. It does not signal the analytical primacy of men. Nor does it imply a covert attack upon women's history or upon women's historians. On the contrary. The change has occurred as a gradual progression. There is extensive overlapping between practitioners. Indeed, it could be argued that the new nomenclature merely reflects what has long been happening in practice. Women's history courses already discuss, without controversy, topics relating to the history of men. Equally, the journal *Gender and History* stressed at its inception in 1989 that it sought to broaden rather than to undermine women's history, by confronting gender relations 'from a feminist perspective'.

Shifting the name has not therefore stemmed from any sudden loss of confidence in female agency. The explicit analysis of gender relationships has instead highlighted new questions. For example, are changing roles for one gender always/often/sometimes/never accompanied by contrapuntal changes for the other? There are, however, no rules for research in this or any other field. Historians of gender can and do focus upon any aspect of men and/or women's history, as they choose. But these issues can all be viewed within a multi-gendered 'humanist' field of study.

Among other things, such ecumenicalism provides a helpful analytical framework for *men's history*, bringing this subject in from the cold. Otherwise, it should presumably be left to languish, awaiting the advent of a separate masculinism.

Knowledge is too multifarious, interactive and ever-expanding to be pigeonholed into a discrete 'malestream' version or rival 'femalestream', just as it does not fall into separate streams for people classified by their race, class, religion, politics, looks, physical ability, intelligence, and so forth.

Lastly, the shift from women's history to gender history will not, in my view, prevent efforts to remedy the regrettable shortage of women among the professoriat. Nor will it silence feminists, whether male or female. What do others think?

PART II

Deconstructing the female subject

Feminist history and 'the linguistic turn'

Joan Wallach Scott

GENDER
A useful category of historical analysis

Joan Scott is recognised internationally as a groundbreaking theorist on gender and history. She is the author of numerous works on feminist theory and history including *Gender and the Politics of History* (1988) and *Only Paradoxes to Offer: French Feminists and the Rights of Man* (1996). Along with the work of Denise Riley (see Reading 8), her name has become synonymous with the advocacy of poststructuralist approaches to writing feminist and gender history. Her 1986 article 'Gender: A Useful Category of Historical Analysis', reproduced here, appears theoretically less radical now than many of her later essays, but that is, in part, an indication of the way in which her germinal multi-part definition of gender as 'a constitutive element of social relationships' and as 'a primary way of signifying relationships of power' has already influenced twenty years of subsequent feminist scholarship. In this pioneering article Scott argues that current theorisations of gender, whether formulated through patriarchal, Marxist or psychoanalytical approaches, do not have the 'analytic power' to transform existing historical paradigms because of their tendency to revert to ahistorical, essentialised notions of sexual difference. Drawing upon Derrida's notion of 'deconstruction' and Foucault's understanding of 'power' as 'dispersed constellations of unequal relationships, discursively constituted', Scott asserts that gender is a 'primary field within which ... power is articulated', thus underscoring the idea of gender as a dynamic process. Four interrelated elements – cultural symbols, normative concepts, political and social institutions and subjective identity – together comprise her definition of gender. According to Scott, the task for the feminist historian is to deconstruct the way in which 'gender', as a powerful system of meaning-making and knowledge, operates historically to reinforce or challenge dominant social formations of femininity and masculinity. Only in this way will feminists effect the transformation of history they desire.

> Gender. n. a grammatical term only. To talk of persons or crea-
> tures of the masculine or feminine gender, meaning of the male
> or female sex, is either a jocularity (permissible or not according
> to context) or a blunder.
>
> *Fowler's Dictionary of Modern English Usage*, Oxford, 1940

THOSE WHO WOULD CODIFY the meanings of words fight a losing
battle, for words, like the ideas and things they are meant to signify, have a
history. Neither Oxford dons nor the Académie Française have been entirely able
to stem the tide, to capture and fix meanings free of the play of human invention
and imagination. Mary Wortley Montagu added bite to her witty denunciation 'of
the fair sex' ('my only consolation for being of that gender has been the assurance
of never being married to any one among them') by deliberately misusing the
grammatical reference.[1] Through the ages, people have made figurative allusions by
employing grammatical terms to evoke traits of character or sexuality. For example,
the usage offered by the *Dictionnaire de la langue française* in 1876 was, 'On ne sait
de quel genre il est, s'il est mâle ou femelle, se dit d'un homme très-caché, dont
on ne connait pas les sentiments.'[2] And Gladstone made this distinction in 1878:
'Athene has nothing of sex except the gender, nothing of the woman except the
form.'[3] Most recently—too recently to find its way into dictionaries or the
Encyclopedia of the Social Sciences—feminists have in a more literal and serious vein
begun to use 'gender' as a way of referring to the social organization of the relationship between the sexes. The connection to grammar is both explicit and full of
unexamined possibilities. Explicit because the grammatical usage involves formal
rules that follow from the masculine or feminine designation; full of unexamined
possibilities because in many Indo-European languages there is a third category—
unsexed or neuter.

In its most recent usage, 'gender' seems to have first appeared among American
feminists who wanted to insist on the fundamentally social quality of distinctions
based on sex. The word denoted a rejection of the biological determinism implicit
in the use of such terms as 'sex' or 'sexual difference.' 'Gender' also stressed the
relational aspect of normative definitions of femininity. Those who worried that
women's studies scholarship focused too narrowly and separately on women used
the term 'gender' to introduce a relational notion into our analytic vocabulary.
According to this view, women and men were defined in terms of one another,
and no understanding of either could be achieved by entirely separate study. Thus
Natalie Davis suggested in 1975, 'It seems to me that we should be interested in
the history of both women and men, that we should not be working only on the
subjected sex any more than an historian of class can focus entirely on peasants.
Our goal is to understand the significance of the *sexes*, of gender groups in the historical past. Our goal is to discover the range in sex roles and in sexual symbolism in
different societies and periods, to find out what meaning they had and how they
functioned to maintain the social order or to promote its change.'[4]

In addition, and perhaps most important, 'gender' was a term offered by those
who claimed that women's scholarship would fundamentally transform disciplinary
paradigms. Feminist scholars pointed out early on that the study of women would
not only add new subject matter but would also force a critical reexamination
of the premises and standards of existing scholarly work. 'We are learning,' wrote

three feminist historians, 'that the writing of women into history necessarily involves redefining and enlarging traditional notions of historical significance, to encompass personal, subjective experience as well as public and political activities. It is not too much to suggest that however hesitant the actual beginnings, such a methodology implies not only a new history of women, but also a new history.'[5] The way in which this new history would both include and account for women's experience rested on the extent to which gender could be developed as a category of analysis. Here the analogies to class (and race) were explicit; indeed, the most politically inclusive of scholars of women's studies regularly invoked all three categories as crucial to the writing of a new history.[6] An interest in class, race, and gender signaled first, a scholar's commitment to a history that included stories of the oppressed and an analysis of the meaning and nature of their oppression and, second, scholarly understanding that inequalities of power are organized along at least three axes. [. . .]

Feminist historians, trained as most historians are to be more comfortable with description than theory, have nonetheless increasingly looked for usable theoretical formulations. They have done so for at least two reasons. First, the proliferation of case studies in women's history seems to call for some synthesizing perspective that can explain continuities and discontinuities and account for persisting inequalities as well as radically different social experiences. Second, the discrepancy between the high quality of recent work in women's history and its continuing marginal status in the field as a whole (as measured by textbooks, syllabi, and monographic work) points up the limits of descriptive approaches that do not address dominant disciplinary concepts, or at least that do not address these concepts in terms that can shake their power and perhaps transform them. It has not been enough for historians of women to prove either that women had a history or that women participated in the major political upheavals of Western civilization. In the case of women's history, the response of most non-feminist historians has been acknowledgment and then separation or dismissal ('women had a history separate from men's, therefore let feminists do women's history, which need not concern us'; or 'women's history is about sex and the family and should be done separately from political and economic history'). In the case of women's participation, the response has been minimal interest at best ('my understanding of the French Revolution is not changed by knowing that women participated in it'). The challenge posed by these responses is, in the end, a theoretical one. It requires analysis not only of the relationship between male and female experience in the past but also of the connection between past history and current historical practice. How does gender work in human social relationships? How does gender give meaning to the organization and perception of historical knowledge? The answers depend on gender as an analytic category.

For the most part, the attempts of historians to theorize about gender have remained within traditional social scientific frameworks, using longstanding formulations that provide universal causal explanations. These theories have been limited at best because they tend to contain reductive or overly simple generalizations that undercut not only history's disciplinary sense of the complexity of social causation but also feminist commitments to analyses that will lead to change. A review of these theories will expose their limits and make it possible to propose an alternative approach.[7]

The approaches used by most historians fall into two distinct categories. The first is essentially descriptive; that is, it refers to the existence of phenomena or realities without interpreting, explaining, or attributing causality. The second usage is causal; it theorizes about the nature of phenomena or realities, seeking an understanding of how and why these take the form they do.

In its simplest recent usage, 'gender' is a synonym for 'women.' Any number of books and articles whose subject is women's history have, in the past few years, substituted 'gender' for 'women' in their titles. In some cases, this usage, though vaguely referring to certain analytic concepts, is actually about the political acceptability of the field. In these instances, the use of 'gender' is meant to denote the scholarly seriousness of a work, for 'gender' has a more neutral and objective sound than does 'women.' 'Gender' seems to fit within the scientific terminology of social science and thus dissociates itself from the (supposedly strident) politics of feminism. In this usage, 'gender' does not carry with it a necessary statement about inequality or power nor does it name the aggrieved (and hitherto invisible) party. Whereas the term 'women's history' proclaims its politics by asserting (contrary to customary practice) that women are valid historical subjects, 'gender' includes but does not name women and so seems to pose no critical threat. This use of 'gender' is one facet of what might be called the quest of feminist scholarship for academic legitimacy in the 1980s.

But only one facet. 'Gender' as a substitute for 'women' is also used to suggest that information about women is necessarily information about men, that one implies the study of the other. This usage insists that the world of women is part of the world of men, created in and by it. This usage rejects the interpretive utility of the idea of separate spheres, maintaining that to study women in isolation perpetuates the fiction that one sphere, the experience of one sex, has little or nothing to do with the other. In addition, gender is also used to designate social relations between the sexes. Its use explicitly rejects biological explanations, such as those that find a common denominator for diverse forms of female subordination in the facts that women have the capacity to give birth and men have greater muscular strength. Instead, gender becomes a way of denoting 'cultural constructions'—the entirely social creation of ideas about appropriate roles for women and men. It is a way of referring to the exclusively social origins of the subjective identities of men and women. Gender is, in this definition, a social category imposed on a sexed body.[8] Gender seems to have become a particularly useful word as studies of sex and sexuality have proliferated, for it offers a way of differentiating sexual practice from the social roles assigned to women and men. Although scholars acknowledge the connection between sex and (what the sociologists of the family called) 'sex roles,' these scholars do not assume a simple or direct linkage. The use of gender emphasizes an entire system of relationships that may include sex, but is not directly determined by sex or directly determining of sexuality.

These descriptive usages of gender have been employed by historians most often to map out a new terrain. As social historians turned to new objects of study, gender was relevant for such topics as women, children, families, and gender ideologies. This usage of gender, in other words, refers only to those areas—both structural and ideological—involving relations between the sexes. Because, on the face of it, war, diplomacy, and high politics have not been explicitly about those relationships, gender seems not to apply and so continues to be irrelevant to the thinking of historians concerned with issues of politics and power. The effect is to endorse a certain functionalist view ultimately rooted in biology and to perpetuate the idea of separate spheres (sex or politics, family or nation, women or men) in the writing of history. Although gender in this usage asserts that relationships between the sexes are social, it says nothing about why these relationships are constructed as they are, how they work, or how they change. In its descriptive usage, then, gender is a concept associated with the study of things related to women. Gender is a new topic, a new department of historical investigation, but it does not have the analytic power to address (and change) existing historical paradigms.

Some historians were, of course, aware of this problem, hence the efforts to employ theories that might explain the concept of gender and account for historical change. Indeed, the challenge was to reconcile theory, which was framed in general or universal terms, and history, which was committed to the study of contextual specificity and fundamental change. The result has been extremely eclectic: partial borrowings that vitiate the analytic power of a particular theory or, worse, employ its precepts without awareness of their implications; or accounts of change that, because they embed universal theories, only illustrate unchanging themes; or wonderfully imaginative studies in which theory is nonetheless so hidden that these studies cannot serve as models for other investigations. Because the theories on which historians have drawn are often not spelled out in all their implications, it seems worthwhile to spend sometime doing that. Only through such an exercise can we evaluate the usefulness of these theories and, perhaps, articulate a more powerful theoretical approach.

Feminist historians have employed a variety of approaches to the analysis of gender, but they come down to a choice between three theoretical positions.[9] The first, an entirely feminist effort, attempts to explain the origins of patriarchy. The second locates itself within a Marxian tradition and seeks there an accommodation with feminist critiques. The third, fundamentally divided between French post-structuralist and Anglo-American object-relations theorists, draws on these different schools of psychoanalysis to explain the production and reproduction of the subject's gendered identity. [. . .]

Theorists of patriarchy have addressed the inequality of males and females in important ways, but, for historians, their theories pose problems. First, while they offer an analysis internal to the gender system itself, they also assert the primacy of that system in all social organization. But theories of patriarchy do not show how gender inequality structures all other inequalities or, indeed, *how* gender affects those areas of life that do not seem to be connected to it. Second, whether domination comes in the form of the male appropriation of the female's reproductive labor or in the sexual objectification of women by men, the analysis rests on physical difference. Any physical difference takes on a universal and unchanging aspect, even if theorists of patriarchy take into account the existence of changing forms and systems of gender inequality.[10] A theory that rests on the single variable of physical difference poses problems for historians: it assumes a consistent or inherent meaning for the human body—outside social or cultural construction—and thus the ahistoricity of gender itself. History becomes, in a sense, epiphenomenal, providing endless variations on the unchanging theme of a fixed gender inequality.

Marxist feminists have a more historical approach, guided as they are by a theory of history. But, whatever the variations and adaptations have been, the self-imposed requirement that there be a 'material' explanation for gender has limited or at least slowed the development of new lines of analysis. Whether a so-called dual-systems solution is proffered (one that posits the separate but interacting realms of capitalism and patriarchy) or an analysis based more firmly in orthodox Marxist discussions of modes of production is developed, the explanation for the origins of and changes in gender systems is found outside the sexual division of labor. Families, households, and sexuality are all, finally, products of changing modes of production. That is how Engels concluded his explorations of the *Origins of the Family*;[11] that is where economist Heidi Hartmann's analysis ultimately rests. Hartmann insisted on the importance of taking into account patriarchy and capitalism as separate but interacting systems. Yet, as her argument unfolds, economic causality takes precedence, and patriarchy always develops and changes as a function of relations of production. When she suggested that 'it is necessary to eradicate the sexual division of labor itself to end male domination,' she meant ending job segregation by sex.[12]

[. . .]

The difficulty for both English and American feminists working within Marxism is [. . .] the opposite of the one posed by patriarchal theory. Within Marxism, the concept of gender has long been treated as the by-product of changing economic structures; gender has had no independent analytic status of its own.

A review of psychoanalytic theory requires a specification of schools, since the various approaches have tended to be classified by the national origins of the founders and the majority of the practitioners. There is the Anglo-American school, working within the terms of theories of object-relations. In the U.S., Nancy Chodorow is the name most readily associated with this approach. In addition, the work of Carol Gilligan has had a far-reaching impact on American scholarship, including history. Gilligan's work draws on Chodorow's, although it is concerned less with the construction of the subject than with moral development and behavior. In contrast to the Anglo-American school, the French school is based on structuralist and post-structuralist readings of Freud in terms of theories of language (for feminists, the key figure is Jacques Lacan).

Both schools are concerned with the processes by which the subject's identity is created; both focus on the early stages of child development for clues to the formation of gender identity. Object-relations theorists stress the influence of actual experience (the child sees, hears, relates to those who care for it, particularly, of course, to its parents), while the post-structuralists emphasize the centrality of language in communicating, interpreting, and representing gender. (By 'language,' post-structuralists do not mean words but systems of meaning—symbolic orders— that precede the actual mastery of speech, reading, and writing.) [. . .]

In recent years, feminist historians have been drawn to these theories either because they serve to endorse specific findings with general observations or because they seem to offer an important theoretical formulation about gender. Increasingly, those historians working with a concept of 'women's culture' cite Chodorow's or Gilligan's work as both proof of and explanation for their interpretations; those wrestling with feminist theory look to Lacan. In the end, neither of these theories seems to me entirely workable for historians. [. . .]

My reservation about object-relations theory concerns its literalism, its reliance on relatively small structures of interaction to produce gender identity and to generate change. Both the family division of labor and the actual assignment of tasks to each parent play a crucial role in Chodorow's theory. The outcome of prevailing Western systems is a clear division between male and female: 'The basic feminine sense of self is connected to the world, the basic masculine sense of self is separate.'[13] [. . .]

This interpretation limits the concept of gender to family and household experience and, for the historian, leaves no way to connect the concept (or the individual) to other social systems of economy, politics, or power. [. . .] How can we account within this theory for persistent associations of masculinity with power, for the higher value placed on manhood than on womanhood, for the way children seem to learn these associations and evaluations even when they live outside nuclear households or in households where parenting is equally divided between husband and wife? I do not think we can without some attention to symbolic systems, that is, to the ways societies represent gender, use it to articulate the rules of social relationships, or construct the meaning of experience. Without meaning, there is no experience; without processes of signification, there is no meaning (which is not to say that language is everything, but a theory that does not take it into account misses the powerful roles that symbols, metaphors, and concepts play in the definition of human personality and human history.)

Language is the center of Lacanian theory; it is the key to the child's induction into the symbolic order. Through language, gendered identity is constructed. [. . .] But, gender identification, although it always appears coherent and fixed, is, in fact, highly unstable. Like words themselves, subjective identities are processes of differentiation and distinction, requiring the suppression of ambiguities and opposite elements in order to assure (and create the illusion of) coherence and common understanding. The idea of masculinity rests on the necessary repression of feminine aspects—of the subject's potential for bisexuality—and introduces conflict into the opposition of masculine and feminine. Repressed desires are present in the unconscious and are constantly a threat to the stability of gender identification, denying its unity, subverting its need for security. In addition, conscious ideas of masculine or feminine are not fixed, since they vary according to contextual usage. Conflict always exists, then, between the subject's need for the appearance of wholeness and the imprecision of terminology, its relative meaning, its dependence on repression.[14] This kind of interpretation makes the categories of 'man' and 'woman' problematic by suggesting that masculine and feminine are not inherent characteristics but subjective (or fictional) constructs. This interpretation also implies that the subject is in a constant process of construction, and it offers a systematic way of interpreting conscious and unconscious desire by pointing to language as the appropriate place for analysis. As such, I find it instructive.

I am troubled, nonetheless, by the exclusive fixation on questions of 'the subject' and by the tendency to reify subjectively originating antagonism between males and females as the central fact of gender. In addition, although there is openness in the concept of how 'the subject' is constructed, the theory tends to universalize the categories and relationship of male and female. The outcome for historians is a reductive reading of evidence from the past. [. . .]

The problem of sexual antagonism in this theory has two aspects. First, it projects a certain timeless quality, even when it is historicized as well as it has been by Sally Alexander. Alexander's reading of Lacan led her to conclude that 'antagonism between the sexes is an unavoidable aspect of the acquisition of sexual identity . . . If antagonism is always latent, it is possible that history offers no final resolution, only the constant reshaping, reorganizing of the symbolization of difference, and the sexual division of labor.'[15] It may be my hopeless utopianism that gives me pause before this formulation, or it may be that I have not yet shed the episteme of what Foucault called the Classical Age. Whatever the explanation, Alexander's formulation contributes to the fixing of the binary opposition of male and female as the only possible relationship and as a permanent aspect of the human condition. [. . .]

It is precisely that opposition, in all its tedium and monotony, that (to return to the Anglo-American side) Carol Gilligan's work has promoted. Gilligan explained the divergent paths of moral development followed by boys and girls in terms of differences of 'experience' (lived reality). It is not surprising that historians of women have picked up her ideas and used them to explain the 'different voices' their work has enabled them to hear. The problems with these borrowings are manifold, and they are logically connected.[16] The first is a slippage that often happens in the attribution of causality: the argument moves from a statement such as 'women's experience leads them to make moral choices contingent on contexts and relationships' to 'women think and choose this way because they are women.' Implied in this line of reasoning is the ahistorical, if not essentialist, notion of woman. [. . .] This use of Gilligan's ideas provides sharp contrast to the more complicated and historicized conceptions of 'women's culture' evident in the *Feminist Studies* 1980 symposium.[17] Indeed, a comparison of that set of articles with Gilligan's formulations reveals the extent to which her notion is ahistorical, defining woman/man as a universal, self-reproducing binary opposition—fixed always in the same way. [. . .]

We need a refusal of the fixed and permanent quality of the binary opposition, a genuine historicization and deconstruction of the terms of sexual difference. We must become more self-conscious about distinguishing between our analytic vocabulary and the material we want to analyze. We must find ways (however imperfect) to continually subject our categories to criticism, our analyses to self-criticism. If we employ Jacques Derrida's definition of deconstruction, this criticism means analyzing in context the way any binary opposition operates, reversing and displacing its hierarchical construction, rather than accepting it as real or self-evident or in the nature of things.[18] In a sense, of course, feminists have been doing this for years. The history of feminist thought is a history of the refusal of the hierarchical construction of the relationship between male and female in its specific contexts and an attempt to reverse or displace its operations. Feminist historians are now in a position to theorize their practice and to develop gender as an analytic category. [. . .]

It seems to me significant that the use of the word gender has emerged at a moment of great epistemological turmoil that takes the form, in some cases, of a shift from scientific to literary paradigms among social scientists (from an emphasis on cause to one on meaning, blurring genres of inquiry, in anthropologist Clifford Geertz's phrase),[19] and, in other cases, the form of debates about theory between those who assert the transparency of facts and those who insist that all reality is construed or constructed, between those who defend and those who question the idea that 'man' is the rational master of his own destiny. In the space opened by this debate and on the side of the critique of science developed by the humanities, and of empiricism and humanism by poststructuralists, feminists have not only begun to find a theoretical voice of their own but have found scholarly and political allies as well. It is within this space that we must articulate gender as an analytic category.

What should be done by historians who, after all, have seen their discipline dismissed by some recent theorists as a relic of humanist thought? I do not think we should quit the archives or abandon the study of the past, but we do have to change some of the ways we have gone about working, some of the questions we have asked. We need to scrutinize our methods of analysis, clarify our operative assumptions, and explain how we think change occurs. Instead of a search for single origins, we have to conceive of processes so interconnected that they cannot be disentangled. Of course, we identify problems to study, and these constitute beginnings or points of entry into complex processes. But it is the processes we must continually keep in mind. We must ask more often how things happened in order to find out why they happened; in anthropologist Michelle Rosaldo's formulation, we must pursue not universal, general causality but meaningful explanation: 'It now appears to me that woman's place in human social life is not in any direct sense a product of the things she does, but of the meaning her activities acquire through concrete social interaction.'[20] To pursue meaning, we need to deal with the individual subject as well as social organization and to articulate the nature of their interrelationships, for both are crucial to understanding how gender works, how change occurs. Finally, we need to replace the notion that social power is unified, coherent, and centralized with something like Foucault's concept of power as dispersed constellations of unequal relationships, discursively constituted in social 'fields of force.'[21] Within these processes and structures, there is room for a concept of human agency as the attempt (at least partially rational) to construct an identity, a life, a set of relationships, a society with certain limits and with language—conceptual language that at once sets boundaries and contains the possibility for negation, resistance, reinterpretation, the play of metaphoric invention and imagination.

My definition of gender has two parts and several subsets. They are interrelated but must be analytically distinct. The core of the definition rests on an integral connection between two propositions: gender is a constitutive element of social relationships based on perceived differences between the sexes, and gender is a primary way of signifying relationships of power. Changes in the organization of social relationships always correspond to changes in representations of power, but the direction of change is not necessarily one way. As a constitutive element of social relationships based on perceived differences between the sexes, gender involves four interrelated elements: first, culturally available symbols that evoke multiple (and often contradictory) representations—Eve and Mary as symbols of woman, for example, in the Western Christian tradition—but also, myths of light and dark, purification and pollution, innocence and corruption. For historians, the interesting questions are, which symbolic representations are invoked, how, and in what contexts? Second, normative concepts that set forth interpretations of the meanings of the symbols, that attempt to limit and contain their metaphoric possibilities. These concepts are expressed in religious, educational, scientific, legal, and political doctrines and typically take the form of a fixed binary opposition, categorically and unequivocally asserting the meaning of male and female, masculine and feminine. In fact, these normative statements depend on the refusal or repression of alternative possibilities, and, sometimes, overt contests about them take place (at what moments and under what circumstances ought to be a concern of historians). The position that emerges as dominant, however, is stated as the only possible one. Subsequent history is written as if these normative positions were the product of social consensus rather than of conflict. An example of this kind of history is the treatment of the Victorian ideology of domesticity as if it were created whole and only afterwards reacted to instead of being the constant subject of great differences of opinion. Another kind of example comes from contemporary fundamentalist religious groups that have forcibly linked their practice to a restoration of women's supposedly more authentic 'traditional' role, when, in fact, there is little historical precedent for the unquestioned performance of such a role. The point of new historical investigation is to disrupt the notion of fixity, to discover the nature of the debate or repression that leads to the appearance of timeless permanence in binary gender representation. This kind of analysis must include a notion of politics as well as reference to social institutions and organizations—the third aspect of gender relationships. [. . .]

The fourth aspect of gender is subjective identity. I agree with anthropologist Gayle Rubin's formulation that psychoanalysis offers an important theory about the reproduction of gender, a description of the 'transformation of the biological sexuality of individuals as they are enculturated.'[22] But the universal claim of psychoanalysis gives me pause. Even though Lacanian theory may be helpful for thinking about the construction of gendered identity, historians need to work in a more historical way. If gender identity is based only and universally on fear of castration, the point of historical inquiry is denied. Moreover, real men and women do not always or literally fulfill the terms of their society's prescriptions or of our analytic categories. Historians need instead to examine the ways in which gendered identities are substantively constructed and relate their findings to a range of activities, social organizations, and historically specific cultural representations. [. . .]

The first part of my definition of gender consists, then, of all four of these elements, and no one of them operates without the others. Yet they do not operate simultaneously, with one simply reflecting the others. A question for historical research is, in fact, what the relationships among the four aspects are. The sketch I have offered of the process of constructing gender relationships could be used to discuss class, race, ethnicity, or, for that matter, any social process. My point was to clarify and specify how one needs to think about the effect of gender in social and institutional relationships, because this thinking is often not done precisely or systematically. The theorizing of gender, however, is developed in my second proposition: gender is a primary way of signifying relationships of power. It might be better to say, gender is a primary field within which or by means of which power is articulated. Gender is not the only field, but it seems to have been a persistent and recurrent way of enabling the signification of power in the West, in Judeo-Christian as well as Islamic traditions. As such, this part of the definition might seem to belong in the normative section of the argument, yet it does not, for concepts of power, though they may build on gender, are not always literally about gender itself. French sociologist Pierre Bourdieu has written about how the 'di-vision du monde,' based on references to 'biological differences and notably those that refer to the division of the labor of procreation and reproduction,' operates as 'the best-founded of collective illusions.' Established as an objective set of references, concepts of gender structure perception and the concrete and symbolic organization of all social life.[23] To the extent that these references establish distributions of power (differential control over or access to material and symbolic resources), gender becomes implicated in the conception and construction of power itself. [. . .]

The legitimizing function of gender works in many ways. Bourdieu, for example, showed how, in certain cultures, agricultural exploitation was organized according to concepts of time and season that rested on specific definitions of the opposition between masculine and feminine. Gayatri Spivak has done a pointed analysis of the uses of gender in certain texts of British and American women writers.[24] Natalie Davis has shown how concepts of masculine and feminine related to understandings and criticisms of the rules of social order in early modern France.[25] Historian Caroline Bynum has thrown new light on medieval spirituality through her attention to the relationships between concepts of masculine and feminine and religious behavior. Her work gives us important insight into the ways in which these concepts informed the politics of monastic institutions as well as of individual believers.[26] Art historians have opened a new territory by reading social implications from literal depictions of women and men.[27] These interpretations are based on the idea that conceptual languages employ differentiation to establish meaning and that sexual difference is a primary way of signifying differentiation.[28] Gender, then, provides a way to decode meaning and to understand the complex connections among various forms of human interaction. When historians look for the ways in which the concept of gender legitimizes and constructs social relationships, they develop insight into the reciprocal nature of gender and society and into the particular and contextually specific ways in which politics constructs gender and gender constructs politics.

Politics is only one of the areas in which gender can be used for historical analysis. I have chosen the following examples relating to politics and power in their most traditionally construed sense, that is, as they pertain to government and the nation-state, for two reasons. First, the territory is virtually uncharted, since gender has been seen as antithetical to the real business of politics. Second, political history— still the dominant mode of historical inquiry—has been the stronghold of resistance to the inclusion of material or even questions about women and gender.

Gender has been employed literally or analogically in political theory to justify or criticize the reign of monarchs and to express the relationship between ruler and ruled. One might have expected that the debates of contemporaries over the reigns of Elizabeth I in England and Catharine de Medici in France would dwell on the issue of women's suitability for political rule, but, in the period when kinship and kingship were integrally related, discussions about male kings were equally pre-occupied with masculinity and femininity.[29] Analogies to the marital relationship provide structure for the arguments of Jean Bodin, Robert Filmer, and John Locke. Edmund Burke's attack on the French Revolution is built around a contrast between ugly, murderous *sans-culottes* hags ('the furies of hell, in the abused shape of the vilest of women') and the soft femininity of Marie-Antoinette, who escaped the crowd to 'seek refuge at the feet of a king and husband' and whose beauty once inspired national pride. (It was in reference to the appropriate role for the feminine in the political order that Burke wrote, 'To make us love our country, our country ought to be lovely.')[30] But the analogy is not always to marriage or even to heterosexuality. In medieval Islamic political theory, the symbols of political power alluded most often to sex between man and boy, suggesting not only forms of acceptable sexuality akin to those that Foucault's last work described in classical Greece but also the irrelevance of women to any notion of politics and public life.[31]

Lest this last comment suggest that political theory simply reflects social organization, it seems important to note that changes in gender relationships can be set off by views of the needs of state. [. . .]

The connection between authoritarian regimes and the control of women has been noted but not thoroughly studied. Whether at a crucial moment for Jacobin hegemony in the French Revolution, at the point of Stalin's bid for controlling authority, the implementation of Nazi policy in Germany, or the triumph in Iran of the Ayatollah Khomeni, emergent rulers have legitimized domination, strength, central authority, and ruling power as masculine (enemies, outsiders, subversives, weakness as feminine) and made that code literal in laws (forbidding women's political participation, outlawing abortion, prohibiting wage-earning by mothers, imposing female dress codes) that put women in their place.[32] These actions and their timing make little sense in themselves; in most instances, the state had nothing immediate or material to gain from the control of women. The actions can only be made sense of as part of an analysis of the construction and consolidation of power. An assertion of control or strength was given form as a policy about women. [. . .] Historically, some socialist and anarchist movements have refused metaphors of domination entirely, imaginatively presenting their critiques of particular regimes or social organizations in terms of transformations of gender identities. Utopian socialists in France and England in the 1830s and 1840s conceived their dreams for a harmonious future in terms of the complementary natures of individuals as exemplified in the union of man and woman, 'the social individual.'[33] [. . .]

These examples are of explicit connections between gender and power, but they are only a part of my definition of gender as a primary way of signifying relationships of power. Attention to gender is often not explicit, but it is nonetheless a crucial part of the organization of equality or inequality. Hierarchical structures rely on generalized understandings of the so-called natural relationship between male and female. [. . .]

The subject of war, diplomacy, and high politics frequently comes up when traditional political historians question the utility of gender in their work. But here, too, we need to look beyond the actors and the literal import of their words. Power relations among nations and the status of colonial subjects have been made comprehensible (and thus legitimate) in terms of relations between male and female. The legitimizing of war—of expending young lives to protect the state—has variously taken the forms of explicit appeals to manhood (to the need to defend otherwise vulnerable women and children), of implicit reliance on belief in the duty of sons to serve their leaders or their (father the) king, and of associations between masculinity and national strength.[34] High politics itself is a gendered concept, for it establishes its crucial importance and public power, the reasons for and the fact of its highest authority, precisely in its exclusion of women from its work. Gender is one of the recurrent references by which political power has been conceived, legitimated, and criticized. It refers to but also establishes the meaning of the male/female opposition. To vindicate political power, the reference must seem sure and fixed, outside human construction, part of the natural or divine order. In that way, the binary opposition and the social process of gender relationships both become part of the meaning of power itself; to question or alter any aspect threatens the entire system.

If significations of gender and power construct one another, how do things change? The answer in a general sense is that change may be initiated in many places. Massive political upheavals that throw old orders into chaos and bring new ones into being may revise the terms (and so the organization) of gender in the search for new forms of legitimation. But they may not; old notions of gender have also served to validate new regimes.[35] [. . .] The emergence of new kinds of cultural symbols may make possible the reinterpreting or, indeed, rewriting of the oedipal story, but it can also serve to reinscribe that terrible drama in even more telling terms. Political processes will determine which outcome prevails—political in the sense that different actors and different meanings are contending with one another for control. The nature of that process, of the actors and their actions, can only be determined specifically, in the context of time and place. We can write the history of that process only if we recognize that 'man' and 'woman' are at once empty and overflowing categories. Empty because they have no ultimate, transcendent meaning. Overflowing because even when they appear to be fixed, they still contain within them alternative, denied, or suppressed definitions.

Political history has, in a sense, been enacted on the field of gender. It is a field that seems fixed yet whose meaning is contested and in flux. If we treat the opposition between male and female as problematic rather than known, as something contextually defined, repeatedly constructed, then we must constantly ask not only what is at stake in proclamations or debates that invoke gender to explain or justify their positions but also how implicit understandings of gender are being invoked and reinscribed. What is the relationship between laws about women and the power of the state? Why (and since when) have women been invisible as historical subjects, when we know they participated in the great and small events of human history? Has gender legitimated the emergence of professional careers?[36] Is (to quote the title of a recent article by French feminist Luce Irigaray) the subject of science sexed?[37] What is the relationship between state politics and the discovery of the crime of homosexuality?[38] How have social institutions incorporated gender into their assumptions and organizations? Have there ever been genuinely egalitarian concepts of gender in terms of which political systems were projected, if not built?

Investigation of these issues will yield a history that will provide new perspectives on old questions (about how, for example, political rule is imposed, or what the impact of war on society is), redefine the old questions in new terms (introducing considerations of family and sexuality, for example, in the study of economics or war), make women visible as active participants, and create analytic distance between the seemingly fixed language of the past and our own terminology. In addition, this new history will leave open possibilities for thinking about current feminist political strategies and the (utopian) future, for it suggests that gender must be redefined and restructured in conjunction with a vision of political and social equality that includes not only sex, but class and race.

Notes

1   *Oxford English Dictionary* (1961 edn.), vol. 4.

2   E. Littré, *Dictionnaire de la langue française* (Paris, 1876).

3   Raymond Williams, *Keywords* (New York, 1983), 285.

4   Natalie Zemon Davis, 'Women's History in Transition: The European Case,' *Feminist Studies*, 3 (Winter 1975–6): 90.

5   Ann D. Gordon, Mari Jo Buhle, and Nancy Shrom Dye, 'The Problem of Women's History,' in Berenice Carroll, ed., *Liberating Women's History* (Urbana, Ill., 1976), 89.

6   The best and most subtle example is from Joan Kelly, 'The Doubled Vision of Feminist Theory,' in her *Women, History and Theory* (Chicago, 1984), 51–64, especially 61.

7   For a review of recent work on women's history, see Joan W. Scott, 'Women's History: The Modern Period,' *Past and Present*, 101 (1983): 141–57.

8   For an argument against the use of gender to emphasize the social aspect of sexual difference, see Moira Gatens, 'A Critique of the Sex/Gender Distinction,' in J. Allen and P. Patton, eds., *Beyond Marxism? Interventions after Marx* (Sydney, 1983), 143–60.

9   For a somewhat different approach to feminist analysis, see Linda J. Nicholson, *Gender and History: The Limits of Social Theory in the Age of the Family* (New York, 1986).

10 For an interesting discussion of the strengths and limits of the term 'patriarchy,' see the exchange between historians Sheila Rowbotham, Sally Alexander, and Barbara Taylor in Raphael Samuel, ed., *People's History and Socialist Theory* (London, 1981), 363–73.

11 Frederick Engels, *The Origins of the Family, Private Property, and the State* (1884; reprint edn., New York, 1972).

12 Heidi Hartmann, 'Capitalism, Patriarchy, and Job Segregation by Sex,' *Signs*, I (Spring 1976): 168. See also 'The Unhappy Marriage of Marxism and Feminism: Towards a More Progressive Union,' *Capital and Class*, 8 (Summer 1979): 1–33; 'The Family as the Locus of Gender, Class, and Political Struggle: The Example of Housework,' *Signs*, 6 (Spring 1981): 366–94.

13 Nancy Chodorow, *The Reproduction of Mothering: Psychoanalysis and the Sociology of Gender* (Berkeley, Calif., 1978), 169.

14 Juliet Mitchell and Jacqueline Rose, eds., *Jacques Lacan and the Ecole Freudienne* (London, 1983); Sally Alexander, 'Women, Class and Sexual Difference,' *History Workshop Journal*, 17 (Spring 1984): 125–35.

15 Alexander, 'Women, Class and Sexual Difference,' 135.

16 Carol Gilligan, *In a Different Voice: Psychological Theory and Women's Development* (Cambridge, Mass., 1982).

17 *Feminist Studies*, 6 (Spring 1980): 26–64.

18 By 'deconstruction,' I mean to evoke Derrida's discussion, which though it surely did not invent the procedure of analysis it describes, has the virtue of theorizing it so that it can constitute a useful method. For a succinct and accessible discussion of Derrida, see Jonathan Culler, *On Deconstruction: Theory and Criticism after Structuralism* (Ithaca, N.Y., 1982), especially 156–79. See also Jacques Derrida, *Of Grammatology* (Baltimore, 1976); Jacques Derrida, *Spurs* (Chicago, 1979); and a transcription of Pembroke Center Seminar, 1983, in *Subjects/Objects* (Fall 1984).

19 Clifford Geertz, 'Blurred Genres,' *American Scholar*, 49 (October 1980): 165–79.

20 Michelle Zimbalist Rosaldo, 'The Uses and Abuses of Anthropology: Reflections on Feminism and Cross-Cultural Understanding,' *Signs*, 5 (Spring 1980): 400.

21 Michel Foucault, *The History of Sexuality*, vol. 1, *An Introduction* (New York, 1980); Michel Foucault, *Power/Knowledge: Selected Interviews and Other Writings, 1972–77* (New York, 1980).

22 Gayle Rubin, 'The Traffic in Women: Notes on the "Political Economy" of Sex,' in Rayna E. Reiter, ed., *Toward an Anthropology of Women* (New York, 1975): 167–8.

23   Pierre Bourdieu, *Le Sens Pratique* (Paris, 1980), 246–7, 333–461, especially 366.

24   Gayatri Chakravorty Spivak, 'Three Women's Texts and a Critique of Imperialism,'
      Critical Inquiry, 12 (Autumn 1985): 243–6. See also Kate Millett, *Sexual Politics* (New
      York, 1969). An examination of how feminine references work in major texts of
      Western philosophy is carried out by Luce Irigaray in *Speculum of the Other Woman*
      (Ithaca, N.Y., 1985).

25   Natalie Zemon Davis, 'Women on Top,' in her *Society and Culture in Early Modern
      France* (Stanford, Calif., 1975), 124–51.

26   Caroline Walker Bynum, *Jesus as Mother: Studies in the Spirituality of the High Middle
      Ages* (Berkeley, Calif., 1982); Caroline Walker Bynum, 'Fast, Feast, and Flesh: The
      Religious Significance of Food to Medieval Women,' *Representations*, 11 (Summer
      1985): 1–25; Caroline Walker Bynum, 'Introduction,' *Religion and Gender: Essays on
      the Complexity of Symbols* (Beacon Press, 1987).

27   See, for example, T. J. Clarke, *The Painting of Modern Life* (New York, 1985).

28   The difference between structuralist and post-structuralist theorists on this question
      rests on how open or closed they view the categories of difference. To the extent
      that post-structuralists do not fix a universal meaning for the categories or the rela-
      tionship between them, their approach seems conducive to the kind of historical
      analysis I am advocating.

29   Rachel Weil, 'The Crown Has Fallen to the Distaff: Gender and Politics in the Age
      of Catharine de Medici,' *Critical Matrix* (Princeton Working Papers in Women's
      Studies), 1 (1985). See also Louis Montrose, 'Shaping Fantasies: Figurations of
      Gender and Power in Elizabethan Culture,' *Representations*, 2 (Spring 1983): 61–94;
      and Lynn Hunt, 'Hercules and the Radical Image in the French Revolution,'
      Representations, 2 (Spring 1983): 95–417.

30   Edmund Burke, *Reflections on the French Revolution* (1892; reprint edn., New York,
      1909), 208–9, 214. See Jean Bodin, *Six Books of the Commonwealth* (1606; reprint
      edn., New York, 1967); Robert Filmer, *Patriarcha and Other Political Works*, ed. Peter
      Laslett (Oxford, 1949); and John Locke, *Two Treatises of Government* (1690; reprint
      edn., Cambridge, 1970). See also Elizabeth Fox-Genovese, 'Property and Patriarchy
      in Classical Bourgeois Political Theory,' *Radical History Review*, 4 (Spring–Summer
      1977): 36–59; and Mary Lyndon Shanley, 'Marriage Contract and Social Contract in
      Seventeenth Century English Political Thought,' *Western Political Quarterly*, 32 (March
      1979): 79–91.

31   I am grateful to Bernard Lewis for the reference to Islam. Michel Foucault, *Historie
      de la Sexualité*, vol. 2, *L'Usage des plaisirs* (Paris, 1984). One wonders in situations of
      this kind what the terms of the subject's gender identity are and whether Freudian
      theory is sufficient to describe the process of its construction. On women in classical
      Athens, see Marilyn Arthur, 'Liberated Woman: The Classical Era,' in Renate
      Bridenthal and Claudia Koonz, eds., *Becoming Visible* (Boston, 1976), 75–8.

32   On the French Revolution, see Darlene Gay Levy, Harriet Applewhite, and Mary
      Johnson, eds., *Women in Revolutionary Paris, 1789–1795* (Urbana, Ill., 1979), 209–20;
      on Soviet legislation, see the documents in Rudolph Schlesinger, *The Family in the
      USSR: Documents and Readings* (London, 1949), 62–71,251–4; on Nazi policy, see
      Tim Mason, 'Women in Nazi Germany,' *History Workshop*, 1 (Spring 1976): 74–113,
      and Tim Mason, 'Women in Germany, 1925–40: Family, Welfare and Work,' *History
      Workshop*, 2 (Autumn 1976): 5–32.

33   On English utopians, see Barbara Taylor, *Eve and the New Jerusalem* (New York, 1983);
      on France, Joan W. Scott, 'Men and Women in the Parisian Garment Trades:
      Discussions of Family and Work in the 1830s and 40s,' in Pat Thane, *et al.*, eds.,
      The Power of the Past: Essays for Eric Hobsbawm (Cambridge, 1984), 67–94.

34   Gayatri Chakravorty Spivak, '"Draupadi" by Mahasveta Devi,' *Critical Inquiry*; 8
      (Winter 1981): 381–402; Homi Bhabha, 'Of Mimicry and Man: The Ambivalence of
      Colonial Discourse,' *October*, 28 (Spring 1984): 125–33; Karin Hausen, 'The Nation's

Obligations to the Heroes' Widows of World War I,' in Margaret R. Higonnet, *et al.*, eds., *Women, War and History* (New Haven, Conn., 1986). See also Ken Inglis, 'The Representation of Gender on Australian War Memorials,' unpublished paper presented at the Bellagio Conference on Gender, Technology and Education, October 1985.

35 On the French Revolution, see Levy, *Women in Revolutionary Paris*; on the American Revolution, see Mary Beth Norton, *Liberty's Daughters: The Revolutionary Experience of American Women* (Boston, 1980); Linda Kerber, *Women of the Republic* (Chapel Hill, N.C., 1980); Joan Hoff-Wilson, 'The Illusion of Change: Women and the American Revolution,' in Alfred Young, ed., *The American Revolution: Explorations in the History of American Radicalism* (DeKalb, Ill., 1976), 383–446. On the French Third Republic, see Steven Hause, *Women's Suffrage and Social Politics in the French Third Republic* (Princeton, N.J., 1984). An extremely interesting treatment of a recent case is Maxine Molyneux, 'Mobilization without Emancipation? Women's Interests, the State and Revolution in Nicaragua,' *Feminist Studies*, 11 (Summer 1985): 227–54.

36 See for example, Margaret Rossiter, *Women Scientists in America: Struggles and Strategies to 1914* (Baltimore, Md., 1982).

37 Luce Irigaray, 'Is the Subject of Science Sexed?' *Cultural Critique*, 1 (Fall 1985): 73–88.

38 Louis Crompton, *Byron and Greek Love: Homophobia in Nineteenth-Century England* (Berkeley, Calif., 1985). This question is touched on in Jeffrey Weeks, *Sex, Politics and Society* (New York, 1983).

Denise Riley

DOES A SEX HAVE A HISTORY?

This reading is taken from the first chapter of Denise Riley's book *Am I That Name? Feminism and the Category of 'Women' in History* (1988). Riley is a feminist theorist and poet whose non-fictional writings include *War in the Nursery: Theories of Child and Mother* (1981), a text on family policy and the history of psychology in postwar Britain. Riley's writing style, uncharitably criticised by some as insufficiently 'historical', illustrates her intellectual position on the borders of philosophy and history. The essay is structured around a series of rhetorical questions and responses on the instability of the category 'woman' for which, according to Riley, there is no 'ontological foundation' or underlying continuity but only a series of historical discursive formations that are themselves always positioned relative to other categories. Anticipating the negative reaction to her assertion that there aren't any 'real concrete women' – given that women's sufferings are all too physically endured – Riley explains that the oppression of women arises not from a social reality of subordination, but from a prior, dominant ideological positing of the category 'woman' that results in such exclusionary and unjust practices. For Riley, the political activism of feminists throughout history is underpinned by 'the systematic fighting-out' of the various unstable, contradictory identifications of 'women'. Women have banded together under the collective noun 'women' at various times in history, of course, but never without conflict or exclusion. Thus, the history of feminism for Riley is a contested history of the instability of the category 'women'. The task of the feminist historian is to map out how and why differing hegemonic definitions of 'women' emerged at particular historical moments. Throughout the remainder of *Am I That Name? Feminism and the Category of 'Women' in History,* from which this extract is taken, Riley certainly paints her centuries with a very broad brush, but nevertheless this essay remains as provocative and challenging as it was almost twenty years ago and repays careful scrutiny and reflection.

Desdemona: Am I that name, Iago?
Iago: What name, fair lady?
Desdemona: Such as she says my lord did say I was.
Shakespeare, *Othello*, Act IV, Scene II, 1622

THE BLACK ABOLITIONIST and freed slave, Sojourner Truth, spoke out at the Akron convention in 1851, and named her own toughness in a famous peroration against the notion of woman's disqualifying frailty. She rested her case on her refrain 'Ain't I a woman?' It's my hope to persuade readers that a new Sojourner Truth might well — except for the catastrophic loss of grace in the wording — issue another plea: 'Ain't I a fluctuating identity?' For both a concentration on and a refusal of the identity of 'women' are essential to feminism. This its history makes plain.

The volatility of 'woman' has indeed been debated from the perspective of psychoanalytic theory; her fictive status has been proposed by some Lacanian work,[1] while it has been argued that, on the other hand, sexual identities are ultimately firmly secured by psychoanalysis.[2] From the side of deconstruction, Derrida among others has advanced what he calls the 'undecidability' of woman.[3] I want to sidestep these debates to move to the ground of historical construction, including the history of feminism itself, and suggest that not only 'woman' but also 'women' is troublesome — and that this extension of our suspicions is in the interest of feminism. That we can't bracket off either Woman, whose capital letter has long alerted us to her dangers, or the more modest lower-case 'woman', while leaving unexamined the ordinary, innocent-sounding 'women'.

This 'women' is not only an inert and sensible collective; the dominion of fictions has a wider sway than that. The extent of its reign can be partly revealed by looking at the crystallizations of 'women' as a category. To put it schematically: 'women' is historically, discursively constructed, and always relatively to other categories which themselves change; 'women' is a volatile collectivity in which female persons can be very differently positioned, so that the apparent continuity of the subject of 'women' isn't to be relied on; 'women' is both synchronically and diachronically erratic as a collectivity, while for the individual, 'being a woman' is also inconstant, and can't provide an ontological foundation. Yet it must be emphasized that these instabilities of the category are the *sine qua non* of feminism, which would otherwise be lost for an object, despoiled of a fight, and, in short, without much life.

But why should it be claimed that the constancy of 'women' can be undermined in the interests of feminism? If Woman is in blatant disgrace, and woman is transparently suspicious, why lose sleep over a straightforward descriptive noun, 'women'? Moreover, how could feminism gain if its founding category is also to be dragged into the shadows properly cast by Woman? And while, given the untidiness of word use, there will inevitably be some slippery margins between 'woman' and 'women', this surely ought not to worry any level-headed speaker? If the seductive fraud of 'woman' is exposed, and the neutral collectivity is carefully substituted, then the ground is prepared for political fights to continue, armed with clarity. Not woman, but women — then we can get on with it.

It is true that socialist feminism has always tended to claim that women are socially produced in the sense of being 'conditioned' and that femininity is an effect.

But 'conditioning' has its limits as an explanation, and the 'society' which enacts this process is a treacherously vague entity. Some variants of American and European cultural and radical feminism do retain a faith in the integrity of 'women' as a category. Some proffer versions of a female nature or independent system of values, which, ironically, a rather older feminism has always sought to shred to bits,[4] while many factions flourish in the shade cast by these powerful contemporary naturalisms about 'women'. Could it be argued that the only way of avoiding these constant historical loops which depart or return from the conviction of women's natural dispositions, to pacifism for example, would be to make a grander gesture – to stand back and announce that there *aren't any* 'women'? And then, hard on that defiant and initially absurd-sounding assertion, to be scrupulously careful to elaborate it – to plead that it means that all definitions of gender must be looked at with an eagle eye, wherever they emanate from and whoever pronounces them, and that such a scrutiny is a thoroughly feminist undertaking. The will to support this is not blandly social-democratic, for in no way does it aim to vault over the stubborn harshness of lived gender while it queries sexual categorization. Nor does it aim at a glorious indifference to politics by placing itself under the banner of some renewed claim to androgyny, or to a more modern aspiration to a 'post-gendered subjectivity'. But, while it refuses to break with feminism by naming itself as a neutral deconstruction, at the same time it refuses to identify feminism with the camp of the lovers of 'real women'.

Here someone might retort that there are real, concrete women. That what Foucault did for the concept of 'the homosexual' as an invented classification just cannot be done for women, who indubitably existed long before the nineteenth century unfolded its tedious mania for fresh categorizations. That historical constructionism has run mad if it can believe otherwise. How can it be overlooked that women are a natural as well as a characterized category, and that their distinctive needs and sufferings are all too real? And how could a politics of women, feminism, exist in the company of such an apparent theoreticist disdain for reality, which it has mistakenly conflated with ideology as if the two were one?

A brief response would be that unmet needs and sufferings do not spring from a social reality of oppression, which has to be posed against what is said and written about women – but that they spring from the ways in which women are positioned, often harshly or stupidly, *as* 'women'. This positioning occurs both in language, forms of description, and what gets carried out, so that it is misleading to set up a combat for superiority between the two. Nor, on the other hand, is any complete identification between them assumed.

It is true that appeals to 'women's' needs or capacities do not, on their own, guarantee their ultimately conservative effects any more than their progressivism; a social policy with innovative implications may be couched in a deeply familial language, as with state welfare provision at some periods. In general, which female persons under what circumstances will be heralded as 'women' often needs some effort of translation to follow; becoming or avoiding being named as a sexed creature is a restless business.

Feminism has intermittently been as vexed with the urgency of disengaging from the category 'women' as it has with laying claim to it; twentieth-century European feminism has been constitutionally torn between fighting against over-feminization and against under-feminization, especially where social policies have been at stake. Certainly the actions and the wants of women often need to be fished out of obscurity, rescued from the blanket dominance of 'man', or 'to be made visible'. But that is not all. There are always too many invocations of 'women', too much visibility, too many appellations which were better dissolved again – or are in need of some accurate and delimiting handling. So the precise specifying of 'women' for feminism might well mean occasionally forgetting them – or remembering them more accurately by refusing to enter into the terms of some public invocation. At times feminism might have nothing to say on the subject of 'women' – when their excessive identification would swallow any opposition, engulfing it hopelessly.

This isn't to imply that every address to 'women' is bad, or that feminism has some special access to a correct and tolerable level of feminization. Both these points could generate much debate. What's suggested here is that the volatility of 'women' is so marked that it makes feminist alliances with other tendencies as difficult as they are inescapable. A political interest may descend to illuminate 'women' from almost anywhere in the rhetorical firmament, like lightning. This may happen against an older, slower backdrop of altering understandings as to what sexual characterizations are, and a politician's fitful concentration on 'women' may be merely superimposed on more massive alternations of thought. To understand all the resonances of 'women', feminist tactics would need to possess not only a great elasticity for dealing with its contemporary deployments, but an awareness of the long shapings of sexed classifications in their post-1790s upheavals.

This means that we needn't be tormented by a choice between a political realism which will brook no nonsense about the uncertainties of 'women', or deconstructionist moves which have no political allegiances. No one needs to believe in the solidity of 'women'; doubts on that score do not have to be confined to the giddy detachment of the academy, to the semiotics seminar rooms where politics do not tread. There are alternatives to those schools of thought which in saying that 'woman' is fictional are silent about 'women', and those which, from an opposite perspective, proclaim that the reality of women is yet to come, but that this time, it's we, women, who will define her. Instead of veering between deconstruction and transcendence, we could try another train of speculations: that 'women' is indeed an unstable category, that this instability has a historical foundation, and that feminism is the site of the systematic fighting-out of that instability – which need not worry us.

It might be feared that to acknowledge any semantic shakiness inherent in 'women' would plunge one into a vague whirlpool of 'postgendered' being, abandoning the cutting edges of feminism for an ostensibly new but actually well-worked indifference to the real masteries of gender, and that the known dominants would only be strengthened in the process. This could follow, but need not. The move from questioning the presumed ahistoricity of sexed identities does not have to result in celebrating the carnival of diffuse and contingent sexualities. Yet this question isn't being proposed as if, on the other hand, it had the power to melt away sexual antagonism by bestowing a history upon it.

What then is the point of querying the constancy of 'men' or 'women'? Foucault has written, 'The purpose of history, guided by genealogy, is not to discover the roots of our identity but to commit itself to its dissipation.'[5] This is terrific – but, someone continues to ask, whatever does feminism want with dissipated identities? Isn't it trying to consolidate a progressive new identity of women who are constantly mis-defined, half-visible in their real differences? Yet the history of feminism has also been a struggle against over-zealous identifications; and feminism must negotiate the quicksands of 'women' which will not allow it to settle on either identities or counter-identities, but which condemn it to an incessant striving for a brief foothold. The usefulness of Foucault's remark here is, I think, that it acts as a pointer to history. It's not that our identity is to be dissipated into airy indeterminacy, extinction; instead it is to be referred to the more substantial realms of discursive historical formation. Certainly the indeterminacy of sexual positionings can be demonstrated in other ways, most obviously perhaps by comparative anthropology with its berdache, androgynous and unsettling shamanistic figures. But such work is often relegated to exoticism, while psychoanalytic investigations reside in the confined heats of clinical studies. It is the misleading familarity of 'history' which can break open the daily naturalism of what surrounds us.

There are differing temporalities of 'women', and these substitute the possibility of being 'at times a woman' for eternal difference on the one hand, or undifferentiation on the other. This escapes that unappetizing choice between 'real women' who are always solidly in the designation, regardless, or post-women, no-longer-women, who have seen it all, are tired of it, and prefer evanescence. These altering periodicities are not only played out moment by moment for the individual person, but they are also historical, for the characterizations of 'women' are established in a myriad mobile formations.

Feminism has recognized this temporality in its preoccupation with the odd phenomenology of possessing a sex, with finding some unabashed way of recognizing aloud that which is privately obvious – that any attention to the life of a woman, if traced out carefully, must admit the degree to which the effects of lived gender are at least sometimes unpredictable, and fleeting. The question of how far anyone can take on the identity of being a woman in a thoroughgoing manner recalls the fictive status accorded to sexual identities by some psychoanalytic thought. Can anyone fully inhabit a gender without a degree of horror? How could someone 'be a woman' through and through, make a final home in that classification without suffering claustrophobia? To lead a life soaked in the passionate consciousness of one's gender at every single moment, to will to be a sex with a vengeance – these are impossibilities, and far from the aims of feminism.

But if being a woman is more accurately conceived as a state which fluctuates for the individual, depending on what she and/or others consider to characterize it, then there are always different densities of sexed being in operation, and the historical aspects are in play here. So a full answer to the question, 'At this instant, am I a woman as distinct from a human being?', could bring into play three interrelated reflections. First, the female speaker's rejections of, adoptions of, or hesitations as to the rightness of the self description at that moment; second, the state of current understandings of 'women', embedded in a vast web of description covering public policies, rhetorics, feminisms, forms of sexualization or contempt; third, behind these, larger and slower subsidings of gendered categories, which in part will include the sedimented forms of previous characterizations, which once would have undergone their own rapid fluctuations.

Why is this suggestion about the consolidations of a classification any different from a history of ideas about women? Only because in it nothing is assumed about an underlying continuity of real women, above whose constant bodies changing aerial descriptions dance. If it's taken for granted that the category of women simply refers, over time, to a rather different content, a sort of Women Through the Ages approach, then the full historicity of what is at stake becomes lost. We would miss seeing the alterations in what 'women' are posed against, as well as established by — Nature, Class, Reason, Humanity and other concepts — which by no means form a passive backdrop to changing conceptions of gender. That air of a wearingly continuous opposition of 'men' and 'women', each always identically understood, is in part an effect of other petrifications. [. . .]

My supposition here — and despite my disclaimer, it may be fired by a conciliatory impulse — is rather that the arrangement of people under the banners of 'men' or 'women' are enmeshed with the histories of other concepts too, including those of 'the social' and 'the body'. And that this has profound repercussions for feminism. [. . .]

I've written about the chances for a history of alternations in the collectivity of 'women'. Why not 'men' too? It's true that the completion of the project outlined here would demand that, and would not be satisfied by studies of the emergence of patriarchs, eunuchs, or the cult of machismo, for example; more radical work could be done on the whole category of 'men' and its relations with Humanity. But nothing will be ventured here, because the genesis of these speculations is a concern with 'women' as a condition of and a trial to feminist history and politics. Nor will the term 'sexual difference' appear as an analytic instrument, since my point is neither to validate it not to completely refuse it, but to look instead at how changing massifications of 'men' and 'women' have thrown up such terms within the armoury of contemporary feminist thought.

How might this be done? How could the peculiar temporality of 'women' be demonstrated? Most obviously, perhaps, by the changing relations of 'woman' and her variants to the concept of a general humanity. The emergence of new entities after the Enlightenment and their implicatedness with the collectivity of women — like the idea of 'the social'. The history of an increasing sexualization, in which female persons become held to be virtually saturated with their sex which then invades their rational and spiritual faculties; this reached a pitch in eighteenth-century Europe. Behind this, the whole history of the idea of the person and the individual, including the extents to which the soul, the mind, and the body have been distinguished and rethought, and how the changing forms of their sexualization have operated. For the nineteenth century, arguments as to how the concept of class was developed in a profoundly gendered manner, and how it in turn shaped modern notions of 'women'.[6] These suggestions could proliferate endlessly; in these pages I have only offered sketches of a couple of them.

What does it mean to say that the modern collectivity of women was established in the midst of other formations? Feminism's impulse is often, not surprisingly, to make a celebratory identification with a rush of Women onto the historical stage. But such 'emergences' have particular passages into life; they are the tips of an iceberg. The more engaging question for feminism is then what lies beneath. To decipher any collision which tosses up some novelty, you must know the nature of the various pasts that have led up to it, and allow to these their full density of otherness. Indeed there are no moments at which gender is utterly unvoiced. But the ways in which 'women' will have been articulated in advance of some prominent 'emergence' of the collectivity will differ, so what needs to be sensed is upon what previous layers the newer and more formalized outcropping has grown.

The grouping of 'women' as newly conceived political subjects is marked in the long suffrage debates and campaigns, which illustrate their volatile alignments of sexed meaning. Demands for the franchise often fluctuated between engagement with and disengagement from the broad category of Humanity – first as an abstraction to be exposed in its masculine bias and permeated, and then to be denounced for its continual and resolute adherence, after women had been enfranchised, to the same bias. An ostensibly unsexed Humanity, broken through political pressures of suffragist and antisuffragist forces into blocs of humans and women, men and women, closed and resealed at different points in different nations. In the history of European socialism, 'men' have often argued their way to universal manhood suffrage through a discourse of universal rights. But for women to ascend to being numbered among Humanity, a severe philosophical struggle to penetrate this category has not eliminated the tactical need to periodically break again into a separately gendered designation. The changing fate of the ideal of a non-sexed Humanity bears witness to its ambiguity.

Yet surely – it could be argued – some definitive upsurge of combative will among women must occur for the suffrage to be demanded in the first place? Must there not, then, be some unambiguously progressive identity of 'women' which the earliest pursuers of political rights had at their disposal? For, in order to contemplate joining yourself to unenfranchised men in their passion for emancipation, you would first have to take on that identity of being a woman among others *and* of being, as such, a suitable candidate too. But there is a difficulty; a dozen qualifications hedge around that simple 'woman', as to whether she is married or not, a property-owner or not, and so forth. 'Women' *en masse* rarely present themselves, unqualified, before the thrones of power; their estates divide them as inequalities within their supposed unity.

Nevertheless, to point to sociological faults in the smoothness of 'women' does not answer the argument that there must be a progressive identity of women. How is it that they ever come to rank themselves together? What are the conditions for any joint consciousness of women, which is more than the mutual amity or commiseration of friends or relations? Perhaps it could be argued that in order for 'women' to speak as such, some formal consolidation of 'men against women' is the gloomy prerequisite. That it is sexual antagonism which shapes sexual solidarity; and that assaults and counter-assaults, with all their irritations, are what make for a rough kind of feminism.

Here there is plenty of ground. We could think of those fourteenth- and fifteenth-century treatises which began to work out a formal alignment of sex against sex. These included a genre of women's defences against their vilification.

[. . .]

Between the fifteenth- and the seventeenth-century compositions, what remains constant is the formal defences of the sex, the many reiterations of 'Women are not, as you men so ignorantly and harshly claim, like that – but as we tell you now, we are really like this, and better than you.' This highly stylized counter-antagonism draws in 'all women' under its banner against 'all men'. Even though its references are to women of a high social standing and grace, nevertheless it is the collectivity which is being claimed and redeemed by debate. [. . .]

Is this in any sense a precondition of feminism; a pre-feminism which is established, indeed raging, in Europe for centuries before the Enlightenment? Certainly seventeenth-century women writers were acutely conscious of the need to establish their claims to enter full humanity, and to do so by demonstrating their intellectual capacities. If women's right to any earthly democracy had to be earned, then their virtues did indeed have to be enunciated and defended; while traces of seemingly sex-specific vices were to be explained as effects of a thoughtless conditioning, an impoverished education – the path chosen by Poulain de la Barre in his *De l'Egalité des Deux Sexes* of 1673. When Mary Wollstonecraft argued that 'the sexual should not destroy the human character'[7] in her *A Vindication of the Rights of Woman*, this encapsulated the seventeenth-century feminist analysis that women must somehow disengage from their growing endemic sexualization.

It is this which makes it difficult to interpret the defences and proclamations of 'women' against 'men' as pre-feminism [. . .] for it suggests that there is some clear continuity between defensive celebrations of 'women' and the beginning of the 1790s claims to rights for women, and their advancement as potential political subjects. But the more that the category of woman is asserted, whether as glowingly moral and unjustly accused, or as a sexual species fully apart, the more its apparent remoteness from 'humanity' is underwritten. It is a cruel irony, which returns at several watersheds in the history of feminism, that the need to insist on the moral rehabilitation of 'women' should have the effect of emphasizing their distinctiveness, despite the fact that it may aim at preparing the way into the category of humanity. The transition, if indeed there is one, from passing consolidations of 'women' as candidates for virtue, to 'women' as candidates for the vote, is intricate and obscure.

When the name of feminism is plunged into disgrace – for example, in Britain immediately after the end of the First World War – then the mantle of a progressive democracy falls upon Humanity; though the resurgences of feminism in the 1920s tore this apart. But before even a limited suffrage is granted, it may have to be sought for a sex in the name of a sex-blind humanism, as an ethical demand. This may work for men, but not for women. Most interesting here are the intricate debates in Britain between socialist and feminist proponents of a universal adult suffrage, and feminists who supported a limited female suffrage instead as the best route to eventual democracy; these are discussed in detail below. But what has Humanity been conjugated against? Must it be endlessly undemocratic because 'gender-blind' – or 'raceblind'? Its democratic possibilities would depend on, for example, how thoroughly, at the time of any one articulation of the idea, the sex of the person was held to infuse and characterize her whole being, how much she was gender embodied. The question of race would demand analogous moves to establish the extent of the empire of racially suffused being over the general existence of the person. A history of several categories, then, would be demanded in order to glimpse the history of one.

If it is fair to speculate that 'women' as a category does undergo a broadly increasing degree of sexualization between the late seventeenth and the nineteenth centuries, what would constitute the evidence? To put clear dates to the long march of the empires of gender over the entirety of the person would be difficult indeed. My suggestion isn't so much that after the seventeenth century a change in ideas about women and their nature develops; rather that 'women' itself comes to carry an altered weight, and that a re-ordered idea of Nature has a different intimacy of association with 'woman' who is accordingly refashioned. It is not only that concepts are forced into new proximities with one another – but they are so differently shot through with altering positions of gender that what has occurred is something more fundamental than a merely sequential innovation – that is, a reconceptualization along sexed lines, in which the understandings of gender both re-order and are themselves re-ordered.

The nineteenth-century collective 'women' is evidently voiced in new ways by the developing human sciences of sociology, demography, economics, neurology, psychiatry and psychology, at the same time as a newly established realm of the social becomes both the exercising ground and the spasmodic vexation for feminism. The resulting modern 'women' is arguably the result of long processes of closure which have been hammered out, by infinite mutual references, from all sides of these classifying studies; closures which were then both underwritten and cross-examined by nineteenth- and twentieth-century feminisms, as they took up, or respecified, or dismissed these productions of 'women'.

'Women' became a modern social category when their place as newly re-mapped entities was distributed among the other collectivities established by these nineteenth-century sciences. 'Men' did not undergo any parallel re-alignments. But 'society' relied on 'man' too, but now as the opposite which secured its own balance. The couplet of man and society, and the ensuing riddle of their relationship, became the life-blood of anthropology, sociology, social psychology – the endless problem of how the individual stood *vis-à-vis* the world. This was utterly different from the ways in which the concept of the social realm both encapsulated and illuminated 'women'. When this effectively feminized social was then set over and against 'man', then the alignments of the sexes in the social realm were conceptualized askew. It was not so much that women were omitted, as that they were too thoroughly included in an asymmetrical manner. They were not the submerged opposite of man, and as such only in need of being fished up; they formed, rather, a kind of continuum of sociality against which the political was set. [. . .]

The ideas of temporality which are suggested here need not, of course, be restricted to 'women'. The impermanence of collective identities in general is a pressing problem for any emancipating movement which launches itself on the appeal to solidarity, to the common cause of a new group being, or an ignored group identity. This will afflict racial, national, occupational, class, religious and other consolidations. While you might choose to take on being a disabled person or a lesbian, for instance, as a political position, you might not elect to make a politics out of other designations. As you do not live your life fully defined as a shop assistant, nor do you as a Greek Cypriot, for example, and you can always refute such identifications in the name of another description which, because it is more individuated, may ring more truthfully to you. Or, most commonly, you will skate across the several identities which will take your weight, relying on the most useful for your purposes of the moment; like Hanif Kureishi's suave character in the film *My Beautiful Laundrette*, who says impatiently, 'I'm a professional businessman, not a professional Pakistani'.

The troubles of 'women', then, aren't unique. But aren't they arguably peculiar in that 'women', half the human population, do suffer from an extraordinary weight of characterization? 'Mothers' also demonstrate this acutely, and interact with 'women' in the course of social policy invocations especially; in Britain after 1945 for instance, women were described as either over-feminized mothers, or as under-feminized workers, but the category of the working mother was not acknowledged.[8] So the general feminine description can be split in such ways, and its elements played off against each other. But the overall effect is only to intensify the excessively described and attributed being of 'women'.

Feminism of late has emphasized that indeed 'women' are far from being racially or culturally homogeneous, and it may be thought that this corrective provides the proper answer to the hesitations I've advanced here about 'women'. But this is not the same preoccupation. Indeed there is a world of helpful difference between making claims in the name of an annoyingly generalized 'women' and doing so in the name of, say, 'elderly Cantonese women living Soho'. Any study of sexual consolidations, of the differing metaphorical weightings of 'women', would have to be alerted to the refinements of age, trade, ethnicity, exile, but it would not be satisfied by them. However the specifications of difference are elaborated, they still come to rest on 'women', and it is the isolation of this last which is in question.

It's not that a new slogan for feminism is being proposed here – of feminism without 'women'. Rather, the suggestion is that 'women' is a simultaneous foundation of and an irritant to feminism, and that this is constitutionally so. It is true that the trade-off for the myriad namings of 'women' by politics, sociologies, policies and psychologies is that at this cost 'women' do, sometimes, become a force to be reckoned with. But the caveat remains: the risky elements to the processes of alignment in sexed ranks are never far away, and the very collectivity which distinguishes you may also be wielded, even unintentionally, against you. Not just against you as an individual, that is, but against you as a social being with needs and attributions. The dangerous intimacy between subjectification and subjection needs careful calibration. There is, as we have repeatedly learned, no fluent trajectory from feminism to a truly sexually democratic humanism; there is no easy passage from 'women' to 'humanity'. The study of the historical development and precipitations of these sexed abstractions will help to make sense of why not. That is how Desdemona's anguished question, 'Am I that name?', may be transposed into a more hopeful light.

Notes

1   See Jacqueline Rose, 'Introduction – II', in J. Mitchell and J. Rose (eds.), *Feminine Sexuality, Jacques Lacan and the École Freudienne* (London: Macmillan, 1982).

2   See Stephen Heath, 'Male Feminism', *Dalhousie Review*, 64/2 (1986).

3   Jacques Derrida, *Spurs: Nietzsche's Styles* (Chicago: University of Chicago Press, 1978), 51, 55.

4   See arguments in Lynne Segal, *Is the Future Female? Troubled Thoughts on Contemporary Feminism* (London: Virago, 1987).

5   Michel Foucault, 'Nietzsche, Genealogy, History', in Donald F. Bouchard and Sherry Simon (eds. and trans.), *Language, Counter-Memory, Practice: Selected Essays and Interviews* (Ithaca, NY: Cornell University Press, 1977), 162.

6   See Joan Scott, '"L'Ouvrière! Mot Impie, Sordide . . .": Women Workers in the Discourse of French Political Economy (1840–1860)', in P. Joyce (ed.), *The Historical Meanings of Work* (Cambridge University Press, 1987).

7   Mary Wollstonecraft, *A Vindication of the Rights of Woman, 1792* (Harmondsworth: Penguin, 1982), 142.

8   Denise Riley, *War in the Nursery: Theories of the Child and Mother* (London: Virago, 1983), 150–5, 195.

Sonya Rose, Kathleen Canning, Anna Clark and Mariana Valverde

GENDER HISTORY/WOMEN'S HISTORY
Is feminist scholarship losing its critical edge?

Two animated exchanges concerning the impact of poststructuralism upon feminist history appeared during the mid-1990s in leading American and British women's history journals. The first roundtable discussion reproduced here between historians Kathleen Canning, Anna Clark and Mariana Valverde, introduced by Sonya Rose, was published in 1993 in the *Journal of Women's History*. The exchange suggests ways in which certain insights derived from poststructuralism may be usefully applied in the differing contexts of German, British and Canadian feminist history. Rose provides a useful overview of the main themes of the discussion. Both Canning and Clark tackle the vexed new 'binary' of discourse and experience elicited by post-structuralist theory. Canning observes that the epistemological crisis created by 'the linguistic turn' in the US and UK has yet to reach Germany, but she envisages its impact as particularly problematic for a national history still haunted by the spectre of the Holocaust. This said, Canning welcomes the destabilisation of the unitary category 'woman' as creating new possibilities to 'rethink our own paradigms and categories'. For Anna Clark, in her study of the nineteenth-century British Chartist movement, the challenge is how to link the postmodernist enshrinement of language with the historical operations of power. Foucauldian notions of power, she argues, evoke passive historical subjects who are merely constituted by professional discourses. Thus she prefers the term 'rhetoric' to 'discourse' to denote the active negotiations present in all historical contestations over gender relations. The Canadian historian Mariana Valverde, probably the most sympathetic towards poststructuralism, is still critical of Scott's overrating of Derridean theory for history-writing. She sees poststructuralism as most productive in its insistence upon the absence of any final or complete constitution of male or female subjectivity. She cites Denise Riley's work approvingly and argues that feminist historians should avoid the trap of presupposing the object of their own enquiry.

————————————

Sonya Rose

THERE HAS NEVER BEEN A PERIOD when feminists have been unified around a single analytical frame. As a number of scholars have pointed out, disunity has marked feminism throughout history. Major fault lines have formed and reformed over the very subject matter of feminist analysis – the category women.

[. . .]

Kathleen Canning, Anna Clark, and Mariana Valverde consider issues raised by post-structuralism. Rather than rejecting the linguistic turn, they respond to it in creative ways, and indicate how they apply their understandings of language, meaning, and subjectivity or identity in their own empirical work. Kathleen Canning explores the controversies among German feminist historians over new directions in feminist inquiry. Her discussion illuminates the markedly different trajectories of scholarship in Germany as contrasted with the United Kingdom and North America. She raises thought provoking questions about the implications of the post-structuralist critique of subjectivity and experience for German historical practice. In her discussion, Canning demonstrates the importance of coming to terms, both theoretically and empirically, with the issue of historical agency and rethinking the analytical categories of discourse and experience and their relationship. She formulates her own understanding of identity as the location in which subjects link experience and discourse. In doing so, she suggests subjects create their own meanings and sometimes resist those that are dominant. It is in this way that they become historical agents.

Anna Clark contends that gender analysis is a step forward in feminist history, because it can make evident different forms of male power, and it can incorporate sexual orientation as a historical dynamic. She situates her own uneasiness with contemporary feminist history in particular aspects of postmodernism, especially in those strands influenced by Foucault. She is particularly concerned with the problem of linking the exercise of power to the instability of meaning created by the play of difference in language and the idea that subjects are created discursively. By turning to history itself, Clark challenges some of the understandings about gender and language in post-structuralism. She suggests, for example, that the idea of gender as constituted by a binary opposition between the masculine and the feminine was an historical construction rather than being a timeless artifact of the operation of language. In order to conceptualize how language is linked to power and political struggle, Clark prefers the term *rhetoric* to the concept of discourse.

Rhetoric, she suggests, implies a dialogue between and among social actors who are attempting to persuade one another.

Mariana Valverde parts company from Canning and Clark by more fully embracing post-structuralism, especially its theory of subjectivity. While Valverde faults Joan Scott for being overly enamored with deconstruction, she applauds post-structuralism for conceptualizing both discourses and subjectivities as fragmented and multiple. She suggests that historical agency resides in how 'the constant work of reproducing the discursive structures subjectively, often subverts and fractures those very structures.' Furthermore, Valverde maintains that gender history can be critical history if feminist historians take as their subject the analysis of gender formations, by which she means studying how 'the two genders are formed and reformed, renegotiated, contested.' Like Joan Scott, Valverde insists that it is crucial that feminist historians 'remember the need for a philosophical critique of the formation of the categories whose history we study qua historians.'

Each of these three essays suggest how feminist history can move forward by encompassing some if not all of the suppositions of post-structuralism. Clark and Canning are both concerned with the problem of agency, especially how subjects can 'talk back' or can exercise power, and they wish for a concept of subjectivity that is not fully determined in and by discourses. Valverde, in contrast, is not at all troubled by the notion that subjectivities are formed through discourse. She conceptualizes historical agency as the process by which subjects, using multivalent language, both reproduce and challenge dominant meanings. Each of them provides imaginative ways of thinking about some of the problems for feminist history posed by post-structuralism.

[. . .]

Kathleen Canning

GERMAN PARTICULARITIES IN WOMEN'S HISTORY/GENDER HISTORY

I **WILL SEEK TO ANSWER** the question posed to this panel today from my own perspective as a social historian of modern Germany, a field marked by an 'Atlantic divide,' by a striking divergence in the ways in which German history is conceptualized and practiced on either side of the Atlantic. This Atlantic divide applies as well to feminist scholarship, which is still working to establish its critical edge within the field, albeit in different ways on each side of the Atlantic. Historians on both sides of the Atlantic have seen the gradual displacement of *Frauengeschichte* (women's history) by *Geschlechtergeschichte* (gender history) in recent years, but the meanings of this shift and the controversies surrounding it are distinct in Germany and the United States. My exploration of this Atlantic divide in German gender history aims to relate the different meanings, methodologies and theories of gender history to the success or failure of feminist history in attaining a 'critical edge.'

Historical practice during the last decade in the United States and Britain has been marked by a fruitful fracturing of disciplinary boundaries – by the interrogation, disassembly, and recasting of these paradigms in light of new histories of women and, gender, of race, ethnicity, and sexuality. By contrast, the social science paradigms of modernization, urbanization, of class and state formation – established in Germany during the 1960s – remain safely in place while the history of women and gender persists in its '*Aussenseiterdasein*' (outsider status). As a result of the 'mutual distancing' that marks the relationship between feminist history and German historical social science, many of the most interesting historical monographs on women's work, everyday lives, and political movements have been produced in relative isolation from the mainstream of historical social science. Most social and labor historians, in turn, regard women's history as too specialized to be relevant to their synthetic histories of social transformations.

A comparison of the various practices of gender history is complicated first by the fact that the German term *Geschlecht* means both sex and gender. Indeed, some of its most prominent practitioners emphatically reject the division, implicit in the Anglo-Saxon term *gender*, between the biological category, sex, and the social structures and ideology of gender. Furthermore, some feminist historians view gender history as a retreat from the more radical claims of women's history. They contend that gender history is more palatable to mainstream male historians because it employs a more compliant language and abandons the confrontational tone of much of women's history. Historian Gisela Bock warns in a recent essay that gender has the potential not only to produce a gender-neutral historical discourse, but also to render women thoroughly invisible.

Yet there are numerous proponents of the opposite view that *Geschlechtergeschichte* has not gone far enough in breaking with the traditions of women's history. In recent articles surveying the current state of *Geschlechtergeschichte*, Ute Frevert, Hanna Schissler, and Dorothee Wierling suggest that the practice of German gender history lags far behind its theoretical aspirations. Frevert and Wierling lament the fact that the shift from women's history to gender history has been mainly a semantic, rather than a methodological or theoretical transition: *Geschlecht*, they point out, is often merely a more fashionable term for women's history and talking about gender continues to mean talking about women. Thus, this shift has done little to change the perception among mainstream historians that gender is something inherently female or to challenge the purported gender-neutrality or universality of their narratives and paradigms.

As a remedy for this impasse, feminist critics envision a new, expanded version of *Geschlechtergeschichte* which disavows the 'separatist' pursuit of women's history in its incorporation of men and masculinity and in its exploration of the relationships *between* the two sexes. While aiming to widen the empirical scope of gender history to include men, this proposal omits any reflection on the methodological-theoretical framework of *Geschlechtergeschichte*, which is, in many respects, still embedded in social science history. Indeed, one of the most interesting aspects of the Atlantic divide in gender history is the way in which *Geschlechtergeschichte* has thus far resisted an exploration of gender as a symbolic system or as a signifier of relations of power. Like the mainstream social historians they critique, German feminist historians have been reluctant to explore cultures, mentalities, or ideologies, or to engage in debates about post-structuralist literary or anthropological theory, which may be explained in part by the absence of an interdisciplinary frame-work for fruitful encounters between the disciplines (such as women's studies programs in the United States).

Instead, Frevert and Wierling express a kind of utopian desire to overcome the 'mutual distance' between gender history and social history by *integrating* the two fields and their two main concepts, gender and class. Thus, social history would integrate gender as a central category of social-historical analysis, while gender history would locate itself in a social-historical and class-specific context, a process which they imply has already occurred in Britain and the U.S. This vision of reciprocity and integration – between feminist history and mainstream social history and between the categories of gender and class – seems to assume that established fields and categories will somehow emerge from this encounter intact. It overlooks the dissension and disorientation, the acute sense of 'epistemological crisis' that has accompanied the feminist interrogation of established categories, narratives, and chronologies in Britain and the United States.

The turn to gender and the challenge of post-structuralism

The turn from German women's history to gender history is no less controversial in the United States, but the issues of contest differ significantly on either side of the Atlantic. Since the late 1960s, when feminist scholarship began to challenge the prevalent paradigms of social science, feminist historians in the United States have upheld a 'doubled vision' of society, one that emphasized the simultaneity of sex and class in shaping social identities in dissolving the myth of natural divisions between public and private, between women and men, and in emphasizing the ways in which these divisions were 'socially constructed and socially imposed,' this doubled vision prepared the way for the shift towards 'the self-conscious study of gender,' which began in the mid-1970s. By the mid-1980s, feminist social scientists began to assail the 'logical mistake of equating *women* with *gender*,' and to argue for a view of gender as 'a system of social, symbolic, and psychic relations, in which men and women are differentially positioned.'

Even as feminists began to distinguish between *women* and *gender*, most refrained from establishing a kind of binary opposition between them, by which one was a valid topic of historical inquiry and the other outmoded or superfluous. Rather, women's history remained vital as a foundation for, and as a prerequisite of gender history. The discovery that women's history broke up 'the smooth narrative of progress . . . confound[ed] the analytical categories' and failed to 'offer an easy alternative or synthesis to replace what it has disrupted' opened the way for gender as a theoretical and methodological intervention. Yet the shift to gender, to a more theorized historical research and writing, did not mean losing sight of female historical actors.

By the late 1980s however, new controversies and 'a new skepticism about the use of gender as an analytical category' had become evident, as the once-unitary category, *woman*, began to fracture in new and complex ways. As women of color challenged racism within feminist movements and in the academy, feminist scholarship in the United States became increasingly aware of the ways in which the 'feminist dream of a common naming of experience,' was a totalizing, imperialist, and racist one. In Germany, by contrast, *woman* – and in its peculiar affinity, *gender* – remain unitary categories, undifferentiated by race or ethnicity.

At the same time, but in a somewhat different vein, historian Joan Wallach Scott's critique of the discipline of history from a post-structuralist perspective also began to transform the debates about *women* and *gender* during the late 1980s. Scott's recognition of the 'difficulty of analyzing gender inequality within the framework of social history' and her sense of frustration at 'the relatively limited impact women's history was having on historical studies generally' prompted her interest in post-structuralism, in particular the theories of Michel Foucault and Jacques Derrida. Scott illustrated the workings of this 'more radical epistemology' in a series of path-breaking theoretical and historical essays which posed important challenges to categories that had long been integral to feminist histories, such as experience, agency, subjectivity, identity, and class. Four years after the publication of *Gender and the Politics of History*, Scott's turn to post-structuralism continues to stimulate spirited debates within (and beyond) the ranks of feminist historians.

Indeed, it is less the shift from women to gender than the uneasy relationship between feminism and post-structuralism, the sense of identities and subjectivities fracturing, of categories and concepts dissolving in a 'new master-narrative' of multiplicity, fluidity, and interdeterminancy, that has prompted this panel to ask whether feminist inquiry is losing its critical edge. While the decentering of the autonomous western white male subject initially appeared to open up a space for the constitution of female subjects, the emancipatory moments have been over-shadowed by the fragmenting effects of multiple and indeterminate identities. Yet, it is important for us to recognize that these controversies and crises (whether of identity or epistemology) and, to some extent, the *theory* that has been formulated to respond to them, originated in the very contradictions and limitations of women's history, as Scott points out. Because most of the debates about the so-called *linguistic turn* in history have centered on Foucault, Lacan, and Derrida, we have lost sight of the ways in which feminist history destabilized the historical canon of social history *before* their works became widely known among historians. When it rejected biological essentialism as an explanation of gender inequalities, feminist history discovered in its own right the power of language, of discourses, to socially construct these inequalities and to anchor them in social practices and institutions. Together, if not hand-in-hand, feminist and post-structuralist critiques of history rendered 'what was previously deemed central' as fragmented – the state, for example – and sought to understand that center in terms of its margins and peripheries.

Feminist scholars have responded to the ongoing encounter with post-structuralism in a variety of ways. Some continue to warn that 'postmodernism represents a dangerous approach for any marginalized group to adopt,' since it undermines the efforts of those 'who have not been allowed to make their own history' to name themselves, to 'act as subjects rather than objects of history.' It is clear that attempts to decenter a subject whose own subjectivity (in an historical sense) is still in the process of being constituted – the white western woman, women and men of color, the gay or lesbian subject – has been far more contested than the first wave of deconstructive history aimed at the white male subject-individual-citizen of western European history. This process of fragmenting, decentering, dissolving narratives and paradigms has created a number of dilemmas for feminist historians.

Perhaps the most important one at present is the ambiguity of the terms *experi-ence* and *agency* and the difficulty of disentangling the discursive aspects from the moments of experience and agency in the shaping of subjectivity or identity. Joan Scott's portrayals of the 'discursive construction' of experiences and identities are convincing and compelling in many respects, but they also appear to create their own binary oppositions in which one of the pair – in this case, discourse – always seems to determine or construct the other (experience). In her essay on the discourse of political economy in nineteenth-century France, for example, women workers are present only as objects of discursive construction: their silence is juxta-posed with the loud and powerful voices of political economists holding forth on the perils of the industrial world as embodied in the figure of the working woman. Scott's recent essay, 'The Evidence of Experience,' emphatically rejects the 'appeal to experience as uncontestable evidence.' In her view, the 'evidence of experience' obscures 'the workings of the ideological system itself [and] its categories of repre-sentation (homosexual/heterosexual, man/woman, black/white as fixed immutable identities).' Here Scott constructs as oppositional, rather than as complementary historical tasks, the analysis of how difference – femininity, for example – was con-stituted and the exploration of how that difference was experienced by women in specific historical settings.

This kind of a critique will pose particular problems for German women's history and *Geschlechtergeschichte* should it be widely circulated there one day. Because German social history has focused mainly on systems and abstract processes in which individual actors figure only seldom, the act of constituting a subject has been an integral part of critical alternative history, in particular women's his-tory and *Alltagsgeschichte* (the history of everyday life). Furthermore, the peculiar-ities and the horrors of modern German history, the ways in which National Socialism and in particular, the Holocaust, serve as 'a limit case for testing difficult questions about historical practice,' make discussions of discursive constructions and representations, and of experience and agency more complicated.

Indeed, one of the most important disputes in recent German women's history revolves around Claudia Koonz's analysis of the agency and complicity of German women who 'lived in/under/through the Third Reich.' Breaking apart the victim/perpetrator dichotomy by which women in most historiography heretofore were viewed somewhat unproblematically as victims of a virulently sexist and racist dicta-torship, Koonz argued in *Mothers in the Fatherland* that women comprised 'half of the Germans who made dictatorship, war and genocide possible. . . . Far from remaining untouched by Nazi evil, women operated at its very center.' The publi-cation of Koonz's book in 1987 unleashed a vitriolic and defensive response from German historian Gisela Bock in which the Atlantic divide in German history again became painfully evident. Bock, whose own work on Nazi sterilization policies underscored the 'profound anti-natalism which potentially victimized all women by threatening their (biological and social) maternal identity' accused Koonz of reducing 'the writing of women's history to an attack on "separate spheres."'

Agency was also at the heart of this debate as it was taken up at a 1990 confer-ence in Würzburg on 'Participation and Resistance: The Problematization of National Socialism in Recent Women's Studies' and discussed in the subsequent volume, *Töchter-Fragen, NS-Frauen-Geschichte (Daughters Ask: National Socialist Women's*

History). The conference opened with a controversial call to feminists to break with the 'understandable wish' to identify with the positive accomplishments of women in history, to put an end to 'the rituals of innocence in the women's movement and in women's history regarding National Socialism.' Instead, feminists should claim the guilt and the responsibility for National Socialism, including Auschwitz, as a negative legacy of German women's history. While one side pointed to the connections between *Fortpflanzungswahn* (the drive to reproduce) and *Vernichtungswille* (the drive to annihilate), recognizing in the cult of the Aryan mothers a profound claim to power on the part of women, the other side pointed out that women's guilt was proportional to their 'access to knowledge, to political power, and to social influence.' Central to the controversies about this negative legacy was the task of constituting the female subject and delineating the boundaries between agency (responsibility) and victimization.

This controversy, a kind of life-and-death issue in German women's history, makes clear the importance of contending with agency historically and theoretically, of seeking to determine how subjects are 'constituted discursively' and the ways in which they are 'subject to definite conditions of existence, conditions of endowment of agents, and conditions of exercise.' It calls for 'a weaving of theory into historical research,' for exploring 'empirical solutions' to theoretical problems. In illustrating the historical specificity of our theoretical problems, this controversy also suggests that the dilemmas of feminist history are mutable: we need to think about not only how these dilemmas change over time but also about how they differ according to the geographical, chronological contexts of our own research projects; according to our own subject positions as historians of modern Germany, urban America, colonial Africa, or ancient Greece and Rome; as historians of labor, religion, or race; of class, state, or identity formation; or of nation, empire, slavery, or war (or any combination thereof). Recognizing the historical specificity of the dilemmas discussed here also shows that there is no one answer to the question posed by this panel, no singular response to post-structuralist feminism.

Yet it is crucial that we take the opportunities presented by dissolving categories and fragmenting identities to rethink them, to respond creatively to Joan Scott's challenge rather than becoming enmeshed in dilemmas or paralyzed by epistemological crisis. This might mean thinking historically about concepts like *discourse* which too often seem fixed in time and detached from processes of historical change, without historical origins or consequences; or seeking not only to expose the hidden meanings of concepts and texts, but also, as Louise Tilly has argued, to construct new meanings, to redefine our concepts, embedding them in the histories we study and create. We might explore, for example, the conflictual meanings of class or examine the meaning of (sexual, ethnic, racial, religious) difference both as ideology and as experience in specific historical settings. In my own work I attempt to break open the binary oppositions between discourse and experience, to counter the silence of 'discursively constructed subjects' by inquiring about the reception, the contestation, the multiple meanings of the texts in question; about the complex ways in which women workers, for example, might have interpreted, subverted, or internalized these constructions. Thus, I attempt to read sources both for the ways that discourses 'position subjects' and for the ways subjects 'talked back,' while remaining fully aware of the discursive context in which they talked and acted.

I explore a notion of identity as a location in which subjects are constituted as they encounter and interact with discourse, as they derive their own meanings and/or resist discourses.

The work of Judith Walkowitz, Mary Poovey, Leonore Davidoff, and Catherine Hall offers diverse examples of feminists reading 'the ways that discursive meanings circulate throughout a culture.' They point to different ways of exploring the 'non-discursive'; of dissolving the oppositions between discourse and experience or agency; of discerning the role of human agency in the production of texts; and of analyzing texts as they 'resonate[d] differently in separate cultural and social settings.' We also have much to learn from feminists, mostly non-historians, who engage post-structuralist theory in a critical and differentiated manner by proposing, for example, to 'rewrite deconstruction' or to conceive a feminist variation of postmodernist social theory.

Indeed, the richness and diversity of feminist history in the United States today offers a compelling reason for us to regard these moments of fragmentation, destabilization, and even deconstruction as fruitful. Even if we do not agree with post-structuralist feminist theories or histories, these conflicts force us to sharpen our historical vision, to rethink our own paradigms and categories. Even if it is not yet clear where we will go from here, we should seriously consider the implications of turning back the clock. The liberating effects of leaving behind the unitary category *woman*, of breaking apart binary oppositions like public and private and 'exposing the artifice inherent in such categories as "nature" and gender,' class and citizen, should banish all nostalgia for old times.

Anna Clark

COMMENT

ONE OF THE QUESTIONS this panel has been asked to address is whether the postmodern or poststructuralist turn to gender and language away from our more traditional focus on women's lives has distracted from the central question of feminist history, in Judith Bennett's words: 'Why and how has the subordination of women endured for so long?'

Postmodernists hold that meaning is determined through binary differences and gender is a prime example of this phenomenon. Masculinity and femininity are not fixed essences, but empty categories determined in opposition to each other. The meaning of masculinity, for instance, is constructed by what it is not: the Other, femininity. Furthermore, these binary differences are very unstable; their meanings are constantly shifting. In fact, postmodernists 'deconstruct' any fixed meaning or essence.

For those of us concerned with gender and class, however, the problem remains of how to link the elegant postmodernist play with language to the grubby historical questions of power. Postmodernists influenced by Foucault have an answer here, too: they reject notions of overarching systems of power, such as class or patriarchy, and instead assert that power is exercised through dispersed networks and nodes, in which subjects are constructed through discourses. The passive voice here is deliberate; they rarely answer the question of who exercises this power. Postmodernists have done us a service in moving us away from a rigid Marxist determinism or a bleak vision of unchanging patriarchy, but I'm not ready to abandon the big questions of how gender structures class. Relations of power were always shifting, but they shifted because real political actors, including women, negotiated and contested them. Today my remarks will focus on these issues in the context of my work on gender and the making of the British working class.

The notion of gender as defined by binary opposites is a historical construction, of course, rather than a fact of human nature or culture. Before the Victorian era, masculinity and femininity were thought of less as binary opposites than as a fragile hierarchy, which also served as a metaphor for other political relationships. Political caricatures and songs used the image of a woman wearing the breeches to undermine the patriarchal authority or the political potency of her husband. The breeches, of course, resembled the phallus as a symbol of male power, but unlike the phallus they were easily removable and worn by a woman. This 'struggle for the breeches' can also be understood as a symbolic representation of a material conflict between women's economic contribution and a patriarchal ideology that mandated their submission.

During the late eighteenth and early nineteenth centuries, as Davidoff and Hall have delineated, the middle class developed a new, contrasting ideology of separate spheres, in which men were to be rational and self-controlled in the public sphere of work and politics, while women were to be passive and nurturing in the private sphere of the home.

Here I would like to demonstrate how a gender analysis can both address different forms of male power and incorporate sexual orientation as a historical dynamic, an issue which Bennett rightly fears is often ignored. Including sexual orientation means not just adding lesbians and gay men to history, but also challenging the assumptions of heterosexuality. As Judith Butler writes, 'heterosexuality is always in the process of imitating and approximating its own phantasmatic idealization of itself – and failing.' For instance, the new middle-class notion of self-controlled masculinity was not suddenly accepted in 1800 – instead, for a long time it competed with an older aristocratic and plebeian manhood of physical prowess and pleasure-seeking. The discovery of an effeminate sodomitical subculture in early nineteenth-century London exposed anxieties about changing definitions of manhood: Was the bachelor journeyman really so manly if he didn't have a wife? Was the pleasure-seeking aristocrat engaging in the suspect effeminacy of corruption? Or, was the middle-class man's prim virtue a cover for womanly emotion?

Moreover, during the early nineteenth century, the idea of separate spheres was not a universal notion of gender but was based on class privilege. Only middle-class men could afford to keep their wives at home. Furthermore, middle-class men justified their claim to political power on a Lockean basis of their status as individual property owners and heads of household whose pure, sheltered wives proved their public, manly virtue. This notion of citizenship was enshrined in the 1832 Reform Act, which gave middle-class men the vote, but excluded the working class.

This era therefore also saw the 'making' of the working class, in E. P. Thompson's terms. Feminist historians have challenged Thompson's heroic narrative to point out that the working class was made in a masculine form. Joan Scott argues that working-class radicals defined citizenship in particularly masculine terms; for her, it doesn't matter that real women participated in the Chartist movement for the working-class vote in the 1830s and 1840s, for when they did, they accepted this masculine definition. However, I would suggest that while there is no doubt radicals eventually defined the working class as masculine, this was not a given, but was the outcome of struggles and negotiations between working-class men and women and between working-class men and the state. For this reason, I prefer to use the term *rhetoric* rather than *discourse* when discussing the radical language of class. *Discourse* evokes the image of professionals scientifically constructing the identity of passive subjects, while rhetoric implies a political *dialogue* that intends to persuade its audience and pressure its opponents. And women were part of the audience who needed to be persuaded.

Radicals used rhetoric to develop new meanings for community, citizenship, and manhood and womanhood. Chartists began to organize the working class on an inclusive community basis, rather than the artisan tradition of organizing just skilled men in the workplace. In response, Chartist women organized alongside men. Chartist rhetoric began to define citizenship as an inherent human right to political representation, rather than a privilege of property. Again, some women pointed out that therefore they also deserved the franchise. Chartists also needed to move away from the old notion of gender as a struggle for the breeches to more harmonious notions of relations between the sexes which would enable working-class men and women to unite. So they developed a rhetoric of domesticity, promising sober, responsible husbands to women and a breadwinner wage to men.

But Chartist political rhetoric also had to contend with its other task – not only unifying its supporters but pressuring its opponents in Parliament. And they had to overcome the fact that the working class had been negatively defined by gendered notions of virtue, such as separate spheres, Malthusianism, and political economy, which demarcated the working class as different and inferior to the middle class. Working-class men were depicted as drunken louts unwilling to support their families and therefore undeserving of political and familial rights. These discourses took a material form in working-class exclusion from the privileges of participation in the state, the imposition of the New Poor Law, and the failure of factory reform.

In response, Chartists challenged the notion that the public manhood of participation in politics and the private womanhood of domestic virtue were middle-class privileges. They demanded that these *class-based* notions of gender become universally available. However, in exploiting the issue of domesticity, Chartists allowed their notion of citizenship to mutate. Moving away from a Painite concept of inherent human rights, they argued that working men needed the vote to protect women and children from the contaminating effects of factories and mines. Parliament conceded the principle of domesticity for women and children, legislatively limiting their work in factories and mines in the 1840s, but it refused to give working men the vote and therefore refused to admit them to the public sphere.

Ultimately, this gendered struggle produced a conservative, masculine version of the working class. Joan Scott ascribes this to a working-class adoption of Enlightenment correlations between masculine/feminine, public/private, rational/expressive, individual/community. However, I would like to take Scott's postmodernism to its logical extreme and undercut the stability of these binary oppositions. There was no fixed correlation between masculine/feminine, public/private, and individual/community. The Chartists could have defined citizenship in gender neutral terms but chose to restrict its meaning to masculine forms, both in order to manipulate middle-class opinion but also because they refused to relinquish an older misogynist artisanal form of male power. These gendered dichotomies were therefore historically constructed, yet repeatedly contested, on the basis of class and gender. We may no longer consider class and gender as tightly constructed systems, but they still resonate as fundamental dynamics of power. I suggest we borrow postmodernism's insistence on the always unstable character of gender relations, yet refuse its apolitical notion of dispersed power. By illuminating different forms of male power, we can thus come closer to, rather than evading, the fundamental question as to why women's subordination has lasted so long.

Mariana Valverde

COMMENT

I **HAVE SOME PREPARED REMARKS** on the issue of whether gender history is more or less politically trenchant, as a banner for feminist historians, than women's history. But before offering these, I feel obliged to quickly respond to some of the comments made by other panelists on the vexing question of discourse analysis. For the sake of convenience I will confine myself hereto differentiating my methodological position from that of Joan Scott, whose name has dominated many of these discussions in the United States, and to a lesser extent in English Canada.

As a feminist historian sometimes engaging in discourse analysis and post-structuralist social theory, I am not aware that Joan Scott has been elected to represent us; I am not even aware that there is anything like an us, as against the empiricist *them*. My view is that Scott vastly overrates what philosophers such as Derrida can offer history, and that both supporters and detractors of Scott's work overrate her role in the debate. Skeptical social historians would do far better to read the work of careful cultural historians such as Mary Poovey or Patrick Brantlinger rather than listen to the exaggerations of recent converts. Scott presents an impoverished view of the possibilities of 'philosophical' history, often using only one technique in her recent 'culturalist' work – Derridean deconstruction. Useful as this souped-up Hegelian trick is, there are a wealth of other techniques devised by narratology, philosophy, and literary studies, and many of the techniques neglected by Scott are, in my view, extremely useful in the interpretation of historical systems of signs.

In any case, post-structuralism is useful to social history not only because of its theorization of sign systems as ongoing struggles over and through meaning, but also because of its theorization of social subjectivity. Taking from structuralism the fundamental insight that subjectivity is constituted rather than originary, more recent theorists have argued that neither discourses nor subjectivities are mono-lithic (as was thought in the days of high structuralism). Discourses produce a plurality of subject positions in tension with one another. Subjectivity is thereby fragmented and, most importantly for those interested in agency, it fragments mean-ings and discourses; the constant work of reproducing the discursive structures subjectively often subverts and fractures those very structures.

This I find quite relevant to the theorization of gender: gender power and gender meanings constitute each of us as men and women, but they never do so finally or completely. Not finally because even in times of relative gender peace there are alternative meanings of masculinity and femininity available in the nooks and crannies of dominant cultures, and not completely because, as Third World feminists are tired of repeating, nobody is *just* a man or a woman.

It may now appear that after having waved the flag of post-structuralism (some-what ambiguously given my quick disassociation from Joan Scott) I am about to wave another perhaps fashionable flag, that of gender studies. As is the case with post-structuralism, however, there are many different positions, theoretical and political, all staking their claim on the new terrain: gender studies is not a single thing with a single meaning. Depending on the context, gender studies can be a liberal humanist appropriation – a cooptation – of feminist radicalism. Some people (mostly men, but some women too) prefer 'gender' because it can include men and is thus more polite than other feminist terms. Used in this way the term can shift attention away from male power and male privilege. The liberal usage of *gender studies* reduces contradiction and oppression to mere difference, acting in a way similar to the way in which *race relations* depoliticizes and coopts antiracist work.

But gender history can be deployed so as to constitute a more radically critical enterprise than women's history – with the term *critical* used here in the strict philosophical sense, not in the popular sense of criticism. It was Kant who first theorized critique as the investigation into the conditions for the possibility of some-thing (knowledge, in his case). This critical method has been taken up by Foucault: *Madness and Civilization* is a book not on the history of mad people but is rather an inquiry into the conditions, social and intellectual, of the emergence of the very category of madness. Before mad people can be treated badly, or well for that matter, there has to be a process of category construction – madness has to be recognized as a social fact.

This neo-Kantian method has been applied by Denise Riley to the category of woman, in her much misunderstood study of how and when the category appears in history. As Riley shows, women's history tends to presuppose the existence of the social object, women, whose history can then be documented. Just as the history of psychiatry takes madness and reason for granted, so women's history takes its own object, women, for granted, even if it is very critical – in the sense of disap-proving – of the way in which women have been positioned. The history of asylums also often criticizes the authorities managing mad people, without thereby becoming truly critical.

Having said that, it needs to be added that the documentation of the status of women and the experiences of women is by no means superseded. It is still neces-sary. But as we continue doing women's history it is, I think, advisable to remember the need for a philosophical critique of the formation of the categories whose history we study qua historians. There is a need for what I would call 'historical critique of gender formation.' Let me explain this phrase word by word.

1) *historical*: by this I mean not merely a theoretical or philosophical critique, but one studying the material as well as the intellectual preconditions for the existence of certain social categories;

2) *critique*: I want to reclaim the Kantian meaning of the term, as outlined above;

3) of *gender* rather than *women*: because the term *gender* allows us to study structures as well as individual experience, and hence points to the structuralist dimension retained in post-structuralist critique; and

4) *gender formation* rather than gender structure: because the concept of *structure* is too static and too divorced from historical agency. Just as poststructuralist historians talk about class formation rather than class structure, which gives class a more dynamic conceptualization, so too I prefer naming our project as the critical study of gender formation. We want to analyze how the two genders are formed and reformed, renegotiated, contested.

But having named what I think is the object of study in the more philosophical dimension of our historical work, how is this done? Difficulties arise immediately because gender formation, though analytically distinct from other processes such as class and racial formation, is only analytically distinct, not ontologically separate. Incidentally, many of our inconclusive discussions about whether race is more important than gender would never happen if we remembered that race and gender are analytical, not ontological, categories. The boundaries of gender formation are constantly being drawn and redrawn and shifted by the very processes that regulate masculinity and femininity.

This means that historical analysis cannot assume *a priori* knowledge of what is and is not a gender issue. Social regulation does not proceed along already formed natural channels – race, class, gender, nationality, sexual identity, and so on. Rather, the terrain of the social is constantly being mapped in conflicting ways at the same time that the identities produced by the mapping are regulated. An issue regulated via racial categories can shift and be later regulated through gender categories, and vice versa, without losing its original meaning or emotional impact. Incest, for example, was considered in the 1890s a class issue, an issue of urban slum overcrowding; now it is considered a gender issue, and yet it has not totally lost its link to social reformers' views of the vices of the poor. Similarly, lynching was a race issue for some and a gender issue for others; the two dimensions of the problem were never as separate as certain groups claimed when they tried to define and take possession of the issue.

That is the current focus of my work, theoretically speaking – what I call fractures in social regulation. The process I am fascinated by is the shifting of social problems from one category to another, a shift which often conceals the previous or alternative meanings of 'the issue', but never wholly successfully. The different currents of power and meaning flowing across social signifiers should not be regarded as mere layers whose cumulative impact is obtained by addition, but rather as processes interacting in unpredictable ways (possibly best approximated by Freud's analysis of primary processes).

Let me give an example from my current work, an article entitled 'Representing Childhood: The Multiple Fathers of the Dionne Quintuplets'. These five baby girls, taken over by the Ontario government soon after their birth in 1934, were not, it turns out, regulated as children: the then embryonic but nevertheless powerful child welfare apparatus was not used even once. Rather, the children were regulated as a natural resource or tourist attraction, as the government-father displayed them like zoo animals and even got a special trademark law copyrighting the noun *quintuplets*. These girls were socially constructed not as neglected children but as that typically Canadian economic entity, the crown corporation, administered by a Board of Guardians that was in practice nothing but a board of directors. Therefore the quintuplets were, for the paternal state, not children to be regulated through family policy, but rather an economic entity. The public debate was about the merits of privatization versus nationalization of this resource. Not all human beings under twelve are necessarily governed as children, it would seem. We cannot assume from the start that a government takeover of children is part of that government's family policy. The boundaries between economic policy and social/family policy, so clear in the apparently fixed division of responsibilities among ministries, turn out to be extremely fluid in governmental practice.

While the women's history aspect of our work documents the changes in the situation of those individuals and groups regulated via categories of gender, the critical philosophical dimension of our work looks at the prior process by which the social terrain was mapped, the process by which the boundaries defining *children*, *women*, or even *gender*, are drawn and redrawn.

Feminist history needs both dimensions. Women's history is not self-sufficient, because it can fall into the trap of presupposing the object of its inquiry; but the critique of the constitution of gender at the level of discourse is not sufficient either, since philosophy's general statements can be methodologically useful but do not, at this late point in the history of western philosophy, provide any ontological certainties that are true underneath or beside history. Contemporary philosophers recognize that, if 'there is nothing outside the text', there is also nothing outside history. A post-ontological philosophy and a critical history can thus, in my opinion, work together fruitfully for feminist purposes in the study of how particular categories of social regulation are formed, stretched, and reformed.

Joan Hoff, Susan Kingsley Kent and Caroline Ramazanoglu

GENDER AS A POSTMODERN CATEGORY OF PARALYSIS

A second, more controversial feminist exchange on poststructuralism was prompted by the American historian Joan Hoff with responses by Susan Kingsley Kent and Caroline Ramazanoglu, published in the British-based *Women's History Review* between 1994 and 1996. Hoff provides an emphatic rejection of poststructuralist readings of gender. She describes poststructuralism as 'the patriarchal ideology for the end of the twentieth century' and as an elitist, obfuscatory set of male 'linguistic gymnastics' which represent a misogynist backlash against feminism. Hoff's analysis is a good example of the polarisation of discourse and agency as she berates those who seek, through deconstruction, to erase 'flesh and blood women' in favour of 'disembodied subjects', to sever women's history from its political roots and to deny women a collective voice and set of experiences around which to mobilise themselves. Most controversially, she equates postmodernist disconnections of women from their experiential base with that of 'violent pornographic' methods, an association that Susan Kingsley Kent, two years later, takes particular exception to. According to Kingsley Kent, Hoff's anti-poststructuralist position is both 'unreasoned and uninformed', ignoring the many recent feminist appropriations of postmodern theory that have produced excellent histories of the relationship between material conditions and ideological systems. Postmodernism is not 'without its troubling aspects', but Hoff misses the point when she describes it as 'politically paralysing' argues Kingsley Kent. The much-vaunted 'collective identity of women' has always been a profoundly political act, excluding all those 'who do not conform to her'. Hoff's 'misplaced rage and fear' towards feminist protagonists of postmodernism is both regretful and damaging she asserts and, given Hoff's reference to the generational tensions underlying these debates, reflects a nostalgia for past political certainties that can never be restored. Ramazanoglu's response is that of the intellectual pragmatist: poststructuralism may have exposed feminism's lack of a clear 'theory of power' that spans the divisions between women, yet feminists should take from it what helps them most to interrogate further the nature of knowledge, experience and the effects of power.

Joan Hoff

THE POTENTIALLY PARALYZING CONSEQUENCES of poststructuralism upon the writing of women's history in the United States arose innocuously enough in the mid-1980s as many scholars in women's history sought to find concepts in French postmodernist theory that would enhance the emphasis already being placed on gender. Unfortunately, most began with Michael Foucault who in his work on sexuality talked extensively about gender, but largely neglected to focus on women. Moving on to other male poststructuralists whose theories were equally insensitive or hostile to half the human population, a male-defined definition of gender that erased woman as a category of analysis emerged as a major component of American poststructuralism.

From the beginning, therefore, American poststructuralism threatened to sever the field of women's history from its political roots by insisting that 'there is no experience outside of the ways that language constructs it'. Valid as such an assertion may be in linguistic terms, it is enraging to feminist activists, especially those representing racial minorities, and unintelligible to the vast majority of history teachers trying to integrate material on women into their classes because it denies retrievable historical 'reality', substituting instead the 'linguistic turn', meaning historical analysis based on analysis of representation. Like all postmodern theories, poststructuralism casts into doubt stable meanings and sees language as so slippery that it compromises historians' ability to identify facts and chronological narratives, and uses gender as a category of analysis to reduce the experiences of women, struggling to define themselves and better their lives in particular historical contexts, to mere subjective stories.

This line of argument is perplexing because leading historians of women have been defining gender as the socially conditioned behavior of both sexes in their research since the late 1970s. Gender as a category of analysis did not need to be reinvented using a special linguistic jargon except to eliminate the category of woman in the much touted new field of gender history. Moreover, this original use of gender, in the hands of early practitioners, did not cut academic analysis off from the realities women face in their daily lives. Instead of promoting women's history into the mainstream, as predicted by some advocates of gender history, poststructuralism leaves activists without generalizations about the commonly shared experiences of women as a basis for activism. It also leaves most historians in the United States and abroad, floundering as they try to convert facts into chronological narratives in the face of what is called the 'linguistic turn'.

Ironically, French postmodernism (of which American poststructuralism and postfeminism appear to be watered-down versions) is either being ignored or subjected to rigorous questioning by feminist activists and scholars abroad. For example, Margaret MacCurtain and Mary O'Dowd, two historians of women, noted in 1991 that 'there are signs of a European reaction against' this distinction between women's and gender history and 'a recognition' that its origins have more to do with the 'way in which women's history has developed in North America', than in any inherent supremacy of the poststructural gender history. They concluded that it 'may not necessarily be helpful in studying the history of women in other countries where, as in Ireland, much basic research still needs to be done'. [. . .]

It must also be remembered that US historians of women now have the luxury of turning to any and all theory *because* a pioneer generation, beginning in the late 1960s produced a number of monographic narratives. This is a luxury historians of women in most other countries do not enjoy.

Moreover, I believe that certain characteristics of postmodern theory make it more difficult and more dangerous for historians of women to adopt it than those scholars in such disciplines as film criticism, semiotics, or literature, which are more tightly tied to textual analysis. Postmodern theory disadvantages the field of women's history in three ways. First, it is hostile to the basic concept of linear time and of cause and effect assumptions which most professionally trained historians continue to honor in their teaching and writings. Second, postmodern theory's misogynist and very specific historical origins among post-World War II Parisian intellectuals – from Lévi-Strauss and Lacan to Foucault and Derrida – require excessive intellectual modification and machinations to include women. Finally, it is politically paralyzing. Let me explain why all of these characteristics may not benefit the field of women's history.

Postmodernism cannot under any circumstances be considered 'history-friendly'. For postmodernists, 'history has no reality' because 'it [history] assumes a material world, an external reality unappropriated by the cultural and aesthetic'. Most historians, as teachers and writers, traditionally organize facts into some kind of chronological narrative rather than fit them into a theoretical framework. Since the Second World War with few exceptions – such as economic and labor history – the discipline of history generally has not been distinguished by its adherence to macro-models of theoretical debates but, rather, by its empiricism. For postmodernists, this traditional history falsely assumes the existence of a real, material world and no linear change over time based on causality. All that can be described using poststructuralist methodology is the moment of observation that has no past, present, or future. Therefore, historical agency – real people having an impact on real events – is both impossible and irrelevant. For poststructuralists, each historical moment is unique and does not necessarily relate to any other one, except that perhaps a series of random possibilities could indirectly shape the next random possibility, but not in a historically causal way. Therefore, history as an unbroken continuum cannot survive the scrutiny of deconstructionist methodology because to see history as linear not only is essentialist, but also requires the interposition of that which postmodernists must deny: that is, praxis, which by definition 'demands commitment and change'. [. . .]

History, according to postmodern theory, is at best chaos and, at worst, does not exist at all in the sense that there is no truth about human actions, human thought, or human experience to be revealed through research. [. . .]

If women's history is 'dissolving', as was asserted at the Eighth Berkshire Conference on the History of Women in 1990, in the USA, it is only doing so in a sea of relativity created on the head of a semiotic pin by deconstructionists, not because the field itself has nothing to offer contemporary feminism except post-feminism. For feminist historians of women (if gender analysis does not include women), it is meaningless both as a methodology and as a material underpinning for political action. [. . .]

But obfuscation is not the only, perhaps not even the major, danger of post-structural theory. Too often, poststructuralism has assumed peculiarly ethnocentric characteristics in the United States. Thus it stresses the scientific, intellectual, and apolitical superiority of gender history, which emphasizes the socially conditioned behavior of both sexes, over women's history, which some gender historians say concentrates too much on identifying 'woman' as a discrete category of gender analysis. Thus, poststructural scholars argue that gender history is in line with today's new theories of how science operates because it critiques the Enlightenment tradition and denies the possibility of any objective truth. Within several academic disciplines they also claim that poststructuralism is more intellectually satisfying because it represents an élite, cutting edge of theoretical interpretation which takes a lot of academic training to understand. And, with confrontational language giving way to linguistic gymnastics, it is far less politically oriented because taking women out of the definition of gender, there is no need (or concern) to describe and better the plight of real women.

My second concern about the impact of poststructuralism on women's history has to do with the sexism of postmodern theory. Here Somer Brodribb's book, *Nothing Mat(t)ers: a feminist critique of postmodernism*, published in 1992, has made my task much easier because she has presented a compendium of radical feminist criticism that demystifies postmodernism, revealing it as 'the cultural capital of late patriarchy'. In other words, it is the patriarchal ideology for the end of the twentieth century. [. . .]

Using feminist, not postmodern language (except when quoting others), Brodribb analyzes and dissects the evolution of various definitions and examples of postmodern, poststructural, deconstruction, and semiotic theory demonstrating that [. . .] male postmodernists since the 1960s have been disguising their failure as revolutionaries to change the post-World War II world by devising an ideology in which, to use Simone de Beauvoir's words, 'appearances are everything . . . [and] the whole real world disappears into thin air'.

How does this disappearing act manifest itself as misogynist? Based on the massaging of 'privileged' texts, deconstructionist methodology has been described as an intellectual form of 'masturbation' that results in an 'endless deferral of sense'. Thus, American poststructuralism defers feminism in two primary ways. First, it defers radical feminism in the same way that violent pornography objectifies women — it dismembers and disconnects women from any material experiential base. By disconnecting women from their factual context, females are annihilated through disassociation and physical violence, just as radical feminism is destroyed by dispossession from its political roots through the phallologocentric theories of postmodernism. This way of deferring radical feminism not only uses the same methods as violent pornographic representations of women, but it also has the same impact on women: it silences or coopts them with the implicit threat of violence, or in everyday life, with [the] threat of not being acceptable to the men with whom they associate. The result is female silence, fear or, at the very least, anxiety. [. . .]

Poststructuralism also defers mainstream feminism by allowing infiltration from within, by 'Tootsie' men. Drawing on the movie in which Dustin Hoffman dressed up as a woman and became a better friend of a real (meaning physiologically) woman than a real woman, sociologist Kathleen Barry has called this phenomenon the 'Tootsie syndrome', whereby 'Tootsie' men become better and more authentic representations of women than real women – better mothers than real women, better feminists than real women, and finally, better women than real women. As a result, male poststructuralists (and their female followers) are becoming part of the backlash movement against both radical and mainstream feminism in the United States. It is not surprising that this has happened since some of the French intellectuals who were the 'fathers' of postmodernism exhibited such misogynist views that at times they seemed to claim that only men could speak for women. [. . .]

As a sophisticated linguistic technique, postmodernism may be a logical and useful methodology for purely textual analysis but, as French feminist Christine Delphy pointed out in a 1993 article in *Women's Studies International Forum*, it is irrelevant for analyzing the socially constructed nature of gender because as a linguistic tool it was not designed to discern the existence of socio-economic hierarchies that give meaning to gender differences. When this pitfall is not recognized, it can lead poststructuralists to deconstruct gender relations in a socio-economic void. In this way gender can become a postmodern category of paralysis, destroying any collective concept of woman or women through the fragmentation of female subjects. By ignoring that difference and dominance go hand-in-hand, poststructuralists deny or mask that gender analysis is, after all, about the authority of men over women, preferring to talk about multiple and indeterminate identities. [. . .]

As Tania Modleski has noted, many poststructuralists use feminism simply as a 'conduit to the more comprehensive field of gender studies' in which the primary emphasis is on the deconstruction of masculinity. Thus, feminist critics of poststructural historians who employ gender as a *postmodern* category of analysis to deconstruct both male and female essentialism, point out that some of these poststructuralists focus so much on 'male sensitivity and male persecution' and 'multiple masculinities' that they downplay male privilege. They also are 'implicitly denying the existence of patriarchy' and espousing theories about the predominance of differences among women in which 'the voice of gender risks being lost entirely'.

Why are poststructural feminists, especially in the United States, so obsessed with showing diversity at the expense of gender identity? Obviously *différence* is an important linguistic tool of deconstruction because it is a linguistic way of showing how meaning arises out of implicit or explicit contrasts (binary opposition) that while represented in opposition are in fact interdependent on one another deriving their meaning from that unstable interdependence and the difference in space and time between them rather than in their apparent antithesis. This highly useful linguistic technique for analyzing texts was developed primarily by the French beginning with Saussure and continuing through Lévi-Strauss to Derrida. However, American poststructuralists adapted their ideas to include a peculiarly ethnocentric concept of gender based on differences that denies any collective concept of woman or women and which implicitly masks its apolitical nature. [. . .]

Initially, this emphasis on differences among women sounded innocuous and familiar – nothing more than diversity within a commonly shared set of socially constructed female characteristics. Instead, poststructuralism has become a way for historians of gender in the United States to impose supposedly benign and neutral diversity on the past because of their legitimate concern with the fragmentation and increasing socioeconomic inequities of contemporary American society. [. . .] What could be more anachronistic than imposing contemporary interest in the diversity of the present on the past so that no sources of patriarchal power or hierarchy can be held responsible for collective oppression in any time period? By replacing historical reality (meaning socially constructed gender, race, and class differences) with a thousand points of power and difference, poststructural historians of gender did not originate the attack on essentialism, or the presumed 'truth' of Enlightenment concepts – it had already been undertaken by historians who placed women at the heart of gender analysis.

Few American historians, regardless of field of specialization, understand the complicated linguistic theories and ahistorical concepts on which poststructuralism is based. Thus when historian Joan W. Scott said that postmodern gender analysis represented a 'methodology and theoretical reformulation . . . especially in the areas of symbolic representation and theories of language', that would change the organization of knowledge in the humanities and social sciences, most historians of women in the United States were impressed, but not disturbed. Scott was sincerely concerned about the 'relatively limited impact women's history was having on historical studies generally'. [. . .] So a more 'radical epistemology' seemed in order to satisfy both needs: (1) the desire for more theoretical sophistication, and (2) the activist desire to exercise more impact on the field of history in general. The solution for some turned out to be the poststructuralism associated in the United States primarily with Jacques Derrida and Michel Foucault.

It was not until historians of gender began to redefine gender along poststructural lines by denying the existence of female culture and female experience based on a male-defined postmodern version of gender, that historians of women began to become concerned about where it would all lead. It soon became evident, however, that for some deconstructionists, *différence* meant that 'the female subject of feminism' consisted of 'each woman's consciousness and subjective limits'. Thus, according to Teresa de Lauretis, women were defined by their differences rather than any commonality derived from subordination under patriarchy over time. Differences among women, de Lauretis has asserted, will prevent feminism from ever again being represented as a 'coherent ideology'. In this sense, deconstruction represents an attack on radical political feminism in the United States. Yet this point of view is what Scott has praised in reviewing de Lauretis's work as a 'crucial breakthrough for feminist theorizing' because of its commitment to antiessential particularism.

There can be no universality about questions or answers, according to postmodernists, and so they cannot ask – let alone answer – what is it about the experiences of women that have contributed for so long to their own subordination? We will never know if we do not consider female experiences and actions as real. In a 1991 essay, Joan Scott went so far in the direction of particularism as to reject emphatically any 'appeal to experience as uncontestable evidence' in historical research because experience makes ideological systems in any time period appear fixed rather than in a constant state of change of mutatable identities. This refusal to recognize the objective reality of certain male-inspired dualities and of cognitive male notions about moral and political development, makes it difficult for poststructuralists to focus on the socio-economic and political implications of patri-archy for our own times, let alone the past. [. . .]

If experience cannot be based on socioeconomic categories and on the diver-sity and variability of common gender identities in different time periods, then there can be no political, visionary (I prefer this word to utopian) history from which contemporary feminist activists can draw sustenance and advice for opposing and critiquing the obvious discrimination against women in the United States and other countries. Instead of remaining simply another useful methodological inno-vation for studying women's history and keeping that history relevant to the Second Women's Movement, as gender analysis was in the 1970s and early 1980s, in the hands of poststructuralists it has become a potentially politically paralyzing and intel-lectually irrelevant exercise for endlessly deconstructing binary oppositions and analyzing myriad representations of cultural forms and discourses – disconnected from material reality. As a result, gender history in the United States is becoming more and more removed from political and legal activism.

Using poststructural jargon to support gender as a category of analysis, histor-ians of gender attempted to go beyond the definition of gender employed by historians and those in other disciplines since the mid-1970s. It was in that decade when many women scholars in the United States began to move toward 'the self conscious study of gender' without the aid of poststructuralism. Initially employed by those feminists writing the new social history in the last half of the 1970s, gender simply meant 'the cultural definition of behavior appropriate to both sexes'. This early definition of gender, which the new social historians began to employ, allowed feminist historians of women to reject biological essentialism as the rationale for women's subordination by concentrating on the ways in which differ-ent societies over time interpreted and attached values to the conditioned behavior and perceptions of women and men. Most importantly, in the hands of feminist social historians, gender analysis from the 1970s also carried with it a promise of change, self-determination, and ultimately emancipation from patriarchal bondage. [. . .]

The apolitical origins of postmodernism have been commented upon by a number of feminist scholars. Even though some poststructural feminists have expressed concern about modifying postmodernism so it can address feminist political issues, they usually have not discussed why it was not more difficult for historians of women to be seduced in the first place by a theory that did not provide any basis for feminist politics. Most simply put, postmodern theories are politically paralyzing because they arose out of a situation that male intellectuals found politic-ally paralyzing in postwar Europe – especially in France and Germany. German scholars developed critical theory and the French, postmodern linguistic theory, to rationalize their own disillusionment. [. . .]

If, indeed, postmodernism is ahistorical and misogynist, as well as politically paralyzing, why has it been taken up by historians of gender in the United States and given such attention in academic journals? A number of reasons come to mind. One I have already mentioned: the impulse among some historians in the 1980s to impose the fragmentation of the present on the past. A related reason can be referred to as the 'delayed disillusionment syndrome' among American academic leftists – not unlike that experienced earlier by French and German intellectuals after World War II. Already familiar with both German critical theory and French postmodernism, older marxist-leninist academics in the United States seemed particularly susceptible to the nihilism present in such theories (be it through re-reading Nietzsche or Foucault and Derrida) during the 1980s.

If some older historians succumbed to the bewildering fragmentation of American life and general disillusionment with politics in an age of conservatism, what attracted the younger ones? Most new or revisionist theories in any discipline usually start out as correctives of old ones by a new generation. In women's history in the United States, I am calling the group of women who began to revive and revitalize women's history in the early 1970s – the pioneer generation of historians of women. It was an historical accident that this pioneer generation of historians of women (in which I include myself) also constitutes the same generation that participated in the formation of the Second Women's Movement in the United States. [. . .]

Such generational conflict within history and other disciplines is common although this is the first time it has occurred primarily among women who are historians of women because until the last 25 years there were not enough of them to constitute a separate subfield. In the process, a debate over women's or feminist history versus gender history has emerged that is not completely unique to North America because similar ones arose in other English-speaking countries such as Australia, New Zealand, Canada, England, and even India. There is no denying, however, that in the United States the revival of the field of women's history was so intertwined with the development of the Second Woman's Movement beginning in the late 1960s, that the controversy over women's history versus gender history assumed complicated ethnocentric linguistic and political overtones – often confounding to those outside the country.

Of the various phases and generations that the writing of women's history in the United States has passed through since the 1960s, each one was more method-ologically and theoretically sophisticated than previous ones. As a result, the subfield of women's history emerged on the cutting edge of theory in the discipline of history in general. It was almost inevitable that there would be more experimentation with interdisciplinary approaches beyond social/cultural, ethnographic, and the sex/gender analysis stage that women's history had already reached by the mid-1980s.

Was it that some older, as well as many younger, historians of gender were simply captivated by the elitist idea of keeping women's history in the theoretical limelight? Possibly, because by privileging the text, poststructuralism is elitist by definition. [. . .]

If this were simply an academic debate over methodology and theory, I would not be so concerned. However, poststructuralism reared its relativistic head in the United States just as women and minorities were beginning to find their voices and speak out with a collective identity. It told them that there could not be such commonality of purpose and that their texts did not mean what they said because they had no reality or purpose outside of being reconstructed by poststructuralism. This privileging of texts has led groups already marginalized by color or ethnicity, or sexual preference, or geographical location (such as minority and Western women) who have not produced many texts to fear that poststructuralism could result in silencing them by denying the presence of real women (and men) as political agents. It is perhaps not coincidental that American poststructuralism and neoconservatism emerged at the very moment when it looked as though such marginal groups in the United States were on the verge of obtaining more civil liberties and the long-sought-after equality with white men.

For all these reasons, academic and activist women of color in the United States have expressed justifiable apprehension over the possibility that poststructuralism may become the dominant mode for interpreting women of the past and present. The concern of minority women about deconstructionist methodology is threefold. First, they suspect that it may be established as a hegemonic practice in élite academic circles, thereby displacing the collective understanding of racism that women of color have struggled to obtain by using African or nationalist modes of analysis and an Afrocentric feminist epistemology rooted in both experience and action. Second, they suspect that postfeminists who use deconstructionist methodology may be unintentionally racist because it prompts them to suggest that race, like gender, is a discursively constructed concept. Finally, they fear that political opportunities in the post-Cold War world will be irrevocably lost if not realized in the 1990s.

As I noted at the beginning of this paper, I think that this same political danger exists for women in other countries who are still in the process of constructing authentic female voices from the past. To skip the traditional stage of historical fact-finding by writing about the experiential histories and memories of various races and classes of women and instead to adopt deconstructionist methodology would mean ignoring the material details and oppression of women's past and present lives. Female scholars attending international conferences, especially from non-English-speaking countries often express anxiety about the apolitical character of postmodernism, especially in recently liberated countries like Poland where women constituted such an important component of Solidarity in the 1980s. For example, I heard Polish women at the Teaching Women's Studies Conferences held in May 1993 in Lódz say that they could not afford to abandon politics for linguistics, especially when their rights were being curtailed by the democratically elected parties in their parliament. [. . .]

Just as activists of the Second Women's Movement by the late 1970s and early 1980s were again beginning to be able to communicate across both class and race lines by developing a unifying language so effectively used by women reformers during the progressive era; just as historians of women were using the new social history and definition of gender as socially constructed behavior to show greater class and race diversity — without deconstructionism — in addition to the shared commonality of subordinated and oppressed female experiences across class and race lines, poststructuralism intervened. Once again a younger generation began to say that they would transform the defects of women's history using not feminist but masculinist theories. 'The master's tools', as Audre Lorde once remarked, 'will never dismantle the master's house'.

Like their predecessors in the 1920s and 1930s, today's female poststructuralists and postfeminists seem likely to fall victim to those very male theories that have already turned Tootsie men into representations and spokesmen for real women. This is much more subtle and seductive than the educated women of the interwar years ever encountered in their attempts to turn Freud and Marx into women-friendly theorists because the latter never pretended they were women. However, the 'fathers' of postmodernism insist on 'aping the feminine . . . [and women who follow in their footsteps often end up] trying to be like Daddy who is trying to be a woman'.

As a stubborn relic from the 1960s and tenured guerrilla to boot, I write these words more in sadness than anger because I regard the current divisions among historians of women over women's versus gender history as counterproductive. While I hope for some intellectual accommodation between the two by the end of this century, if poststructuralism prevails, it could effectively sever the connection between women academics and women activists, harm the teaching of women's history, and hamper the study of women in countries where such scholarship is just beginning.

One of the original goals actually achieved by early American practitioners of women's history in the 1960s and 1970s was to write so as to encourage the integration of the new material into general history classes and to provide facts and figures that would be useful in the struggle for women's rights in the United States and abroad. Until recently, that goal was being met. However, the various paralyzing aspects of postmodern theory make it, and especially its use of gender analysis to deny the category woman, a very 'dangerous supplement' for the future of women all over the world who are still struggling for their rights – to say nothing of the future of women's history in the United States, and the future of the Women's Movement in the last decade of the twentieth century.

Susan Kingsley Kent

MISTRIALS AND DIATRIBULATIONS: A REPLY TO JOAN HOFF

IN 1993, A CRITIQUE of postmodernism entitled 'If "woman" is just an empty category, then why am I afraid to walk alone at night?' appeared in *Comparative Studies in Society and History*. The allusion to sexual violence, coupled with the author's references to deconstruction as 'a sharp sword' and to 'troubling elements lurk[ing] on the edges' of Joan Scott's essay in *Gender and the Politics of History*, betrayed a profound, if vague sense of personal danger that was displaced, somehow, onto poststructuralism. Now comes Joan Hoff's equation of poststructuralist or 'gender' historians with violent pornographers in the intemperate and ill-considered 'Gender as a postmodern category of paralysis', to which I have been asked to reply.

The invitation poses a dilemma. On the one hand, to reply means to legitimate Hoff's arguments, to endow them with a seriousness and intelligibility they do not possess. On the other, to allow the article to go unchallenged is to let an unreasoned and uninformed treatment of poststructuralism pass as a responsible critique. Faced with such unattractive alternatives, I chose to risk the former in order to prevent the latter.

[. . .]

What Hoff describes is not an accurate portrayal either of the variety of post-modern theory or of the important and thoughtful criticism that has been brought to bear upon it. Mary Poovey's critique of one aspect of postmodernism, decon-struction, acknowledges that it 'undermines identity, truth, being as such', which 'renders the experience women have of themselves and the meaning of their social relations problematic, to say the least'. But Poovey is also persuaded that decon-struction as formulated by Jacques Derrida offers a way out of essentialist thinking that has helped to trap women in subservient positions and, by grouping all women in one category, has obscured the workings of power that divide women as much as bring them together. In *Uneven Developments: the ideological work of gender in mid-Victorian England*, she demonstrates how deconstruction's demystification of identity based on binary oppositions can be used to produce good history, in which real women, operating under historically specific material conditions, act both to uphold and to resist the ideological system that gives meaning to and constrains their lives. Poovey does not believe that there is nothing outside the text; she argues that texts and subjects are produced by material conditions 'in the ever elusive last instance', even as she insists that the 'last instance *is* ever elusive' because 'the material and economic relations of production can only make themselves known through representation'. Because material conditions and representations are inter-dependent, cause and effect do not work necessarily in one direction. But that does not mean there is no such thing as cause and effect, only that it is or can be multidirectional.

Moreover, Hoff has caricatured and misrepresented the positions gender histor-ians hold. (On the most superficial level, anyone who thinks that 'Michael' Foucault's *History of Sexuality* is about gender hasn't read it.) Mary Louise Roberts's *Civilization Without Sexes*, 1995 winner of the American Historical Association's Joan Kelly prize, is just one example of the kind of fine historical work utilizing gender as a category of analysis being done by scholars. These studies are historical, they contain real women, and those women act. [. . .]

Historians who use the tools of deconstruction to write about gender have aban-doned neither history nor women. They seek 'to understand the operations of the complex and changing discursive processes by which identities are ascribed, resisted, or embraced'. They seek, in short, to be more historical in their approach to the study of women and gender.

Hoff's claim of poststructuralism's essential misogyny, based upon an insup-portable association of deconstruction and pornography, is, simply, irresponsible. Where Laura Lee Downs endowed poststructuralism with the power to rape, Hoff has rendered it capable of torture and dismemberment. Its practitioners, by implication, do serious harm to women. The lumping together of poststructuralist and gender historians with those who commit sexual violence against women may well be an effective rhetorical strategy, but it constitutes what Jane Flax describes as a disquieting tendency for 'feminists to demonize others. Some recent criticism creates the impression that adherents to often-misconstrued but disliked positions – whether "individualism" or "postmodernism" – represent a greater danger to femi-nist aims than those with the power, for example, to outlaw abortion'. Hoff would do well to direct her energies to the real culprits in the backlash against feminism and civil rights.

Hoff has ignored the work of scholars who have sought to challenge the view that the poststructuralist critique of the myth of a stable, unitary subject obviates a feminist politics. As Judith Butler, Denise Riley, Joan Scott, Jane Flax, Donna Haraway and others have pointed out, the epistemological project that assigns autonomy, unity, and stability to the individual subject is itself profoundly political. Poovey has noted that the binary thinking that constitutes our symbolic order has acted to create a stable category of women that '*could* be collectively (although not uniformly) oppressed'. Its deconstruction is a political act, capable of revealing the exclusions – women and people of color – that are necessary in the fashioning of the liberal subject, and of exposing the operations of power that maintain systems of dominance. 'If feminism took deconstruction at its word', Poovey argues, 'we could begin to dismantle the system that assigns to all women a single identity and a marginal place'.

Hoff's rehearsal of the plagues of poststructuralism breaks no new intellectual ground, but for anti-intellectualism, disingenuousness, and sheer incivility, Hoff's article stands apart. The anti-intellectualism of Hoff's piece appears in at least two areas. First, her choice of the rhetorical cudgel over the gentler instruments of persuasion eschews the development of careful reasoning or case-building that historians depend upon to make ourselves clear and convincing. Assertions such as that above about poststructuralists and pornographers; tautological claims that postmodernism is paralyzing because it emerged out of the politically paralyzing conditions of post-war Europe – these involve leaps of logic and lapses in critical thinking that we would not tolerate in our undergraduates. Hoff's use of evidence, about which more later, is also questionable. When she wishes to support an assertion about the nature of poststructuralism, she cites not the work in which the offense is to be found, but that of critics of poststructuralism. These are not the careful methods of argumentation from the evidence that we seek to instil in our students.

Secondly, Hoff insists that gender history is a bad thing because scholars in Eastern Europe and the Third World cannot understand it. They have not yet proceeded through the 'traditional stage of historical fact-finding by writing about the experiential histories and memories of various races and classes of women' that American scholars have had the 'luxury' to enjoy by virtue of the efforts of a 'pioneer generation' of women's historians. Poor benighted academics in Ireland and Poland, as Hoff would tell it, cannot get on with the business of writing their histories as long as gender historians in the USA continue along their disastrous poststructuralist path. A more patronizing and condescending attitude is difficult to imagine; perhaps, worse is the assumption that intellectual endeavors going on in one part of the world should be held hostage to developments in other parts of the world, as if they could not possibly have any relevance or benefit. Substantively, Hoff suggests that privilege has put US scholars ahead, that those in the Third World or Eastern Europe need time to catch up. But rather than complacently pursuing the luxurious pastime of producing gender history, poststructuralist historians are exposing the very premises upon which our privilege is based, cognizant of the ways in which our participation in the maintenance of a particular form of global dominance has enabled us to write the history we write. [. . .]

For, as poststructuralists have consistently pointed out, the unitary subject whose loss Hoff so bitterly laments depends for its very being on the exclusion of all of those who do not conform to her. 'A unitary voice requires the suppressing of many differences', notes Flax, and the privileging of usually white, middle-class, heterosexual women. Indeed, it was precisely when women of color began to subject this unitary white middle-class woman thrown up by the white middle-class feminist movement to scrutiny and criticism that alternative ways of thinking about identity, subjectivity, epistemology, and power began to take hold among feminist historians. Instead of, as Hoff maintains, poststructuralism appearing among US academics as an attempt to counter the emergence of women and minorities who 'were beginning to find their voices and speak out with collective identity', poststructuralism offered white women a way to respond to the challenge of women of colour to 'confront problems of difference and the relations of domination that are the conditions of possibility for the coherence of our own theorizing and category formation'. [. . .]

Second, Hoff claims that women of color believe that those of us who use deconstructionist methodologies in our work 'may be unintentionally racist' because we have extended our thinking about the constructed nature of identity to include race. (Where that leaves people like Toni Morrison, Evelyn Brooks Higginbotham, Henry Louis Gates Jr., Stuart Hall, Zakia Pathak, and Rajeswari Sunder Rajan, to name only a handful of scholars of color involved in deconstructing 'race', Hoff does not say.) Hoff's insinuations of racism against the very people seeking to examine the constructed, contingent nature of whiteness are cynical and dishonest, and have to be seen as part of an effort to silence or cow the individuals whose work she so disdains.

Finally, the vitriol with which Hoff addresses those engaged in gender history cannot go unremarked. Disagreement is the *sine qua non* of our profession; without it our debates and scholarly work would be sterile and, well, academic. Moreover, as many sympathizers have pointed out, poststructuralism contains much with which historians can and should take issue; indeed, the *Journal of Women's History*, which Hoff co-edits, has carried many fine, thoughtful pieces on the uses of poststructuralism for historians and on the relative merits of gender and women's history. This is why Hoff's slurs against those of us who embrace the opportunities afforded by poststructuralism to write history are all the more perplexing and doubly to be regretted: they cannot come from ignorance of the substance and terms of the debates. [. . .]

What are we to make of these critiques, in which philosophers and scholars who utilize the intellectual tools they made possible are turned into monsters, capable – indeed guilty – of collaborating with rapists, axe murderers, and other, more garden-variety oppressors of women? Where does the anxiety that motivates such incommensurable expenditures of affect come from? Jane Flax has suggested one such source: the nostalgic desire for a return to a unified female subjectivity that would obviate both the need to acknowledge conflicts between women and an analysis of the power relations that render white women complicit in the oppression of women of color. 'Our guilt and anxieties about racism (and our anger at the "others" for disturbing the initial pleasure and comfort of "sisterhood")', says Flax:

> partially account for the discomfort and difficulties we white women have in rethinking differences and the nature of our own theorizing and social locations. . . . Directly attacking women of color or voicing our

resentment of them (in public) would be politically unthinkable. Is it easier and more acceptable for white women to express our discomfort with difference discourses and the politics of knowledge claims by categorically rejecting postmodernism and branding it politically incorrect?

This is not to say, as Flax and others readily concede, that postmodernism is beyond reproach or without its troubling aspects, but Flax does offer one way of understanding the misplaced rage and fear that seem to dog so many of its critics.

Caroline Ramazanoglu

UNRAVELLING POSTMODERN PARALYSIS: A RESPONSE TO JOAN HOFF

JOAN HOFF HAS GOOD GROUNDS for worrying about the political impact of poststructuralism and postmodernism on US women's history. Similar developments are occurring in the United Kingdom, and across a number of disciplines. Once the material realities of women's lives become transformed into deconstructions of gender, women's complex and contradictory experiences can become reduced to debates about the limits and possibilities of knowing. While feminists have responded productively to these debates, poststructuralists are much more resistant to recognising the challenge that feminism offers them.

One meaning of paralysis is powerlessness. Joan Hoff usefully shows how feminist knowledge is being disempowered, as questions of *how* we know what we know, displace questions about *what* needs to be known and *why*. A critical problem in fighting back, and in convincing a diversity of younger women that feminism is not yet past its sell-by date, is that postmodern and poststructural critiques have caught feminism on a weak spot. Feminists, like other scholars and activists, have not always thought through problems of why they think as they do; feminists are entangled in, as well as critical of, Enlightenment thought; feminism does not have a clear theory of power that cuts across political differences within feminism; the validity of feminist knowledge is always problematic because of the social divisions between women. But the extensive feminist debates on methodology, rationality, binary thinking, the social construction of gender, the commonalities and differences between women and how gendered power affects people's lives cannot sensibly be ignored. [. . .]

Once on the poststructuralist wavelength, scholars are freed from the need to attend to what feminists are saying or have said, since feminist thought can be dismissed as essentialist, fundamentalist or extra-discursive. I find now when teaching and examining, but also in scholarly comments, the practice of reducing feminism to two or three lines of unreason: naïve claims to absolute truth; uncritical belief in essential sex/gender/body; assumptions that 'raw' experience constitutes a source of general knowledge. Judith Grant, for example, takes feminism as having a fundamentalist belief in the validity of experience. She opposes this on the grounds that experience cannot be a source of feminist knowledge since it is feminist theory that makes sense of experience. The limitations of a poststructuralist approach to history are further illustrated in Joan W. Scott's criticisms of historians' reliance on 'documenting the experience of others'.

Scott allows that historians recognize that evidence only counts as evidence within the framework of a particular way of telling the stories that are discovered, i.e. theory. But she denies that a historian's appeal to experience as 'uncontestable evidence' can stand up, because appealing to experience does not take into account the language through which historians make sense of experience. She contests claims to knowledge about *what* the world is like and *why* it is this way, because she claims that what matters is *how* knowledge is produced and made powerful. [. . .]

A feminist response to Scott need not lie in universal claims to experience simply as knowledge. A white feminist who denies that she is privileged by her whiteness, will not understand colonial history in the same way as a woman who has experienced British rule as her 'other', a 'non-white' colonial subject. This is not just a matter of the effects of power of colonial discourses and their silences, but the fact that different *theories* have different grasps of the complexity of life and the reality of power relations. Social realities such as gender relations may be discursively constituted, but this does not mean that they do not really exist. This raises a further problem that poststructuralist relativism rules out – the fact that some theories are better at grasping gendered power than others. The disintegration of history into a multiplicity of voices does not make all narratives equal. Historians (like scholars in other disciplines) fall out primarily because their theories of *what* is the case differ.

Joan Scott, then, is not producing historical knowledge to challenge feminist knowledge, but is wondering about how best to analyze language. From this point, history can become an endless process of substituting one interpretation for another. However, at the end of her article 'Experience', she arrives at a somewhat contradictory position that touches on the problems raised by feminist politics: 'Experience is not a word we can do without . . .'. She argues that experience 'serves as a way of talking about what has happened, of establishing difference and similarity, of claiming knowledge that is "unassailable"'. Therefore we should work with it, and work out the politics of its construction. [. . .] Joan Scott claims that this does not '. . . undercut politics by denying the existence of subjects, it instead interrogates the processes of their creation . . .'.

This recognition of the interpretation of history as politically contested seems closer to Joan Hoff's feminist concern with the historical 'realities' of gendered lives. But, if in Scott's view the subjects of history only exist as they are created through language, the material grounding of politics goes missing. The feminist and the misogynist will always read the same documents differently; the maid and the mistress will understand the reality of domestic labour differently, but these differences need not mean abandoning experience to the irresolution of multiple readings. Feminists have a case for claiming a better reading of women's history than misogyny or silence. [. . .]

Hoff makes the case that feminists should hang on to the validity of women's experiences (although establishing validity will remain problematic, contested, political, and context-dependent). Feminist history cannot avoid being informed by political anger, a sense of justice, and ethical stances against subordination (including subordination of others by women). It must logically then resist relativism.

Rosi Braidotti has argued that poststructuralism 'calls into question the very foundations and premises of what we recognise as thinking'. But we can take shake off paralysis by standing the ground that postmodernism and poststructuralism are rocking, and re-examining the foundations. Feminism can afford to take from post-structuralism and postmodernism what it is useful to ask about *how* we know what we know, why we think as we do, and how else we might think about the nature and effects of power. We also need to confront historians and other scholars with the moral, political, and intellectual implications of degendering power. If we want to understand embodied lives and how and *why* gender relations have been and are *lived*, then feminists need to continue to work on the difficult problems of using feminist theory to interrogate data, and justifying ways of taking accounts of experience as sources of knowledge.

bell hooks

POSTMODERN BLACKNESS

A prolific and leading historian of black women, bell hooks has published classic texts on African-American feminist theory including 'Ain't I a Woman': Black Women and Feminism (1981), Feminist Theory from Margin to Center (1984) and Sisters of the Yam: Black Women and Self-Recovery (1993). This reading on 'Postmodern Blackness' is taken from hooks's volume Yearning: Race, Gender and Cultural Politics (1990) and is a series of reflections on postmodernism that centre around two main themes: the exclusionary practices of the conventional language used by white, middle-class academic elites, and postmodernism's critique of essentialism. Given the elevated status of 'difference and otherness' in postmodernist discourse, hooks finds it particularly ironic that it engages in an effective silencing of black women's experience such that she finds herself 'on the outside of the discourse looking in'. Any meaningful radical 'politics of difference', she argues, should incorporate the voices of those most displaced, marginalised and exploited. Despite this criticism, however, hooks finds much to recommend in the post-modern critique of essentialist subjectivities, especially those aspects that challenge 'static, over-determined' and frequently racist identities of blackness. Postmodernist approaches, she believes, can act as a process of intellectual decolonisation, opening up new possibilities for the construction of oppositional and liberating notions of black identity as well as creating opportunities for 'new and varied forms of bonding' in the black community. Finally, hooks urges black intellectuals to engage with postmodern theory and relate that theory to black life. Because of postmodernism's engagement with popular cultural forms, it may yet be the best opportunity to open up spaces for 'new and radical happenings'.

POSTMODERNIST DISCOURSES ARE OFTEN exclusionary even as they call attention to, appropriate even, the experience of 'difference' and 'Otherness' to provide oppositional political meaning, legitimacy, and immediacy when they are accused of lacking concrete relevance. Very few African-American intellectuals have talked or written about postmodernism. At a dinner party I talked about trying to grapple with the significance of postmodernism for contemporary black experience. It was one of those social gatherings where only one other black person was present. The setting quickly became a field of contestation. I was told by the other black person that I was wasting my time, that 'this stuff does not relate in any way to what's happening with black people.' Speaking in the presence of a group of white onlookers, staring at us as though this encounter were staged for their benefit, we engaged in a passionate discussion about black experience. Apparently, no one sympathized with my insistence that racism is perpetuated when blackness is associated solely with concrete gut level experience conceived as either opposing or having no connection to abstract thinking and the production of critical theory. The idea that there is no meaningful connection between black experience and critical thinking about aesthetics or culture must be continually interrogated.

My defense of postmodernism and its relevance to black folks sounded good, but I worried that I lacked conviction, largely because I approach the subject cautiously and with suspicion.

Disturbed not so much by the 'sense' of postmodernism but by the conventional language used when it is written or talked about and by those who speak it, I find myself on the outside of the discourse looking in. As a discursive practice it is dominated primarily by the voices of white male intellectuals and/or academic elites who speak to and about one another with coded familiarity. Reading and studying their writing to understand postmodernism in its multiple manifestations, I appreciate it but feel little inclination to ally myself with the academic hierarchy and exclusivity pervasive in the movement today.

Critical of most writing on postmodernism, I perhaps am more conscious of the way in which the focus on 'Otherness and difference' that is often alluded to in these works seems to have little concrete impact as an analysis or standpoint that might change the nature and direction of postmodernist theory. Since much of this theory has been constructed in reaction to and against high modernism, there is seldom any mention of black experience or writings by black people in this work, specifically black women (though in more recent work one may see a reference to Cornel West, the black male scholar who has most engaged postmodernist discourse). Even if an aspect of black culture is the subject of postmodern critical writing, the works cited will usually be those of black men. A work that comes immediately to mind is Andrew Ross's chapter 'Hip, and the Long Front of Color' in *No Respect*: *Intellectuals and Popular Culture*; while it is an interesting reading, it constructs black culture as though black women have had no role in black cultural production. At the end of Meaghan Morris' discussion of postmodernism in her collection of essays *The Pirate's Fiance*: *Feminism and Postmodernism*, she provides a bibliography of works by women, identifying them as important contributions to a discourse on postmodernism that offer new insight as well as challenging male theoretical hegemony. Even though many of the works do not directly address postmodernism, they address similar concerns. There are no references to works by black women.

The failure to recognize a critical black presence in the culture and in most scholarship and writing on postmodernism compels a black reader, particularly a black female reader, to interrogate her interest in a subject where those who discuss and write about it seem not to know black women exist or even to consider the possibility that we might be somewhere writing or saying something that should be listened to, or producing art that should be seen, heard, approached with intellectual seriousness. This is especially the case with works that go on and on about the way in which postmodernist discourse has opened up a theoretical terrain where 'difference and Otherness' can be considered legitimate issues in the academy. Confronting both the absence of recognition of black female presence that much postmodernist theory re-inscribes and the resistance on the part of most black folks to hearing about real connection between postmodernism and black experience, I enter a discourse, a practice, where there may be no ready audience for my words, no clear listener, uncertain then, that my voice can or will be heard.

During the sixties, [the] black power movement was influenced by perspectives that could easily be labeled modernist. Certainly many of the ways black folks addressed issues of identity conformed to a modernist universalizing agenda. There was little critique of patriarchy as a master narrative among black militants. Despite the fact that black power ideology reflected a modernist sensibility, these elements were soon rendered irrelevant as militant protest was stifled by a powerful, repressive postmodern state. The period directly after the black power movement was a time when major news magazines carried articles with cocky headlines like 'Whatever Happened to Black America?' This response was an ironic reply to the aggressive, unmet demand by decentered, marginalized black subjects who had at least momentarily successfully demanded a hearing, who had made it possible for black liberation to be on the national political agenda. In the wake of the black power movement, after so many rebels were slaughtered and lost, many of these voices were silenced by a repressive state; others became inarticulate. It has become necessary to find new avenues to transmit the messages of black liberation struggle, new ways to talk about racism and other politics of domination. Radical postmodernist practice, most powerfully conceptualized as a 'politics of difference,' should incorporate the voices of displaced, marginalized, exploited, and oppressed black people. It is sadly ironic that the contemporary discourse which talks the most about heterogeneity, the decentered subject, declaring breakthroughs that allow recognition of Otherness, still directs its critical voice primarily to a specialized audience that shares a common language rooted in the very master narratives it claims to challenge. If radical postmodernist thinking is to have a transformative impact, then a critical break with the notion of 'authority' as 'mastery over' must not simply be a rhetorical device. It must be reflected in habits of being, including styles of writing as well as chosen subject matter. Third world nationals, elites, and white critics who passively absorb white supremacist thinking, and therefore never notice or look at black people on the streets or at their jobs, who render us invisible with their gaze in all areas of daily life, are not likely to produce liberatory theory that will challenge racist domination, or promote a breakdown in traditional ways of seeing and thinking about reality, ways of constructing aesthetic theory and practice. [. . .]

The postmodern critique of 'identity', though relevant for renewed black liberation struggle, is often posed in ways that are problematic. Given a pervasive politics of white supremacy which seeks to prevent the formation of radical black subjectivity, we cannot cavalierly dismiss a concern with identity politics. Any critic exploring the radical potential of postmodernism as it relates to racial difference and racial domination would need to consider the implications of a critique of identity for oppressed groups. Many of us are struggling to find new strategies of resistance. We must engage decolonization as a critical practice if we are to have meaningful chances of survival even as we must simultaneously cope with the loss of political grounding which made radical activism more possible. I am thinking here about the postmodernist critique of essentialism as it pertains to the construction of 'identity' as one example.

[. . .]

Considering that it is as subject one comes to voice, then the postmodernist focus on the critique of identity appears at first glance to threaten and close down the possibility that this discourse and practice will allow those who have suffered the crippling effects of colonization and domination to gain or regain a hearing. Even if this sense of threat and the fear it evokes are based on a misunderstanding of the postmodernist political project, they nevertheless shape responses. It never surprises me when black folks respond to the critique of essentialism, especially when it denies the validity of identity politics by saying, 'Yeah, it's easy to give up identity, when you got one.' Should we not be suspicious of postmodern critiques of the 'subject' when they surface at a historical moment when many subjugated people feel themselves coming to voice for the first time. Though an apt and often-times appropriate comeback, it does not really intervene in the discourse in a way that alters and transforms.

Criticisms of directions in postmodern thinking should not obscure insights it may offer that open up our understanding of African-American experience. The critique of essentialism encouraged by postmodernist thought is useful for African-Americans concerned with reformulating outmoded notions of identity. We have too long had imposed upon us from both the outside and the inside a narrow, constricting notion of blackness. Postmodern critiques of essentialism which challenge notions of universality and static over-determined identity within mass culture and mass consciousness can open up new possibilities for the construction of self and the assertion of agency.

Employing a critique of essentialism allows African-Americans to acknowledge the way in which class mobility has altered collective black experience so that racism does not necessarily have the same impact on our lives. Such a critique allows us to affirm multiple black identities, varied black experience. It also challenges colonial imperialist paradigms of black identity which represent blackness one-dimensionally in ways that reinforce and sustain white supremacy. This discourse created the idea of the 'primitive' and promoted the notion of an 'authentic' experience, seeing as 'natural' those expressions of black life which conformed to a pre-existing pattern or stereotype. Abandoning essentialist notions would be a serious challenge to racism. Contemporary African-American resistance struggle must be rooted in a process of decolonization that continually opposes re-inscribing notions of 'authentic' black identity. This critique should not be made synonymous with a dismissal of the struggle of oppressed and exploited peoples to make ourselves subjects. Nor should it deny that in certain circumstances this experience affords us a privileged critical location from which to speak. This is not a re-inscription of modernist master narratives of authority which privilege some voices by denying voice to others. Part of our struggle for radical black subjectivity is the quest to find ways to construct self and identity that are oppositional and liberatory. The unwillingness to critique essentialism on the part of many African-Americans is rooted in the fear that it will cause folks to lose sight of the specific history and experience of African-Americans and the unique sensibilities and culture that arise from that experience. An adequate response to this concern is to critique essentialism while emphasizing the significance of 'the authority of experience.' There is a radical difference between a repudiation of the idea that there is a black 'essence' and recognition of the way black identity has been specifically constituted in the experience of exile and struggle.

When black folks critique essentialism, we are empowered to recognize multiple experiences of black identity that are the lived conditions which make diverse cultural productions possible. When this diversity is ignored, it is easy to see black folks as falling into two categories: nationalist or assimilationist, black-identified or white-identified. Coming to terms with the impact of postmodernism for black experience, particularly as it changes our sense of identity, means that we must and can rearticulate the basis for collective bonding. Given the various crises facing African-Americans (economic, spiritual, escalating racial violence, etc.), we are compelled by circumstance to reassess our relationship to popular culture and resistance struggle. Many of us are as reluctant to face this task as many non-black postmodern thinkers who focus theoretically on the issue of 'difference' are to confront the issue of race and racism.

Music is the cultural product created by African-Americans that has most attracted postmodern theorists. It is rarely acknowledged that there is far greater censorship and restriction of other forms of cultural production by black folks – literary, critical writing, etc. Attempts on the part of editors and publishing houses to control and manipulate the representation of black culture, as well as the desire to promote the creation of products that will attract the widest audience, limit in a crippling and stifling way the kind of work many black folks feel we can do and still receive recognition. Using myself as an example, that creative writing I do which I consider to be most reflective of a postmodern oppositional sensibility, work that is abstract, fragmented, non-linear narrative, is constantly rejected by editors and publishers. It does not conform to the type of writing they think black women should be doing or the type of writing they believe will sell. Certainly I do not think I am the only black person engaged in forms of cultural production, especially experimental ones, who is constrained by the lack of an audience for certain kinds of work. It is important for postmodern thinkers and theorists to constitute themselves as an audience for such work. To do this they must assert power and privilege within the space of critical writing to open up the field so that it will be more inclusive. To change the exclusionary practice of postmodern critical discourse is to enact a postmodernism of resistance. Part of this intervention entails black intellectual participation in the discourse.

In his essay 'Postmodernism and Black America,' Cornel West suggests that black intellectuals 'are marginal – usually languishing at the interface of Black and white cultures or thoroughly ensconced in Euro-American settings.' He cannot see this group as potential producers of radical postmodernist thought. While I generally agree with this assessment, black intellectuals must proceed with the understanding that we are not condemned to the margins. The way we work and what we do can determine whether or not what we produce will be meaningful to a wider audience, one that includes all classes of black people. West suggests that black intellectuals lack 'any organic link with most of Black life' and that this 'diminishes their value to Black resistance.' This statement bears traces of essentialism. Perhaps we need to focus more on those black intellectuals, however rare our presence, who do not feel this lack and whose work is primarily directed towards the enhancement of black critical consciousness and the strengthening of our collective capacity to engage in meaningful resistance struggle. Theoretical ideas and critical thinking need not be transmitted solely in written work or solely in the academy. While I work in a predominantly white institution, I remain intimately and passionately engaged with [the] black community. It's not like I'm going to talk about writing and thinking about postmodernism with other academics and/or intellectuals and not discuss these ideas with underclass non-academic black folks who are family, friends, and comrades. Since I have not broken the ties that bind me to [the] underclass poor black community, I have seen that knowledge, especially that which enhances daily life and strengthens our capacity to survive, can be shared. It means that critics, writers, and academics have to give the same critical attention to nurturing and cultivating our ties to [the] black community that we give to writing articles, teaching, and lecturing. Here again I am really talking about cultivating habits of being that reinforce awareness that knowledge can be disseminated and shared on a number of fronts. The extent to which knowledge is made available, accessible, etc. depends on the nature of one's political commitments.

Postmodern culture with its decentered subject can be the space where ties are severed or it can provide the occasion for new and varied forms of bonding. To some extent, ruptures, surfaces, contextuality, and a host of other happenings create gaps that make space for oppositional practices which no longer require intellectuals to be confined by narrow separate spheres with no meaningful connection to the world of the everyday. Much postmodern engagement with culture emerges from the yearning to do intellectual work that connects with habits of being, forms of artistic expression, and aesthetics that inform the daily life of writers and scholars as well as a mass population. On the terrain of culture, one can participate in critical dialogue with the uneducated poor, the black underclass who are thinking about aesthetics. One can talk about what we are seeing, thinking, or listening to; a space is there for critical exchange. It's exciting to think, write, talk about, and create art that reflects passionate engagement with popular culture, because this may very well be 'the' central future location of resistance struggle, a meeting place where new and radical happenings can occur.

Judith Butler

CONTINGENT FOUNDATIONS
Feminism and the question of 'postmodernism'

Judith Butler, although not a historian, is an internationally acclaimed theorist of feminism, gender and sexuality whose critical re-readings of the sex/gender distinction and of subjectivity have exercised a strong influence upon feminists across many academic disciplines. She has published extensively, notably *Gender Trouble: Feminism and the Subversion of Identity* (1990), *Bodies that Matter: On the Discursive Limits of 'Sex'* (1993) and *Excitable Speech: A Politics of the Performative* (1997). Reading 12 is a short extract taken from an essay in a collection that Butler edited with Joan Scott entitled *Feminists Theorize the Political* (1992). I include it here because it tackles the concerns of many feminists surrounding postmodernism's perceived denial of the agency of the subject, as discussed in the Introduction. Butler explains that to assume the agency of the subject in advance is itself an act of political power because 'subjects are constituted through exclusion'. (In this *Reader* for example we have already seen the constitution of the normative white, heterosexual female subject through the exclusion of black, Third World and lesbian women, among others.) It is not a case of postmodernism desiring to eliminate the subject and her opportunity for political agency, argues Butler, for 'to call a presupposition into question is not to do away with it'. Rather, a postmodernist reading of (feminist) agency seeks to free the (female) subject from its 'metaphysical lodgings' into a future myriad of as yet unimagined opportunities for political agency. For Butler, therefore, the discursively constituted subject might well enable an *enhanced* sense of agency. And anyway, she asks, why would feminists wish to continue working with the same epistemological and ontological premises that have so successfully established the subordination of women?

[. . .]

W E MAY BE TEMPTED to think that to assume the subject in advance
is necessary in order to safeguard the *agency* of the subject. But to claim that
the subject is constituted is not to claim that it is determined; on the contrary, the
constituted character of the subject is the very precondition of its agency. For what
is it that enables a purposive and significant reconfiguration of cultural and political
relations, if not a relation that can be turned against itself, reworked, resisted?
Do we need to assume theoretically from the start a subject with agency *before* we
can articulate the terms of a significant social and political task of transformation,
resistance, radical democratization? If we do not offer in advance the theoretical
guarantee of that agent, are we doomed to give up transformation and meaningful
political practice? My suggestion is that agency belongs to a way of thinking about
persons as instrumental actors who confront an external political field. But if we
agree that politics and power exist already at the level at which the subject and its
agency are articulated and made possible, then agency can be *presumed* only at the
cost of refusing to inquire into its construction. Consider that 'agency' has no formal
existence or, if it does, it has no bearing on the question at hand. In a sense, the
epistemological model that offers us a pregiven subject or agent is one that refuses
to acknowledge that *agency is always and only a political prerogative.* As such, it seems
crucial to question the conditions of its possibility, not to take it for granted as an
a priori guarantee. We need instead to ask, what possibilities of mobilization are
produced on the basis of existing configurations of discourse and power? Where
are the possibilities of reworking that very matrix of power by which we are constituted, of reconstituting the legacy of that constitution, and of working against each
other those processes of regulation that can destabilize existing power regimes? For
if the subject is constituted by power, that power does not cease at the moment
the subject is constituted, for that subject is never fully constituted, but is subjected
and produced time and again. That subject is neither a ground nor a product, but
the permanent possibility of a certain resignifying process, one which gets detoured
and stalled through other mechanisms of power, but which is power's own possibility of being reworked. It is not enough to say that the subject is invariably engaged
in a political field; that phenomenological phrasing misses the point that the subject
is an accomplishment regulated and produced in advance. And is as such fully
political; indeed, perhaps *most* political at the point in which it is claimed to be
prior to politics itself. To perform this kind of Foucaultian critique of the subject
is not to do away with the subject or pronounce its death, but merely to claim that
certain versions of the subject are politically insidious.

For the subject to be a pregiven point of departure for politics is to defer the
question of the political construction and regulation of the subject itself; for it is
important to remember that subjects are constituted through exclusion, that is,
through the creation of a domain of deauthorized subjects, presubjects, figures of
abjection, populations erased from view. This becomes clear, for instance, within
the law when certain qualifications must first be met in order to be, quite literally,
a claimant in sex discrimination or rape cases. Here it becomes quite urgent to
ask, who qualifies as a 'who,' what systematic structures of disempowerment make
it impossible for certain injured parties to invoke the 'I' effectively within a court
of law? Or less overtly, in a social theory like Albert Memmi's *The Colonizer and*

the Colonized, an otherwise compelling call for radical enfranchisement, the category of women falls into neither category, the oppressor or the oppressed.[1] How do we theorize the exclusion of women from the category of the oppressed? Here the construction of subject-positions works to exclude women from the description of oppression, and this constitutes a different kind of oppression, one that is effected by the very *erasure* that grounds the articulation of the emancipatory subject. As Joan Scott makes clear in *Gender and the Politics of History*, once it is understood that subjects are formed through exclusionary operations, it becomes politically necessary to trace the operations of that construction and erasure.[2]

The above sketches in part a Foucaultian reinscription of the subject, an effort to resignify the subject as a site of resignification. As a result, it is not a 'bidding farewell' to the subject *per se*, but, rather, a call to rework that notion outside the terms of an epistemological given. But perhaps Foucault is not really postmodern; after all, his is an analytics of *modern* power. There is, of course, talk about the death of the subject, but *which* subject is that? And what is the status of the utterance that announces its passing? What speaks now that the subject is dead? That there is a speaking seems clear, for how else could the utterance be heard? So clearly, the death of that subject is not the end of agency, of speech, or of political debate. There is the refrain that, just now, when women are beginning to assume the place of subjects, postmodern positions come along to announce that the subject is dead (there is a difference between positions of poststructuralism which claim that the subject *never* existed, and postmodern positions which claim that the subject *once* had integrity, but no longer does). Some see this as a conspiracy against women and other disenfranchised groups who are now only beginning to speak on their own behalf. But what precisely is meant by this, and how do we account for the very strong criticisms of the subject as an instrument of Western imperialist hegemony theorized by Gloria Anzaldua,[3] Gayatri Spivak[4] and various theorists of postcoloniality? Surely there is a caution offered here, that in the very struggle toward enfranchisement and democratization, we might adopt the very models of domination by which we were oppressed, not realizing that one way that domination works is through the regulation and production of subjects. Through what exclusions has the feminist subject been constructed, and how do those excluded domains return to haunt the 'integrity' and 'unity' of the feminist 'we'? And how is it that the very category, the subject, the 'we,' that is supposed to be presumed for the purpose of solidarity, produces the very factionalization it is supposed to quell? Do women want to become subjects on the model which requires and produces an anterior region of abjection, or must feminism become a process which is self-critical about the processes that produce and destabilize identity categories? To take the construction of the subject as a political problematic is not the same as doing away with the subject; to deconstruct the subject is not to negate or throw away the concept; on the contrary, deconstruction implies only that we suspend all commitments to that to which the term, 'the subject,' refers, and that we consider the linguistic functions it serves in the consolidation and concealment of authority. To deconstruct is not to negate or to dismiss, but to call into question and, perhaps most importantly, to open up a term, like the subject, to a reusage or redeployment that previously has not been authorized.

Within feminism, it seems as if there is some political necessity to speak as and for *women*, and I would not contest that necessity. Surely, that is the way in which representational politics operates, and in this country, lobbying efforts are virtually impossible without recourse to identity politics. So we agree that demonstrations and legislative efforts and radical movements need to make claims in the name of women.

But this necessity needs to be reconciled with another. The minute that the category of women is invoked as *describing* the constituency for which feminism speaks, an internal debate invariably begins over what the descriptive content of that term will be. There are those who claim that there is an ontological specificity to women as childbearers that forms the basis of a specific legal and political interest in representation, and then there are others who understand maternity to be a social relation that is, under current social circumstances, the specific and cross-cultural situation of women. And there are those who seek recourse to [Carol] Gilligan and others to establish a feminine specificity that makes itself clear in women's communities or ways of knowing. But every time that specificity is artic-ulated, there is resistance and factionalization within the very constituency that is supposed to be *unified* by the articulation of its common element. In the early 1980s, the feminist 'we' rightly came under attack by women of color who claimed that the 'we' was invariably white, and that that 'we' that was meant to solidify the movement was the very source of a painful factionalization. The effort to charac-terize a feminine specificity through recourse to maternity, whether biological or social, produced a similar factionalization and even a disavowal of feminism alto-gether. For surely all women are not mothers; some cannot be, some are too young or too old to be, some choose not to be, and for some who are mothers, that is not necessarily the rallying point of their politicization in feminism.

I would argue that any effort to give universal or specific content to the category of women, presuming that that guarantee of solidarity is required *in advance*, will necessarily produce factionalization, and that 'identity' as a point of departure can never hold as the solidifying ground of a feminist political movement. Identity categories are never merely descriptive, but always normative, and as such, exclu-sionary. This is not to say that the term 'women' ought not to be used, or that we ought to announce the death of the category. On the contrary, if feminism pre-supposes that 'women' designates an undesignatable field of differences, one that cannot be totalized or summarized by a descriptive identity category, then the very term becomes a site of permanent openness and resignifiability. I would argue that the rifts among women over the content of the term ought to be safeguarded and prized, indeed, that this constant rifting ought to be affirmed as the ungrounded ground of feminist theory. To deconstruct the subject of feminism is not, then, to censure its usage, but, on the contrary, to release the term into a future of multiple significations, to emancipate it from the maternal or racialist ontologies to which it has been restricted, and to give it play as a site where unanticipated meanings might come to bear.

Paradoxically, it may be that only through releasing the category of women from a fixed referent that something like 'agency' becomes possible. For if the term permits of a resignification, if its referent is not fixed, then possibilities for new configurations of the term become possible. In a sense, what women signify has been taken for granted for too long, and what has been fixed as the 'referent' of the term has been 'fixed,' normalized, immobilized, paralyzed in positions of sub-ordination. In effect, the signified has been conflated with the referent, whereby a set of meanings have been taken to inhere in the real nature of women themselves. To recast the referent as the signified, and to authorize or safeguard the category of women as a site of possible resignifications is to expand the possibilities of what it means to be a woman and in this sense to condition and enable an enhanced sense of agency. [. . .]

In the final part of this paper, I would like to turn to a related question, one that emerges from the concern that a feminist theory cannot proceed without presuming the materiality of women's bodies, the materiality of sex. The chant of antipostmodernism runs, if everything is discourse, then is there no reality to bodies? How do we understand the material violence that women suffer? In responding to this criticism, I would like to suggest that the very formulation misconstrues the critical point.

I don't know what postmodernism is, but I do have some sense of what it might mean to subject notions of the body and materiality to a deconstructive critique. To deconstruct the concept of matter or that of bodies is not to negate or refuse either term. To deconstruct these terms means, rather, to continue to use them, to repeat them, to repeat them subversively, and to displace them from the contexts in which they have been deployed as instruments of oppressive power. Here it is of course necessary to state quite plainly that the options for theory are not exhausted by *presuming* materiality, on the one hand, and *negating* materiality, on the other. It is my purpose to do precisely neither of these. To call a presupposition into question is not the same as doing away with it; rather, it is to free it up from its metaphysical lodgings in order to occupy and to serve very different political aims. To problematize the matter of bodies entails in the first instance a loss of epistemological certainty, but this loss of certainty does not necessarily entail political nihilism as its result.[5]

[. . .]

If there is a fear that, by no longer being able to take for granted the subject, its gender, its sex, or its materiality, feminism will founder, it might be wise to consider the political consequences of keeping in their place the very premises that have tried to secure our subordination from the start.

Notes

1 'At the height of the revolt,' Memmi writes, 'the colonized still bears the traces and lessons of prolonged cohabitation (just as the smile or movements of a wife, even during divorce proceedings, remind one strangely of those of her husband).' Here Memmi sets up an analogy which presumes that colonizer and colonized exist in a parallel and separate relation to the divorcing husband and wife. The analogy simultaneously and paradoxically suggests the feminization of the colonized, where the colonized is presumed to be the subject of men, and the exclusion of the women from the category of the colonized subject. Albert Memmi, *The Colonizer and the Colonized* (Boston: Beacon Press, 1965), p. 129.

2 Joan W. Scott, *Gender and the Politics of History* (New York: Columbia University Press), 1988, introduction.

3 Gloria Anzaldua, *La Frontera/Borderlands* (San Francisco: Spinsters Ink, 1988).

4   Gayatri Spivak, 'Can the Subaltern Speak?' in *Marxism and the Interpretation of Culture*, eds. Nelson and Grossberg (Chicago: University of Illinois Press, 1988).

5   The body posited as prior to the sign, is always *posited* or *signified* as prior. This signification works through producing an *effect* of its own procedure, the body that it nevertheless and simultaneously claims to discover as that which *precedes* signification. If the body signified as prior to signification is an effect of signification, then the mimetic or representational status of language, which claims that signs follow bodies as their necessary mirrors, is not mimetic at all; on the contrary, it is productive, constitutive, one might even argue *performative*, inasmuch as this signifying act produces the body that it then claims to find prior to any and all signification.

PART III

Searching for the subject

Lesbian history

Lillian Faderman

WHO HID LESBIAN HISTORY?

'Heterocentric biographies' of lesbian women 'are generally not to be trusted' declares Lillian Faderman in this article which first appeared in the *Journal of Lesbian Studies* in 1979. I have included this brief extract by Faderman because it illustrates very well the various 'techniques of bowdlerization and avoidance of the obvious' utilised by post-sexological, post-Freudian biographers of women who engaged in intimate friendships with other women. Of all the various methods of the effacement of lesbianism, '*cherchez l'homme*' (hunting for the elusive male lover in a woman's life) has been, according to Faderman, the most common. Whether or not twentieth-century biographers have been well intentioned (concerned to 'save' the reputation of their female subject) or downright homophobic is of little interest to Faderman; either way the oppressive weight of intellectual and methodological heterocentrism continues to distort extant historical records of affection and love between women. Faderman provides four examples here of the erasure of the 'lesbian-like' behaviour of women such as Lady Mary Montagu, Anna Seward, Mary Wollstonecraft and Emily Dickinson. The extract provides some sense of the enormity of the recuperative task that faced, and still faces, the historian of lesbianism. Even in these more perceptive days argues Faderman, lesbian and feminist scholars must remain vigilant in their reading of primary source materials to ensure that the biographies that are produced are 'divested of the heterocentric perspective'.

BEFORE THE RISE of the lesbian–feminist movement in the early 1970s, twentieth-century women writers with great ambitions were generally intimidated into silence about the lesbian experiences in their lives. In their literature, they gave male personae the voice of their most autobiographical characters, and they were thus permitted to love other women; or they disguised their homoerotic subject matter in code which is sometimes all but unreadable, or when they wrote of love most feelingly and even laid down rules for loving well, as Margaret Anderson did, they left out gender altogether. We cannot blame them for not providing us with a clear picture of what it was like for a woman to love other women in their day. If they had they would have borne the brunt of anti-lesbian prejudice which followed society's enlightenment by late-nineteenth-century and early-twentieth-century sexologists about love between women,[1] and they knew that if they wished to be taken seriously they had to hide their arrested development and neuropathic natures. But we might expect that before the twentieth century, before love between women was counted among the diseases, women would have had little reason to disguise their emotional attachments; therefore, they should have left a record of their love of other women. And they did. However, it is impossible to discover that record by reading what most of their twentieth-century biographers have had to say about their lives.

While pre-twentieth century women would not have thought that their intensest feelings toward other women needed to be hidden, their twentieth-century biographers, who were brought up in a post-Krafft-Ebing, Havelock Ellis, Sigmund Freud world, did think that, and they often altered their subjects' papers. Other twentieth-century biographers have refused to accept that their subjects 'suffered from homosexuality,' and have discounted the most intense expressions of love between their subjects and other women. And where it was impossible to ignore the fact that their subjects were despondent over some love relationship, many twentieth-century biographers frantically searched for some hidden man who must have been the object of their subject's affection, even though a beloved woman was in plain view. These techniques of bowdlerization, avoidance of the obvious, and *cherchez l'homme* appear in countless pre-1970s biographies about women of whom there is reason to suspect lesbian attachments.

In our heterocentric society, the latter technique is the most frequent. What can it mean when a woman expresses great affection for another woman? It means that she is trying to get a man through that woman. What can it mean when a woman grieves for years over the marriage or death of a woman friend? It means that she is really unhappy because she had hoped to procure her friend's husband for herself, or she is unhappy because there must have been another man somewhere in the background who coincidentally jilted her at the same time—only all concrete evidence has been lost to posterity. So why did Lady Mary Montagu write to Anne Wortley in 1709 letters which reveal a romantic passion?

> My dear, dear, adieu! I am entirely yours, and wish nothing more than it may be some time or other in my power to convince you that there is nobody dearer (to me) than yourself. . . .[2]
>
> I cannot bear to be accused of coldness by one whom I shall love all my life. . . . You will think I forget you, who are never out of my thoughts. . . . I esteem you as I ought in esteeming you above the world.[3]
>
> . . . your friendship is the only happiness of my life; and whenever I lose it, I have nothing to do but to take one of my garters and search for a convenient beam.[4]
>
> Nobody ever was so entirely, so faithfully yours. . . . I put in your lovers, for I don't allow it possible for a man to be so sincere as I am.[5]

Lady Mary's 1920s biographer admits that Mary's letters to Anne carry 'heart-burnings and reproaches and apologies' which might make us, the readers, 'fancy ourselves in Lesbos,'[6] but, she assures us, Lady Mary knew that Anne's brother, Edward, would read what she wrote to Anne, 'and she tried to shine in these letters for him.'[7] Thus, Mary was not writing of her love for Anne; she was only showing Edward how smart, noble, and sensitive she was, so that he might be interested in her.

Why did Anna Seward, the eighteenth-century poet, grieve for thirty years over the marriage of Honora Sneyd? Why in a sonnet of 1773 does she accuse Honora of killing 'more than life—e'en all that makes life dear'?[8] Why in another does she beg for merciful sleep which would 'charm to rest the thoughts of whence, or how/Vanish'd that priz'd Affection'?[9] Why in still another poem does she weep because the 'plighted love' of the woman she called 'my life's adorner'[10] has now 'changed to cold disdain'?[11] Well, speculates her 1930s biographer, it was probably because Anna Seward wished to marry the recently widowed Robert Edgeworth (whom Honora ensnared) herself. After all, 'She was thirty years old— better suited to him in age and experience than Honora. Was she jealous of the easy success of [Honora]? Would she have snatched away, if she could have done so, the mature yet youthful bridegroom, so providentially released from his years of bondage?'[12]

But surely such distortions could not be made by a biographer of Mary Wollstonecraft. Even her husband, William Godwin, admitted in his memoirs of her that Mary's love for Fanny Blood had been 'so fervent, as for years to have constituted the ruling passion of her mind.'[13] But what was regarded as a fact of life by an eighteenth-century husband, boggles the mind of a twentieth-century scholar. For example, how was one biographer of the early 1950s to deal with the information that in 1785 Mary underwent a terrible depression and that she complained in a letter to Fanny Blood's brother, George, 'My harassed mind will in time wear out my body. . . . I have lost all relish for life—and my almost broken heart is only cheered by the prospect of death. . . . I almost hate the Green [her last home with Fanny] for it seems that grave of all my comforts.'?[14] The biographer states himself that at the Green Fanny's health worsened and she could no longer teach, and for that reason Mary urged her to marry a man who would take her to a warm climate where she might recover. Then he asks, quoting the above letter to George Blood, 'What had happened [to cause her great depression]? Surely her father's difficulties could not have suddenly plunged her into such a despondent state; nor could loneliness for Fanny or George.'[15] His explanation is that Mary must have been madly in love with the Reverend Joshua Waterhouse and had been spurned by him. The biographer admits that there is no evidence he can offer to prove his hypothesis, and even that 'On the surface Waterhouse seems like the last man in the world who would have attracted Mary Wollstonecraft.' But he was the only man around at the time so 'apparently he did.'[16] 'Something drastic,' the biographer points out, must have happened 'to provoke such despair,' and the loss of a much-loved woman friend cannot be seen as 'drastic' by a heterocentric scholar.

When there is no proof that a subject was involved in a heterosexual relationship, such biographers have been happy enough to accept circumstantial evidence rather than acknowledge the power of a same-sex attachment. Characteristically, the same Wollstonecraft scholar quotes a letter to George Blood which Mary wrote six months after Fanny's death ('My poor heart still throbs with selfish anguish.

It is formed for friendship and confidence—yet how often it is wounded') and then points out that the next sixteen lines have been obliterated by a later hand and suggests that they must have referred to her affair with Waterhouse. 'Surely the censor did not go to such pains to conceal Mary's lamentations on the death of her friends,' he asserts. It must have been Mary's love of a man the censor was trying to hide.[17] However, considering Godwin's complete honesty regarding Mary's affairs with Fuseli, Imlay, and himself, it is doubtful that a considerate censor would wish to spare her the embarrassment of one more youthful affair. What is more likely is that the letter was censored by someone from our century, aware of the twentieth-century stigma regarding lesbianism, who wished to spare Mary that more serious accusation.

Despite that biographer's flimsy proof of the Waterhouse affair, subsequent Wollstonecraft biographers, uncomfortable with the evidence of her attachment to Fanny, have been happy to accept Waterhouse as fact. The myth is even propagated in a 1970s biography of Wollstonecraft by a woman. After discussing Mary's attachment to Fanny and pointedly distinguishing it from 'lesbianism,' she introduces Mary's 'affair' with Waterhouse with the statement, 'In spite of these emotions and professions [to Fanny], a certain secret disloyalty to Fanny did take place. It is rather a relief to discover it [sic].'[18]

The *cherchez l'homme* technique has been used most frequently by biographers of Emily Dickinson who have filled up tomes looking for the poet's elusive lover and have come up with no fewer than ten candidates, generally with the vaguest bits of 'evidence.' Concrete evidence that the ruling passion of Dickinson's life may well have been Sue Gilbert was eradicated from Dickinson's published letters and has become available only within the last couple of decades through Thomas Johnson's complete edition of her correspondence.[19] The earlier publications of a sizable number of Dickinson's letters was the work of her niece, Martha Dickinson Bianchi, the author of *The Life and Letters of Emily Dickinson* (1924) and *Emily Dickinson Face to Face* (1932). Bianchi, a post-Freudian, felt compelled to hide what her aunt expressed without self-consciousness. Therefore, Bianchi reproduced a February 16, 1852 (Johnson date) letter to Sue thus:

> Sometimes I shut my eyes and shut my heart towards you and try hard to forget you, but you'll never go away. Susie, forgive me, forget all that I say.[20]

What she did not produce of that letter tells a much more potent story:

> Sometimes I shut my eyes, and shut my heart towards you, and try hard to forget you because you grieve me so, but you'll never go away, Oh, you never will—say, Susie, promise me again, and I will smile faintly—and take up my little cross of sad—*sad* separation. How vain it seems to *write*, when one knows how to feel—how much more near and dear to sit beside you, talk with you, hear the tones of your voice; so hard to 'deny thyself, and take up thy cross, and follow me'!—give me strength, Susie, write me of hope and love, and of hearts that *endured*, and great was their reward of 'Our Father who art in Heaven.' I don't

know how I shall bear it, when the gentle spring comes; if she should come and see me and talk to me of you, Oh it would surely kill me! While the frost clings to the windows, and the World is stern and drear; this absence is easier; the Earth mourns too, for all her little birds; but when they all come back again, and she sings and is so merry— pray, what will become of me? Susie, forgive me, forget all that I say. . . . [. . .]

Sue Gilbert was later to marry Austin Dickinson, Emily's brother, and Martha Dickinson Bianchi was the daughter of Sue and Austin. As anxious as she was to prove that Sue played a great part in making Emily a poet and to show that they were the closest of friends, she was even more anxious to prove that Emily and Sue were *only* friends. Thus, she includes in *Face to Face* an affectionate note that Emily sent Sue on June 27, 1852 (Johnson date):

> Susie, will you indeed come home next Saturday? Shall I indeed behold you, not 'darkly, but face to face' or am I *fancying* so and dreaming blessed dreams from which the day will wake me? I hope for you so much and feel so eager for you—feel I cannot wait. Sometimes I must have Saturday before tomorrow comes.[21]

But what Emily really said in that note, as Johnson shows, places their relationship in quite a different light:

> Susie, will you indeed come home next Saturday, and be my own again, and kiss me as you used to? Shall I indeed behold you, not 'darkly, but face to face' or am I *fancying* so, and dreaming blessed dreams from which the day will wake me? I hope for you so much, and feel so eager for you, feel I *cannot* wait, feel that *now* I must have you—that the expectation once more to see your face again, makes me feel hot and feverish, and my heart beats so fast—I go to sleep at night, and the first thing I know, I am sitting there wide awake, and clasping my hands tightly, and thinking of next Saturday, and 'never a bit' of you. Sometimes I must have Saturday before tomorrow comes.

Where biographers have been too scrupulous to bowdlerize they have nevertheless managed to distort lesbian history by avoiding the obvious. Sometimes this has been done to 'save' the reputations of their subjects (e.g., Emma Stebbins, Alice B. Toklas, and Edith Lewis were the 'companions,' respectively, of Charlotte Cushman, Gertrude Stein, and Willa Cather), although illicit heterosexual affairs are seldom treated with such discretion by even the most sensitive biographers. Sometimes this has been done out of willful ignorance. For example, Amy Lowell so obviously made her 'companion,' Ada Russell, the subject of her most erotic love poetry that even a casual acquaintance could observe it, and Lowell herself admitted 'How could so exact a portrait remain unrecognized?'[22] It did remain unrecognized by those who saw Lowell only as an overweight unmarried woman whose 'sources of inspiration are literary and secondary rather than primarily the expression of emotional experience,'[23] and whose characters thus never breathe, except for those 'few frustrated persons such as the childless old women in "The Doll,"' who share Lowell's 'limited personal experiences.'[24]

Although many biographers of the 1970s have been much more perceptive and honest with regard to their subjects' lesbian loves (e.g., Jean Gould's *Amy: The World of Amy Lowell and the Imagist Movement* [New York: Dodd, Mead, 1975]) and Virginia Spencer Carr's *The Lonely Hunter: A Biography of Carson McCullers* [Garden City, NY: Doubleday, 1975]) we cannot assume that lesbian history will never again be hidden by scholars who live in this heterocentric world. One otherwise careful, contemporary feminist critic totally ignores Margaret Anderson's successive passionate relationships with Jane Heap, Georgette LeBlanc, and Dorothy Caruso, and explains that ambitious women of Anderson's day were forced into loveless existences. But even where lesbian relationships are admitted in biographies of the 1970s, their importance is often discounted. A recent author of an Edna St. Vincent Millay biography squeezes Millay's lesbian relationships into a chapter entitled 'Millay's Childhood and Youth' and organizes each of the subsequent chapters around a male with whom Millay had some contact, all of them ostensibly her lovers. Six who had relatively short contact with her are treated together in a chapter entitled 'Millay's Other Men,' although the author admits in that chapter that three of 'Millay's other men' were homosexual.

This essay no doubt reads like a long complaint. It is. But it is also a warning and a hope. It is as difficult for heterocentric biographers to deal with love between women in their subjects' lives as it is for ethnocentric white scholars to deal with Third World subject matter, and their products are generally not to be trusted. If we wish to know about the lives of women it is vital to get back to their diaries, letters (praying that they have not already been expurgated by some well-meaning heterosexist hand), and any original source material that is available. It is also vital to produce biographies divested of the heterocentric perspective. Women's lives need to be reinterpreted, and we need to do it ourselves.

Notes

1   See my article, 'The Morbidification of Love between Women by Nineteenth Century Sexologists,' *Journal of Homosexuality* 4 (Fall 1978): 73–90.

2   *The Complete Letters of Mary Wortley Montagu*, vol. 1, edited by Robert Halsband (Oxford: Clarendon Press, 1965), 4.

3   Ibid., 5.

4   Ibid., 12.

5   Ibid.

6   Iris Barry, *Portrait of Lady Mary Wortley Montagu* (Indianapolis: Bobbs-Merrill, 1928), 61.

7   Ibid., 54.

8   Walter Scott, ed., *The Poetical Works of Anna Seward with Extracts from Her Literary Correspondence*, volume 3 (Edinburgh: John Ballantyne and Co., 1810), 135.

9   Ibid., vol. 3, 134.

10   Ibid., vol. 1, 76–7.

11   Ibid., vol. 3, 133.

12   Margaret Ashmun, *The Singing Swan: An Account of Anna Seward and Her Acquaintances with Dr. Johnson, Boswell, and Others of Their Time* (New Haven, CT: Yale University Press, 1931), 28–9.

13   William Godwin, *Memoirs of Mary Wollstonecraft*, edited by W. Clark Durant (1798; reprinted London: Constable and Co., 1927), 18.

14   Quoted in Ralph M. Wardle, *Mary Wollstonecraft: A Critical Biography* (Lawrence: University of Kansas Press, 1951), 40–1.

15   Ibid., 41.

16   Ibid., 37.

17   Ibid., 41–2.

18   Claire Tomalin, *The Life and Death of Mary Wollstonecraft* (London: Harcourt Brace Jovanovich, 1974), 18.

19   Thomas Johnson and Theodora Ward, eds., *The Letters of Emily Dickinson* (Cambridge, MA: Harvard University Press, 1958).

20   Martha Dickinson Bianchi, *Emily Dickinson Face to Face* (Boston: Houghton Mifflin, 1932), 184.

21   Ibid., 218. I discuss these letters at greater length in 'Emily Dickinson's Letters to Sue Gilbert,' *Massachusetts Review* 18 (Summer 1977).

22   Letter, John Livingston Lowes, February 13, 1918, in S. Foster Damon, *Amy Lowell: A Chronicle, with Extracts from Her Correspondence* (Boston: Houghton Mifflin, 1935), 441.

23   Hervey Allen, 'Amy Lowell as a Poet,' *Saturday Review of Literature* 3 (February 5, 1927): 558. See also Horace Gregory; *Amy Lowell: Portrait of the Poet in Her Time* (New York: Thomas Nelson and Sons, 1958), 212; and Walter Lippman, 'Miss Lowell and Things,' *New Republic* 6 (March 18, 1916), 178–9.

24   Ibid., 568.

Sheila Jeffreys

DOES IT MATTER IF
THEY DID IT?

Sheila Jeffreys is a radical feminist theorist who has written several books on the history of sexuality, most recently *Unpacking Queer Politics. A Lesbian Feminist Perspective* (2004), and who has been active in lesbian feminist politics since the 1970s. In this article she assesses the merits of sexualised and non-sexualised definitions of lesbianism. Jeffreys begins with an outline of the controversies arising from Faderman's celebrated thesis of romantic female friendships, notably Faderman's ambivalence towards the necessity of 'compulsory genital activity' in any lesbian relationship. According to Jeffreys, many contemporary lesbian women felt betrayed by this desexualised reading of lesbian relations that appeared to undercut the very specificity of their own daily experiences of oppression. Jeffreys also notes the blatant sexual double standard operating in any historical demand for genital proof of lesbianism given the absence of any such requirement for heterosexual historical subjects. Her view of heterosexuality as an 'organizing principle of male supremacy' means that, for Jeffreys, lesbianism is best understood as 'a passionate commitment to women, a culture, a political alternative to . . . male supremacy . . . [which] is more than likely to include a sensual component, which may or may not take a genital form'. Jeffreys concludes with a critical assessment of Faderman's book *The Scotch Verdict* (1985) and suggests that feminists need to continue to interrogate sexualised and non-sexualised readings of lesbian identity in order to challenge male-defined norms of women's sexuality and propose instead an identity that is 'strong, revolutionary and *lesbian*'.

I N H E R B O O K *Surpassing the Love of Men*,[1] Lillian Faderman showed that passionate friendships with other women were a crucial part of the lives of middle-class women in the eighteenth and nineteenth centuries. She, in common with other American feminist historians, found that the diaries and letters of these women would almost inevitably reveal a same-sex friendship which was likely to have involved passionate embraces and kisses, declarations of love, sharing a bed for a night of cuddles and intimacies, and which would last, often, from childhood to old age. These relationships were so socially acceptable to contemporaries that a woman could write to the fiancé of the woman she loved and tell him that she felt just like a husband to his betrothed, and loved her to distraction and could not help but be very jealous. Men tended to see these relationships as very good practice for their future wives in the habit of loving. Sometimes the women friends could not bear to be parted even on the honeymoon and the husband would have to spend his honeymoon with both of them.

To modern eyes the passionate declarations of eternal devotion and descriptions of highly sensual interaction are startling because we have been trained to see such behaviour as indicative of lesbianism and not part of the everyday lifestyle of the majority of married middle-class women. Faderman shows how sexologists in the late nineteenth century started to create a stereotype of the lesbian in which such passionate interactions were included, and how the acceptable form of friendships between women became more and more circumscribed. Strong emotional and physical intimacy was allowed only to those who were classified as lesbian. She attributes this change to the greater necessity of controlling woman which resulted from the development of a really strong women's movement, and social and economic changes which threatened men's power over women. Emotional relationships between women were harmless only when women had no chance to be independent of men, and became dangerous when the possibility of women avoiding heterosexuality became a reality. Faderman's work deservedly earned her many admirers, but it also provoked some critics to a storm of protest. It is important to our understanding of ourselves that we understand what the controversy was all about.

The problem seems to be that Faderman includes these passionate friendships specifically within the history of lesbianism. She assumes that the women involved were unlikely, because of nineteenth-century views on women's lack of an active sexuality, to have engaged in genital contact, and her definition of lesbianism does not include compulsory genital activity:

> 'Lesbian' describes a relationship in which two women's strongest emotions and affections are directed toward each other. Sexual contact may be a part of the relationship to a greater or lesser degree, or it may be entirely absent. By preference the two women spend most of their time together and share most aspects of their lives with each other. 'Romantic friendship' described a similar relationship.[2]

Faderman is aware that the suggestion that lesbian identity need not include genital contact is controversial. She recognises that 'It is no doubt unlikely that many women born into a sex-conscious era can conduct a lesbian relationship today without some sexual exchange. The pressure is on in our culture if we want to be physically and mentally healthy . . . '.[3] She quotes a number of lesbian writers who reject what they see as the male definition of lesbianism as defined by and focused upon genital contact.

In discussions, workshops, on the pages of the *Guardian* and elsewhere, lesbians have voiced hostile reactions to Faderman's assumptions. There seem to be two main grounds for the opposition. One objection is that Faderman has made a false reading of history and has somehow been disloyal to the memories of the women she describes as having passionate friendships by imputing to them lesbianism when they would not have recognised themselves as lesbians. Another is a sense of betrayal. Faderman's definition is seen as watering down lesbianism by playing down the sexual content. An example of a fairly standard attack is an article by Sonja Ruehl in the Women's Press collection *Sex and Love* (1983) in which she dismisses Faderman's work as being of any use to feminist theory because, she says, Faderman 'desexualises' lesbianism.[4]

Ruehl and other critics take a particular contemporary definition of lesbianism – the one which lies closest to the hearts of the male sexologists – and they deny that women's passionate friendships can have anything to do with lesbianism because, not surprisingly, they don't match up to this definition. They want to uphold a particular lesbian identity and subculture which they see as being threatened by admitting those who have not gone through the initiation ceremony of genital contact. (They clearly define 'sex' as genital contact.) All the intense sensual activity, kissing and fondling which nineteenth-century passionate friends went in for is classed as wishy-washy and 'not' lesbianism.

Some of their anxiety is well grounded. It is true that the uniqueness of lesbianism and the lesbian identity has been under threat from the concept of sisterhood. During the 1970s and 1980s lesbians within the women's liberation movement have considered it necessary to play down their passions and sexuality so as not to give offence to the heterosexual women who are still the bulk of the movement; and little attention has been given to lesbianism or any issues connected with it. Lesbianism cannot be subsumed beneath the good feelings of handholding sisterhood. This leaves no space to talk about specifically lesbian oppression and gives us little chance to build up the history and culture of lesbianism which we need for our pride and our survival. In this context Adrienne Rich's idea of the lesbian continuum is problematic; her argument that all women's friendships with women are some shade or gradation of lesbianism inevitably confuses attempts to analyse lesbian oppression.[5] Women who simply have 'best friends' who are women share neither lesbian oppression nor lesbian experience. So long as we keep the definition of lesbianism open enough to include heterosexual women who love their women friends, it will be hard to articulate what is specific about the experience and oppression of lesbians and to develop the strength to fight compulsory heterosexuality and the invisibility of lesbians.

Passionate friendships and the history of lesbianism

However, if we accept that proof of genital contact is required before we may include any relationship between two women in the history of lesbianism, then there is a serious possibility that we will end up with no lesbian history at all. The history of heterosexuality – and that is the only history we have been offered to date – does not rely on proof of genital contact. Men and women are assumed to be heterosexual unless there is 'genital' proof to the contrary. Women who have lived in the same house and slept in the same bed for thirty years have had their lesbianism strongly denied by historians. But men and women who simply take walks together are assumed to be involved in some sort of heterosexual relationship.

If we see the creation of a lesbian history as important then we must be prepared to assert that certain women were involved in relationships which have some relationship to lesbianism, even though in any historical period before the 1920s we are likely to have difficulty locating women who would be recognisably part of a subculture and lesbian identity which would fit with current definitions. It is surely dubious to argue that it is insulting and unfair to identify as lesbian those women who did not see themselves as lesbian. First, if they lived in periods before sexological theories became fashionable, their general frames of reference, as well as their particular views regarding love between women, must necessarily have differed from those now current. Secondly, such an argument assumes that a lesbian identity is of itself shameful; a view not held by lesbians now and not one which should be imputed to women in the past.

Heterosexuality has changed its form too, yet we are prepared to assume women to be heterosexual in the past who had no interest in sexual activity with men and may have endured it with total repugnance. Many nineteenth-century women, so far as we can tell, were in this position. For the married middle-class woman in the nineteenth century, a heterosexual identity based upon a positive choice of sexual activity with men, or indeed upon any concept of desire for men, would have been unintelligible. Can we include these women in the history of heterosexuality?

Heterosexuality is, of course, much more than a sexual practice. It is an institution documented by written statutes and is a cultural universe sustained by, and signified in, countless rituals, histories, art, literature, and religious and social ideology. Trying to pretend that heterosexuality or homosexuality are simply, or mainly, sexual practices, is to ignore politics entirely. There is now an enormous and growing body of published work written by feminist theorists: historians, philosophers, sociologists, literary critics and others, which explains and illustrates the ways in which society is organised to conform to heterosexual stereotypes. Heterosexuality, it becomes clear, is the organising principle of male supremacy.

Since that is so, women who won't take part drift in a limbo or form an identity for themselves which can enable them to survive with a sense of self, a culture and a social life. Lesbianism can therefore never be simply a sexual practice. The genital sexual practices currently identified by many people as characterising lesbianism have been taking place for centuries, for example between prostitutes; but in that context their function has been (and still is) to titillate and excite men. They have also been tried out by women whose commitment to the heterosexual system has never been in doubt. By contrast, lesbianism as understood by lesbian feminists is a passionate commitment to women, a culture, a political alternative to the basic institution of male supremacy, a means through which women have always gained self-respect and pursued their own goals and achievements with the support of other women. It is more than likely to include a sensual component, which may or may not take a genital form.

Whose interests does it serve to regard lesbianism solely as a sexual practice? If lesbianism is reduced to part of a list in sexological textbooks, together with bestiality and paedophilia, the emotional, cultural and political dimensions disappear. This clearly serves the status quo. Lesbianism as a sexual practice is not a threat. If it were, then it would not be the stock in trade of brothels and men's pornography. Lesbianism as an emotional universe which provides an alternative to women from slotting into the heterosexual system, on the other hand, is a threat. It is then anarchic and threatens the organising principle of male supremacy.

'The Scotch Verdict'

With these problems in mind, it becomes crucial to decide how to assess Faderman's second book, *The Scotch Verdict*.[6] The book treats in greater depth an incident given briefly in *Surpassing the Love of Men*. This is the case of Miss Woods and Miss Pirie against Dame Helen Cummings Gordon in Edinburgh in 1811. Dame Cummings Gordon's grandchild (the illegitimate daughter of a Scottish imperialist and an Indian woman) was a pupil at the school run by Woods and Pirie. She told her grandmother that the mistresses had sex together, and Cummings Gordon saw that all the other children were removed from the school and the teachers ruined. Woods and Pirie then brought a case against Cummings Gordon, which they won largely as a result of the inability of the judges to believe that two ladies would do such things. The book includes large chunks from the trial transcripts translated into contemporary English. These offer us tantalising glimpses of how women and girls in the period saw their relationships with each other.

Faderman chooses to rest the book on the interesting question of what Pirie and Woods were doing with each other. Were they involved in genital contact, as some witnesses in the trial suggested? Faderman is certain they were not. Her lover, Ollie, who travelled to Edinburgh with her when Faderman did her research, was just as convinced that they did. I admit to being puzzled by both their versions of events, and to being puzzled as to why the question of whether they had genital contact is a matter of such importance that it needs to be proved or disproved. I'm not sure that it's sufficient subject matter for the detective story that *The Scotch Verdict* becomes. Faderman and Ollie's versions are interspersed amongst Faderman's translations of the trial transcripts.

Faderman considers it unlikely that the two women had genital sex, for the following reasons: they lived in an era when women were likely to repress sexual feelings or at least not interpret them in a genital way; and they were unlikely to have done it (as they were accused of doing) whilst sharing beds with school students. It is quite possible to sympathise with Faderman's belief that they did not have genital sex. What is hard to accept is the energy she devotes to proving this. Here is part of her explanation:

> Almost everything Jane Cumming and Janet Munro (schoolgirls) described had its counterpart in a gesture or remark that was entirely innocuous. Where there was no innocent counterpart it was because Jane Cumming invented that particular detail from a stock of misinformation and half-understood images. These she had gathered from one or two girls at Elgin school, shopkeepers' daughters who had been out in the world before they were sent to learn a trade. . . . From September to November they came to each other's beds more than a dozen times to talk. . . . Sometimes they came to argue, in subdued tones – but the strength of their emotion was so powerful that if it could not find vent through the voice, it would be expressed through the body;

they might shake each other or pound the pillow or tear at the bed-clothes. Sometimes they sobbed, breathing high and fast. . . . In October Miss Pirie's rheumatism would have been bad. Sometimes, when they were on good terms, Miss Woods would have gone to Miss Pirie's bed to massage her friend's back.[7]

And so on.

Ollie's version is very different. She uses a very contemporary model of lesbianism to explain for herself what these women were doing. For that reason I find it hard to accept. It does seem that she was simply transposing her own experience and definitions on to those of women in a very different time and place. Here is part of her explanation:

They became lovers – not in the romantic friendship sense, but as we would use that word today – shortly after they met, eight or nine years before the breakup of the school. . . . And there they were in bed together for over a year perhaps, maybe longer. Miss Cumming snored loudly. They had not intended to, but they found themselves making love. The long abstinence, and the necessity to be covert, the risk, all together made it more exciting than it had ever been.[8]

The strength of Faderman's determination to prove that they were not doing genital sex rang so strangely to me that I began to question her confidence in her earlier book that nineteenth-century women in passionate friendships would never have had genital sex.

I think there is a third possibility which may give credit to the fact that these women were living in a very different world with different definitions, whilst allowing some flexibility. I think it is possible that two women, engaged in passionate embraces as a usual part of a passionate friendship, might discover the interesting sensations attendant on genital friction and explore the possibility of improving on the sensations. Women do sometimes discover sex with other women in this way now, so it does not seem impossible that they would have done in the nineteenth century. I think we must be flexible and avoid transplanting on to the experience of our foresisters either a contemporary lesbian identity or a determinedly non-genital one.

What is very interesting about the book is that it shows that girls at 'nice' boarding schools in 1811 seem to have been as keenly aware of and as likely to chatter about lesbians as they are today. They talked of lesbianism with maids and nannies who all seem to have known something about it. This suggests to me that an assumption that all passionate friendships were non-genital is unwise when so many girls and women were aware of the genital possibilities of such relationships.

The Scotch Verdict is a book well worth reading in conjunction with *Surpassing the Love of Men* because it raises the question of how we are to interpret passionate friendships so acutely. Faderman's work has provided a foundation for all other lesbian–feminist history writing. She has overturned both traditional heterosexual history and more recent 'gay' interpretations. Her work helps us to enter upon the debate that is crucial to the writing of lesbian history, the debate about what lesbianism means for us now and the exploration of our differing definitions. This is a process long overdue. The subject of passionate friendships rouses passionate controversy and this suggests that it must touch on some very important political issues. Any heretical questioning of the traditional twentieth-century stereotype of lesbianism, such as was done in 1979 in a paper later published in *Love Your Enemy*, which called on feminists to withdraw from men and define themselves as political lesbians even before they had had a love affair with a woman, leads to a storm of protest.[9]

How can we question that definition whilst protecting our identity as lesbians? If we do not question it, then lesbians will remain a tiny minority of women, defined by genital contact, fitting neatly into the category the lords and masters have assigned to us. The ramparts of heterosexuality will not be breached, and the heterosexual foundations of male supremacy will remain firm. If we do question it, then we question our own security too, inasmuch as our security and identity have been based on this definition. We need an identity that is strong, revolutionary and *lesbian*.

Notes

1   Faderman, Lillian, *Surpassing the Love of Men: Romantic Friendship and Love between Women from the Renaissance to the Present*, The Women's Press, London, 1985.
2   Ibid., p. 18.
3   Ibid., p. 329.
4   Ruehl, Sonja, 'Sexual Theory and Practice: Another Double Standard', in Sue Cartledge and Joanna Ryan (eds), *Sex and Love*, The Women's Press, London, 1983.
5   Rich, Adrienne, 'Compulsory Heterosexuality and Lesbian Existence', in Ann Snitow *et al.* (eds), *Desire: The Politics of Sexuality*, Virago, London, 1984.
6   Faderman, Lillian, *The Scotch Verdict*, Quartet, London, 1985.
7   Ibid., p. 246.
8   Ibid., p. 247.
9   Leeds Revolutionary Feminist Group, 'Political Lesbianism: The Case Against Hetero-sexuality', in Onlywomen Press (eds), *Love Your Enemy*, Onlywomen Press, London, 1981.

Martha Vicinus

LESBIAN HISTORY
All theory and no facts or all facts and no theory?

Martha Vicinus is a leading theorist on the history of lesbianism and has written extensively on Victorian women and sexuality. Her numerous works include *Independent Women: Work and Community for Single Women, 1850–1920* (1985, reprinted 1994) and, most recently, *Intimate Friends: Women Who Loved Women, 1778–1928* (2004). In her important 1994 survey article reproduced here, Vicinus seeks, above all, to make a case for the centrality of lesbians in history. In her review of the main trends and assumptions underlying lesbian history to date, she bemoans the tendency of scholars to privilege the visible, self-identified lesbian, arguing that such an approach has led to an over-hasty and reductionist categorisation of women's sexual behaviours as well as an excessive concern with 'knowing-for-sure'. Even the advent of queer theory, she observes, with its emphasis on gender as performance, still privileges the visibly marked lesbian. By way of contrast, Vicinus offers two new approaches to the writing of lesbian history. First, she argues for the analytical possibilities of the 'not said' and 'not seen' as conceptual tools. This is because historically lesbian relations have so often been based upon fragmentary evidence and suspicion, upon silence and ambiguity of meaning such as that left to us by the trial of Miss Woods and Miss Pirie in Lillian Faderman's *The Scotch Verdict*. Second, she calls for a 'more open definition of women's sexual subjectivity' encompassing a continuum of sexual behaviours, in recognition of the fact that women have frequently moved back and forth between hetero- and homosexual experiences. In this way, 'the lesbian is never absent from any definition of woman, whatever her avowed sexual preference' Vicinus asserts; only through an exploration of 'the complex threads' that bind women's lesbian desires to their wider relationships in family and society will lesbian history become central to rather than peripheral to women's history in general.

IN 1980 THE PIONEERING lesbian historian Blanche Wiesen Cook wrote of 'The historical denial of lesbianism [that] accompanies the persistent refusal to acknowledge the variety and intensity of women's emotional and erotic experience.'[1] This 'historical denial' has been overtaken by a cacophony of voices; the growth in cultural studies in the academy has made the study of homosexuality seem like the hottest property in intellectual ideas – or at the very least, the most exciting site of marginality. The lesbian is a popular subject for scrutiny – she exists, but how are we to define her history, who do we include and when did it begin? Our own literalism, a paucity of sources, and what Judith Bennett has called 'definitional uncertainty' have inhibited all too many of us from undertaking the painstaking excavational work necessary to understand the variety of women's sexual subjectivities, and the ways in which different societies have permitted, forbidden, and interpreted these experiences.[2]

I want to review briefly the main currents in lesbian history, and to question some of the assumptions and definitions that have become common parlance. I believe that lesbian history is currently under-theorized and under-researched. We are also excessively concerned with knowing-for-sure.[3] Lesbian history has always been characterized by a 'not knowing' what could be its defining core. Over a decade ago I pointed out the tendency to categorize and define women's sexual behaviors too hastily; unfortunately this still remains true.[4] Our current models all privilege either the visibly marked mannish woman or the self-identified lesbian; romantic friendships, once the leading example of a lesbian past, are now either reconfigured in terms to fit these categories or labeled asexual. We seem to accept only what is seen and what is said as evidence.

These limitations have shaped both how we know and how we imagine the lesbian. I want to argue for the possibilities of the 'not said' and the 'not seen' as conceptual tools for the writing of lesbian history. Recognizing the power of not naming – of the unsaid – is a crucial means for understanding a past that is so dependent upon fragmentary evidence, gossip, and suspicion. A present limited to the visible, self-identified lesbian reduces our understanding of both the daily life of the homosexual and her multiple relationships with the dominant heterosexual society and its cultural productions. A more open definition of women's sexual subjectivity, and of same-sex desire, will enable us not only to retrieve a richer past, but also to understand the complex threads that bind women's actions and desires to the larger world.

The binaries that have dominated our conceptualization of sex and gender have been rigorously questioned recently, but too often this questioning has yielded either polymorphous play or an unstable 'third sex' defined by cross-dressing and marginal sexualities.[5] In contrast, I believe that the lesbian is never absent from any defin-ition of woman, whatever her avowed sexual preference. I am arguing here for the primacy of a continuum of women's sexual behaviors, in which lesbian or lesbian-like conduct can be both a part of, and apart from, normative heterosexual marriage and childbearing. I am not calling for a return to Adrienne Rich's notion of a continuum of 'woman-identified experience,' in which all-female bonding is defined as unproblematic nurturance and love, in opposition to the divisions wrought by compulsory heterosexuality.[6] Instead, I seek to understand a continuum of women's sexual experiences that also contains an irreducible sense of the dangerous difference implicit in homosexuality. Perhaps no image – continuum, circle, or margin – can embody a subject as pervasive as sexual desire. But I contend that the lesbian is at the center rather than the periphery of any study of women and men. Women's same-sex love always remains a threatening affront to male sexual prerogatives; it is also a hazardous act that can both unite and divide women.[7] Lesbian history should not be a marginal preoccupation of lesbians; rather it is pivotal to our understanding of women. By implication, this must include men, for we live in a gendered world in which the subordinate gender can never escape the dominant. We need more lesbian history, but we also need lesbians and lesbian-like women in history.

As Eve Kosofsky Sedgwick has said in regard to male homosexuality, ignorance is not an empty box waiting to be filled by knowledge.[8] Ignorance now and in prior times can be willed. Every lesbian has an anecdote about someone – often a family member or teacher – who failed to recognize what was going on between her and a best friend. But perhaps this was not a failure to know, but a refusal to know. Knowing – recognizing a woman's sexual autonomy – may be simply too threatening. I want to suggest that lesbianism can be everywhere without being mentioned; the sustained withholding of the name can actually be the very mechanism that reinforces its existence as a defined sexual practice.[9] In effect, we have what was unnamed in the past and our own reluctance to name that past; this determined ignorance reinforces homophobia and impoverishes both lesbian history and the writing of history itself.

I find it ironic that 'lesbianism' continues to depend upon the evidence of sexual consummation, whereas heterosexuality is confirmed through a variety of diverse social formations. For example, we know of several unconsummated marriages among middle-class British intellectuals – I draw your attention to the Ruskins, Carlyles, and George Bernard Shaw and Charlotte Payne Townshend; these spouses may be failed heterosexuals, but they are not stripped of their sexual identity. Conversely, even when we have evidence of homosexual practices, it has often been reinterpreted as asexual sentimentality. The American sculptor Harriet Hosmer (1830–1908) made a specific distinction in her letters between kissing her close friends and the pleasures of 'Laöcooning' in bed with her lover. But her most recent biographer insists that Hosmer was not like her lesbian friend, Charlotte Cushman (1816–76), the internationally admired American actress.[10] However difficult it may be to interpret the flowery language of letters written between friends by both women and men during the nineteenth century, are we not relying too much on a literal language of either sex or sentimentality? Why is an explicit statement seen as a true statement and elision as uncertainty?

This insistence upon explicitness has led to a privileging of an identity model of lesbian history. We have focused on two obvious categories of same-sex love: romantic friendships and butch-femme role playing. The former depends upon our present-day identification of these friendships as homoerotic, if not homosexual, while the latter depends upon self-identification by the women themselves. Romantic friends can be called the 'good girls' – educated, monogamous, and gently loving of women. Numerous examples of these Sapphic loves can be documented throughout European and American history, for they were an established phase of a young girls initiation into emotional maturity. As a result, it has been repeatedly claimed that 'once upon a time' women could love each other and society approved.[11] This rosy picture of social acceptance, while never fully endorsed by historians, has seemed boringly asexual to many lesbians of today. They preferred in Alice Echols' phrase, the 'bad girls' from an immediate, retrievable past.[12] These 1950s working-class butches drank, fought, and had fun; among young lesbians a romantic nostalgia for the bar-dyke culture of this period is pervasive. Self-identification as either butch or femme has become the defining sign of one's true identity.[13]

I want to suggest that limiting lesbian sexuality to these two categories, romantic friendships and butch-femme roles, has led to a dreary narrowing of historical possibilities. Both are conceptualized, so as to leave little room for women who might behave differently at different times, or who might belong to both categories of romantic friendship and butch-femme passion – or neither. How are we to define a married woman who falls in love with a woman? Or a lesbian who falls in love with a man?[14] Charlotte Cushman fashioned for herself a visibly mannish appearance while writing letters to her lovers in a romantic friendship style. She and her partners wore matching jackets and dresses, so that they looked alike, but different from heterosexual women.[15] The 'randy widow' of medieval literature seems to have disappeared from the lesbian overview perhaps because, with historical primness, we have refused to call anybody a lesbian before the late nineteenth century, arguing that the word was not used before then. Actually, if we wish to be literal-minded – which I am arguing strenuously against – 'lesbian' is used in its modern sense as early as 1736, in a virulent attack on the widowed Duchess of Newburgh.[16]

Present-day concerns with self-identification have led to a fetishization of *difference* visibly inscribed on the physical appearance of a woman – and its seemingly inevitable accompaniment, the coming-out story. One might say that scholars of romantic friendships, such as Carroll Smith-Rosenberg and myself, have 'outed' forgotten nineteenth-century middle-class women whose diaries and letters so eloquently describe their erotically charged emotional involvements with women.[17] Elizabeth Lapovsky Kennedy and Madeline D. Davis pioneered interviewing women who participated in the bar community of Buffalo in the '40s and '50s; numerous local studies of lesbian-dominated softball leagues, bars, and other venues have followed their efforts.[18] Anthologies of coming-out autobiographies have given ordinary women of all ethnicities an opportunity to speak their sexual preference.[19] However important these political gestures have been – and I do not wish to minimize them – they all depend upon a notion of lesbian visibility – of recognition *and* then the speaking what has previously been suppressed, ignored, or denied.

Given the conceptual impasse of lesbian history by the mid-1980s, it is hardly surprising that 'queer theory,' based in cultural studies, has come to the fore as the most exciting way to think about sexual-object choice. It posed a new set of questions that could be more easily answered – or deployed – than a history dependent upon certifiable homoeroticism. The queer perspective is most eloquently argued by Eve Kosofsky Sedgwick in *The Epistemology of the Closet*, which is based upon the premise that 'an understanding of virtually any aspect of modern Western culture must be, not merely incomplete, but damaged in its central substance to the degree that it does not incorporate a critical analysis of modern homo-heterosexual definition.'[20] Queer theorists, led by the philosopher Judith Butler, have fought vigorously against the notion of homosexuality as a miming of heterosexuality – as if the latter were the legitimate original and homosexuality an imitation. Moreover, as Lisa Duggan has pointed out, 'queer theories' refuse the marginality of both civil-rights style liberal gay politics, and the ghettoizing of gay studies. They provide a means of analyzing the here and now, giving fresh impetus to political action at a time when many left-leaning academics have felt the lack of any viable political arena.[21] These are heady claims for a sub-discipline just gaining academic credibility. But they have freed us from previously reductive notions of sexual identity, as well as the tedious essentialist (sexual identity rooted in biology) versus social construction (sexual identity determined by social factors) debate that agitated homosexuals in the late 1980s.[22]

Few queer theorists have been centrally concerned with historical questions, but instead have focused upon the cultural construction of gays and lesbians at the present time. One of the new questions the queer theorist Judith Butler asked was, 'Does gender exist?' Her answer is 'yes and no,' because all gender is performance. Revising the psychoanalytic notion first advanced by Joan Rivière, that femininity itself is a masquerade, she argues that no one can be defined by or limited to a single gendered identity; even the process of speaking as a lesbian, is, in her words, 'a production . . . an identity that, once produced, sometimes functions as a politically efficacious phantasm,' but which, as an 'identity category' suggests 'a provisional totalization.'[23] For Butler, the performance of gender, and especially the practices of butch-femme and drag, offer a more viable politics in our post-modern world, than identity-based politics, which depends upon privileging one identity over another.[24] In effect, she has taken the definitional uncertainty about 'what is a lesbian' and argued for its radical potential. If all gender is a performance, then we historians need not seek a coherent lesbian identity in the past or present. Lesbians are a social construct produced in the process of relating to others. This is, of course, an immensely freeing notion for historians.

Nevertheless, as Kath Weston has pointed out, butch and femme roles today may be a 'playful, irreverent, anti-essentialist approach to gender, but this association is confined to a limited number of "players" in relatively specialized historical circumstances.'[25] As she goes on to argue, people do not always experience themselves as being in control of gendered representations, which involve their immersion in social and material relations.[26] While a woman may play at being femme one night, in her heart she feels butch, or vice-versa. For Weston, a troubling residue of an essentialized, instrinsic role remains in lesbian sexuality.

Biddy Martin has argued that much queer theory posits a dichotomy between race and sexuality, whereby race becomes the stable identity in opposition to a playful, postmodern sexual sensibility.[27] In effect, it places sexuality outside such variables as race and class, giving it a kind of false independence. Martin, like Weston, points to the impossibility of sustaining a metaphoric performance independent of the social context that shapes and constrains all of us, whatever our current sexual choice. But for her, and implicitly I would argue, for historians, Butler's argument about the performative nature of gender 'underscores the importance of rendering visible complexities that already exist but are rendered unthinkable, invisible, or impossible by discursive-institutional orderings with deep investments in defining viable subjects.'[28] It is precisely these 'discursive-institutional orderings' that historians need to examine – to render visible – for they reveal the pervasive denial of lesbian practices.

My own criticism of 'queer theory,' as defined by Judith Butler and Sue-Ellen Case, rests in part on its ahistorical nature. The wholesale embracing of a theatrical metaphor denies the historicity of all lesbian roles, and their specific meanings at different historical times – indeed, even the possibility of their nonexistence in the past.[29] Modern sexual behavior cannot be divorced from its intersection with race, class, and other social variables, nor can it be wholly a matter of fashionable, presentist metaphorizing. Moreover, the focus of queer theory upon performance is also a privileging of the visible, which returns us to some of the same difficulties that have characterized identity-based history. It is as if 'what is gender?' is still confined to 'what is *visibly* gendered?' From its very inception lesbian studies has been concerned with 'making visible' the lesbian of the present and the past. This process of reclamation has focused almost entirely upon the mannish woman because she has been the one most obviously different from other women – and men. What does this insistence on visibility do to notions of both femininity and feminism? Are we fixated on visibly marked difference, whether it be a 'performed' gender or a gendered identity, because the explicitness of our age demands clear erotic signals? No wonder so many postmodernist lesbians when they dress for a party go in butch drag or a campy femininity – the theatricality of each role provides the necessary erotic marker.

Historians are especially well situated to problematize the privileging of the visible as sexual sign. Did this defining of external physical signs as the crucial referent for sexual difference begin with the nineteenth-century medical profession? Early sexologists argued for an enlarged clitoris or excessive bodily hair, or similar physical 'deformations.'[30] Freud's theory of sexual difference depends directly upon the male child's *seeing* its mother's lack of a penis.[31] Carroll Smith-Rosenberg has pointed out that Richard von Krafft-Ebing 'made gender inversion physiologically manifest. The women who "aped" men's roles looked like men. But even more, having rooted social gender in biological sexuality, Krafft-Ebing then made dress analogous to gender. "Only by her dress you would know her."'[32] There is a curious elision from presumed bodily deformities to the clothes one wears. In effect, difference becomes defined by what is visibly different – if we can't see the bodily hair or the deformed pudenda, we can see the cigarette, long stride, and tie. But what we see as different means, for the sexologists, the mannish lesbian.

The sexologists' insistence upon defining homosexuality as inversion meant that the effeminate man and the masculine woman shared the same definitional space as identifiable 'inverts.' But if only the visual marker of mannishness could signify sexual preference, a so-called femme could be distinct from a heterosexual woman only by her performance of an extreme form of femininity, as if to counteract Havelock Ellis's claim that such women were the homely leftovers rejected by men.[33] Teresa de Lauretis has tackled 'what cannot be seen,' in her analysis of Radclyffe Hall's *The Well of Loneliness* (1928). The mannish Stephen's lover, Mary, 'in most representations' 'would be either passing lesbian or passing straight,' for she can be seen as lesbian only on the arm of her lover.[34] Recently self-identified political femmes have refused an identity based solely on their relationship to a butch lover. As Lisa M. Walker has said, 'because subjects who can "pass" exceed the categories of visibility that establish identity, they tend to be peripheral to the understanding of marginalization.' Like Biddy Martin, she too examines the implicit racism of writers who reify marginalization in terms of 'the visible signifier of difference,' whether it be race, class, or 'mannishness.'[35]

Even a cursory glance at lesbian history shows that many couples dressed alike in a manner that would repel men, and remind onlookers of their distinct interest in each other. I have already mentioned Charlotte Cushman, who, with her partner Mathilda Hays, in 1852 was described by Elizabeth Barrett Browning as a couple who had 'made vows of celibacy & of eternal attachment to each other – they live together, dress alike . . . it is a female marriage.'[36] The famous late-eighteenth early-nineteenth-century Ladies of Llangollen wore identical Irish riding habits and powdered wigs. Observers repeatedly sought to differentiate the two women; a scurrilous journalist described the fifty-one year old, dumpy Lady Eleanor Butler as 'tall and masculine,' and 'in all respects a young man.'[37] His preconception of their relationship demanded a visible differentiation between the two women, even if they themselves eschewed such marking. Seemingly a popular model of 'inversion' predates the sexologists, though this has not yet been sufficiently explored by historians. Sartorial sameness as practiced by the Ladies and Cushman and Hays may well have been an upper-class defense against the well-known lower-class 'female soldier' who passed as a man; these women conveyed a sense of their distinct difference from heterosexual women without losing respectability.[38]

The alternative to 'making visible' the lesbian is, of course, language itself. Some feminists have found Jacques Lacan's theory of the construction of the subject through language to be an especially powerful way to theorize feminine desire, however much they may disagree with his notion of desire for the phallus. By concentrating on the psychological importance of our entry into a socially constructed language, he has drawn our attention to the ways in which language is an intrinsic part of our sexual selves. Moreover, Lacan's notion that the individual subject is constituted in a world of language and symbols eliminates a strict boundary between the self and society – a point that could be potentially valuable for historians. But as Jeffrey Weeks has warned, 'The problem remains of how to theorise the relationship between desire and the social, between the ideological categories which address and construct a particular subject and the processes, real historical processes, by which individual meanings and identities are shaped.'[39]

Nevertheless, language theories remain a powerful means for understanding the formation of a self. But I want to suggest some of the ways in which we may be in danger of magnifying their importance in lesbian studies. For both Lillian Faderman and Esther Newton, the late nineteenth-century sexologists' language of genital sex made women sexually self-conscious. For Newton, this 'new vocabulary built on the radical idea that women apart from men could have autonomous sexual feeling,' and thereby freed lesbians from the asexuality of romantic friendships.[40] Radclyffe Hall seemed to confirm Newton's generalization; her heroine, Stephen, cannot understand what is wrong with her until she stumbles upon an annotated copy of the sexologist Richard von Kraft-Ebing in her father's study. For Faderman, this provision of a sexual language was a disaster that took away the innocence of romantic friends. She describes late nineteenth-century women as 'fledgling human beings' who lacked the self-confidence to resist the sexologists' language of neurosis.[41] Both interpretations, though diametrically opposed, give inordinate power to language as either a freeing or a disabling means of self-identification for lesbians. Both critics also reinforce the common assumption that until middle-class women had a sexual vocabulary, their relationships were asexual or guiltily furtive.

These two influential critics both denied homosexual agency to pre-twentieth-century women. It is therefore no surprise that many lesbians greeted with pleasure and relief the 1988 publication of excerpts from the diary of the early nineteenth-century English gentlewoman, Anne Lister (1791–1840). Lister had developed a complete vocabulary to define her lesbian behavior, including such words as 'kiss' to describe her orgasms and those of her partners. Entries written in code are quite explicit about what she did in bed, as well as what she suspected numerous other women of doing. At last we had evidence that women in the past not only knew what to do in bed with each other, they actually did it – and then created their own sexual vocabulary. Lister seems to have had no trouble in recognizing other women who enjoyed sexual relations with each other; she may not have inhabited a modern lesbian subculture, but she knew that many other women of her own social class shared her proclivities.

Yet I don't believe that similar diaries lie waiting to be found, or that we only need better skills to decode the language of the past in order to know what women did with each other. Indeed, I want to caution against focusing on what is said – either by others or by a woman herself. By doing so we may fall into the trap of the same literalism that has characterized our search for the visible markers of lesbian sexuality. The analysis of romantic friendships in particular has been bedeviled by the assumption that because Victorian women from upper-class backgrounds did not use the language of sex, they could not know what to do in bed.[42] Just because Anne Lister reverses this widespread generalization, this does not free us to assume unproblematically – and unhistorically – that every time two women slept together they were disporting themselves. The time has come to stop concentrating on what might have been said or done in private and to focus on other issues.

As Terry Castle has noted, the lesbian is repeatedly treated as if she were a ghost, whose sexuality cannot be pinned down, and yet she repeatedly reappears, haunting the heterosexual imaginary. This ghosting of lesbian desire has enabled historians to deny its reality for too long. We need to learn from Castle that the 'apparitional lesbian' is not absent from history, but to be found everywhere, and as she suggests, 'to focus on presence instead of absence, plentitude instead of scarcity.'[43] As part of that plenitude, I return to my earlier argument: if we begin with the possibility of a continuum of sexual behaviors for all women, then the lesbian is neither marginal nor phantasmic, but central. We need to remind ourselves again – as queer theorists have claimed – that sexual behavior is poly-morphous, changeable and impossible to define absolutely. It can only be understood in relation to the multifarious elements that make up a human identity. At the same time, we should not lose that sense of 'dangerous love,' so eloquently defended by Elizabeth Wilson a decade ago; risk-taking, romantic idealism, and passionate hedonism are not limited to a heterosexual imagination.[44] Many more women from the past will be part of this sexual world, temporarily or permanently, when we recognize the sheer variety and richness of women's sexual desires – and actions. Truth-claims cannot be made, but a fuller history can be constructed.

My disagreements with fellow scholars in the nascent field of lesbian studies spring from a sense of shared concerns. My criticism is reserved for those historians who complacently ignore the lesbian, confident that she is either irrelevant to their own historical project or that she can be relegated to specialists. To paraphrase Judith Bennett, I am not making a case for lesbian history, but for the central place of lesbians in history.[45] It is the presumed heterosexuality of women, past and present, which needs to be overcome, if we are to understand how lesbians and lesbian-like behavior is intrinsic to the study of women and men. Lesbians and lesbian-like women have had a profound influence upon women and men, challenging them to rethink and alter their behavior. Economic independence, alternative life-styles, and sometimes nontraditional political and cultural activities characterize these women. Why then do they remain so peripheral to our definition of the past?

Let me turn to a well-known example, the trial *Miss Marianne Woods and Miss Jane Pirie against Dame Helen Cumming Gordon*, to demonstrate how definitional uncertainty is at the core of lesbian studies. It also illustrates the complex connections among sexual expression, economics, and social status for single women. The case is easily summarized.[46] In 1811 two school teachers sued the grandmother of one of their students for libel. The illegitimate, half-Indian Jane Cumming had accused her teachers of having sexual relations while she shared a bed with Miss Jane Pirie. Lady Cumming Gordon, one of the most influential noblewomen in Edinburgh, removed her granddaughter from the school; she also convinced other parents to remove their children. The economically ruined teachers persisted for over nine years in their legal efforts to regain their reputations and to receive compensation. Although they were found innocent by a margin of one vote, Lady Cumming Gordon appealed to the House of Lords, and when she lost yet again, delayed payment of their claim. The two women, their friendship broken, disappear from history without our knowing if they ever received compensation. The whereabouts of Jane Cumming is also unknown.

I chose this example because it has been recognized as a key source for lesbian history. To date no one seems to have thought it odd that a cornerstone of lesbian history is a libel case brought by two teachers who adamantly denied any carnal knowledge – of each other, of their students, or of men.

[. . .]

All of the judges, regardless of how they voted, distrusted the instigator of the case, and concluded that Jane Cumming, having spent her early years in India with her mother, was guilty of imagining practices that could only occur in a hot country. She could not be held to the same standards of honesty as a British woman, and therefore might be lying. The sexualized colonial body often stands in for the deviant sexual desires of British women. In this trial, these desires were confronted, made foreign, and then denied as existing in Britain. In effect, middle-class women could not be capable of lesbian sex and remain British.

This lawsuit epitomizes the interpretative difficulties inherent in romantic friendships. The counsel for the defence insisted that 'it was the general opinion in the school that the pursuers [plaintiffs] caressed and fondled each other more than was consistent with ordinary female friendship.'[47] But what was ordinary female friendship? At what stage did fondling become extraordinary? Was it possible to impugn 'unnatural lewdness' if one woman asked another into her bed on a cold night, so that they might discuss the days events in reasonable comfort? To answer this question in the affirmative strained the credulity of Lord Gillies, who rhetorically asserted, 'Are we to say that every woman who has formed an early intimacy, and has slept in the same bed with another, is guilty? Where is the innocent woman in Scotland?'[48]

[. . .]

The case represents not only definitional uncertainty, but also the social danger inherent in women's economic and sexual independence.

Miss Marianne Woods and Miss Jane Pirie against Dame Helen Cumming Gordon is situated in the *locus classicus* of female autonomy. The boarding-school story has been repeated in various forms for over 150 years; Lillian Hellman's *The Children's Hour* (1934) is only the best-known example.[49] Lesbian sexuality, whether found in a legal case, a twentieth-century melodrama, or numerous pornographic fantasies, can repeatedly evaporate into denial, concealment, or displacement. But it also never disappears. I would claim Miss Woods and Miss Pirie as lesbian-like, even if they were as innocent as they declared themselves to be. We can maintain the undecidability of their case and still insist upon their centrality in any history of lesbians. The reactions of the male judges, of heterosexual women (ranging from Dame Cumming Gordon to the pregnant servant), and of those few outsiders who heard of the case, tell us a good deal about contemporary attitudes toward women's sexual and economic autonomy. As a representative plot in our cultural imagination, the trial of Miss Woods and Miss Pirie deserves center stage. Finally, no one writes history only from facts, whatever they may be. What richer image do we need than an invitation to join a beloved friend in bed on a cold night?

Notes

1   Review of Doris Faber, *The Life of Lorena Hickok: ER's Friend* (New York: Morrow, 1980), in *Feminist Studies* 6, 3 (Fall 1980): 510–2.

2   Judith Bennett, 'The L-word in Women's History,' unpub. papers (October 1990 and September 1993). I have not mentioned bisexuality. As Elisabeth D. Daümer has recently said, for a bisexual, falling in love with a women does not seem like 'a truer, more authentic self ha[s] surfaced,' but instead it is 'the exhilaration of being offered a choice that she had not known – or felt – to exist.' See her 'Queer Ethics, or The Challenge of Bisexuality to Lesbian Ethics,' *Hypatia* 7, 4 (Fall 1992): 99.

3   Sheila Jeffreys makes this point from a different political perspective from mine in 'Does It Matter If They Did it?' *Not a Passing Phase: Reclaiming Lesbians in History, 1840–1985*, ed. Lesbian History Group (London: The Woman's Press, 1989), 19–28.

4   'Sexuality and Power: A Review of Current Work in the History of Sexuality,' *Feminist Studies* 8 (Spring 1982): 150–1.

5   The most influential critics for these perspectives have been Judith Butler in *Gender Trouble: Feminism and the Subversion of Identity* (New York: Routledge, 1990); and Sue-Ellen Case, 'Towards a Butch-Femme Aesthetic,' *Discourse* 11, 1 (1988–9): 55–73. For a discussion of the importance of 'the third sex,' see Majorie Garbar's *Vested Interests* (New York: Routledge, 1991).

6   Adrienne Rich, 'Compulsory Heterosexuality and Lesbian Existence,' *Signs* 5, 4 (Summer 1980): 649.

7   See Elizabeth Wilson's important intervention on behalf of the erotic power of deviance in 'Forbidden Love,' *Feminist Studies* 10, 2 (Summer 1984): 213–26. She also critiques Rich's lesbian continuum.

8   Eve Kosofsky Sedgwick, *Epistemology of the Closet* (Berkeley: University of California Press, 1990), 7–8.

9   Annamarie Jagose, 'Springing Miss Wade: *Little Dorrit* and a Hermeneutics of Suspicion,' unpub. paper (December 1993).

10 Doris Sherwood, *Harriet Hosmer: American Sculptor, 1830–1908* (Columbia: University of Missouri, 1991), 169–71, 270–3.

11 The best-known argument for this position is Lillian Faderman's in *Surpassing the Love of Men: Romantic Friendship and Love between Women from the Renaissance to the Present* (New York: William Morrow, 1981), and her essentially unchanged position in *Odd Girls and Twilight Lovers: A History of Lesbian Life in Twentieth-Century America* (New York: Columbia University Press, 1991). See also the ways in which these generalizations have been unproblematically accepted by literary critics such as Tess Cosslett, *Woman to Woman: Female Friendship in Victorian Fiction* (Brighton: Harvester, 1988); and Betty T. Bennett in *Mary Diana Dods: A Gentleman and A Scholar* (New York: William Morrow, 1991).

12 See her *Daring to be Bad: Radical Feminism in America, 1967–75* (Minneapolis: University of Minnesota Press, 1989).

13 A sense of finding one's 'true identity' as a butch or as a femme, particularly in opposition to 1970s' feminism, characterizes many of the 'coming out' stories in *The Persistent Desire: A Femme-Butch Reader*, ed. Joan Nestle (Boston: Alyson Publications, 1992).

14 See Jan Clausen's 'My Interesting Condition: What Does it Mean When a Lesbian Falls in Love with a Man?' *Outlook* 2, 3 (Winter 1990): 10ff.

15 Joseph Leach, *Bright Particular Star: The Life and Times of Charlotte Cushman* (New Haven: Yale University Press, 1970), 188, and passim.

16 William King's *The Toast*, a mock-heroic epic written after he had lost a debt case to the Duchess, is discussed by Emma Donoghue, 'Imagined More than Women: Lesbians as Hermaphrodites, 1671–1766,' *Women's History Review* 2, 2 (1993): 210.

17 See Smith-Rosenberg's groundbreaking 'The Female World of Love and Ritual: Relations Between Women in Nineteenth-Century America,' originally published in 1975, and reprinted in her *Disorderly Conduct: Visions of Gender in Victorian America* (New York: Knopf, 1985), 53–76; and my 'Distance and Desire: English Boarding School Friendships, 1870–1920,' originally published in 1984, and reprinted in *Hidden from History: Reclaiming the Gay and Lesbian Past*, ed. Martin Bauml Duberman, Martha Vicinus, and George Chauncey, Jr. (New York: New American Library, 1989), 212–29.

18 See their 'Oral History and the Study of Sexuality in the Lesbian Community: Buffalo. New York, 1940–1960,' *Feminist Studies* 12, 1 (Summer 1986): 7–26, and their *Boots of Leather, Slippers of Gold: The History of a Lesbian Community* (New York: Routedge, 1993).

19 See especially the highly influential *This Bridge Called My Back: Writings of Radical Women of Color*, ed. Cherrie Moraga and Gloria Anzaldúa (Watertown, MA: Persephone Press, 1981). See also the critique of coming-out stories by Biddy Martin, 'Lesbian Identity and Autobiographical Difference[s],' *The Lesbian and Gay Studies Reader*, ed. Henry Abelove, Michèle Aina Barale, and David M. Halperin (New York: Routledge, 1993), 274–93.

20 Sedgwick, *The Epistemology of the Closet*, 1.

21 Lisa Duggan, 'Making It Perfectly Queer,' *Socialist Review* 22, 1 (January–March 1992): 26–7.

22 This debate is summarized in the introduction to *Hidden from History*, 1–13. Eve Kosofsky Sedgwick suggests that most of us hold two contradictory notions of

homo-sexuality simultaneously, essentialist 'minoritizing' and a constructivist 'universalizing.' See Sedgwick, 1, 9, 86–7.

23   Judith Butler, 'Imitation and Gender Insubordination,' *Inside/Out: Lesbian Theories, Gay Theories*, ed. Diana Fuss (New York: Routledge, Chapman & Hall, 1991), 13–15. The running head to this article gives a better sense of its contents than the title: 'Decking Out. Performing Identities.'

24   See not only 'Imitation and Gender Subordination,' but also her *Gender Trouble*. See also Sue-Ellen Case.

25   Kath Weston, 'Do Clothes Make the Woman?: Gender, Performance theory, and Lesbian Eroticism,' *Genders* 17 (Fall 1993): 7.

26   Weston, 13.

27   Biddy Martin, 'Sexual Practice and Changing Lesbian Identities,' *Destabilizing Theory: Contemporary Feminist Debates*, ed. Michèle Barrett, and Anne Phillips (Stanford: Stanford University Press, 1992), 106–7. I am indebted to Marlon Ross for reminding me of Martin's argument.

28   Martin, 'Sexual Practice,' 104–5.

29   In 'Critically Queer,' *GLQ*, 1, 1(1993): 17–32, Butler partially responds to critics who have called her work ahistorical.

30   See George Chauncey, Jr., 'From Sexual Inversion to Homosexuality: Medicine and the Changing Conceptualization of Female Desire,' *Salmagundi* 58–9 (Fall/Winter 1982–3): 114–46.

31   For a discussion of the implications of this, see Jacqueline Rose, *Sexuality in the Field of Vision* (London: Verso, 1986), 227–8.

32   'The New Woman as Androgyne: Social Disorder and Gender Crisis, 1870–1936,' *Disorderly Conduct*, 272.

33   See Esther Newton's discussion of Ellis's conceptual contradictions in 'The Mythic Mannish Lesbian: Radclyffe Hall and the New Woman,' *Hidden from History*, 288–9.

34   Teresa de Lauretis, 'Sexual Indifference and Lesbian Representation,' *Theatre Journal* 40, 2 (May 1988): 177.

35   Lisa M. Walker, 'How to Recognize a Lesbian: The Cultural Politics of Looking Like What You Are,' *Signs* 18, 4 (Summer 1993): 868, 888. See also Shane Phelan, '(Be)Coming Out: Lesbian Identity and Politics', *Signs* 18, 4 (Summer 1993): 765–90; and Daümer's critique of lesbian identity ethics from a bisexual's perspective (n. 2).

36   Elizabeth Barrett Browning to Arabel Moulton-Browning, her sister, October 22, 1852. Quoted in Sherwood, 41.

37   Quoted in Elizabeth Mavor, *The Ladies of Llangollen* (London: Michael Joseph, 1971), 74.

38   For a discussion of the female soldier, see Julie Wheelwright, *Amazons and Military Maids: Women Who Dressed as Men in Pursuit of Life, Liberty and Happiness* (London: Pandora, 1989); and Dianne Dugaw, Warrior Women and Popular Balladry, 1650–1850 (Cambridge: Cambridge University Press, 1989).

39   Jeffrey Weeks, *Sexuality and Its Discontents: Meanings, Myths & Modern Sexualities* (London: Routledge & Kegan Paul, 1985), 171–2.

40   Esther Newton, 'The Mythic Mannish Lesbian: Radclyffe Hall and the New Woman,' *Hidden from History*, 286.

41   Faderman, 249. This section reprints her well-known 'The Morbidification of Love Between Women by 19th-Century Sexologists,' *The Journal of Homosexuality* 4 (1978), 73–90.

42   See Faderman, passim, as well as the scholars mentioned in n. ii. But see also my own cautious 'Distance and Desire: English Boarding School Friendships, 1870–1920,' in Duberman, *et al.*, 212–29.

43   Terry Castle, *The Apparitional Lesbian: Female Homosexuality and Modern Culture* (New York: Columbia University Press, 1993), 19.

44   Wilson, 220–3.

45   Judith Bennett, unpub. paper, 'The L-Word in Women's History.'

46   The trial is most readily available in Lillian Faderman's fictionalized *Scotch Verdict* (New York: Quill, 1983). Faderman found a few details about Marianne Woods' aunt, Anne Quelch Woods, a minor actress married to a well-known local actor, who had died in 1802. The original transcript of the trial has been reprinted: *Miss Marianne Woods and Miss Jane Pirie against Dame Helen Cumming Gordon* (New York: Arno, 1975). Each section is numbered separately, and is, therefore, quoted here by section title and page number. In Scotland at this time, a libel case went first to a hearing Judge, the Lord Ordinary. If he felt that the case merited a hearing, as Lord Meadowbank ruled in this instance, it went forward to the Lords of Session (seven judges). Each was expected to prepare a brief, explaining his decision, though all did not do so.

47   'State of the Process,' *Miss Marianne Woods . . .*, 56

48   'Speeches of the Judges,' *Miss Marianne Woods . . .*, 92

49   The many stories of lesbian love situated in a boarding school is beyond the scope of this paper. But see Mary Titus, 'Murdering the Lesbian: Lillian Hellman's The Children's Hour,' *Tulsa Studies in Women's Literature* 10, 2 (Fall 1991): 215–32.

Donna Penn

QUEER
Theorizing politics and history

This article by Donna Penn sets out to examine 'both the promises and limitations of queer to political and historical practices'. She begins with a critical analysis of the congenital interpretation of homosexuality represented in Radclyffe Hall's celebrated novel *The Well of Loneliness* (1928) and the enduring popularity of essentialist arguments for gay rights activists and scholars. Essentialised and trans-historicised models of lesbian identity have performed their own work of erasure argues Penn. In an argument not dissimilar to that of Vicinus's in Reading 15, she suggests that the privileging of an identity model over a behavioural model of lesbianism has limited the knowledge base and analytical framework of historians by excluding certain categories of women in the past who may not have identified themselves as lesbians or been part of visible lesbian subcultures but who, never-theless, have acted upon homoerotic desires for other women. 'Queer' may provide a more imaginative theoretical framework for achieving this reconstruction, argues Penn, by 'retheorizing categories of inclusion and exclusion that guide our historical work'. Queering lesbian history means foregrounding the construction of hetero-normativity and, in the process, mapping sexual deviance through sources that may not be explicitly about lesbianism at all. As to whether or not the term 'queer' is any less elisive than the more conventional identity politics model, Penn suggests that the breadth of forms of sexual deviancy covered by 'queer' means that the term may perform precisely the same type of erasure of difference as essentialist approaches. Penn criticises contemporary queer theory for its dismissal of radicals of the past and its failure to recognise the 'specific challenges posed by differently constituted deviants in particular cultural and historical contexts'.

THE ARRIVAL OF A NEW MOMENT in our political, social, sexual, theoretical, and cultural lives is announced in the proliferation of references to 'queer.' 'Queer Nation,' *Making Things Perfectly Queer*, 'Making It Perfectly Queer,' 'Queer Theory,' 'Queer Studies,' 'I Can See Queerly Now,' 'On a Queer

Day You Can See Forever,' *Fear of a Queer Planet*.[1] The use of the term 'queer' in the names of an organization, recent books, articles, film series, and academic sub-disciplines represents more than a remedy for the increasingly cumbersome designation 'gay, lesbian, bisexual, and transgendered.' More than a term of convenience, 'queer' and the interventions it seeks to make into academic and political practices is intentional and remains highly contested. Academics and activists continue to disagree over its benefits and liabilities as an intellectual category of analysis and as a strategy for political organizing.

This article is intended as a meditation on these queer matters. My purpose is to consider both the promises and limitations of queer to political and historical practices. In order to place this queer moment in a larger historical context of theoretical visions and revisions, I will first sketch out an example of the political application of a once new and challenging theory from an earlier historical period to demonstrate how inextricably theories and political investments are bound. For example, early twentieth-century theories that understood homosexuality as congenital sexual inversion posed a political challenge to previous theories that treated homosexuality as a criminally degenerate act.[2] I will examine the political implications of this theoretical move as evidenced in Radclyffe Hall's novel of sexual inversion, *The Well of Loneliness*.[3]

To firmly locate queer in historical, historiographical, political, and intellectual contexts and to identify the problematic that queer, at least in part, intends to remedy, I will consider the theoretical debates in the history of sexuality that preceded its arrival. By tracing the by-now-familiar political promises and liabilities of essentialism and constructionism, we can more readily appreciate how and why queer theory arrived when it did and the intellectual knot it may help unravel. By providing an admittedly cursory rendition of a genealogy of the sexually deviant subject formations that prefigured this queer moment, I will examine how the current political and intellectual battlefield over identity politics and a politics of fractured identities has taken shape.[4] Finally, my purpose is to consider what queer analysis permits and inhibits, both in our scholarship—specifically historical studies—and in our movement politics.[5] Determining the possibilities that the conceptual category 'queer' offers to our analysis of the present and to our interpretations of the past necessarily brings us one step closer to a design for the future.

The lure of essentialism and the challenge of constructionism

Sixty-five years after its publication, Radclyffe Hall's *The Well of Loneliness* remains one of the most important historical documents on early twentieth-century constructions of homosexuality. Despite her somewhat depressing portrait of homosexuality, Hall made two very important political interventions. First, by insisting that sexual inversion was a congenital defect rather than a character flaw, Hall argued that homosexuality was a 'who,' an identity, a noun. Rejecting theories that defined homosexuality as criminal or immoral behavior that theoretically should be curbed by one's free will, Hall instead suggested that it described a type of person—in Foucauldian terms, the homosexual was a 'species of being.'[6] Although Hall's notion of homosexuality never fully replaced older understandings of homosexuality as sin, crime, or sickness, it was nonetheless politically inspired, permitting Hall to assert that the homosexual ought to be left in peace. In the context of a culture that viewed homosexuality as either a crime, sin, or sickness, Hall defended homo-sexuality on the grounds that it, like heterosexuality, was an immutable part of the natural world, not subject to change or cure.

Furthermore, by insisting that homosexuality was a biological, congenital fact of nature, Hall reframed the so-called problem of homosexuality. For Hall, if homo-sexuality was 'natural,' the 'problem of the homosexual' resided with the society that deemed him or her 'unnatural' and persecuted him or her on that basis. Instead of individual remedies for—or social control of—this phenomenon of nature, the logic of Hall's argument dictated that the onus of responsibility for the plight of sexual inverts belonged to the society that condemned them. Hall's homosexual sought either society's compassion or its benign neglect. In posing this argument, Hall added a new dimension to what had been perceived as a medical, criminal, or psychological problem—she made it a sociological one. It is not surprising that Havelock Ellis provided prefatory remarks that accompanied the original and every subsequent publication of *The Well of Loneliness*. As one of the earliest sexologists and 'defenders' of homosexuality and sexual inversion as natural, Ellis appreciated the political implications of recognizing society's assault upon the homosexual as a significant problem facing the homosexual.[7]

At least since Hall's time, arguments on behalf of the 'essential homosexual' have been politically attractive for many of the same reasons that they were for Hall. Viewing homosexuality as a natural, biologically determined phenomenon invites defenses of homosexuality based on its inevitability and 'naturalness' for a class of individuals. Essentialist arguments posit homosexuality as an immutable fact of nature that, at the very least, ought to be tolerated. This approach fur-ther implies that attempts to cure and/or discriminate against the homosexual are wholly inappropriate responses to an immutable genetic phenomenon over which homosexuals have no choice. Consequently, activists have often feared and resisted arguments about homosexuality and social change rooted in construc-tionism. Construction theory posits sexuality as a product of social relations and thereby suggests the history of sexuality to be 'the history of the subject whose meaning and content are in a continual process of change.'[8] By attending to the shifting meanings assigned to homosexuality, social constructionism challenges the notion of the essential, natural, transhistorical, congenital, pre-social homosexual. Although the constructionists' belief in social change is implicit, and although the very theoretical basis of constructionism requires, in Carole Vance's words, 'imag-ining that things could be different, other, better than they are,' constructionists have nevertheless been viewed as traitors whose arguments threaten the movement.[9] Lured by the seeming political expediency in arguments grounded in biological determinism, many gay men and lesbians have allied themselves with essentialist positions.

While essentialist notions concerning homosexuality have formed the foun-dation of much political organizing, constructionism, alternately, has guided our theory-making. In 1968, British sociologist Mary McIntosh introduced an almost unprecedented way of thinking about the homosexual and homosexuality. Describing a number of historically and culturally diverse anthropological accounts of same-sex sexual behavior, McIntosh declared '[I]n all of these societies there may be much homosexual behavior, but there are no "homosexuals."'[10] She argued that homosexuality, as well as the homosexual, acquired meaning only in cultural, social, and historical context. Divorced from a particular cultural context that ascribes meaning to same-sex acts, homosexuality merely describes a particular set or choreography of sexual acts, a gymnastics of orgasm. Similarly, in 1974, Jonathan Ned Katz suggested that '[b]eyond the most obvious fact that homosexual relations involve persons of the same gender, and include feelings as well as acts, there is no such thing as homosexuality in general, only particular historical forms of homosexuality.'[11] [. . .]

The problem of identity politics for historical investigation

This question—Who is a homosexual?—has concerned historians of lesbians for over a decade. From Blanche Cook's 'woman-loving-woman' and Adrienne Rich's 'lesbian continuum' to Joan Nestle's 'sexual warriors' and Elizabeth Kennedy and Madeline Davis's 'working-class butch-fem bar dykes,' scholars in lesbian history have debated about the guidelines that determine who is a lesbian.[12]

The lesbian scholars of the pre-sex war generation of the 1970s and early 1980s employed definitions appropriate to the task of retrieving historical foresisters. Seeking to recapture a lost 'herstory,' their guidelines for determining legitimate subjects of inquiry were not unlike those recently suggested by Martha Vicinus as 'lesbian and lesbian-like.'[13] An unfortunate result of these efforts to address and remedy the 'historical denial of lesbianism' by expanding our understanding of who might constitute the historicized lesbian is the essentialized and transhistoricized lesbian. By failing to distinguish between the particular oppressions faced by, for example, passing women and 'particular friends,' these definitions obfuscated the distinctions between differently deviant subjects. Further, according to these definitions, sex between women is no longer necessary to the definition of lesbianism. Finally, these recuperative historical accounts identify as lesbian many women, both in the past and present, who would not identify themselves as such.

Yet, more circumscribed definitions of lesbians pose their own problems. An especially significant weakness that has resulted from the application of more precise guidelines for identifying the historical lesbian is the obscuring of the lesbian femme. As the 'feminine' partner of the butch lesbian, the femme confounded turn-of-the-century sexologists, whose focus on congenital and constitutional gender and sexual defects, abnormalities, or confusion as the signposts for lesbianism drew them to the butch or 'true' lesbian, but blinded them to her 'wife.' If feminine women were recognized as lesbians at all, it was as 'latent' homosexuals or as unfortunate victims of predatory butches into whose clutches they fell. Although historians have decried the sexologists' erasure of femmes, their efforts have often been similarly thwarted. Despite the best efforts of recent historians to make the femme visible in lesbian history, her recuperation remains a formidable challenge. Elizabeth Kennedy and Madeline Davis make a valiant effort to place the femme in the post-World War II lesbian community of Buffalo, New York. Yet, they explain that, of the forty-five narrators upon whose stories the book is based, only eight were femmes. This imbalance is, in large part, an unintended consequence of their decision to interview only those women who, at the time of the interview, 'were still lesbians.' They admit in their introduction that: '[A]t the time, we didn't realize how many fems we were excluding.'[14]

These examples illustrate some of the problems that accompany various answers to the question: how do historians of lesbians determine who is an appropriate historical subject? Do we require evidence of genital contact for someone to fit into the parameters of the research group under investigation?[15] Or, depending on the historical moment, is an indication of primary emotional attachment to another of the same sex enough? Furthermore, do we examine a type of behavior, the perpetration of certain acts, or a species of being, a type of person possessing a particular sexual identity? Each choice we make carries liabilities and benefits for the larger project. For example, Tomás Almaguer has suggested that for Chicano men a focus on inverted gender identity or specific sexual aims, rather than sexual identity or object choice, more accurately reflects that culture's guidelines for determining homosexuality.[16] Given this example, we must consider whether, in privileging identity over behavior, we inadvertently narrow our scope to a largely white, relatively urban, North American homo-history. Applying homosexual *identity* as the determining feature of homosexuality uncritically to other peoples and cultural contexts may level differences in the interest of deriving a theoretically coherent unifying principle.

What I am suggesting, then, is that basing the production of knowledge on homosexuality on definitions that depend upon homosexual identity will limit that knowledge. For example, I have recently begun rethinking how the fixity of definitional categories performs particular elisions in my own work. By relying on a strategy that presumes identity, however broadly or strictly defined, to guide our determination of who is and who isn't included in historical accounts, we fail to recognize the variety of challenges to the sex/gender system posed by various subjects. By privileging identity over behavior, how will we account for suburban white women of the postwar years who 'played' around with each other during the day while their husbands toiled to provide for perfect suburban lives? The question confronting historians remains how to retrieve the histories of women who may or may not have identified as lesbians, dykes, or daggers; who may or may not have lived exclusively homosexual lives; who may or may not have associated themselves with local or national lesbian subcultures, organizations, or communities; but whose lives nonetheless help flesh out the idea, experience, and consequences of homoerotic desire among women. And, yet, how do we achieve this recuperation of variously sexually deviant women without blurring or masking the distinctions between them and the different prices paid by those in each category? Was the woman who renounced married, heterosexual life to take up with a factory-working urban butch any more transgressive than the suburban housewife who, by remaining married while indulging her homoerotic desires, fundamentally destabilized the intended ideology of postwar American female domesticity and family values?

The grip of the identity paradigm on our scholarly as well as political imaginings has made it extremely difficult to address these questions. As a theory and politics of multiple and deviant subjectivities, it is possible that 'queer' provides new ways of thinking. The challenge of 'queer' to the hegemony of the 'normal' might provide the space in which to begin retheorizing categories of inclusion and exclusion that guide our historical work. By reframing the project, queer may provide an interpretative strategy that can free the historian from the bondage of rigid definitions that, necessarily if unintentionally, limit the historical imagination.

[. . .]

Queer and the historical imagination

While queer nationals organized on the streets, gay and lesbian intellectuals and academics began rethinking the project of gay and lesbian studies. No longer satisfied with merely restorative solutions such as adding gays to the curriculum, scholars working in this field began reconsidering the very purpose of their work. Whereas previous scholarship in gay and lesbian studies tended to assume a hetero-homo dyad and to generate accounts of homosexual resistance to dominant cultural oppression, 'queer' approaches attempt to reframe the subject. Like queer nationalists, scholars in gay and lesbian studies are increasingly interested in investigating the operations of what Michael Warner has called 'regimes of the normal.'[17] By shifting the scholarly lens off of homosexuality per se—its invention, discovery, subcultural formations—as the object to be examined, queer scholars invert the equation, thereby scrutinizing the production, construction, and investment in the so-called 'normal.'

Therefore, as a theoretical intervention, Teresa de Lauretis insists that 'the term "queer," juxtaposed to . . . "lesbian and gay," . . . is intended to mark a certain critical distance from the latter, by now established and often convenient, formula. For the phrase "lesbian and gay" or "gay and lesbian" has become the standard way of referring to what only a few years ago used to be simply "gay" or, just a few years earlier still, "homosexual."'[18] Yet, these are not a catalogue of terms from which we choose randomly but, in fact, are frequently employed with specific historical and political intent. Furthermore, the notion that the phrase 'lesbian and gay' is now considered an 'established and often convenient, formula,' sometimes arrogantly dismissed as 'retro' by queer activists and theorists alike, diminishes the courage exhibited by those who daily risk personal and professional relationships and reputations by writing, teaching, taking courses in, and living gay and lesbian lives. In the academy, where de Lauretis' arguments are directed, queer may be the latest in intellectual chic, but to indulge the presumption that 'lesbian and gay' has somehow become mainstreamed and assimilated is, at best, wishful thinking. At worst, it is a gross misrepresentation of the place occupied by most lesbians and gay men in the academy and the larger culture.

De Lauretis explains how each of these discursive shifts rectifies an elision produced by the previously used term. 'In a sense,' she states, 'the term "Queer Theory" was arrived at in the effort to avoid all of these fine distinctions in our discursive protocols, not to adhere to any one of the given terms, not to assume their ideological liabilities, but instead to both transgress and transcend them—or at the very least problematize them.'[19] She continues, 'our "differences," such as they may be, are less represented by the discursive coupling of those two terms in the politically correct phrase "lesbian and gay" than they are elided by most of the contexts in which the phrase is used; that is to say, differences are implied in it but then simply taken for granted or even covered over by the word "and."'[20]

However, the question remains, is 'queer' any less elisive? However true de Lauretis's observation concerning the elisive nature of 'and' in 'lesbian and gay' may be, what remedy does 'queer' offer? Despite the barrier-crossing queer intends, can it do so without also masking difference? My fear is that 'queer' might flatten the social, cultural, and material distinctions and liabilities confronting each type of queer and the different stakes for each. While, in theory, queer invites the possibility of building alliances based on our common identity on the fringes, it is equally possible that it performs the same elision it was intended to remedy. [. . .]

Rich's continuum has been criticized for failing to distinguish between the different experiences of those situated variously along it, thus glossing over difference. My concern is whether 'queer,' like the continuum, could be charged with performing a similar kind of erasure. Because many locations on the grid of sexual deviancy are sufficient for inclusion as queer, for example, we have the phenomenon of 'queer straights.'[21] For queers, same-sex sexual activity is only one element among many that permits one access to or the adoption of queer. This begs the question: what does it mean that claiming the label 'queer' no longer requires identification with or engagement in homo-sex?

To avoid the various elisions produced by the use of 'queer,' one must account for precisely that which is unique to each queer's transgression. We need to be able to analyze the varying geographies of deviance specific to each category of dissenter from the dominant sex/gender system. Only by recognizing, acknowledging, and engaging these differences can coalitions be built that can withstand the strains of those differences.

Regardless of these shortcomings, queer should not be casually dismissed. Just as queer promises to refocus the lens of politics, foregrounding heteronormativity rather than homophobia, so too might queer alter the way in which we conceptualize history and the subject(s) of inquiry. As such, it opens up new possibilities for thinking through the projects before us. Instead of aiming to find homosexuality in history, the notion of 'queer' asks that we examine the construction of the normal and, in the process, map the deviant.

What benefits might accrue to lesbian history by queering historical research? Historians of lesbians have long bemoaned the scarcity of sources due to the relative absence of lesbians from much of the public discourse and the consequent invisibility of lesbians in much of the historical record. A queer approach might permit reading lesbianism where, initially, it doesn't seem to be. An application of queer theory to the historical investigation of lesbianism need not require sources that are explicitly about lesbianism for them to shed light on the operations of the normal.

For example, when I set out to conduct my first interview for a project on lesbianism in postwar America, I found myself facing an unanticipated problem for which, at the time, I had no contingency plan. Although a woman who had agreed to meet with me knew in advance the research topic, she announced before I even sat down, 'You know, I'm not sure I'm a very good subject for you. I mean, I'm not a . . .' and she trailed off. Since she did not view herself as a lesbian, she was not altogether sure she was an appropriate research subject. Because she viewed 'lesbians' as a 'predatory lot' and 'incredibly fickle in their relationships,' she didn't think of herself as one, despite the fact that she has remained for forty years with a woman whom she described as 'very male.' I proceeded with the interview without any clear idea of how or whether to accommodate this woman into my project. [. . .]

Very shortly after, I read a letter written by Lorraine Hansberry in 1957, in which she pleaded the case for the heterosexually married lesbian. She suggested that her particular situation resulted from social and economic pressures that bound some women to a life that is what '. . . they have been taught all their lives to believe was their "natural" destiny—AND—their only expectation for . . . security.'[22] Hansberry's defense of heterosexually married lesbians was a plea for understanding for both herself and many others like her. As a historical document, it reminds us that particular racial, social, economic, and cultural factors permit, inhibit, and otherwise shape the choices available for living socially and/or sexually deviant lives. More implicitly, it warns us that if we do not loosen the identity categories with which we examine history, we will overlook many sources that can develop our understanding of the construction of deviance, of homosexuality, and of queer.

The conceptual category of 'queer' makes it possible to include discussion of these [. . .] women because it reframes the very thing we are examining. 'Queer' is an analytical tool that allows us to reread personal experiences and cultural prescriptions and proscriptions through a lens focused on how the *normal* gets constructed and maintained.

While providing new recuperative possibilities for our scholarship, queer also poses a political challenge to that very same scholarship. Just as 'queer' politics intends an oppositional relationship to the normal, so too must queer history. Just as queer politics is intended to counter assimilationist tendencies associated with gay and lesbian politics, so too must the queer historian recognize those same tendencies as they have operated in different historical and cultural contexts. Just as queer nationalists insist that 'we are NOT just like you except for who we sleep with,' so too must the deviant historiographer attend to the varieties of sexual subject formations subsumed under the label queer and identify and account for each.[23]

In doing so, some questions remain: How does the politics of queer shape the history of same-sex eroticism? How might queering history affect our readings and writings, interpretations and analyses? To investigate the usefulness of queer to historical work, I will illustrate by way of example. Women's prisons have been largely overlooked as a valuable site for studying the historical construction of lesbianism.[24] Evidence from prisons, like that from the annals of psychiatry, has been shunted aside with arguments that it does not represent the lives of 'normal,' 'well-adjusted,' 'average' lesbians. Furthermore, homosexual activity among inmates, or between inmates and prison personnel, can be easily dismissed as examples of 'situational' rather than 'true' homosexuality, the 'unnatural' consequence of isolation in single-sex institutions. By approaching the subject of lesbianism queerly, however, prison documents can become a valuable source for the investigation of lesbianism. Insofar as crime indicates the perpetration of some kind of rebellion from the socially prescribed dictates of and standards for 'proper' womanhood, incarcerated women are absolutely appropriate queer subjects. By failing to measure up to the dominant cultural norm for women, investigations concerning incarcerated women shed significant light on the construction and maintenance of the norm.

Second, dismissing women's prison relationships as somehow not representative of 'true' homosexuality is to believe implicitly in the existence of the 'true homosexual.' While the notion of the 'true' homosexual reflects the need for rigid regulation and strict policing of the borders between true and false to even exist as a conceptual category, queer captures and retrieves the stories from across the border.

Finally, by defining itself in a direct and oppositional relationship to the normal, a queer approach has no interest in sanitizing the image of the lesbian. By investing deviance with pride instead of shame, the notion of cleansing the lesbian for public consumption runs counter to queer interests. Furthermore, sanitizing the historical homosexual also smacks of the kind of assimilationist tendencies rejected by queers both politically and intellectually.

[. . .]

Drawing the line

[. . .] Determining, accounting for, and effecting change in how and where the line between acceptable and unacceptable sexual practices are drawn, when they are drawn, and by whom is the job of the critic, activist, and scholar. It is also a decidedly political task. The line itself may be inevitable, but where it is drawn is not.

As a politics of sexual deviance, queer must attend to the shifting of the line, to the remapping of the borders. Whereas queer politics tend to associate 'gay and lesbian' politics with attempts to redraw the line so that 'normal' homosexuals are no longer on the 'other' side of the DMZ [demilitarized zone], queers tribadically choose to rub up against the boundary in the hopes of destabilizing, denaturalizing, and perhaps dissolving it.

However, during this most recent period of contestation over the placement of the line, a 'queer and present danger' has emerged. While working to distinguish itself politically and intellectually from earlier examples of oppositional sexual politics, particularly gay and lesbian politics, the move to queer has engendered a problematic revisionist history. This revisionism is most clearly indicated in the tendency among queers to strip the radical oppositional nature of gay and lesbian political work of the 1970s and 1980s from their accounts. 'Gay and lesbian,' whether describing politics, organizations, frames of reference, visions of the future, or scholarship, have, for queers, come to be equated with assimilationist, accommodationist, mainstream, conservative, and 'retro.' Similarly and not unrelatedly, lesbian, like feminist, has been reduced to a description for anti-porn, anti-sex, vanilla-licking 'wimmin.' In effect, queer politics, rather than dissolving the line, redraws it in a fashion that hierarchizes deviance, thereby purging lesser deviants, whether literally or conceptually, from its ranks.

Rather than permitting these terms to continue serving as codes for a kind of 'straight queer' (read: more normal), the movement might be better served by historicizing the politics of drawing the line. In other words, by analyzing the ways in which deviance is mapped, contested, and then remapped in historically specific ways, we can identify the formations that challenge heteronormativity in particular contexts and under specific conditions.[25] For example, the homophile movement's theorizing of homosexuals as an 'oppressed minority, sharing an identity that subjected them to systematic injustice,' can be easily dismissed as bound by the limitations of identity politics.[26] Instead, I would suggest that we assess that movement's vision in the context of the time and under the circumstances in which it was produced.

I am criticizing the failure to recognize the specific challenges posed by differently constituted deviants in particular cultural and historical contexts. To the extent that the practice of history interprets and explains social, cultural, and political change, it must also delineate how those changes are produced, when and by whom, if they are to serve as 'lessons of history.' Ultimately, effective and progressive organizing, theorizing, and strategizing in the interests of a queer future can only profit from understanding rather than dismissing radicals of the past, as well as writing itself as a history of the present.

Notes

1   Alexander Doty, *Making Things Perfectly Queer: Interpreting Mass Culture* (Minneapolis: University of Minnesota Press, 1993); Lisa Duggan, 'Making it Perfectly Queer,' *Socialist Review* 22 (January–March, 1992): 11–31; 'On a Queer Day You Can See Forever' refers to the Lesbian, Gay, Queer Film Series at the Massachusetts Institute of Technology, 1992–3; Michael Warner, ed., *Fear of a Queer Planet: Queer Politics and Social Theory* (Minneapolis: University of Minnesota Press, 1993).

2   For the seminal work that linked homosexuality to degeneracy, see Richard von Krafft-Ebing, *Psychopathia Sexualis, With a Special Reference to the Antipathic Sexual Instinct*, trans. S. J. Redman (Brooklyn: Physician's and Surgeon's Book Company, 1908).

3   Radclyffe Hall, *The Well of Loneliness* (New York: Avon Books, 1981). Originally published in 1928.

4   Jennifer Terry, 'Theorizing Deviant Historiography,' *differences* 3 (Summer 1991): 55–74.

5   For a useful discussion of the terms of the battle in which the tensions and challenges facing queer theorists and historians (as well as between queer theorists and historians) are explained, see Lisa Duggan, 'The Discipline Problem: Queer Theory Meets Lesbian and Gay History,' paper presented at the annual meeting of the American Historical Association in San Francisco, January 1994, *GLQ: A Journal of Lesbian and Gay Studies*, 2, 3 (1995): 179–91. Duggan explains that 'Queer theorists are engaged in at least three areas of critique: (a) the critique of Humanist narratives which posit the progress of the self and of history, and thus tell the story of the heroic progress of gay liberationists against forces of repression, (b) the critique of empiricist methods which claim directly to represent the transparent "reality" of "experience," and claim to relate, simply and objectively, what happened, when and why, and (c) the critique of identity categories presented as stable, unitary or "authentic"'. 'These critiques,' she continues, 'applied to lesbian and gay history texts, might produce a fascinating discussion—but so far, they haven't. Queer theorists have generally either ignored lesbian/gay history texts, or treated them with condescension. Lesbian and gay historians, in turn, have largely ignored the critical implications of queer theory for their scholarly practice.'

6   Michel Foucault, *History of Sexuality, Volume 1: An Introduction*, trans. Robert Hurley (New York: Random House, 1978), 101.

7   In his preface to *The Well of Loneliness*, Ellis writes, '. . . so far as I know, it is the first English novel which presents, in a completely faithful and uncompromising form, one particular aspect of sexual life as it exists among us to-day. The relation of certain people—who, while different from their fellow human beings, are sometimes of the highest character and the finest aptitudes—to the often hostile society in which they move, presents difficult and still unsolved problems. . . .' On Ellis's place in early sexological discussions on the etiology and prospects for sexual inverts, see George Chauncey, 'From Sexual Inversion to Homosexuality: The Changing Medical Conceptualization of Female "Deviance,"' *Salmagundi*: 58–9 (Fall 1982–Winter 1983): 114–46; Paul Robinson, *The Modernization of Sex: Havelock Ellis, Alfred Kinsey, William Master, and Virginia Johnson* (Ithaca: Cornell University Press, 1976); Janice Irvine, *Disorders of Desire: Sex and Gender in Modern American Sexology* (Philadelphia: Temple University Press, 1990); Jennifer Terry, 'Lesbians Under the Medical Gaze: Scientists Search for Remarkable Differences,' *Journal of Sex Research* 27 (August 1990): 317–39; Phyllis Grosskurth, *Havelock Ellis: A Biography* (New York: New York University Press, 1985).

8   Robert A. Padgug, 'Sexual Matters: On Conceptualizing Sexuality in History,' *Radical History Review* 20 (Spring/Summer, 1979): 11.

9   Carole S. Vance, 'Social Construction Theory: Problems in the History of Sexuality: Keynote Address,' in *Homosexuality, Which Homosexuality?: International Conference on Gay and Lesbian Studies*, ed. Dennis Altman *et al.* (London: GMP Publishers, 1989), 30.

10   Mary McIntosh, 'The Homosexual Role,' *Social Problems* 16 (Fall 1968): 187.

11   Jonathan Ned Katz, *Gay American History: Lesbians and Gay Men in the U.S.A.* (New York: Thomas Y. Crowell Company, 1976), 6.

12   Blanche Cook advises that 'Women who love women, who choose women to nurture and support and to form a living environment in which to work creatively and independently are lesbians.' (Blanche Wiesen Cook, 'The Historical Denial of Lesbianism,' *Radical History Review* 20 (1979): 64.) See also, Cook, 'Women Alone Stir My Imagination,' *Signs* 4 (1979): 718–39; Frances Doughty, 'Lesbian Biography, Biography of Lesbians,' *Frontiers* 4 (1979): 76–9; Adrienne Rich, 'Compulsory Heterosexuality and Lesbian Existence,' in *Powers of Desire*, ed. Ann Snitow *et al.* (New York: Monthly Review, 1983), 177–205; Nancy Sahli, 'Smashing: Women's Relationships Before the Fall,' *Crysalis* 8 (1979): 17–27; Bonnie Zimmerman, 'On Writing Biography of Lesbians,' *Sinister Wisdom* 9 (1979): 95–7; Judith Schwarz, 'Yellow Clover: Katharine Lee Bates and Katharine Coman,' *Frontiers* 4 (1980): 59–67; Leila Rupp, 'Imagine My Surprise,' *Frontiers* 5 (1981): 61–70. For challenges to these approaches, see Gayle Rubin, 'Thinking Sex: Notes for a Radical Theory of the Politics of Sexuality,' in *Pleasure and Danger: The Politics of Sexuality*, ed. Carole Vance (Boston: Routledge and Kegan Paul, 1984), 267–319; and Alice Echols, 'Taming of the Id,' in *Pleasure and Danger*, 50–72; Joan Nestle, *A Restricted Country* (Ithaca: Firebrand Books, 1987); Elizabeth Kennedy and Madeline Davis, *Boots of Leather, Slippers of Gold: The History of A Lesbian Community* (New York: Routledge, 1993).

13   Martha Vicinus, 'Lesbian History: All Theory and No Facts or All Facts and No Theory?', *Radical History Review* 60 (Fall 1994): 57–75.

14   Kennedy and Davis, *Boots of Leather, Slippers of Gold*.

15   See Cook, 'Historical Denial of Lesbianism,' for a critique of requiring evidence of genital contact as proof of lesbianism.

16   Tomás Almaguer, 'Chicano Men: A Cartography of Homosexual Identity and Behavior,' *differences* 3 (Summer 1991): 75–100.

17   Michael Warner, 'Introduction', *Fear of a Queer Planet*, xxvi.

18   Teresa de Lauretis, 'Queer Theory: Lesbian and Gay Sexualities, An Introduction,' *differences* 3 (Summer 1991): iv–v.

19   Ibid., iv–v.

20   Ibid., iv–vi.

21   Ann Powers, 'Queer in the Streets, Straight in the Sheets: Notes on Passing,' *The Village Voice* (June 29, 1993), 24.

22   Lorraine Hansberry, 'Letter to the Editor,' *The Ladder* (August 1957), 28.

23   See Terry, 'Theorizing Deviant Historiography.'

24   For an exception, see Estelle Freedman, *Their Sisters' Keepers: Women's Prison Reform in America, 1830–1930* (Ann Arbor: University of Michigan Press, 1984), and her continuing work on Superintendent of the Massachusetts Reformatory for Women during the mid-twentieth century, Miriam Van Waters.

25   Comments by Melani McAlister on an earlier draft of this essay greatly helped in my thinking on this matter.

26   John D'Emilio, *Sexual Politics, Sexual Communities: The Making of a Homosexual Minority in the United States, 1940–70* (Chicago: University of Chicago Press, 1983), 4.

Judith M. Bennett

'LESBIAN-LIKE' AND THE SOCIAL
HISTORY OF LESBIANISMS

According to Judith Bennett, medieval gay and lesbian studies has, until recently, been dominated by a focus on elite theological, medical, literary and legal views of lesbianism. Much of this scholarship has also focused on mystical texts, the opaqueness of which have often enabled medievalists to resist explicitly lesbian readings. In the second extract by Bennett in this *Reader,* she aims to complement existing imaginative 'intellectual' approaches to lesbian history with a more social-historical research agenda in which the lives of ordinary women as opposed to those of the privileged and powerful are foregrounded. Bennett argues that historians can only achieve a wider lesbian reconstruction by broadening their perspective to include all those women who engaged in 'lesbian-like' behaviour. These are women whose lifestyles offered particular opportunities for same-sex love, who resisted feminine, marital norms of behaviour, or whose circumstances allowed them to provide support for other women. For Bennett, the term 'lesbian-like' simultaneously names '"lesbian" and destabilizes it'. It therefore avoids the assumption of a core identity and introduces a 'productive uncertainty', relocating the focus of research from persons to practices. The analytical categories of lesbian history may thus be extended to include single women, widows, cross-dressers, sexual rebels and marriage-resisters, in other words all those women with some autonomy from male sexual control. The term is not perfect, admits Bennett, for if over-used, it could 'create a lesbian history that lacks lesbians'. Nevertheless, its greater open-endedness might encourage scholars to imagine an interplay of lesbian identity and non-identity that rethinks the lives of single women for example (seen through a traditional heteronormative lens as embittered, lonely and failed female subjects) as lives of emotional richness and women-identified relationships. The term 'lesbian-like' will not resolve lesbian history's definitional dilemmas alone, she concludes, but it will expand 'the purview and evidence of lesbian history' and promote the writing of women's histories less hindered by heteronormative myopias.

IN QUEER STUDIES, SOCIAL HISTORY is 'queer.' Gay and lesbian histories abound with insightful analyses of texts produced by the powerful and privileged, but they are relatively poor in scholarship about the ordinary lives of average people.[1] I offer here a proposal that might adjust this balance a bit. The rich insights brought by intellectual, cultural, and literary studies of same-sex love are invaluable, but I seek to complement these with more complete understandings of the same-sex relations of people who were more real than imagined and more ordinary than extraordinary.[2] For example, I have been delighted to read in recent years about how medieval theologians conceptualized (or failed to conceptualize) same-sex relations between women; about how medieval nuns might have expressed same-sex desire in their kissing of images of Christ's wound; about how a lesbian character might have lurked in the thirteenth-century *Roman de Silence*, a story with a cross-dressed heroine; and about how a fourteenth-century Parisian play explored the meanings of accidental marriage between two women.[3] But I want more. I want to know about the actual practices and lives of ordinary women – more than ninety percent of medieval women – who never met a theologian, contemplated Christ's wound, heard a romance, or even saw a Parisian play.

This challenge is not peculiar to either women's history or medieval history. I shall not explore in this essay the ways in which my suggestion – a category of 'lesbian-like' – might (or might not) have analogous applications to the histories of gay men, but it is certainly clear that gay studies have been dominated by the words and writings of elite men – from Plato and Aelred of Rievaulx to Oscar Wilde and Armistead Maupin. Before the twentieth century, ordinary gay men can be traced most often in records of legal or religious persecution, records whose terse and sad entries compete poorly with the often rich and illuminating writings of philosophers, monks, diarists, and novelists. Lesbian histories are, of course, even more challenging to construct, for even fewer documents tell of past lesbians among either privileged or ordinary folk. Women wrote less; their writings survived less often (Sappho's works are the classic example); and they were less likely than men to come to the attention of civic or religious authorities. For more recent times, it is certainly easier to locate lesbians of ordinary circumstances – one need only think of the love shared by Addie Brown and Rebecca Primus in late nineteenth-century Hartford or of the culture of Buffalo's lesbian bars in the mid-twentieth century.[4] But even recent lesbian history is dominated by women who were wealthier, better educated, more powerful, and more articulate than most: Anne Lister, Radclyffe Hall, Gertrude Stein, M. Carey Thomas, Eleanor Roosevelt, Rita Mae Brown. I shall argue my case using medieval evidence, which I know best, but the particular difficulties of this evidence make it exemplary, not peculiar. If 'lesbian-like' can allow us to create a social history of poorly documented medieval lesbianisms, it might be even more useful for better documented peoples and times.

The medieval problem is bleak and simply stated. We can find information about medieval lesbian practices in the writings of theologians and canonists, in some very suggestive literary texts, and even in a few artistic representations, but if we want to write about actual women whom extant sources explicitly associate with same-sex genital contact, we have, as best I can tell, about a dozen women for the entire medieval millennium: all of them from the fifteenth century, and all of them, either imprisoned or executed for their activities.[5] This is material for only a *very* modest social history, and no matter how carefully we scour the religious and cultural remains of medieval Europe, it leaves us with a haunting problem. Where were the women who loved other women and how can we now recover their histories?

As always, these questions have things at stake behind them, things that make their answers more than a mere academic exercise.[6] My objectives are two-fold. First, I want to participate in the creation of histories that can have meaning for those women who today identify as lesbians, bisexuals, queers, or otherwise. This search has parallels in the social histories of other minorities, and it speaks to the emancipatory possibilities of history. Some historians would downplay this aspect of their work; I am not among them. History is not mere antiquarianism, fascinated with the past for its sake alone and assuming, naively, that there is a unitary past reality that can be approached, albeit not fully uncovered. In its best forms, history transcends the antiquarian impulse, seeking, of course, to understand the past in its proper contexts but seeking also to play with the ways in which the past illumines the present and the present illumines the past. As V. A. Kolve recently noted, 'we have little choice but to acknowledge our modernity, admit that our interest in the past is always (and by no means illegitimately) born of present concerns.'[7]

Second, I seek ways better to resist the heterosexist bias of history writing, especially as seen in the history of women. This queering, if you like, of women's history is essential and long overdue. In recent years, one feminist historian has bewailed the 'distorted and unhappy life' of medieval nuns, seen by her as forced to choose between the joys of heterosexual sex and motherhood, on the one hand, and a life of learning and contemplation, on the other. For Gerda Lerner, both heterosexual intercourse and childbearing were (and presumably still are) normal and desirable for women, and medieval nuns – as well as many early feminists – are to be pitied for having had to do without these purported joys.[8] Another feminist historian has produced an impassioned history of female monasticism, a history that nowhere notes the evidence – as discussed by Ann Matter and others – of intense emotional and homoerotic relations between medieval nuns. For Jo Ann McNamara, the celibacy of medieval nuns seems to have been threatened only by men.[9] And a third feminist historian has written about ordinary women in the medieval countryside in ways that normalize the heterosexual lifestyle. For myself, when I studied peasant women in the 1980s, the marriage-defined roles of not-yet-wed daughter, married wife, and bereaved widow loomed deceptively large.[10] Women's history must not continue along this road, simply must not continue to view women – from whatever time or place – through such a distorting hetero-normative lens.

* * *

Where, then, were the medieval women who loved other women and how can we recover their histories? To date, medievalists have responded to the sparse evidence for actual lesbian practices by focusing on intellectual or cultural approaches, not social history. The intellectual approach has focused mostly on why lesbianism was so underplayed – compared to male homosexuality – in the literatures of the Middle Ages. Most medieval physicians discussed male homosexuality much more fully than lesbianism; most authors of penitentials (that is, handbooks designed to guide priests in assigning penance during confession) either ignored lesbianism or rated it a lesser sin than male homosexuality; most theologians similarly either overlooked or trivialized same-sex relations between women. Why was lesbian practice so relatively untroubling? To John Boswell, the answer lies in the importance of women as conduits of bloodlines; since same-sex intimacy between women neither produced bastards nor introduced false heirs into lineages, it was relatively unproblematic.[11] To Jacqueline Murray, the phallocentric sexuality of the Middle Ages best explains its obfuscation of lesbian activity; as long as women-loving women did not use dildoes or other devices that seemingly mimicked penises, their same-sex relations were not seen by many medieval writers as being fully sexual.[12] To Harry Kuster and Raymond Cormier, sperm loom larger than phalluses; Kuster and Cormier suggest that in the 'spermatic economy' of medieval understandings of sex, little harm was done in same-sex relations between women – since no sperm were spilled.[13] To Joan Cadden, lesbian invisibility is part of the subordinate place of all women in the Middle Ages; seen as lesser, more passive, and secondary players in reproduction, women were easily overlooked by physicians and natural philosophers.[14]

These explanations are plausible and intriguing, and they are not mutually exclusive. But they too often construe a tiny group of authors as representing a broad medieval reality, reconstructing medieval attitudes about same-sex love between women mostly from the ideas of clerics – that is, the most male and most sexually anxious segment of medieval society. The observations and speculations of this clerical minority are certainly impressive, but their world view too often becomes, in modern interpretations, the medieval world view.[15] I am delighted to know what medieval theologians, canonists, and physicians thought about lesbianism, but their thoughts represent their sex, their education, their class privilege, and their professional contexts, as well as their time. In this sense, I am sympathetic with Catharine MacKinnon's comment that in most histories of sexuality 'the silence of the silenced is filled by the speech of those who have it and the fact of the silence is forgotten.'[16]

Still, in comparing how medieval theologians, physicians, canonists, and other authors treated male homosexuality and lesbianism, this intellectual approach has usefully delineated differences between elite perceptions of male same-sex relations, on the one hand, and female same-sex relations, on the other. To these medieval writers, same-sex love between women seemed less sexual than male homosexuality; it more often prompted explanations based on purported physical deformities; it was doubly perverse for positing love not only of the *same* sex but also of the *lesser* sex; and if it resulted in marriage resistance, it could be profoundly disruptive.[17] Among these authors, same-sex relations between women or men in the Middle Ages were not entirely unrelated, but they were certainly distinct. These elite understandings usefully remind us that when a medieval woman had sex with another woman, she did so within physical, social, familial, sexual, and gendered contexts quite different from those of a medieval man who had sex with another man.[18]

Literary and cultural scholars have also responded in creative ways to the virtual absence of actual women from the sources of medieval lesbianisms. In their playful and provocative readings of medieval texts, these critics have found homoerotic possibilities not only in the sources cited at the beginning of this essay but also in the music of Hildegarde of Bingen; in the piety of the mystic Hadwijch of Brabant;

in the admonitions of the anonymous author of *Holy Maidenhead*; in the ragings of Margery Kempe; and even in the cross-dressing of Joan of Arc.[19] Although these analyses offer insightful commentaries on how we might better imagine the sexual mentalities of the Middle Ages, even the best of them can give me pause. As literary criticism, these readings reach plausible conclusions, but as guides to social history, they are considerably less convincing.

To begin with, many of these readings draw on mystical texts – that is, texts that were profoundly obscure at the time of their composition and are profoundly hard to interpret today. As Ulrike Wiethaus has suggested, the obscurity of these texts *might* have allowed female mystics to express and still mask same-sex desires.[20] But the obscurity of these texts *might* also encourage modern scholars to read desires into them that would have been foreign to their authors: fascinating readings, in other words, rather than historically plausible ones. Caroline Bynum, whose opinions have considerable authority in studies of mysticism, female spirituality, and conceptions of the body, has resisted lesbian readings of such texts, arguing that we too readily sexualize medieval somatic experiences and expressions. Others, such as Karma Lochrie, vehemently disagree, arguing that Bynum resolutely sees maternity where same-sex affections might, in fact, have been at play.[21] The debate on this issue has only just begun, but in the meantime, those who, like myself, are interested in actual people and plausible behaviors might best respond with caution – as well as pleasure – to literary readings of same-sex expressions in mystical texts.

Moreover, in other cases, I have been more impressed by the cleverness of modern critics than by the historicity of their arguments. It is great fun, for example, to read Lochrie's impressive exploration of the artistic, literary, and linguistic ties between Christ's wound and female genitalia, and to speculate, therefore, that the kissing of images of Christ's wound by medieval nuns somehow paralleled lesbian oral sex. Yet Lochrie very wisely does not claim that any medieval nun who contemplated Christ's wound ever, in fact, was really thinking about last night's tumble in bed with a sister nun.[22] Within the traditions of literary scholarship, readings such as Lochrie's can stand on their own, properly appreciated for their careful and insightful explication of interpretive possibilities. Yet they sometimes speak less convincingly about the historical issues that concern me – the possibilities of same-sex love between actual women in the Middle Ages.

If we are to move beyond elite understandings of lesbian relations in the Middle Ages and beyond intriguing-but-not-fully-historicized readings that interrupt, redirect, or even queer the canonical texts of medieval studies, we need to complement – and I *do* mean complement, not supplant – intellectual and cultural approaches with social historical study. To accomplish this, we need much more than the brief and depressing notices we have about the dozen or so women who found themselves in legal trouble for same-sex relations in the fifteenth century. These might be the only women for whom we can be reasonably confident about same-sex genital contact, but they need not be the only women whose stories are relevant to lesbian history.[23] To approach the social history of lesbianisms in the Middle Ages, I suggest that we try broadening our perspective to include women whom I have chosen to call 'lesbian-like': women whose lives might have particularly offered opportunities for same-sex love; women who resisted norms of feminine behavior based on heterosexual marriage; women who lived in circumstances that allowed them to nurture and support other women (to paraphrase

Blanche Wiesen Cook's famous formulation).[24] I first coined the term 'lesbian-like' in a paper presented in 1990; Martha Vicinus adopted it to good effect in an article published in 1994, and it is now being used by such other historians as Alison Oram.[25] Thus far, however, the term has been more evoked than explored, and in this essay, I would like to undertake that exploration. What might 'lesbian-like' really mean? How might it enhance the ways in which we approach the history of lesbianisms?

* * *

It may seem crazy to create yet another piece of jargon and to link to it a troubled term like 'lesbian.' After all, no one today is really sure what 'lesbian' means. Are lesbians born or made? Do lesbians delight in sex with women exclusively or can the term encompass those who enjoy sex with men as well as women? What defines lesbian sex – genital contact, 'bosom sex,' or an even more amorphous 'erotic in female terms'?[26] And, indeed, might sexual practice be less determinative of lesbianism than *desire* for women, *primary love* for women (as in 'women-identified women'), or even *political* commitment to women (especially as manifested in resistance to 'compulsory heterosexuality')? Lesbian theorists offer us debate on these questions, not firm agreement, and this definitional fluidity has been a source of both anxiety and flexibility.

Nevertheless, the ever-changing contemporary meanings of 'lesbian' have often been belied by a persistent assumption of a core lesbian identity, especially when used in such expressions as 'she came out as a lesbian.' This invocation of identity is both affirming and embarrassing. To me, it still speaks powerfully about the revelation of self I felt when I first had sex with another woman in 1973, but it also, in 2000, seems to be unduly naive, simple, and maybe even silly. Still worse, it can work to obfuscate critical differences. Do various sorts of women who love women – femmes and butches, lesbian feminists and lipstick lesbians, vanilla lesbians and sexual radicals, American lesbians and Jamaican lesbians, rich lesbians and poor ones, 15-year-old lesbians and 55-year-old ones, African-American lesbians and Asian-American lesbians – really share enough to fit comfortably under the rubric 'lesbian'? Are 'we,' in other words, really a 'we'?

These are troubles enough, but for historians, 'lesbian' is also troubled by its apparent contemporaneity. To many scholars, the use of 'lesbian' to describe women before the late nineteenth century reeks of ahistoricism, and especially of the naive search for past heroines plucked out of historical context and reclaimed for presentist uses. For some (mostly pre-modernists), it is important to preserve the past from presentist concerns. For others (mostly modernists), it is important to preserve the distinctiveness of modernity, especially as represented by a pseudo-Foucaultian paradigm that restricts sexual identities and, indeed, sexuality itself to the modern era.[27] Strange bedfellows, traditional medievalist and queer theorists, and their coalition is powerful enough to encourage many historians to abandon 'lesbian' in favor of terms less laden with contemporary identities, such as 'homo-erotic' or 'same-sex relations.' This concession is, I think, both unnecessary and counterproductive.[28]

In the first place, 'lesbian' has considerable antiquity, and its use by historians accords well with long-accepted professional practices. More than a thousand years

ago, the Byzantine commentator Arethas associated 'lesbian' with same-sex relations between women. By equating *Lesbiai* with *tribades* and *hetairistriai*, Arethas
indicated that, to at least one person in the tenth century, the term 'lesbian' roughly
signified what it roughly signifies today.[29] In English, the first uses of 'lesbian' to
denote same-sex relations between women date at least as early as the 1730s.[30]
Unlike 'gay' or 'queer,' then, 'lesbian' has deep historical roots. Yet even without
these roots, 'lesbian' can, with due care, apply just as well to the past as do many
other terms that have recent origins or meanings. In historical writing, it is not
uncommon to find, for example, that Jakob Fugger was a 'capitalist' (long before
Adam Smith and Karl Marx), that Thomas Aquinas was 'Catholic' (although he lived
several centuries before Catholicism took on its post-Reformation meaning), or that
the Black Prince prepared for 'kingship' (even though it was kingship of a different
sort than that anticipated today by Charles Windsor). Historians are accustomed to
using modern words to investigate past times, to assessing the changing meanings
of words over time, and to weighing differences as well as similarities in their uses
of such words. We should try to allow the same historical range, with the same
comparative cautions, for 'lesbian.'

Indeed, to do otherwise might do more harm than good. First, the refusal to
use 'lesbian' defers to homophobia and thereby promotes heteronormative misconceptions
of the past. To some people, 'lesbian' is a more upsetting word than
'capitalist,' 'Catholic,' or 'king,' and it can seem rude or slanderous to suggest that
such women as Margery Kempe or Hildegarde of Bingen had feelings or experiences that we might associate with modern lesbianisms. This homophobic anxiety
works on many levels, some articulated and others unacknowledged. Its main effect
is bad history, history driven by heteronormative imperatives. For example, our
modern tendency to classify women according to sex of lovers – and thereby labeling
them as lesbian, heterosexual, bisexual, queer, or whatever – does not seem to
work well for the European Middle Ages. Penitentials suggest that medieval theologians thought in terms of a wide range of sexual activities, among which choosing
a lover of the same sex was only one of many possible sexual sins. Romances suggest
that aristocratic husbands worried more that their wives might produce illegitimate
heirs and less that their wives might love others or, indeed, might play with lovers
in non-reproductive ways. And a wide variety of sources indicates that medieval
people identified themselves less by sexual practice and more by other criteria –
willful or repentant sinner; householder or dependent; serf, free, or wellborn;
Christian or Jew. Insofar as there *were* sexual identities in the Middle Ages, the best
articulated might have been those of the celibate and the virginal.[31] These are
important and profound differences that separate the world of medieval Europe
from our world today, but they can disappear in history-writing that seeks out
heterosexuality as pervasive, natural, and ideal.

Second, a refusal to apply 'lesbian' to the distant past stabilizes things that are
better kept in a state of productive instability. Is there such a stable entity as a
modern lesbian? Clearly not. Was there such a stable meaning to 'lesbian' in any
past time? Probably not. We should play with these instabilities and learn from
them, not reify one in order to deny relationship with the other. For example,
medieval sexual regimes look very different from our own, but our information is,
as yet, very preliminary and even contradictory. Some scholars are finding that
medieval people operated on a one-sex system that saw the male body as the sole

standard, others that medieval people embraced a two-sex binary that rigidly separated male and female; and still others that medieval people played readily with ideas about intermediate genders or third sexes.[32] Are these differences a matter of method or reading? A matter of sources or genre? A matter of competing or complementary medieval ideologies? We cannot yet say. We need more readings, more research, and more speculations before we can sort out even the most basic aspects of medieval sexual practices. In these circumstances, it would be counterproductive to create a tidy discrimination between the abundance of modern lesbianisms and what we still have to learn about medieval sexualities.[33] In short, one of our first steps toward understanding the antecedents of modern sexual identities must be to examine how well and how poorly our modern ideas of 'lesbians' and 'heterosexual women' and 'bisexuals' and 'queers' work for the past. If we avoid these terms altogether, we will create a pure inviolable, and irrelevant past: a fetish instead of a history.[34] And we will risk doing the same to the present. No word has transparent meaning, now or in the past.

In any case, I am suggesting not the use of 'lesbian,' but instead the use of 'lesbian-like,' a hyphenated construction that both names 'lesbian' and destabilizes it.[35] The 'lesbian' in 'lesbian-like' articulates the often-unnamed, forcing historians who might prefer otherwise to deal with their own heterosexist assumptions and with the possibility of lesbian expressions in the past. Yet at the same time as the term forthrightly names the unnamed, the 'like' in 'lesbian-like' decenters 'lesbian,' introducing into historical research a productive uncertainty born of likeness and resemblance, not identity. It might therefore allow us to expand lesbian history beyond its narrow and quite unworkable focus on women who engaged in certifiable same-sex genital contact (a certification hard to achieve even for many contemporary women), and to incorporate into lesbian history women who, regardless of their sexual pleasures, lived in ways that offer certain affinities with modern lesbians. In so doing, we might incorporate into lesbian history sexual rebels, gender rebels, marriage-resisters, cross-dressers, singlewomen. It struck me as a 'herstory' sort of invention until I read below that this was the term used in early England, that there were women who found special sustenance in female worlds of love and ritual.[36] I hope that, in such ways, 'lesbian-like' might speak to our modern need for a useable past, for what Margaret Hunt has called the 'cautious kinship' that can link our many lives with the histories of those long dead.[37]

As a social historian, I am most interested in exploring affinities that are broadly sociological – affinities related to social conduct, marital status, living arrangements, and other behaviors that might be traced in the archives of past societies. I would therefore like to play with the implications of naming as lesbian-like a range of practices that impinge on our own modern – and very variable – ideas about lesbianism. If women had genital sex with other women, regardless of their marital or religious status, let us consider that their behavior was lesbian-like. If women's primary emotions were directed toward other women, regardless of their own sexual practices, perhaps their affection was lesbian-like. If women lived in single-sex communities, their life circumstances might be usefully conceptualized as lesbian-like. If women resisted marriage or, indeed, just did not marry, whatever the reason, their singleness can be seen as lesbian-like. If women dressed as men, whether in response to saintly voices, in order to study, in pursuit of certain careers, or just to travel with male lovers, their cross-dressing was arguably lesbian-like.

And if women worked as prostitutes or otherwise flouted norms of sexual propriety, we might see their deviance as lesbian-like.

Unlike Adrienne Rich, I do not wish to label all woman-identified experience – from maternal nurturance and lesbian sadomasochism to the esprit de corps of an abortion rights march – on a lesbian continuum.[38] The essence of Rich's continuum is 'primary intensity between and among women,' an intensity that involves both 'sharing of a rich inner life' and 'bonding against male tyranny.' Some behaviors that I would identify as lesbian-like – such as singleness – were not necessarily based in the female bonding at the center of Rich's analysis. To my mind, a single-woman in a sixteenth-century European town, regardless of her emotional life, lived in ways relevant to lesbian history: she tended to be poor, in part because her household was not supported by the better earning power of men; she was viewed by her neighbors with some suspicion and concern; she could expect to be tolerated, *if* her conduct was above reproach in other respects. This singlewoman might have shared neither an emotional life nor any political commitment with other women, but her life circumstances were, in some respects, lesbian-like.

Unlike Martha Vicinus, I do not wish to privilege sexual behaviors in defining lesbians past or present.[39] Many lesbian-like behaviors – such as the deep attachments formed between some medieval nuns – were not necessarily sexual in expression. I certainly am not eager to wash sexuality out of lesbian-like, but same-sex relations are not a sine qua non of lesbianism (as the debates of lesbian theorists make clear), and if we treat lesbianism as rooted primarily or even exclusively in sexuality, we create very limited histories (as rehearsed above for the Middle Ages). In thinking about both 'lesbian' and 'lesbian-like,' sexual behavior is certainly important, but it need not be defining.

I am hesitant to restrict the purview of 'lesbian-like,' for, as Greta Christina has argued so well, patrolling the borders of any loaded term is a divisive and elitist business.[40] But I am also cognizant of the risk of 'lesbian-*lite*,' and I hope we might use 'lesbian-like' playfully and wisely. Obviously, 'lesbian-like' can be extended to ridiculous dimensions, by arguing, for example, that since some modern lesbians wear sandals, all sandal-wearers in past times were lesbian-like.[41] Let us stick to essentials that will allow us to construct histories that have meaning to sexual minorities today. I shall not define those essentials, for to do so would be as pointless as trying to secure the meaning of 'lesbian' or 'sexual minorities' or even, indeed, 'history with meaning.' We stand on shifting sands, but we need not lose our balance. Obviously, 'lesbian-like' will overlook some lesbians in past times, particularly those who conformed to social norms. Let us remember that although 'lesbian-like' can usefully broaden the field, it cannot cover it. And, obviously, 'lesbian-like' speaks more about circumstance than choice; some singlewomen in pre-modern Europe willfully schemed to avoid marriage, but most found themselves unmarried thanks to poor luck, family circumstances, religious imperatives, or plain poverty. Let us appreciate the sociological uses of 'lesbian-like' without endowing it with motivational meanings.

To my mind, 'lesbian-like' offers not an endless set of possibilities but a set that is multidimensional, allowing any one of several criteria to call forth 'lesbian-like' as an analytical tool. In playing with the possibilities of 'lesbian-like,' I am more comfortable applying it to *practices* than to *persons*, for most women whom I might label 'lesbian-like' seem to have engaged in some lesbian-like behaviors (such

as living in single-sex communities) but not others (such as indulging in sexual relations with other women). But perhaps we will eventually come to decide that we
can call some of these women 'lesbian-like' – maybe, for example, those whose
behaviors evoked several criteria at once. Certainly, I would think that a woman
who never married and shared an emotionally rich life with another woman might
be more 'lesbian-like' *as a person* than one who cross-dressed to follow her husband
to war. But, then, I would call the *behavior* of the Delany sisters lesbian-like, not
their *persons*.[42] Again, the sands shift; again, wise play is necessary.

[. . .]

'Lesbian-like' is not a perfect term: it adds new jargon to our field; it is as
impossible as 'lesbian' to define precisely; it highlights deviance more than
conformity; it stresses circumstances over motivations; and if over-used, it might
even create a lesbian history that lacks lesbians (however defined). Yet, 'lesbian-
like' might offer two critical uses for lesbian history. First, it can add nuance to
behaviors that we might too readily identify as lesbian [. . .] Second, it can add
many sorts of behaviors to the historical study of lesbianisms: cross-dressing; pious
autonomy from male control; singleness; monastic same-sex community; prostitution; unremarried widowhood. Each of these practices shares affinities with
contemporary lesbianisms, and insofar as lesbian history, like all history, plays with
the interplay between past and present, these lesbian-like behaviors are arguably as
important as sexual practices. [. . .]

'Lesbian-like' can allow us to imagine in plausible ways the opportunities for
same-sex love that actual women once encountered, and it can allow us to explore
those plausibilities without asserting a crude correlation between our varied experiences today and the varied lives of those long dead. In the process, of course, we
might understand ourselves better, for through exploring likeness, resemblance,
and difference with past times, we might better understand the fraught interplay
of identity and non-identity in our own lives. [. . .]

Consider, for just one example, the singlewomen whose never-married state
has prompted me to incorporate them under the rubric of lesbian-like. No doubt,
many singlewomen never enjoyed sex with other women, but 'lesbian-like' might
nevertheless help us view them more clearly. Singlewomen have usually been seen
through a heteronormative lens – and therefore seen as pathetic, sexless, and lonely
failures in a game of heterosexual courtship and marriage. If we use 'lesbian-like'
to put aside this distorting lens, we can discover that, although singlewomen might
have often been pathetically poor, their lives were not devoid of either sexual possibility or emotional richness. Many singlewomen were sexually active, and since
procreative sex was problematic for the not-married, singlewomen might have
particularly engaged in forms of sexual pleasure that easily accommodated partners
of either sex. Similarly, although singlewomen lived without husbands and (often)
children, their emotional lives could be quite full – and woman-identified. Some
lived together in what demographers have dubbed 'spinster clusters'; many congre-
gated in specific neighborhoods or streets; most worked in occupations – as servants,
spinsters, lacemakers, laborers, or hucksters – that brought them into daily contact
with more women than men; and many had close female relatives and friends with
whom they shared life's sorrows and joys.[43] If we do not use 'lesbian-like' to see

singlewomen in new ways – if we do not thereby startle ourselves out of our own heterosexist assumptions – we might continue to interpret their lives, as did Gerda Lerner, as 'distorted and unhappy.'[44] In this sense, 'lesbian-like' is shock therapy for a women's history – modern as well as medieval – that not only has long over-looked lesbian possibilities but also has resolutely defined 'women' as 'heterosexual women.'[45]

'Lesbian-like' will not yield real-life lesbians in past times; it will not help us identify every past instance of same-sex relations; it will not address motivation as much as situation; it will not resolve the definitional dilemmas that both plague and enrich the term 'lesbian'; and if used as a blunt instrument, it will produce blunt results. But if used in playful, wise, and careful ways, 'lesbian-like' can address difficult problems that now confront lesbian historians, on the one hand, and women's historians, on the other. In helping us imagine possibilities and plausibil-ities that have hitherto been closed off from lesbian history, 'lesbian-like' can expand the purview and evidence of lesbian history. And in encouraging us to see past soci-eties in more complex ways, 'lesbian-like' can promote the writing of women's histories that are less hindered by heteronormative blinders, sexist ideologies, or modernist assumptions. As a new way of thinking about the past, 'lesbian-like' might both enrich lesbian history and reform women's history.

Notes

1   Social history is not, of course, confined to the study of ordinary people, for it is perfectly possible to write a social history of aristocrats or other privileged folk. Yet social history is distinguished from most historical approaches by its relatively greater interest in average people. In the case of queer studies, social history is 'queer' not only in its greater emphasis on ordinary people but also in its questions (about actual practices and lives) and its greater reliance on documentary sources.

2   The 'real' is, of course, always apparitional, always a reductionist fantasy. See particu-larly Joan Scott, 'The Evidence of Experience,' *Critical Inquiry* 17 (1991): 773–97. Yet acknowledging the fantasy of 'reality' does not, I think, reduce history to fiction; historians can still seek out the more multivalent and still substantial 'actual' and 'plausible.' In this regard, I am indebted to Charles Zita who introduced me to Greg Dening's distinction between the possibilities of 'actuality' and the reductionism of 'reality.' See especially Greg Dening, *Performances* (Melbourne: Melbourne University Press, 1996), p. 60.

3   Jacqueline Murray, 'Twice Marginal and Twice Invisible: Lesbians in the Middle Ages,' in *Handbook of Medieval Sexuality*, ed. Vern L. Bullough and James A. Brundage (New York: Garland, 1996), pp. 191–223; Karma Lochrie, 'Mystical Acts, Queer Tendencies,' in *Constructing Medieval Sexuality*, ed. Karma Lochrie, *et al.* (Minneapolis: University of Minnesota Press, 1997), pp. 180–200; Kathleen M. Blumreich, 'Lesbian Desire in the Old French *Roman de Silence*,' *Arthuriana* 7:2 (1997): 47–62; Robert L. A. Clark and Claire Sponsler, 'Queer Play: The Cultural Work of Cross-dressing in Medieval Drama,' *New Literary History* 28:2 (1997): 319–44.

4   Karen V. Hansen, '"No *Kisses* is Like Youres": An Erotic Friendship between Two African-American Women during the Mid-Nineteenth Century,' *Gender and History* 7:2 (1995): 153–82; Elizabeth Lapovsky Kennedy and Madeline D. Davis, *Boots of Leather, Slippers of Gold: The History of a Lesbian Community* (New York: Routledge, 1993).

5   Unlike historians of more modern eras, who might find information about the same-sex relations of ordinary women in letters, diaries, and other personal memorabilia

or even through oral interviews, medievalists must rely on criminal accusations. This especially limits our purview, for it allows us to see lesbians only in scripted contexts that emphasize deviance, disorder, and danger. The pre-1500 cases identified thus far are as follows: (a) seven women executed in Bruges in 1482–3. Marc Boone, 'State Power and Illicit Sexuality: The Persecution of Sodomy in Late Medieval Bruges,' *Journal of Medieval History* 22:2 (1996): 135–53 at 151, n. 62 (Boone also cites some cases in the early sixteenth century); (b) a reputed lesbian drowned in Speier in 1477. Louis Crompton, 'The Myth of Lesbian Impunity: Capital Laws from 1270 to 1791,' *Journal of Homosexuality* 6:1/2 (1980–1): 11–25 at 17; (c) two women charged with a 'vice against nature which is called sodomy' in Rottweil in 1444. Helmut Puff, 'Localizing Sodomy: The "Priest and Sodomite" in Pre-Reformation Germany and Switzerland,' *Journal of the History of Sexuality* 8:2 (1997): 165–95, at 182–3; (d) two women cited in a French royal register of 1405. Joan Cadden, *Meanings of Sex Difference in the Middle Ages: Medicine, Science, and Culture* (Cambridge: Cambridge University Press, 1993), p. 224. Some of these cases are examined more fully in two forthcoming articles: Helmut Puff, 'Female Sodomy: The Trial of Katherina Hetzeldorfer, 1477,' *Journal of Medieval and Renaissance Studies*, 30:1 (2000): 41–61 and Edith J. Benkov, 'The Erased Lesbian: Sodomy and the Legal Tradition in Medieval Europe,' in *Same-Sex Love and Desire Among Women in the Middle Ages*, ed. Francesca Canadé Sautman and Pamela Sheingorn (Basingstoke and New York: Palgrave, 2001). Since I have argued elsewhere that 1500 marks an artificial divide in women's history, I would like to stress that my reliance on it here is purely rhetorical. It is striking how many forays into the study of medieval lesbianisms rely on non-medieval cases (especially the early seventeenth-century case of Benedetta Carlini), but even these extensions of the Middle Ages do not result in many more cases. See, for example, the relative paucity of female same-sex relations prosecuted in eighteenth-century Amsterdam: Theo Van der Meer, 'Tribades on Trial: Female Same-Sex Offenders in Late Eighteenth-Century Amsterdam,' *Journal of the History of Sexuality* 1:3 (1991): 424–45. For Benedetta Carlini, see Judith C. Brown, *Immodest Acts: The Life of a Lesbian Nun in Renaissance Italy* (New York: Oxford University Press, 1986). For my argument on chronology, see 'Medieval Women, Modern Women: Across the Great Divide,' in *Culture and History 1350–1600: Essays on English Communities, Identities, and Writing*, ed. David Aers (London: Harvester Wheatsheaf, 1992), pp. 147–75 (revised version in *Feminists Revision History*, ed. Ann-Louise Shapiro [New Brunswick: Rutgers University Press, 1994], pp. 47–72).

6   For the importance of stressing strategic considerations in discussions such as these, see Shane Phelan, '(Be)coming Out: Lesbian Identity and Politics,' *Signs* 18:4 (1993): 765–90.

7   V. A. Kolve, 'Ganymede/*Son of Getron*: Medieval Monasticism and the Drama of Same-Sex Desire,' *Speculum* 73:4 (1998): 1014–67, at 1016.

8   Gerda Lerner, *The Creation of Feminist Consciousness* (New York: Oxford University Press, 1993), p. 179. This phrase is applied to female writers before the mid-nineteenth century, a group that implicitly includes the medieval nuns and mystics discussed earlier. Lerner also describes medieval mystics in terms of 'sacrifices' (p. 65) and 'insecurity, sickness' (p. 83). On p. 30, she concludes that the single, cloistered, or widowed status of many learned women suggests that women were unable to 'combine a sexual and reproductive life with the life of the intellect' and were 'forced to choose between the life of a woman and the life of the mind.'

9   Jo Ann Kay McNamara, *Sisters in Arms: Catholic Nuns through Two Millennia* (Cambridge, MA: Harvard University Press, 1996). McNamara speaks briefly about emotional attachments between women on pp. 76 and 113, and she cursorily mentions medieval fears of same-sex attractions between women on pp. 144 and 380. As best I can tell, these references are her only considerations of the possibility of emotional and/or sexual intimacy between medieval nuns. For fuller attention to same-sex desire

between nuns, see Ann Matter, 'My Sister, My Spouse: Woman-identified Women in Medieval Christianity,' *Journal of Feminist Studies in Religion* 2:2 (1986): 81–93; Karma Lochrie, 'Mystical Acts.'

10   Judith M. Bennett, *Women in the Medieval English Countryside: Gender and Household in Brigstock before the Plague* (New York: Oxford University Press, 1986).

11   John Boswell, *Same-Sex Unions in Premodern Europe* (New York: Villard Books, 1994), pp. xxvii–xxx.

12   As Murray phrases it on p. 199 of 'Twice Marginal,' for medieval people, '[s]exual activity without a penis was difficult to imagine.'

13   Harry J. Kuster and Raymond J. Cormier, 'Old Views and New Trends: Observations on the Problem of Homosexuality in the Middle Ages,' *Studi Medievali*, ser. 3, 25 (1984): 587–610, esp. 600–1, 609.

14   Joan Cadden, *Meanings of Sex*, p. 224.

15   Hence, for example, Jacqueline Murray writes about 'the devaluation of physical relations across medieval society' ('Twice Marginal,' p. 206). This was perhaps true for theologians, philosophers, and other clerics, but it was certainly not true for ordinary medieval people – peasants, laborers, artisans, merchants – whose appreciation of physical relations is manifestly clear in their bawdy tales and songs. For just two examples of such alternative discourses, see two songs copied into the commonplace book of an Oxford student in the fifteenth century, 'Led I the Dance a Midsummer's Day' and 'All this Day I have Sought,' both printed in Richard Leighton Greene, *The Early English Carols*, 2nd edition (Oxford: Clarendon Press: 1977), items 453 and 452 respectively. The latter has been rendered in modern English by P. J. P. Goldberg in his *Women in England c. 1275–1535* (Manchester: Manchester University Press, 1995), pp. 88–90, but he left out the sexually explicit stanzas.

16   Catharine MacKinnon, 'Does Sexuality Have a History?' in *Discourses of Sexuality: From Aristotle to AIDS*, ed. Donna C. Stanton (Ann Arbor: University of Michigan Press, 1992), pp. 117–36 at 121.

17   Bernadette J. Brooten has similarly observed that the 'highly gendered, social arrangements' of same-sex love in ancient Rome distinguished male homosexuality and lesbianism. See her *Love Between Women: Early Christian Responses to Female Homoeroticism* (Chicago: University of Chicago Press, 1996), quote at p. 14. For the greater physicality of elite understandings of lesbianism, see Helen Rodmite Lemay, 'William of Saliceto on Human Sexuality,' *Viator* 12 (1981): 165–81, at 178–9, and also Katharine Park, 'The Rediscovery of the Clitoris: French Medicine and the Tribade, 1570–1620,' in *The Body in Parts: Fantasies of Corporeality in Early Modern Europe*, ed. David Hillman and Carla Mazzio (New York: Routledge, 1997), pp. 170–93. There is some evidence that the bodies of male homosexuals were occasionally also seen as marked by their acts. See: Steven F. Kruger, 'Racial/Religious and Sexual Queerness in the Middle Ages,' *Medieval Feminist Newsletter* 16 (Fall, 1993): 32–6, esp. 34 (to me, his evidence suggests physical revulsion on the part of medieval commentators, not an attribution of physical deformity to male homosexuals); Joan Cadden, 'Sciences/Silences: The Natures and Languages of "Sodomy" in Peter of Abano's *Problemata* Commentary,' in *Constructing Medieval Sexuality*, pp. 40–57; Mark D. Jordan, *The Invention of Sodomy in Christian Theology* (Chicago: University of Chicago Press, 1997), esp. pp. 114–35.

18   As Judith Butler has made very clear, it would be a mistake to overlook matters of gender difference when studying sexuality. See her 'Against Proper Objects,' *differences* 6:2/3 (1994): 1–26.

19   Bruce Holsinger, 'The Flesh of the Voice: Embodiment and the Homoerotics of Devotion in the Music of Hildegarde of Bingen (1098–1179),' *Signs* 19:1 (1993): 92–125; Matter, 'My Sister, My Spouse'; Ulrike Wiethaus, 'Female Homoerotic Discourse and Religion in Medieval Germanic Culture,' in *Gender and Difference in the*

Middle Ages, ed. Sharon Farmer and Carol Pasternak (Minneapolis: University of Minnesota Press, 2002); Mary Anne Campbell, 'Redefining Holy Maidenhead: Virginity and Lesbianism in Late Medieval England,' *Medieval Feminist Newsletter*, 13 (1992): 14–15; Kathy Lavezzo, 'Sobs and Sighs between Women: The Homoerotics of Compassion in *The Book of Margery Kempe*,' in *Premodern Sexualities*, ed. Louise Fradenburg and Carla Freccero (New York: Routledge, 1996), pp. 175–98; Susan Crane, 'Clothing and Gender Definition: Joan of Arc,' *Journal of Medieval and Early Modern Studies* 26:2 (1996): 297–320.

20 Wiethaus, 'Female Homoerotic Discourse.'

21 This maternal interpretation runs throughout Bynum's *Holy Feast and Holy Fast: The Religious Significance of Food to Medieval Women* (Berkeley: University of California Press, 1987), but see also her explicit statement in *Fragmentation and Redemption: Essays on Gender and the Human Body in Medieval Religion* (New York: Zone, 1992), p. 86. For Karma Lochrie's critique, see 'Mystical Acts' in *Constructing Medieval Sexuality*, and 'Desiring Foucault,' *Journal of Medieval and Early Modern Studies* 27:1 (1997): 3–46.

22 Lochrie, 'Mystical Acts.' In public discussion at the 1998 conference on the Queer Middle Ages, Karma Lochrie indicated her willingness to entertain the possibility that medieval nuns did, in fact, venerate Christ's wound in ways that spoke to their own same-sex desires and actions.

23 Although same-sex sexual contact was the issue in these cases, legal records do not, of course, constitute truthful records. Moreover, in many cases [. . .] one woman asserted her innocence by accusing the other of unnatural aggression toward her – that is, one was scripted as 'normal' and the other as 'abnormal.' Still, most other indicators of lesbian relations in medieval records are less transparently sexual, and they are also more susceptible to erasure through interpretation. See, for example, Angelica Rieger's argument that Bieris de Romans, author of a love song addressed to another woman, was not, in fact, a lesbian. Angelica Rieger, 'Was Bieris de Romans Lesbian? Women's Relations with Each Other in the World of the Troubadours,' in *The Voice of the Trobairitz: Perspectives on Women Troubadours*, ed. William D. Paden (Philadelphia: University of Pennsylvania Press, 1989), pp. 73–94. Given the hetero-normativity of modern scholarship and the homophobia of many modern scholars, almost all citations to lesbian or gay practices can, of course, be interpreted out of existence – and done so in ways that suit academic culture particularly well. As a result, each instance of the interpretive denial of same-sex relations must be approached with careful skepticism.

24 Blanche Wiesen Cook, 'The Historical Denial of Lesbianism,' *Radical History Review* 20 (1979): 60–5.

25 Martha Vicinus, 'Lesbian History: All Theory and No Facts or All Facts and No Theory?' *Radical History Review* 60 (1994): 57–75. Alison Oram, '"Friends", Feminists and Sexual Outlaws: Lesbianism and British History,' in *Straight Studies Modified: Lesbian Interventions in the Academy*, ed. Gabriele Griffin and Sonya Andermahr (London: Cassell, 1997), pp. 168–83.

26 I am grateful to Emily McLain for helping me see how a focus on genital contact can rest in heterosexist and phallocentric assumptions. For 'bosom sex,' see Hansen, 'No Kisses.' For the 'erotic in female terms,' see Adrienne Rich, 'Compulsory Heterosexuality and Lesbian Existence,' *Signs* 5 (1980), pp. 631–60 at 650.

27 As I understand David Halperin's new essay in *Representations*, we need no longer flounder on the shoals of the distinction between sex acts and sexual identities. Even Halperin – perhaps the most fervent of social constructionists – now agrees that there were, indeed, sexual *identities* before the nineteenth century; our job is to try to understand the very different constituents of these past sexual identities. David Halperin, 'Forgetting Foucault: Acts, Identities, and the History of Sexuality,' *Representations* 63 (1998): 93–120. This project has perhaps been best illustrated, to date, by Anna Clark's essay on Anne Lister which shows how, long before sexolo-

gists like Havelock Ellis or Richard von Krafft-Ebing could have provided her with a ready-made identity, Anne Lister fashioned one for herself, from her 'inherent desires,' from her 'material circumstances,' and from the 'cultural representations' available to her. Anna Clark, 'Anne Lister's Construction of Lesbian Identity,' *Journal of the History of Sexuality* 7:1 (1996): 23–50, at p. 27.

28   Refusal to apply the term 'lesbian' to historical subjects often serves to affirm the historical professionalism of the author, and for those researching as undervalued a field as the historical study of lesbians, this affirmation can be both strategic and appealing. For an example, see Hansen, 'No Kisses': 173.

29   Bernadette Brooten, *Love Between Women*, p. 5. For the original modern reference, see Albio Cesare Cassio, 'Post-Classical Λέσβίοί,' *The Classical Quarterly*, n.s., 33:1 (1983), pp. 296–7. Scholars debate Arethas' precise meaning – he might, for example, have used 'lesbian' more as an eponym than as a classification – but the link between 'lesbian' and 'female same-sex relations' seems quite clear.

30   Emma Donoghue, *Passions between Women: British Lesbian Culture 1668–1801* (London: Scarlet Press, 1993), p. 3.

31   I am grateful to Ruth Karras for stressing this point to me. For further discussion of medieval sexual identities, see Ruth Mazo Karras, 'Prostitution and the Question of Sexual Identity in Medieval Europe,' *Journal of Women's History* 11:2 (1999): 159–77, with comments by Theo van der Meer and Carla Frecerro and response by Karras, 179–98.

32   Carol Clover has argued that Norse sagas suggest 'a one-sex, one-gender model with a vengeance.' Carol J. Clover, 'Regardless of Sex: Men, Women and Power in Early Northern Europe,' in *Studying Medieval Women*, ed. Nancy F. Partner (Cambridge, MA: Medieval Academy of America, 1993), pp. 61–87, quote at 84. Joan Cadden has argued that medical texts suggest so strong a commitment to a two-gender binary that variations could only be understood within that binary (for example, as a female man rather than a third sex), Joan Cadden, *The Meanings of Sex Difference*, esp. pp. 221–7. Jane Burns has argued that medieval romances so play with 'gender indeterminacy' as to create characters of mixed male and female qualities. E. Jane Burns, 'Refashioning Courtly Love: Lancelot as Ladies' Man or Lady/Man?' in *Constructing Medieval Sexuality*, pp. 111–34, quote at 134. See also Cary J. Nederman and Jacqui True, 'The Third Sex: The Idea of the Hermaphrodite in Twelfth-Century Europe,' *Journal of the History of Sexuality* 6:4 (1996): 497–517.

33   A useful analogy can be made here with women's history, which rushed far too readily, in my opinion, to assuming and thereby finding radical discontinuities in gender relations, past and present. Only now are women's historians starting to reconsider these early and over-hasty judgments, and we are finding, in the process, some quite remarkable continuities in the histories of women, ancient, medieval, and modern. Judith M. Bennett, 'Confronting Continuity,' *Journal of Women's History* 9:3 (1997): 73–94.

34   As medievalists know well, the desire to create an inviolate past runs strong and deep along the line that separates 'medieval' and 'modern' – and it usually imagines 'medieval' as the evil twin of modernity, as the repository of all that is 'not-modern.' This pernicious construction has been recently interrogated by so many medievalists that I need not belabor its difficulties. See, among others, Lee Patterson, 'On the Margin: Postmodernism, Ironic History, and Medieval Studies,' *Speculum* 65:1 (1990): 87–108; Louise O. Fradenburg with Carla Freccero, 'The Pleasures of History,' *GLQ1* (1995): 371–84; Judith M. Bennett, 'Medieval Women, Modern Women.' Almost every contributor to the special issues of the *Medieval Feminist Newsletter* 13 (1992) on 'Gay and Lesbian Concerns in Medieval Studies and *GLQ1* (1995) on 'Premodern Sexualities in Europe' rejected the medieval/modern distinction.

35   I am grateful to Sarah Ferber for explicating for me the useful instabilities of this term.

36   Carroll Smith-Rosenberg, 'The Female World of Love and Ritual: Relations between

Women in Nineteenth-Century America,' as reprinted in her *Disorderly Conduct: Visions of Gender in Victorian America* (New York: Oxford University Press, 1985), pp. 53–76.

37 Margaret Hunt, 'Afterword,' in *Queering the Renaissance*, ed. Jonathan Goldberg (Durham, NC: Duke University Press, 1994), pp. 359–77, at 372.

38 Rich, 'Compulsory Heterosexuality.'

39 Vicinus, 'Lesbian History: All Theory' focuses especially on the issue of 'knowing for sure' about *sexual* contact between women.

40 Greta Christina, 'Loaded Words,' *PomoSexuals: Challenging Assumptions about Gender and Sexuality*, ed. Carol Queen and Lawrence Schimel (San Francisco: Cleis Press, 1997), pp. 29–35.

41 I am grateful to David Halperin for this example. Paul Halsall offered me another: lesbian potlucks which might lead us, *ad absurdum*, to characterize church potlucks as lesbian-like.

42 Sarah L. Delaney and A. Elizabeth Delany, *Having Our Say: The Delany Sisters' First 100 Years* (New York: Delta, 1993). Sarah and Elizabeth Delany, two African-American sisters well known not only for their memoir but also for the play and movie produced from it, provide a deliberately provocative example. I am not accusing the Delany sisters of incest, nor am I suggesting that they were lesbians. I am suggesting, however, that in both their singleness and their emotional partnership, the Delany sisters behaved in ways that offer affinities with modern lesbian behaviors and that are, therefore, lesbian-like.

43 Judith Bennett and Amy Froide (eds.) *Singlewomen in the European Past, 1250–1800* (Philadelphia: University of Philadelphia Press, 1999).

44 Lerner, *Creation of Feminist Consciousness*, p. 179.

45 Cheshire Calhoun, 'The Gender Closet: Lesbian Disappearance under the Sign "Women,"' *Feminist Studies* 21:1 (1995), pp. 7–34.

Leila J. Rupp

TOWARD A GLOBAL HISTORY
OF SAME-SEX SEXUALITY

What happens to our existing analytical framework of lesbian and gay histories when scholars turn their attention to more global patterns of same-sex desire? Leila Rupp attempts an initial exploratory response to this question in this reading, prompted by a context of increasing international research into same-sex relations. Rupp is a prolific theorist and historian of feminism and sexuality. Although she prefers the phrase 'same-sex sexuality' as one that moves historians beyond the more ubiquitous terms 'lesbian', 'gay' or 'queer', her article reproduced here is committed to problematising the phrase. Rupp reminds us that sexuality is a relatively modern concept that may have narrowed our conceptual frameworks in unhelpful ways. Citing examples of male homosexual relations from places and periods as diverse as Ancient Athens, seventeenth-century Japan and modern New Guinea, Rupp contends that these transgenerational relationships performed an educative rite of passage from boyhood to adulthood for young men. In similar ways Melanesian women nourished girls on their breast milk as a ritual of maturity into womanhood. To construct these practices as primarily sexual ones is to miss the point argues Rupp. Age is the determinative analytical factor here, for it is the privilege of age that legitimates sexual access to, and domination over, the younger generation. Relations between genitally alike bodies may have religious or spiritual origins as among the Mohave Indians, she suggests, or, as in the case of women who passed as men, may alternatively be better defined as 'different-gender' rather than 'same-sex' relations. Although not entirely satisfied with the term 'same-sex sexuality' because so many genitally alike behaviours manifest themselves along other lines of difference, Rupp argues that the phrase at least allows scholars to raise important questions about the historical and global context of same-sex interactions. Ultimately the history of 'same-sex sexuality' may be able to tell us just as much about class, age, religion, culture and other significant social formations.

THIS IS THE PRESUMPTUOUS TITLE of a paper I delivered for what I believe was the first-ever session on 'Gay and Lesbian History/L'histoire de l'homo-sexualité' at the International Congress of Historical Sciences, held in August 2000 in Oslo. As I did there, let me hasten to say here that I do not claim knowledge of same-sex sexuality in every time and every place. But the blossoming of research on a wide range of manifestations of same-sex sexuality calls for an attempt at global thinking. Although my own work is rooted in U.S. and European history, I would like to make use of the work of scholars focusing on different parts of the world to reflect on what patterns might emerge. I take up this task from the perspective of one firmly committed to a social constructionist perspective on sexuality. Thus, I recognize that making transhistorical comparisons can be a risky business. Nevertheless, I think we can learn something by thinking about same-sex sexuality from a global viewpoint.

I favor the term 'same-sex sexuality' as one that gets beyond the use of terms such as 'queer,' 'gay,' 'lesbian,' or 'homosexual.' Yet I would like to proceed by looking at manifestations of what we call 'same-sex sexuality' in different times and places both to explore global patterns and to consider how those patterns make the two parts of the term 'same-sex sexuality' problematic. That is, sometimes such manifestations cannot really be considered 'same-sex,' and sometimes they should not really be labeled 'sexuality.' These complications suggest that even the attempt to avoid assumptions about the meanings of desires, acts, and relationships by using a term such as 'same-sex sexuality' may inadvertently lump together phenomena that are quite different. This is the difficulty of thinking about a global history of same-sex sexuality.

There are various ways that sexual acts involving two genitally alike bodies may in fact not be best conceptualized as 'same-sex.' In some cases, what is more important than genital similarity is the fact of some kind of difference: age difference, class difference, gender difference. As numerous scholars have pointed out, across time and space those differences have in more cases than not structured what we call same-sex acts in ways that are far more important to the people involved and to the societies in which they lived than the mere fact of the touching of similar bodies.[1] (My favorite way to explain this to my students is through the story of my colleague's five-year-old son, who was one day playing with the family dog and a girl from his school. The girl said, 'I love Lily [the dog] so much I wish I could marry her. But I can't because she's a girl.' My colleague's son, viewing the relevant categories in a different way, responded, 'That's not the reason you can't marry Lily. You can't marry Lily because she's a dog!') Looking at the whole question of sameness and difference from an entirely different angle, Jens Rydström's work on homosexuality and bestiality in rural Sweden reminds us that these two categories of deviant acts were not conceptually distinct in the past.[2] Thus, the lines between same-sex and different-species acts were not clearly drawn.

To start, probably the most familiar example is from ancient Athenian society where age difference between older and younger men determined the ways they engaged in sex acts, and such relationships had educative functions that were as much the point as the sex. Furthermore (although this is a bit controversial), the lack of an age or other differential was considered deviant, while same-sex and different-age (or different-status) relationships were not. Adult male citizens of Athens could penetrate social inferiors, including women, boys, foreigners, and slaves.[3]

The privilege of elite men to penetrate anyone other than their equals lingered on into early modern Europe. 'Missing my whore, I bugger my page,' wrote the Earl of Rochester in Restoration England.[4] Were such men 'bisexual,' or was the whole notion of sexual object choice irrelevant? Was this 'same-sex sex'? Or are such relations or acts best described as 'different-status sex'?

We find examples of age differences structuring sexual acts in other parts of the world as well. In seventeenth-century Japan, men expected to desire sexual relations with both women and boys.[5] Two different words described love of women and love of boys. Styles of dress and distinct haircuts differentiated youths from men, thus creating visible categories of difference based on age. When a youth became a man, ceremonially donning the proper garment and having his forelocks shaved, he would cease his role as the anally penetrated partner and take on the adult male penetrator role in a new relationship.

Yet age itself could become a socially constructed category. That is, although it was a violation of the norms, men might keep the boy role well past youth. In *The Great Mirror of Male Love*, a collection of short stories published in Japan in 1687, 'Two Old Cherry Trees Still in Bloom' tells of two samurai lovers in their sixties who had first met when one was sixteen and the other nineteen. 'Han'emon still thought of Mondo as a boy of sixteen. Though his hair was thinning and had turned completely white, Mondo sprinkled it with "Blossom Dew" hair oil and bound it up in a double-folded topknot anyway. . . . There was no sign that he had ever shaved his temples; he still had the rounded hairline he was born with.'[6] John Boswell, who vehemently denied that age difference structured male same-sex relations in ancient Athens and the Roman Empire, suggests that the term 'boy' might simply mean 'beautiful man' or one who was beloved.[7] Boswell took this to signify that age difference was irrelevant, but it is also possible that this means, as in Japan, that age difference was crucial but that the concept of age might be only loosely tied, or not tied at all, to the number of years a person had lived.

In some societies, transgenerational same-sex relations are thoroughly institutionalized. We know the most about a number of cultures in New Guinea in which boys cannot grow into men without incorporating the semen of older men into their bodies, either through oral sex, anal sex, or simply smearing it on the skin.[8] Such 'boy-inseminating rituals' transmit life-giving semen, which produces masculinity and a warrior personality. What is critical here is that all boys take part in the ritual, and once they become men (sometimes through marriage, sometimes through fathering a child), they take on the adult role. Different cultures prescribe different lengths of time for such same-sex relations, different rules for which men should penetrate which boys (sometimes a mother's brother, sometimes a sister's husband), and different ways to transmit the semen.

Note that almost all of the information we have about age-differentiated relationships is about men. True, the construction of Sappho as the mistress of a girls' school falling in love with her students hints at age difference, but this seems a bit far-fetched.[9] Martha Vicinus and Karin Lützen have both told tales about passion between students and teachers in English and Danish schools in the nineteenth century, but this is still a far cry from the evidence about men.[10] Perhaps more comparable is a ritual among the Baruya in Melanesia in which lactating mothers nourish young girls who are not their own daughters by offering a breast, believing that breast milk is produced from men's semen and thus essential to womanhood.[11]

A young girl at the breast, however, is reminiscent of motherhood, while a boy enclosing a penis has nothing to do with traditional men's roles. A more convincing, if still very sketchy, example can be found in Big Nambas society in the New Hebrides, where higher-ranking women took younger girls as sexual partners.[12]

The point here, of course, is that our construction of these interactions as same-sex may be totally foreign to the people involved. That is even more true for transgenderal relations, which can be found in a variety of cultures throughout history and around the globe. For a number of reasons – spiritual, political, economic, social, cultural – individuals take on (or are forced to take on) the social role, dress, and other markers of the (here our language fails us) 'other' sex. Sexual relations may then occur between biological males of female gender and biological males of male gender, or biological females of male gender and biological females of female gender. (Here again, our language describes just two genders where other cultures may see three or more.) Such 'gender-transformed relationships' can be found in many parts of the world.

We know the most about transgenderal relations among North American native peoples. The term 'berdache,' a derogatory French word bestowed by the horrified European invaders, emphasized the sexual aspects of the role, but in fact the spiritual characteristics of what some scholars now call the 'two-spirit person' were sometimes more important.[13] The male transgendered role could be found in over a hundred American Indian tribes, the female in about thirty.[14] Among the Mohave Indians in the western United States, both male (*alyha*) and female (*hwame*) two-spirit roles existed. A two-spirit male would take a female name, engage in female occupations, and even enact menstruation and childbirth. 'Manly-hearted women' would take on male characteristics and have children with their wives through adoption. Men-women sought orgasm through anal sex, while women-men engaged in tribadism or genital rubbing, with the two-spirit on top.[15] [. . .]

Not all cases of transgenderal relations have spiritual or religious origins or implications. The *travestis* of Brazil are transgendered prostitutes who, beginning at a young age, take female names and wear women's clothes as a result of their desire to attract men.[16] Although they do not, like the *hijras*, remove their genitals, they do take female hormones and inject silicone in order to enlarge their buttocks, thighs and breasts. They work as prostitutes, attracting men who define themselves as resolutely heterosexual.

In the case of women who passed as men in early modern Europe, the motivation may have been a desire for occupational or literal mobility, although this is undoubtedly something we will never know for sure.[17] Women who dressed in men's clothing in order to join the army or take a man's job had to impersonate men in all ways, including in their relations with women. When discovered, punishment could be swift and severe for the usurpation of male privilege, particularly if it involved the use of what were called 'material instruments' to 'counterfeit the office of a husband,' as a 1566 case put it.[18] In Germany in the early eighteenth century, a woman named Catharine Margaretha Linck dressed as a man, served in the army, and, after discharge, worked as a cotton dyer. She married a woman who, following a quarrel, confessed to her mother that her husband was not what he seemed. When the outraged mother took Linck to court and produced what another trial transcript in a similar case described as 'the illicit inventions she used to supplement the shortcomings of her sex,' Linck was sentenced to death for her crimes.[19] Were women who risked death looking only for better job prospects, or were these gender-crossers what we would today consider transgendered?

The connection between women's cross-dressing and same-sex desire becomes tighter over time. Lisa Duggan, in her analysis of the case of Alice Mitchell, a nineteen-year-old Memphis woman who murdered the girl she loved when their plans to elope came to naught, ties together the threads of romantic friendship, gender transgression, and the emerging definitions of lesbianism.[20] Jennifer Robertson's pathbreaking work on cross-dressing women in the Japanese Takarazuka Revue, founded in 1913, does much the same thing in a very different context. Exploring a rash of lesbian double suicides in Japan in the 1930s, Robertson details the erotics of fandom inspired by the Revue.[21] Like Duggan and Robertson, Lucy Chesser, in her dissertation on cross-dressing in Australia, shows the development over time of the idea that cross-dressing had something to do with same-sex desire.[22]

The point of all these examples is, once again, that sexual relations between two genitally alike (or originally alike) bodies are in many cases better defined as different-gender than same-sex relations. This seems clear in the case of two-spirit people [. . .] but as the spectrum of transgendered relations moves from those who alter their bodies to those who simply take on some characteristics traditionally associated with the other/another gender, the lines get blurry. What about the 'mollies' of eighteenth-century London? Like men in subcultures in other large European cities, including Paris and Amsterdam, 'mollies' were effeminate men who frequented taverns, parks, and public latrines; sought out male sexual partners; and shared a style of feminine dress and behavior.[23] An agent of the English Societies for the Reformation of Manners entered a London club in 1714 and found men 'calling one another my dear, hugging and kissing, tickling and feeling each other, as if they were a mixture of wanton males and females; and assuming effeminate voices, female airs.'[24] What about the 'roaring girls' of London or the 'randy women' of Amsterdam, cross-dressed but not entirely? Mary Frith, known by her pseudonym, Moll Cutpurse, the model for a number of early-seventeenth-century English accounts, struck one observer as 'both man and woman.'[25] Examples of gender-differentiated pairings – the *bichas* (faggots) and *bofès* (real men) of Brazil, the *jotas* (homosexuals) and *mayates* (men who have sex with *jotas*) of Mexico City, the butches and fems of 1950s American bar culture, the 'mine wives' and 'husbands' of South Africa – can be found in many parts of the world, and how much they are perceived within their own cultures as different-gender and how much as same-sex is a tricky question.[26]

In the narrowest sense, then, 'same-sex sexuality' may best refer to modern Western notions of relations between individuals undifferentiated by gender, age, class, or any other factors: in other words, those (or some of those) who adopt a 'gay' or 'lesbian' identity. That is an irony of a term designed to do just the opposite.

The second part of my critique of the term 'same-sex sexuality' is already implicit here. That is, how do we determine what is 'sexuality' and what is something else in these different interactions? Scholars have argued that 'sexuality' itself is a relatively modern concept, that, for example, acts of fellatio or anal penetration in ancient Athens were expressions of power, acts of domination and submission, not 'sexuality.'[27] [. . .]

How can we know for sure what is a sexual act? There are really two questions here. How do we think about acts – such as fellatio, cunnilingus, anal penetration

– that seem clearly sexual yet may have other meanings? What do we make of acts – such as kissing, hugging, cuddling – that may or may not be considered 'sex'? These questions in turn raise a third: Are certain acts associated with specific forms of relationships?

We have already considered the possibility that fellatio and a girl's mouth on the breast of a woman not her mother may be about a kind of spiritual nutrition rather than sexuality; and even that a whole range of acts might be the assertion of elite male privilege a sign of power. [. . .] If these are accurate conclusions (and I know that a chorus of voices will be raised to shout that they are not!), can we think of such interactions as 'same-sex sexuality' at all, or are they, rather, 'same-sex domination'?

What about societies that make room for loving relations that seem sexual to outsiders but not to the participants? In Basotho society in contemporary Lesotho, girls and women exchange long kisses, putting their tongues in each others' mouths; they fondle each other and endeavor to lengthen the labia minora; they rub their bodies together and engage in cunnilingus without defining any of this as sexual. They fall in love and form marriage-like unions. In this context sex requires a penis and marriage means sex with a man, so there is no such concept as lesbian sex or lesbian relationships.[28] Are these sexual acts? [. . .]

Part of the problem of evaluating what counts as sex between women is that we have so little evidence of what women did with each other, in contrast to how they felt about each other. Some of this can be accounted for because religious and civil authorities – that is, male religious and civil authorities – could not really understand sex without a penis, so they were themselves never really sure what was taking place.

Consider the evidence we do have. Marie-Jo Bonnet has collected a range of images in European art from ancient times to the present, images of what she calls the 'female couple,' many of them engaged in what look to be quite explicitly sexual encounters.[29] The question remains, however, what such representations mean. At the very least, they make female same-sex acts visible.

Potentially sexual activities between women fall into several different categories across time. In written as well as visual sources, one kind of act that we find is the caressing of breasts. A twelfth-century nun in the monastery of Tegernsee in Bavaria wrote to another nun, 'When I recall the kisses you gave me, / And how with tender words you caressed my little breasts, / I want to die / Because I cannot see you.'[30] Centuries later across the Atlantic, Addie Brown, a domestic servant, and Rebecca Primus, a schoolteacher, both African American women who met in Hartford, Connecticut, in the 1860s, also engaged in what Karen Hansen calls 'bosom sex.' Addie worked at a girls' school and wrote Rebecca that the 'girls are very friendly towards me. One of them wants to sleep with me. Perhaps I will give my consent some of these nights.' In response to Rebecca's lost reply, Addie explained, 'If you think that is my bosom that captivated the girl that made her want to sleep with me, she got sadly disappointed injoying it, for I had my back towards [her] all night and my night dress was butten up so she could not get to my bosom. I shall try to keep your favored one always for you. Should in my excitement forget [sic], you will pardon me I know.' Like other romantic friends, and like the twelfth-century nuns, Rebecca and Addie also enjoyed kissing. 'No kisses is like youres,' Addie told Rebecca in another letter.[31]

Then we also have some evidence of genital contact, either tribadism or manual stimulation of the clitoris and/or vagina. Judith Brown recounts the story of Benedetta Carlini, the seventeenth-century Italian 'lesbian nun.' In the course of an investigation into Carlini's mystical claims of being the bride of Christ, Bartolomea Crivelli, a younger and less powerful sister in the convent where Carlini was abbess, testified that Carlini had forced her into 'the most immodest acts.' 'Benedetta would grab her by the arm and throw her by force on the bed. Embracing her, she would put her under herself and kissing her as if she were a man, she would speak words of love to her. And she would stir on top of her so much that both of them corrupted themselves.'[32] [. . .]

Perhaps the most extensive account we have of such sexual acts comes from the diary of Anne Lister, a nineteenth-century, upper-class, independent, mannish English woman. Anne recorded numerous sexual affairs with women, some of them married. In 1819, she detailed an encounter with the love of her life, Marianne, who married for economic and social status but continued her affair with Lister, passing on a venereal disease contracted from her husband through his own extra-marital exploits. *Kiss* in Lister's diary is a code word for 'orgasm.' 'From the kiss she gave me it seemed as if she loved me as fondly as ever. By & by, we seemed to drop asleep but, by & by, I perceived she would like another kiss & she whispered, "Come again a bit, Freddy." But soon, I got up a second time, again took off, went to her a second time &, in spite of all, she really gave me pleasure, & I told her no one had ever given me kisses like hers.' Fed up with waiting for Marianne's all-too-healthy husband to die, Lister went to Paris in 1824, where she began to court a widow staying in the same pension. One night the widow came to her room and climbed into bed with her: 'I was contented that my naked left thigh should rest upon her naked left thigh and thus she let me grubble her over her petticoats. All the while I was pressing her between my thighs. Now and then I held my hand still and felt her pulsation, let her rise towards my hand two or three times and gradually open her thighs, and felt that she was excited.'[33]

Which of these descriptions qualify as 'sex'? What is required? This question has been, historically, particularly difficult in the case of women, but even for men we are sometimes in the dark. At the same time that romantic friendship flourished among women, men in the United States might also kiss, hug, and share a bed with no sense that they were violating sexual norms. Jonathan Katz argues that the separation between love and lust – the notion not only that love between men had no connotations of sexuality, but also that sodomy was perceived as only sexual, with no connection to love – confused men who might have felt both.[34]

[. . .]

Although I am bold enough to dare to address a global history of same-sex sexuality, I am not foolish enough to pretend to have answers to all of these questions. As the Euramerican nature of most of the evidence I use to consider the nature of sexual acts makes plain, we (or, certainly, I) do not know enough about such questions in other parts of the world to say anything even suggestive. But I do think these are good questions for future research.

I have spent all this time undermining the term 'same-sex sexuality,' but, in fact, I think that it is the best one we have. I have focused on the problems that arise from the term not because I think it is flawed, but because it in fact allows us to raise these very important questions about global patterns of love and desire between genitally alike bodies. I think we can see a limited number of patterns of same-sex interactions: differentiated by age or gender or class, or not differentiated in any of these ways; with spiritual or practical implications or based on desire and/or love; totally determining or determined by social roles, or not; clearly associated with specific acts, or not.[35] As we pursue our specific research projects, we would do well to remember that we need to consider carefully the ways that love, desire, and relationships are structured by differences or similarities, and the meaning of sex acts in their historical contexts. There are rich stories of same-sex sexuality out there that will tell us a great deal about gender, class, ethnicity, nationality, bodies, emotions, social relations, religion, law, identity, community, activism, culture, and just about every other thing that is part of what we think of as history.

Notes

1   Stephen O. Murray, 'Homosexual Categorization in Cross-Cultural Perspective,' in *Latin American Male Homosexualities*, ed. Stephen O. Murray (Albuquerque: University of New Mexico Press, 1995), 3–32, cites a number of schemes for the social structuring of homosexuality and adopts that of Barry Adam, 'Age, Structure, and Sexuality,' *Journal of Homosexuality* 11 (1986): 19–33. This includes age-structured, gender-defined, profession-defined, and egalitarian. In Murray's most recent book, *Homosexualities* (Chicago: University of Chicago Press, 2000), he includes 'profession-defined' under 'gender-defined.' John Howard, in his comment on the paper I delivered at Oslo, added race and ethnicity to this list, citing Nayan Shah's work on Indian and Chinese men arrested in British Columbia for their sexual relations with Anglo-Canadian men, and his own work on African American and white same-sex interactions in the U.S. South. See Nayan Shah, 'The Race of Sodomy: Asian Men, White Boys, and the Policing of Sex in North America' (paper presented at the Organization of American Historians conference, St. Louis, April 2000); John Howard, *Men Like That: A Southern Queer History* (Chicago: University of Chicago Press, 1999).

2   Jens Rydström, 'Beasts and Beauties: Bestiality and Male Homosexuality in Rural Sweden, 1880–1950' (paper presented at the 19th International Congress of Historical Sciences, Oslo, Norway, August 2000).

3   The classic work is K. J. Dover, *Greek Homosexuality* (New York: Vintage, 1978). More recent studies include Eva C. Keuls, *The Reign of the Phallus: Sexual Politics in Ancient Athens* (New York: Harper and Row, 1985); David Halperin, *One Hundred Years of Homosexuality and Other Essays on Greek Love* (New York: Routledge, 1990); Eva Cantarella, *Bisexuality in the Ancient World* (New Haven, CT: Yale University Press, 1992); and Wayne R. Dynes and Stephen Donaldson, eds., *Homosexuality in the Ancient World* (New York: Garland, 1992). See also Craig A. Williams, *Roman Homosexuality: Ideologies of Masculinity in Classical Antiquity* (New York: Oxford University Press, 1999). John Boswell, 'Revolutions, Universals, and Sexual Categories,' in *Hidden From History: Reclaiming the Gay and Lesbian Past*, ed. Martin Bauml Duberman, Martha Vicinus, and George Chauncey, Jr. (New York: New American Library, 1989), 17–36, disputes the notion that an age or status difference was essential to same-sex relations in Athenian society, and, more recently, Murray, in *Homosexualities*, has

argued that undifferentiated (what he calls 'egalitarian') relationships between men existed in ancient Greece and Rome (as well as in other premodern places) and that age difference did not always determine sexual role.

4   Quoted in James M. Saslow, 'Homosexuality in the Renaissance: Behavior, Identity, and Artistic Expression,' in *Hidden From History*, 90–105, quotation on 92. See Alan Bray, *Homosexuality in Renaissance England* (New York: Columbia University Press, 1982); Michael Rocke, *Forbidden Friendships: Homosexuality and Male Culture in Renaissance Florence* (New York: Oxford University Press, 1996); Louise Fradenburg and Carla Freccero, eds., *Premodern Sexualities* (New York: Routledge, 1996); Carolyn Dinshaw, *Getting Medieval: Sexualities and Communities, Pre- and Postmodern* (Durham, NC: Duke University Press, 1999); James M. Saslow, *Pictures and Passions: A History of Homosexuality in the Visual Arts* (New York: Viking, 1999); Glenn Burger and Steven F. Kruger, eds., *Queering the Middle Ages* (Minneapolis: University of Minnesota Press, 2001).

5   Paul Gordon Schalow, ed., *The Great Mirror of Male Love* (Stanford, CA: Stanford University Press, 1990); Stephen O. Murray, 'Male Homosexuality in Japan before the Meiji Restoration,' in *Oceanic Homosexualities*, ed. Stephen O. Murray (New York: Garland, 1992), 363–70; Gary P. Leupp, *Male Colors: The Construction of Homosexuality in Tokugawa Japan* (Berkeley: University of California Press, 1995).

6   Quoted in Paul Gordon Schalow, 'Male Love in Early Modern Japan: A Literary Depiction of the "Youth",' in *Hidden from History*, 118–28, quotation on 126.

7   John Boswell, *Christianity, Social Tolerance, and Homosexuality* (Chicago: University of Chicago Press, 1980), 28–30.

8   David F. Greenberg, *The Construction of Homosexuality* (Chicago: University of Chicago Press, 1988, 26–40; Gilbert Herdt, *Same Sex, Different Cultures* (Boulder, CO: Westview Press, 1997), 64, 88; Murray, *Oceanic Homosexualities*.

9   See Judith P. Hallett, 'Sappho and Her Social Context: Sense and Sensuality,' *Signs: Journal of Women in Culture and Society* 4: 447–64 (1979).

10   Martha Vicinus, 'Distance and Desire: English Boarding School Friendships,' *Signs: Journal of Women in Culture and Society* 9: 600–22 (1984); Karin Lützen, *Was das Herz begehrt: Liebe und Freundschaft zwischen Frauen* (Hamburg, Germany: Ernst Kabel Verlag, 1990).

11   Greenberg, *Construction of Homosexuality*, 29.

12   Herdt, *Same-Sex, Different Cultures*, 86.

13   Herdt, *Same-Sex, Different Cultures*, 90–102; Walter L. Williams, *The Spirit and the Flesh: Sexual Diversity in American Indian Culture* (Boston: Beacon Press, 1986); Sue-Ellen Jacobs, Wesley Thomas, and Sabine Lang, eds., *Two-Spirit People: Native American Gender Identity, Sexuality, and Spirituality* (Urbana: University of Illinois Press, 1997). There is disagreement about the status of transgendered individuals in the Americas. For a contrary view to those cited above, see Richard C. Trexler, *Sex and Conquest: Gendered Violence, Political Order, and the European Conquest of the Americas* (Ithaca, NY: Cornell University Press, 1995).

14   Herdt, *Same Sex, Different Cultures*, 91.

15   Herdt, *Same Sex, Different Cultures*, 92–4.

16   Don Kulick, *Travesti: Sex, Gender and Culture among Brazilian Transgendered Prostitutes* (Chicago: University of Chicago Press, 1998).

17   See Rudolf M. Dekker and Lotte C. van de Pol, *The Tradition of Female Transvestism in Early Modern Europe* (London: Macmillan Press, 1989).

18   Quoted in Lillian Faderman, *Surpassing the Love of Men* (New York: William Morrow, 1981), 51.

19   Faderman, *Surpassing the Love of Men*, 51–2.

20   Lisa Duggan, *Sapphic Slathers: Sex Violence, and American Modernity* (Durham, NC: Duke University Press, 2001).

21   Jennifer Robertson, *Takarazuka: Sexual Politics and Popular Culture in Modern Japan* (Berkeley: University of California Press, 1998); Jennifer Robertson, 'Dying to Tell:

Sexuality and Suicide in Imperial Japan,' *Signs: Journal of Women in Culture and Society* 25: 1–36 (1999).

22   Lucy Sarah Chesser, '"Parting with My Sex for a Season": Cross-Dressing, Inversion and Sexuality in Australian Cultural Life, 1850–1920,' (Ph.D. diss., La Trobe University, 2001). See also Lucy Chesser, '"A Woman Who Married Three Wives": Management of Disruptive Knowledge in the 1879 Australian Case of Edward De Lacy Evans,' *Journal of Women's History* 9: 53–77 (winter 1998).

23   Rictor Norton, *Mother Clap's Molly House: The Gay Subculture in England* 1700–1830 (London: GMP Publishers, 1992); Michael Rey, 'Parisian Homosexuals Create a Lifestyle, 1700–1750: The Police Archives,' *Eighteenth-Century Life 9*, new series 3: 179–91 (1985); Jeffrey Merrick, 'Sodomitical Scandals and Subcultures in the 1720s,' *Men and Masculinities* 1: 365–84 (April 1999); Arend H. Huussen, Jr., 'Sodomy in the Dutch Republic during the Eighteenth Century,' *Unauthorized Sexual Behavior during the Enlightenment* ed. Robert P. Maccubbin (Williamsburg, VA: College of William and Mary Press, 1985), 169–78.

24   Randolph Trumbach, 'The Birth of the Queen: Sodomy and the Emergence of Gender Equality in Modern Culture, 1660–1750,' in *Hidden from History*, 129–40, quotation on 137. See also Randolph Trumbach, *Sex and the Gender Revolution: Heterosexuality and the Third Gender in Enlightenment London* (Chicago: University or Chicago Press, 1998).

25   Quoted in Faderman, *Surpassing the Love of Men*, 57. 'Randy women' is a rough translation of *lollepotten*, a term analyzed by Myriam Everard in 'Ziel en zinnen: Over liefde en lust tussen vrouwen in de tweede helft van de achttiernde eeuw' (Ph.D. diss., Rijksuniversiteit Leiden, 1994).

26   See James N. Green, *Beyond Carnival: Male Homosexuality in Twentieth-Century Brazil* (Chicago: University of Chicago Press, 1999); Annick Prieur, *Mema's House, Mexico City: On Transvestites, Queens, and Machos* (Chicago: University of Chicago Press, 1998); Elizabeth Lapovsky Kennedy and Madeline D. Davis, *Boots of Leather, Slippers of Gold: The History of a Lesbian Community* (New York: Routledge, 1993); Stephen O. Murray and Will Roscoe, eds., *Boy-Wives and Female Husbands: Studies of African Homosexualities* (New York: St. Martin's, 1998).

27   David M. Halperin, 'Sex before Sexuality: Pederasty, Politics, and Power in Classical Athens,' in *Hidden from History*, 37–53.

28   Kendall, '"When a Woman Loves a Woman" in Lesotho: Love, Sex, and the (Western) Construction of Homophobia,' in Murray and Roscoe, *Boy-Wives and Female Husbands*, 223–41.

29   Marie-Jo Bonnet, *Les deux amies: Essai sur le couple de femmes dans l'art* (Paris: Èditions Blanche, 2000). See also Marie-Jo Bonnet, *Les relations amoureuses entre les femmes du XVIème au XXè siècle* (Paris: Odile Jacob, 1995).

30   Quoted in Boswell, *Christianity, Social Tolerance, and Homosexuality*, 220.

31   Quoted in Karen V. Hansen, '"No Kisses Is Like Youres": An Erotic Friendship between Two African-American Women during the Mid-Nineteenth Century,' *Gender and History* 7: 153–82 (1995). See also Farah Jasmine Griffin, ed., *Beloved Sisters and Loving Friends: Letters from Rebecca Primus of Royal Oak, Maryland, and Addie Brown of Hartford, Connecticut, 1854–1868* (New York: Knopf, 1999).

32   Quoted in Judith Brown, *Immodest Acts: The Life of a Lesbian Nun in Renaissance Italy* (New York: Oxford University Press, l986), 117–18.

33   Anne Lister, *I Know My Own Heart: The Diaries of Anne Lister (1791–1840),* ed. Helena Whitbread (New York: Virago, 1988), 104; Anne Lister, *No Priest but Love: The Journals of Anne Lister from 1824–1826,* ed. Helena Whitbread (New York: New York University Press, 1992), 65. On Lister, see Jill Liddington, 'Anne Lister of Shibden Hall, Halifax (1791–1840): Her Diaries and the Historians,' *History Workshop* 35: 45–77(1993); and Anna Clark, 'Anne Lister's Construction of Lesbian Identity,' *Journal of the History of Sexuality* 7: 23–50 (1996).

34   Jonathan Ned Katz, *Love Stories: Sex between Men before Homosexuality* (Chicago: University of Chicago Press, 2001).

35 In his comments at the Oslo conference, John Howard suggested that if we combine the myriad hierarchies of sexuality with the categories of age, gender, class, race, ethnicity, and so on, 'we see a system of distinction-making that is virtually limitless in its permutations, in its capacity for normalizing and marginalizing.' I think this is an important point, but I am still struck, as is Stephen Murray, by the fact that there 'are not hundreds or even dozens of different social organizations of homosexual relations in human societies.' See his 'Homosexual Categorization in Cross-Cultural Perspective' in *Latin American Male Homosexualities*, ed. Stephen O. Murray (Albuquerque: University of New Mexico Press, 1995), 3–32, quotation on 4, and the introduction to *Homosexualities*.

PART IV

Centres of difference

Decolonising subjects, rethinking boundaries

Elizabeth V. Spelman

GENDER & RACE
The ampersand problem in feminist thought

This reading is taken from Chapter 5 of Elizabeth Spelman's influential work *Inessential Woman: Problems of Exclusion in Feminist Thought* (Beacon Press, 1988) which provided a pioneering critical examination of feminist theorising on racial difference. I have placed this essay at the head of the readings in Part IV because it leads us into the following debates with a clear exposition of the sometimes problematic attempts of feminists to consider the relationship between race, class and gender. As a philosopher, Spelman is well placed to analyse the intersection of the various aspects of women's identity and her observations have rightly been much-quoted and referred to by historians working in the field. In this reading Spelman presents a strong case against the white solipsism – the tendency to 'think, imagine and speak as if whiteness described the world' – practised by eminent white feminist theorists such as Kate Millett and Mary Daly, among others. She argues that this has led to an additive model of women's identity in which sexism is 'elevated' as the primary form of women's oppression, rendering the racial and class identities of women as subsidiary and 'inessential'. To suggest that black women experience sexism in the same way as white women and then experience racism in addition to this fails to recognise the important 'differences between the contexts in which Black women and white women experience sexism', declares Spelman. It is simply not possible to subtract a woman's racial identity from her sexual identity as if human identity formations were constructed in neatly compartmentalised layers. Spelman does not believe that women's identities are equatable with their physiologies but that, on the other hand, they cannot be fully comprehended without the significance attached to bodily features. The persistent feminist strategy of somatophobia or 'body denial' as a means to liberation could therefore have important ramifications for black women by compounding a dismissal of blackness as of 'temporary and negative importance'. Ultimately, Spelman warns, analyses of women's identity must recognise that gender, race and class oppression are always experienced in interlocking and interrelated ways.

You don't really want Black folks, you are just looking for yourself with a little color to it.

Bernice Johnson Reagon

[. . .]

IT IS NOT EASY to think about gender, race, and class in ways that don't
obscure or underplay their effects on one another. The crucial question is how
the links between them are conceived. So, for example, we see that [Simone] de
Beauvoir tends to talk about comparisons between sex and race, or between sex
and class, or between sex and culture; she describes what she takes to be comparisons between sexism and racism, between sexism and classism, between sexism
and anti-Semitism. In the work of [Nancy] Chodorow and others influenced by her,
we observe a readiness to look for links between sexism and other forms of oppression depicted as distinct from sexism. In both examples, we find an additive analysis
of the various elements of identity and of various forms of oppression: there's
sex *and* race *and* class; there's sexism *and* racism *and* classism. In both examples,
attempts to bring in elements of identity other than gender, to bring in kinds of
oppression other than sexism, still have the effect of obscuring the racial and class
identity of those described as 'women,' still make it hard to see how women not
of a particular race and class can be included in the description.

In this chapter we shall examine in more detail how additive analyses of identity
and of oppression can work against an understanding of the relations between
gender and other elements of identity, between sexism and other forms of oppression. In particular we will see how some very interesting and important attempts
to link sexism and racism themselves reflect and perpetuate racism. Ironically, the
categories and methods we may find most natural and straightforward to use as we
explore the connections between sex and race, sexism and racism, confuse those
connections rather than clarify them.

As has often been pointed out, what have been called the first and second waves
of the women's movement in the United States followed closely on the heels of
women's involvement in the nineteenth-century abolitionist movement and the
twentieth-century civil rights movement. In both centuries, challenges to North
American racism served as an impetus to, and model for, the feminist attack on sexist
institutions, practices, and ideology. But this is not to say that all antiracists were
antisexists, or that all antisexists were antiracists. Indeed, many abolitionists of
the nineteenth century and civil rights workers of the twentieth did not take sexism
seriously, and we continue to learn about the sad, bitter, and confusing history of
women who in fighting hard for feminist ends did not take racism seriously.[1]

Recent feminist theory has not totally ignored white racism, though white feminists have paid much less attention to it than have Black feminists. Much of feminist
theory has reflected and contributed to what Adrienne Rich has called 'white solipsism': the tendency 'to think, imagine, and speak as if whiteness described the
world.'[2] While solipsism is 'not the consciously held belief that one race is inherently superior to all others, but a tunnel-vision which simply does not see nonwhite
experience or existence as precious or significant, unless in spasmodic, impotent
guilt-reflexes, which have little or no long-term, continuing momentum or political
usefulness.'[3]

In this chapter I shall focus on what I take to be instances and sustaining sources of this tendency in recent theoretical works by, or of interest to, feminists. In particular, I examine certain ways of comparing sexism and racism in the United States, as well as habits of thought about the source of women's oppression and the possibility of our liberation. I hope that exposing some of the symptoms of white solipsism—especially in places where we might least expect to find them—will help to eliminate tunnel vision and to widen the descriptive and explanatory scope of feminist theory. Perhaps we might hasten the day when it will no longer be necessary for anyone to have to say, as Audre Lorde has, 'How difficult and time-consuming it is to have to reinvent the pencil every time you want to send a message.'[4] [. . .]

I

It is perhaps inevitable that comparisons of sexism and racism include, and often culminate in, questions about which form of oppression is more 'fundamental.'[5] [. . .] To begin, I will examine some recent claims that sexism is more fundamental than racism, a highly ambiguous argument. In many instances the evidence offered in support turns out to refute the claim; and this way of comparing sexism and racism often presupposes the nonexistence of Black women, insofar as neither the description of sexism nor that of racism seems to apply to them. This is a bitter irony indeed, since Black women are the victims of both sexism and racism.

We need to ask first what 'more fundamental' means in a comparison of racism and sexism. It has meant or might mean several different though related things:[6]

> It is harder to eradicate sexism than it is to eradicate racism.

> There might be sexism without racism but not racism without sexism: any social and political changes that eradicate sexism will eradicate racism, but social and political changes that eradicate racism will not eradicate sexism.

> Sexism is the first form of oppression learned by children.

> Sexism predates racism.

> Sexism is the cause of racism.

> Sexism is used to justify racism.

> Sexism is the model for racism. [. . .]

In *Sexual Politics*, Kate Millett seems to hold that sexism is more fundamental than racism in three senses: it is 'sturdier' than racism and so presumably is harder to eradicate; it has a more 'pervasive ideology' than racism, and so those who are not racists may nevertheless embrace sexist beliefs; and it provides our culture's 'most fundamental concept of power.'[7] But as Margaret Simons has pointed out, Millett ignores the fact that Black women and other women of color do not usually describe their own lives as ones in which they experience sexism as more fundamental than racism.[8] There is indeed something very peculiar about the evidence Millett offers on behalf of her view that sexism is the more endemic oppression.

On the one hand, she states that everywhere men have power over women. On the other hand, she notes with interest that some observers have described as an effect of racism that Black men do not have such power over Black women, and that only when racism is eradicated will Black men assume their proper position of superiority. She goes on to argue that 'the military, industry, technology, universities, science, political office, and finance—in short, every avenue of power within the society, including the coercive force of the police, is entirely in male hands.'[9] But surely that is white male supremacy. Since when did Black males have such institutionally based power, in what Millett calls 'our culture'? She thus correctly describes as sexist the hope that Black men could assume their 'proper authority' over Black women, but her claim about the pervasiveness of sexism is belied by her reference to the lack of authority of Black males.

[. . .]

II

If Millett's [. . .] account tends to ignore facts about the status of Black men, other similar accounts ignore the existence of Black women. In the process of comparing racism and sexism, Richard Wasserstrom describes the ways in which women and Blacks have been stereotypically conceived of as less fully developed than white men: In the United States, 'men and women are taught to see men as independent, capable, and powerful; men and women are taught to see women as dependent, limited in abilities, and passive.'[10] But who is taught to see Black men as 'independent, capable, and powerful,' and by whom are they taught? Are Black men taught that? Black women? White men? White women? Similarly, who is taught to see Black women as 'dependent, limited in abilities, and passive'? If this stereotype is so prevalent, why then have Black women had to defend themselves against the images of matriarch and whore?

Wasserstrom continues:

> As is true for race, it is also a significant social fact that to be a female is to be an entity or creature viewed as different from the standard, fully developed person who is male as well as white. But to be female, as opposed to being black, is not to be conceived of as simply a creature of less worth. That is one important thing that differentiates sexism from racism: the ideology of sex, as opposed to the ideology of race, is a good deal more complex and confusing. Women are both put on a pedestal and deemed not fully developed persons.[11]

He leaves no room for the Black woman. For a Black woman cannot be 'female, as opposed to being Black'; she is female *and* Black. Since Wasserstrom's argument proceeds from the assumption that one is either female or Black, it cannot be an argument that applies to Black women. Moreover, we cannot generate a composite image of the Black women from Wasserstrom's argument, since the description of women as being put on a pedestal, or being dependent, never generally applied to Black women in the United States and was never meant to apply to them.

Wasserstrom's argument about the priority of sexism over racism has an odd result, which stems from the erasure of Black women in his analysis. He wishes to claim that in this society sex is a more fundamental fact about people than race. Yet his description of women does not apply to the Black woman, which implies that being Black is a more fundamental fact about her than being a woman and hence that her sex is not a more fundamental fact about her than her race. I am not saying that Wasserstrom actually believes this is true, but that paradoxically the terms of his theory force him into that position. If the terms of one's theory require that a person is either female or Black, clearly there is no room to describe someone who is both.

[. . .]

III

First of all, sexism and racism do not have different 'objects' in the case of Black women. It is highly misleading to say, without further explanation, that Black women experience 'sexism and racism.' For to say merely that suggests that Black women experience one form of oppression, as Blacks (the same thing Black men experience) and that they experience another form of oppression, as women (the same thing white women experience). While it is true that images and institutions that are described as sexist affect both Black and white women, they are affected in different ways, depending upon the extent to which they are affected by other forms of oppression. [. . .]

Reflection on the experience of Black women also shows that it is not as if one form of oppression is merely piled upon another. As Barbara Smith has remarked, the effect of multiple oppression 'is not merely arithmetic.'[12] This additive method informs Gerda Lerner's analysis of the oppression of Black women under slavery: 'Their work and duties were the same as that of the men, while childbearing and rearing fell upon them as an added burden.'[13] But as Angela Davis has pointed out, the mother/housewife role (even the words seem inappropriate) doesn't have the same meaning for women who experience racism as it does for those who are not so oppressed:

> In the infinite anguish of ministering to the needs of the men and chil-
> dren around her (who were not necessarily members of her immediate
> family), she was performing the only labor of the slave community which
> could not be directly and immediately claimed by the oppressor.[14]

[. . .] All of these factors are left out in a simple additive analysis. How one form of oppression is experienced is influenced by and influences how another form is experienced. An additive analysis treats the oppression of a Black woman in a society that is racist as well as sexist as if it were a further burden when, in fact, it is a different burden. As the work of Davis, among others, shows, to ignore the difference is to deny the particular reality of the Black woman's experience.

If sexism and racism must be seen as interlocking, and not as piled upon each other, serious problems arise for the claim that one of them is more fundamental than the other. [. . .] In this connection, racism is sometimes seen as something that is both derivative from sexism and in the service of it: racism keeps women from uniting in alliance against sexism. This view has been articulated by Mary Daly in *Beyond God the Father*. According to Daly, sexism is the 'root and paradigm' of other forms of oppression such as racism. Racism is a 'deformity *within* patriarchy. . . . It is most unlikely that racism will be eradicated as long as sexism prevails.'[15]

Daly's theory relies on an additive analysis, and we can see again why such an analysis fails to describe adequately Black women's experience. Daly's analysis makes it look simply as if both Black women and white women experience sexism, while Black women also experience racism. Black women, Daly says, must come to see what they have in common with white women—shared sexist oppression—and see that they are all 'pawns in the racial struggle, which is basically not the struggle that will set them free as women.'[16] But insofar as she is oppressed by racism in a sexist context and sexism in a racist context, the Black woman's struggle cannot be compartmentalized into two struggles—one as a Black and one as a woman. Indeed, it is difficult to imagine why a Black woman would think of her struggles this way except in the face of demands by white women or by Black men that she do so. This way of speaking about her struggle is required by a theory that insists not only that sexism and racism are distinct but that one might be eradicated before the other. Daly rightly points out that the Black woman's struggle can easily be, and has usually been, subordinated to the Black man's struggle in antiracist organizations. But she does not point out that the Black woman's struggle can easily be, and usually has been, subordinated to the white woman's struggle in antisexist organizations.

Daly's line of thought also promotes the idea that, were it not for racism, there would be no important differences between Black and white women. Since, according to her view, sexism is the fundamental form of oppression and racism works in its service, the only significant differences between Black and white women are differences that men (Daly doesn't say whether she means white men or Black men or both) have created and that are the source of antagonism between women. What is really crucial about us is our sex; racial distinctions are one of the many products of sexism, of patriarchy's attempt to keep women from uniting. According to Daly, then, it is through our shared sexual identity that we are oppressed together; it is through our shared sexual identity that we shall be liberated together.

This view not only ignores the role women play in racism and classism, but it seems to deny the positive aspects of racial identities. It ignores the fact that being Black is a source of pride, as well as an occasion for being oppressed. It suggests that once racism is eliminated, Black women no longer need be concerned about or interested in their Blackness—as if the only reason for paying attention to one's Blackness is that it is the source of pain and sorrow and agony. [. . .]

In sum, according to an additive analysis of sexism and racism, all women are oppressed by sexism; some women are further oppressed by racism. Such an analysis distorts Black women's experiences of oppression by failing to note important differences between the contexts in which Black women and white women experience sexism. The additive analysis also suggests that a woman's racial identity can be 'subtracted' from her combined sexual and racial identity: 'We are all women.' But this does not leave room for the fact that different women may look to different forms of liberation just because they are white or Black women, rich or poor women, Catholic or Jewish women.

IV

[. . .] In the rest of the chapter I will explore how some ways of conceiving women's oppression and liberation contribute to the white solipsism of feminist theory.

As I have argued in detail elsewhere, feminist theorists as politically diverse as Simone de Beauvoir, Betty Friedan, and Shulamith Firestone have described the conditions of women's liberation in terms that suggest that the identification of woman with her body has been the source of our oppression, and hence that the source of our liberation lies in sundering that connection.[17] For example, de Beauvoir introduces *The Second Sex* with the comment that woman has been regarded as 'womb'; and she later observes that woman is thought of as planted firmly in the world of 'immanence,' that is, the physical world of nature, her life defined by the dictates of her 'biologic fate.'[18] In contrast, men live in the world of 'transcendence,' actively using their minds to create 'values, mores, religions.'[19] Theirs is the world of culture as opposed to the world of nature. [. . .]

This view comes out especially clearly in Firestone's work. According to her, the biological difference between women and men is at the root of women's oppression. It is woman's body—in particular, our body's capacity to bear children—that makes, or makes possible, the oppression of women by men. Hence we must disassociate ourselves from our bodies—most radically—by making it possible, or even necessary, to conceive and bear children outside the womb, and by otherwise generally disassociating our lives from the thankless tasks associated with the body.[20]

In predicating women's liberation on a disassociation from our bodies, Firestone oddly enough joins the chorus of male voices that has told us over the centuries about the disappointments entailed in being embodied creatures. What might be called 'somatophobia' (fear of and disdain for the body) is part of a centuries-long tradition in Western culture. [. . .]

Insofar as feminists ignore, or indeed accept, negative views of the body in prescriptions for women's liberation, we will also ignore an important element in racist thinking. For the superiority of men to women (or, as we have seen, of some men to some women) is not the only hierarchical relationship that has been linked to the superiority of the mind to the body. Certain kinds, or 'races,' of people have been held to be more body-like than others, and this has meant that they are perceived as more animal-like and less god-like. [. . .]

We need to examine and understand somatophobia and look for it in our own thinking, for the idea that the work of the body and for the body has no part in real human dignity has been part of racist as well as sexist ideology. That is, oppressive stereotypes of 'inferior races' and of women (notice that even in order to make the point in this way, we leave up in the air the question of how we shall refer to those who belong to both categories) have typically involved images of their lives as determined by basic bodily functions (sex, reproduction, appetite, secretions, and excretions) and as given over to attending to the bodily functions of others (feeding, washing, cleaning, doing the 'dirty work'). [. . .]

Finally, if one thinks—as de Beauvoir, Friedan, and Firestone do—that the liberation of women requires abstracting the notion of woman from the notion of woman's body, then one might logically think that the liberation of Blacks requires abstracting the notion of a Black person from the notion of a black body. Since the body, or at least certain of its aspects, may be thought to be the culprit, the solution may seem to be: Keep the person and leave the occasion for oppression behind. Keep the woman, somehow, but leave behind her woman's body; keep the Black person but leave the Blackness behind. Once one attempts to stop thinking about oneself in terms of having a body, then one not only will stop thinking in terms of characteristics such as womb and breast, but also will stop thinking in terms of skin and hair. We would expect to find that any feminist theory based in part on a disembodied view of human identity would regard blackness (or any other physical characteristic that may serve as a centering post for one's identity) as of temporary and negative importance.

Once the concept of woman is divorced from the concept of woman's body, conceptual room is made for the idea of a woman who is no particular historical woman—she has no color, no accent, no particular characteristics that require having a body. She is somehow all and only woman; that is her only identifying feature. And so it will seem inappropriate or beside the point to think of women in terms of any physical characteristics, especially if their oppression has been rationalized by reference to those characteristics.

None of this is to say that the historical and cultural identity of being Black or white is the same thing as, or is reducible to, the physical feature of having black or white skin. Historical and cultural identity is not constituted by having a body with particular identifying features, but it cannot be comprehended without such features and the significance attached to them.

V

Adrienne Rich was perhaps the first well-known contemporary white feminist to have noted 'white solipsism' in feminist theorizing and activity. I think it is no coincidence that she also noticed and attended to the strong strain of somatophobia in feminist theory. [. . .] But unlike de Beauvoir or Firestone, Rich refuses to throw out the baby with the bathwater: she sees that the historical negative connection between woman and body (in particular, between woman and womb) can be broken in more than one way. [. . .] She asks us to think about whether what she calls 'flesh-loathing' is the only attitude it is possible to have toward our bodies. Just as she explicitly distinguishes between motherhood as experience and motherhood as institution, so she implicitly asks us to distinguish between embodiment as experience and embodiment as institution. [. . .]

I think it is not a psychological or historical accident that having examined the way women view their bodies, Rich also focused on the failure of white women to see Black women's experiences as different from their own. For looking at embodiment is one way (though not the only one) of coming to recognize and understand the particularity of experience. Without bodies we could not have personal histories. Nor could we be identified as woman or man, Black or white. This is not to say that reference to publicly observable bodily characteristics settles the question of whether someone is woman or man, Black or white; nor is it to say that being woman or man, Black or white, just means having certain bodily characteristics (that is one reason some Blacks want to capitalize the term; 'Black' refers to a cultural identity, not simply a skin color). But different meanings are attached to having certain characteristics, in different places and at different times and by different people, and those differences affect enormously the kinds of lives we lead or experiences we have. Women's oppression has been linked to the meanings assigned to having a woman's body by male oppressors. Blacks' oppression has been linked to the meanings assigned to having a black body by white oppressors. (Note how insidiously this way of speaking once again leaves unmentioned the situation for Black women.) We cannot hope to understand the meaning of a person's experiences, including her experiences of oppression, without first thinking of her as embodied, and second thinking about the particular meanings assigned to that embodiment. If, because of somatophobia, we think and write as if we are not embodied, or as if we would be better off if we were not embodied, we are likely to ignore the ways in which different forms of embodiment are correlated with different kinds [of] experience. [. . .]

VI

I have been discussing the ways in which some aspects of feminist theory exhibit what Adrienne Rich has called 'white solipsism.' In particular, I have been examining ways in which some prominent claims about the relation between sexism and racism ignore the realities of racism. I have also suggested that there are ways of thinking about women's oppression and about women's liberation that reflect and encourage white solipsism, but that thinking differently about women and about sexism might lead to thinking differently about Blackness and about racism.

First, we have to continue to reexamine the traditions which reinforce sexism and racism. Though feminist theory has recognized the connection between somatophobia and misogyny/gynephobia, it has tended to challenge the misogyny without challenging the somatophobia, and without fully appreciating the connection between somatophobia and racism.

Second, we have to keep a cautious eye on discussions of racism versus sexism. They keep us from seeing ways in which what sexism means and how it works is modulated by racism, and ways in which what racism means is modulated by sexism. Most important, discussions of sexism versus racism tend to proceed as if Black women—to take one example—do not exist. None of this is to say that sexism and racism are thoroughly and in every context indistinguishable. [. . .] But as long as Black women and other women of color are at the bottom of the economic heap (which clearly we cannot fully understand in the absence of a class analysis), and as long as our descriptions of sexism and racism themselves reveal racist and sexist perspectives, it seems both empirically and conceptually premature to make grand claims about whether sexism or racism is 'more fundamental.' For many reasons, then, it seems wise to proceed very cautiously in this inquiry.

Third, it is crucial to sustain a lively regard for the variety of women's experiences. On the one hand, what unifies women and justifies us in talking about the oppression of women is the overwhelming evidence of the worldwide and historical subordination of women to men. On the other, while it may be possible for us to speak about women in a general way, it also is inevitable that any statement we make about women in some particular place at some particular time is bound to suffer from ethnocentrism if we try to claim for it more generality than it has. [. . .]

In short, the claim that all women are oppressed is fully compatible with, and needs to be explicated in terms of, the many varieties of oppression that different populations of women have been subject to. After all, why should oppressors settle for uniform kinds of oppression, when to oppress their victims in many different ways—consciously or unconsciously—makes it more likely that the oppressed groups will not perceive it to be in their interest to work together?

Finally, it is crucial not to see Blackness only as the occasion for oppression—any more than one sees being a woman only as the occasion for oppression. No one ought to expect the forms of our liberation to be any less various than the forms of our oppression. We need to be at least as generous in imagining what women's liberation will be like as our oppressors have been in devising what women's oppression has been.

Notes

1   See Eleanor Flexner, *Century of Struggle* (New York: Atheneum, 1972), especially chapter 13, on the inhospitality of white women's organizations to Black women, as well as Aileen S. Kraditor's *The Ideas of the Woman Suffrage Movement, 1890–1920* (Garden City, N.Y.: Doubleday, 1971). See also Ellen Carol DuBois, *Feminism and Suffrage* (Ithaca: Cornell University Press, 1978); Sara Evans, *Personal Politics* (New York: Vintage, 1979), on sexism in the civil rights movement; Dorothy Sterling, *Black Foremothers* (Old Westbury, N.Y.: Feminist Press, 1979), 147, on Alice Paul's refusal to grant Mary Church Terrell's request that Paul endorse enforcement of the Nineteenth Amendment for all women; Angela Davis, *Women, Race, and Class* (New York: Random, 1981); Bettina Aptheker, *Women's Legacy: Essays on Race, Sex, and Class in American History* (Amherst: University of Massachusetts Press, 1982); Paula Giddings, *When and Where I Enter: The Impact of Black Women on Race and Sex in America* (New York: Morrow, 1984).

2   Adrienne Rich, 'Disloyal to Civilization: Feminism, Racism, Gynephobia,' in her *On Lies, Secrets, and Silence* (New York: Norton, 1979), 299 and passim. In the philosophical literature, solipsism is the view according to which it is only one's self that is knowable, or it is only one's self that constitutes the world. Strictly speaking, of course, Rich's use of the phrase 'white solipsism' is at odds with the idea of there being only the self, insofar as it implies that there are other white people; but she is drawing from the idea of there being only one perspective on the world—not that of one person, but of one 'race.' [. . .]

3   Ibid., 306.

4   Audre Lorde, 'Man Child: A Black Lesbian Feminist's Response,' *Conditions* 4 (1979): 35. My comments about racism apply to the racism directed against Black people in the United States. I do not claim that all my arguments apply to the racism experienced by other people of color.

5   See Margaret A. Simons, 'Racism and Feminism: A Schism in the Sisterhood,' *Feminist Studies* 5, no. 2 (1979): 384–401.

6   A somewhat similar list appears in Alison M. Jaggar and Paula Rothenberg's introduction to part 2 of *Feminist Frameworks*, 2nd ed. (New York: McGraw-Hill, 1984), 86.

7   Kate Millett, *Sexual Politics* (New York: Ballantine, 1969), 33–4.

8   Simons, 'Racism and Feminism.'

9   Millett, *Sexual Politics*, 33–4.

10 Richard A. Wasserstrom, 'Racism and Sexism,' in *Philosophy and Women*, ed. Sharon Bishop and Marjorie Weinzweig (Belmont, Cal.: Wadsworth, 1979), 8. Reprinted from 'Racism, Sexism, and Preferential Treatment: An Approach to the Topics,' *UCLA Law Review* (February 1977): 581–615.

11   Ibid.
12   Barbara Smith, 'Notes For Yet Another Paper on Black Feminism, Or Will the Real
     Enemy Please Stand Up,' *Conditions* 5 (1979): 123–32. See also 'The Combahee River
     Collective Statement,' *Capitalist Patriarchy and the Case for Socialist Feminism*, ed. Zillah
     Eisenstein (New York: Monthly Review Press, 1979), 362–72.
13   Gerda Lerner, ed., *Black Woman in White America* (New York: Vintage, 1973), 15.
14   Angela Davis, 'Reflections on the Black Woman's Role in the Community of Slaves,'
     Black Scholar 3 (1971), 7. Davis revises this slightly in *Women, Race, and Class*.
15   Mary Daly, *Beyond God the Father* (Boston: Beacon Press, 1975), 56–7.
16   Ibid.
17   Elizabeth Spelman, 'Woman as Body: Ancient and Contemporary Views,' *Feminist
     Studies* 8, no. 1 (1982).
18   Simone de Beauvoir, *The Second Sex* (New York: Knopf, 1953), xii, 57.
19   Ibid., 119.
20   Shulamith Firestone, *The Dialectic of Sex* (New York: Bantam, 1970), chap. 10.

Valerie Amos and Pratibha Parmar

CHALLENGING IMPERIAL FEMINISM

'Challenging Imperial Feminism' by Valerie Amos and Pratibha Parmar presents, within a British context, one of the earliest critiques of white feminist theory and its relevance, or lack of it, to the development of black feminist scholarship. Amos and Parmar argue that historically both American and British feminism has been rooted in theories of racial superiority. Feminist theory has therefore been unable to speak meaningfully to the experiences of black and working-class women because of this fundamentally imperial and colonial past. Black women's experience is essentially dualistic they argue, their identities shaped by an allegiance to both the black community and to the wider community of women. To date, however, white feminist scholarship has either ignored black women or represented them as 'exotic' contrasts. Nor has the tokenistic inclusion of black women as additional 'subject content' influenced the reshaping of feminism's theoretical centre-ground, for white feminist theories have failed to prioritise race or difference as a primary theoretical agenda. Amos and Parmar examine three key areas – the family, sexuality and the women's peace movement – to illustrate further the theoretical implications of black women's differing historical and contemporary experiences. They find that white feminist analyses of sexuality and the family have continued to reinforce dominant stereotypes of the subordinate Asian wife, the dominant matriarchal African-Caribbean head of the household and of 'aggressive' black male sexuality. In addition, the attitudes of feminist peace campaigners at Greenham Common are regarded by Amos and Parmar as essentially parochial. British feminists' unwillingness to take up corresponding issues against the arms race on a more global level is prohibitive of meaningful conversation with black women. This is a hard-hitting article that clearly defines the boundaries of 'sisterhood' in the early 1980s and, as a clarion call to black feminists to construct their own contextually specific theories of liberation, it highlights important issues destined to be played out more fully during the following decades.

OUR TASK HERE IS TO begin to identify the ways in which a particular tradition, white Eurocentric and Western, has sought to establish itself as the only legitimate feminism in current political practice. [. . .]

The growth of the Black feminist movement in Britain in the last decade has forced the question of the centrality of Black women's oppression and exploitation onto the political and theoretical agendas. The political energy of Black women who have organized at the grassroots within our communities against the myriad of issues engendered by the racism of the British state has inspired and pointed to the urgent need to challenge many of the theoretical conceptualizations and descriptions of Black and Third World women existing within white feminist literature. [. . .]

It is our aim in this article to critically examine some of the key theoretical concepts in white feminist literature, and discuss their relevance or otherwise for a discussion and development of Black feminist theory.

It would be naive of us to suggest in any way that the white women's movement is a monolithic structure or organization, indeed we recognize that it is a variety of groups with a diversity of interests and perspectives.

However, our concern here is to show that white, mainstream feminist theory, be it from the socialist feminist or radical feminist perspective, does not speak to the experiences of Black women and where it attempts to do so it is often from a racist perspective and reasoning. [. . .]

Our starting point then is the oppressive nature of the women's movement in Britain both in terms of its practice and the theories which have sought to explain the nature of women's oppression and legitimize the political practices which have developed out of those analyses. In describing the women's movement as oppressive we refer to the experiences of Black and working class women of the movement and the inability of feminist theory to speak to their experience in any meaningful way.[1]

In arguing that most contemporary feminist theory does not begin to adequately account for the experience of Black women we also have to acknowledge that it is not a simple question of their absence, consequently the task is not one of rendering their visibility.

On the contrary we will have to argue that the process of accounting for their historical and contemporary position does, in itself, challenge the use of some of the central categories and assumptions of recent mainstream feminist thought. This work has already begun; Black women are not only making history but rewriting it.

The publication in recent years of a number of books by Black feminists in the US marks the beginning of a systematic documentation of Black women's individual and collective histories. Dominant among these are the rediscovery of ourselves; our place in the Black movement; the boundaries of our sisterhood with white feminists.

These are important areas for us Black women, for our experience is the shared experience of Black people but it is also the shared experience of women within different class contexts. Our political responses have been and will continue to be shaped by that duality, the range of political options available to us will depend on the social context in which we experience that dualism. To date, the majority of work available by Black women addresses itself to the situation in the USA or to the situation in the Third World countries from which our ancestors are drawn. Although comparisons can be made between Britain and the USA and although it is important to draw on the histories of the communities and countries of the Third World which have contributed to our world view, it is important that Black women in Britain locate their experiences within the context of what is happening to Black people here.

There is little recognition in the women's movement of the ways in which the gains made by white women have been and still are at the expense of Black women. Historically white women's sexuality has been constructed in oppositional terms to that of Black women and it is to this history that white women refer as their starting point, it is with this history that they seek to come to terms but in an uncritical way – the engagement with it is essentially selective. The 'herstory' which white women use to trace the roots of women's oppression or to justify some form of political practice is an imperial history rooted in the prejudices of colonial and neo-colonial periods, a 'herstory' which suffers the same form of historical amnesia of white male historians, by ignoring the fundamental ways in which white women have benefited from the oppression of Black people. [. . .]

Thus the perception white middle-class feminists have of what they need liberating from has little or no relevance to the day to day experience of the majority of Black women in Britain and the ways in which they determine the political choices which have to be made. Nowhere is this more apparent than in the oppositional terms in which women's liberation and Black people's liberation has been and still is posed. In her analysis of the women's suffrage movement in the USA and the Abolition of Slavery Campaigns, Angela Davis pointed to the opportunistic and racist arguments of some white women who made simplistic comparisons between the position of Black men and white women in 19th century America. One such woman Elizabeth Cady Stanton wrote in 1865:

> The representation of women of the nation have done their uttermost for the last 30 years to secure freedom for the negroes and as long as he was the lowest in the scale of being we were willing to press his claims but now, as the celestial gate to civil rights is slowly moving on its hinges, it becomes a serious question whether we had better stand aside and see 'sambo' walk into the kingdom first.

This line of reasoning was not only limited to the USA; the movement for female emancipation in Britain was closely linked to theories of racial superiority and Empire.

It would appear that although feminists and indeed Marxists invoke the spectre of history/herstory at will in an attempt to locate the articulation of class and gender oppression at the point at which that very history is called into question and challenges the bases of their analyses there is a curious kind of amnesia. The past is invoked at will, but differentially, to make sense of the range of political options open to socialists and feminists.[2]

Few white feminists in Britain and elsewhere have elevated the question of racism to the level of primacy, within their practical political activities or in their intellectual work. The women's movement has unquestioningly been premised on a celebration of 'sisterhood' with its implicit assumption that women qua women have a necessary basis for unity and solidarity; a sentiment reflected in academic feminist writings which is inevitably influenced by the women's movement and incorporates some of its assumptions.

While one tendency has been for Black women to have either remained invisible within feminist scholarship or to have been treated purely as women without any significance attached to our colour and race, another tendency has been the idealization and culturalism of anthropological works. Often we have appeared in cross cultural studies which under the guise of feminist and progressive anthropology, renders us as 'subjects' for 'interesting' and 'exotic' comparison. [. . .]

Furthermore, when Black and Third World women are being told that imperialism is good for us, it should be of no great surprise to anyone when we reject a feminism which uses Western social and economic systems to judge and make pronouncements about how Third World women can become emancipated. Feminist theories which examine our cultural practices as 'feudal residues' or label us 'traditional', also portray us as politically immature women who need to be versed and schooled in the ethos of Western feminism. They need to be continually challenged, exposed for their racism and denied any legitimacy as authentic feminists.

Strength in differences

The failure of the academic feminists to recognize difference as a crucial strength is a failure to reach beyond the first patriarchal lesson. Divide and conquer in our world must become define and empower.

Many white feminists' failure to acknowledge the differences between themselves and Black and Third World women has contributed to the predominantly Eurocentric and ethnocentric theories of women's oppression. Recently, some white feminist academics have attempted to deal with the question of differences but again this has raised many problems and often perpetuated white feminist supremacy. [. . .]

Historically, it was [. . .] Black women themselves who instigated the debates on our differences. For instance in America, many Black women were involved in the women's movement from its beginnings, and they struggled to bring home the following to their Black sisters who were pessimistic about the viability of joint political work with white feminists. [. . .]

Black women were also raising the issue of feminism and feminist demands within the Black movement and such questions were continually raised in the civil rights movement well before Black women were engaging in debate within the predominantly white women's movement in the 1960s. [. . .]

We now turn to look at three critical areas in which Black women's experience is very different from that of white women. As we have already stated, white women have benefited fundamentally from the oppression of Black women and before any kind of collective action takes place it is necessary to reassess the basis on which we ally ourselves to the white feminist movement. The three areas we have chosen as illustrations of our thesis are the family, sexuality and the women's peace movement. Each of these areas, in very different ways point to the 'imperial' nature of feminist thought and practice.

Family

[. . .] The family, rightly, has been the object of much debate in the women's move-ment and has been cited as one of the principle sites of women's oppression — women's role in reproducing the labour force, their supposed dependence on men and the construction of a female identity through notions of domesticity and mother-hood have all been challenged. Indeed within that questioning there have been attempts to elevate domestic labour to the same level of analysis as the Marxist analysis of the mode of production and the relations between capital and labour. The family and its role in the construction of a consensual ideology remains central to discussions of feminism. We would question however the ways in which white academics, particularly sociologists and anthropologists, have sought to define the role of Black women in the family.

Much work has already been done which shows the ways in which sociology, especially the sociology of 'ethnicity', pathologizes and problematizes the Black communities in Britain. Our concern here is the impact the above analyses have had on Euro-American contemporary feminist thought, particularly socialist femi-nists. Although it is true to say that some of these feminists have distanced themselves from the crude stereotyping common in such analyses, some stereo-types do stick and they are invariably linked to colonial and historical interpretations of the Black woman's role. The image is of the passive Asian woman subject to oppressive practices within the Asian family with an emphasis on wanting to 'help' Asian women liberate themselves from their role. Or there is the strong, dominant Afro-Caribbean woman, the head of the household who despite her 'strength' is exploited by the 'sexism' which is seen as being a strong feature in relationships between Afro-Caribbean men and women. So although the crude translation of theories of ethnicity which have become part and parcel of the nation's common sense image of Black people may not be accepted by many white feminists, they are influenced by the ideas and nowhere is this more apparent than in debates about the family, where there has certainly been a failure to challenge particular patho-logical ideas about the Black family. There is little or no engagement by white feminists with the contradictions which constitute and shape our role as women in a family context, as sisters, aunts or daughters. For both Black and white women, it is a critical issue which has to be addressed, but in this area of struggle it is Black women who have sought to look critically at the family, its strengths and weak-nesses, its advantages and disadvantages, its importance for certain women in class and race terms.

[. . .]

White feminists have fallen into the trap of measuring the Black female experi-ence against their own, labelling it as in some way lacking, then looking for ways in which it might be possible to harness the Black women's experience to their own. Comparisons are made with our countries of origin which are said to funda-mentally exploit Black women. The hysteria in the western women's movement surrounding issues like arranged marriages, purdah, female headed households, is often beyond the Black woman's comprehension — being tied to so called feminist notions of what constitutes good or bad practice in our communities in Britain or the Third World.

In rejecting such analyses we would hope to locate the Black family more firmly in the historical experiences of Black people – not in the romantic idealized forms popular with some social anthropologists, and not merely as a tool of analysis. There are serious questions about who has written that history and in what form, questions which have to be addressed before we as Black people use that history as an additional element of our analysis. Black women cannot just throw away their experiences of living in certain types of household organization; they want to use that experience to transform familial relationships. Stereotypes about the Black family have been used by the state to justify particular forms of oppression. The issue of fostering and adoption of Black kids is current: Black families are seen as being 'unfit' for fostering and adoption. Racist immigration legislation has had the effect of separating family members, particularly of the Asian community, but no longer is that legislation made legitimate just by appeals to racist ideologies contained in notions of 'swamping'. Attempts have actually been made by some feminists to justify such legislative practices on the basis of protecting Asian girls from the 'horrors' of the arranged marriage system. White feminists beware – your unquestioning and racist assumptions about the Black family, your critical but uninformed approach to 'Black culture' has found root and in fact informs state practice.

Sexuality

Sexuality has been and continues to be a central issue of discussion and debate within the white women's movement, and much political energy has been spent on understanding and questioning sexuality and sexual oppression:

> . . . feminism has thrown up enormous challenges in the whole field of sexuality. We have challenged the 'rights' of men to women's bodies; the compulsory nature of heterosexuality; the stigma and invisibility of lesbianism; the primacy of the nuclear family; rigid gender roles – patriarchal definitions of what is 'natural'; the violence of rape; the exploitation of pornography; sexist imagery and symbolism. Even the importance and priority given to sexual relationships have been questioned.

While such debates rage virulently amongst white feminists, many Black women have rightly felt that we do not have the 'luxury' of engaging in them in the context of the intense racism of the British state. But the fact that Black women have been peripheral to these debates that have taken place within the women's movement, does not mean that we have not always thought about and discussed these issues with each other. The ways in which we have discussed and prioritized issues around sexuality have differed markedly from white women.

Such theoretical debates, while important components in any theory and discussion of women and sexuality, have not been areas of focus for Black women's energy and action because in many ways our theoretical and political agendas have already been circumscribed and defined for us.

Our very position as Black women in a racist society has meant that we have been forced to organize around issues relating to our very survival. The struggle for independence and self determination and against imperialism has meant that for Black and Third World women in Britain and internationally, sexuality as an issue has often taken a secondary role and at times not been considered at all.

As we have increasingly grown confident in our feminism, some of us have begun to look at the area of sexuality in ways that are relevant to us as Black women. The absence of publicly overt debates on and around sexuality by Black women does not mean that such discussions have not been taking place. As illustrated in Brixton Black women's group's analysis of the demise of the Organisation of Women of Asian and African Descent (OWAAD), this was and continues to be one area which has been recognized as an essential element of Black feminist practice and theory. [. . .]

More specifically when challenging heterosexuality as the norm many Black lesbians have had to face the profound homophobia of both Blacks and whites. As Barbara Smith comments when talking about the American situation:

> Implicit in our communities attitudes towards Black lesbians is the notion that they have transgressed both sexual and racial norms. Despite all the forces with which we must contend, Black women have a strong tradition of sexual self determination.

Black women's continued challenges to the question of forced sterilization and the use of the contraceptive drug Depo Provera has meant that such campaigns as the National Abortion Campaign have been forced to reassess the relevance of their single issue focus for the majority of working class, Black women, and to change the orientation of their campaigns and actions. [. . .]

It is worthwhile at this point to look back at history and highlight the fact that some of the unquestioned assumptions inherent in contemporary feminist demands have remained the same as those of the nineteenth and early twentieth-century feminists who in the main were pro-imperialist. One strand of early feminism in Britain has its roots in the radical liberal and social purity campaign work of Josephine Butler who drew on religious rhetoric with its notions of purity and impurity, virtue and vice and linked her analysis to aspects of contemporary theories of evolution. Christabel Pankhurst, a leading light at the time, echoed her agreement with the growing eugenic lobby when she said, 'sex powers are given . . . as a trust to be used not for . . . immorality and debauchery, but . . . reverently and in a union based on love for the purpose of carrying on the *race*'. [. . .]

Many suffragists campaigned around slogans such as 'votes for women, chastity for men' and created new spaces for women but their compliance with the development of an ideology of women as mothers and reproducers of the race highlighted their interest in upholding white supremacy.

At the beginning of the nineteenth century a healthy and growing population was seen as a national resource and neo-Malthusians alongside eugenists recommended contraception not only as an artificial check on population but also as a means of selective limitation of population growth to prevent the 'deterioration' of the 'race' and decline as an imperial nation through the proliferation of those they regarded as 'unfit' (to breed). It must however be said that there was a small section of women who attempted to counter the Eugenicist movement, such as Stella Brown.

[. . .] Within this context developed a new definition of women's role and the pressures which led to the formation of an ideology of motherhood:

> In many cases the terms in which reforms to do with marriage, child rearing and bearing were proposed also involved reference to the nation, the empire, or the race. . . .

White feminists have attacked this for its oppressiveness to them but not on the grounds of race and anti-imperialism.

Such a development of an ideology of women as mothers duty bound to reproduce for the race went alongside the development of an imagery of them as vulnerable creatures who needed protection not only at home but also in the colonies.

There are historical counterparts of contemporary white male use of the image of vulnerable and defenceless white women being raped and mugged by Black men, images which are reinforced by racist ideologies of black sexuality. Also in responding to the use of physical violence to control white women's sexuality white feminists have singularly failed to see how physical violence to control the sexuality of Black men is a feature of our history (eg lynching). This has implications for analyses and campaigning around sexual violence. [. . .]

The racist ideology that black and immigrant men are the chief perpetrators of violent crimes against women permeates not only the racist media fed regularly by police 'revelations' of 'racial' crime statistics as in 1982 but also sections of the white women's liberation movement as illustrated by their actions and sometimes their non-action.

For example, the compliance of many white feminists with the racist media and the police is shown in their silence when public hysteria is periodically whipped up through images of white women as innocent victims of black rapists and muggers. When white feminists have called for safer streets, and curfew of men at nights they have not distanced themselves from the link that exists in common sense racist thinking between street crime and Black people. Again, when women marched through Black inner city areas to 'Reclaim the Night' they played into the hands of the racist media and the fascist organizations, some of whom immediately fanned vigilante groups patrolling the streets 'protecting' innocent white women by beating up black men. Therefore we would agree that 'any talk, of male violence that does not emphatically reject the idea that race or colour is relevant automatically reinforces these racist images'.

Black women's sexuality has been used in various oppressive ways throughout imperialist history. For instance, during slavery women were forced to breed a slave labour force, raped, assaulted and experimented on; practices that still continue today under 'scientific' and sophisticated guises.

For Asian women, one such historical example of control over them was in the form of the Contagious Diseases Act passed in India in 1868. Throughout the nineteenth century the British military in India was only concerned with maintaining an efficient and 'healthy' army who had 'natural' sexual desires which needed to be fulfilled. Prostitution was encouraged and local Indian women were either taken on as 'mistresses' or regularly visited in the brothels both within and outside of the cantonments. Such practices were so widespread that venereal disease increased rapidly. What the Act did was call for compulsory registration of brothels and prostitutes and periodical medical examinations and compulsory treatment of such 'diseases'. The soldiers were not required to do this. This is just one example of state regulation of prostitutes which was a result of imperialist policies which required the maintenance of huge and 'healthy' armies.

In identifying the institution of the family as a source of oppression for women, white feminists have again revealed their cultural and racial myopia, because for Asian women in particular, the British state through its immigration legislation has done all it can to destroy the Asian family by separating husbands from wives, wives from husbands and parents from children.

But while many Black feminists would agree that the ideology of mother/wife roles is oppressive to women and that marriage only serves to reinforce and institutionalize that oppression, in a political climate where the state is demanding proof of the 'genuine' nature of 'arranged marriages' as a blatant attack on Asian-culture, and Asian people's right to enter this country, we demand the right to choose and struggle around the issue of family oppression ourselves, within our communities without state intervention, and without white feminists making judgements as to the oppressive nature of arranged marriages.

Many white feminists have argued that as feminists they find it very difficult to accept arranged marriages which they see as reactionary. Our argument is that it is not up to them to accept or reject arranged marriages but up to us to challenge, accept, or reform, depending on our various perspectives, on our own terms and in our own culturally specific ways.

Nuclear power on the north London line

With the setting up of the Greenham Common Women's Peace camp in 1981, world attention has focussed on the women's peace movement in Britain. Thousands of women have identified the threat of a nuclear war as a priority issue to organize around. [. . .]

The women's peace movement is and continues to remain largely white and middle-class because yet again their actions and demands have excluded any understanding or sensitivity to Black and Third World women's situations.

Black women's political priorities have not been to organize around the siting of American cruise missiles at Greenham or to focus on the disarmament campaigns. This has been inevitable given the implicit and often explicit nationalist sentiments of its campaigns as much as the overall framework within which they have addressed these questions. The patriotic cries of 'We want to protect our country' which extend both to the mixed left anti-nuclear groups as much as sections of the women's peace movement is not one with which many Black people seek to or want to identify with, particularly when we know that we are not recognized or accepted as legitimate and equal inhabitants of this island and are continuously fighting for our right to be here. The parochial concerns of the Campaign for Nuclear Disarmament (CND) and the women's peace movement are manifest in their unwillingness to take up any international issues. Why, for instance, are they not exposing, campaigning and mobilizing against Britain's role in illegal mining of uranium in Namibia for fuel for its Trident submarines? Why are connections not being made with people in the Pacific who are fighting for land rights? Why is there continued silence and inaction on the war going on in Britain's own 'back-yard', Northern Ireland? Why is it that some white women who have sought to involve Black women in their peace campaigns at Greenham can only include them by asking them to service them yet again and play the role of caterers?

It is inevitable that such questions and issues do not feature on the agendas of either the women's peace movement or the CND, because both these move-ments are imbued with the uncritical acceptance of the concept of 'the nation', in particular the 'British nation'. Their failure to distance themselves or be critical of anti-Americanism prevalent in public opinion which supports nuclear arms but opposes American nuclear arms is a result of their deepseated and entrenched patriotism. In Britain, there is not a single social or political institution that has not been fundamentally affected by the ideology of Empire and its corollary of British superiority. [. . .]

The slogan 'Yanks out' and 'Yankees go home' has been widely adopted by many women peace activists and is an illustration of racism arising out of a confu-sion of collapsing the American state with individual Americans. An example of such a tactic is an incident witnessed recently when a group of white, middle-class women began to shout and chant 'Yanks out' and 'Yankees go home' at a Black American soldier walking through the train carriage they were sitting in. To some of the Black women present this was reminiscent of 'Blacks go home' and 'wogs out'. When confronted with the racism of their action one woman justified their actions by saying that in an individual situation, such confrontations are necessary and legitimate. Necessary and legitimate to whom? [. . .]

The choice to demonstrate 'peacefully' or take non-direct action has never been available to us. When thousands of Black people marched against the National Front racists in Southall, in Lewisham, police were ready to do battle with their truncheons, riot shields and horses. Self defence in such instances has been the only option and the armoury available to us has consisted of bricks, dustbinlids, chilli bombs and petrol bombs. The question of deliberating over how best to fight our oppressor is not an abstract one for us nor for people involved in national liberation struggles around the world.

In saying that as Black women we have sought not to prioritize our political energies on organizing around 'peace' and disarmament, does not in any way mean we do not consider these as crucial political issues.

Indeed, the arms race is fundamentally political and the complexities of the new cold war and the increasing drive for American global supremacy are crucial questions of importance which concern us all. But, it is only when western peace activists, be they male or female, begin to broaden the parameters of their campaigns and integrate an international perspective within their frameworks, will there be a radical shift away from the predominantly white composition of these movements.

Conclusion

For us the way forward lies in defining a feminism which is significantly different to the dominant trends in the women's liberation movement. We have sought to define the boundaries of our sisterhood with white feminists and in so doing have been critical not only of their theories but also of their practice. True feminist theory and practice entails an understanding of imperialism and a critical engagement with challenging racism – elements which the current women's movement significantly lacks, but which are intrinsic to Black feminism. We are creating our own forms and content. As Black women we have to look at our history and at our experiences at the hands of a racist British state. We have to look at the crucial question of how we organize in order that we address ourselves to the totality of our oppression. For us there is no choice. We cannot simply prioritize one aspect of our oppression to the exclusion of others, as the realities of our day to day lives make it imperative for us to consider the simultaneous nature of our oppression and exploitation. Only a synthesis of class, race, gender and sexuality can lead us forward, as these form the matrix of Black women's lives.

Black feminism as a distinct body of theory and practice is in the process of development and debate both here in Britain and internationally and has begun to make significant contribution to other movements of liberation, as well as challenging the oppression and exploitation of Black women.

Notes

1   Some attempts have been made to look at both racism and feminism. For example Jenny Bourne in her essay 'Towards an anti-racist feminism' *Race and Class*, vol. 25 (1983), no. 1, pp. 1–22 attempts to locate anti racist practice within a (white) feminist context. However Jenny Bourne's essay fails adequately to address contemporary debates within feminism and ignores the contribution of black feminists to the broader debate around issues of racism, feminism, class and sexuality.

2   There have been a range of debates around socialism and feminism which have ignored the issue of race. See for example Rowbotham, Sheila, Segal, Lynne, and Wainwright, Hilary, *Beyond the Fragments. Feminism and the Making of Socialism*, London: Merlin (1979) and Sargent, Lydia, ed. *The Unhappy Marriage of Marxism and Feminism*, London: Pluto (1981) which has only one essay on 'The Incompatible Menage aTrois'.

Audre Lorde

AN OPEN LETTER TO MARY DALY

Audre Lorde, a self-described 'Black lesbian, mother, warrior and poet', is not a historian but, as a critically acclaimed novelist and poet, her penetrating exegeses on racism, difference, power and sexuality have galvanised the feminist scholarly community in influential and theoretically productive ways. Her 'Open Letter', reproduced here, is addressed to the lesbian feminist theologian and philosopher Mary Daly. It is a moving yet sharply expressed warning against the misappropriation of black women's words and history. Lorde begins with a generous acknowledgement of the impact of Daly's thinking upon her own work. She then goes on to describe how, in reading Daly's volume *Gyn/Ecology: The Metaethics of Radical Feminism* (1978), the exclusion of any images of black female power and the representation of non-European women as solely victims of various patriarchal forms of subordination leads to a painful recognition of the distortion of her own words, as well as the trivialisation of her history and 'mythic background'. 'So the question arises in my mind Mary', asks Lorde, 'do you ever really read the work of Black women? Did you read my words, or did you merely finger through them for quotations which you thought might valuably support an already conceived idea?' As in Reading 19 by Elizabeth Spelman, Lorde vehemently refutes any suggestion that all women suffer the same oppression by virtue of their gender. This, she remarks, is 'to lose sight of the many and varied tools of patriarchy'. Instead, 'difference' exposes women to diverse forms of suffering, some of which they share but many which they do not. Daly's 'un-recognizing' and dismissal of black women's history elicits a potential rupturing for Lorde of any meaningful communication between them. Although impatient of having to convince white women of the existence of racism within the sisterhood of feminism yet again, Lorde signs off in hopeful anticipation of future connectivities.

DEAR MARY,

WITH A MOMENT OF SPACE in this wild and bloody spring, I want to speak the words I have had in mind for you. I had hoped that our paths might cross and we could sit down together and talk, but this has not happened.

I wish you strength and satisfaction in your eventual victory over the repressive forces of the University in Boston. I am glad so many women attended the speak-out, and hope that this show of joined power will make more space for you to grow and be within.

Thank you for having *Gyn/Ecology* sent to me. So much of it is full of import, useful, generative, and provoking. As in *Beyond God The Father*, many of your analyses are strengthening and helpful to me. Therefore, it is because of what you have given to me in the past work that I write this letter to you now, hoping to share with you the benefits of my insights as you have shared the benefits of yours with me.

This letter has been delayed because of my grave reluctance to reach out to you, for what I want us to chew upon here is neither easy nor simple. The history of white women who are unable to hear Black women's words, or to maintain dialogue with us, is long and discouraging. But for me to assume that you will not hear me represents not only history, perhaps, but an old pattern of relating, sometimes protective and sometimes dysfunctional, which we, as women shaping our future, are in the process of shattering and passing beyond, I hope.

I believe in your good faith toward all women, in your vision of a future within which we can all flourish, and in your commitment to the hard and often painful work necessary to effect change. In this spirit I invite you to a joint clarification of some of the differences which lie between us as a Black and a white woman.

When I started reading *Gyn/Ecology*, I was truly excited by the vision behind your words and nodded my head as you spoke in your First Passage of myth and mystification. Your words on the nature and function of the Goddess, as well as the ways in which her face has been obscured, agreed with what I myself have discovered in my searches through African myth/legend/religion for the true nature of old female power.

So I wondered, why doesn't Mary deal with Afrekete as an example? Why are her goddess images only white, western european, judeo-christian? Where was Afrekete, Yemanje, Oyo, and Mawulisa? Where were the warrior goddesses of the Vodun, the Dahomeian Amazons and the warrior-women of Dan? Well, I thought, Mary has made a conscious decision to narrow her scope and to deal only with the ecology of western european women.

Then I came to the first three chapters of your Second Passage, and it was obvious that you were dealing with noneuropean women, but only as victims and preyers-upon each other. I began to feel my history and my mythic background distorted by the absence of any images of my foremothers in power. Your inclusion of African genital mutilation was an important and necessary piece in any consideration of female ecology, and too little has been written about it. To imply, however, that all women suffer the same oppression simply because we are women is to lose sight of the many varied tools of patriarchy. It is to ignore how those tools are used by women without awareness against each other.

To dismiss our Black foremothers may well be to dismiss where european women learned to love. As an African–american woman in white patriarchy, I am used to having my archetypal experience distorted and trivialized, but it is terribly painful to feel it being done by a woman whose knowledge so much touches my own.

When I speak of knowledge, as you know, I am speaking of that dark and true depth which understanding serves, waits upon, and makes accessible through language to ourselves and others. It is this depth within each of us that nurtures vision.

What you excluded from *Gyn/Ecology* dismissed my heritage and the heritage of all other noneuropean women, and denied the real connections that exist between all of us.

It is obvious that you have done a tremendous amount of work for this book. But simply because so little material on nonwhite female power and symbol exists in white women's words from a radical feminist perspective, to exclude this aspect of connection from even comment in your work is to deny the fountain of non-european female strength and power that nurtures each of our visions. It is to make a point by choice.

Then, to realize that the only quotations from Black women's words were the ones you used to introduce your chapter on African genital mutilation made me question why you needed to use them at all. For my part, I felt that you had in fact misused my words, utilized them only to testify against myself as a woman of Color. For my words which you used were no more, nor less, illustrative of this chapter than 'Poetry Is Not a Luxury' or any number of my other poems might have been of many other parts of *Gyn/Ecology*.

So the question arises in my mind, Mary, do you ever really read the work of Black women? Did you ever read my words, or did you merely finger through them for quotations which you thought might valuably support an already conceived idea concerning some old and distorted connection between us? This is not a rhetorical question.

To me, this feels like another instance of the knowledge, crone-ology and work of women of Color being ghettoized by a white woman dealing only out of a patriarchal western european frame of reference. Even your words on page 49 of *Gyn/Ecology*, 'The strength which Self-centering women find, in finding our Background, is our *own* strength, which we give back to our Selves,' have a different ring as we remember the old traditions of power and strength and nurturance found in the female bonding of African women. It is there to be tapped by all women who do not fear the revelation of connection to themselves.

Have you read my work, and the work of other Black women, for what it could give you? Or did you hunt through only to find words that would legitimize your chapter on African genital mutilation in the eyes of other Black women? And if so, then why not use our words to legitimize or illustrate the other places where we connect in our being and becoming? If, on the other hand, it was not Black women you were attempting to reach, in what way did our words illustrate your point for white women?

Mary, I ask that you be aware of how this serves the destructive forces of racism and separation between women – the assumption that the herstory and myth of white women is the legitimate and sole herstory and myth of all women to call upon for power and background, and that nonwhite women and our herstories are noteworthy only as decorations, or examples of female victimization. I ask that you be aware of the effect that this dismissal has upon the community of Black women and other women of Color, and how it devalues your own words. This dismissal does not essentially differ from the specialized devaluations that make Black women prey, for instance, to the murders even now happening in your own city. When patriarchy dismisses us, it encourages our murderers. When radical lesbian feminist theory dismisses us, it encourages its own demise.

This dismissal stands as a real block to communication between us. This block makes it far easier to turn away from you completely than to attempt to understand the thinking behind your choices. Should the next step be war between us, or separation? Assimilation within a solely western european herstory is not acceptable.

Mary, I ask that you re-member what is dark and ancient and divine within yourself that aids your speaking. As outsiders, we need each other for support and connection and all the other necessities of living on the borders. But in order to come together we must recognize each other. Yet I feel that since you have so completely un-recognized me, perhaps I have been in error concerning you and no longer recognize you.

I feel you do celebrate differences between white women as a creative force toward change, rather than a reason for misunderstanding and separation. But you fail to recognize that, as women, those differences expose all women to various forms and degrees of patriarchal oppression, some of which we share and some of which we do not. For instance, surely you know that for nonwhite women in this country, there is an 80 percent fatality rate from breast cancer; three times the number of unnecessary eventrations, hysterectomies and sterilizations as for white women; three times as many chances of being raped, murdered, or assaulted as exist for white women. These are statistical facts, not coincidences nor paranoid fantasies.

Within the community of women, racism is a reality force in my life as it is not in yours. The white women with hoods on in Ohio handing out KKK literature on the street may not like what you have to say, but they will shoot me on sight. (If you and I were to walk into a classroom of women in Dismal Gulch, Alabama, where the only thing they knew about each of us was that we were both Lesbian/Radical/Feminist, you would see exactly what I mean.)

The oppression of women knows no ethnic nor racial boundaries, true, but that does not mean it is identical within those differences. Nor do the reservoirs of our ancient power know these boundaries. To deal with one without even alluding to the other is to distort our commonality as well as our difference.

For then beyond sisterhood is still racism.

We first met at the MLA panel, 'The Transformation of Silence Into Language and Action.' This letter attempts to break a silence which I had imposed upon myself shortly before that date. I had decided never again to speak to white women about racism. I felt it was wasted energy because of destructive guilt and defensiveness, and because whatever I had to say might better be said by white women to one another at far less emotional cost to the speaker, and probably with a better hearing. But I would like not to destroy you in my consciousness, not to have to. So as a sister Hag, I ask you to speak to my perceptions.

Whether or not you do, Mary, again I thank you for what I have learned from you.

This letter is in repayment.

In the hands of Afrekete,

Audre Lorde

Elsa Barkley Brown

'WHAT HAS HAPPENED HERE'
The politics of difference in women's history and feminist politics

Elsa Barkley Brown is a historian of African-American political culture with a particular focus on gender. In this article, published in the journal *Feminist Studies* in 1992, she argues that aspects of African-American culture can provide feminists with a conceptual framework that may help them think beyond western linear, symmetrical narratives of history. By way of illustration she highlights the Creole term 'gumbo ya ya', meaning 'everybody talks at once', to develop her manifesto for a women's history that prioritises simultaneous dialogue and the need for a rela-tional analysis of difference. Most scholars write history as if they were classically trained musicians, argues Brown, foregrounding a particular tune (historical subject or theme) against a surrounding context of silence. Feminists need to think and theorise like jazz musicians, however, with differing strands running in tandem with each other. As she explains, 'the events and people we write about did not occur in isolation, but in dialogue with a myriad of other people and events'. Despite femi-nist theory's complacency about its inclusive approach to the analytical categories of race, class and gender, there is still a tendency for feminists to assume 'race' as significant for black women only, just as we might assume that sexuality is only relevant to lesbian women. Until white heterosexual women acknowledge the way in which race and sexuality have shaped their own 'normative' lives she asserts, they will not reconstruct their own history adequately. Nor is this simply a matter of academic debate. Rather, it has serious political implications with regard to racial stereotyping and racial solidarity, as the legal case of Anita Hill cited by Brown illustrates. Feminists may be apprehensive of the potential chaos and disorder arising from 'multiple and asymmetrical stories' of women, but we must learn to think differently about 'difference' she argues, for we live in a world that is neither linear nor symmetrical.

My work is not traditional. I like it that way. If people tell me to turn my ends under, I'll leave them raggedy. If they tell me to make my stitches small and tight, I'll leave them loose. Sometimes you can trip over my stitches they're so big. You can always recognize the traditional quilters who come by and see my quilts. They sort of cringe. They fold their hands in front of them as if to protect themselves from the cold. When they come up to my work they think to themselves, 'God, what has happened here – all these big crooked stitches.' I appreciate these quilters. I admire their craft. But that's not my kind of work. I would like them to appreciate what I'm doing. They are quilters. But I am an artist. And I tell stories.

Yvonne Wells, quoted in *Stitching Memories:*
African American Story Quilts

QUESTIONS OF DIFFERENCE loom large in contemporary intellectual and political discussions. Although many women's historians and political activists understand the intellectual and political necessity, dare I say moral, intellectual, and political correctness, of recognizing the diversity of women's experiences, this recognition is often accompanied with the sad (or angry) lament that too much attention to difference disrupts the relatively successful struggle to produce and defend women's history and women's politics, necessary corollaries of a women's movement. Like the traditionalists who view Yvonne Wells's quilts,[1] many women's historians and feminist activists cringe at the big and loose rather than small and tight stitches that now seem to bind women's experiences. They seek a way to protect themselves and what they have created as women's history and women's politics, and they wonder despairingly, 'God, what has happened here.' I do not say this facetiously; the fear that all this attention to the differences among women will leave us with only a void, a vacuum, or chaos is a serious concern. Such despair, I believe, is unnecessary, the product of having accepted the challenge to the specifics of our historical knowledge and political organizing while continuing to privilege a linear, symmetrical (some would say Western) way of thinking about history and politics themselves.

I am an optimist. It is an optimism born of reflecting on particular historical and cultural experiences. [. . .]

And it is here that I think African American culture is instructive as a way of rethinking, of reshaping our thinking processes, our understandings of history and politics themselves. [. . .]

[I]nstructive is the work of Luisah Teish. In *Jambalaya: The Natural Woman's Book of Personal Charms and Practical Rituals*, she writes about going home to New Orleans for a visit and being met by her family at the airport: 'Before I can get a good look in my mother's face, people begin arranging themselves in the car. They begin to talk gumbo ya ya, and it goes on for 12 days. . . . Gumbo ya ya is a creole term that means "Everybody talks at once."' It is through gumbo ya ya that Teish learns everything that has happened in her family and community and she conveys the essential information about herself to the group.[2] That is, it is through gumbo ya ya that Teish tells the history of her sojourn to her family and they tell theirs to her. They do this simultaneously because, in fact, their histories are joined

– occurring simultaneously, in connection, in dialogue with each other. To relate their tales separately would be to obliterate that connection.

To some people listening to such a conversation, gumbo ya ya may sound like chaos. We may better be able to understand it as something other than confusion if we overlay it with jazz, for gumbo ya ya is the essence of a musical tradition where 'the various voices in a piece of music may go their own ways but still be held together by their relationship to each other.'[3] In jazz, for example, each member has to listen to what the other is doing and know how to respond while each is, at the same time, intent upon her own improvisation. [. . .]

History is also everybody talking at once, multiple rhythms being played simultaneously. The events and people we write about did not occur in isolation but in dialogue with a myriad of other people and events. In fact, at any given moment millions of people are all talking at once. As historians we try to isolate one conversation and to explore it, but the trick is then how to put that conversation in a context which makes evident its dialogue with so many others – how to make this one lyric stand alone and at the same time be in connection with all the other lyrics being sung.

Unfortunately, it seems to me, few historians are good jazz musicians; most of us write as if our training were in classical music. We require surrounding silence – of the audience, of all the instruments not singled out as the performers in this section, even often of any alternative visions than the composer's. That then makes it particularly problematic for historians when faced with trying to understand difference while holding on to an old score that has in many ways assumed that despite race, class, ethnicity, sexuality, and other differences, at core all women do have the same gender; that is, the rhythm is the same and the conductor can point out when it is time for each of us to play it. Those who would alter the score or insist on being able to keep their own beat simultaneously with the orchestrated one are not merely presenting a problem of the difficulty of constructing a framework that will allow for understanding the experiences of a variety of women but as importantly the problem of confronting the political implications of such a framework, not only for the women under study but also for the historians writing those studies.

I think we still operate at some basic levels here. This is an opinion which may not be widely shared among women's historians. For I am aware that there is a school of thought within women's history that believes that it, more than any other field of history, has incorporated that notable triumvirate – race, class, and gender – and has addressed difference. But my point is that recognizing and even including difference is, in and of itself, not enough. In fact, such recognition and inclusion may be precisely the way to avoid the challenges, to reaffirm the very traditional stances women's history sees itself as challenging, and to write a good classical score – silencing everyone else until the spotlight is on them but allowing them no interplay throughout the composition. We need to recognize not only differences but also the relational nature of those differences. Middle-class white women's lives are not just different from working-class white, Black, and Latina women's lives. It is important to recognize that middle-class women live the lives they do precisely because working-class women live the lives they do. White women and women of color not only live different lives but white women live the lives they do in large part because women of color live the ones they do.

Let me here grossly simplify two hundred years of Black and white women's history in the United States. Among the major changes we have seen has been the greater labor force participation of white middle-class women; the increasing movement of white middle-class women from the home to voluntary associations within the larger society to formal public political roles; the shift among Black women from agricultural labor to industrial, service, and clerical work; the emergence of Black working-class women from the kitchens of white women to jobs in the private sector; and the shift of middle-class Black women to jobs in the public sector. We could, and often do, set these experiences side by side, thus acknowledging the differences in the experiences of different women. And most often, whether stated or not, our acknowledgment of these differences leads us to recognize how Black women's life choices have been constrained by race – how race has shaped their lives. What we are less apt to acknowledge (that is, to make explicit and to analyze) is how white women's lives are also shaped by race.[4] Even less do I see any real recognition of the relational nature of these differences.

But white middle-class women moved from a primary concern with home and children to involvement in voluntary associations when they were able to have their homes and children cared for by the services – be they direct or indirect – of other women. [. . .] The increased labor force participation of white middle-class women has been accompanied, indeed made possible, by the increased availability outside the home of services formerly provided inside the home – cleaning, food, health, and personal services. These jobs are disproportionately filled by women of color – African American, Latina, Asian American.[5] [. . .]

We are likely to acknowledge that white middle-class women have had a different experience from African American, Latina, Asian American, and Native American women; but the relation, the fact that these histories exist simultaneously, in dialogue with each other, is seldom apparent in the studies we do, not even in those studies that perceive themselves as dealing with the diverse experiences of women. The overwhelming tendency now, it appears to me, is to acknowledge and then ignore differences among women. [. . .]

We have still to recognize that all women do not have the same gender. In other words, we have yet to accept the fact that one cannot write adequately about the lives of white women in the United States *in any context* without acknowledging the way in which race shaped their lives. One important dimension of this would involve understanding the relationship between white women and white men as shaped by race. This speaks not just to the history we write but to the way we understand our own lives. And I believe it challenges women's history at its core, for it suggests that until women's historians adequately address difference and the causes for it, they have not and can not adequately tell the history of even white middle-class women.

The objections to all of this take many forms but I would like to address two of them. First, the oft-repeated lament of the problems of too many identities; some raise this as a conceptual difficulty, others as a stylistic one. In either case, such a discussion reinforces the notion that women of color, ethnic women, and lesbians are deviant, not the norm. And it reinforces not just the way in which some histories are privileged but also the way in which some historians are privileged. In fact, in women's history difference means 'not white middle-class heterosexual,' thus renormalizing white middle-class heterosexual women's experiences. One result of this is that white middle-class heterosexual women do not often have to think about difference or to see themselves as 'other.'[6] Not only do people of color not have the luxury in this society of deciding whether to identify racially but historians writing about people of color also do not have the privilege of deciding whether to acknowledge, at least at some basic level, their multiple identities. No editor or publisher allows a piece on Black or Latina women to represent itself as being about 'women.' On the other hand, people who want to acknowledge that their pieces are about 'white' women often have to struggle with editors to get that in their titles and consistently used throughout their pieces – the objection being it is unnecessary, superfluous, too wordy, awkward. Historians writing about heterosexual women seldom feel compelled to consistently establish that as part of their subjects' identity whereas historians writing about lesbian women must address sexuality. Does this imply that sexuality is only a factor in the lives of lesbian women, that is, that they are not only different from but deviant? These seem to me to be issues that historians cannot address separately from questions of the privilege some people have in this society and the way in which some historians have a vested interest in duplicating that privilege within historical constructions.

Another objection to the attention to difference is the fear, expressed in many ways, that we will in the process lose the 'voice of gender.'[7] This reifies the notion that all women have the same gender and requires that most women's voices be silenced and some privileged voice be given center stage. But that is not the only problem with this assumption for it also ignores the fact that gender does not have a voice; women and men do. They raise those voices constantly and simultaneously in concert, in dialogue with each other. Sometimes the effect may seem chaotic because they respond to each other in such ways; sometimes it may seem harmonic. But always it is polyrhythmic; never is it a solo or single composition. [. . .]

This is not merely a question of whether one prefers jazz to classical music. Like most intellectual issues, this one, too, has real political consequences. We have merely to think about the events surrounding Anita Hill's fall 1991 testimony before the Senate Judiciary Committee. When Professor Hill testified, a number of women, individually and collectively, rallied to her support and to advance awareness of the issue of sexual harassment. Many of Hill's most visible supporters, however, ignored the fact that she is a Black woman, the thirteenth child of Oklahoma farmers, or treated these as merely descriptive or incidental matters.[8] [. . .]

In the end, I would argue, the ignoring of these racialized and class-specific histories became a political liability. Having constructed Anita Hill as a generic or universal woman with no race or class, and having developed an analysis of sexual harassment in which race and class were not central issues, many of Hill's supporters were unable to deal with the racialized and class-specific discussion when it emerged. [. . .] Once Clarence Thomas played the race card and a string of his female supporters raised the class issue, they had much of the public discussion to themselves.[9] Thomas [. . .] constructed himself as a Black man confronting a generic (read, for many people, 'white' or 'whitened') woman assisted by white men. 'Thomas outrageously manipulated the legacy of lynching in order to shelter himself from Anita Hill's allegations'; by 'trivializ[ing] and misrepresent[ing] this painful part of African American people's history,' Thomas was able 'to deflect attention away from the reality of sexual abuse in African American women's lives.'[10] Such a strategy could only have been countered effectively by putting the experience of sexual harassment for Anita Hill in the context of her being a Black woman in the United States.[11] [. . .]

Few Black women of Anita Hill's age and older grew up unaware of the frequency of sexual abuse as part of Black women's employment history. Many of us were painfully aware that one reason our families worked so hard to shield us from domestic and factory work was to shield us from sexual abuse. [. . .]

A collective memory of sexual harassment runs deep in African American communities and many Black women, especially those both before the 1960s' civil rights movement, would likely recognize sexual harassment not as a singular experience but as part of a collective and common history. [. . .]

Anita Hill experienced sexual harassment not as a woman who had been harassed by a man but as a Black woman harassed by a Black man. Race is a factor in all cases of sexual abuse – inter- or intraracial – although it is usually only explored in the former. When white middle-class and upper-class men harass and abuse white women they are generally protected by white male privilege; when Black men harass and abuse white women they may be protected by male privilege, but they are as likely to be subject to racial hysteria; when Black men harass and abuse Black women they are often supported by racist stereotypes which assume different sexual norms and different female value among Black people.[12] I think we understand this only if we recognize that race is operative even when all the parties involved are white.

But, recognizing race as a factor in sexual harassment and sexual abuse requires us particularly to consider the consequences of the sexual history and sexual stereotypes of African Americans, especially African American women. 'Throughout U.S. history Black women have been sexually stereotyped as immoral, insatiable, perverse; the initiators in all sexual contacts – abusive or otherwise.' A result of such stereotyping as well as of the political, economic, and social privileges that resulted to white people (especially white men but also white women) from such stereotyping is that 'the common assumption in legal proceedings as well as in the larger society has been that black women cannot be raped or otherwise sexually abused.'[13] This has several effects. One is that Black women are most likely not to be believed if they speak of unwarranted sexual advances or are believed to have been willing or to have been the initiator. Both white and Black women have struggled throughout the nineteenth and twentieth centuries to gain control of their sexual selves. But while white elite women's sexual history has included the long effort to break down Victorian assumptions of sexuality and respectability in order to gain control of their sexual selves, Black women's sexual history has required the struggle to be accepted as respectable in an effort to gain control of their sexual selves.[14] Importantly, this has resulted in what Darlene Clark Hine has described as a culture of dissemblance – Black women's sexuality is often concealed, that is, Black women have had to learn to cover up all public suggestions of sexuality, even of sexual abuse. Black women, especially middle-class women, have learned to present a public image that never reveals their sexuality.[15]

Further, given the sexual stereotyping of Black men, a young Anita Hill may also have recognized that speaking of the particularities of Thomas's harassment of her had the potential to restigmatize the whole Black community – male and female. This is not merely, as some have suggested, about protecting Black men or being 'dutiful daughters.' Black women sought their own as well as the larger community's protection through the development of a politics of respectability.[16] Respectable behavior would not guarantee one's protection from sexual assault, but the absence of such was certain to reinforce racist notions of Black women's greater sexuality, availability, or immorality, as well as the racist notions of Black men's bestiality which were linked to that.

Thomas exploited these issues. Only a discussion which explored the differences and linkages in Black and white women's and working-class and middle-class women's struggles for control of their sexual selves could have effectively addressed his manipulation of race and class and addressed the fears that many Black people, especially women, had at the public discussion of what they perceived as an intraracial sexual issue. Dismissing or ignoring these concerns or imposing a universal feminist standard which ignores the differential consequences of public discourse will not help us build a political community around these issues.

Attending to the questions of race and class surrounding the Thomas hearings would have meant that we would not have had a linear story to tell. The story we did have would not have made good quick sound bites or simple slogans for it would have been far more complicated. But, in the end, I think, it would have spoken to more people's experiences and created a much broader base of understanding and support for issues of sexual harassment. Complicating it certainly would have allowed a fuller confrontation of the manipulation and exploitation of race and class on the part of Thomas and his supporters. The political liability here and the threat to creating a community of struggle came from *not* focusing on differences among women and *not* seriously addressing the race and class dimensions of power and sexual harassment. It would, of course, have been harder to argue that things would have been different if there were a woman on the committee.[17] But then many Black working-class women, having spent their days toiling in the homes of white elite women, understood that femaleness was no guarantee of support and mutuality. Uncomplicated discussions of universal women's experiences cannot address these realities. Race (and yes gender, too) is at once too simple an answer and at the same time a more complex answer than we have yet begun to make it.

The difficulty we have constructing this more complicated story is not merely a failure to deal with the specifics of race and class; the difficulty is also, I believe, in how we see history and politics in an underlying focus on linear order and symmetry which makes us wary, fearing that layering multiple and asymmetrical stories will only result in chaos with no women's history or women's story to tell, that political community is a product of homogeneity, and that exploring too fully our differences will leave us void of any common ground on which to build a collective struggle. These are the ideas/assumptions which I want to encourage us to think past.

I suggest African American culture as a means to learning to think differently about history and politics. I do this not merely because these are cultural forms with which I am familiar and comfortable. Rather, I do this because there is a lot that those who are just confronting the necessity to be aware of differences can learn from those who have had always to be aware of such. Learning to think non-linearly, asymmetrically, is, I believe essential to our intellectual and political developments. A linear history will lead us to a linear politics and neither will serve us well in an asymmetrical world.

Notes

1   See *Stitching Memories: African American Story Quilts*, Gallery Guide, Eva Grudin, curator (Williamstown, Mass.: Williams College Museum of Art, 1989), 1.

2   Luisah Teish, *Jambalaya: The Natural Woman's Book of Personal Charms and Practical Rituals* (San Francisco: Harper & Row, 1985), 139–40.

3   Lawrence Levine, *Black Culture and Black Consciousness: Afro-American Folk Thought from Slavery to Freedom* (New York: Oxford University Press, 1977), 133.

4   We need historical studies of white women in the United States comparable to the work begun by Alexander Saxton, David Roediger, Vron Ware, and Ann Laura Stoler – work which takes seriously the study of the racial identity of white U.S. men and white European women and men. See, Alexander Saxton, *The Rise and Fall of the White Republic: Class Politics and Mass Culture in Nineteenth-Century America* (New York: Verso, 1990); David R. Roediger, *The Wages of Whiteness: Race and the Making of the American Working Class* (New York: Verso, 1991); Vron Ware, *Beyond the Pale: White Women, Racism, and History* (London: Verso, 1992); Ann Laura Stoler, 'Carnal Knowledge and Imperial Power: Gender, Race, and Morality in Colonial Asia,' in *Gender at the Crossroads of Knowledge: Feminist Anthropology in the Postmodern Era*, ed. Micaela di Leonardo (Berkeley: University of California Press, 1991), 51–101.

5   Evelyn Nakano Glenn, 'From Servitude to Service Work: Historical Continuities in the Racial Division of Reproductive Labor,' *Signs* 18, 1 (1992): 1–43.

6   One result of this is that women of color often come to stand for the 'messiness' and 'chaos' of history and politics much as an 'aesthetic of uniformity' led the Radio City Music Hall Rockettes to perceive the addition of Black dancers to their chorus line as making 'it ugly ("unaesthetic"), imbalanced ("nonuniform"), and sloppy ("imprecise").' See Patricia J. Williams's wonderful discussion in *The Alchemy of Race and Rights* (Cambridge: Harvard University Press, 1991), 116–18.

7   See, for example, 'Editor's Notes,' *Journal of Women's History* 1 (Winter 1990): 7.

8   The discussion which follows should not be read as a critique of Hill's testimony but rather of those who set themselves out as political and intellectual experts able to speak with authority on 'women's issues.' It is concerned with public discussion in mainstream media by those identifying themselves as feminist activists, primarily white. My focus on such is a reflection of the scope of this essay and is not intended to hold white women solely or even primarily responsible for the state of public discussion. For my analysis that addresses and critiques developments within the Black community and among Black organizations, see 'Imaging Lynching: African American Communities, Collective Memory, and the Politics of Respectability,' in *African-American Women Speak Out on Anita Hill-Clarence Thomas*, ed. Geneva Smitherman (Detroit: Wayne State University Press, 1995). Finally, I am not naive enough to think the conclusion of the Thomas confirmation process would have been different if these issues had been effectively addressed. I do believe public discussion and political mobilization then and in the future could have been shaped differently by these discussions. Given that for two decades Black women have, according to almost all polls, supported feminist objectives in larger numbers than white women, I think we have to look to something other than Black women's reported antifeminism or

privileging of race over gender for the answer to why an effective cross-race, cross-class political mobilization and discussion did not develop.

9 Thomas did this most significantly in his dramatic calling up of the lynching issue and situating himself, for the first time in the hearings, as a Black man, and also in his efforts to portray Hill as a Black woman who felt inferior to and threatened by lighter skinned and white women. Those who testified for him, most notably J. C. Alvarez, in her venomous references to Hill as a Black female Yale Law School graduate who, by Alvarez's account, could have gotten any job anywhere that she wanted. The following analysis, for reasons of space, addresses the manipulation of issues of race; for a more extensive analysis of the class issues, see my 'Imaging Lynching,' and 'Can We Get There from Here? The Contemporary Political Challenge to a Decade of Feminist Research and Politics' (paper prepared for 'What Difference Does Difference Make? The Politics of Race, Class and Gender Conference,' Duke University, University of North Carolina Center for Research on Women, Chapel Hill, May 31, 1992).

10 'African American Women in Defense of Ourselves,' Guest Editorial in *New York Amsterdam News*, Oct. 26, 1991 and Advertisement in *New York Times*, Nov. 17, 1991; San Francisco *Sun Reporter*, Nov. 20, 1991; *Capitol Spotlight* (Washington, D.C.), Nov. 21, 1991; *Los Angeles Sentinel*, Nov. 21, 1991; *Chicago Defender* Nov. 23, 1991; *Atlanta Inquirer*, Nov. 23, 1991; *Carolinian* (Raleigh, N.C.), Nov. 28, 1991.

11 The following discussion is not meant to speak for or analyze specifically Anita Hill's personal experience but to suggest the ways in which complicating the issues was essential to a discussion which would engage women from differing racial and class backgrounds.

12 One of the most egregious examples of the latter as related to this particular case can be seen in Orlando Patterson's argument that if Thomas said the things Hill charged he was merely engaging in a 'down-home style of courting' which would have been 'immediately recognizable' to Hill 'and most women of Southern working-class backgrounds, white or black, especially the latter' but which would have been 'completely out of the cultural frame of [the] white upper-middle-class work world' of the senators who would vote on his confirmation. See, 'Race, Gender, and Liberal Fallacies,' *New York Times*, Oct. 20, 1991, and the even more obnoxious defense of his position in *Reconstruction* 1, 4 (1992): 68–71, 75–7.

13 'African American Women in Defense of Ourselves.' For a good discussion of the sexual stereotypes of African American women in the late nineteenth and early twentieth centuries, see Beverly Guy-Sheftall, *Daughters of Sorrow: Attitudes toward Black Women, 1880–1920* (Brooklyn: Carlson Publishing, 1990), esp. chaps. 3 and 4. See also Patricia Morton, *Disfigured Images: The Historical Assault on Afro-American Women* (New York: Praeger, 1991).

14 Kimberle Crenshaw, 'Roundtable: Sexuality after Thomas/Hill,' *Tikkun*, January/February 1992, 29.

15 Darlene Clark Hine, 'Rape and the Culture of Dissemblance: Preliminary Thoughts on the Inner Lives of Black Midwestern Women,' *Signs* 14 (Summer 1989): 912–20.

16 The implications of this are explored in my 'Imaging Lynching.'

17 This became a common argument during and in the days following the hearings; see, for example, Barbara Ehrenreich, 'Women Would Have Known,' *Time*, Oct. 21, 1991, 104.

Ania Loomba

DEAD WOMEN TELL NO TALES

Issues of female subjectivity, subaltern agency and tradition in colonial and post-colonial writings on widow immolation in India

Ania Loomba is a literary and cultural critic of gender, colonialism and the nation from the early modern period to the present. Although this article, first published in the *History Workshop Journal* in 1993, does not address the development of feminist history specifically, it does provide an insightful overview of the difficulties encountered in the recovery of the subaltern subject through the figure and practice of sati. According to Loomba, the immolated widow 'provides the most suitable language for talking about silence: she is after all, a conceptual and social category that comes into being only when the subject dies'. Three main bodies of writing on sati are examined – colonial debates, feminist analyses and the diverse responses to the burning of the young woman Roop Kanwar in 1987. Loomba seeks to move beyond historical, dualistic conceptualisations of sati as either an oppressed female victim (sign of Hindu barbarism) or a heroic free agent who chooses to burn beside her husband on his funeral pyre (sign of the ideal devoted wife). That sati became a major emblem of Hindu tradition and national resistance to nineteenth-century colonial law is beyond doubt, but as Loomba observes, 'nowhere is the sati herself a subject of the debate' in these conflicts. On the one hand, we have an over-representation of sati by colonial authorities, nationalist reformers, pro-sati lobbies and feminists. On the other, we have scholars such as Gayatri Spivak who, as seen in the Introduction to this *Reader,* declares that the subaltern woman herself cannot speak and cannot be represented. Loomba explores a number of ways out of this dilemma. These include rethinking the categories of the experiencing subject, the fuller historicisation of the political conditions that produced such brutal events and ideologies, and the conditions under which we discuss them today. Feminist historians must 'suppose a presence which at first cannot be found', she argues, they must try to recover the writings of those women who escaped the potential threat of immolation and lived 'to tell the tale'.

S ATI HAS BEEN A FOCAL POINT not only for the colonial gaze on India, but also for recent work on post-coloniality and the female subject, for nineteenth- and twentieth-century Indian discourses about tradition, Indian culture and femininity, and, most crucially, for the women's movement in India.[1] Reading these various discourses against each other and in the context of the specific cultural moments and inter-cultural tensions in which they are produced is often a frustrating task because of the astounding circularity of language, arguments and even images that marks discussions on sati from the late eighteenth century till today. This circularity has sometimes been used to indicate the enormous shaping power of a colonial past on contemporary Indian society, or 'to question', as Lata Mani puts it, 'the "post" in "post-colonial"'.[2] While such an emphasis has been useful in indicating the continued economic, cultural and epistemological hegemony of the West, and salutary in questioning Eurocentric intellectual paradigms, it has also contributed to a lack of focus on the crucial shifts from colonial to post-colonial governance and culture. To isolate the study of colonialism from that of its later evolution is to deflect attention from the narratives of nationalism, communalism and religious fundamentalism which are the crucibles within which gender, class, caste, or even neo-colonialism function today.[3]

Widow immolation is one of the most spectacular forms of patriarchal violence; each burning was and is highly variable, and is both produced by and helps to validate and circulate other ideologies that strengthen the oppression of women. But for the most part, representations of sati have tended to homogenize the burnings and to isolate them from the specific social, economic and ideological fabric in which they are embedded. Thus the spectacularity of widow immolation lends itself to a double violence: we are invited to view sati as a unique, transhistorical, transgeographic category and to see the burnt widow as a woman with special powers to curse or bless, as one who feels no pain, and one who will be rewarded with everlasting extra-terrestrial marital bliss. She is marked off from all other women by her will; thus her desire, her 'decisions' are to be revered by the community even as theirs are consistently erased. Paradoxically but necessarily, this process also casts the burning widow as a sign of normative femininity: in a diverse body of work, she becomes the privileged signifier of either the devoted and chaste, or the oppressed and victimized Indian (or sometimes even 'third world') woman.

In this essay, I will attempt to locate, within the apparent repetitions of arguments, the differences in what is at stake in the three most substantial bodies of writings on sati: the first being the colonial debate on widow immolation, the second the work of feminists working in the Western academy (both diasporic Indians and non-Indians), and the third is the spate of writings produced in India following the burning of a young woman, Roop Kanwar, in the village of Deorala, Rajasthan, in October 1987. These historical and conceptual differences, I shall suggest, are crucial to our reconceptualizing the burning widow as neither an archetypal victim nor a free agent, and to analysing the inter-connections between colonialism and its aftermath. In order to trace the roots and trajectories of the different ideologies and representations of widow immolation, I shall move freely between these three sets of writings.

Despite widespread references to sati, there were surprisingly few extended studies of it between Edward Thompson's well-known colonial commentary on the subject published in 1928 and the Deorala episode in 1987.[4] Even now, apart from

Lata Mani's work, the most thought-provoking accounts have been shorter essays, although several book-length studies are now available.[5] Curiously too, the most prestigious historians of colonial India (either British or Indian) have not written at any length on the subject, and nor does the influential revisionist series Subaltern Studies deal with it.[6] There is no conclusive evidence for dating the origins of sati, although Romilla Thapar points out that there are growing textual references to it in the second half of the first millenium A.D.[7] [. . .]

The growth of colonial enterprises in India shaped the tone as well as frequency of comments by Europeans on the idea as well as the spectacle of sati.[8] With increasing English involvement, the accounts proliferate; simultaneously, the commentator becomes enmeshed in the scenario he describes, and the burning widow herself is progressively pictured as reaching out to the white man watching her: 'I stood close to her, she observed me attentively,' writes William Hodges;[9] Mandelso claims that she gives him a bracelet; Thomas Bowery receives some flowers from another's hair. By the late eighteenth/early nineteenth century, the recurrent theme of what Spivak calls 'white men saving brown women from brown men' has crystallized.[10] Legend has it that Job Charnock, the founder of Calcutta, rescued from the flames a Brahmin widow and lived with her for 14 years till her death; European fiction from Jules Verne's *Around the World in Eighty Days* to M. M. Kaye's *The Far Pavilions* is obsessed with such rescues. Sati became, as is well known, simultaneously the moral justification for empire and an ideal of female devotion. Katherine Mayo's *Mother India* had blamed all of India's ills on the Indian male's 'manner of getting into the world and his sex-life thenceforward'. London's *New Statesman and Nation* said that the book demonstrated 'the filthy personal habits of even the most highly educated classes in India – which, like the denigration of Hindu women, are unequalled even among the most primitive African or Australian savages'.[11] Sati was emblematic of this denigration; at the same time, even the harshest colonial criticism included a sneaking admiration for the sati as the ideal wife who represented 'the wholly admirable sentiment and theory, that the union of man and woman is lifelong and the one permanent thing in the world'.[12] [. . .]

These contradictory responses to sati – as a powerful male fantasy of female devotion, and an instance of Hindu barbarism – both fuelled the voyeuristic fascination of the colonial gaze and impelled the narrative division, in the first half of the colonial debate on widow immolation in nineteenth-century India, of satis into good and bad ones. [. . .]

The final abolition in 1829 is regarded as a sort of landmark in the history of Indian women; commentators allot the credit for it to different people according to their own ideological positions: hence Thompson attributes it entirely to the efforts of William Bentinck, the then Governor General, as does V. N. Datta; Ashis Nandy predictably gives [Raja Ram Mohan] Roy pride of place,[13] and only Lata Mani traces the complex interpenetration of interests in a way that takes into account the entire spectrum of positions on this subject. Comments on the increase of satis in 1818 are also significant; many British officials simply attributed it to a cholera epidemic. Edward Thompson, like some others, read it as a sign of excessive native obedience to British law: 'I think there can be no doubt that the sanction of the Government was sometimes misrepresented as an order that widows should burn'.[14] Ashis Nandy interprets the increase as precisely the opposite of this, as a form of subaltern disobedience: 'the rite', he suggests, 'became popular in groups made psychologically marginal by their exposure to Western impact . . . the opposition to sati constituted . . . a threat to them. In their desperate defence of the rite they were also trying to defend their traditional self-esteem'.[15] [. . .] [Nandy's analysis] remains important for at least two reasons.

First, by arguing that the colonial conflict calcified indigenous patriarchal practices, Nandy's was one of the pioneering attempts to trace the multiple connections between colonial power and gender relations. Later feminist work on British India has considered in greater depth and with more sophistication how the colonial disenfranchisement of Indian men led to a situation whereby women became the grounds and signs for the colonial struggle. Indian nationalisms of different shades produced their own versions of the good Hindu wife, each of which became emblematic of Indian-ness and tradition, a sign of rebellion against colonial authority and a symbol of the vision of the future.[16] In the process, women's own questioning of patriarchal authority – both indigenous and colonial – were specifically marginalised. [. . .]

The *second* outcome of [Nandy's] work has not been as felicitous; it is worth tracing its somewhat involved trajectory here because it warns against the dangers of easy explanations of indigenous patriarchies as merely responses to colonial power and also because it encodes the problems – of separating colonial and post-colonial histories, and of recovering and theorizing female agency – with which I began this essay. [. . .]

Nandy had, as I have pointed out, been one of the pioneers of historicizing sati, of analysing sati as a form of specifiable political economic social and psychic cultures. This, ironically, was the thrust of feminist writings following the Deorala episode of 1987. Feminists insisted that the death of Roop Kanwar should be viewed not as a remnant of a feudal past but as an expression of distinctly modern economies and the contemporary denigration of women. They pointed out that huge amounts of money had been made following the murder of Roop Kanwar by those who turned the sati into a commercial spectacle involving hundreds of thousands of people; that Roop Kanwar was an educated girl, not a simple embodiment of rural femininity (a fact that pro-sati lobbyists used to argue that it was a case of 'free choice'); and that the leaders of the pro-sati movement 'constitute a powerful regional elite' who had much to gain from constructing sati anew as emblematic of their 'tradition'.[17] [. . .]

Now, these are almost exactly the terms in which Lata Mani, in essays written before the Deorala incident, had described the colonial discourse on the subject. Brilliantly unravelling the rhetorical and ideological overlaps between seemingly opposed views in the debates between the colonial government, the nationalist reformers and the indigenous pro-sati lobby, Mani points out that 'the entire issue was debated within the framework of the scriptures'.[18] Even Indian reformers, epitomised by Raja Ram Mohan Roy, argued against sati by contending that it had no scriptural sanction and that it was custom and not the Hindu religion that had fostered the practice.

At first glance, then, it seems that little has changed between the colonial situation and 1987. But Nandy's own analytical moves – towards *subscribing* to a division that he had earlier *analysed*, and invoking an ideal of mythical sati that represents an Indian tradition, a tradition that he had earlier seen as constructed out of the tensions of colonialism – help us identify the definitive contextual shifts.

His conflation of 'respect' for an ideal sati with rural India, native authenticity and the canny cultural instincts of the average Indian clearly positions him as a sophisticated example of the nativism which Gayatri Spivak has repeatedly targeted as a major pitfall for the post-colonial intellectual. [. . .]

Significantly too, the target of Nandy's anger today is not the colonial state but Indian feminists who are seen as deculturalised, inauthentic, westernised and alienated from an appreciation of their own culture, which their village sisters embody in the act of immolating themselves. Here Nandy has a wide range of allies [. . .]. American sociologist Patrick Harrigan too launched his defence of sati on the shoulders of an attack on westernised feminists who were out of touch, he claimed, with the sentiments of their rural sisters, who in turn were emblematic of 'Bharat Mata' or Mother India.[19] The conservative Hindi press spoke in similar terms, as did various pundits and sadhus.[20] All of them zeroed in on 'azad kism ki auratein' [types of free woman] and pitted them against both archetypes of the good Hindu woman and the present-day average/authentic rural woman. The Rajput lobby was vociferous in condemning women in trousers and with short hair who were now going to tell 'their' women what not to do. As we can see, the division between the west and India, crass materialism and spirituality, is angrily and sanctimoniously re-worked to guard against the spectre of organized women's movements.

Thus, while the post-Deorala debate seems cast entirely in the mould of the tradition/modernity dichotomy Mani speaks of, the distinctively new factor is the women's movement, a movement which has 'been the single most important factor in changing the terms of the public debate on issues like rape, domestic violence, women's employment [etc.] . . . if it were not for this, the incident at Deorala would not have been a national issue'.[21] [. . .]

While discussions of the textual tradition figured after Deorala, the question of the widow's choice was at the core of all debates. The idea of the voluntary sati as an expression of a peculiarly Indian mode of femininity was repeated ad nauseam by the pro-sati lobby – contradictorily invoked both via Roop Kanwar's modern education as well as via her supposed distance from other educated Indian women. The struggle now was clearly over female volition – with feminists claiming that the entire notion of a voluntary sati is retrogressive and the pro-sati lobby insisting on the freedom of choice. This brings us to the frustrating core of past and present representations of, and debates over, sati.

Female subjectivity and the subject of sati

For the Indian woman to be cast as Mother India and to serve a wide spectrum of political interests in colonial times, she had to be rewritten as more-than-victim. As an agent of Hindu tradition, or nationalist interests, a certain amount of volition, and even desire had to be attributed to her. This rewriting is evident in the drama of sati abolition.

Two petitions were put forward by the Indian pro-sati lobby protesting the abolition in 1828, one to the King and the second to William Bentinck, the then Governor-General. In both a death-wish on the part of the loving, faithful widow becomes the emblem of Hindu resistance to colonial law. [. . .]

Here, the *desire* of the Hindu wife for her husband is accorded a recognition that is otherwise entirely absent in patriarchal discourses. Ironically but hardly surprisingly, this recognition of desire and of subjectivity, and of agency, leads to the annihilation of the woman; hence female desire is allowed but a spectacular moment, a swan's song that announces her ceasing to be.[22]

After the Deorala incident, it was not only the pro-sati lobby that invoked the widow's desire. The new legislations on sati introduced by the Indian Government and the Rajasthan State Government, both of which were avowedly concerned with effectively eradicating widow immolation as well as its 'glorification', implicitly cast the woman herself as agent of the crime. [. . .]

As Vasudha Dhagamwar, a feminist legal expert pointed out, the relevant clauses 'do not distinguish between voluntary and involuntary sati. But in effect they treat all sati as voluntary. That is why the woman is punished and that is why those who kill her are punished for abetment and not for murder'.[23] The invocation of female will here can be seen to work against the woman herself.

Lata Mani's central argument has been that the entire colonial debate on sati was concerned with re-defining tradition and modernity, that 'what was at stake was not women but tradition' (p. 118) and that women 'become sites on which various versions of scripture/tradition/law are elaborated and contested' (p. 115). Hence, she argues, nowhere is the sati herself a subject of the debate, and nowhere is her subjectivity represented. Thus, we learn little or nothing about the widows themselves, or their interiority, or in fact of their pain, even from reformers such as Ram Mohan Roy.

Mani's conclusions have set the terms for subsequent work on sati, especially that which is concerned with the relationship between gender and colonialism. The critical recovery of the sati's consciousness and subjectivity has become a recurrent but fraught project, consonant with the recent preoccupation in writings on colonial discourse in general and South Asian historiography in particular with the agency of the oppressed subject.[24] Anand Yang laments the lack of focus on the satis themselves in existing writings, but largely repeats statistical data about the womens' age, caste and region.[25] Gayatri Spivak, in at least three influential essays, reads the absence of women's voices in the colonial debate as representative of the difficulty of recovering subject positions in general and as indicative of the violence of colonialism and of indigenous patriarchy in particular: the discourses on sati are read as proof that 'there is no space from where the subaltern [sexed] subject can speak'.[26]

The silence of Spivak's subaltern is both a critique and, more disturbingly, an echo of a notoriously recurrent theme in the writings of British colonialists, Indian nationalists, Hindu orthodoxy, and indeed British feminists of the nineteenth century. The silence of Indian women enabled British feminists to claim a speaking part for themselves.[27] In an editorial comment in *The Storm-bell* of June 1898, Josephine Butler commented that Indian women were:

> indeed between the upper and nether millstone, helpless, voiceless, hopeless. Their helplessness appeals to the heart, in somewhat the same way in which the helplessness and suffering of a dumb animal does, under the knife of a vivisector. Somewhere, halfway between the Martyr Saints and the tortured 'friend of man', the noble dog, stand, it seems

to me, these pitiful Indian women, girls, children, as many of them are. They have not even the small power of resistance which the western woman may have . . . [28]

Butler and others could thus claim the necessity of representing their mute sisters, and hence legitimize themselves as 'the imperial authorities on "Indian woman-hood"'.[29] Although she contests precisely the legacy of such politics, it is not surprising that the silence of Spivak's subaltern is a pre-condition for her own project of representation. She writes:

> As Sarah Kofman has shown, the deep ambiguity of Freud's use of women as a scapegoat is a reaction-formation to an initial and contin-uing desire to give the hysteric a voice, to transform her into the subject of hysteria. The masculist-imperialist ideological formation that shaped that desire into 'the daughter's seduction' is part of the same formation that constructs the monolithic 'third world woman'. . . . Thus, when confronted with the questions, Can the subaltern speak? and Can the subaltern (as woman) speak?, our efforts to give the subaltern a voice in history will be doubly open to the dangers run by Freud's discourse.[30]

Spivak contends that both Foucault and the Subaltern school of South Asian histor-ians succumb to these dangers in trying to recover the voice of the marginalised subject. In both cases the idea of a sovereign subject creeps back and undercuts their own concerns – in the case of Foucault, s/he is imperialist, in the case of the subaltern historians, a nativist. Spivak thus signals the necessity of adapting the Gramscian maxim – 'pessimism of the intellect, optimism of the will' – by combining a philosophical scepticism about recovering any subaltern agency with a political commitment to making visible the positioning of the marginalised. Thus she makes her case for the validity of the representation of the subaltern by the post-colonial feminist intellectual:

> The subaltern cannot speak. There is no virtue in global laundry lists with 'woman' as a pious item. Representation has not withered away. The female intellectual as intellectual has a circumscribed task which she must not disown with a flourish.[31]

The intellectual whom Spivak here calls to arms is almost by definition the Indian woman academic working in the metropolitan academy, a woman who must struggle against the neo-colonial impulses of that space without succumbing to the nostalgic gestures of her counterpart in the third world.

It is no accident that such a project focuses on the immolated widow, who, in Spivak's work, becomes the ground for formulating a critique of colonialism, of indigenous patriarchy, of contemporary critical and cultural theories and of revi-sionist historiographies. She provides the most suitable language for talking about silence: she is, after all, a conceptual and social category that comes into being only when the subject dies. The to-be-sati is merely a widow, the sati is by definition a silenced subject. Caught between a notion of representation that comes too easily, as in the case of nineteenth-century British feminists, and another that recognises its contingencies and difficulties, like Spivak's, the Indian woman remains silent: she still 'cannot speak'. An insistence on subaltern silence is disquieting for those who are engaged in precisely the task of recovering such voices; it can be linked to Spivak's curious detachment, in these essays, from the specificities of post-colonial politics. But her argument for the validity, indeed necessity, of repre-sentation ironically takes on, as I hope to show below, a specially urgent resonance in the very arena she does not address: the struggles of third world feminists in their own countries, and in this case, India.

From the earliest commentaries onwards, only two options are offered for the dead widow: she either wanted to die or was forced to. Each option marks a dead end for feminist investigations. In the first case, we are dangerously close to the 'radiant heroism' of the willing widow which is suggested by both British and Indian male commentators. In the second case, fears have been voiced that if we refuse to 'grant sati the dubious status of existential suicide' we will find ourselves 'in another bind, that of viewing the sati as inexorably a victim and thereby emptying her subjectivity of any function or agency'.[32] [. . .]

Rajeswari Sunder Rajan attempts to break this impasse by drawing on Elaine Scarry's work on the 'radical subjectivity' of pain.[33] Arguing that neither colonial commentators, nor Indian reformers, nor even the feminist work on sati have suffi-ciently focused on the pain of the dying woman, and showing also how the pro-sati lobby has always insisted that the sati feels none, Sunder Rajan claims that 'an inherent resistance to pain is what impels the individual or collective suffering subject towards freedom. It is therefore as one who acts/reacts, rather than as one who invites assistance, that one must regard the subject in pain' (p. 9). A recent essay by Lata Mani can be read as in dialogue with Sunder Rajan and other femi-nists working in India.[34] Mani now mines colonial eyewitness accounts of widow burning for signs of the struggles and vacillations of potential satis and shows how pain may impel a woman to try to escape the pyre, contrary to her own earlier resolution to die. She thereby moves beyond her earlier notion of 'complex subjectivity' for satis, which had seemed to merely oscillate between various static states of being. Significantly, she now clearly states that there is no such thing as a voluntary sati and is anxious, too, that we avoid 'globalizing the local . . . granting colonialism more power than it achieved'. She wants also to 'make sure that the things in my work that speak to the context of the U.S. are not . . . counter-productive in the struggle of progressives in India'.[35] Such a note is rare in work on colonial discourse within the Western academy and it leads Lata Mani to a crucial reformulation:

> The question 'can the subaltern speak?' then, is better posed as a series of questions: Which groups constitute the subalterns in any text? What is their relationship to each other? How can they be heard to be speaking or not speaking in a given set of materials? With what effects? Rephrasing the question in this way enables us to retain Spivak's insight regarding the positioning of women in colonial discourse *without conceding to colonial discourse what it, in fact, did not achieve – the erasure of women.*[36]

Let me attempt to answer these questions by returning to the question of the subaltern's experience and her pain as they figure in Sunder Rajan's essay, which searches the post-colonial discourse on sati for representations of the widow's pain. Analysing the law, the media, feminist analyses, and the Indian women's movement, she finds that the pain of the sati is represented only in 'forms of agitprop representations in theater, film and posters' which bring 'us closer to the "reality" of sati than does either the liberal discourse denouncing it or the popular and religious discourse glorifying it' (p. 16). It is significant, I think, that an essay which begins with an inquiry into subjectivity and the individual subject ends up with what in fact is one of the most succinct accounts of the political situation after the Deorala sati. Sunder Rajan discusses how the Indian media and others writing on the Deorala incident persistently attempted to re-construct the subjectivity of Roop Kanwar, and shows how the assumption that the 'answer to such a complex mystery is to be sought in knowing the sati herself, leads all too often to a closure of analysis, her death creating a condition of definitional unknowability'.[37] She herself is forced to conclude 'that an exclusive focus on choice and motivation in constructing the subjectivity of the sati in some representations leads either to mystification or to cognitive closure'. [. . .]

Even though I find her use of the subject-in-pain model somewhat problematic, I think Sunder Rajan's essay is crucial in implicitly moving towards a collective subjectivity of agents – in this case this would not be a collectivity of satis or even of widows but rather of huge, if not all, sections of Indian women who suffer from the consequences of the ideology of sati. I would like to suggest that 'the subaltern' 'in the text of sati', if we must locate one, cannot be understood simply as the immolated widow. The sati is produced by and functions to recirculate ideologies which target and seek to position a larger body of women, whose experiences, articulations and silences are crucial to understanding the relations of power and insubordination which are central to any analysis of 'the subaltern'.

It is entirely true that to focus on the pain of the burning widow is at once to draw attention to the shared indifference to women on the part of both defenders and abolitionists of sati, then and now, and to remind ourselves that sati is not just a symbol and a figuration, but a tortuous experience. However, recovering that experience, or locating agency within the temporal and experiential boundaries of the act of widow immolation is fraught with the dangers of succumbing to its grotesque power and its ideal authenticity at the expense of understanding how and why it is produced in the first place. Joan Scott's critique of 'experience' as a foundational historical category is useful in drawing attention to the dangers of Scarry's epistemology of pain even when it is used as cautiously as it is by Sunder Rajan. Scott points out that:

> experience works as a foundation providing both a starting point and a conclusive kind of explanation beyond which few questions need to or can be asked. And yet it is precisely the questions precluded – questions about discourse, difference and subjectivity as well as about what counts as experience and who gets to make that determination – that would enable us to historicize experience, to reflect critically on the history we write about it, rather than to premise our history upon it.[38]

If we are not to take either identity or experience for granted, we should look at how they are 'ascribed, resisted or embraced', she writes.

Such an exercise points to several directions in which work on sati still needs to be done. Colonial accounts voyeuristically focus on the spectacle of burning and obsessively describe the beautiful young widow as she strips herself of clothes and ornaments to ascend the fire.[39] An alternative view that exposes the pain and ugliness of the event must also guard against sealing it off from what precedes or follows it. The sati's experience is not limited to the pain of a death: a whole life is brought to the violence of that event, which, if unpacked, can be seen as constructed – not just crudely by her fears of a miserable life as a widow, not just by familial economic designs on her property, not even by male anxieties about her sexuality, but by social and ideological interactions, pressures and configurations that connect her immediate situation to the politics of her community, and indeed of the nation, and to the crucial articulations of gender within each of them. Some feminist work produced in India has been moving towards making these connections visible. Kumkum Sangari and Sudesh Vaid have meticulously documented specific cases of sati and delineated their 'contexts'.[40] Their writings certainly speculate on the ideologies that connect one burning to another, but they also focus on what was at stake in staging each immolation. [. . .]

The 1987 episode of sati was particularly frightening for feminists in India precisely because it was embedded within a context in which various types of murders are constructed as questions of female choice. When wives are burnt for dowry it is alleged that they committed suicide. The systematic abortion of female foetuses in contemporary India, it has been argued, is only a question of 'choice' on the part of the mothers-to-be. The debate over these amniocentesis-determined abortions also highlights the dubious status of women's experience and of a feminist politics that valorises it.[41] [. . .]

The debate on sati, then, signals the need to take into account two sorts of collective subjects in order to reposition the individual subject within them – the first is the collectivity of women at large, and the second a politically organized collectivity of women. The first would highlight that, despite its spectacular nature, the sati is not an isolated event; the second would indicate the ways in which female agency is wrought out of precariously achieved political intervention. Taken together, the two collectivities do not seek to bypass, devalue or erase the suffering, the pain or the determinations of the individual subject. They do, however, extend Spivak's notion of representation: the 'truth' about Roop Kanwar is not exclusively or best represented by the post-colonial feminist intellectual, but by an intersection of the two collectivities mentioned above. In the post-Deorala debates, statements by rural women showed that they often believed in sati as a possibility even as they questioned that Roop Kanwar was a 'true' sati. But at the same time, they questioned various aspects of women's oppression in India, and showed an awareness of women's movements even when these had not touched their own lives.[42]

Such an exercise, of listening to other women's voices to position the individual sati, and of detailing the individual circumstances and nuances of each immolation, is obviously easier to attempt in the present context. But I want to suggest here that if we look back, from the vantage point of a contemporary widespread backlash against the women's movement, at the bedfellows of the colonial controversy, and find that women are somehow erased there, we should not simply suppose that they were merely the grounds on which other concerns were articulated. We may modify Lata Mani's conclusions to suggest that women were, *then as now*, the targets as well as the grounds of the debates over tradition.

This, however, calls for us to *suppose a presence which at first cannot be found*, an exercise that Spivak critically endorses in the case of the subaltern school of Indian historians. If women are and have always been at stake, we must look for them, both within discourses which seek to erase their self-representation and elsewhere. The writings of women who worked alongside, within or in opposition to the nationalist movements are increasingly becoming available for feminist scholars and invaluable in understanding what was at stake in nineteenth-century widow immo-lations.[43] These writings help us understand that the debate over traditional and modernity did not merely use *woman* as a 'site', but specifically targeted those who challenged or critiqued the patriarchal underpinnings of nationalist discourses. The more feminist research uncovers these hitherto hidden and erased voices, the clearer it becomes that the precursors of today's feminists, as individuals and as a potential collectivity, constituted a threat and were thus at least partially the target of earlier rewritings of 'tradition'. [. . .]

I have been arguing that we can re-position the sati by looking not just at the widow who died but at those who survived to tell the tale. This tale, however, will only underline that subaltern agency, either at the individual level or at the collective, cannot be idealised as pure opposition to the order it opposes; it works both within that order and displays its own contradictions. Finally, identity is not just a matter of self-perception. In an article called 'The Plight of Hindu Widows as Described by a Widow Herself', which first appeared in *The Gospel of All Lands* in April 1889, the writer describes the misery of a wife following the death of her husband:

> None of her relatives will touch her to take her ornaments off her body. That task is assigned to three women from the barber caste . . . those female fiends literally jump all over her and violently tear all the orna-ments from her nose, ears etc. In that rush, the delicate bones of the nose and ear are sometimes broken. Sometimes . . . tufts of hair are also plucked off . . . At such times grief crashes down on the poor woman from all sides . . . there is nothing in our fate but suffering from birth to death. When our husbands are alive, we are their slaves; when they die, our fate is even worse . . . Thousands of widows die after a husband's death. But far more have to suffer worse fates throughout their lives if they stay alive. Once, a widow who was a relative of mine died in front of me. She had fallen ill before her husband died. When he died, she was so weak that she could not even be dragged to her husband's cremation. She had a burning fever. Then her mother-in-law dragged her down from the cot onto the ground and ordered the servant to pour bucketfuls of cold water over her. After some eight hours, she died. But nobody came to see how she was when she was dying of the cold. After she died, however, they started praising her, saying she had died for the love of her husband . . . If all [such] tales are put together they would make a large book. The British government

put a ban on the custom of sati, but as a result of that several women who could have died a cruel but quick death when their husbands died now have to face an agonizingly slow death.[44]

The widows in this narrative come close to those constructed by colonial records and accounts. The speaker herself offers a functionalist explanation of the sati's desire to die. And yet, she herself, a potential sati, did not die. In speaking, she reveals not just a tremulous or vacillating subjectivity but an awareness of the traumatic constructedness of one's own 'experience'. Identity is both self-constructed, and constructed for us.

To conclude, feminist theory is still working out the connections between social determinations and individual subjectivity. The work on sati demonstrates how the contexts of utterance and intervention still determine which of these two will be stressed, but it also marks a space where a fruitful dialogue has begun to emerge. Widow immolation is thus neither the burning of the exceptional woman nor the sign of the special devotion/victimisation of the average Indian or 'third world' woman; in becoming a vanishing point for a theory of female subjectivity, it signals both worthwhile directions in which revisionist histories of Indian women and theories of subaltern agency might move, and the problems they will encounter.

Notes

1   I would like to thank Rajeswari Sunder Rajan and Rukun Advani for their generous help with materials; Nivedita Menon, Priyamvada Gopal and Andrew Parker for their responses, and above all, Suvir Kaul for his extensive comments and his illuminating editorial pencil. I use the term 'sati', which has itself been the subject of much debate, for the act as well as the practice of widow immolation, as well as for the woman who dies. Colonial writings spelt it as 'suttee'; and recently, Sudesh Vaid and Kumkum Sangari 'use the words "widow immolation" to designate the primary violence and the word "sati" to indicate those structures of belief and ideology which gain consent for widow immolation', 'Institutions, Beliefs, Ideologies: Widow Immolation in Contemporary Rajasthan', *Economic and Political Weekly*, Vol. XXVI, no. 17, 27 April 1991, p. WS-3. 'Dead women tell no tales' in my title refers both to Pamela Philipose and Teesta Setalvad's casual use of the phrase ('Demystifying Sati', *The Illustrated Weekly of India*, 13 March 1988, p. 41) and to the obsession of the dead widow's desire in discourses on sati.

2   Lata Mani, 'Contentious Traditions: The Debate on Sati in Colonial India', in *Recasting Women* edited by Kumkum Sangari and Sudesh Vaid, New Delhi, 1989, p. 126 n. 97.

3   For an elaboration of this argument, see my 'Overworlding the "third world"', *Oxford Literary Review*, 3: 1–2, 1991, pp. 164–92.

4   Edward Thompson, *Suttee: A Historical and Philosophical Enquiry into the Hindu Rite of Widow-Burning*, 1928.

5   See for example, Arvind Sharma, *Sati, Historical and Phenomenological Essays*, Delhi, 1988; VN Datta, *Sati: a Historical, Social and Philosophical Enquiry into the Hindu Rite of Widow Burning*, New Delhi, 1988. I have been unable to review *Sati, the Blessing and the Curse; The Burning of Wives in India*, edited by John Stratton Hawley, New York, 1993.

6   *Subaltern Studies*, Vols 1–8, edited by Ranajit Guha, Delhi, 1982–92.

7   Romila Thapar, 'Traditions Versus Misconceptions', in *Manushi*, no. 42–3, 1987, p. 8. See also her essay, 'In History', in *Seminar*, no. 342 ('Sati: a symposium on widow immolation and its social contexts'), February 1988. pp. 14–19.

8   A translation of 'M. Caesar Fredericke [Federici], Marchant of Venice' in 1558 describes with puzzlement the Indian Women who 'so wilfully burne themselves against nature and law' (quoted by Thomas Hahn, 'Indians East and West: Primitivism and Savagery in English Discovery Narratives of the Sixteenth Century', *The Journal of Medieval and Renaissance Studies*, 8: 1 1978, p. 103.) The (16th-century) Jesuit Missionary, de Nobili, was impressed 'by the ecstatic devotion with which many of these young widows went to their deaths'.

9   Quoted in Lata Mani, 'Cultural Theory, Colonial Texts: Reading Eyewitness Accounts of Widow Burning', in *Cultural Studies* edited by Lawrence Grossberg, Cary Nelson and Paula Treichler, New York and London, 1992, p. 400.

10 Gayatri Chakravorty Spivak, 'Can the Subaltern Speak?' in *Marxism and the Interpretation of Culture*, edited by Cary Nelson and Lawrence Grossberg, Urbana and Chicago, 1988, p.297.

11 Katherine Mayo, *Mother India*, New York, 1927 p. 22; the review is quoted by Rama Joshi and Joanna Liddle, *Daughters of Independence: Gender, Caste and Class in India*, 1986, p. 31.

12 George Macmun, *The Religious and Hidden Cults of India*, 1931, p. 174.

13 Ashis Nandy, 'Sati: A Nineteenth Century Tale of Women, Violence and Protest', in *At the Edge of Psychology: Essays in Politics and Culture*, Delhi, 1980, pp. 1–31.

14 Thompson, *Suttee*, p. 65. The presence of British officers at the immolations are supposed to have 'thrown the ideas of the Hindoos upon the subject into a complete state of confusion', according to one Mr. C. Smith, a second judge of the Sudder Court, '. . . they conceive our power and our will to be commensurable' (pp. 64–5). The ironies attendant upon policing sati do not stop there: in 1987, the Indian government passed The Commission of Sati (Prevention) Act which sought to intensify the existing ban on sati by outlawing its spectacle: hence witnessing a sati became a potential abetment of the crime. Ironically, where the British half-measure necessitated that each sati event be policed, watched, observed and documented, the latest act has led to a paradoxical situation where surveillance is criminal; now, as Rajeswari Sunder Rajan has acutely observed, to report sati is to render oneself vulnerable to law so that today, when a woman dies, a 'collective amnesia' suggests that 'her death never occurred', 'The Subject of Sati: Pain and Death in the Contemporary Discourse on Sati', *Yale Journal of Criticism*, 3: 2, 1990, p. 13.

15 Nandy, 'Sati', p. 7.

16 See for example, Partha Chatterjee, 'The Nationalist Resolution of the Women's Question' in *Recasting Women*, pp. 233–53.

17 It is significant that now the tradition or culture being defended by the pro-sati lobby was that of the Rajputs, whereas once the pan-Indian-ness of sati was stressed. Of course, in this instance, the 'Rajput' became encoded as the essence of Indian-ness.

18 Mani, 'Contentious Traditions', p. 110.

19 'Tyranny of the Elect? Bringing Bharat Mata Up to Date', *Statesman*, Delhi Edition, Nov. 5, 1987.

20 For an analysis of some of these positions see Kumkum Sangari, 'Perpetuating the Myth', *Seminar* no 342, Feb. 1988, pp. 24–30.

21 Pamela Philipose and Teesta Setalvad, 'Demystifying Sati', p. 41.

22 In contemporary pro-sati discourses, the sati is repeatedly spoken of in terms of her love for her husband, a love whose everyday expression is subjection and service to him and which is marked by a consistent erasure of the self. All other forms of female desire are, within such discourses, repellant and abnormal.

23 Vasudha Dhagamwar, 'Saint, Criminal or Victim', *Seminar*, no 342, Feb. 1988, p. 38.

24   Rosalind O'Hanlon's essay, 'Recovering the Subject: *Subaltern Studies* and Histories of Resistance in Colonial South Asia', *Modern Asian Studies*, 22:1, 1988, pp. 189–224, perceptively reviews these materials.

25   Anand Yang, 'Whose Sati? Widow Burning in 19th century India', *Journal of Women's History*, pp. 8–33 and 'The Many Faces of Sati in The Early Nineteenth Century', *Manushi*, no. 42–3, 1987, pp. 26–9.

26   Gayatri Chakravorty Spivak, 'Can the Subaltern Speak? Speculations on Widow-Sacrifice', *Wedge*, Winter/Spring 1985, pp. 120–30, p. 120, and p. 129. The other two essays are, 'Can the Subaltern Speak?' in *Marxism and the Interpretation of Culture*, pp. 271–313 and 'The Rani of Sirmur', *History and Theory*, 24: 3, 1987, pp. 247–72.

27   Antoinette M. Burton, 'The White Woman's Burden, British Feminists and "The Indian Woman", 1865–1915', in *Western Women and Imperialism* edited by Nupur Chaudhuri and Margaret Strobel, Bloomington, 1992, pp. 137–57, suggests that feminists in Britain constructed 'the Indian woman' as a foil against which to gauge their own progress; for them empire was an integral and enabling part of 'the woman question' (p. 139). See also Barbara N. Ramusack, 'Cultural Missionaries, Maternal Imperialists, Feminist Allies, British Women Activists in India, 1865–1945' in the same volume, pp. 119–36.

28   Burton, 'The White Woman's Burden', p. 144.

29   Ibid., p. 148.

30   Spivak, 'Can the Subaltern Speak?', *Marxism and the Interpretation of Culture*, p. 296.

31   Ibid., 308. See also her 'Subaltern Studies: Deconstructing Historiography' in *Subaltern Studies IV: Writings on South Asian History and Society* edited by Ranajit Guha, Delhi, 1985.

32   Sunder Rajan, 'The Subject of Sati: Pain and Death in the Contemporary Discourse on Sati', *Yale Journal of Criticism* 3:2, 1990, p. 5.

33   Elaine Scarry, *The Body in Pain: The Making and Unmaking of the World*, New York and Oxford, 1985.

34   Lata Mani, 'Cultural Theory, Colonial Texts: Reading Eyewitness Accounts of Widow Burning', in *Cultural Studies* edited by Lawrence Grossberg, Cary Nelson and Paula A. Treichler, New York and London, 1992, pp. 392–408.

35   Ibid., p. 408. See also Mani's discussion of the different resonances of her work in the US, in India and in Britain in 'Multiple Mediations: Feminist Scholarship in the Age of Multinational Reception', *Feminist Review*, no. 36, 1989, pp. 24–41.

36   Mani, 'Cultural Theory, Colonial Texts', p. 403.

37   Sunder Rajan, 'The Subject of Sati', p. 14.

38   Joan Scott, 'Experience', in *Feminists Theorize the Political* edited by Judith Butler and Joan W. Scott, New York and London, 1992, p. 33.

39   Satis were of course not always or even mostly the nubile young things they are portrayed as in such accounts, as Anand Yang and Lata Mani both indicate.

40   See Sudesh Vaid and Kumkum Sangari, 'Sati in Modern India: A Report', *Economic and Political Weekly*, 16: 31, August 1, 1981, pp. 1284–8, and 'Institutions, Beliefs, Ideologies, Widow Immolation in Contemporary Rajasthan', *Economic and Political Weekly*, 26: 17, 27 April 1991, pp. WS-2–WS-18.

41   See Nivedita Menon, 'Abortion and the Law: Problems for Feminism', *Canadian Journal of Women and the Law*, 6:1, 1993, pp. 103–18.

42   See Kavita, Shobha, Shobita, Kanchan and Sharad, 'Rural Women Speak', *Seminar* no. 342, February 1988, pp. 40–4.

43   *Women Writing in India*, edited by Susie Tharu and K. Lalita, Volume 1, New Delhi, 1991 and Volume 2, New York, 1993 are valuable recent resources for feminists working in this area.

44   *Women Writing in India*, pp. 359–63.

Mrinalini Sinha

GENDER AND NATION

Mrinalini Sinha's wide-ranging chapter 'Gender and Nation' taken from Bonnie Smith's edited collection, *Women's History in Global Perspective* (2004), presents some of the key themes explored by feminist historians in a gendered analysis of the formation of national identities. Sinha's acclaimed expertise in gender studies and colonial Indian history has already produced some important works on colonial masculinity, as well as feminism and internationalism. Here she indicates the diverse ways in which feminist historians have begun to move beyond the coloniser/colonised paradigm to examine the multiple national contexts of gender difference. According to Sinha, Third World feminist scholarship has frequently taken the lead on this, prompted by the coterminous struggles of anticolonialism and women's emancipation. The symbiotic relationship between gender and nation has been analysed through several approaches. First, feminists have recovered women's contributions to nationalist struggles as participants in social reform and revolutionary campaigns in contexts as culturally diverse as Japan, Ireland and Kenya. Second, the constitution of the nation itself through constructions of gender has been explored. Third, Sinha investigates the ubiquitousness of gendered imagery and symbolism in discourses of nationalism through the language of family, marriage and sacrifice. Finally, as we have already seen in Ania Loomba's article in Reading 23, Sinha notes the use of women's bodies, dress-codes and sexual behaviour as symbolic sites of nationalist traditions. This extract from Sinha illustrates feminist history's move away from a focus on imperialism to a far more complex and contextualised reading of 'difference' as scholars seek to articulate the gendered construction of the nation and its impact on the experience of women and men.

[. . .]

IN THE WAKE OF MORE THAN A DECADE of feminist scholar-
ship on the subject it is no longer possible to ignore that nations have been, and
are, constituted around culturally specific constructions of gender difference. This
scholarship has gone a long way toward not only establishing the gendered character
of the nation but also suggesting the mutual constitution of discourses of the nation
and of modern gender identities themselves. It has been no coincidence, as some
scholars have suggested, that attachments to modern gender and national identities
have developed together and reinforced each other. What has followed is precisely
a questioning of the seeming 'naturalness' of, and an establishment of the connections between, the almost ubiquitous construction of people's identities in the
modern world along the lines of gender and national difference.

Not so long ago, it would have been difficult to foresee the emergence of even
this fragile scholarly consensus on the connections between discourses of gender
and the nation. That was partly because, until the 1980s, much of the scholarship
on both gender and nation had developed along separate and independent lines.
Most theories of nationalism were thus quite content with an apparently gender-
neutral analysis of the subject. On the one hand, this scholarship tended to minimize
the contribution of women, whether in nationalist movements or in the construction and maintenance of national identities and communities, and to assume that
the experience of modern nationhood was basically similar for men and women.
On the other hand, this apparently gender-neutral analysis of nationalism treated
men and masculinity as unmarked 'universal' categories and tended to ignore the
ways in which nationalism constitutes both 'men' and 'women.'[1] While some were
willing to acknowledge that gender, like race, class, and ethnicity, was a constituent
element of the nation, they, too, tended to underestimate the potential of gender
as a category of analysis.[2] [. . .]

If the scholarship on nationalism had demonstrated a certain indifference to
gender as a category of analysis, feminist scholarship was equally guilty of neglecting
the study of the nation and of nationalism. That was especially true of certain
strands within feminist scholarship shaped by an assumption of the apparent naturalness of the nation for women in North America and Northwestern Europe. This
scholarship tended to assume that women's relation to the nation was best summed
up in that famous quotation from a character in Virginia Woolf's novel *Three Guineas*:
'[A]s a woman I have no country. As a woman I want no country. As a woman my
country is the whole world.'[3]

The quotation invokes, of course, the history of Europe and North America,
where women had to wage a separate struggle for the right to vote and to be
included as citizens of the nation. On the basis of this particular history, moreover,
the quotation also assumes that feminism has an apparently natural antipathy for,
and an ability to transcend, the nation. A feminist scholarship that took this history
as axiomatic tended to dismiss the salience of the nation and of nationalism for
women and for feminism.

Here again, it was feminist scholarship of the 'third world' (the colonized and
semiperipheral areas of the world) that took the lead in engaging the study of nationalism as a feminist concern. Women's engagement in nationalist struggles against
imperialism often led to a very different trajectory for feminism in the third world.

[. . .] In many colonized and semiperipheral areas of the world, the struggle for women's emancipation occurred in tandem with anticolonial nationalist struggles. It should come as no surprise, therefore, that third-world feminist scholarship once again was at the forefront in engaging with the phenomenon of nationalism.[4] More recently, feminist scholarship more generally has recognized the equally important ways in which the nation has also shaped, and been shaped by, gender relations and gender identities in the older, more established nation-states of the world. Indeed, the history of anticolonial nationalisms has played a formative role in shaping the scholarly agenda on gender and nation more generally.

[. . .]

Contributions of feminist scholarship

[. . .]

One important contribution of feminist scholarship has been the considerable body of work on women and the nation that reverses the neglect of women by previous scholarship on nationalism. This scholarship has demonstrated women's contributions to, and the nature of women's integration in, the project of modern nationhood. Although women may have been marginalized from the domain of the public, they have clearly played a significant role in the production and maintenance of national communities and national identities all over the world. Women, for example, are conspicuous in nationalist discourses as symbols of national culture and, through the control of women's sexuality, as the markers of community boundaries. Hence concerns about interracial and intercommunal sexual relations have typically centered on the access to, and availability of, women.

The most visible contribution of women to nationalist projects, of course, has been the mobilization of women, along with men, as active participants in various nationalist projects. From the peasant women whose bread riots ignited the French Revolution (1789) and the Russian Revolution (1917) to the contribution of elite and bourgeois women in various nationalist movements, the range of women's activities has been varied. Women have contributed to social reform and public education movements, they have participated in various public rituals and protests that constitute the 'national public,' and they have mobilized on behalf of national liberation and revolutionary struggles.

A Japanese journalist who witnessed the 1911 uprisings that brought down the Qing dynasty in China was impressed by the impact of the nationalist project on middle-class women. Compared with 'modern Chinese women,' he wrote, 'the militant London suffragette is nothing. Daily she supplies arms and ammunitions to her brother revolutionaries and is occasionally arrested with her tunic lined with dynamite.'[5] At times, moreover, women's contributions to the nationalist struggle have been more radical than men's. During the Irish Land War in 1881 and 1882, for example, the uncompromising stand of Anna Parnell's Ladies Land League, with its membership extending from Catholic middle-class to peasant women, against evictions and in favor of Irish self-determination became an embarrassment to many of the male leaders who were ready to compromise with the British.[6] Similarly, women fought alongside men as guerillas in the Land and Freedom Army during the Mau Mau uprising in Kenya (1952–9). For Elizabeth Gachika, who was in the guerilla camps in the Nyandura forest from 1952 to 1953, the experience challenged traditional gender roles: 'We were doing just like men. We could shoot and so forth . . . I shot many [Europeans] . . . I went with the men on the raids.'[7] Equally significant, however, is the invocation of the supposedly 'traditional' roles of women – as mothers, as objects of reverence and of protection, and as signifiers or markers of a group's innermost identity – in projects of nationalism.

Feminist scholarship, indeed, has demonstrated a variety of ways in which women contribute to the project of the nation:

- as biological reproducers of the members of ethnic collectivities;
- as reproducers of the boundaries of ethnic/national groups;
- as participants in the ideological reproduction of the collectivity and as transmitters of its culture;
- as signifiers of ethnic/national difference – as a focus and symbol in ideological discourses used in the construction, reproduction, and transformation of ethnic/national categories; and
- as participants in national, economic, political, and military struggles.[8]

Yet women are themselves always differentiated by race, class, age, education, religion, ethnicity, and urban/rural residence, all of which affect the nature and extent to which they are included in the national embrace. Their contributions and commitments to the nation have been shaped not just by their difference from men but by differences among women themselves. Insofar as this scholarship has focused on women and their relation to the nation it has also raised important questions about the implications of nationalist projects for women. While some scholars emphasize the oppressive results of nationalism on women, others focus on the contribution of nationalism in creating a space for the empowerment of women. What this scholarship, despite its difference in emphasis, seems to suggest is that women's experience of the project of modern nationhood has been distinct from that of men's.

Because gender is not a synonym for women, however, a gendered analysis of the nation does not rest simply on making women visible in the project of nationalism. The challenge posed by feminist scholarship has to do not just with the visibility of 'women' but, more important, with the constitution of the nation itself in the 'sanctioned institutionalization of gender *difference*.'[9] The discourse of the nation is implicated in particular elaborations of masculinity as much as of femininity. As such, it contributes to their normative constructions. It becomes a privileged vehicle in the consolidation of dichotomized notions of 'men' and 'women' and of 'masculinity' and 'femininity.' We thus have 'fathers' and 'mothers,' and 'sons' and 'daughters,' of the nation, each with their own gendered rights and obligations. This is the sense in which the discourses of gender and the nation can be seen as symbiotic. On the one hand, national narratives rely heavily on the supposedly natural logic of gender differences to consolidate new political identities around the nation. On the other hand, the discourse of nationalism provides legitimacy to normative gendered constructions of masculinity and femininity.[10]

The concern of many a feminist scholar, therefore, has been as much with men and masculinity as with women and femininity.[11] Indeed, some scholars have argued that the nation – typically imagined as a gendered fraternity – is essentially a masculinist or a heterosexual male construct. Nationalisms, they argue, have 'typically sprung from masculinized memory, masculinized humiliation and masculinized hope.'[12] So, for example, nationalist movements often involve reasserting masculinity and reclaiming male honor, and moments of nationalist fervor frequently center around a remasculinization of national culture.[13] At the same time, as many studies have shown, women have enthusiastically supported the nation and nationalism. Although we may thus debate the extent to which nations are best understood as inherently masculinist constructs, nations in one form or another have relied on a discourse of gender difference. [. . .]

Nations, indeed, are not only gendered but also simultaneously 'raced' and constituted by other axes of difference. The discourse of race – the fiction of a 'racial identity' – is no less constitutive than the discourse of gender in the construction of nations.[14]

The further point, however, is that the various axes of difference – of gender, race, ethnicity, class, sexuality, and of colonizer and colonized – are not only mutually constitutive but also differently constituted. Hence they often intersect in the articulation of nations in uneven and unpredictable ways. The construction of Australian national identity, for example, mobilized various forms of difference – colonizer versus colonized, elitist versus populist, urban versus rural, settlers versus indigenous populations, and men versus women – whose interaction played out in unexpected ways. The creation of the Commonwealth of Australia in 1901 from a federation of six former British colonies was frequently represented as the coming of age of a white Australian masculinity. On the one hand, the colonial context led to an elaboration of Australia's difference from the 'mother-country' in a populist narrative of the nation around the 'mateship' of rough and virile men in a white frontier society. The cultural representation of the nation was centered around a white masculinity that privileged the white 'bushmen' at the expense of both non-Aboriginal and Aboriginal women as well as Aboriginal men. On the other hand, the heavily masculinist rhetoric of the nation was also tempered by the specific context of a colonial settler society. White Australian women were thus enfranchised only one year after the creation of the Commonwealth, well before their counterparts in Britain. The political rights and representation of white Australian women as 'citizen mothers' was closely tied to a state apparatus designed to maintain a 'white' Australia.[15]

To ignore the various modes of organizing 'difference' in the articulation of the nation, therefore, would reproduce the 'gender blindness of previous historians of nations and nationalism in another key.'[16] One of the most challenging and rewarding agendas for feminist scholarship, indeed, has been to account for the mutual constitution, and the often contradictory and uneven mediation, of multiple axes of difference in the articulation of both genders and nations.

[. . .]

The constitution of the nation in gender difference

One of the most striking features of nationalist discourses, as numerous scholars have observed, is the pervasiveness of familial and gendered imagery. All nations are imagined as 'domestic genealogies.'[17] The very term *nation* comes from the Latin *natio* (to be born). People are 'born' into a nation, and foreigners 'adopt' a nation or are 'naturalized' into national citizenship.[18] Individuals are assigned their place within the national family, and nations themselves belong within the global family of nations. The nation is often constituted as *Heimat* (homeland). The relations of people to specific lands, languages, cultures, or shared histories are expressed as motherlands or fatherlands, mother tongues, mother cultures, and 'founding fathers' or 'mothers of the nation.' Feminist scholars, therefore, justifiably raise questions about the reasons for, and implications of, the ubiquitousness of gendered and familial imagery in nationalist discourses.

[. . .]

The imposition of a Western bourgeois ideology of gender and family [. . .] informed such colonial initiatives as the British slave emancipation in the Western Cape of South Africa. The project of emancipation was shaped by the view of ostensibly 'liberating the family' so free African men could take up their 'proper' roles as fathers and heads of households, and free African women could, as wives and mothers, be brought under the natural authority of the male head of the family.[19] The pervasiveness of that ideal – to which many freed African men and women contributed – helped maintain the power of former slaveowners, missionaries, and the colonial state over African men and women even after emancipation. The ideology of gender, family, and sexuality similarly framed the colonial policies and practices of the other European nations, such as the French, the Dutch, and the Germans in their respective empires.[20] The marriage between European nationalisms and bourgeois respectability, therefore, was cemented not just in Europe but also in the imperial-nationalist process of 'domesticating the empire.'

[. . .]

The language of kinship plays a very important role in allowing the nation to appropriate for itself the kind of elemental passions hitherto associated with the ties of blood. Thus the nation in the form of an abused or humiliated mother appeals to her sons and daughters, albeit often in differently gendered ways, to come to her protection and restore her honor. Similarly, the nation as fatherland calls upon its sons and daughters to obey the father and fulfill their respective gendered duties to the nation. The representation of the nation through a language of love – an 'eroticized nationalism' – helps account for the distinctiveness of nationalism as a discourse capable of arousing enormous passions from the members of nations.[21]

In this context, therefore, heterosexual desire is often mapped onto political desire as *amor patrie* (love of country). In Latin America during the nineteenth century, for example, romance novels inspired 'passionate patriotism' toward the new nations.[22] The new national ideals in Latin America were reflected in tales of heterosexual desire and marriage. These 'foundational fictions,' through stories of love that conquers all, offered a figurative conciliation for the many political and social tensions that beset the new nation states. Most often, perhaps, the nation is represented as a female body – 'to love, to possess, and to protect' – in the discourse of nationalism. That was the form in which the nation was represented, for example, in nineteenth-century Iran.[23] Iranian nationalist discourse offered a new hetero-sexual love – transforming the tradition of the divine and homoerotic love of classical Perso-Islamic literature – in which the *vatan* (homeland/Iranian nation) was con-structed as the female paramour of nationalist men. The image of the vatan as female lover coexisted with another, equally powerful, female incarnation of the vatan as mother. It is as female lover/mother that the vatan/Iran insinuated itself into the emotions of the people, with different implications, of course, for men and women's relation to this feminized nation. The eroticization of nationalism through the iden-tification of the nation with a female body – and the prominence of metaphors of the feminine in the discourse of the nation – allowed women to create a place for themselves within the national family, and it also fixed them in certain relations within the national collectivity. The nation's hold on the emotions of people, indeed, would be hard to understand outside of its investment in gendered kinship relations and in the poetics of heterosexual love.

[. . .]

Women – more often than not – have had to carry the more complex burden of representing the colonized nation's 'betweenness' with respect to precolonial traditions and 'Western' modernity.[24] The nationalist project both initiated women's access to modernity and set the limits of the desirable modernity for women. In this context, several early-twentieth-century feminists, such as Halide Edibe in Turkey or Hudá Sha'rawi in Egypt, constructed their dynamic public roles as a duty to the nation rather than as a right.[25] As signifiers of the nation, women needed to be modern, but they could not mark a complete break from tradition. The woman of the anticolonial nationalist imagination, then, was not necessarily a 'traditional' woman. She was more likely the 'modern-yet-modest' woman who both symbolized the nation and negotiated its tension between tradition and modernity.[26]

Even cultural-revivalist and fundamentalist movements in the third world are seldom traditionalist in any simple way. The call to tradition in these movements is more precisely a response to the modernization of gender relations and to the transformation of gender roles that have already been underway. As one scholar so aptly puts it, 'if fundamentalists are calling for the return to the veil, it must be because women have been taking off the veil.'[27] The fundamentalist attack against the modernization of gender roles, moreover, is often fueled by class tensions produced by the failure of socioeconomic development and the effects of neo-colonialism. The critique of *gharbzahdegi* ('Westoxification') under Ayatollah Khomeini in the Islamic Republic of Iran, for example, reflected both gender and class conflict. The objects of that critique were mainly upper-middle-class and educated women, who, compared with poor and peasant women, had benefited under the previous Pahlavi regime.[28] The important point is that as the 'true essence' of national and cultural identity – whether as signifiers of tradition or of modernity – women become vulnerable to different political agendas of the nation.

Gendered modes of national belonging

If the ideology of gender difference has been important in the constitution of the nation, then the nation has been equally important for the construction of gender and the performance of masculinity and femininity. Hence, as various scholars have demonstrated, the nation always relates to its members differently as 'men' and 'women.' The project of modern nationhood has largely cast men as 'metonymic' (as causes of national history) and women as 'metaphorical' or symbolic (analogues of the national soul).[29] In other words, men are defined as consequential to the nation and as its agents, but women are defined as its iconic embodiments. [. . .]

The trope of sacrifice – one of the most powerful in the narrative of the nation – is similarly gendered. Men are usually called to give their life or die for the nation, and women willingly to surrender their sons and husbands to die for the nation. To be sure, women have historically been agents in the project of the nation and, in some cases, have also died along with men on the battlefields for the sake of the nation. Vietnam, with a tradition of women leading armed resistance against foreign oppression going back to the famous Trung sisters (Trung Trac and Trung Nhi) in 39 C.E., produced a long list of women martyrs during all stages of its nationalist struggles against the Japanese, the French, and the United States.[30] Furthermore, not all men (and not all women) are constructed in similar ways in the project of the nation.

Yet the belief in the 'natural' difference between men and women has been fairly constant in the constitution of nations, and the nation itself has helped construct the normative constructions of 'men' and 'women' and of 'masculinity' and 'femininity.'

The focus on the nation as a site for the construction of gender difference has, first, called attention to the hitherto neglected question of the construction of 'men' and 'masculinity' in nationalist discourse. The nation is implicated in the construction of 'men' in various ways. The nation itself is largely modeled as a brotherhood or a fraternity. This, of course, has never included all men. The homosociality of the national brotherhood has depended in large part on the exclusion of homosexuals and men otherwise constructed as deviants.

[. . .]

The production of nationalist masculinity in national discourse is also enacted via the control/protection of women. The politics of 'colonial masculinity' (which informed both colonizers and colonized) in the British Empire illustrates the multiple dimensions in the performance of masculinity.[31] On the one hand, elite 'white' British masculinity was constructed both through its difference from feminized or effeminate native men and through its role as the benevolent protector of women. The protection of 'Oriental' women – the idea of 'white men saving brown women from brown men' – was an important component in the self-definition of white British masculinity in the colonial context.[32] The real or imagined threat to white women from the alleged assaults of native men provided, perhaps, the most dramatic demonstrations of white imperial masculinity in the colonial domain. Even rumors of attacks on white women – as, for example, during the Rebellion of 1857–8 in India – produced a call to arms to white men to avenge the 'honor' of the English race.[33] On the other hand, however, 'native' men also sought to reclaim their honor and masculinity – from negative representations in colonial discourse – by claiming the right to control/protect 'our' women from foreigners and foreign influence. The rhetoric of the protection of women as well as the protection of the nation – itself often represented as a woman – was thus an important component in the production of masculinity.

The nationalist constructions of 'women' and 'femininity,' and women's complicity in those constructions, have also been the subject of much scholarly attention. Despite the historical marginalization of women from the sphere of formal national politics, women are not absent from the domain of the national public. [. . .] Women have emerged as national actors – as mothers, educators, workers, and fighters – in various nationalist projects. The myriad ways in which they contribute to the nationalist project have been discussed. A further point, however, is that the construction of femininity within nationalist discourse has had important implications for women.

The pervasiveness of powerful female figures – especially the figure of the mother – in the discourse of nationalism provides an important context for understanding the cooperation and complicity of women with such constructions. The image of 'motherhood,' both in the cultural representation of the nation as 'mother' and in women's roles as 'mothers of the nation,' has been among the most powerful and exalted images of the feminine. [. . .]

The complementary construction of machismo and *marianismo* in Latin America similarly emphasized the maternal qualities of women, mainly elite, white, and creole women in the national narratives of the various nations.[34] Yet this glorification of motherhood in nationalist discourse has also justified the exclusion of women from the civic virtues that made formal political participation in national politics possible. Nationalist projects, indeed, demonstrate tension between the exaltation of powerful female figures – especially the mother – and the marginalization of women from national politics. [. . .]

The meaning of motherhood is also constructed differently in different nationalist projects. In South Africa, for example, 'motherhood' was deployed very differently, despite its superficial similarities, by the racially exclusive Afrikaner nationalist project and the multiracial nationalism of the African National Congress.[35] Whereas in the former the construction of motherhood remained limited to the domestic domain and did not engage the broader issues of women's situation, women in the African National Congress were able to deploy the focus on motherhood to raise general concerns about women's emancipation. Women in both nationalist projects were active in the articulation of motherhood and also deployed it to sanction their own participation in nationalist movements. The Argentine Madres de la Plaza de Mayo is, perhaps, the most famous example of women's mobilization of motherhood. This movement had counterparts not only in several Latin American countries reeling under the effects of military dictatorships in the 1970s but also in the Mothers Fronts in Sri Lanka in the 1980s.[36] Women powerfully invoked the image of 'motherhood' to denounce political torture and the 'disappearance' of political activists. In this sense, then, the construction of powerful female figures in nationalist projects may also empower the mobilization of women. [. . .]

Finally, nationalist projects construct 'women' primarily through a heterosexual relationship to men that emphasizes a supposedly 'natural' hierarchy between
men and women. The identification of women mainly with the private and familial
sphere has been the basis for the exclusion of women as citizens or from full
membership of the community. The most obvious, of course, is the denial of
political rights to women as citizens. In most states in Europe and the Americas,
women's suffrage followed well after most men's. It was not until the twentieth
century that most of these states granted national female suffrage. Many Asian and
African states, however, extended universal suffrage to men and women at the same
time during the period of national independence in the twentieth century.

Yet the political disabilities in women's status as citizens go beyond the denial
of the right to vote. The history of discrimination against women in relation to
education, professional employment, economic independence, and rights within
marriage, divorce, inheritance, and the custody of children – all the things that have
qualified men for public roles – have constructed women's disqualification from a
variety of public roles and made them dependent on fathers and husbands. The
legacy continues to haunt women's relations to the nation and the state, well after
the granting of formal legal equality.

[. . .]

The relation between feminisms and nationalisms

The contemporary scholarship on gender and nationalism has raised questions about
the compatibility of feminisms and nationalisms. Although some scholars have
suggested that these are necessarily incompatible, the history of feminisms and
nationalisms in different locations belies such easy generalizations.[37] What emerges
instead is the recognition that the relationship between feminisms and nationalisms
is not given but rather shaped in specific historical conjunctures.

In Europe, feminist movements for suffrage and other rights for women generally emerged after, and in response to, the projects of modern nationhood. As such,
therefore, they called attention to the inequality of women in the constitution of
the nation as a community. In revolutionary France, for example, modern French
feminism developed against a background of the construction of a sexually differentiated national public and private and the resulting gendered exclusions in the
idea of republican citizenship. In her *Declaration of the Rights of Women* in 1791,
Olympe de Gouges made a case for the rights of women and challenged the exclusion of women from national politics. In doing so she stressed the fundamental
complementarity between men and women based on their sexual 'difference.' At
the same time, however, Gouges also sought to transcend the construction of sexual
difference by claiming equality for men and women. Herein lay the 'paradox' of
feminism: Even as it challenged the construction of sexual difference on the basis
of which women were excluded from political rights, it could not help calling attention to these differences and in the process securing sexual difference.[38] [. . .]

Because the nationalist programs of most Western European countries had an
overall negative impact on women, some scholars have assumed that feminism and
nationalism in the European context are 'almost always incompatible ideological

positions,' with only two examples from Western European history – that of nineteenth-century Italy and twentieth-century Finland – of a temporary confluence between feminism and nationalism.[39]

Although the self-representation of European feminism may be aligned with radical ideologies that were often explicitly international – and even antinational – in orientation, that does not mean that early European feminists were not staunchly nationalist or that their feminist project was not invested in the racial and imperial politics of their nations. European feminists, as much as their counterparts in the United States and elsewhere, articulated their feminisms as explicitly racialized and imperialist projects precisely for the sake of acceptance and inclusion in the imperial nation. [. . .]

Other scholars have similarly demonstrated that the internationalism of European and U.S. feminists did not necessarily entail the transcendence of nationalist politics. In the United States, where an organized antiblack women suffrage strategy had already emerged by the 1890s, white suffragists readily identified with the racial and imperial priorities of the nation. At the Inter-American Women's Congress in Panama in 1926, for example, feminists representing the United States abstained from voting on a resolution for woman suffrage in all American nations on the grounds that Latin American women were not ready to exercise political rights.[40]

The point is, notwithstanding the inhospitable climate for feminism within many nationalist projects in Europe, that the feminism of middle-class white European feminists, like that of their counterparts in the United States, was informed by the racial and imperial politics of their respective projects of nationhood.

In many colonized and semiperipheral regions, as also in some Eastern European countries, the development of feminism and nationalism was often self-consciously connected.[41] That was partly because here the nationalist projects stimulated the transformation of women's position through a broader concern with national rejuvenation and social reforms. These projects often sought to counter colonial portrayals of the plight of women by turning to a golden age in the ancient past where women supposedly enjoyed equality with men. The project of nineteenth-century Czech nationalism entailed a similar construction of a golden age of gender equity in the past. The mythical figures of Libuse, founder of Prague, and Vlasta, a woman warrior and leader of a woman's revolt, became appropriated as real historical persons from the nation's past. This past was then contrasted favorably to the masculinist culture of German oppressors.[42] The 'woman question,' therefore, has been an important component of the national agenda for national reconstruction in some projects. These projects afforded enhanced opportunities to bourgeois women.

The development of feminism alongside nationalism, however, does not necessarily provide safeguards. In many third-world nationalist projects the articulation of women's interests has often been subordinated to the interests of the nation. Feminist demands, for example, are expected to be framed only within the parameters of anticolonial nationalism. In some nationalist movements, moreover, feminists are advised to shelve demands until the nationalist emergency is over; they are told 'not now, later.'[43] In other cases, feminists have been portrayed as 'traitors to the nation' and feminism identified as a bourgeois and Westernized project that is irrelevant to the more urgent concerns of the nation. Ironically, the nationalist project in post-Soviet Russia has similarly delegitimized feminism for its association with the 'old order' and with state emancipation. The end of women's emancipation is thus hailed as a positive result of the collapse of the USSR.[44] In still others, the hospitable climate for feminism created during nationalist liberation struggles has been overturned with the attainment of independence. The most famous example is of the Algerian war of liberation against the French, in which approximately eleven thousand Algerian women participated as *moudjahidates* (freedom fighters), with some two thousand involved in the armed wing of the struggle. Whatever openings emerged for a new gender politics in the course of the struggle were quickly foreclosed in its aftermath. Women were pushed back from the political sphere and officially subordinated to men with the adoption of the Family Code based on the *Shariah* (Islamic canonical law).[45] There was a similar trajectory in the relation between feminism and nationalism in Ireland. The commitment to progressive gender politics, and the contributions of Irish women in the nationalist struggle, were conveniently forgotten in the repressive gender regime instituted by the Irish constitution of 1937.[46] [. . .]

Although the relation between feminism and nationalism has almost always been complex, there is no necessary outcome of this relationship. The more important point is that nowhere has feminism ever been autonomous of the national context from which it has emerged. This has been clearly evident in the history of the international feminist movement. The major liberal-feminist international organizations of the first half of the twentieth century were dominated by women from the United States and Northwestern Europe, many of whom not only assumed feminism's ostensible transcendence of national politics but were also invested in an ideology that insisted on the apparent separation of feminist from nationalist concerns.[47] Feminists from other parts of the world contested and exposed that view. Indian feminists such as Kamaladevi Chattopadhyay, Shareefah Hamid Ali, Dhanvanthi Rama Rau, and others, for example, never missed an opportunity to raise the question of the struggle against imperialism at international feminist conferences like the International Alliance of Women and the Women's International League for Peace and Freedom conferences, throughout the interwar period.[48]

Feminists from different parts of the world not only challenged the 'maternalism' that often underwrote the ideology of the international feminist movement but also insisted on making national self-determination into a feminist issue. The real possibility of transnational feminist alliances lies in recognition, rather than transcendence, of the unequal power relations and disparate histories that divide women. That is the kind of hard political work that some women's projects are undertaking in order to build alliances between women of polarized ethnonational groups by challenging the mobilization of their ethnonational identities for war: the Women's Support Network in Belfast in Northern Ireland of Protestant and Catholic women; the Medica Women's Therapy Centre in Zenica in central Bosnia of Bosnian Serb, Croatian, and Muslim women, and Bat Shalom in Israel of Jewish and Palestinian women.[49]

Conclusion

It should be clear by now that the gendered articulation of the nation can be examined only in specific historical contexts and always in relation to a variety of forms of organizing difference. Catherine Hall's study of a critical moment in the formation of British national identity — the passage of the English Parliamentary Reform Act of 1832 — is in many ways exemplary in this respect.[50] [. . .] The settlement of 1832 was shaped precisely by the historical conjuncture of the moment and entailed new definitions of citizens and subjects and of different modes of belonging in, and identifying with, the nation and the Empire. This brings together a web of relations that include Britain and Jamaica; England and Ireland; Catholics and Protestants; and aristocratic, middle-class, and working-class men and women as well as former slave men and women in the making of the settlement of 1832.

The strength of this approach comes from attention to the significance of the historical conjuncture of the 1820s and 1830s and deployment of the 'rule of difference' to explore the multiple articulation of the nation. We thus see a variety of intersecting but uneven modes of identification with and belonging in the imperial nation: Protestant women claiming their right to participate in the public sphere by signing petitions to the Parliament against Catholic emancipation; Catholic Irish women succeeding in their campaign on behalf of their men in the passage of the Catholic Emancipation Act; Catholic men gaining the right to enter some public offices at the same time as many Irish Catholic men had lost the franchise; former slave men and women being partially freed as they were made apprentices for a fixed term until they could 'learn' to be free; freed black women being made the property of their husbands; working-class men and women active in reform demonstrations and female political unions; and new groups of men claiming their political fitness by the assertion of their manly independence against the effeminacy of the aristocracy. [. . .]

This multilayered analysis of the 1832 Reform Act underscores the potential for recasting the study of gender and of the nation. The future of the scholarship on gender and the nation, indeed, may lie precisely in such densely historicized analysis of the articulation of the nation in specific historical moments. Only then will we begin to make visible the multiple, and often uneven, ways in which particular forms of difference inform, and are produced by, the nation in any given historical moment.

Notes

1   For a critique of this literature, see Nira Yuval-Davis, *Gender and Nation* (Thousand Oaks: Sage, 1997).

2   Anthony D. Smith, *National Identity* (London: Penguin, 1991). Smith recognizes gender as significant for social identity but dismisses its role in collective mobilization.

3   Virginia Woolf, *Three Guineas* (1938, repr. London: Hogarth Press, 1947), 197.

4   Kumari Jayawardena, *Feminism and Nationalism in the Third World* (London: Zed Books, 1986).

5   Quoted in Jayawardena, *Feminism and Nationalism in the Third World*, 182; also see Tani Barlow, *Gender Politics in Modern China* (Durham: Duke University Press, 1993); and Christina K. Gilmartin *et al.*, eds., *Engendering China: Women, Culture, and State* (Cambridge: Harvard University Press, 1994).

6   Margaret Ward, 'The Ladies Land League and the Irish Land War 1881/1882: Defining the Relation between Women and Nationalism,' in *Gendered Nations: Nationalisms and Gender Order in the Long Nineteenth Century,* ed. Ida Blom, Karen Hagemann, and Catherine Hall (New York: Berg, 2000), 229–48.

7   Cora Ann Presley, *Kikuyu Women, the Mau Mau Rebellion and Social Change in Kenya* (Boulder: Westview Press, 1992), 136.

8   The list is from the Introduction in *Woman-Nation-State,* ed. Nira Yuval Davis and Floya Anthias (New York: St. Martin's Press, 1989), 7.

9   Anne McClintock, '"No Longer in a Future Heaven": Gender, Race, and Nationalism,' in *Dangerous Liaisons: Gender, Nation and Postcolonial Perspectives,* ed. Anne McClintock, Aaamir Mufti, and Ella Shohat, (Minneapolis: University of Minnesota Press, 1997), 89.

10   Tamar Mayer, 'Gender Ironies of Nationalism: Setting the Stage' in *Gender Ironies of Nationalisms* ed. Tamar Mayer (New York: Routledge, 2000), 1–24.

11   Joanne Nagel, 'Masculinity and Nationalism: Gender and Sexuality in the Making of Nations,' *Ethnic and Racial Studies* 21 (March 1998): 242–69.

12   Cynthia Enloe, *Bananas, Beaches and Bases: Making Feminist Sense of International Politics* (Berkeley: University of California Press, 1989), 44.

13   For some examples, see Joseph Massad, 'Conceiving the Masculine: Gender and Palestinian Nationalism,' *Middle East Journal* 49 (Summer 1995): 467–83; Frances Gouda, 'Gender and Hyper-Masculinity as Postcolonial Modernity during Indonesia's Struggle for Independence, 1945–1949,' in *Gender, Sexuality and Colonial Modernities,* ed. Antoinette Burton (New York: Roudedge, 1999), 161–74; and Susan Jeffords, *The Remasculinization of America: Gender and the Vietnam War* (Bloomington: Indiana University Press, 1989).

14   Etienne Balibar, 'The Nation-Form,' in Etienne Balibar and Immanuel Wallerstein, *Race, Nation, Class: Ambiguous Identities*, trans. Chris Turner (London: Verso Press, 1991), 86–106. Some scholars, most notably [Benedict] Anderson, *Imagined Communities: Reflections on the Origin and Spread of Nationalism* (1983 rev. ed., London: New Left Books, 1991) separate the history of racism from the principle, as opposed to the actual practices, of the nation.

15   The discussion is from Marilyn Lake, 'Frontier Feminism and the Marauding White Man: Australia, 1890s to 1940s,' in *Nation, Empire, Colony: Historicizing Gender and Race*, ed. Ruth Roach Pierson and Nupur Chaudhury (Bloomington: Indiana University Press, 1998), 94–105; and Marilyn Lake, 'Mission Impossible: How Men Gave Birth to the Australian Nation: Nationalism, Gender and other Seminal Acts,' *Gender and History* 4, no. 3 (1992): 305–22.

16   Quoted in Ruth Roach Pierson, 'Nations: Gendered, Racialized, Crossed with Empire,' in *Gendered Nations*, p. 42.

17   Anne McClintock, *Imperial Leather: Race, Gender and Sexuality in the Colonial Contest* (New York: Routledge, 1995), 357.

18   McClintock, '"No Longer in a Future Heaven,"' 90–1.

19   This discussion is from Pamela Scully, *Liberating the Family? Gender and British Slave Emancipation in the Rural Western Cape, South Africa, 1823–1853* (Portsmouth: Heinemann, 1997).

20   Julia Clancy-Smith and Frances Gouda, eds., *Domesticating the Empire: Languages of Gender, Race, and Family Life in French and Dutch Colonialism* (Charlottesville: University of Virginia Press, 1998); Lora Wildenthal, 'Race, Gender, and Citizenship in the German Colonial Empire,' in *Tensions of Empire*, ed. Frederick Cooper and Ann Laura Stoler (Berkeley: University of California Press, 1997), 263–86.

21   Andrew Parker *et al.* eds, *Nationalisms and Sexualities* (New York: St Martin's Press, 1989): 1.

22   Doris Sommer, *Foundational Fictions: The National Romances of Latin America* (Berkeley: University of California Press, 1991).

23   The following discussion is from Afshaneh Najmabadi, 'The Erotic Vatan [Homeland] as Beloved and Mother: To Love, to Possess, and to Protect,' *Comparative Studies in Society and History* 39 (July 1997): 442–67.

24   Winifred Woodhull cited in Madhu Dubey, 'The "True Lie" of the Nation: Fanon and Feminism,' *Differences* 10 (Summer 1998): 1–29.

25   This point is made in D. Kandiyoti, 'Identity and Its Discontents: Women and the Nation', *Millennium: Journal of International Studies* 20 no. 3 (1991): note 17; see also Hudá Sha'rawi, *Harem Years: The Memoirs of an Egyptian Feminist (1879–1924)*, ed. and trans. by Margot Badran (1986, repr. New York: Feminist Press, 1987); and Margot Badran, *Feminists, Islam and Nation: Gender and the Making of Modern Egypt* (Princeton: Princeton University Press, 1995).

26   Afshaneh Najmabadi cited in Kandiyoti, 'Identity and Its Discontents,' 432.

27   Fatima Mernissi, *Beyond the Veil*, quoted in Valentine E. Moghadam, 'Introduction: Women and Identity Politics in Theoretical and Comparative Perspective,' in *Identity Politics and Women: Cultural Assertions and Feminisms in International Perspectives*, ed. Valentine E. Moghadam (Boulder: Westview Press, 1994), 15.

28   Nayareh Tohidi, 'Modernity, Islamization and Women in Iran,' in *Gender and National Identity: Women and Politics in Muslim Societies*, ed. Valentine M. Moghadam (London: Zed Books, 1994), 110–47; see also Valentine E. Moghadam, 'Introduction and Overview,' in *Identity Politics and Women: Cultural Assertions and Feminisms in International Perspectives*, ed. Valentine E. Moghadam (Boulder: Westview Press, 1994), 1–17.

29   Elleke Boehmer, cited in McClintock, '"No Longer in a Future Heaven,"' 91.

30   For examples, see Karen Gottshchang Turner with Phan Thank Hao, *Even the Women Must Fight: Memories of War from North Vietnam* (New York: John Wiley, 1998); Thi Tuyet Mai Nguyen, *The Rubber Tree: Memoir of a Vietnamese Woman Who Was an Anti-French Guerilla, a Publisher and a Peace Activist*, ed. Monique Senderowicz (Jefferson: McFarland, 1994).

31   Mrinalini Sinha, *Colonial Masculinity: The 'Manly Englishman' and the 'Effeminate Bengali' in the Late Nineteenth Century* (New York: St Martin's Press, 1995).

32   The phrase is from Gayatri Chakravorty Spivak, 'Can the Subaltern Speak? Speculations on Widow Sacrifice,' *Wedge* 7–8 (Winter–Spring 1985): 121.

33   Jenny Sharpe, *Allegories of Empire: The Figure of Woman in the Colonial Text* (Minneapolis: University of Minnesota Press, 1993).

34   S. Radcliffe and S. Westwood, *Remaking the Nation: Place, Ideology and Politics in Latin America* (New York: Routledge, 1996), cited in Rick Wilford, 'Women, Ethnicity and Nationalism: Surveying the Ground' in *Women, Ethnicity and Nationalism: The Politics of Transition,* ed. Rick Wilford and Robert C. Miller (New York: Routledge, 1998), 11–12.

35   Deborah Gaitskill and Elaine Unterhalter, 'Mothers of the Nation: A Comparative Analysis of Nation, Race and Motherhood in Afrikaner Nationalism and the African National Congress,' in *Woman-Nation-State*, ed. Nira Yuval Davis and Floya Anthias (NewYork: St. Martin's Press, 1989), 58–78.

36   Asuncion Lavrin, 'International Feminisms: Latin American Alternatives,' and Mary E. John, 'Feminisms and Internationalisms: A Response from India,' both in *Feminisms and Internationalism*, ed. Mrinalini Sinha, Donna Guy, and Angela Woollacott (Oxford: Blackwell, 1999), 175–91, 195–204; see also Malathi de Alwis, 'Motherhood as a Space of Protest: Women's Political Participation in Contemporary Sri Lanka,' in *Appropriating Gender: Women's Activism and the Politicization of Religion in South Asia*, ed. Amrita Basu and Patricia Jeffrey (NewYork: Routledge, 1997), 185–202.

37   The claim about the incompatability of nationalism and feminism is implicitly endorsed in the editor's introduction – although in not all the essays – in *Feminist Nationalism*, ed. Lois A. West (New York: Routledge, 1997), xi–xxxv.

38   Joan Scott, *Only Paradoxes to Offer: French Feminists and the Rights of Man* (Cambridge: Harvard University Press, 1996).

39   Gisela Kaplan, 'Feminism and Nationalism: The European Case,' in *Feminist Nationalism*, ed. Lois A. West (New York: Routledge, 1997), 3–40.

40   Rosalyn Terborg-Penn, 'Enfranchising Women of Color: Woman Suffragists as Agents of Imperialism,' in *Nation, Empire, Colony: Historicizing Gender and Race*, ed. Ruth Roach Pierson and Nupur Chaudhury (Bloomington: Indiana University Press, 1998), 4 1–56.

41   Jayawardena, *Feminism and Nationalism in the Third World*.

42   Jitka Maleckova, 'Nationalizing Women and Engendering the Nation: The Czech Nationalist Movement,' in *Gendered Nations: Nationalisms and Gender Order in the Long Nineteenth Century*, ed. Ida Blom, Karen Hagemann, and Catherine Hall (NewYork: Berg, 2000), 293–310.

43   Enloe, *Bananas, Beaches and Bases*, 62.

44   Rosalind March, 'Women in Contemporary Russia,' in *Women, Ethnicity and Nationalism: The Politics of Transition*, ed. Rick Wilford and Robert C. Miller (New York: Routledge, 1998), 87–119.

45   Cherifa Boutta, 'Feminine Militancy: Moudjahidates During and After the Algerian War,' in *Gender and National Identity: Women and Politics in Muslim Societies*, ed. Valentine M. Moghadam (London: Zed Books, 1994), 18–39.

46   Breda Gray and Louise Ryan, 'The Politics of Irish Identity and the Interconnections between Feminism, Nationhood, and Colonialism,' in *Nation, Empire, Colony: Historicizing Gender and Race*, ed. Ruth Roach Pierson and Nupur Chaudhury (Bloomington: Indiana University Press, 1998), 121–38.

47   Leila J. Rupp, *Worlds of Women: The Making of an International Women's Movement* (Princeton: Princeton University Press, 1997); see also *Feminisms and Internationalism*, ed. Sinha *et al.*

48   Mrinalini Sinha, 'Suffragism and Internationalism: The Enfranchisement of British and Indian Women under an Imperial State,' *Indian Economic and Social History Review* 36 (Dec. 1999): 461–84, reprinted in *Women's Suffrage in the British Empire: Citizenship, Race, and Nation*, ed. Ian Fletcher, Laura E. Nym Mayhall, and Philippa Levine (New York: Routledge, 2000), 224–40.

49   Cynthia Cockburn, *The Space between Us: Negotiating Gender and National Identities in Conflict* (London: Zed Books, 1998).

50   Catherine Hall, 'The Rule of Difference: Gender, Class and Empire in the Making of the 1832 Reform Act,' in *Gendered Nations: Nationalisms and Gender Order in the Long Nineteenth Century*, ed. Ida Blom, Karen Hagemann, and Catherine Hall (New York: Berg, 2000), 107–36.

Catherine Hall

'INTRODUCTION' TO
CIVILISING SUBJECTS

Catherine Hall is internationally renowned for her work on feminist history, gender and the British empire. Her numerous publications include *Family Fortunes: Men and Women of the English Middle Classes, 1780–1850* (new edn 2002) co-authored with Leonore Davidoff, *Defining the Nation: Class, Race, Gender and the Reform Act of 1867* (2000) co-authored with Keith McLelland and Jane Rendall, and an edited collection entitled *Cultures of Empire. Colonizers in Britain and the Empire in the Nineteenth and the Twentieth Centuries* (2000). This reading is taken from the introduction to her *Civilising Subjects. Metropole and Colony in the English Imagination, 1830–1867* (2002) in which Hall outlines the origins and gestation of her project to trace the interconnected and mutually constitutive histories of Jamaica and England in the first half of the nineteenth century. The extract reproduced here is not specifically concerned with the future direction of feminist history, but I include it as a fine example of the theoretically accomplished and innovative work on 'difference' now being undertaken by feminist historians. Hall's 'Introduction' is an evocative combination of the autobiographical and the theoretical. Her self-reflexive, critical interrogation of her own 'whiteness' both as a feminist historian and as a white woman living with a black partner in late twentieth-century Britain has particular resonance for those of us who are members of racially mixed families. The essay also draws together many of the significant features of post-colonialist feminist theory. Drawing upon the scholarship of Frantz Fanon, Gayatri Chakravorty Spivak and Jacques Derrida among others, Hall expounds upon the psychological underpinnings of racialised identities, rejecting the binary construction of the coloniser and the colonised relationship in favour of the mutual constitution of metropole and colony – a position for which she has become particularly well known in the rethinking of the history of Britain and its empire.

> People are trapped in history and history is trapped in them.
>
> James Baldwin, 'Stranger in the Village'

THE ORIGINS OF THIS BOOK lie in my own history. I was born in Kettering, Northamptonshire, in 1946. My father, John Barrett, was a Baptist minister, my mother a budding historian who had become a clergyman's wife. My father was at that time the minister of Fuller Baptist Chapel, named after the nonconformist divine and first secretary of the Baptist Missionary Society, Andrew Fuller.

[. . .]

In 1949, when I was three, we left Kettering. My father had been appointed superintendent of the north-eastern area of the Baptist Union, and we went to live in Leeds. We returned to Kettering to visit on a very regular basis, and Fuller continued to be a place of belonging, of warmth and acceptance, where our family was loved and my parents revered. Leeds was a very different experience. My father now had no church of 'his own', and travelled across the north-east preaching in different chapels every Sunday, but the rest of the family attended the local Baptist church, South Parade. [. . .]

At home the sense of a Baptist family stretching across the globe was always part of domestic life: missionaries from 'the field', 'on furlough', bringing me stamps for my collection; African students studying at the university who were invited for Christmas or Sunday tea; the small concerts we held to raise money for 'good causes' both near and far. My mother's involvement in the United Nations Association meant that some of the specifically Christian dimensions of a connection with other parts of the world could be displaced by a focus on internationalism. But there were uncomfortable moments as to quite what the nature of these connections were. A visiting West African student was upset with me when I exclaimed about the 'funny' feel of her hair and kept wanting to touch it. A great United Nations enthusiast, an acquaintance of my mother's, was deeply disapproving of my sister's friendship with some Trinidadian students. What was the nature of this supposedly universal family? And how were black people and white people placed within it?

Living in a city made it much easier to find other forms of identity, other kinds of belonging, beyond that of the church. There was school and the political activities to which I became attached: YCND (the Youth Campaign for Nuclear Disarmament) in particular, an extension of my parents' radical sentiments. It was the political aspects of my parents' thinking that I took up, while the religious dimensions were cast off. At one of the CND Easter marches to demonstrate against the nuclear base at Aldermaston, I met my partner-to-be, Stuart Hall, a Jamaican who had come to England in 1951 to study. He had never gone home but settled, one of the first post-war generation of West Indians to 'come home' to the mother country.

In 1964, now married, I arrived in Birmingham as a student in the Department of History. Birmingham was not a city that appealed to me. Leeds in the 1950s was proud of its radical traditions and its labour movement. Birmingham, represented by Liberals from its inception as a parliamentary borough, had followed Joseph

Chamberlain and turned conservative and imperialist at the end of the nineteenth century. [. . .] This was a foretaste of things to come, and the ripples were all too apparent in Birmingham. Travelling on the bus as a mixed-race couple, or looking for a flat to rent, was a difficult venture, to say the least.

In the late 1960s and 1970s, however, it was student politics and then being a mother to my daughter and son, feminist politics and feminist history, which absorbed my energies. My 'Englishness' and my 'whiteness', as I have written elsewhere, seemed irrelevant to my political project.[1] Of course I knew about Enoch Powell's 'Rivers of Blood' speech in Birmingham in April 1968. I watched the burgeoning of far-right groups demanding an end to immigration and the repatriation of the black and Asian migrants already here. I followed the development of the many organisations based in the West Indian, Indian, Pakistani and Bangladeshi communities across Birmingham, from Sparkbrook, Sparkhill and Balsall Heath to Handsworth. There were groups based in churches, dealing with housing, welfare youth, police harassment, employment. What is more, they became preoccupied in different ways with the question of what it means to be a migrant, how to create some new kind of place for themselves in postcolonial Britain. For some the issue became how to construct a new way of being, that of the black Briton, and here black was an inclusive political identity.[2] But the division of labour in our household was that Stuart worked on race, which meant black men, and I worked on gender, which meant white women: a variation on that common phenomenon on the Left, where men dealt with class and women with gender. At moments of crisis, it was taken for granted that 'we' – anti-racists, women's groups, trade unionists, Labour movement activists, socialists – would all be out for the demonstrations against the National Front. Anti-racism was assumed as part of the socialist feminism with which I was engaged: what might be characterised as a humanist universalism, an assumption that all human beings are equal, was integral to the shared vocabulary of the Left. 'Black and White together, we shall not be moved,' we sang, just as once I had sung those missionary hymns which celebrated the Christian family across the empire. But the unspoken racial hierarchy which was the underlying assumption of that humanist universalism had not been confronted in my psyche, any more than I had worked through just what was meant by the Baptist family of man.

I first visited Jamaica in 1964, soon after independence, but thereafter went only irregularly until the late 1980s. I found it a difficult place because it meant encountering my whiteness, meeting hostility simply because I was white, being identified with the culture of colonialism in a way which stereotyped me and left no space for me as an English woman to define a different relation to Jamaica. A new experience for a white woman, albeit one of the defining experiences of being black, as Frantz Fanon has so eloquently explored.[3] But it was also an exciting place, so different from England, so profoundly connected: yet that connection was colonialism and slavery. Africa was being rediscovered in Jamaica, in part through Rastafarianism and the music of Bob Marley. But in white England, amnesia about empire, which was so characteristic of the period of decolonisation, was prevalent. The empire was best forgotten, a source of embarrassment and guilt, or alternatively a site of nostalgia.[4] [. . .]

'It is a very charged and difficult moment', argues James Baldwin, when the white man confronts his own whiteness and loses 'the jewel of his naiveté'.

Whiteness carries with it authority and power, the legacy of having 'made the modern world', of never being 'strangers anywhere in the world'.[5] White women carry this legacy in different ways from men, but they carry it none the less. The white construction of 'the African', the black man or the black woman, depends on the production of stereotypes which refuse full human complexity. When the black man insists, wrote Baldwin, 'that the white man cease to regard him as an exotic rarity and recognise him as a human being', then that difficult moment erupts, and the naiveté of not knowing that relation of power is broken. 'The white man prefers', he argued, 'to keep the black man at a certain human remove because it is easier for him thus to preserve his simplicity and avoid being called to account for crimes committed by his forefathers, or his neighbours'. The Christian version of the family of man and the Left's universal humanism had both acted as screens for me, allowing me to avoid the full recognition of the relations of power between white and black, the hierarchies that were encoded in those two paradigms. But the dismantling of those screens was not simply a matter of personal will-power (though that is necessarily a part of the process): rather, it was something which became possible in a particular conjuncture, the postcolonial moment, a moment of crisis for the whole culture. [. . .]

It was the time when the new nations which had become independent began to recognise the limits of nationalism, and in the old centres of empire the chickens came home to roost: in the case of Britain, in the guise of those once imperial subjects who 'came home'. White first-generation migrants felt compelled for the most part to make the best they could of the inhospitable mother country, their children, born here, made very different claims.[6] At this point of transition, [Simon] Gikandi suggests, the foundational histories of both metropolitan and decolonised nations began to unravel: a disjunctive moment when 'imperial legacies' came 'to haunt English and postcolonial identities'.[7] This was also the time when questions of culture, of language and of representation began to be understood as central to the work of colonialism. [. . .] In the metropole this was the moment when second-generation black Britons asked what it meant to be black and British, when black feminists asked who belonged, and in what ways, to the collective 'we' of a feminist sisterhood. That question was posed very sharply in the editorial meetings of *Feminist Review*, a journal which I had worked on for some years and which was forced to rethink its practice at every level by the group of black feminists who had agreed to join the collective. How inclusive were those humanist visions that white feminists took for granted? The idea of the unity of black and white could not simply be taken for granted: its founding assumptions needed radical re-examination. Whiteness was problematised for me in a way that it had never been before. My assumption that my black husband and mixed-race children somehow made me different, that I need not think about the privilege and power associated with my white skin and white self, was challenged and undermined, particularly in my encounters with Gail Lewis, Avtar Brah and Ann Phoenix.[8] At the same time, in the wider society, Powellite formulations regarding the threat to 'our island race' had passed into the common sense of Thatcherism and conservatism, provoking more explicit racial antagonisms. Race was an issue for British society in new ways by the late 1980s: racial thinking had been around for a very long time, but the bringing of it to consciousness, the making explicit of the ways in which the society is 'raced', to use Toni Morrison's term, is another matter.

Driving along the north coast of Jamaica that summer of 1988, on the main road from Falmouth, once the prosperous port at the centre of a trade in enslaved peoples and the market for a complex of sugar plantations, to Ocho Rios, with its modern economy tied to tourism, we came to the small village of Kettering. I was immediately struck by its name, and by the large Baptist chapel with the name of William Knibb, the Emancipator, blazoned upon it. Why was this village called Kettering? What was its relation to the Northamptonshire town in which I was born? And why did the Baptist chapel occupy pride of place in the village? Who was William Knibb, and why was he remembered? What part did nonconformists play in the making of empire? This was the beginning of an unravelling of a set of connected histories linking Jamaica with England, colonised with colonisers, enslaved men and women with Baptist missionaries, freed people with a wider public of abolitionists in the metropole. [. . .] My project as I elaborated it, was to try to understand the making of this particular group of colonisers: that was my task, from where I stood, the politics of my particular location, driven by my 'trans-generational haunting'.[9]

[. . .]

The imperative of placing colony and metropole in one analytic frame, as Frederick Cooper and Ann Stoler have succinctly phrased it, has been one of the starting points for this study.[10] I was a historian of Britain who assumed that Britain could be understood in itself, without reference to other histories: a legacy of the assumption that Britain provided the model for the modern world, the touchstone whereby all other national histories could be judged. World history had been constructed as European histories, and the division of labour that academics made in the nineteenth century has left deep legacies. As a result, historians took on the ancient Mediterranean and Europe; orientalists dealt with Mesopotamia, Egypt, Persia, India and China; and the 'peoples without history' in Africa, South-East Asia, tropical America and Oceania fell to anthropologists.[11] I have become a historian of Britain who is convinced that, in order to understand the specificity of the national formation, we have to look outside it. A focus on national histories as constructed, rather than given, on the imagined community of the nation as created, rather than simply there, on national identities as brought into being through particular discursive work, requires transnational thinking. We can understand the nation only by defining what is not part of it, for identity depends on the outside, on the marking both of its positive presence and content and of its negative and excluded parts. Being English means being some things, and definitely not others – not like the French, the Irish or the Jamaicans. 'I cannot assert a differential identity', as Ernesto Laclau argues, 'without distinguishing it from a context and in the process of making the distinction, I am asserting the context at the same time'.[12] Identities are constructed within power relations, and that which is external to an identity, the 'outside', marks the absence or lack which is constitutive of its presence.[13] We need, then, to consider how modernity begins, in Paul Gilroy's phrase, 'in the constitutive relationships with outsiders that both found and temper a self-conscious sense of western civilisation'.[14]

[. . .]

There is already a considerable literature both on the Baptists in Jamaica and on the shift in racial thinking in the metropole which has been invaluable to me.[15] But my focus is different.

My questions concern the ways in which a particular group of English men and women, mainly Baptists and other varieties of nonconformists, constituted themselves as colonisers both in Jamaica and at home. Did nonconformists, in their own particular ways, conceive of themselves as 'lords of human kind', superior to others? I take the development of the missionary movement, one formative moment in the emergence of modern racial thinking, as my point of departure. What difference did the missionary enterprise, the anti-slavery movement and emancipation make to thinking about race? What vision of metropole and colony did these men and women have? What did people in England know about Jamaica in the heady days of abolitionism? And what happened when those days were over? What other sites of empire were significant for them, and why? And how did they know what they knew? Which forms of representation mattered? [. . .]

Through a focus on the Baptist missionaries who went to Jamaica and the men and women of Birmingham, I explore the making of colonising subjects, of racialised and gendered selves, both in the empire and at home.[16]

In thinking about the mutual constitution of coloniser and colonised, Fanon has been an important influence. A child of the French Caribbean, Fanon left his native Martinique to train as a psychiatrist in Paris. There he encountered the meanings of blackness in a new way. Best known for his thinking about the black male subject, Fanon is less often cited for his recognition of the double inscription of black and white. Deeply troubled by the psychic dimensions of colonialism, he explored his own fractured sense of himself as a black man. 'The black is not a man', he believed, until he was liberated from himself. [. . .]

But Fanon did not dissect only the psyche of the colonised. If blackness was constituted as a lack, what was whiteness? In his work as a psychiatrist in Algeria and Tunisia, treating victims from both sides of the conflict over decolonisation, he studied the torturers as well as the tortured. Those torturers were formed by a culture of settlement. Settlers had to become colonisers, had to learn how to define and manage the new world they were encountering. Whether as missionaries, colonial officials, bounty hunters, planters, doctors or military men, they were in the business of creating new societies, wrenching what they had found into something different. As Sartre noted in his introduction to *The Wretched of the Earth*, 'the European has become a man only through creating slaves and monsters'. Europeans made history and made themselves through becoming colonisers. For Fanon, decolonisation was inevitably a violent phenomenon, for it meant 'the replacing of a certain "species" of men by another species of men'. This involved the 'veritable creation of new men . . . the "thing" which has been colonised becomes man', and the coloniser in his or her turn had to be made anew. In Fanon's mind the world which the settlers created was a Manichean world. 'The settler paints the native as a sort of quintessence of evil'. 'Natives' could become fully human again only by violently expelling their colonisers, both from their land and from their own psyche. The settlers meanwhile were the heroes of their stories, the champions of a modern world, expunging savagery and barbarism, as they construed it, in the name of civilisation and freedom. [. . .]

'Europe', he insisted in a critical formulation, 'is literally the creation of the Third World'. Europeans made themselves and made history through becoming colonisers, becoming new subjects. Without colonialism, there would have been no Europe.[17]

Fanon's Manichean binary, coloniser/colonised, was in part a product of anti-colonial wars. From his own position in one such war, the struggle for Palestine, Edward Said also emphasised the hegemonic identities of 'the West' and 'the Orient'. Said's utilisation of Foucault's theory of the relation between knowledge and power was critical to the development of a new field of study. His insistence on the cultural dimensions of imperialism and the impetus he gave to the analysis of colonial discourse ('an ensemble of linguistically-based practices unified by their common deployment in the management of colonial relationships') have contributed to the breakdown of the idea of a common vision and a single colonial project, of Manichean binaries and hegemonic blocs.[18]

An important shift in understanding has taken place as anthropologists, cultural critics, geographers, art historians and historians have struggled to describe, analyse and define the complex formations of the colonial world. There were the colonialisms associated with the different European empires and the different forms of colonialism which operated within the British empire. On each of those sites different groups of colonisers engaged in different colonial projects. Travellers, merchants, traders, soldiers and sailors, prostitutes, teachers, officials and missionaries – all were engaged in colonial relations with their own particular dynamics. [. . .]

And then there is gender. Feminist scholars have been in the forefront of the effort to write new imperial histories, cognisant of the centrality of masculinity, femininity and sexuality to the making of nations and empires. Both men and women were colonisers, both in the empire and at home. Their spheres of action were delineated, their gendered and racialised selves always in play.[19] In the postcolonial moment we are perhaps more aware of the multiplicity of positionalities located across the binary of coloniser/colonised: the distinctions of gender, of class, of ethnicity. The distinctions between one kind of coloniser and another, one colonised subject and another, were indeed significant. Colonial officials, planters and missionaries had very different aims and preoccupations. An enslaved man acting as gang leader on a plantation exercised forms of power over others which an enslaved woman serving as maid-of-all-work in an urban household could not hope to emulate. The black lover of a white plantation owner was entirely subject to his power in some respects, although their sexual relationship meant that power might not flow only one way.[20] The times when the collective identity of coloniser or colonised overrode all other distinctions were rare, and were the effect of particular political articulations: the rebellion of 1831 in Jamaica or the aftermath of Morant Bay, for example. But even then there were those who refused to be positioned in that way. The framework of them/us, or what is absolutely the same versus what is absolutely other, will not do. It is not possible to make sense of empire either theoretically or empirically through a binary lens: we need the dislocation of that binary and more elaborate, cross-cutting ways of thinking.[21] [. . .]

Nineteenth-century discourses of sexual identity and difference, as Joanna de Groot has argued, drew upon, and contributed to, discourses of ethnic and racial identity and difference; these analogous languages drew on understandings of both domination and subordination.[22] The scientific theorising which was so strategic to understanding human variation, Nancy Stepan notes depended heavily on an analogy linking race to gender: women became a racialised category, and non-white peoples were feminised.[23] Similarly, class divisions were racialised, the poor constructed as 'a race apart'.[24] In the colonial order of things, as Ann Stoler argues, the Dutch, the British and the French all made new bourgeois selves, across colony and metropole. Each defined 'their unique civilities through a language of difference that drew on images of racial purity and sexual virtue'.[25] Marking differences was a way of classifying, of categorising, of making hierarchies, of constructing boundaries for the body politic and the body social. Processes of differentiation, positioning men and women, colonisers and colonised, as if these divisions were natural, were constantly in the making, in conflicts of power. The most basic tension of empire was that 'the otherness of colonised persons was neither inherent nor stable: his or her difference had to be defined and maintained'. This meant that 'a grammar of difference was continuously and vigilantly crafted as people in colonies refashioned and contested European claims to superiority'.[26] The construction of this 'grammar of difference' was the cultural work of both colonisers and colonised.

Fanon's settlers were men. But women were colonisers too. The mental world of a Birmingham middle-class female abolitionist was peopled with numerous others: imagined 'sisters' suffering under slavery, her male relatives – husband, father and brothers – and the female servants working in her household, to name a few. Gayatri Chakravorty Spivak has drawn attention to the gendered constitution of imperial subjects and the making of the white feminist woman. This is a woman constituted and interpellated not only as bourgeois individual but as 'individualist'. 'This stake is represented', she continues, 'on two registers: child bearing and soul making. The first is domestic-society-through-sexual-reproduction cathected as "companionate love"; the second is the imperialist project cathected as civil-society-through-social mission'.[27] The imperialist project, Spivak insists, was at the heart of this white woman's subjecthood. It is family and empire which are proposed here as the constitutive agents in the construction of the female bourgeois subject, and it is the discourses of race which form the Western female as an agent of history, while the 'native' woman is excluded. The social mission is as important at home as in the empire: the civilising of others had to take place on multiple fronts, from the civilising work which women did on men in the drawing-room or parlour, to their work with servants in the back kitchen, fallen women in the city, or the enslaved women of their imaginations. No binary, whether of class, race, or gender, is adequate to the multiple constructions of difference.

Spivak is working with Jacques Derrida's notion of *différance*. Derrida argues that, rather than meaning being produced through binary oppositions, it is produced through endless proliferation and constant deferral: the 'logic of the supplement'. As Deborah Cherry puts it: 'Alluding to the double meaning in French of *supplement* as addition and replacement, Derrida writes in *La dissemination* that the supplement is dangerous precisely because its textual movement is unstable and slippery, disrupting binary oppositions and securities of meaning.'[28] *Différance* is 'a playing movement' across a continuum of similarities and differences which refuses to separate into fixed binary oppositions. *Différance* characterises a system in which 'every concept [or meaning] is inscribed in a chain or in a system within which it refers to the other, to other concepts [meanings], by means of the systematic play of differences'.[29] Meanings, then, cannot be fixed, but are always in process. Cherry utilises these insights in her analysis of egalitarian feminism in the 1850s. The term 'sister', she argues, widely adopted by feminists, was doubly inscribed. It slipped between registers of meaning, marking both kinship and a gap, between philanthropic ladies at home and those they supported and helped. 'As it conjured a communality', she writes, 'it denied differences and disavowed the violence of colonial conquest'. The term hinted at proximity, but established a distance between 'the native female', 'not quite/not white', and the Western feminist, 'not quite/not male'. Far from fixing 'native women' in a close sibling relationship to white feminists, 'sister' destabilised and unsettled, leaving meanings ambiguous and unresolved.[30]

Working with these same issues, John Barrell utilises a notion of 'this/that/the other' in his analysis of de Quincy's psychopathology of imperialism. He draws on the distinction which Spivak makes between 'self-consolidating other' and 'absolute other'. The difference between self and other in de Quincy's writing, he suggests,

> though in its own way important, is as nothing compared with the difference between the two of them considered together, and that third thing, way over there, which is truly *other* to them both . . . what at first seems other can be made over to the side of the self – to a subordinate position on that side – only so long as a new, and a newly absolute 'other' is constituted to fill the discursive space that has thus been evacuated.

These are the mechanisms, he argues, through which an imperial power produces a sense of national solidarity; 'for it enables the differences between one class and another to be fully acknowledged', only then to be recognised as trivial in comparison with the civilisation which they share and which is not shared by 'whatever oriental other, the sepoys or the dervishes, is in season at the time'. De Quincy was constantly terrorised by his fear of infection from the East, argues Barrell, and inoculated himself by splitting, taking in something of the East, projecting whatever he could not acknowledge on to the East beyond the East, the absolute other. But there was always something of the East inside himself, precluding any possibility of a metropolitan identity safe from colonial invasions.[31] Splitting is central, then, to thinking 'otherness', splitting between good and bad, taking in or identifying with those aspects which are seen as good, projecting the bad on to absolute others.

These insights have helped me to think about the nineteenth-century men and women whose mental worlds and structures of feeling I have tried to make sense of. In tracing some of the shifts and turns in racial thinking over three decades, the historical specificity of the distinctions made between such pairs of terms as good/bad, docile/hostile, industrious/lazy, civilisation/barbarism, are very apparent. The 'good negro' of the abolitionists became the 'nigger' of the mid-Victorian imagination; the docile sepoy became the terrifying mutineer. The mapping of difference, I suggest, the constant discursive work of creating, bringing into being or reworking these hieratic categories, was always a matter of historical contingency. The map constantly shifted, the categories faltered, as different colonial sites came into the metropolitan focus, as conflicts of power produced new configurations in one place or another.[32] Generation mattered too. Those who came to adulthood in the early 1830s tended to share an optimism about the possibilities for reform and change. It was a different moment for those growing up in the 1850s: a different political culture, a more defensive relationship to the world outside, a bleaker view of racial others. Both coloniser and colonised were terms the meaning of which could never be fixed. Yet this did not mean that these terms did not have political effectivity: far from it. This mapping of difference across nation and empire had many dimensions: subjects were constituted across multiple axes of power, from class, race, and ethnicity, to gender and sexuality.[33] The map provided the basis for drawing lines as to who was inside and who was outside the nation or colony, who were subjects and who were citizens, what forms of cultural or political belonging were possible at any given time.

[. . .]

My title, *Civilising Subjects,* has a double meaning. The nonconformist men on whom I have focused – and there are more men than women because of the sources available and the period on which I have concentrated – believed that they could make themselves anew and become new subjects. That was their most important task. An aspect of that new self would be a more civilised self, for Christianity and civilisation were intimately linked in their minds. But they also carried the responsibility to civilise others, to win 'heathens' for Christ, whether at home or abroad. The 'heathen' subjects of the empire were a particular responsibility for those in the metropole, since they had a special relation to other British subjects. But 'heathen', 'subject' and 'civilisation' were all terms with complex meanings: each apparently named one category while masking ambivalent understandings. Colonial subjects were, and were not, the same as those of the metropole, 'not quite/not white': colonial heathens were, and were not, more in need of civilisation than heathens at home. And there was no certainty that England was civilised: even Dickens, in his moments of harshest racial thinking, could turn the categories around, terrified of the savage within.[34] In constructing imagined worlds across colony and metropole, the men and women who are the subject of this book were struggling with questions of difference and power. As Baldwin so eloquently puts it, they were trapped in history, and history was trapped in them.[35] [. . .]

Notes

1   Catherine Hall, 'Feminism and Feminist History', in *White, Male and Middle Class: Explorations in Feminism and History* (Polity, Cambridge, 1992), pp. 1–42.

2   Stuart Hall, 'Minimal Selves', in *Identity* (Institute of Contemporary Arts, London, 1997), vol. 6, p. 45.

3   Frantz Fanon, *Black Skins, White Masks,* 1st edn 1952 (Pluto Press, London 1968).

4   On the remembering of empire see Bill Schwarz, *Memories of Empire* (Verso, London, 2002).

5   James Baldwin, 'Stranger in the Village', 1st edn 1953, repr. in *Notes of a Native Son* (Penguin, Harmondsworth, 1995), pp. 151–65. Special thanks to Bill Schwarz for pointing me in the direction of this eloquent essay. There is now a considerable literature on whiteness. See, e.g., Vron Ware, *Beyond the Pale. White Women, Racism and History* (Verso, London, 1992); David Roediger, *The Wages of Whiteness: Race and the Making of the American Working Class* (Verso, London, 1992); Virginia R. Dominguez, *White by Definition. Social Classification in Creole Louisiana* (Rutgers University Press, New Brunswick, NJ, 1994); Bronwen Walter, *Whiteness, Place and Irish Women Inside: Outsiders* (Routledge, London, 2001).

6   See, e.g., Mike Phillips and Trevor Phillips, *Windrush. The Irresistible Rise of Multi-Racial Britain* (Harper Collins, London, 1998).

7   Simon Gikandi, *Maps of Englishness. Writing Identity in the Culture of Colonialism* (Columbia University Press, New York, 1996), p.19.

8   'Editorial', *Feminist Review*, 40 (Spring 1992), pp. 1–5, explores the shift which took place in the politics of the journal.

9   '[A] form of remembrance – most often of hidden and shameful family secrets – which hover in the space between social and psychic history, forcing and making it impossible for the one who unconsciously carried them to make the link': Jacqueline Rose, *States of Fantasy* (Clarendon Press, Oxford, 1996), p. 5.

10   Frederick Cooper and Ann Laura Stoler, 'Between Metropole and Colony: Rethinking a Research Agenda', in their edited collection *Tensions of Empire: Colonial Cultures in a Bourgeois World* (University of California Press, Berkeley, 1997), p. 4.

11   Jerry H. Bentley, Introduction to 'Perspectives on Global History: Cultural Encounters between the Continents over the Centuries', in *Proceedings of the Nineteenth Congress of Historical Sciences* (Oslo, 2000), pp. 29–45; Eric R. Wolf's book, *Europe and the People without History* (University of California Press, Berkeley, 1982), was very important to encouraging rethinking of the global nature of capitalist development.

12   Ernesto Laclau, *Emancipations* (Verso, London, 1996), cited in Stuart Hall, 'The Multi-Cultural Question', in Barnor Hesse (ed.), *Un/settled Multiculturalisms. Diasporas, Entanglements, Disruptions* (Zed, London, 2001), pp. 209–41, 234.

13   S. Hall, 'Multi-Cultural Question', p. 234.

14   Paul Gilroy, *The Black Atlantic: Modernity and Double Consciousness* (Verso, London, 1993), p. 17.

15   Philip D. Curtin, *Two Jamaicas: The Role of Ideas in a Tropical Colony 1830–1865* (Harvard University Press, Cambridge, Mass., 1955); Douglas Hall, *Free Jamaica, 1936–65: An Economic History* (Yale University Press, New Haven, 1959); Bernard Semmel, *The Governor Eyre Controversy* (MacGibbon and Kee, London, 1962); Christine Bolt, *The Anti-Slavery Movement and Reconstruction. A Study in Anglo-American Cooperation 1833–77* (Oxford University Press, Oxford, 1969); *idem, Victorian Attitudes to Race* (Routledge & Kegan Paul, London, 1971); Douglas Lorimer, *Colour, Class and the Victorians. English Attitudes to the Negro in the Mid Nineteenth Century* (Leicester University Press, Leicester, 1978); Mary Turner, *Slaves and Missionaries. The Disintegration of Jamaican Slave Society, 1787–1834* (University of Illinois Press, Urbana, 1982); Thomas C. Holt, *The Problem of Freedom: Race, Labor and Politics in Jamaica and Britain 1832–1938* (Johns Hopkins University Press, Baltimore, 1992); Robert J. Stewart, *Religion and Society in Post-Emancipation Jamaica* (University of Tennessee Press, Knoxville, 1992); Gad J. Heuman, *'The Killing Time': The Morant Bay Rebellion in Jamaica* (Macmillan, London, 1994).

16   'What kind of racialised, gendered selves get produced at the conjuncture of the transnational and the postcolonial?': M. Jacqui Alexander and Chandra Talpade Mohanty (eds), *Feminist Genealogies, Colonial Legacies, Democratic Futures* (Routledge, New York, 1997), Introduction, p. xviii.

17   Frantz Fanon, *The Wretched of the Earth* (Penguin, Harmondsworth, 1967), introduction by Jean-Paul Sartre, pp. 21–3; 'Concerning Violence', pp. 27, 39–40, 81.

18   Edward W. Said, *Orientalism. Western Conceptions of the Orient* (Routledge, London, 1978); *idem, Culture and Imperialism* (Chatto & Windus, 1993); the definition of colonial discourse is that of Peter Hulme, *Colonial Encounters: Europe and the Native Caribbean 1492–1797* (Metheun, London, 1986), p. 2.

19   There is substantial literature here, but see, e.g., K. Sangari and S. Vaid (eds), *Recasting Women: Essays in Indian Colonial History* (Rutgers University Press, New Brunswick, NJ, 1990); Nupur Chaudhuri and Margaret Stroebel (eds), *Western Women and Imperialism: Complicity and Resistance* (Indiana University Press, Bloomington, 1992); Moira Ferguson, *Subject to Others: British Women Writers and Colonial Slavery,*

1670–1834 (Routledge, London, 1992); Clare Midgley, *Women against Slavery: The British Campaigns, 1780–1870* (Routledge, London, 1992); Antoinette Burton, *Burdens of History: British Feminists, Indian Women and Imperial Culture, 1865–1915* (University of North Carolina Press, Chapel Hill, 1994); idem, *At the Heart of the Empire: Indians Colonial Encounter in Late Victorian Britain* (University of California Press, Berkeley, 1998); Mrinalini Sinha, *Colonial Masculinity: The 'Manly Englishman' and the 'Effeminate Bengali' in the Late Nineteenth Century* (Manchester University Press, Manchester, 1995); Ann Laura Stoler, *Race and the Education of Desire: Foucault's 'History of Sexuality' and the Colonial Order of Things* (Duke University Press, Durham, NC, 1995); Anne McClintock, *Imperial Leather: Race, Gender and Sexuality in the Colonial Context* (Routledge, New York, 1995); Wilson, *Sense of the People;* Susan Thorne, *Congregational Missions and the Making of an Imperial Culture in Nineteenth-Century England* (Stanford University Press, Stanford, Calif., 1999); Madhavi Kale, *Fragments of Empire: Capital, Slavery and Indian Indentured Labor Migration in the British Caribbean* (University of Pennsylvania Press, Philadelphia, 1999).

20   Douglas Hall, *In Miserable Slavery. Thomas Thistlewood in Jamaica 1750–1786* (Macmillan, Basingstoke, 1989).

21   Alexander and Mohanty (eds), *Feminist Genealogies; Avtar Brah, Cartographies of Diaspora: Contesting Identities* (Routledge, London, 1996); Gail Lewis, *'Race', Gender, Social Welfare: Encounters in a Postcolonial Society* (Polity, Cambridge, 2000); Ann Phoenix, *(Re)Constructing Gendered and Ethnicised Identities: Are We All Marginal Now?* (University for Humanist Studies, Utrecht, 1998).

22   Joanna de Groot, ' "Sex" and "Race": The Construction of Language and Image in the Nineteenth Century', in Susan Mendus and Jane Rendall (eds), *Sexuality and Subordination* (Routledge, London, 1989), pp. 89–128; repr. in Catherine Hall (ed.), *Cultures of Empire: A Reader. Colonizers in Britain and the Empire in the Nineteenth and Twentieth Centuries* (Manchester University Press, Manchester, 2000), pp. 37–60.

23   Nancy Leys Stepan, 'Race and Gender: The Role of Analogy in Science', in David Theo Goldberg (ed.), *Anatomy of Racism* (University of Minnesota Press, Minneapolis, 1990), p. 43.

24   Thorne, *Congregational Missions*, esp. ch. 5.

25   Stoler, *Race and the Education of Desire*, pp. 5, 10.

26   Cooper and Stoler (eds), *Tensions of Empire*, pp. 3–4, 7.

27   Gayatri Chakravorty Spivak, 'Three Women's Texts and a Critique of Imperialism', in *In Other Worlds. Essays in Cultural Politics* (Routledge, New York, 1985), p. 244.

28   Deborah Cherry, 'Shuttling and Soul Making: Tracing the Links between Algeria and Egalitarian Feminism in the 1850s', in Shearer West (ed.), *The Victorians and Race* (Scholar Press, Aldershot, 1994), pp. 156–70. See also idem, *Beyond the Frame. Feminism and Visual Culture, Britain 1850–1900* (Routledge, London, 2001).

29   Cited in S. Hall, 'Multi-Cultural Question', p. 216.

30   Cherry, 'Shuttling and Soul Making', p. 168. As Cherry notes, Spivak's use of the phrase 'not quite/not male' (Spivak, 'Three Women's Texts', p. 244) rewrites, as she acknowledges, Homi Bhabha's 'not quite/not white', which he elaborated in 'Of Mimicry and Man', in *The Location of Culture* (Routledge, London, 1994), pp. 85–92.

31   John Barrell, *The Infection of Thomas de Quincy. A Psychopathology of Imperialism* (Harvard University Press, London, 1991), pp. 10–11, 18–19.

32   For one excellent study of this process see Sinha, *Colonial Masculinity*.

33   Anne McClintock argues in her study *Imperial Leather* that the categories class, race and gender came into existence in relation to each other.

34   Charles Dickens, 'The Noble Savage', 1st edn 1853, in *The Works of Charles Dickens,* 34 vols (Chapman and Hall, London, 1899), vol. 34: *Reprinted Pieces*, pp. 120–7.

35   Baldwin, 'Stranger in the Village', p. 154.

Sanjam Ahluwalia and Antoinette Burton

RETHINKING BOUNDARIES
Feminism and (inter)nationalism in early-twentieth-century India

This exchange on transnational feminist histories between Sanjam Ahluwalia and Antoinette Burton forms part of a larger roundtable discussion on 'Women and Gender in Modern India: Historians, Sources and Historiography' published in the *Journal of Women's History* in 2003. Ahluwalia is a feminist theorist and scholar of Indian women's history and comparative histories of birth control and colonialism. Burton is an eminent historian of modern Britain, feminism and the empire, and the author of many influential works including *Burdens of History: British Feminists, Indian Women and Imperial Culture, 1865–1915* (1994), *At the Heart of the Empire: Indians and the Colonial Encounter in Late-Victorian Britain* (1998) and *Dwelling in the Archives: Women Writing House, Home and History in Late Colonial India* (2003). Ahluwalia argues for interconnected feminist histories that dismantle national boundaries. She cites her own work on the dialogue between the birth control movements of India, Britain and the United States as a salient example of just such an international approach. Ahluwalia's research shows how birth control discourse was constructed in such a way that it 'successfully marginalized the experiences of subordinate social groups' and exposed the complicity of the Indian elite in the regulation of subaltern women's fertility patterns. In interviewing non-elite rural Jaunpuri women about their resistance to various birth control agendas, Ahluwalia admits to having her own assumptions of contraceptive knowledge as empowering as profoundly challenged. Writing cross-national histories means taking seriously 'alternative imaginings' she concludes, 'even if they sit uncomfortably with our own ideas or politics'. Antoinette Burton's response to Ahluwalia acknowledges the importance of her research, particularly Ahluwalia's use of oral history as a noteworthy way of circumventing the limitations of the official colonial archive. Yet Burton also inserts a note of caution into the rush to tell transnational feminist stories. Globalism has the potential to create new hegemonies she argues, underpinned by the urgent, powerful demands of western capitalism. Just how Indian women's history will resist such agendas is the compelling, but as yet unanswered, question.

Sanjam Ahluwalia

THIS ESSAY INTERROGATES THE BOUNDARIES within which we locate our historical narratives to suggest a move towards interconnected histories. I argue for the need to rethink the interactions among feminisms and their relationships to imperial and national politics. Drawing upon my research on the history of birth control in colonial India from 1871 to 1946, this essay demonstrates connections among the birth control movements in India, Britain, and the United States.[1] Recent feminist scholarship has moved toward such interconnected histories and dismantled the idea of hegemony of the nation as a historical category. Furthermore, feminists scholars have demonstrated that intellectual and social movements are interactive and evolve across national boundaries, thus linking international, national, and local politics, and 'public' as well as 'private' concerns.[2] Emphasis on interconnected histories also permits us to recognize how complex historical agencies operate within non-Western societies, and challenges the ubiquitous all-knowing Western subject. Within Indian historiography, this move will enable feminist historians to rescue the past from metanarratives of nationalism and from that of its other, communalism, making room for alternative narratives.

To challenge the dominant metanarratives that restrict our understanding of feminist history, however, the move toward interconnected histories is insufficient. We must also take seriously alternative imaginings, even if they sit uncomfortably with our own ideas or politics. Voices from the local fringes of Jaunpur, a tribal block in the Tehri Gaharwal district of Uttar Pradesh, allowed me to recognize the elitist assumptions that have shaped and continue to shape the project of determining and policing fertility behaviors. Moreover, Jaunpuri women's voices expanded my range of sources, allowing me to construct a more inclusive narrative for the history of birth control in India and elsewhere.

I focus on the discourse of birth control to investigate the history of gender politics and its intersection with the emergence of the middle-class-dominated nationalist politics in colonial India. My research has shown me the limitations of trying to understand the discourse of birth control in colonial India in isolation from birth control movements in Britain and the United States. Therefore, I examine the dialogue between Indian birth control activists and their British and American counterparts to understand the interconnected workings of power locally, nationally, and globally. Focusing on dialogues among Indian activists and their cohorts in Britain and United States has allowed me to foreground the interlocking dimensions of global birth control politics. I argue for the need to comprehend birth control politics in the early twentieth century as what historian Adele E. Clarke has called a 'shared commitment of multiple worlds and individuals to the production of new knowledge.'[3]

The issue of sources is important for historians trying to restore subaltern/ marginal social groups to accounts of the past. In my own work, I began with traditional colonial state records and elite writings and then went on to do ethnographic fieldwork. Among the elite writings I examined were the records of such Western women birth control advocates as Margaret Sanger, Marie Stopes, Edith How-Martyn, Eileen Palmer, and Margaret Cousins. Among elite Indian men, Gopaljee Ahluwalia, A. P. Pillay, N. S. Phadke, and Radhakamal Mukherjee ardently supported birth control. Kamaladevi Chattopadhyaya, Rani Lakshmi Rajwade, Begum Hamid Ali, and Lakshmi Menon were leading Indian middle-class women supporters of birth control who debated the issue within their organizations—the Women's India Association (WIA) and All-India Women's Conference (AIWC).[4] Together, writings of these Western and Indian advocates are important sources for reconstructing the debates among elites on birth control, a subject that remains largely unexamined in Indian historiography.

The writings of Western birth control advocates allowed me to highlight cross-border interactions. For example, on the one hand, Sanger visited India and tried to 'convert' Mahatma Gandhi into a supporter of birth control. Stopes, on the other hand, wrote scathingly about Gandhi's views against the use of contraceptives in her journal *Birth Control News*. Although they employed different tactics, both women recognized the significance of Gandhi's views in determining public acceptance for birth control in India. Sanger and Stopes exchanged correspondence with Indian supporters of birth control from the 1920s onward, eagerly promoting their respective 'products' as the most suitable contraceptive method for Indians.[5] Stopes sent letters to some Maharajas in Princely India, requesting them to provide funding for her birth control organization in Britain—the Society for Constructive Birth Control and Racial Progress—and setting up appointments to meet with them when they visited Britain.[6]

Indian supporters of birth control selectively embraced the ideas and contraceptive technologies available to them in the early twentieth century. Pillay took the initiative and began publishing an international journal, *Marriage Hygiene*, in Bombay in 1937; he was the editor-in-chief, with co-editors in Britain and the United States. Both Stopes and Sanger contributed to Pillay's journal, writing articles and placing advertisements for their products and books in the publication. Stopes also wished to have her books advertised in other important Indian journals that addressed the subject of birth control, such as the *Madras Birth Control Bulletin*.[7] Indian media carried reports on work done by Sanger and How-Martyn during their visits to India. The publicity accorded to international birth control activists in the Indian press caused contention among competing international advocates.[8] Even while there was an international community espousing the cause of birth control, the movement was not unified or homogenous. Conflicts arose among prominent international figures, and some of these tensions were expressed in struggles over how to exercise influence on birth control politics and practices in India.[9]

The presence of international women advocates in India was more complex than a gesture of shared sisterhood. Sanger and Stopes supported a eugenicist understanding of population; for them the non-West represented dysgenic populations needing lower fertility rates than whites in Western nations. In a letter to C. P. Blacker of the London Eugenic Society requesting funds for her international trip, Sanger wrote, 'In my coming campaign I hope to do the preliminary work for realizing two aims—first, to bring to the poorer and biologically worse endowed stocks the knowledge of birth control that is already prevalent among those who are both genetically and economically better favored, and secondly, to bring the birth rates of the East more in line with those of England and the civilizations of the West.'[10]

How-Martyn's letter to Sanger from India in February 1935 reflects her intolerance and racist attitude toward the people on whose behalf this international advocate claimed to be working. When writing about India she said, 'But how humanity breeds here. No registration of deaths, so infanticide, abortion and stealthy murders can go on unchecked. Sanitation they will not understand. Cows and other animals wander almost anywhere unmolested. They bathe in the Ganges. Yet for most part they are attractive good looking, quite and have the animals unquestioning acceptance of life as it is and its surroundings. So far we have been there has been no beautiful scenery and nothing like the color and glamour I expected.'[11]

Such racist attitudes evidently did not outrage early-twentieth-century birth control advocates in India, as they do historians at the beginning of the next one. Sanger attended the 1935 AIWC meeting at Trivandrum where the birth control resolution was passed, and presented her views on the subject along with Indian middle-class women, some of whom were opposed to introducing birth control as part of their own feminist politics.

Connections among indigenous and international elites, however, contributed to the construction of a discourse on birth control that successfully marginalized the aspirations of subordinate social groups. By making population control the principle objective, middle-class and elite birth control reformers, whether Western or Indian, displaced the agency of subaltern women, particularly as it related to fertility patterns and sexual mores. The discourse of birth control constructed by reformers enabled the identification of poor Indian working classes, lower castes, and, in some cases, Muslims as sexually irresponsible and immoral because of the high fertility rates found among them. In this framework, subalterns were portrayed as unfit to be 'national' citizens because of their supposed inability or unwillingness to regulate sexual behavior and fertility practices to conform to new ideals promoted by the international community of birth control advocates. For instance, Begum Hamid Ali advocated the need to sterilize the 'unfit.' This measure, she argued, 'needed to be counted among those compulsions which are necessary for larger social interest especially in a country like India where perhaps the most fundamental of all problems is that of improving racial breed.'[12] Ali's position demonstrates her complicity with the elite modernist project of producing and reproducing fit, healthy, and virile bodies for a newly emerging Indian nation.[13]

It is important to point out that international activists sought to associate themselves with movements in India and other parts of the world partly to enhance their work in their home countries and to establish a powerful international voice, giving their cause greater visibility and acceptance at home.[14] The strategy of international advocates was to create alternative communities of support that could be called upon to justify their work in the face of domestic apathy. The timing of Sanger's trip to India was important in her attempt to seek international prominence to help bolster her work in the United States in the face of President Franklin D. Roosevelt's political hesitation to embrace the cause of birth control.[15] This recognition of mutual sustenance of birth control movements in India and the West also allows us to challenge the illusion of autonomy assumed by dominant, uncritical, Western historical narratives.

From the above examples it would be safe to conclude that interactions among Indian and international birth control advocates were far from simple, unidirectional exchanges. Sanger and Stopes, for example, looked to India as a site for greater publicity and acceptance for their project, just as Indian advocates saw in such reformers international endorsement of their agenda for disseminating contraceptive information. Western birth control advocates also viewed India and other non-Western countries as profitable markets for promoting their respective contraceptive technologies. Indian advocates found in the international community a major support base for their politics; by bringing in international reformers to address public meetings, they hoped to gain greater acceptance for their controversial cause, especially in the face of Gandhi's opposition to mechanical or chemical contraceptives.[16]

Do Gandhi, Sanger, and Stopes, even with Ali or Chattopadhyaya thrown in for good measure, however, really constitute the entire history of birth control in India? How can we retrieve subaltern agency, which at once allows for both the recognition and disavowal of main/malestream ideas of family, sexuality, and the nation? If elite sources do not allow subalterns to speak, may one remedy this by searching for non-elite sources that record alternative stories? The answer is yes and no. I agree with historian Kalpana Ram's argument that there is a profound social distance between women writing and the women written about. A feminist enterprise necessarily reaches out to the women it studies, even if the objects of that study will never completely identify with feminist researchers who study them. According to Ram, relations of utter identity cannot be made the prerequisite for writing and speaking.[17] My conversations with traditional midwives—*dais* working in Jaunpur—helped me understand how women both consented to and contested ideas of regulating female sexuality to ensure lower national birth rates. Despite the plethora of writings by Indian and Western birth control activists stating the need for introducing birth control devices for poor Indian working-class women, very little of their propaganda actually 'trickled down' to alter fertility behaviors among the women whom advocates intended to enlist as consumers for their technology. Attempts by malestream Indian nationalists, Indian middle-class feminists, and Western birth control advocates together to inscribe meticulously onto the bodies of subaltern women the ideals of progress and modernization have been resisted, especially in Jaunpur.

Close attention to the Jaunpuri lexicon of reproduction, motherhood, family, and self highlights tensions and negotiations between elite agendas of surveillance and subaltern resilience in the face of such domination. For instance, in contemporary rural Jaunpur, in opposition to the state slogan 'One is Fun,' the ideal family size is considered to be three children, preferably two sons and one daughter.[18] Only once this ideal family size has been achieved are some of the younger women willing to adopt birth control methods.

The greatest challenge to my own underlying liberal assumptions came through my fieldwork in Jaunpur. I visited Jaunpur hoping to 'unearth' some of the indigenous contraceptive methods circulating within what I fondly believed were its 'subversive female subcultures.' As a Western-trained feminist, I had accepted the teleological construction of birth control as an empowering knowledge and technology. However, Jaunpuri women challenged my assumptions, narrating their different experiences, perceptions, and needs for fertility control. Many of these women regard children as *bhagvan ki deen* (a gift from God) and, according to them, abortion is a crime against God. However difficult it was for me as a Western-trained feminist historian to accept these views, incorporating women's perspectives from the margins of the Indian mainstream compelled me to recognize the elitist assumptions that have shaped the project of controlling and policing fertility. The conversations in Jaunpur ultimately helped me recognize the elitism of the demand for birth control that the different proponents in colonial and postcolonial India articulated.

Conclusion

This essay pushes the boundaries of existing scholarship and calls for a rethinking of our approaches to the study of feminist subjects. I argue that feminist historians need to adopt cross-national approach to question the agenda of those we are often tempted to celebrate because they forwarded a cause we understand as necessarily progressive. Whether observing Margaret Sanger, A. P. Pillay, or Begum Hamid Ali, looking at the history of birth control as a transnational history provides a different perspective, not only about these individual figures but also their agendas. Thus, we may appreciate how the transnational interaction of birth control activists produced—perhaps against the wishes of these individuals—a discourse that was more concerned with population control than it was with women's well being. Only an interconnected narrative on the history of birth control can open up space to question the legitimacy of middle-class and elite activists from a feminist perspective. The radically different and sometimes disturbing position taken by Jaunpuri women regarding sexuality and birth control fueled my reexamination of existing feminist assumptions about the body and individualism, raising fundamental questions about my own preconceived notions about what constitutes feminism and feminist historiography. The voices of these women helped me write a history of birth control that questions the Western feminist shibboleth that the demand for birth control necessarily functions as a liberatory enterprise, revealing instead the darker, more oppressive, and hegemonic potential of this discourse.

Notes

1   See my dissertation, Sanjam Ahluwalia, 'Controlling Births, Policing Sexualities: History of Birth Control in Colonial India, 1871–1946' (Ph.D. diss., University of Cincinnati, 2000).

2   I found the work of Antoinette Burton and Mrinalini Sinha helpful in trying to rethink the parameters within which traditional national histories are located and in understanding the interrelated histories of British colonialism and Indian nationalism. Antoinette Burton, *At the Heart of the Empire: Indians and the Colonial Encounter in Late-Victorian Britain* (Berkeley: University of California Press, 1998); and Mrinalini Sinha, *Colonial Masculinity: The 'Manly Englishman' and the 'Effeminate Bengali' in the Late Nineteenth Century* (Manchester: Manchester University Press, 1995).

3   Adele E. Clarke, *Disciplining Reproduction: Modernity, American Life Sciences, and 'The Problems of Sex'* (Berkeley: University of California Press, 1998), 29.

4   Barbara N. Ramusack, 'Embattled Advocates: The Debates over Birth Control in India, 1920–40,' *Journal of Women's History*, 1, no. 2 (1989): 34–64.

5   For more details on the competing assertions by Sanger and Stopes on the 'ideal' contraceptive method for Indian women see Ahluwalia, 'Controlling Births, Policing Sexualities,' chap. 2.

6   Ibid.

7   Ibid., esp. 97.

8   Ibid., 98.

9   See Peter Neushul's article for details on the professional and personal conflicts between the two leading international birth control enthusiasts. Peter Neushul, 'Marie C. Stopes and the Popularization of Birth Control Technology,' *Journal of Technology and Culture* 39, no. 4 (1998): 245–72.

10 Margaret Sanger to C. P. Blacker, 14 November 1935, Eugenic Society Papers, SA/EUG/D.21, Box 26, Contemporary Medical Archives Center, Wellcome Institute, London.

11 Edith How-Martyn to Margaret Sanger, date, Margaret Sanger Papers, Box 56, folder 530, Sophia Smith Collection, Schlesinger Library, Radcliffe College, Cambridge, Mass.

12 'Section 111: Marriage, Maternity, and Succession.' 20 February 1940, Begum Hamid Ali Papers, All India Women's Conference Archives, New Delhi.

13 I examine the middle-class elitist bias underlying early-twentieth-century Indian feminist politics in Ahluwalia, 'Controlling Births, Policing Sexualities,' chap. 3.

14 Ahluwalia, 'Controlling Births, Policing Sexualities,' 94–6.

15 This point has been made by historian Ellen Chesler in her biography of Sanger. See Ellen Chesler, *Woman of Valor: Margaret Sanger and the Birth Control Movement in America* (New York: Anchor Books, 1992), 352.

16 Mahatma Gandhi discussed his views on birth control in Mahatma Gandhi, *Self Restraint versus Self Indulgence* (Ahmedabad: Navajivan Publishing House, 1947).

17 Kalpana Ram, 'Maternal Experience and Feminist Body Politics: Asian and Pacific Perspectives,' in *Maternities and Modernities: Colonial and Postcolonial Experiences in Asia and the Pacific*, ed. Margaret Jolly and Kalpana Ram (Cambridge: Cambridge University Press, 1998), 275–98, esp 287.

18 I saw this slogan posted on billboards and buses and in government hospitals in Delhi in 1997 and 1998. It was adopted by the Health Ministry in 1997, when Renuka Choudhary was Union Health Minister of the United Front Government.

Antoinette Burton

SOUTH ASIAN WOMEN, GENDER, AND TRANSNATIONALISM

[. . .]

S ANJAM AHLUWALIA'S ESSAY GLOSSES her innovative dissertation research in order to make a plea for history-writing that exceeds national boundaries, because she sees those very boundaries as a lingering effect of imperial power and territorial conquest. The topic of birth control in the twentieth century would seem to be especially well disposed to this task, not least because, again, the question of population control that undergirded it was one of global, imperial, and, as she demonstrates, anticolonial nationalist concern as well. Ahluwalia's principled complaint against the tendency of much historiography, even feminist history, to reproduce the erasure of the non-elite subject [. . .] is a methodological and political dilemma that none of us can afford to ignore. And yet I cannot help but feeling that Ahluwalia's well-placed outrage at this recurrent phenomenon enables her to occlude an equally important question: that is, the complicity of middle-class Indian feminists qua middle class in the hierarchies of subordination and invisibility that we are left to deal with when we face the official archive. Here the recent work of Mrinalini Sinha is apposite.[1] She examines the rhetoric and writing of feminists in the All-India Women's Conference around both modernity and internationalism, arguing that middle-class Indian women actively took up these discourses in the 1920s and 1930s precisely in order to align themselves with the bourgeois project of Indian anti-imperialism. Sinha, courageous and historically astute as always, challenges the rather triumphalist narratives forged in the 1980s that represent Indian feminists as the failed opponents of British feminist imperialism and the equally unsuccessful critics of male Indian nationalism. It makes much more sense, it seems to me, to read their agency, as Sinha does, not inevitably as resistance, but as the complex desire for participation in the public sphere under the sign of 'Indian modernity' and all that it entailed for motherhood, conjugality, and sexuality in the pre-1947 period. Ahluwalia's account is uncannily in line with Sinha's recent work, insofar as it adds birth control to the stock of rhetorically available discourses that enabled some Indian women to stake power and authority over the bodies and lives of other Indian women. The multisited audiences for these discourses must be attended to, not least because such a move furthers Ahluwalia's claims for transnational history as one pathway out of history-writing's entanglement with the mechanisms of the nation-state.

Ahluwalia's use of oral history is evidence of how scholars interested in Indian women's history in the generations following upon [Geraldine] Forbes's and [Barbara] Ramusack's important early work have taken up the cudgels they raised, and continue to raise, against the official archive. For this reason, Ahluwahlia's work on the politics of doing oral history, of recovering unrecorded memories and experiences, also deserves our attention—especially since the archive she is creating is no less politically charged or transparent than the official one. One wonders what the women she talked with made of this America-returned feminist scholar; one wonders too how she represented herself, in what contexts those conversations happened, and what kind of archive she has generated. [. . .] At the very least, Ahluwalia's work pushes Forbes and Ramusack and indeed all of us to consider the nation—both in its Western incarnation and in its postcolonial Indian one—as an insufficient investigative category for capturing the complex dynamics of issues such as birth control in their fullest historicity. As compelling as that call is, and as sympathetic as my own work and politics are with the investigative frameworks of transnationalism, I want to end on a somewhat agnostic note by wondering whether all historical subjects necessarily have a transnational genealogy, or can tell a transnational story. I ask this because I worry, frankly, about the new hegemonies that globalism has the capacity to make not just powerful, but also fashionable and commodifiable in the ever-more urgent context of transnational capital flow. How South Asian women's history will engage these concerns—and to what extent they are the function of North American agendas of globalization—remains a compelling question for feminist historians in the decades to come.

Note

1   Mrinalini Sinha, 'The Lineage of the "Indian" Modern: Rhetoric, Agency, and the Sarda Act in Late Colonial India,' in *Gender, Sexuality, and Colonial Modernities*, ed. Antoinette Burton (London: Routledge, 1999), 207–21; Mrinalini Sinha, 'Suffragism and Internationalism: The Enfranchisement of British and Indian Women under an Imperial State,' in *Women's Suffrage in the British Empire: Citizenship, Race, and Nation*, ed. Ian Christopher Fletcher, Laura B. Nym Mayhall, and Philippa Levine (London: Routledge, 2000), 224–39; and Mrinalini Sinha, 'Refashioning Mother India: Feminism and Nationalism in Late-Colonial India,' *Feminist Studies*, 28, no. 3 (autumn 2000): 623–44.

Cheryl Johnson-Odim

ACTIONS LOUDER THAN WORDS
The historical task of defining feminist consciousness in colonial West Africa

Originally published in Ruth Roach Pierson's and Nupur Chaudhuri's successful 1998 edited collection *Nation, Empire, Colony: Historicizing Gender and Race*, this chapter by Cheryl Johnson-Odim provides an illustration of a fully contextualised reading of 'difference' between women in her study of twentieth-century Nigerian women's anticolonial protest movements. Johnson-Odim, a renowned scholar of African-American and Sub-Saharan African history, argues that only by investigating 'models and agendas of feminism' beyond those of Euro-American women can we engage in meaningful comparative women's history. It is now essential for scholars of West African women to 'generate theory and construct paradigms' that are thoroughly grounded in African historical, social and cultural developments as opposed to appropriating western feminist concepts and themes. Johnson-Odim's study of two women's protest groups in colonial Nigeria – the Lagos Market Women's Association and the Nigerian Women's Party – demonstrates the traditional, indigenous forms of protest adopted by the women towards men (both colonial and indigenous) antipathetic to their cause. 'Action itself is a kind of theory' observes Johnson-Odim, thus, in their various protests against female taxation, the price of commodities and women's right to vote, Nigerian women made theoretical statements about themselves, their identities and their version of feminism. In Reading 28 Chandra Talpade Mohanty argues that a genuinely comparative feminist history must be located in the particular historical experiences of women, even if their strategies do not cohere with dominant readings of feminism. Johnson-Odim's article is therefore a prescient example of an indigenous Third World/South reading of female activism that may yet displace the western hegemonic model.

THE TERM 'FEMINISM' IS LAYERED with multiple meanings, interpretations, and perspectives. In recent years, primarily due to research and writing emanating from and being conducted in the non-western world, and to the contribution of women of color in the western world, some scholars have begun to speak of feminism in the plural, as feminisms. Others have elected not to use the term feminism at all, but to coin other terms, such as womanist.[1] Still others, as I have done elsewhere, have attempted to redefine feminist philosophy in a way in which women remain integral to it but that includes activity and thought aimed at eliminating structural inequalities (racism, imperialism) that oppress both women and men.[2]

As a result, in recent years much of feminist theory originating in the West has reached out to include analyses of nonwhite, non-western women of varying classes and in various places. Some feminist theory has begun to embrace what historian Joan Wallach Scott has termed 'an historicizing approach [that] stresses differences among women and even within the concept of "women".'[3] Yet, Scott acknowledges two things. First, that women of color, in both national and international fora, have been responsible for, in her words, 'exposing the implicit whiteness of [western] feminism' as well as its essentializing and ahistorical tendencies.[4] And two, that the historicizing and acknowledgment of the salience of difference is still working its way into western feminist theory and is seen as divisive by some western feminist theoreticians.

The tremendous growth (at least if we judge by publications) in post-1960s theories of feminism mostly took place in the United States and western Europe. In part due to the fact that they proliferated as fast as or even faster than specific research, theories of feminism often proceeded from the theoretical to the concrete; hypotheses went in search of examples. Moreover, much of the specific research on which theories were based was undertaken in western, Christian, industrialized, capitalist societies. This sometimes engendered a reductionist reasoning that resulted in two equally unsatisfactory conclusions vis-à-vis the study of the lives of women outside the West. First, it defined feminism in a cultural context and along a historical continuum that were western. Secondly, it looked to the 'Third World' with a western eye in search of examples of western feminism, or anthropological antecedents of women's preindustrial, precapitalist power that could fit someplace along a western historical continuum that could be defined as universal. Nancy Hewitt telescopes the point in observing that:

> Without intending to, Western women's historians may become mere raiders of a lost ark—seeking out the telling anecdote, the apparent parallel, the seeming sisterhood; exploring the primitive, the pre-capitalist, the pre-patriarchal; searching for either the pre-modern and traditional or the mythic and matriarchal, with which or against which to define ourselves, still at the center.[5]

There were problems with this logic even among some women resident in the West. Among women of color long resident in the West, African American women for example, debate has often ensued over whether race or sex took precedence in African American women's struggles—as if African American women could separate the two, given that they are indivisibly nonwhite and female in a society that locates nonwhites and females at its lowest rungs.[6] For instance, the debate over whether African American women were doing 'race work' or 'feminist work' in their anti-lynching campaigns seems a false dichotomy, even granted that most victims of lynching were men. The popular perception of the justification for lynching was that Black men had sexually assaulted white women. But the construction of Black men as sexually uncontrolled and savage was linked to the construction of Black women as promiscuous and lascivious.[7] If the struggle of African American women against lynching was 'race work,' given that it focused on a concern particular to African Americans, was the struggle of white women to pass a white-woman-only suffrage bill also 'race work' rather than feminist struggle?

African American and African women share common terrain in relating women's struggle against oppression to the struggles of their communities against oppression. African women who opposed colonialism, for instance, opposed it on the dual grounds of its oppression of their *people* (both male and female) and its rendering of women, to use Fran Beale's phrase of over twenty years ago, as 'slaves of slaves.'[8] Interestingly enough, when the Nigerian woman's rights and anticolonial activist Funmilayo Ransome-Kuti took her message to London in the 1940s, she accused colonialism of making women slaves.[9]

The historicizing and contextualizing of women's actions allow us to locate 'difference' in a useful way—such that it can be understood in relation to conditions. Thus we can make meaningful comparisons about those things that seem to oppress or liberate women and delineate connections between women's different statuses in different places. We can also investigate other models and agendas of feminism beyond those located in the activities of European and Euroamerican women.

In my dissertation, written over fifteen years ago, I went in search of Yoruba women's roles in the anticolonial struggle in Nigeria.[10] I believe I did important work in uncovering women's activity on behalf of women and in elucidating the important and powerful role of the 'community of women' in the lives of Yoruba women and girls. Among the precolonial Yoruba (and actually far beyond for most women), it was the community of women that would make as many decisions affecting the lives of girls and women as men. This was primarily a result of the sexual division of labor, women's important roles in the productive and distributive sectors of the economy, the proliferation of dual male and female societies and offices, and a cultural ethos that placed the group above the individual. Still, I paid less attention to the complexity of the web in which women's identities and actions were constructed—including the extent to which women operated (and often continue to operate) in a dialectic of oppression and power.

Africanist scholars have long resisted (and I believe rightly so) the extension to Africa of the public/private dichotomous analysis of women's productivity.[11] Women were (most still are) employed directly in production that crossed such boundaries, and they derived a certain autonomy and status from their roles as cultivators, traders, artisans, and providers of other marketplace services. Yet there is a discrepancy, a contradiction, in the autonomous ways women behaved collectively and in women's obeisance as daughters-in-law and especially as wives. Women are far more subordinated to men privately than publicly, and even to other women such as mothers-in-law or senior wives (wives entering a polygamous marriage before other wives).

More and more I realize the difficulty of describing women's statuses in West Africa in cultures that sometimes simultaneously oppressed, venerated, and feared women, in whose economies women were integrally productive workers in both the home and the marketplace, in whose philosophical/spiritual cosmologies women were often centered, and that provided space in which even nonelite women exercised power. Thus, it is no wonder that we so often have contradictory pictures of women in 'traditional' West African societies. Whether it is the legendary market women, the women's 'wars,' or the anticolonial activists, we are presented with ample evidence that ordinary, nonelite women exercised autonomy and planned massive grass-roots responses aimed at directing and controlling their collective and shared destinies.

This contradiction, combined with the historical juncture at which much of West African women's history begins to be produced, affects the way that history is written. In fact, the 'modern' (post-1960s) historiography of West African women doesn't seem to have passed through any real 'women as victims' stage of development, with the possible exception of some of the recent historiography on the continental enslavement and pawnship of women.[12]

In fact, the idea that writing women's history proceeds along a linear trajectory of development, one defined by the methodological, conceptual, and theoretical models of the development of women's history in Europe and the United States, is often assumed by western scholars. Nancy Hewitt has observed:

> By rendering Western women's history more cohesive and complete in retrospect than it has been in its making we will find it easy to 'add 'n stir' other 'marginal' women into existing frameworks and will resist their transformative power the way men's history resisted ours.[13]

The writing of the histories of women in West Africa has the opportunity to shape and to gender the writing of West African history at an earlier juncture in the development of that historiography than did that of European or American women's history in the development of those historiographies.

The construction of gender in much of West Africa depended as much on life-cycle as it did on sex, wealth, or status. A woman's order as wife in a polygamous marriage (for example, as first or second wife), her ability to bear children, her status as mother and as mother-in-law, or her being postmenopausal resulted in often radically different constructions of 'gender privilege' or 'gender oppression.'

The need for historians of women in West Africa to generate theory and construct paradigms that are rooted in African historical developments, modes of production, and cultures (surely related to the first two) is clear. Given differences in West African settings, this will not essentialize African women's history but rather provide us with the interpretive data to inform gender theories in Africa and elsewhere.

In some arenas, the colonial period in Africa can provide us with a window on the commingling of gender constructions and consciousness. That is, in urban areas where the colonized and the colonizers (both women and men) intermingled regularly and were drawn into one another's world views, we can see mutually transformative processes at work. It is useful in such settings to locate 'difference' and 'sameness' and 'hybridity' to aid in our understanding of how gender is constructed and to allow 'difference' to inform our theory and paradigms relating to the construction of gender and to models of feminism.

One way of doing this lies in examining West African women's anticolonial protest movements. In these movements a partnership often existed between 'traditional' women and 'westernized' women.[14] These protests took place under circumstances where colonialism was much in evidence but not more so than 'traditional' culture and 'traditional' socioeconomic and political organization.

There are a number of well-documented studies of such movements, including their leadership.[15] Though arguments are sometimes made that westernized women activists were taking their cue from the West and even from the nationalist men of their cohort group, and that they supplied the real 'leadership' to many of these activities, I think this is of limited significance and a false dichotomy. Such an argument ignores the fact that the base of support for most of these movements was among nonwesternized, non-elite women; that these women used 'traditional' women's protest tactics such as ridiculing men (both the colonizers and indigenous men whom they considered to be in sympathy with the colonizers) in song and dance, camping en masse in vigils outside the homes and offices of men and refusing to let them pass; that they referred to the 'good old days' when they considered that some 'traditional' power or right of theirs was being trespassed upon; and that they *assumed*, in a time when political activity by women was disparaged and considered unnatural by the colonizers and their supporters, that they had a right as women to engage in public, political activity. Much of West African women's anticolonial protest arose from a philosophical point of departure that was not anything they learned from the colonizers, and they employed tactics that were historically their own.

My own work has been biographical studies of women leaders. Information uncovered in these studies has led me to rethink interpretations of their evidence and to speculate about uses of biographical evidence, particularly in the colonial West African setting. Doing biographical studies of feminist women in colonial Nigeria identified the extent to which women's leadership revolved around actual interaction with, and empowerment by, other women. I am using the term feminist here based on at least *two* of its most universally agreed upon components: women who seek to challenge both the restriction of women's rights, and women's marginalization from centers of power and decision making.

What I am suggesting is that we reexamine the biographical approach for things it can tell us about the creation of feminist theory, and moreover, about what *counts* as theory. The relationship between sociopolitical theory and praxis ought to be organic. That is, theory is not only *writing* that emerges from careful observation and analysis of *action*, but action itself is a kind of theory. It is through action that theory is both created and realized. The anticolonial actions of West African women made a theoretical statement about their gender consciousness, about their definition of feminism. And, it was a theoretical statement rooted in their own traditions rather than being imported from the West.

Even if we examine the 'leadership' (where it is identifiable) of women's anticolonial protests, we see that it is tied to a historically indigenous mode of action.

That 'leadership' is characterized by being at the forefront of all-women's protest movements as much, or more, than by any individual interactions with anticolonial organizations led by men, or by individual interaction with foreign and indigenous members of the colonial hierarchy. Women, especially urban women in direct contact with colonialism, despite their increasing class, ethnic, and religious differences, continued to identify gender qua gender as an important organizing base, as they had done historically. It was not *new* to them to see their collective destiny embodied in gender solidarity, it was *old*. Though not monolithic in their aims, they *assumed* gender as a primary bond and organizing base as they most certainly had for centuries.

The class development, and the ethnic and religious diversity created by the colonial experience provided new challenges to an old way of organizing, but the West had nothing to teach African women about organizing as women. Whether 'traditional' or members of the newly emerging westernized elite, women activists looked primarily to their *past* modes of protest to help remake their future. But, looking to the future, they appropriated those aspects of external ideolgies that seemed most likely to benefit women. They sought to align themselves closely with ideas that were the most consonant with their own cosmologies—the struggle for women's right to vote, for instance, resonated with the 'traditional' notion that women had a role to play in the political sphere.

The struggle against women's taxation separately from their husbands was both a reaction to the transgression of this policy against the family-based taxation of the formerly independent African societies and states, and the desire of women to couple their taxation with the right to vote. The struggle against the power of the colonial bureaucracy to decide the placement of markets and the prices of commodities traded therein was intended to maintain women's power in their roles in production and distribution. Even among the westernizing elite, the struggle for equal pay for equal work, and for access to all grades of the civil service, was an extension of women's historical role of working outside the home, which was as much an obligation of adulthood as a right for most of the women of West Africa.

I will examine, in brief, two women's protest groups of the colonial era in Nigeria. These groups are illustrative of the points I have made above, and they are different from one another.

The first, the Lagos Market Women's Association (LMWA), was an organization of at least ten thousand market women in Lagos, Nigeria. Lagos was the center of the colonial bureaucracy in Nigeria after 1914, when the protectorates of Northern and Southern Nigeria were joined to be the British colony of Nigeria. Though the exact date for the formation of the LMWA is not clear, by the 1920s it was active and a powerful organization that represented the market women before both the 'traditional' African authorities such as the various chiefs, and the colonial hierarchy. Guilds predated the organization of the LMWA, which represented a collectivity of markets. In addition, at least as early as 1908, ad hoc groups of market women's guilds had united to protest the imposition of taxes on the selling and use of water in the city. The formation of associations of women representing various markets, and of women's guilds representing various occupations (such as hairdressers, sellers of cooked food, shea-butter producers), predated colonialism by centuries.

The most well-known head of the LMWA during the colonial period was Madam Alimotu Pelewura. A fish trader in Ereko market at least as early as 1900, Pelewura shared several other characteristics of the market women: she was unlettered, a Muslim, and poor. Pelewura was the elected *Alaga* (head) of Ereko market, which in a 1932 colonial government study was reported as one of the most efficiently run markets in Lagos.[16] [. . .]

By 1932 Pelewura was appointed a member of the *Ilu* committee by the traditional African (Yoruba) authorities of Lagos. The *Ilu* committee was a component of traditional government, a body of chiefs and others who advised the *Oba* (king). With their policy of indirect rule for Lagos (and other parts of Nigeria), the British did not dismantle indigenous political institutions but rather sought to undermine and manipulate them in ways which rendered them primarily titular and consultative when it came to decision making, as well as helpful when it came to implementation of colonial directives. A representative of the market women had historically sat on the *Ilu* to ensure that women's concerns were voiced and considered. At the time of her appointment, Pelewura was a spokeswoman for eighty-four market women's organizations. As will be seen, the *Ilu* would deeply disappoint the colonial authorities when, in a confrontation with the market women, the *Oba* would make it plain that there was no historical precedent for his (or the *Ilu's*) contravening a decision that the women made about their spheres of power.

Between 1932 and 1951, there were several major confrontations between the market women and the colonial authorities. These had to do with the taxation of women, the location of markets, the price of commodities, and women's right to vote.

In 1932 rumors spread that the colonial government intended to tax women in Lagos. Though a limited tax on women had been inaugurated in the nearby town of Abeokuta in 1918, the market women of Lagos were prepared to resist such taxation. They sent a delegation to see the Administrator of the Colony, C. T. Lawrence, who assured them the government had no intention of taxing women in Lagos. Despite that assurance, in 1940 the colonial government enacted an Income Tax Ordinance which proposed to tax women whose incomes exceeded fifty pounds per annum. Immediately the market women began to organize, and on December 16, 1940, within days of the enactment of the Ordinance, over a hundred women assembled outside the office of the Commissioner of the Colony. The women were adamant that the tax be repealed and, receiving no assurance to that effect, left to report to the *Oba* Falolu. In a petition formulated by the women (drawn up by a hired clerk) and 'signed' with over two hundred of their thumbprints, they stated that female taxation had to be repealed because it violated 'native law and custom' and was untimely due to the hardship created by World War II. The petition further reported that the *Oba* Falolu and his chiefs agreed with them that female taxation was not only contrary to custom but undesirable.

On December 18, the markets of Lagos were nearly deserted as the women marched in the thousands. They first went to the Office of the Commissioner of the Colony. Receiving no satisfaction there, they then marched to Government House, where soldiers barred the door. Eventually two women, one of whom was Pelewura, were admitted by Governor Bourdillon. Pelewura later reported in an interview with the *Daily Times* newspaper that Bourdillon apologized that Lady Bourdillon was out that day and could not receive them. She said she replied they were not particular about reception that day. They delivered their petition and later in the evening held a mass meeting at Glover Memorial Hall. Both Pelewura and the Commissioner addressed the crowd, which ranged in estimates from one thousand to seven thousand women. When the Commissioner, in his address, stated that women in England paid tax, it was reported that Pelewura responded that she was not surprised, since England was where the money was made and that Africans were poor 'owing to many factors over which they had no control.' She went on to state that 'Europeans should not interfere with native custom and impose taxation on women' and, according to official reports, wound up with a Yoruba version of 'votes for women or alternatively no taxation without representation.'[17]

Within two days, the government raised the ceiling for women's taxation from fifty pounds income per annum to two hundred pounds. Clearly, this meant that almost no market woman would be taxed. A letter was dispatched to the market women and delivered to Pelewura, advising her of the new policy. Pelewura reportedly responded that once the principle of female taxation was conceded, it was only a matter of time before all women had to pay tax. History proved her prophetic.

During the World War II years, the Nigerian colonial government instituted a system of price controls on food that came to be known as the Pullen Marketing Scheme, named after Captain A. P. Pullen, who was appointed as its director in 1941. The Pullen scheme had expanded by 1943 to such an extent that the government not only sought to cap the prices of food sold in the markets but wanted to send agents to buy food outside of Lagos and bring it to Lagos to sell in the market at designated centers at government-set prices.

The Lagos market women had several objections to the Pullen scheme. As the primary distributors and retailers of food, they had historically exercised control over its pricing. Moreover, most of the market women were petty traders operating on the smallest profit margin and were unable to sustain even short-term losses. Government prices for foodstuffs were unrealistic, often amounting to less than retailers had to pay to purchase them for resale. A vigorous black market developed, and by 1944 the official estimate of the number of Lagosians fed by the black market was as high as two-thirds. When arrests were made for black market profiteering, employees of European firms received lesser sentences than market women arrested for the same offense.

The market women were determined to resist the price controls. The women proposed that, rather than prices being set by the government, a committee composed of twelve experienced market women of the LMWA should regulate prices. When the women farina sellers of Ijebu-Ode (a town near Lagos that supplied much of Lagosians' supply of farina) stationed themselves on the main road between Ijebu-Ode and Lagos and refused to allow any lorries carrying farina to pass, the LMWA supported their actions. Early in 1944, Pelewura was summoned to several meetings with the Deputy Controller of Native Foodstuffs and the Commissioner of the Colony to discuss the possibility of finding a way for the market women to support the price controls. At one such meeting, Captain Pullen proposed that Pelewura assist him and offered to pay her to do so. According to official reports, Pelewura refused and accused Pullen of 'seeking to break and starve the country where she was born.'[18]

A meeting of the market women (reportedly three thousand of them) with the *Oba* and chiefs was also unhelpful to the colonial authorities. At that meeting, Chief

Oluwa informed Pullen that no market woman would go against the LMWA prohibition on abiding by the price controls. The LMWA achieved a limited success in August 1945, when the government agreed to decontrol the price of gari, a staple food of the population of Lagos and the one in greatest scarcity. By September 1945, the government decontrolled food prices. The war was over, the protest was mounting, and there seemed to be no logic to keeping them in place. [. . .]

This brief description of some of the activities of the LMWA is indicative of the market women's awareness of the acute frustrations of the colonial period. More importantly, it is evidence that they had in place conceptual formulations and practical mechanisms to represent themselves, and that they drew on their history as much as their present reality of colonialism/westernization to promote their interests in being active agents in decision making about their lives. The assumptions they made about the proper spheres for women's activity were solidly rooted in their history and in fact contravened colonial notions of 'woman's sphere.'

The second major women's organization in colonial Lagos that I will discuss is the Nigerian Women's Party (NWP). The NWP was founded by a group of women who were members of the newly emerging Christianized, westernized elite. Its most prominent member, and its president from its inception until its demise around 1956, was Lady Oyinkan Ajasa Abayomi. Abayomi's father was the first Nigerian knight (Sir Kitoye Ajasa), and her mother (Oyinkan Bartholomew) was the daughter of first treasurer to the Egba United Government.[19] Abayomi was sent to Britain for postsecondary education. Though both of her parents were relatively conservative, after the death of her first husband, Abayomi married Dr. (later Sir) Kofoworola Abayomi, who was a leader of the Nigerian Youth Movement (NYM), an early nationalist organization founded in 1935. Even before this marriage in 1934, Abayomi had distinguished herself as a freethinker and a political activist who was more radical than her parents, albeit less revolutionary than some other Nigerian women activists.[20] [. . .]

On May 10, 1944, Abayomi held a meeting in her Lagos home to discuss women's political situation. The twelve women gathered there decided to form the Nigerian Women's Party. In an interview the following day in the African-run *Daily Service* newspaper, Abayomi, and another NWP founder, Tinuola Dedeke, addressed the reasons for the founding of the NWP. Abayomi decried the fact that, though women owned property and paid taxes, they had no political representation because they could not vote. She specifically criticized the lack of any women on the Lagos Town Council or the Legislative Council, the two bodies on which the colonial government had allowed some African representation. She also pointed out the lack of government scholarships for girls to study in Britain, comparing the Nigerian situation to that of the British colony of Sierra Leone, where such scholarships existed. Dedeke implored women to 'cast away all feelings of religious and tribal differences and present a united front for the sake of their motherland.'[21]

Within a short time, the NWP had drawn up its Constitution that set forth its goals:

> The Women's Party makes its strongest appeal to the women of Nigeria irrespective of class or any other distinction, reminding them of their

backward and unenviable position among the women of other races and calling them to action. It appeals to those who may be outside the ranks of the Women's Party for sympathy and cooperation:

1. To shape the whole future is not our problem, but only to shape faithfully a small part of it according to rules laid down.

2. To seek by constitutional means the rights of British citizenship in its full measure on the people.

3. To work assiduously for the educational, agricultural and industrial development of Nigeria with a view to improve the moral, intellectual and economic condition of the country.

4. To work for the amelioration of the condition of the women of Nigeria not merely by sympathy for their aspirations but by recognition of their equal status with men.[22]

[. . .] [T]hough the Party sought to solicit membership among the market women, it was not nearly as successful in recruiting them as members as were the market women's own associations, particularly the LMWA. One prominent market woman, Rabiatu Alaso Oke, who was unlettered and Muslim, did serve on the executive committee of the NWP. Though Pelewura had a working relationship with the NWP and shortly after its founding announced her personal willingness to cooperate with the Party, she never appears to have held any official status and it is not even clear if she was actually a member. There was at least one major disagreement between the NWP and the market women over remarks made by Funmilayo Ransome-Kuti, a leftist and leader of the Abeokuta Women's Union.[23] Still, the NWP cooperated with the market women during the resistance to the Pullen price controls and conducted free literacy classes in the evening for market women at the CMS Grammar School.

The NWP took up four major issues during its most active phase: (1) girls' education and literacy classes for adult women; (2) the employment of women in the civil service; (3) the right of female minors to trade freely in Lagos; and (4) the securing of women's rights in general, but particularly the right to vote.

Many in the NWP leadership were schoolteachers and were seriously concerned by the lack of educational facilities for girls' education, particularly at the secondary level. Moreover, the NWP fought to have the curriculum offered to girls expanded; they wanted science and foreign languages added to the curriculum. The Party advocated the provision of government scholarships for Muslim girls, who were at a particular disadvantage since both primary and secondary education was dominated by various Christian church denominations. Last but not least, the Party sought to have the government provide adult literacy education, particularly for women.

The second issue, employment of women in the colonial civil service, had been a major concern since the 1930s, when Charlotte Olajumoke Obasa and her Lagos Women's League (defunct by the 1940s) had battled for African women's employment. The NWP argued not only for women's employment but for equal pay with men in the same grade of the service. Female teachers, for instance, were paid

33 percent less than men employed in the same rank. There was other discrimination. Particularly rankling was the apparent preference by the government for hiring European women, usually wives of administrative officers, as nurses and secretaries.

In 1946 the legislature passed the Children and Young Persons Ordinance, which struck at the heart of African traditions. The Ordinance prohibited children under fourteen from engaging in street trading, required parental permission for girls between fourteen and sixteen to trade, and limited to daylight the hours in which young girls were allowed to trade. Though this legislation may have had as its intention the protection of child labor, it was crafted without consultation with the African community and contravened local customs, in which girls were apprenticed to trade for their mothers and other relatives as a kind of vocational training in preparation for economic independence as adult women. The police force exceeded acceptable behavior when it began meeting trains entering Lagos and removing all girl traders who seemed below age, and arresting young girls, including young married women with babies on their backs. In a letter to the *Daily Service*, the NWP expressed the fear that the authorities intended to introduce a pass system similar to that in effect in South Africa. The NWP worked with the market women's associations in succeeding in having the ordinance suspended.

The NWP constantly agitated for the right of women to vote. In 1950 southern Nigerian women were finally enfranchised. That year, the NWP ran four candidates in the Lagos Town Council election. All four NWP candidates lost. After this election, the NWP began its gradual demise. The Party continued to advocate for girls' education and health care reforms, but by 1956 it effectively disappeared when it joined other Nigerian women's groups to establish the National Council of Women's Societies, a decidedly less politically oriented group.

Most of the active membership of the NWP straddled the 'traditional' and the 'new,' the indigenous and the foreign. Though often much acculturated in western ways, these women also maintained an allegiance to their own culture. They were that middle strand who sometimes opted for slower and less radical change by exhorting colonialism to improve itself rather than end immediately. It was particularly in their advocacy of women's rights that they were a thorn in the side of the colonizers, and often in the side of African men as well. The NWP was clearly a champion of women's rights, especially those of poor women. While there may have been some noblesse oblige in their actions, they were sincere in their desire to see all women treated as equals with men. Their notion of the political sphere as a proper arena for women's activity was certainly nothing they learned from the West.

These two organizations, the Lagos Market Women's Association and the Nigerian Women's Party are examples of feminist activity in the colonial setting in the capital city of the most populous British colony in Africa. The feminist activity they represent was inspired not by western models, but by their own models. Though their activity may have gone unnamed as feminism, and unarticulated in ideological terms, their modes of organization and their language of protest are transparent in their advocacy of women's equal status with men and women's right to power over their own lives and participation in the general political sphere. In actions louder than words, they created theory.

Notes

1   Alice Walker appears to be among the first to use this term. In her book *In Search of Our Mother's Gardens* (New York: Harcourt, Brace, Jovanovich, 1983) she describes a womanist as a Black feminist or feminist of color and says, 'womanist is to feminist as purple is to lavender.'

2   Cheryl Johnson-Odim, 'Common Themes, Different Contexts,' in Chandra T. Mohanty, Ann Russo, and Lourdes Torres, eds., *Third World Women and the Politics of Feminism* (Bloomington: Indiana University Press, 1991).

3   Joan Wallach Scott, 'Introduction,' in Joan Wallach Scott, ed., *Feminism and History* (New York: Oxford University Press, 1996), 1.

4   Ibid., 6.

5   Nancy Hewitt, 'Uneven Developments: Women's History Reaches Puberty,' unpublished paper delivered at the Social Science History Association Conference, Minneapolis, 1990. A version of this paper has been published as 'Reflections from a Departing Editor: Recasting Issues of Marginality' *Gender and History* 4, no. 1 (Spring 1992): 3–9.

6   Joan Wallach Scott writes, 'Some kind of analysis is needed of a complicated and highly specific relationship of power. . . . Does race take priority over class and class over gender, or are there inseparable connections among them?' See Scott, 'Introduction,' 8.

7   For a brilliant discussion of this connection, see Angela Davis, 'Rape, Racism and the Myth of the Black Rapist,' in Angela Davis, *Women, Race and Class* (New York: Random House, 1981). See also Cheryl Johnson-Odim, 'Common Themes, Different Contexts.'

8   Fran Beale, 'Slave of a Slave No More: Black Women in Struggle,' *Black Scholar* 6, no. 6 (March 1975): 2–10.

9   See the quotation in the British newspaper the *Daily Worker*, August 10, 1947. Funmilayo Ransome-Kuti is among the most important women leaders in Nigeria's history. She was the most radical Nigerian woman of the colonial period. For more on her, see Cheryl Johnson-Odim, 'On Behalf of Women and the Nation: Funmilayo Ransome-Kuti and the Struggles for Nigerian Independence and Women's Equality,' in C. Johnson-Odim and M. Strobel, eds., *Expanding the Boundaries of Women's History* (Bloomington: Indiana University Press, 1992); and Cheryl Johnson-Odim and Nina Mba, *For Women and the Nation: A Biography of Funmilayo Ransome-Kuti of Nigeria* (Urbana: University of Illinois Press, 1997).

10 Cheryl Johnson, 'Nigerian Women and British Colonialism: The Yoruba Example with Selected Biographies' (Ph.D. dissertation, Northwestern University, Evanston, IL, 1978).

11 See, for example, Ife Amadiume, *Male Daughters, Female Husbands* (London: Zed Press, 1987); Niara Sudarkassa, *Where Women Work: A Study of Yoruba Women in the Marketplace and in the Home* (Ann Arbor: University of Michigan Press, 1973); Kamene Okonjo, 'The Dual-Sex Political System in Operation: Igbo Women and Community Politics in Midwestern Nigeria,' in N. Hafkin and F. Bay, eds., *Women in Africa* (Stanford: Stanford University Press, 1976), 45–58; Karen Sacks, *Sisters and Wives* (Westport, CT: Greenwood Press, 1979); Simi Afonja, 'Land Control, A Critical Factor in Yoruba Gender Stratification,' in C. Robertson and I. Berger, eds., *Women and Class in Africa* (New York: Holmes and Meier, 1986), 78–91; Leith Mullings, 'Women and Economic Change in Africa,' in Nancy J. Hafkin and Edna G. Bay, eds., *Women in Africa* (Stanford: Stanford University Press, 1976), 239–64; and Nancy J. Hafkin and Edna G. Bay, 'Introduction' to *Women in Africa*, 1–18.

12 I do not include in this discussion the explosive literature on female circumcision/ genital mutilation since this is a literature not primarily written by historians and frequently not even historicized.

13   Hewitt, 'Uneven Developments.'

14   By 'traditional,' I mean the way people did things before the arrival of colonialists external to the region who brought western culture. For an important discussion of false dichotomies between 'traditional' and 'modern,' see Cheryl Johnson-Odim and Margaret Strobel, 'Conceptualizing the History of Women in Africa, Asia, Latin America and the Caribbean, and the Middle East,' *Journal of Women's History* 1, no. 1 (Spring 1989): 36–7.

15   See, for example, Nina Mba, *Nigerian Women Mobilized: Women in Southern Nigerian Political History 1900–1965* (Berkeley, CA: Institute of International Studies, 1982); Cora Ann Presley, 'Labor Unrest among Kikuyu Women in Colonial Kenya,' in Robertson and Berger, eds., *Women and Class in Africa*, 255–73; Cora Ann Presley, *Kikuyu Women, the Mau Mau Rebellion and Social Change in Kenya* (Denver, CO: Westview Press, 1993); Jean O'Barr, 'Making the Invisible Visible: African Women in Politics and Policy,' *African Studies Review* 18, no. 3 (1975): 19–27; Judith Van Allen, 'Sitting on a Man: Colonialism and the Lost Political Institutions of Igbo Women,' *Canadian Journal of African Studies* 6, no. 2 (1972): 168–81; and Cheryl Johnson-Odim, 'Madam Alimotu Pelewura and the Lagos Marketwomen,' *Tarikh* 7, no. 1 (1981): 1–10.

16   For more information on Pelewura, see Johnson-Odim, 'Madam Alimotu Pelewura and the Lagos Marketwomen,' in *Tarikh*, 7, no. 1 (1981): 1–10.

17   *Daily Times*, December 18, 1940, cited in Johnson-Odim, 'Madam Alimotu Pelewura.'

18   Macaulay Papers Collection, University of Ibadan Manuscripts Collection, Box 13, File 5, llbadan, Nigeria. For further discussion of the struggle between Pelewura and Pullen, see *Daily Service* newspaper for September 23, 1942, National Archives, Ibadan, and Colonial Secretary's Office Files #2516 and #2686, National Archives, Ibadan.

19   For more information on Abayomi, see Cheryl Johnson-Odim, 'Lady Oyinkan Abayomi: A Profile,' in Bolanie Awe, ed., *Nigerian Women in Historical Perspective* (Lagos, Nigeria: Sankore Publishers, 1992).

20   The most radical Nigerian woman of the colonial period was certainly Funmilayo Ransome-Kuti. For her story and that of the Abeokuta Women's Union that she founded see Johnson-Odim, 'On Behalf of Women and the Nation'; Johnson-Odim and Mba, *For Women and the Nation*.

21   *Daily Service* newspaper, May 11, 1944, National Archives, Ibadan, Nigeria.

22   The NWP's Constitution was among the private papers of Tinuola Dedeke in Lagos, Nigeria. I am uncertain as to what happened to this collection following her death in the 1990s. The Constitution is also cited in Johnson-Odim, 'Nigerian Women and British Colonialism,' and in Mba, *Nigerian Women Mobilized*.

23   For details, see Johnson-Odim, 'Lady Oyinkan Abayomi.' The bulk of the research on which this chapter is based was done in Lagos, Ibadan, and Abeokuta, Nigeria, in 1975–6 and in 1989. I used several Nigerian newspapers, particularly the *Daily Service, Daily Times*, and *West African Pilot*; the Colonial Secretary's Office Files and the Commissioner of the Colony Files at the National Archives, Ibadan; the Macaulay Papers Collection at the University of Ibadan Manuscripts Collection; the private papers of Tinuola Dedeke and Funmilayo Ransome-Kuti (the Ransome-Kuti papers are available at the University of Ibadan Library); and interviews with Oyinkan Abayomi, Tinuola Dedeke, and Funmilayo Ransome-Kuti, For additional references, please refer to Johnson-Odim, 'Nigerian Women and British Colonialism.'

Chandra Talpade Mohanty

'UNDER WESTERN EYES'
REVISITED
Feminist solidarity through anticapitalist struggles

Chandra Talpade Mohanty is an acclaimed feminist theorist who has worked extensively on transnational feminisms and the legacy of colonialism, co-editing two important collections – *Third World Women and the Politics of Feminism* (1991) and *Feminist Genealogies, Colonial Legacies, Democratic Futures* (1997). This reading is taken from her most recent anthology *Feminism Without Borders: Decolonizing Theory, Practicing Solidarity* (2003). '"Under Western Eyes" Revisited' identifies several points at which Mohanty is rethinking the theoretical project of decolonisation twenty years after she first wrote her classic article 'Under Western Eyes' (1986). Whereas she initially sought to expose the false universalisation of western feminist narratives and prioritise 'difference' as a theoretical and political tool, she now finds herself 'wanting to reemphasise the connections between local and universal' and to articulate women's potential to build new connections, commonalities and solidarities across borders. This shift in Mohanty's emphasis has been brought about by the urgent context of a development that Antoinette Burton warned about in Reading 26, namely, increasingly oppressive forms of western global capitalism. These have exacerbated racist, patriarchal and heterosexist relations in ways that demand, for Mohanty, the organisation of an anticapitalist transnational feminist practice. In order to analyse the operations of capitalism she advocates a historical materialist approach that is located firmly within the communities of Third World/South women. As it is 'on the bodies and lives of women and girls from the Third World/South . . . that global capitalism writes its script' most particularly, Mohanty argues, so it is that anticapitalist feminist theorising should begin with the struggles and experiences of these disenfranchised groups. The standpoint of these women provides 'the most inclusive viewing of systemic power' she contends and therefore the most expansive vision of social justice. Finally, Mohanty sets out an important manifesto for feminist history in this extract, proposing a 'feminist solidarity or comparative feminist studies' model of pedagogy that prioritises mutuality and common interests between women and the need to formulate questions about connection and disconnection that range across the borders of nation and culture.

[. . .]

Decolonizing feminist scholarship: 1986

I WROTE 'UNDER WESTERN EYES' to discover and articulate a critique of 'Western feminist' scholarship on Third World women via the discursive colonization of Third World women's lives and struggles. I also wanted to expose the power-knowledge nexus of feminist cross-cultural scholarship expressed through Eurocentric, falsely universalizing methodologies that serve the narrow self-interest of Western feminism. As well, I thought it crucial to highlight the connection between feminist scholarship and feminist political organizing while drawing attention to the need to examine the 'political implications of our analytic strategies and principles.' I also wanted to chart the location of feminist scholarship within a global political and economic framework dominated by the 'First World.'

[. . .]

In 1986 I wrote mainly to challenge the false universality of Eurocentric discourses and was perhaps not sufficiently critical of the valorization of difference over commonality in postmodernist discourse. Now I find myself wanting to re-emphasize the connections between local and universal. In 1986 my priority was on difference, but now I want to recapture and reiterate its fuller meaning, which was always there, and that is its connection to the universal. In other words, this discussion allows me to reemphasize the way that differences are never just 'differences.' In knowing differences and particularities, we can better see the connections and commonalities because no border or boundary is ever complete or rigidly determining. The challenge is to see how differences allow us to explain the connections and border crossings better and more accurately, how specifying difference allows us to theorize universal concerns more fully. It is this intellectual move that allows for my concern for women of different communities and identities to build coalitions and solidarities across borders.

So what has changed and what remains the same for me? What are the urgent intellectual and political questions for feminist scholarship and organizing at this time in history? First, let me say that the terms 'Western' and 'Third World' retain a political and explanatory value in a world that appropriates and assimilates multi-culturalism and 'difference' through commodification and consumption. However, these are not the only terms I would choose to use now. With the United States, the European Community, and Japan as the nodes of capitalist power in the early twenty-first century, the increasing proliferation of Third and Fourth Worlds within the national borders of these very countries, as well as the rising visibility and struggles for sovereignty by First Nations/indigenous peoples around the world, 'Western' and 'Third World' explain much less than the categorizations 'North/ South' or 'One-Third/Two-Thirds Worlds.'

[. . .]

[N]ow, as in my earlier writings, I straddle both categories. I am of the Two-Thirds World in the One-Third World. I am clearly a part of the social minority now, with all its privileges; however, my political choices, struggles and visions for change place me alongside the Two-Thirds World. Thus I am for the Two-Thirds World, but with the privileges of the One-Third World. I speak as a person situated in the One-Thirds World, but from the space and vision of, and in solidarity with, communities in struggle in the Two-Thirds World.

Under and (inside) Western eyes: at the turn of the century

[. . .]

The politics of feminist cross-cultural scholarship from the vantage point of Third World/South feminist struggles remains a compelling site of analysis for me. Eurocentric analytic paradigms continue to flourish, and I remain committed to reengaging in the struggles to criticize openly the effects of discursive colonization on the lives and struggles of marginalized women. My central commitment is to build connections between feminist scholarship and political organizing. My own present-day analytic framework remains very similar to my earliest critique of Eurocentrism. However, I now see the politics and economics of capitalism as a far more urgent locus of struggle. I continue to hold to an analytic framework that is attentive to the micropolitics of everyday life as well as to the macropolitics of global economic and political processes. The link between political economy and culture remains crucial to any form of feminist theorizing – as it does for my work. It isn't the framework that has changed. It is just that global economic and political processes have become more brutal, exacerbating economic, racial, and gender inequalities, and thus they need to be demystified, reexamined, and theorized.

While my earlier focus was on the distinctions between 'Western' and 'Third World' feminist practices, and while I downplayed the commonalities between these two positions, my focus now is on what I have chosen to call an anticapitalist transnational feminist practice – and on the possibilities, indeed on the necessities, of cross-national feminist solidarity and organizing against capitalism. While 'Under Western Eyes' was located in the context of the critique of Western humanism and Eurocentrism and of white, Western feminism, a similar essay written now would need to be located in the context of the critique of global capitalism (on anti-globalization), the naturalization of the values of capital, and the unacknowledged power of cultural relativism in cross-cultural feminist scholarship and pedagogies.

'Under Western Eyes' sought to make the operations of discursive power visible, to draw attention to what was left out of feminist theorizing, namely, the material complexity, reality, and agency of Third World women's bodies and lives. This is in fact exactly the analytic strategy I now use to draw attention to what is unseen, undertheorized, and left out in the production of knowledge about globalization. While globalization has always been a part of capitalism, and capitalism is not a new phenomenon, at this time I believe the theory, critique, and activism around antiglobalization has to be a key focus for feminists. This does not mean that the patriarchal and racist relations and structures that accompany capitalism are any less problematic at this time, or that antiglobalization is a singular phenomenon. Along with many other scholars and activists, I believe capital as it functions now depends on and exacerbates racist, patriarchal, and heterosexist relations of rule.

Feminist methodologies: new directions

What kinds of feminist methodology and analytic strategy are useful in making power (and women's lives) visible in overtly nongendered, nonracialized discourses? The strategy discussed here is an example of how capitalism and its various relations of rule can be analyzed through a transnational, anticapitalist feminist critique, one that draws on historical materialism and centralizes racialized gender. This analysis begins from and is anchored in the place of the most marginalized communities of women – poor women of all colors in affluent and neocolonial nations; women of the Third World/South or the Two-Thirds World. I believe that this experiential and analytic anchor in the lives of marginalized communities of women provides the most inclusive paradigm for thinking about social justice. This particularized viewing allows for a more concrete and expansive vision of universal justice.

This is the very opposite of 'special interest' thinking. If we pay attention to and think from the space of some of the most disenfranchised communities of women in the world, we are most likely to envision a just and democratic society capable of treating all its citizens fairly. Conversely, if we begin our analysis from, and limit it to, the space of privileged communities, our visions of justice are more likely to be exclusionary because privilege nurtures blindness to those without the same privileges. Beginning from the lives and interests of marginalized communities of women, I am able to access and make the workings of power visible – to read up the ladder of privilege. It is more necessary to look upward – colonized peoples must know themselves and the colonizer. This particular marginalized location makes the politics of knowledge and the power investments that go along with it visible so that we can then engage in work to transform the use and abuse of power. [. . .] I believe there are causal links between marginalized social locations and experiences and the ability of human agents to explain and analyze features of capitalist society. Methodologically, this analytic perspective is grounded in historical materialism. My claim is not that all marginalized locations yield crucial knowledge about power and inequity, but that within a tightly integrated capitalist system, the particular standpoint of poor indigenous and Third World/South women provides the most inclusive viewing of systemic power. In numerous cases of environmental racism, for instance, where the neighborhoods of poor communities of color are targeted as new sites for prisons and toxic dumps, it is no coincidence that poor black, Native American, and Latina women provide the leadership in the fight against corporate pollution. Three out of five Afro-Americans and Latinos live near toxic waste sites, and three of the five largest hazardous waste landfills are in communities with a population that is 80 percent people of color. Thus, it is precisely their critical reflections on their everyday lives as poor women of color that allow the kind of analysis of the power structure that has led to the many victories in environmental racism struggles. Herein lies a lesson for feminist analysis.

[. . .]

Women and girls are still 70 percent of the world's poor and the majority of the world's refugees. Girls and women comprise almost 80 percent of displaced persons of the Third World/South in Africa, Asia and Latin America. Women own less than one-hundredth of the world's property, while they are the hardest hit by the effects of war, domestic violence, and religious persecution. Feminist political theorist Zillah Eisenstein says that women do two-thirds of the world's work and earn less than one-tenth of its income. Global capital in racialized and sexualized guise destroys the public spaces of democracy, and quietly sucks power out of the once social/public spaces of nation states. Corporate capitalism has redefined citizens as consumers – and global markets replace the commitments to economic, sexual, and racial equality.

It is especially on the bodies and lives of women and girls from the Third World/South – the Two-Thirds World – that global capitalism writes its script, and it is by paying attention to and theorizing the experiences of these communities of women and girls that we demystify capitalism as a system of debilitating sexism and racism and envision anticapitalist resistance. Thus any analysis of the effects of globalization needs to centralize the experiences and struggles of these particular communities of women and girls.

[. . .]

Antiglobalization struggles

Although the context for writing 'Under Western Eyes' in the mid-1980s was a visible and activist women's movement, this radical movement no longer exists as such. Instead, I draw inspiration from a more distant, but significant, antiglobalization movement in the United States and around the world. Activists in these movements are often women, although the movement is not gender-focused. So I wish to redefine the project of decolonization, not reject it. It appears more complex to me today, given the newer developments of global capitalism. Given the complex interweaving of cultural forms, people of and from the Third World live not only under Western eyes but also within them. This shift in my focus from 'under Western eyes' to 'under and inside' the hegemonic spaces of the one-Third World necessitates recrafting the project of decolonization.

My focus is thus no longer just the colonizing effects of Western feminist scholarship. This does not mean the problems I identified in the earlier essay do not occur now. But the phenomenon I addressed then has been more than adequately engaged by other feminist scholars. While feminists have been involved in the antiglobalization movement from the start, however, this has not been a major organizing locus for women's movements nationally in the West/North. It has, however, always been a locus of struggle for women of the Third World/South because of their location. Again, this contextual specificity should constitute the larger vision. Women of the Two-Thirds World have always organized against the devastations of globalized capital, just as they have always historically organized anticolonial and antiracist movements. In this sense they have always spoken for humanity as a whole. [. . .]

Antiglobalization pedagogies

Let me turn to the struggles over the dissemination of a feminist cross-cultural knowledge base through pedagogical strategies 'internationalizing' the women's studies curriculum. [. . .]

[T]he question I want to foreground is the politics of knowledge in bridging the 'local' and the 'global' in women's studies. [. . .] After all, the way we construct curricula and the pedagogies we use to put such curricula into place tell a story — or tell many stories. It is the way we position historical narratives of experience in relation to each other, the way we theorize relationality as both historical and simultaneously singular and collective that determines how and what we learn when we cross-cultural and experiential borders.

Drawing on my own work with U.S. feminist academic communities, I describe three pedagogical models used in 'internationalizing' the women's studies curriculum and analyze the politics of knowledge at work. Each of these perspectives is grounded in particular conceptions of the local and the global, of women's agency, and of national identity, and each curricular model presents different stories and ways of crossing borders and building bridges. I suggest that a 'comparative feminist studies' or 'feminist solidarity' model is the most useful and productive pedagogical strategy for feminist cross-cultural work. It is this particular model that provides a way to theorize a complex relational understanding of experience, location, and history such that feminist cross-cultural work moves through the specific context to construct a real notion of universal and of democratization rather than colonization. It is through this model that we can put into practice the idea of 'common differences' as the basis for deeper solidarity across differences and unequal power relations.

Feminist-as-Tourist Model. This curricular perspective could also be called the 'feminist as international consumer' or, in less charitable terms, the 'white women's burden or colonial discourse' model. It involves a pedagogical strategy in which brief forays are made into non-Euro-American cultures, and particular sexist cultural practices addressed from an otherwise Eurocentric women's studies gaze. In other words, the 'add women as global victims or powerful women and stir' perspective. This is a perspective in which the primary Euro-American narrative of the syllabus remains untouched, and examples from non-Western or Third World/South cultures are used to supplement and 'add' to this narrative. The story here is quite old. The effects of this strategy are that students and teachers are left with a clear sense of the difference and distance between the local (defined as self, nation, and Western) and the global (defined as other, non-Western, and transnational). Thus the local is always grounded in nationalist assumptions – the United States or Western European nation state provides a normative context. This strategy leaves power relations and hierarchies untouched since ideas about center and margin are reproduced along Eurocentric lines.

For example, in an introductory feminist studies course, one could include the obligatory day or week on dowry deaths in India, women workers in Nike factories in Indonesia, or precolonial matriarchies in West Africa, while leaving the fundamental identity of the Euro-American feminist on her way to liberation untouched. Thus Indonesian workers in Nike factories or dowry deaths in India stand in for the totality of women in these cultures. These women are not seen in their everyday lives (as Euro-American women are) just in these stereotypical terms. Difference in the case of non-Euro-American women is thus congealed, not seen contextually with all of its contradictions. This pedagogical strategy for crossing cultural and geographical borders is based on a modernist paradigm, and the bridge between the local and the global becomes in fact a predominantly self-interested chasm. This perspective confirms the sense of the 'evolved U.S./Euro feminist.' While there is now more consciousness about not using an 'add and stir' method in teaching about race and U.S. women of color, this does not appear to be the case in 'internationalizing' women's studies. Experience in this context is assumed to be static and frozen into U.S. or Euro-centered categories. Since in this paradigm feminism is always/already constructed as Euro-American in origin and development, women's lives and struggles outside this geographical context only serve to confirm or contradict this originary feminist (master) narrative. This model is the pedagogical counterpart of the orientalizing and colonizing Western feminist scholarship of the past decades. In fact it may remain the predominant model at this time. Thus implicit in this pedagogical strategy is the crafting of the 'Third World difference,' the creation of monolithic images of Third World/South women. This contrasts with images of Euro-American women who are vital, changing, complex, and central subjects within such a curricular perspective.

Feminist-as-Explorer Model. This particular pedagogical perspective originates in area studies, where the 'foreign' woman is the object and subject of knowledge and the larger intellectual project is entirely about countries other than the United States. Thus, here the local and the global are both defined as non-Euro-American. The focus on the international implies that it exists outside the U.S. nation state. Women's, gender, and feminist issues are based on spatial/geographical and temporal/historical categories located elsewhere. Distance from 'home' is fundamental to the definition of international in this framework. This strategy can result in students and teachers being left with a notion of difference and separateness, a sort of 'us and them' attitude, but unlike the tourist model, the explorer perspective can provide a deeper, more contextual understanding of feminist issues in discretely defined geographical and cultural spaces. However, unless these discrete spaces are taught in relation to one another, the story told is usually a cultural relativist one, meaning that differences between cultures are discrete and relative with no real connection or common basis for evaluation. The local and the global are here collapsed into the international that by definition excludes the United States. If the dominant discourse is the discourse of cultural relativism, questions of power, agency, justice, and common criteria for critique and evaluation are silenced.

In women's studies curricula this pedagogical strategy is often seen as the most culturally sensitive way to 'internationalize' the curriculum. For instance, entire courses on 'Women in Latin America' or 'Third World Women's Literature' or 'Postcolonial Feminism' are added on to the predominantly U.S.-based curriculum as away to 'globalize' the feminist knowledge base. These courses can be quite sophisticated and complex studies, but they are viewed as entirely separate from the intellectual project of U.S. race and ethnic studies. The United States is not seen as part of 'area studies,' as white is not a color when one speaks of people of color. [. . .]

The problem with the feminist-as-explorer strategy is that globalization is an economic, political, and ideological phenomenon that actively brings the world and its various communities under connected and interdependent discursive and material regimes. The lives of women are connected and interdependent, albeit not the same, no matter which geographical area we happen to live in.

Separating area studies from race and ethnic studies thus leads to understanding or teaching about the global as a way of not addressing internal racism, capitalist hegemony, colonialism, and heterosexualization as central to processes of global domination, exploitation, and resistance. Global or international is thus understood apart from racism – as if racism were not central to processes of globalization and relations of rule at this time. An example of this pedagogical strategy in the context of the larger curriculum is the usual separation of 'world cultures' courses from race and ethnic studies courses. Thus identifying the kinds of representations of (non-Euro-American) women mobilized by this pedagogical strategy, and the relation of these representations to implicit images of First World/North women are important foci for analysis. What kind of power is being exercised in this strategy? What kinds of ideas of agency and struggle are being consolidated? What are the potential effects of a kind of cultural relativism on our understandings of the differences and commonalities among communities of women around the world? Thus the feminist-as-explorer model has its own problems, and I believe this is an inadequate way of building a feminist cross-cultural knowledge base because in the context of an interwoven world with clear directionalities of power and domination, cultural relativism serves as an apology for the exercise of power.

The Feminist Solidarity or Comparative Feminist Studies Model. This curricular strategy is based on the premise that the local and the global are not defined in terms of physical geography or territory but exist simultaneously and constitute each other. It is then the links, the relationships, between the local and the global that are foregrounded, and these links are conceptual, material, temporal, contextual, and so on. This framework assumes a comparative focus and analysis of the directionality of power no matter what the subject of the women's studies course is – and it assumes both distance and proximity (specific/universal) as its analytic strategy.

Differences and commonalities thus exist in relation and tension with each other in all contexts. What is emphasized are relations of mutuality, co-responsibility, and common interests, anchoring the idea of feminist solidarity. For example, within this model, one would not teach a U.S. women of color course with additions on Third World/South or white women, but a comparative course that shows the interconnectedness of the histories, experiences, and struggles of U.S. women of color, white women, and women from the Third World/South. By doing this kind of comparative teaching that is attentive to power, each historical experience illuminates the experiences of the others. Thus, the focus is not just on the intersections of race, class, gender, nation, and sexuality in different communities of women but on mutuality and coimplication, which suggests attentiveness to the interweaving of the histories of these communities. In addition the focus is simultaneously on individual and collective experiences of oppression and exploitation and of struggle and resistance.

Students potentially move away from the 'add and stir' and the relativist 'separate but equal' (or different) perspective to the coimplication/solidarity one. This solidarity perspective requires understanding the historical and experiential specificities and differences of women's lives as well as the historical and experiential connections between women from different national, racial, and cultural communities. Thus it suggests organizing syllabi around social and economic processes and histories of various communities of women in particular substantive areas like sex work, militarization, environmental justice, the prison/industrial complex, and human rights, and looking for points of contact and connection as well as disjunctures. It is important to always foreground not just the connections of domination but those of struggle and resistance as well. [. . .]

I refer to this model as the feminist solidarity model because, besides its focus on mutuality and common interests, it requires one to formulate questions about connection and disconnection between activist women's movements around the world. Rather than formulating activism and agency in terms of discrete and disconnected cultures and nations, it allows us to frame agency and resistance across the borders of nation and culture. [. . .]

Feminist pedagogies of internationalization need an adequate response to globalization. Both Eurocentric and cultural relativist (postmodernist) models of scholarship and teaching are easily assimilated within the logic of late capitalism because this is fundamentally a logic of seeming decentralization and accumulation of differences. What I call the comparative feminist studies/feminist solidarity model on the other hand potentially counters this logic by setting up a paradigm of historically and culturally specific 'common differences' as the basis for analysis and solidarity. Feminist pedagogies of antiglobalization can tell alternate stories of difference, culture, power, and agency. They can begin to theorize experience, agency, and justice from a more cross-cultural lens. [. . .]

Antiglobalization scholarship and movements

[. . .] Women workers of particular caste/class, race, and economic status are necessary to the operation of the capitalist global economy. Women are not only the preferred candidates for particular jobs, but particular kinds of women – poor, Third and Two-Thirds World, working-class, and immigrant/migrant women – are the preferred workers in these global, 'flexible' temporary job markets. The documented increase in the migration of poor, One-Third/Two-Thirds World women in search of labor across national borders has led to a rise in the international 'maid trade' and in international sex trafficking and tourism. Many global cities now require and completely depend on the service and domestic labor of immigrant and migrant women. The proliferation of structural adjustment policies around the world has reprivatized women's labor by shifting the responsibility for social welfare from the state to the household and to women located there. The rise of religious fundamentalisms in conjunction with conservative nationalisms, which are also in part reactions to global capital and its cultural demands has led to the policing of women's bodies in the streets and in the workplaces.

[. . .]

While feminist scholarship is moving in important and useful directions in terms of a critique of global restructuring and the culture of globalization, I want to ask some of the same questions I posed in 1986 once again. In spite of the occasional exception, I think that much of present-day scholarship tends to reproduce particular 'globalized' representations of women. Just as there is an Anglo-American masculinity produced in and by discourses of globalization, it is important to ask what the corresponding femininities being produced are. Clearly there is the ubiquitous global teenage girl factory worker, the domestic worker, and the sex worker. There is also the migrant/immigrant service worker, the refugee, the victim of war crimes, the woman-of-color prisoner who happens to be a mother and drug user, the consumer-housewife, and so on. There is also the mother-of-the-nation/ religious bearer of traditional culture and morality.

Although these representations of women correspond to real people, they also often stand in for the contradictions and complexities of women's lives and roles. Certain images, such as that of the factory or sex worker, are often geographically located in the Third World/South, but many of the representations identified above are dispersed throughout the globe. Most refer to women of the Two-Thirds World, and some to women of the One-Third World. And a woman from the Two-Thirds World can live in the One-Third World. The point I am making here is that women are workers, mothers, or consumers in the global economy, but we are also all those things simultaneously. Singular and monolithic categorizations of women in discourses of globalization circumscribe ideas about experience, agency, and struggle. While there are other, relatively new images of women that also emerge in this discourse – the human rights worker or the NGO advocate, the revolutionary militant and the corporate bureaucrat – there is also a divide between false, overstated images of victimized and empowered womanhood, and they negate each other. We need to further explore how this divide plays itself out in terms of a social majority/minority, One-Third/Two-Thirds World characterization. The concern here is with whose agency is being colonized and who is privileged in these pedagogies and scholarship. These then are my new queries for the twenty-first century. [. . .]

While women are present as leaders and participants in most of these antiglobalization movements, a feminist agenda only emerges in the post-Beijing 'women's rights as human rights' movement and in some peace and environmental justice movements. In other words, while girls and women are central to the labor of global capital, antiglobalization work does not seem to draw on feminist analysis or strategies. Thus while I have argued that feminists need to be anticapitalists, I would now argue that antiglobalization activists and theorists also need to be feminists. Gender is ignored as a category of analysis and a basis for organizing in most of the antiglobalization movements, and antiglobalization (and anticapitalist critique) does not appear to be central to feminist organizing projects, especially in the First World/North. In terms of women's movements, the earlier 'sisterhood is global' form of internationalization of the women's movement has now shifted into the 'human rights' arena. This shift in language from 'feminism' to 'women's rights' has been called the mainstreaming of the feminist movement – a successful attempt to raise the issue of violence against women to the world stage. [. . .]

Women have been in leadership roles in some of the cross-border alliances against corporate injustice. Thus, making gender, and women's bodies and labor visible, and theorizing this visibility as a process of articulating a more inclusive politics are crucial aspects of feminist anticapitalist critique. Beginning from the social location of poor women of color of the Two-Thirds World is an important, even crucial, place for feminist analysis; it is precisely the potential epistemic privilege of these communities of women that opens up the space for demystifying capitalism and for envisioning transborder social and economic justice.

The masculinization of the discourses of globalization [. . .] seems to be matched by the implicit masculinization of the discourses of antiglobalization movements. While much of the literature on antiglobalization movements marks the centrality of class and race and, at times, nation in the critique and fight against global capitalism, racialized gender is still an unmarked category. Racialized gender is significant in this instance because capitalism utilizes the raced and sexed bodies of women in its search for profit globally, and, as I argued earlier, it is often the experiences and struggles of poor women of color that allow the most inclusive analysis as well as politics in antiglobalization struggles. [. . .]

The critique and resistance to global capitalism, and uncovering of the naturalization of its masculinist and racist values, begin to build a transnational feminist practice.

A transnational feminist practice depends on building feminist solidarities across the divisions of place, identity, class, work, belief, and so on. In these very fragmented times it is both very difficult to build these alliances and also never more important to do so. Global capitalism both destroys the possibilities and also offers up new ones.

Feminist activist teachers must struggle with themselves and each other to open the world with all its complexity to their students. Given the new multi-ethnic racial student bodies, teachers must also learn from their students. The differences and borders of each of our identities connect us to each other, more than they sever. So the enterprise here is to forge informed, self-reflexive solidarities among ourselves.

I no longer live simply under the gaze of Western eyes. I also live inside it and negotiate it every day. I make my home in Ithaca, New York, but always as from Mumbai, India. My cross-race and cross-class work takes me to interconnected places and communities around the world – to a struggle contextualized by women of color and of the Third World, sometimes located in the Two-Thirds World, sometimes in the One-Third. So the borders here are not really fixed. Our minds must be as ready to move as capital is, to trace its paths and to imagine alternative destinations.

Afterword

Joan W. Scott

FEMINISM'S HISTORY

'Have we won or lost?' 'Has our presence transformed the discipline or have we simply been absorbed into it?' 'Does women's history have a future . . . [a]nd how might we imagine that future?' These are some of the questions posed in the Afterword to this *Reader*, which is taken from a roundtable discussion on 'The Future of Women's History: Feminism's History', published in the *Journal of Women's History* in 2004. Joan Scott's reflective and thought-provoking essay takes a retrospective look at the last few decades of feminist history within an American context and critically assesses the gains and losses made. Not unlike Judith Bennett in Reading 2, Scott views the impact of the institutionalisation of feminist history as a somewhat ambiguous one, the source of both tremendous success and corresponding melancholy, as the heady days of early political struggles become part of history themselves, and as radical insurgency is exchanged for academic credibility. The critical edge that came from being on the margins thirty years ago, admits Scott, has now been dulled through the inclusion of feminist and gender scholarship into mainstream academe. Feminists now work in heterosocial as opposed to homosocial worlds and the field itself no longer propounds 'a grand teleological narrative of emancipation'. Indeed, as this *Reader* has shown throughout, it has already been examined and found wanting by the next wave of feminists, by queer, postcolonial and ethnic studies. But this is not the end of the story! For Scott, feminism has always been, at heart, a critical operation 'that uses the past to disrupt the certainties of the present and so opens the way to imagining a different future'. This desire to continuously defamiliarise the historians' terrain is driven by a sense of dissatisfaction and restlessness that characterises the feminist critical spirit, moving in unexpected directions to work with and against prevailing foundational assumptions. This continued critical interrogation of categories (including that of feminism itself), a radical openness of mind and a preparedness to follow (or fly as the Muses did) wherever future historical debates might take us is, for Scott, the open-ended future of feminist history. 'Passion, after all, thrives on the pursuit of the not-yet-known.'

I N 1974, LOIS BANNER and Mary Hartman published a book of essays they called *Clio's Consciousness Raised*.[1] Consisting of papers from the 1973 Berkshire Conference on Women's History, it was a rallying cry for many of us, an assertion of our intention to make women proper objects of historical study. If the Muse of History had too long sung the praises of men ('glorifying the countless mighty deeds of ancient times for the instruction of posterity'[2]), it was time now to bestow a similar glory on women. The second of the nine daughters of Zeus and Mnnemosyne (Memory), Clio's special province was history (and according to some accounts also epic poetry – a version of history). Our challenge to her seemed simple: to make women's stories central to the memory she transmitted to mortal humans. In order to ease her task, we would supply the materials she needed: histories of the lives and activities of women in the past. [. . .]

Our goal was not so much to compete with Clio as to emulate her, although there is always an element of competition in such identification. Like her, we wanted to tell edifying stories whose import went beyond their literal content to reveal some larger truth about human relationships – in our case, about gender and power. Like her, we wanted to be recognized as the just source of those stories, although for us there was no classical myth to authorize the claim. Like her, too, we wanted all of history as our province: we were not just adding women to an existing body of stories, we were changing the way the stories would be told. In our identification with Clio, we revealed the double aspect of our feminist project: to change the discipline fundamentally by writing women into history and by taking our rightful place as historians.

The last several decades have seen the realization of both these aims. Of course the achievement is not perfect; neither women's history nor women historians are fully equal players in the discipline and we have by no means rewritten all the stories. Indeed, the temporal and geographic unevenness of our accomplishment – far greater success in Euro-American modern history than in ancient, medieval, early Modern, and non-Western history; far more success in introducing women into the picture than in reconceiving it in terms of gender – suggests there is more to be done. Still, the gains are undeniable. Unlike Clio, we cannot punish those who would deny our accomplishment, nor can we be only amused by the folly of those brothers of Prometheus who claim to be the real innovators, treating us as imitators or usurpers. (We still get angry.) We can, however, point to an enormous corpus of writing, an imposing institutional presence, a substantial list of journals, and a foothold in popular consciousness that was unimaginable when Banner and Hartman published their book almost thirty years ago. If we have not taken over history, we have claimed a portion of the field; once viewed as transgressors, we are now in possession of legitimate title.

But ownership, for those who began as revolutionaries, is always an ambiguous accomplishment. It is at once a victory and a sell-out, the triumph of critique and its abandonment. This is difficult for feminists who, despite all the derision cast upon them by socialists in the nineteenth and twentieth centuries, have been revolutionaries dedicated to overturning patriarchy, breaking the oppressive chains of sexism, liberating women from the stereotypes that confine them, and bringing them onto the stage of history. The realization of at least some positive change over the past decade – which I have just characterized for historians as gaining ownership of a piece of the field – has produced some ambivalence and uncertainty about the future. Have we won or lost? Have we been changed by our success? What does the move from embattled outsider to recognized insider portend for our sense of self? Has our presence transformed the discipline or have we simply been absorbed into it? Ought we to be content with maintaining and reproducing what we have gained? Or should we be responding to new challenges that may threaten our proprietary standing? Does women's history have a future, or is it history? And how might we imagine that future? [. . .]

Why would the future of a successful movement be so difficult to envision? In some ways we already know the answer – it is a form of social movement analysis. An aging generation of feminist scholar-activists looks back nostalgically on its wild youth, wondering (but not daring to ask aloud) if all the gains we have made were worth it. The institutionalization of women's history means its end as a campaign. Our research and professional activities seem to have lost their purposive political edge and their sense of dedication to building something larger than an individual career. The community of feminist scholars, whose vitality was manifest in fierce divisions no less than in shared commitments, seems diffused now. And at least among historians of women, the theoretical and political stakes no longer seem as high, disagreements seem more personal or generational. If there is relief at the end of the need to conspire in late-night strategy sessions, to have constantly to justify one's scholarship and that of one's students to skeptical or hostile colleagues, and to take pleasure, too, in the quantity, quality, and diversity of work produced under the rubric of women's history, there is nonetheless a sense of loss. For many of us, being embattled was energizing – it elicited strategic and intellectual creativity unmatched by our earlier graduate school experiences. Aspiring to be Clio, we became a subversive version of her: activism confirmed agency. We were producers of new knowledge, transmitters of revised memory, fashioning tales to inspire ourselves and the generations to come – all in the face of opponents more formidable than the Pierides or the Sirens, opponents who had the power to discipline us for what they took to be our pretensions and misdeeds. From insurgents, we have now become disciplinarians and it is inevitable, I think, that there is something of a let down in this exchange of subject identities. It is one thing to criticize disciplinary power from the outside, but quite another to be on the inside, committed to the teaching of established bodies of scholarship. That kind of teaching necessarily seeks to reproduce feminist history in rising generations of students, but it is often resistant to the kind of critical challenges that were its defining characteristic.

As academic feminism has gained institutional credibility, it has also seemed to lose its close connection to the political movement that inspired it. In the 1970s and 1980s, we were the knowledge-producing arm of a broad-based feminist movement devoted to radical social change. During the 1990s, there were critical attacks on, and guilt-ridden condemnations of, the diminished contact between scholars and the grassroots, as well as injunctions to maintain or rebuild those ties. But that effort has foundered, not (as is sometimes alleged) because feminist scholars have retreated to ivory towers (the opposition between academic and political feminism was always a mischaracterization), but because the political movement itself has become fragmented, dispersed into specific areas of activism. This does not mean, as some journalists have claimed, that feminism is dead. Rather, concerns about the status and condition of different kinds of women have infiltrated many more realms of law and policy than was the case at the height of the movement, just as questions about gender have bled into areas of study that were resistant to feminism in the early days of women's studies.[3]

Discontinuous, coordinated, strategic operations with other groups have replaced the sense of a continuous struggle on behalf of women represented as a singular entity. This change is tied to the loss of a grand teleological narrative of emancipation, one that allowed us to conceive of the cumulative effect of our efforts: freedom and equality were the inevitable outcomes of human struggle, we believed, and that belief gave coherence to our actions, defined us as participants in a pro-gressive 'movement.' (We were on the side of redemptive history.) Although discontinuity and dispersed strategic operations are eminently political in nature (and for a younger generation, a familiar way of operating), the loss of the conti-nuity that came with the notion of history as inevitably progressive helps explain the difficulty an older generation has in imagining a future. (They take discontinuity to be regressive – the opposite of progressive, which it was for those who watched fascism in Europe destroy liberal institutions in the 1930s – when, in fact, now in the twenty-first-century context, discontinuity seems to me to be more closely allied to radical (left) critiques.)

Another aspect of the successful institutionalization of women's history is the dulling of the critical edge that comes with being on the margin. There was much debate in the 1980s (perhaps a bit more among literary scholars than historians) about the ultimate benefits of integration. Was the absence of women in the curriculum simply a gap in knowledge that needed to be filled? Or did it reveal something more perni-cious about the patriarchal (or phallocentric) organization of knowledge itself? What kind of impact would women's studies have on the university? Would we simply provide information now lacking, or change the very nature of what counted as knowledge? And were these necessarily contradictory aims? 'As long as women's studies doesn't question the existing model of the university,' Jacques Derrida told a meeting of the Pembroke Center seminar in 1984, 'it risks to be just another cell in the university beehive.'[4] Some insisted that, by definition, a feminine presence (in history textbooks and history departments from which women were usually excluded) was a subversion of the status quo. Wasn't 'becoming visible' itself a challenge to the prevailing historical orthodoxy that maintained women's absence from politics and history? Others of us argued that the radical potential of a women's history would be lost without a thoroughgoing critique of the presumptions of the discipline (its notion, for example, that agency is somehow inherent in the wills of individuals; its inattention to language in the construction of subjects and their iden-tities; its lack of reflection on the implicit interpretive powers of narrative). It is significant, I think, that the lively reform-versus-revolution debate has receded from discussions among women's historians. With at least some measure of reform achieved, the troubling questions are more mundane: overspecialization, overpro-duction, and fragmentation, which undermine the cohesiveness of the community of feminist scholars and make impossible any mastery of the entire corpus of women's history. Even those who do share a common reading list are more likely to debate the merits of a particular interpretation than to ask how it advances a feminist critical agenda. Preoccupied with the details of administering programs,

the implementation or adjustment of curricular offerings, the supervision of undergraduate majors, and the placement of doctoral candidates, we imagine the future
as a continuation of the present rather than as liberation from it.

[. . .]

Some of the difficulty we have now in thinking about the future is, I think, a
symptom of melancholy, an unwillingness to let go of the highly charged affect of
the homosocial world we have lost, indeed an unwillingness even to acknowledge
that it has been lost. The melancholic wants to reverse time, to continue living as
before. Melancholia, Freud tells us, is a 'reaction to the loss of a loved person, or
to the loss of some abstraction which has taken the place of one, such as one's
country, liberty, an ideal, and so on.'[5] Unlike mourning, which consciously
addresses the loss, melancholy is an unconconscious process; the lost object is not
understood as such. Instead, the melancholic identifies with the lost object and
displaces her grief and anger onto herself. In the melancholic, 'the shadow of the
object fell upon the ego, and the latter could henceforth be judged . . . as though
it were . . . the forsaken object.'[6] The judgment is harsh, and the normal process
by which sexual energy (libido) is directed to another object is interrupted. Turned
in upon herself, the melancholic dwells only in the past. To be able to think the
future means to be willing to separate oneself from the lost object, avow the loss,
and find a new object for passionate attachment.[7]

There is no question that when women's history came of age, the intensity of
the passion associated with the campaign to secure its legitimacy waned. However
much remains to be done in this unevenly developed field, the early thrills of
discovery do not now drive our work in the same way. For one thing, the world
of history departments (as that of the university more generally) is heterosocial
(even if women's studies programs remain homosocial); our world is no longer
exclusively female. For another, the expansion of the field has brought some remarkable innovation. It is not only that, having heeded the criticism of women of color,
of Third World women, and of lesbians in the 1980s, we have taken differences
among women to be axiomatic; it is also that, having refined our theory we have
increasingly substituted gender for women as the object of our inquiry. The scholarship we produce is thus no longer focused uniquely on women as a singular category.
And this has meant that the satisfying cohesiveness of the movement – women as
subjects and objects of their own history – has disappeared, if indeed it ever existed.
(I will suggest later that this cohesiveness has largely been established retrospec-
tively, as part of the nostalgia of melancholy.)[8]

[. . .]

Feminism's History has been a variable, mutable endeavor, a flexible strategic
instrument not bound to any orthodoxy. The production of knowledge about the
past, while crucial, has not been an end in itself, but rather (at certain moments –
and not always in the service of an organized political movement) has provided the
substantive terms for a critical operation that uses the past to disrupt the certainties of the present and so opens the way to imagining a different future. This critical
operation is the dynamic that drives feminism; in Lacanian terms it is an operation

of desire, unsatisfied by any particular object, 'constant in its pressure,' ever in search of an elusive fulfillment (elusive because attainment of the utopian aim of abolishing sexual difference altogether would mean the death of feminism).[9]

Desire, Lacan tells us, is driven by lack, ruled by dissatisfaction; it is 'unsatisfied, impossible, misconstrued.'[10] Its existence exposes the insufficiency of any conclusive settlement; something more is always wanted. Desire moves metonymically; relations among its objects are characterized by unexpected contiguities. The movements are lateral, and they do not follow a single direction. [. . .]

Conceiving of feminism as a restless critical operation, as a movement of desire, detaches it from its origins in Enlightenment teleologies and the utopian promise of complete emancipation. It does not, however, assume that desire operates outside of time; rather it is a mutating historical phenomenon, defined as and through its displacements. Feminism emerged in the context of liberal democracy's proclamation of universal equality, discursively positioned in and as contradiction – not just in the arena of political citizenship, but in most areas of economic and social life. Despite many changes in the meanings and practices of liberal democracy, its discursive hegemony remains, and feminism remains one of its contradictions. By calling attention to itself as contradiction, feminism has challenged the ways in which differences of sex have been used to organize relations of power. Feminism's historical specificity comes from the fact that it works within and against whatever are the prevailing foundational assumptions of its time. Its critical force comes from the fact that it exposes the contradictions in systems that claim to be coherent (republicanism that excludes women from citizenship; political economy that attributes women's lower wages to their biologically determined lower value as producers; medical teaching that conflates sexual desire with the natural imperatives of reproduction; exclusions within women's movements that press for universal emancipation) and calls into question the validity of categories taken as first principles of social organization (*the* family, *the* individual, *the* worker, masculine, feminine, Man, Woman).[11]

One example from our own times of the critical operation of feminism is the relationship of women's history to social history. It is often said, with a certain sense of inevitability, that women's history became acceptable with the rise to prominence of social history. The emphasis on everyday life, ordinary people, and collective action made women an obvious group to include. I would put it differently: there was nothing inevitable about women's history arising from social history. Rather, feminists argued, within the terms and against the grain of behaviorism and new left Marxism, that women were a necessary consideration for social historians. If they were omitted, key insights were lost about the ways class was constructed. While male historians celebrated the democratic impulses of the nascent working class, historians of women pointed to its gender hierarchies. We did not only correct for the absence of women in labor histories – although we surely did do that (we showed that 'worker' was an exclusionary category; that women were skilled workers, not just a cheap source of labor; that women called strikes and organized unions, were not just members of the ladies' auxiliary) – we also offered a critique of the ways in which labor historians reproduced the machismo of trade unionists. This did not always sit well, indeed feminists found themselves (still find themselves) ghettoized at meetings of labor historians. But there was certain thrill of discovery as we tried to lead our colleagues to unknown territory. In the process, we did convince some of them to consider the ways in which gender consolidated men's identity as workers and as members of a working class, and the ways in which nature was used not only to justify differential treatments of male and female workers, but also to regulate family structure and patterns of employment.

In labor history (as in other areas of history, from diplomatic to cultural), Liz Faue comments, 'women's history has "defamiliarized" the terrain of other historians.' Defamiliarized is exactly right – the meanings taken for granted, the terms by which historians had explained the past, the lists of so-called appropriate topics for historical research, were called into question and shown to be neither as comprehensive nor as objective as was previously believed. What was once unthinkable – that gender was a useful tool of historical analysis – has become thinkable. But that is not the end of the story. Now a received disciplinary category, gender is being critically examined by the next wave of feminists and others, who rightly insist that it is only one of several equally relevant axes of difference. Sex does not subsume race, ethnicity, nationality, or sexuality; these attributions of identity intersect in ways that need to be specified. To restrict our view to sexual difference is thus to miss the always complex ways in which relations of power are signified by differences. The newly safe terrain of gender and women's history is now itself being defamiliarized as queer, postcolonial, and ethnic studies (among others) challenge us to push the boundaries of our knowledge, to slide (or leap?) metonymically to contiguous domains. For some, it seems premature to branch out before we have fully consolidated our gains, but that is the wrong way to think about Feminism's History. The impulse to reproduce what is already known is profoundly conservative, whether it comes from traditional political historians or historians of women. What makes – has made – Feminism's History so exciting is precisely its radical refusal to settle down, to call even a comfortable lodging a 'home.'

Melancholy rests on a fantasy of a home that never really was. Our idealization of the intensely political, woman-oriented moment of recent feminist history and our desire to preserve it (by speaking of it as the essence of women's history) has prevented us from appreciating the excitement and energy of the critical activity that was then and is now the defining characteristic of feminism. Feminist history was never primarily concerned with documenting the experiences of women in the past, even if that was the most visible means by which we pursued our objective. The point of looking to the past was to destabilize the present, to challenge patriarchal institutions and ways of thinking that legitimated themselves as natural, to make the unthinkable thought (to detach gender from sex, for example). In the 1970s and 1980s, women's history was part of a movement that consolidated the identity of women as political subjects, enabling activism in many spheres of society and winning unprecedented public visibility and, eventually, some success. [. . .] Women's status as subjects of history, subject-producers of historical knowledge, and subjects of politics seems to have been secured in principle if not always in practice.

The public acceptance of women's identity as political subjects made redundant the historical construction of that identity – there was nothing new to be championed in this realm. Stories designed to celebrate women's agency began to seem predictable and repetitive, more information garnered to prove a point that had already been made. Moreover, the politics of identity took a melancholic, conservative turn in the last decades of the twentieth century (as Wendy Brown has so persuasively demonstrated).[12] Victims and their injuries came to the fore and, although a good deal of effort was expended on their behalf, the situation of women as wounded subjects does not inspire either creative politics or history. Increasingly, too, differences among women became more difficult to reconcile in a single category, even if it was pluralized. 'Women' (however modified) seemed too much a universalization of white, Western, straight women, not capacious enough a category to alone do the work that considerations of differences among women required. The emergence of new political movements seemed to call for new kinds of political subjects. Singular identities did not work as they once did for the construction of multiple and mutable strategic alliances. In this context, a new generation of feminists turned their critical lens on the construction of identity itself as an historical process. Seeking to defamiliarize identity's contemporary claims, they emphasized the complex ways in which the identity 'women' operates, and not exclusively to signify gender. If race, sexuality, ethnicity, and nationality play equally significant parts in the definition of 'women,' then gender is not a useful enough category of analysis.

But to tell the story as I have implies a singular narrative that actually was not the case. We did not move neatly from identity to gender to a critique of subject formation. Feminism's History in these years is not a story of a unified assault (Clio brandishing gender, singing of women). Even as the identity of 'women' was being consolidated, even as women seemed the primary object of our inquiry, there were critical, conflicting voices pointing out the limits of 'women' and 'gender,' introducing other objects and theorizing different ways of considering the historical significances of sexual difference. Gayle Rubin, in 1975, opening the way for (among other things) the rethinking and historicizing of normative heterosexuality.[13] Natalie Davis cautioning us in 1976 to study not women, but gender groups, and refusing reductive readings of the symbols of masculine and feminine, reminding us of the multiple and complex historical meanings of those categories.[14] The IX Barnard Conference on the Scholar and the Feminist in 1982 blown apart by debates about the place of sex in representations of women's agency.[15] Denise Riley in 1988 suggesting that the category of women was not foundational, but historical.[16] The following year, Ann Snitow pointing out that feminism was divided by irreconcilable desires for both sameness and difference.[17] Evelyn Brooks Higginbotham, looking to escape the totalizing effects of simple oppositions between white and black women, theorizing 'the metalanguage of race' in 1992. 'By fully recognizing race as an unstable, shifting, and strategic reconstruction,' she wrote, 'feminist scholars must take up new challenges to inform and confound many of the assumptions currently underlying Afro-American history and women's history. We must problematize much more of what we take for granted. We must bring to light and to coherence the one and the many that we always were in history and still actually are today.'[18] Afsaneh Najmabadi in 1997 declaring her 'not-so-hidden pleasure at being unable or unwilling to identify myself in [recognizable identity terms] no matter how many times hybridized,' and confounding those terms, too, in her work on gender and nation-building in Iran.[19]

I offer these examples with dates attached not to demonstrate a cumulative process through which our work got smarter or more sophisticated. Precisely the opposite is the case. The critical questioning of prevailing categories of both mainstream and feminist work is consistently present; and its object keeps changing (these are illustrations of the metonymic slippage I referred to earlier). In fact, in a riot of promiscuous exploration [. . .] many objects overlap and coexist (among these are sexuality, race, symbols of masculine and feminine, the changing representation and uses of gender and racial difference, the intersections of race, ethnicity, and gender in the building of nations). It is this critical activity – the relentless interrogation of the taken-for-granted – that always moves us somewhere else, from object to object, from the present to the future. Those accounts that insist that 'women' are (have been and must ever be) the sole subject/object of feminist history tell a highly selective story that obscures the dynamic that makes thinking the future possible. There have been, of course, strenuous efforts at boundary keeping, and these selective stories are among them, but they have been of little avail: heedless of the broken hearts left in its wake, feminist critical desire keeps moving. This is not a betrayal or a defection, but a triumph; it is the way the passion of the feminist critical spirit is kept alive.

I have been arguing that the primary role of feminist history has not been to produce women as subjects but to explore and contest the means and effects of that subject production as it has varied over time and circumstance. To rest content with any identity – even one we have helped produce – is to give up the work of critique. That goes for our identity as historians as well as feminists: having won entry into the profession by exposing its politics of disciplinary formation, it will not do now to settle down and enforce the existing rules, even if we have helped create some of them. It is not a matter of an anarchic refusal of discipline, but a subversive use of its methods and a more self-conscious willingness to entertain topics and approaches that were once considered out of bounds. It is what we do not know that entices us; it is new stories we yearn to tell. Our passion for women's history was a desire to know and to think what had hitherto been unthinkable. Passion, after all, thrives on the pursuit of the not-yet-known.

Interdisciplinarity has been one of ways we have learned to tell new stories. That is why it has been a hallmark of feminist scholarship. Women's studies seminars, programs, and departments have been the proving grounds for the articulation of new knowledge. They have provided sustenance for research considered untenable in traditional departments; legitimation for those who might otherwise have been untenurable. It was questions posed from elsewhere (from outside one's own disciplinary problematic) that often prodded historians (such as myself) to seek unconventional answers; it was the engaged response from other feminist scholars that made the work seem worthwhile. We had at least two things in common: questions about women, gender, and power, and (because simply comparing data about women did not get us very far) a quest for theories that could provide alternative ways of seeing and knowing. 'Theory,' Stuart Hall has famously stated, 'makes meanings slide.'[20] And it was exactly that destabilization of received meaning that was feminism's aim. The exploration of theory (Marxism, psychoanalysis, liberalism, structuralism, poststructuralism) and the attempt to formulate something we could call feminist theory were ways of overcoming disciplinary barriers, finding a common language despite our different academic formations. Although many historians of women, echoing their disciplinary colleagues, worried that theory and history were incompatible, in fact it was 'theory' that enabled the critique of a history that assumed a singular knowing subject (*the* historian) and some topics more worthy of investigation than others. Whether it is now acknowledged or not, some commonly accepted axioms of feminist historical analysis are in fact theoretical insights about how differences are constructed: there is neither a self nor a collective identity without an other (or others); there is no inclusiveness without exclusion; no universal without a rejected particular; no neutrality that does not privilege an interested point of view; and power is always at issue in the articulation of these relationships. Taken as analytic points of departure, these axioms have become the foundation of an ongoing and far-reaching critical historical inquiry.

Feminist history thrives on interdisciplinary encounters. It has incorporated some of the teachings of theory, but it has rightly considered its primary focus to be the discipline of history itself. (After all, it is Clio who turns us on.) The tension between feminism and history (between subversion and establishment) has been difficult and productive, the one pushing the limits of orthodoxy, the other policing the boundaries of acceptable knowledge. Whether we know it or not, the relationship is not one-sided, but interdependent. Feminism transforms the discipline by critically addressing its problematics from the perspective of gender and power, but without the disciplinary problematic there would be no feminist history. Since these problematics change (only partly because feminism transforms them), feminist history changes as well. In this sense, Feminism's History is always parasitic in relation to the discipline of history. The future depends in large part on the direction the discipline takes. Where is the feminist critique of cultural history? Of rationalist interpretations of behavior? What are the limits of now-accepted disciplinary understandings of gender? What are the histories of the uses of the categories of difference (racial, sexual, religious, ethnic, national, and more) that historians take to be self-evident characterizations of people in the past? These questions, relentless interrogations of accepted knowledges and approaches to them, are the signs of an active, future-oriented feminist critical desire.[21]

If our relationship to our discipline is as a kind of critical gadfly, so it is to our colleagues in other disciplines and in newer areas of interdisciplinary study. It is we who introduce the difference of time into the categories employed by queer, postcolonial, transnational, and global studies. Strategic affiliations are not without their critical dimensions; feminist historians specialize in the temporal dimension. We are relativists when it comes to meanings – we know they vary over time. That makes us particularly good cultural critics. We can historicize the present's fundamental truths and expose the kinds of investments that drive them, in this way using the past not as the precursor to what is (typically the task of official history), but as its foil. Here we are double agents: practicing history to deepen and sharpen the critiques of new oppositional studies while slyly repudiating the discipline's emphasis on continuity and the unidirectionality of causality (past to present). There is a great future for double agents of this kind and a certain thrill in the job. It is destabilizing both to those we engage with and to ourselves. There is no worry that our identity will become fixed or our work complacent; there are always new strategic decisions to be made. To be sure, there are risks involved when orthodoxies (left and right) are challenged. But those are the risks that have characterized Feminism's History from the beginning, the source both of pleasure and danger, the guarantee of an opening to the future. Robyn Wiegman calls her new series of feminist scholarship at Duke University Press, 'The Next Wave,' suggesting that there's no end to Feminism's History – the passionate pursuit of the not-yet-known.[22] [. . .]

Since Clio has from the beginning been our inspiration, it is important to learn some things about her that are not so well known. The Muses had no permanent home: they danced on Mount Olympus; Mount Helicon was also their haunt. And they did not sit or walk – they flew. '. . . wherever they go they may go flying; for in such a way goddesses usually travel, as King Pyreneus of Daulis, who attempted to rape them, too late learned. For he perished when he leapt from the pinnacle of a tower trying to follow the flying Muses who escaped him.'[23] Those who fly escape the dangers of domination, the tyrannical powers of orthodoxy. Flight is also a positive course, a soaring; it traces the path of desire. When melancholy is left behind, that path opens for us. And passion returns as it readies itself for its latest pursuit of what has not yet been thought.

Notes

1   Lois Banner and Mary Hartman, *Clio's Consciousness Raised: New Perspectives on the History of Women, Sex and Class in Women's History* (New York: Harper & Row, 1974).

2   Plato, *Phaedrus*, 245a, trans. R. Hackforth (Cambridge: Cambridge University Press, 1952), 57.

3   This is the case both domestically and internationally, evident most visibly in the work of the United Nations Commission for the Elimination of All Forms of Discrimination Against Women (CEDAW). See Françoise Gaspard, 'Les femmes dans les relations internationales,' *Politique Étrangère* 3–4 (2000): 731–41.

4   Jacques Derrida, 'Women in the Beehive: A Seminar,' in *Men in Feminism*, ed. Alice Jardine and Paul Smith (New York: Methuen, 1987), 190.

5   Sigmund Freud, 'Mourning and Melancholia', SEX IV, trans. James Strachey (London: Hogarth Press, 1995), 243.

6   Ibid., 249.

7   Judith Butler, *Gender Trouble* (New York: Routledge, 1990), 57–66.

8   For a trenchant analysis of the current state of women's studies, see Wendy Brown, 'Women's Studies Unbound: Revolution, Mourning, Politics,' *parallax* 9, no. 2 (2003): 3–16.

9   Jacques Lacan, 'Subversion of the subject and the dialectic of desire in the Freudian unconscious,' in *Ecrits* (New York: Norton, 1977), 292–324. See also Dylan Evans, *An Introductory Dictionary of Lacanian Psychoanalysis,* s.v. 'desire' (London: Routledge 1996), 37.

10   Jacques Lacan, *The Four Fundamental Concepts of Psycho-Analysis* (New York: Norton, 1981), 154.

11   Joan W. Scott, *Only Paradoxes to Offer: French Feminists and the Rights of Man* (Cambridge, MA: Harvard University Press, 1996).

12   Wendy Brown, *States of Injury: Power and Freedom in Late Modernity* (Princeton, NJ: Princeton University Press, 1995).

13   Gayle Rubin, 'The Traffic in Women: Notes on the "Political Economy" of Sex,' reprinted in Joan W. Scott, *Feminism and History*, Oxford Readings in Feminism (Oxford: Oxford University Press, 1996), 105–51.

14   Natalie Zemon Davis, 'Women's History in Transition: The European Case,' reprinted in *Feminism and History*, 79–104.

15   The collected papers of the conference appeared in Carole S. Vance, ed., *Pleasure and Danger: Exploring Female Sexuality* (New York: Routledge, 1984).

16   Denise Riley, *Am I That Name? Feminism and the Category of 'Women' in History* (London: Macmillan, 1988).

17   Ann Snitow, 'A Gender Diary,' in *Conflicts in Feminism*, ed. Marianne Hirsch and Evelyn Fox Yeller (London: Routledge, 1990), 9–43.

18   Evelyn Brooks Higginbotham, 'African-American Women's History and the Metalanguage of Race,' reprinted in *Feminism and History*, 183–208, esp. 202.

19   Afsaneh Najmabadi, 'Teaching and Research in Unavailable intersections,' *differences: A Journal of Feminist Cultural Studies* 9, no. 3 (1997): 76.

20   Stuart Hall, cited in Wendy Brown, *Politics Out of History* (Princeton, NJ: Princeton University Press, 2001), 41.

21   See Ellen Rooney, 'Discipline and Vanish: Feminism, The Resistance to Theory, and the Politics of Cultural Studies,' *differences: A Journal of Feminist Cultural Studies* 2 (Fall 1990): 14–28.

22   Robyn Wiegman, 'What Ails Feminist Criticism?: A Second Opinion,' *Critical Inquiry* 25 (winter 1999); and Robyn Wiegman, 'Feminism, Institutionalism, and the Idiom of Failure,' *differences: A Journal of Feminist Cultural Studies* 11 (autumn 1999/2000): 107–36.

23   <http://homepage.mac.com/cparada/GML/MUSEShtmI>, consulted November 13, 2002.

Guide to further reading

(This guide excludes the articles and chapters contained in *The Feminist History Reader*. Full references for these can be found in the Acknowledgements.)

General theoretical surveys of feminist history

Alberti, Joanna, *Gender and the Historian* (London: Longman, 2002)

Angerman, Arina, Geerte Binnema, Annemieke Keunen, Vefie Poels and Jacqueline Zirkzee (eds) *Current Issues in Women's History* (London and New York: Routledge, 1989)

Bridenthal, Renate, Claudia Koonz and Susan Stuard (eds) *Becoming Visible. Women in European History* (Boston, MA: Houghton Mifflin Company, 1987)

Carroll, Berenice, A. (ed.) *Liberating Women's History: Theoretical and Critical Essays* (Urbana, IL: University of Illinois Press, 1976)

Downs, Laura Lee, 'From Women's History to Gender History' in Stefan Berger, Heiko Feldner and Kevin Passmore (eds) *Writing History: Theory and Practice* (London: Hodder Arnold, 2003): 261–80

Downs, Laura Lee, *Writing Gender History* (London: Hodder Arnold, 2004)

Gallagher, Ann-Marie, Cathy Lubelska and Louise Ryan (eds) *Re-presenting the Past. Women and History* (London: Longman, 2001)

Hartman, Mary S. and Lois Banner (eds) *Clio's Consciousness Raised: New Perspectives in the History of Women* (New York: Harper & Row, 1974)

Kleinberg, Jay (ed.) *Retrieving Women's History: Changing Perceptions of the Role of Women in Politics and Society* (Oxford and New York: Berg/UNESCO, 1998)

Offen, Karen, Ruth Roach Pierson and Jane Rendall (eds) *Writing Women's History: International Perspectives* (Bloomington, IN: Indiana University Press, 1991)

Purvis, June, 'From "Women Worthies" to Poststructuralism? Debate and Controversy in Women's History in Britain' in June Purvis (ed.) *Women's History: Britain, 1850–1945* (London: UCL Press, 1995): 1–22

Rendall, Jane, 'Uneven Developments: Women's History, Feminist History and Gender History in Great Britain' in Karen Offen, Ruth Roach Pierson and Jane Rendall (eds) *Writing Women's History: International Perspectives* (Bloomington, IN: Indiana University Press, 1991): 45–57

Scott, Joan, 'Women's History' in Peter Burke (ed.) *New Perspectives on Historical Writing* (Cambridge: Polity Press, 1991): 42–66

Scott, Joan (ed.) *Feminism and History* (Oxford: Oxford University Press, 1996)

Shapiro, Ann-Louise (ed.) *Feminists Revision History* (New Brunswick, NJ: Rutgers University Press, 1994)

Shoemaker, Robert and Mary Vincent (eds) *Gender and History in Western Europe* (London: Arnold, 1998)

Spongberg, Mary, *Writing Women's History Since the Renaissance* (London: Palgrave Macmillan, 2002)

Thurner, Manuela, 'Subject to Change: Theories and Paradigms of U.S. Feminist History', *Journal of Women's History* 9:2 (Summer, 1997): 122–46

Part I: Bringing the female subject into view

Clegg, Sue, 'The Feminist Challenge to Socialist History', *Women's History Review* 6:2 (1997): 201–13

Dauphin, Cécile, Arlette Farge, Genevieve Fraisse, Christine Klapisch-Zuber, Rose-Marie Lagrave *et al.*, 'Women's Culture and Women's Power: Issues in French Women's History', *Journal of Women's History* 1:1 (Spring, 1989): 63–107

Davidoff, Leonore and Catherine Hall, *Family Fortunes: Men and Women of the English Middle Class 1780–1850* (London: Routledge, 2002 edition)

Davidoff, Leonore, Keith McLelland and Jane Rendall (eds) *Gender and History: Retrospect and Prospect* (Oxford: Blackwell, 2000)

Davis, Natalie Zemon, '"Women's History" in Transition: the European Case', *Feminist Studies* 3:3/4 (Spring/Summer, 1976): 83–103

Hall, Catherine, *White, Male and Middle-Class: Explorations in Feminism and History* (Oxford: Polity Press, 1992)

Hunt, Lynn, 'The Challenge of Gender' in Hans Medick and Anne-Charlotte Trepp (eds) *Geschlechtergeschichte und Allgemeine Geschichte* (Goettingen, Wallstein, 1998): 59–97

Kelly, Joan, 'The Social Relations of the Sexes: Methodological Implications of Women's History', *Signs* 1:4 (Summer, 1976): 809–82

Maynard, Mary, 'Beyond the "Big Three": the Development of Feminist Theory in the 1990s', *Women's History Review* 4:3 (1995): 259–81

Rendall, Jane, 'Women and the Public Sphere', *Gender and History* 11:3 (1999): 475–88

Rowbotham, Sheila, *Hidden from History* (London: Pluto Press, 1973)

Smith-Rosenberg, Carroll, 'The Female World of Love and Ritual: Relations Between Women in Nineteenth Century America', *Signs* 1 (1975): 1–29

Part II: Deconstructing the female subject: feminist history and 'the linguistic turn'

Brown, Wendy, 'Feminist Hesitations, Postmodern Exposures', *differences: A Journal of Feminist Cultural Studies* 3:1 (1991): 63–84

Brown, Wendy, 'Women's Studies Unbound: Revolution, Mourning, Politics', *parallax* 9:2 (2003): 3–16

Butler, Judith, *Gender Trouble: Feminism and the Subversion of Identity* (New York: Routledge, 1990)

Butler, Judith and Joan Scott (eds) *Feminists Theorize the Political* (New York and London: Routledge, 1992)

Canning, Kathleen, 'Feminist History after the Linguistic Turn: Historicizing Discourse and Experience', *Signs* 19:2 (Winter 1994): 368–404

Downs, Laura Lee, 'If "Woman" is Just an Empty Category, Then Why Am I Afraid to Walk Alone at Night? Identity Politics Meets the Postmodern Subject', *Comparative*

Studies in Society and History: An International Quarterly 35:3 (April 1993): 414–51 with a response by Joan Scott, 'The Tip of the Volcano', pp. 438–43

Friedman, Susan Stanford, 'Making History: Reflections on Feminism, Narrative and Desire' in Diane Elam and Robyn Wiegman (eds) *Feminism Beside Itself* (New York and London: Routledge, 1995): 9–53

Gordon, Linda, Review of *Gender and the Politics of History* by Joan Wallach Scott and Joan Scott, Review of *Heroes of Their Own Lives*, by Linda Gordon in *Signs* 15:4 (Summer, 1990): 848–60

Hall, Catherine, 'Politics, Post-structuralism and Feminist History', *Gender & History* 3:2 (Summer, 1991): 204–10

Jackson, Stevi, 'The Amazing Deconstructing Woman', *Trouble and Strife* 25 (1992): 25–31

Newman, Louise M., 'Dialogue: Critical Theory and the History of Women: What's At Stake in Deconstructing Women's History', *Journal of Women's History* 2:3 (Winter, 1991): 58–68

Riley, Denise, *'Am I that Name?' Feminism and the Category of 'Women' in History* (Basingstoke: Macmillan, 1988)

Scott, Joan, 'Deconstructing Equality-Versus-Difference: Or, the Uses of Poststructuralist Theory for Feminism', *Feminist Studies* 14:1 (Spring, 1988): 33–50

Scott, Joan, *Gender and the Politics of History* (New York: Columbia University Press, 1988)

Scott, Joan, 'The Evidence of Experience', *Critical Inquiry* 17:3 (Winter, 1991): 773–97

Scott, Joan, *Only Paradoxes to Offer: French Feminists and the Rights of Man* (Cambridge, MA: Harvard University Press, 1996)

Stanley, Liz, 'Recovering Women in History from Feminist Deconstructionism', *Women's Studies International Forum* 13:1/2 (1990): 151–7

Part III: Searching for the subject: lesbian history

Auchmuty, Rosemary, Sheila Jeffreys and Elaine Miller, 'Lesbian History and Gay Studies: Keeping a Feminist Perspective', *Women's History Review* 1:1 (1992): 89–108

Butler, Judith, 'Imitation and Gender Insubordination' in Diana Fuss (ed.) *Inside/Out: Lesbian Theories, Gay Theories* (New York: Routledge, 1991): 13–31

Calhoun, Cheshire, 'The Gender Closet: Lesbian Disappearance under the Sign "Women"', *Feminist Studies* 21:1 (Spring, 1995): 7–35

Clark, Anna, 'Anne Lister's Construction of Lesbian Identity', *Journal of the History of Sexuality* 7:1 (1996): 23–50

Cook, Blanche Wiesen, 'The Historical Denial of Lesbianism', *Radical History Review* 20 (Spring/Summer, 1979): 60–5

Duberman, Martin, Martha Vicinus and George Chauncey (eds) *Hidden from History: Reclaiming the Gay and Lesbian Past* (New York: New American Library, 1989)

Duggan, Lisa, 'The Discipline Problem: Queer Theory Meets Lesbian and Gay History', *Gay and Lesbian Quarterly* 2 (1995): 179–91

Faderman, Lillian, *Surpassing the Love of Men: Romantic Friendship and Love between Women from the Renaissance to the Present* (New York: William Morrow & Co., 1981)

Gowing, Laura, 'History' in Andy Medhurst and Sally Munt (eds) *Lesbian and Gay Studies* (London: Cassell, 1997): 53–66

Hall Carpenter Archives Lesbian Oral History Group, *Inventing Ourselves: Lesbian Life Stories* (London: Routledge, 1989)

Lesbian History Group (eds) *Not a Passing Phase: Reclaiming Lesbians in History, 1840–1985* (London: The Women's Press, 1989)

Malinowitz, Harriet, 'Lesbian Studies and Postmodern Queer Theory' in Bonnie Zimmerman and Toni A. H. McNaron (eds) *The New Lesbian Studies: Into the Twenty-first Century* (New York: Feminist Press, 1996): 262–8

Oram, Alison, '"Friends, Feminists and Sexual Outlaws": Lesbianism and British History' in Gabrielle Griffin and Sonya Andermahr (eds) *Straight Studies Modified: Lesbian Interventions in the Academy* (London: Cassell, 1997): 168–83

Oram, Alison, and Annmarie Turnbull (eds) *The Lesbian History Sourcebook: Love and Sex Between Women in Britain 1780–1970* (London: Routledge, 2001)

Rich, Adrienne, 'Compulsory Heterosexuality and Lesbian Existence', *Signs* 5:4 (1980): 631–60

Smith, Barbara, 'African-American Lesbian and Gay History: An Exploration' in Barbara Smith, *The Truth that Never Hurts: Writings on Race, Gender and Freedom* (New Brunswick, NJ: Rutgers University Press, 1998): 82–92

Stanley, Liz, 'Romantic Friendship? Some Issues in Researching Lesbian History and Biography', *Women's History Review* 1:2 (1992): 193–216

Terry, Jennifer, 'Theorizing Deviant Historiography', *differences: A Journal of Feminist Cultural Studies* 3:2 (1991): 55–74

Vicinus, Martha, '"They Wonder to Which Sex I Belong": The Historical Roots of the Modern Lesbian Identity,' *Feminist Studies* 18 (1992): 467–97

Vicinus, Martha, *Lesbian Subjects: A Feminist Studies Reader* (Bloomington, IN: Indiana University Press, 1995)

Vicinus, Martha, *Intimate Friends: Women Who Loved Women, 1778–1928* (Chicago, IL: University of Chicago Press, 2004)

Part IV: Centres of difference: decolonising subjects, rethinking boundaries

Bannerji, Himani, 'Politics and the Writing of History' in Ruth Pierson and Nupur Chaudhuri (eds) *Nation, Empire, Colony: Historicizing Gender and Race* (Bloomington, IN: Indiana University Press, 1998): 287–301

Berg, Ida, Karen Hagemann and Catherine Hall (eds) *Gendered Nations: Nationalism and Gender Order in the Long Nineteenth Century* (Oxford: Berg, 2000)

Bhavnani, Kum-Kum (ed.) *Feminism and 'Race'* (Oxford: Oxford University Press, 2001)

Brown, Elsa Barkley, 'Polyrhythms and Improvisation: Lessons for Women's History', *History Workshop Journal* 31 (Spring, 1991): 85–90

Burton, Antoinette, 'History is Now: Feminist Theory and the Production of Historical Feminisms', *Women's History Review* 1:1 (1992): 25–38

Burton, Antoinette, *Burdens of History: British Feminists, Indian Women and Imperial Culture* (Chapel Hill, NC: University of North Carolina Press, 1994)

Burton, Antoinette, 'Some Trajectories of "Feminism" and "Imperialism"', *Gender and History* 10:3 (November 1998): 558–68

Burton, Antoinette, 'Thinking Beyond the Boundaries: Empire, Feminism and the Domains of History', *Social History* XXVI (2001): 60–71

Carby, Hazel V., 'White Women Listen! Black Feminism and the Boundaries of Sisterhood' in Centre for Contemporary Cultural Studies (ed.) *The Empire Strikes Back: Race and Racism in 70s Britain* (London: Hutchinson, 1982): 212–35

Chaudhuri, Nupur and Margaret Strobel (eds) *Western Women and Imperialism: Complicity and Resistance* (Bloomington, IN: Indiana University Press, 1992)

Cooper, Frederick and Ann Laura Stoler (eds) *Tensions of Empire, Colonial Cultures in a Bourgeois World* (Berkeley, CA: University of California Press, 1997)

Curthoys, Ann, 'Identity Crisis: Colonialism, Nation, and Gender in Australian History', *Gender and History* 5:2 (Summer, 1993): 165–76

Haggis, Jane, 'Gendering Colonialism or Colonising Gender?', *Women's Studies International Forum* 13:2 (1990): 105–15

Haggis, Jane, 'Women and Imperialism: Towards a Non-recuperative History' in Clare Midgley (ed.) *Gender and Imperialism* (Manchester: Manchester University Press, 1998): 45–75

Hall, Catherine, *Civilising Subjects: Metropole and Colony in the English Imagination, 1830–1867* (Cambridge: Polity Press, 2002)

Hall, Catherine (ed.) *Cultures of Empire. A Reader. Colonizers in Britain and the Empire in the Nineteenth and the Twentieth Centuries* (Manchester: Manchester University Press, 2000)

Higginbotham, Evelyn Brooks, 'Beyond the Sound of Silence: Afro-American Women in History', *Gender and History* 1:1 (1989): 50–67

Higginbotham, Evelyn Brooks, 'African-American Women's History and the Metalanguage of Race', *Signs* 17 (Winter, 1992): 251–74

Hine, Darlene Clark, 'Black Women's History, White Women's History: The Juncture of Race and Class', *Journal of Women's History* 4:2 (Fall, 1992): 125–33

Hine, Darlene Clark, Wilma King and Linda Reed, *'We Specialize in the Wholly Impossible': A Reader in Black Women's History* (Brooklyn, NY: Carlson, 1995)

hooks, bell, *Feminist Theory: From Margin to Center* (Boston, MA: South End Press, 1984)

Hunt, Nancy, Tessie R. Liu and Jean Quataert (eds) 'Gendered Colonialisms in African History', *Gender and History: Special Issue* 8:3 (November 1996)

Lake, Marilyn, 'Colonised and Colonising: the White Australian Feminist Subject', *Women's History Review* 2:3 (1993): 377–86

Levine, Philippa, (ed.) *Gender and Empire: The Oxford History of the British Empire* (Oxford: Oxford University Press, 2004)

Lewis, Reina and Sarah Mills (eds) *Feminist Postcolonial Theory* (Edinburgh: Edinburgh University Press, 2003)

McClintock, Anne, *Imperial Leather: Race, Gender and Sexuality in the Colonial Context* (London: Routledge, 1995)

Mani, Lata, *Contentious Traditions: The Debate on Sati in Colonial India* (Berkeley, CA: University of California Press, 1998)

Midgley, Clare (ed.) *Gender and Imperialism* (Manchester: Manchester University Press, 1998)

Mitchell, Michele, 'Silences Broken, Silences Kept: Gender and Sexuality in African-American History' in Leonore Davidoff, Keith McLelland and Jane Rendall (eds) *Gender and History: Retrospect and Prospect* (Oxford: Blackwell, 2000): 15–26

Mohanty, Chandra Talpade, *Feminism without Borders. Decolonizing Theory, Practicing Solidarity* (Durham, NC and London: Duke University Press, 2003)

Pierson, Ruth Roach, 'International Trends in Women's History and Feminism: Colonization and Canadian Women's History', *Journal of Women's History* 4:2 (Fall, 1992): 134–56

Pierson, Ruth Roach and Nupur Chaudhuri (eds) *Nation, Empire, Colony: Historicizing Gender and Race* (Bloomington, IN: Indiana University Press, 1998)

Ruiz, Vicki L. and Ellen Dubois (eds) *Unequal Sisters: A Multicultural Reader in US Women's History* (London: Routledge, 2002 edition)

Sangari, Kum Kum and Sudesh Vaid (eds) *Recasting Women: Essays in Indian Colonial History* (New Brunswick, NJ: Rutgers University, 1990)

Shepherd, Verene, Bridget Brereton and Barbara Bailey (eds) *Engendering History: Caribbean Women in Historical Perspective* (London: James Currey Publishers, 1995)

Sinha, Mrinalini, *Colonial Masculinity: The 'Manly Englishman' and the 'Effeminate Bengali' in the Late Nineteenth Century* (Manchester: Manchester University Press, 1995)

Sinha, Mrinalini, Donna Guy and Angela Woollacott (eds) *Feminisms and Internationalism* (Oxford: Blackwell, 1999)

Smith, Bonnie G. (ed.) *Global Feminisms Since 1945* (London: Routledge, 2000)

Smith, Bonnie G. (ed.) *Women's History in Global Perspective* (Urbana, IL and Chicago, IL: University of Illinois Press, 2004)

Spelman, Elizabeth, *Inessential Woman: Problems of Exclusion in Feminist Thought* (Boston, MA: Beacon Press, 1988)

Spivak, Gayatri Chakravorty, 'Can the Subaltern Speak?' in Cary Nelson and Lawrence Grossberg (eds) *Marxism and the Interpretation of Culture* (London: Macmillan, 1988): 271–313

Ware, Vron, *Beyond the Pale: White Women, Racism and History* (London: Verso, 1992)

Index

Routledge History

Women's History, Britain 1700–1850
Hannah Barker and Elaine Chalus

Here for the first time is a comprehensive history of the women of Britain during a period of dramatic change. Placing women's experiences in the context of these major social, economic and cultural shifts that accompanied the industrial and commercial transformations, Hannah Barker and Elaine Chalus paint a fascinating picture of the change, revolution, and continuity that were encountered by women of this time.

A thorough and well-balanced selection of individual chapters by leading field experts and dynamic new scholars, combine original research with a discussion of current secondary literature, and the contributors examine areas as diverse as enlightenment, politics, religion, education, sexuality, family, work, poverty, and consumption.

Providing a captivating overview of women and their lives, this book is an essential purchase for the study of women's history, and, providing delightful little gems of knowledge and insight, it will also appeal to any reader with an interest in this fascinating topic.

ISBN10: 0–415–29176–3 (hbk)   ISBN13: 978–0–415–29176–7 (hbk)
ISBN10: 0–415–29177–1 (pbk)   1SBN13: 978–0–415–29177–4 (pbk)

Women and Work in Britain since 1840
Gerry Holloway

The first book of its kind to study this period, Gerry Holloway's essential student resource works chronologically from the early 1840s to the end of the twentieth century and examines over 150 years of women's employment history and the struggles they have faced in the workplace.

With suggestions for research topics, an annotated bibliography to aid further research and a chronology of important events which places the subject in a broader historical context, Holloway considers how factors such as class, age, marital status, race and locality, along with wider economic and political issues, have affected women's job opportunities and status.

Students of women's studies, gender studies and history will find this a fascinating and invaluable addition to their reading material.

ISBN10: 0–415–25910–X (hbk)   ISBN13: 978–0–415–25910–1 (hbk)
ISBN10: 0–415–25911–8 (pbk)   ISBN13: 978–0–415–25911–8 (pbk)

Available at all good bookshops
For ordering and further information please visit
www.routledge.com

Routledge History

Outspoken Women

Edited by Lesley A. Hall

Outspoken Women brings together the many and varied non-fictional writings of British women on sexual attitudes and behaviour, beginning nearly a hundred years prior to the 'second wave' of feminism and coming right up to the sexual revolution of the 1960s.

Commentators cover a broad range of perspectives and include Darwinists, sexologists, and campaigners against the spread of VD, as well as women writing about their own lives and experiences. Covering all aspects of the debate from marriage, female desire and pleasure to lesbianism, prostitution, STDs and sexual ignorance, Lesley A. Hall studies how the works of this era didn't just criticise male-defined mores and the 'dark side' of sex, but how they increasingly promoted the possibility of a brighter view and an informed understanding of the sexual life.

Hall's remarkable anthology is an engaging examination of this fascinating subject and it provides students and scholars with an invaluable source of primary material.

ISBN10: 0-415-25371-3 (hbk)   ISBN13: 978-0-415-25371-0 (hbk)
ISBN10: 0-415-25372-1 (pbk)   ISBN13: 978-0-415-25372-7 (pbk)

Students: A Gendered History

Carol Dyhouse

This compelling and stimulating book explores the gendered social history of students in modern Britain.

From the privileged youth of Brideshead Revisited to the scruffs at 'Scumbag University' in The Young Ones, representations of the university undergraduate have been decidedly male. But since the 1970s the proportion of women students in universities in the UK has continued to rise so that female undergraduates now outnumber their male counterparts.

Drawing upon wide-ranging original research including documentary and archival sources, newsfilm, press coverage of student life and life histories of men and women who graduated before the Second World War, this text provides rich insights into changes in student identity and experience over the past century.

For students of gender studies, cultural studies and history, this book will have meaningful impact on their degree course studies.

ISBN10: 0-415-35817-5 (hbk)   ISBN13: 978-0-415-35817-0 (hbk)
ISBN10: 0-415-35818-3 (pbk)   ISBN13: 978-0-415-35818-7 (pbk)

Available at all good bookshops
For ordering and further information please visit
www.routledge.com